£40

£15

POLICY COHERENCE IN
DEVELOPMENT CO-OPERATION

EADI BOOK SERIES 22

POLICY COHERENCE
IN DEVELOPMENT
CO-OPERATION

edited by

JACQUES FORSTER and OLAV STOKKE

FRANK CASS
LONDON • PORTLAND, OR

in association with

EADI European Association of Development Research
and Training Institutes, Geneva

First published in 1999 in Great Britain by
FRANK CASS PUBLISHERS
Newbury House, 900 Eastern Avenue
London IG2 7HH, England

and in the United States of America by
FRANK CASS PUBLISHERS
c/o ISBS
5804 N.E. Hassalo Street
Portland, Oregon 97213–3644

Website: www.frankcass.com

British Library Cataloguing in Publication Data

Policy coherence in development co-operation. – (EADI book
series; 22)
1. Economic assistance – Developing countries –
International cooperation 2. Economic assistance –
Developing countries – Government policy 3. Economic
assistance – Developing countries – Case studies
I. Stoke, Olav II. Forster, Jacques
327.1'11'091724
ISBN 0 7146 4914 7 (cloth)
ISBN 0 7146 4464 1 (paperback)
ISSN 1462–219X

Library of Congress Cataloging-in-Publication Data

Policy coherence in development co-operation / edited by
Olav Stokke and Jacques Forster.
    p. cm. – (EADI-book series, ISSN 1462–2181 ; 22)
    Results from a research project organisesd, with the auspices
of the European Association of Development Research and
Training Institutes (EADI) Working Group on Aid Policy and
Performance, by the Institut universitaire d'études du
developpment (IUED), Geneva, and the Norwegian Institute of
International Affairs (NUPI), Oslo.
    Includes bibliographical references and index.
    ISBN 0-7146-4914-7 (cloth) – ISBN 0-7146-4464-1 (paper)
    1. Economic assistance – Developing countries – Case studies.
I. Stokke, Olav, 1934–. II. Forster, Jacques. III. European
Association of Development Research and Training Institutes.
IV. Series.
HC60.P56   1999
338.91'09172'4–dc21   99–14823
                                                             CIP

Printed in Great Britain by
Antony Rowe Ltd, Chippenham, Wilts

Contents

Introduction

JACQUES FORSTER AND OLAV STOKKE

The end of the cold war in the late 1980s had profound effects on international relations in the 1990s. Some of the basic framework conditions for North–South relations were altered, although more in the case of some donor governments than of others [*Stokke, 1996*]. In 1991, the High-level Meeting of the Development Assistance Committee (DAC) of the Organisation for Economic Co-operation and Development (OECD) called for greater coherence in the policies of industrialised countries *vis-à-vis* developing countries. This demand, followed up by the DAC during subsequent years, must be seen against the background of the international system transformation that has been taking place, although the need for better co-ordination in the aid policies of member governments has always been emphasised by the DAC.

The present volume results from a research and publishing project under the auspices of the Working Group on Aid Policy and Perform-ance of the European Association of Development Research and Training Institutes (EADI). The proposal to focus on aid and political conditionality was made in advance of EADI's Eight General Confer-ence, which took place in Vienna in September 1996, and the Working Group decided to take it up. At that time, it had just completed its third major programme, also focusing on evolving North–South relations since the cold war, with particular reference to development co-operation: aid and political conditionality. Two volumes in the EADI Book Series (Nos. 16 and 18) came out of that effort.[1] Earlier in the 1990s, its second major programme, focusing on evaluation, had been finalised; the outcome was a series of three

---

1. Olav Stokke (ed.), *Aid and Political Conditionality*, London: Frank Cass; and Olav Stokke (ed.), *Foreign Aid Towards the Year 2000: Experiences and Challenges*, London: Frank Cass.

volumes in the EADI Book Series (Nos. 11, 12 and 14).[2] Previously, the Group had examined the aid policies of European countries, a task completed in 1984 with the publication of two volumes in the EADI Book Series (No. 4).[3]

Over the years, the Working Group on Aid has established a mode of work, which has been followed this time, too. Usually, a project design is worked out by the Convenor(s) and outstanding researchers in the field are invited to comment on the position paper. These consultations are followed by invitations to specialists to contribute component studies. The draft studies are presented at an international workshop to which, in addition to the authors, a selected group of experts are invited, representing the immediate environment of the chosen theme (researchers, top administrators and others in the specific field). It is the refined and revised versions of selected drafts scrutinised through this process and edited that are finally published, after having been through another referee process organised by the EADI committee on publications as a basis for deciding whether or not to include the volume in the EADI Book Series.

Although the concept of policy coherence is new, the ideas behind it are not new in international development co-operation. In Chapter 1, *the editors* provide a state-of-the-art outline of the concept and its setting, beginning with a definition. They explain that the aspiration to attain greater policy coherence is based on a rational choice approach. In order to attain the main aims set for development co-operation, policy objectives should be formulated in clear terms and harmonised. Objectives set for development co-operation should be internally consistent, and those pursued within other policy frameworks of the system – such as trade, the environment and security – should be harmonised with them or at least not be conflicting. Strategies and mechanisms should be attuned to objectives and the outcome should correspond to the intentions and objectives.

Four systemic frameworks of policy coherence are identified. One framework is (i) *the development co-operation policy of a donor*

---

2.   Edward Clay and Olav Stokke (eds.), 1991, reprinted 1995, *Food Aid Reconsidered: Assessing the Impact on Third World Countries*, London: Frank Cass; Olav Stokke (ed.), 1991, *Evaluating Development Assistance: Policies and Performance*, London: Frank Cass; and Lodewijk Berlage and Olav Stokke (eds.), 1992, *Evaluating Development Assistance: Approaches and Methods*, London: Frank Cass.
3.   Olav Stokke (ed.), 1984, *European Development Assistance: Policies and Performance*, Volume I, Tilburg: EADI Secretariat/University of Tilburg; and Olav Stokke (ed.), 1984, *European Development Assistance: Third World Perspectives on Policies and Performance*, Volume II, Tilburg: EADI Secretariat/University of Tilburg.

government. Its bilateral aid, for a variety of different purposes, is channelled through many recipient governments, each with framework conditions special to that country, through the private sector, non-governmental organisations (NGOs) and international non-governmental organisations (INGOs). Likewise its multilateral aid is provided for a variety of purposes and channelled through many different multilateral aid agencies and development finance institutions. This multitude of purposes and aid channels constitutes a great challenge to the internal coherence of the aid policy. However, aid constitutes only one dimension of the relations between an industrial (donor) country and developing countries. Several policies within other areas (trade, migration, arms sales) affect countries in the South, directly or indirectly, and these policies may counteract objectives set for development co-operation policy. The wider challenge, therefore, concerns (ii) *the coherence of the various policies towards the South*. Internationally, the most burning issue has been that of (iii) *the coherence of industrialised countries' policies vis-à-vis developing countries*. The last framework relates to (iv) *donor–recipient policy coherence*, with particular reference to development policies.

The rationale for policy coherence – and incoherence – within these four frameworks is discussed. Incoherence of policy – emerging from conflicting interests and values and reinforced by compartmentalisation of politics and public administration – is considered the main rationale for seeking policy coherence. Although driven by a rational choice logic from the centre of a political system, the logic of subsystems may lead to different conclusions than those of the centre. From the DAC perspective, member governments' aid should be better co-ordinated so as to be more effective and efficient *vis-à-vis* its development objectives. The commitment to greater policy coherence was, however, coupled with a vision that combined a strong moral imperative to respond to the extreme poverty and human suffering that still afflict more than one billion people in the South and a strong self-interest in fostering increased prosperity in developing countries.

However, conflicting interest – both at the national level of individual donor countries and among nations – may explain why policy coherence at this level is such a tall order. Against this background, mechanisms to attain policy coherence are explored. At the level of international politics, including development co-operation, only fragments of an international regime exist today although several components are established in some issue areas (human rights in particular). However, less ambitiously norm-setting in terms of policy

3

assessment, discussion, consultation and co-ordination takes place both at the level of global and regional organisations and bilaterally.

The key to greater policy coherence – in international as in national politics – remains in the hands of the governments of nation states. The crucial role of the political and administrative centre of these systems is emphasised and inter-ministerial and intra-ministerial restructuring and co-ordination are seen as important mechanisms to this end.

Against this background, future prospects and the effects of greater coherence on aid policy are assessed and discussed. The conclusion is ambivalent: outcomes of an integrated approach within individual donor countries will depend on the context and the relative strength of stakeholders in and out of government administration. From an overall perspective, the focus may contribute to a more systematic policy-making process. Given the original DAC perspective, it may identify the impact of the various policies on developing countries and, accordingly, open up a discussion on how compatible they are *vis-à-vis* overall objectives set by industrialised countries in the North for development in the South. It may also result in more transparency both in the policy-making and in the implementation of policies towards the South and in North–South relations generally.

Although coherence has always been an issue in the field of development co-operation, why has this term emerged as significant and relevant only in recent years? To throw light on this *Göran Hydén*, in Chapter 2, examines how the ground for policy coherence in the field of development co-operation has shifted since the 1960s, and discusses its usefulness in the current context.

Policy coherence is considered a measure of institutional effectiveness. Outlining the various general reasons for policy incoherence, the author addresses the following questions: why is policy coherence important? how is policy coherence achieved? and for whom is coherence being sought? To understand the many dimensions of policy coherence it is necessary to examine in whose interest coherence is being sought, he argues, observing that in some cases a certain measure of policy incoherence may be necessary to achieve a greater degree of policy coherence at another, and more important, level.

With particular reference to development co-operation, the author discusses policy coherence under shifting aid paradigms since the 1960s, when the notion of comprehensive national development planning was expected to guide inputs from outside donors. This phase was followed, in the 1970s, by the paradigm of integrated development, seeking to bring together divergent policy objectives

4

under a single institutional umbrella. The structural adjustment policy of the 1980s brought a whole new way of looking at policy coherence in development – bringing economics back in. In the 1990s, structural adjustment has had to take second place to concerns with political reform – governance and democratisation. Policy coherence is sought on terms set by the principal donor governments. It follows that, compared to previous decades when policy coherence was taken for granted because the institutional set-up was relatively simple, it has become a more manifest concern in the 1990s since so many factors tend to undermine efforts to achieve better results from development co-operation activities. It is argued that if policy coherence is to be achieved, it must increasingly be sought with the institutional requirements of the recipient country in mind, rather than primarily those within the donor bureaucracy, whether at governmental or inter-governmental level.

The following chapters (3–9) focus on the problematique of policy coherence from the perspective of seven donor countries – Canada, France, Germany, the Netherlands, Norway, Sweden and Switzerland. This selection includes governments that place great emphasis on policy coherence within the four frameworks we have identified, and governments that – in practice – are less enthusiastic about it.

In Canada, greater policy coherence has been emphasised at different times in three quite different ways. In the 1980s, it stressed the importance of greater coherence between the macro-economic policies of recipient governments and those advocated by the Bretton Woods institutions (BWIs), in the hope of lessening the risk of good aid programmes being undermined by recipient governments' faulty economic policies. Greater policy coherence within the aid agency (CIDA) was championed, especially in the early 1990s, as a means of increasing the development impact of aid. Moreover, greater coherence between CIDA's policies and other Canadian policies with an impact on the developing countries has been advocated almost as self-evidentially desirable. In Chapter 3, *Cranford Pratt* subjects these expectations to critical analysis, with particular focus on the effects of the drive towards a more coherent aid policy and greater coherence between it and other policies that have an impact on developing countries.

It is argued that CIDA's use of aid to exert pressure on recipient governments to implement structural adjustment programmes can be viewed positively only if one discounts the importance of recipient countries fully 'owning' the development policy they pursue, and accepts that the minimal government neo-liberalism then being pres-

5

sed on Third World governments is in fact essential to sustained development in their countries; these are highly contentious propositions. He concludes in a similar vein with regard to the drive for greater coherence within the Canadian aid policy: the likely consequences of the efforts of the CIDA leadership in recent years to increase coherence between the various separate activities supported by CIDA have diminished rather than improved the Canadian contribution to the development of the economies and the welfare of the populations of developing countries.

The greater coherence of Canadian aid policies and Canadian foreign policy, which the Department of Foreign Affairs hoped to accomplish by seeking a greater subordination of CIDA to it, would almost certainly have diminished the quality of Canada's international development assistance had its efforts succeeded, Pratt concludes. He draws a similar conclusion with regard to the new efforts made by the Ministry of Foreign Affairs in 1997 to increase coherence between Canada's aid policies with its foreign policy: it seems very likely that had greater policy coherence been achieved through the conversion of CIDA into a policy-neutral agency subordinate to Foreign Affairs there would have been a further deterioration in Canada's commitment to the long-term development of the least-developed countries. It might, therefore, be more effective for those concerned to advance equitable international development to stress the importance, not of greater policy coherence, but of giving greater weight to development considerations as against narrowly self-interested trade and international political objectives in the determination of both non-aid and aid policies.

In Chapter 4, *Philippe Hugon* examines both French and European Union (EU) development co-operation policy. After defining the terms and stakes of coherence, he presents, first of all, the new context of French and European development co-operation. The lack of coherence in French development co-operation policy is analysed and recent reforms presented. Finally, the author examines the problems of coherence and co-ordination between French and European policies.

In Chapter 5, *Guido Ashoff* focuses on the degree of coherence between Germany's development co-operation policy and its other policies that affect developing countries. He begins with a discussion of policy coherence, arguing that for several political reasons, complete policy coherence is neither theoretically conceivable nor practically feasible. It follows that a realistic goal would be to remove the most obvious inconsistencies and strive for greater coherence, wherever a need for this is felt, by deepening the understanding of how different policies affect the development process, mobilising greater political consensus on the need for coherence and, to this end, improving the way the political decision-making system is organised.

The author then turns to the evidence of policy incoherence in Germany and the debate on this issue. The most important policy areas that have caused incoherence are found to be the foreign trade policy, agricultural and fisheries policies, the treatment of corruption by German tax and criminal laws, the policy on arms exports and German environmental policies. The evidence emerging from the German case leads to, *inter alia*, the following conclusions. First, the ability to overcome political incoherence will be highly dependent on the complexity and type of incoherence. The evidence suggests that a distinction should be made between 'single-issue incoherence' and 'systemic incoherence', and a further distinction between the incoherence of policies that belong to the national level and the contradictions that exist between the national development co-operation policy and EU policies. Second, NGOs and the media can play a major role in raising public awareness of policy incoherence and in mobilising support for coherence that is guided by a development co-operation perspective. Third, to achieve greater policy coherence will require joint action by several donor countries; co-ordinated action by some donor governments may, on the other hand, put pressure on governments that are less enthusiastic to co-ordinate policies. And fourth, developing countries may, in some cases, be able to mitigate the negative impact of donors' policy incoherence by adjusting their own policies.

The author then outlines the procedures adopted by Germany in order to attain policy coherence. Six proposals to improve policy coherence which have been raised in the German debate are presented and assessed. Three conclusions emerge from this discussion. First, the way the German policy-making system is organised is fairly conducive to coherence because it has a fully-fledged ministry for development co-operation and because the procedural rules of the Federal Government ensure that any ministry can put any issue on the agenda for inter-ministerial co-ordination. Second, all attempts to achieve greater policy coherence by legal, administrative or bureaucratic means cannot change the fact that policy coherence is, by its very nature, a highly political matter and ultimately to be dealt with in the political arena. And finally, the six proposals may nevertheless be helpful in reducing the impact of factors that cause policy incoherence.

In Chapter 6, *Paul Hoebink* gives a historical outline of the Nether-lands' development policy, with particular reference to the coherence problematique, based on the major white papers on development co-operation since the first substantial one appeared in 1966. The drive for integral policies started in 1976 with the first white paper on development co-operation signed by Jan Pronk, although alluded to in pre-vious budget papers. Coherence was sought within aid policy and also within foreign policy where the concern for Third World development became an integral part, with particular reference to the call for a new international economic order. However, the coherence concept as such did not appear until 1989, in a white paper on the quality of aid; it was brought to the forefront in two major white papers in the early 1990s signed by Jan Pronk – back as a minister for development co-operation. He called for a decompartmentalisation of approaches and policies, both within development co-operation and between development co-operation and other dimension of foreign and inter-national policy. This call was strongly reiterated in a major white paper in 1995.

The author reviews several dimensions of Dutch development co-operation with a potential for policy incoherence, starting with the conflict between stated altruistic objectives and (unstated) economic interests in export promotion through, *inter alia*, tying of aid. The concern for human rights is another area of potential conflict between ethics and economic and foreign policy concerns which may lead to incoherence within the aid policy; the shifts of policy within this area are reviewed, with particular reference to relations with Indonesia. The author also scrutinises the degree of coherence over the years within three other policy areas: those of development policy and the environment; the conflicting concerns of human rights, development and conflict prevention on the one hand and those of arms trade on the other; and, finally, the conflicting concerns of development policy and trade policy, with particular reference to the least developed countries and the case of cocoa.

During the first part of the 1990s, Norway's policy towards developing countries, and its North–South policy in general, were reviewed by an government-appointed commission and in two government white papers; the policies were adopted by Parliament in 1996. Norway is committed to greater policy coherence within all four frameworks identified nationally and internationally. In Chapter 7, *Olav Stokke* identifies the prescriptions for greater policy coherence on the basis of these policy documents. The follow-up is described and analysed from a process perspective: to what extent have mechanisms already established to ensure policy co-ordination been strengthened and new ones created? The effects of the prescriptions are then explored, with particular reference to aid policy. The stated and implemented policy towards the South is scrutinised both for its elements of continuity and of change.

During the late 1980s and early 1990s, there was a proliferation of the objectives set for Norway's development co-operation – concerns for the environment, democratic development and human rights have been integrated in the aid policy and increasingly come to the fore. These new components became core components of a high-profile humanitarian foreign policy, reinforcing the general trend: as a share of ODA, humanitarian aid has increased to a level almost three times higher than the DAC average. A major conclusion is that the improved coherence of Norway's policies towards developing countries has almost exclusively taken place in areas that are financed from the aid budget: promotion of new objectives have occurred at the expense of traditional objectives related to long-term sustainable development. The poverty profile of Norway's bilateral aid in terms of the share channelled to the least developed countries (LLDCs) has been negatively affected, although comparing well with other DAC countries. However, poverty alleviation remains task number one in the declared policy.

In Chapter 8, *Anders Danielson* assesses the coherence of Swedish development co-operation policy. After a brief description of the pattern and volume of Swedish aid, he examines Swedish policies *vis-à-vis* developing countries from five different angles. First, the internal consistency of different policy instruments is explored. He finds that the composition of aid has changed: programme aid has increased at the expense of project aid. Second, the internal consistency of policy objectives is discussed. It is suggested that the explicit objectives of Swedish aid may be mutually inconsistent. In particular, the objective that states that aid seeks to promote 'economic and political autonomy' may conflict with the objective of 'growth of resources'. However, the analysis also suggests that such an inconsistency is more or less necessary: it is the price paid for flexibility.

The author then looks at Swedish development co-operation policies *vis-à-vis* other Swedish policies, notably trade and immigration. The review suggests that these policies are fairly coherent, basically because Sweden has very few non-aid relations with low-income countries. The fourth policy dimension explored is Swedish development co-operation policy *vis-à-vis* domestic policies in recipient countries. The most fundamental change within the aid policy has probably occurred here. In the 1960s and early 1970s, Sweden selected main recipient countries on the basis of the development vision of their governments (providing ODA to be used very much at the recipient's discretion). In the 1990s, the situation is different: the donor–recipient relationship is characterised by conditionality with regard to their policies, including explicit demands for democratisation and a market-oriented economic system. Finally, Sweden's development co-operation policies *vis-à-vis* the aid policies of other donor countries are examined. The major conclusion is that a gradual harmonisation has taken place – especially since the introduction of first-generation conditionality in the early 1980s related, in particular, to the IMF/World Bank-supported structural adjustment programmes. This harmonisation has taken place with respect to aid instruments (programme aid has gained ground), prioritising among sectors (social sectors have been emphasised) and the selection of recipient countries (sub-Saharan Africa receives a smaller proportion of aid).

Over the past few years, Switzerland has given emphasis to the issue of policy coherence in its relations with developing countries; in March 1994, the government issued a report on 'Switzerland's North–South Relations in the 1990s' to that effect. In Chapter 9, *Jacques Forster* describes the emergence of this new approach in Switzerland's policy towards developing countries, and discusses the objectives of Swiss development policy and the concept of coherence as they are presented in government policy papers. He then makes a first appraisal of the implementation of this new approach by describing the mechanisms set up to implement it within the federal administration and the role played by other actors.

Although it is premature to make a full assessment of this new policy, the chapter examines examples of its implementation since 1994 (export promotion versus ecology and human rights; the fight against corruption and illegal transfers of capital; arms exports versus employment). These examples illustrate the dilemma that confronts governments in their pursuit of greater policy coherence towards developing countries.

The debate on how the development objectives set out in the Maastricht Treaty may be implemented revolves around three concepts – co-ordination, coherence and complementarity. In Chapter 10, *Paul Hoebink* addresses the policy within one of these areas, that of coherence, as defined in the Treaty on European Union. It refers not only to the coherence within the development co-operation policy but also to coherence between the development objectives set in the Union Treaty and other policies of the Community.

Three categories of policy coherence are identified. First, there may be incoherence between the development policy objectives of the Maastricht Treaty and the external policy of the EU such as (other elements of) the foreign policy and the trade policy. Second, incoherence may exist between the EU's development policy and its 'domestic' policies (such as agricultural and industrial policies). Further, there may be incoherence between the development policy of the Community and policies of individual member states, and between the EU's development policy and the policies of developing countries. Examples of incoherent policies within these categories are provided and discussed.

Focus is then directed to the institutional set-up, with particular reference to the relations between the sections of the EU bureaucracy in Brussels (conflict between horizontal units that can lead to policy incoherence), and their relations with counterparts in member states (involving blurred delimitations with regard to competence) and with developing countries, which may also result in incoherent policies. A distinction is made between intended and unintended incoherence.

The author presents the debate within the EU and measures taken so far to attain greater policy coherence, with particular reference to the case of meat export subsidies (with negative effects on the West African market) and the case of overfishing in West Africa. In both cases, it was European NGOs that drew attention to the incoherent policies. Finally, some mechanisms to promote greater coherence of development policy, proposed by the Netherlands' National Advisory Council for Development Cooperation and others, are examined.

The 1992 Maastricht Treaty, establishing the European Union (EU), stipulated in its Article C that the external policies of the Union should be consistent with each other. This consistency provision was further enhanced in Article 130v which requires the European Community (EC) to take into account development policy objectives in the other policies it implements. Two main factors accounted for this 'coherence' requirement. First, there was the necessity to enhance the credibility of the EU's external actions, in spite of the three-pillar structure introduced in the Treaty on European Union (TEU). Second, the Treaty gave the 33-year old EC development policy a legal foundation and introduced a requirement of coherence, since experience had showed that development policy efforts were often undermined by EC measures in other areas. In Chapter 11, *Andrea Koulaïmah-Gabriel* examines the efforts to achieve policy coherence in the EU, especially between common foreign and security policy (CFSP) and development co-operation.

A certain degree of policy incoherence is a feature of governance structures, for a number of reasons: interest-based politics and the need to compromise, lack of information, difficulty in prioritising and policy fragmentation. It is argued that at the EU level, incoherence is increased by institutional differentiation, a fragmented decision-making system and the co-existence of two levels of policy determination: European and national. An 'institutional' explanation of EU policy incoherence is put forward.

Beyond these difficulties, the integration of a common foreign and security policy, albeit in a different pillar within the areas of competence of the EU, is a source of enhanced consistency. The author looks into three areas of 'interaction' between development and foreign policy since Maastricht: economic sanctions, conflict prevention, and geographical policy articulation. This geographical screening shows the declining status of development co-operation as a driving force of the EU's relations with the developing world. It raises an important question, that of the place of development co-operation and more particularly of the EU–ACP relationship in future EU foreign policy.

In Chapter 12, *Oliver Morrissey* introduces a general framework for identifying the ways in which trade policy and interests may conflict with aid policy objectives. The framework borrows from entitlement theory and identifies how a poor country can meet its basic needs through production (direct entitlement), trade (exchange entitlement) and aid (external entitlement). If, given its resources and ability to trade, a country is unable to meet the basic needs of its populace, the country can be said to have an entitlement deficit, or an aid entitlement (the ultimate purpose of which should be to reduce the deficit). Any elements of aid policy that have the effect of increasing (or at least not helping to reduce) the deficit can be interpreted as sources of incoherence within the aid policy. Any elements of policies that interact with aid policy that have the effect of increasing the deficit can be interpreted as sources of incoherence of donor policies towards the South. The cases of the United Kingdom and the European Union are used to illustrate how the approach can be applied to highlight instances of policy incoherence. The conclusion offers suggestions as to measures that could reduce incoherence in European aid policy.

Economic linkages between the OECD countries and developing countries have become more complex today than they were some ten years ago, with regional variations. This was the background for the OECD to reassess the development co-operation efforts of OECD member countries and three regions with low- and middle-income member countries – ASEAN (Indonesia, Malaysia, the Philippines and Thailand), South Asia (Bangladesh, India, Pakistan and Sri Lanka), and North Africa (Algeria, Morocco and Tunisia). In Chapter 13, *Kiichiro Fukasaku* presents a synthesis of the main results of these three studies, carried out at the OECD Development Centre, with special focus on the coherence of the OECD countries' economic relations with these regions.

It is argued that the contrasting experience of ASEAN and South Asia over the past decade indicates that aid programmes appear to be working better when domestic policy reforms in recipient countries are put on the right track. The recent development of EU–Maghreb relations also points to the importance of seeking a synergy between trade and aid policies in today's more competitive market environment. The magnitude of adjustment to trade openings could be substantial in South Asia and North Africa, and aid programmes should be more targeted to the problems of poverty alleviation and social cohesion in these countries. The notion of policy coherence is important for policy-makers in both donor and recipient countries in assessing the impact of aid policy under different economic and social conditions. However, its practical relevance depends crucially on the capacity of national aid agencies, NGOs and international donor communities to carry out policy surveillance.

The political character of donor policies on democracy, human rights and good governance creates the potential for conflict between competing aid objectives on the part of individual donors, between aid policy objectives and domestic policy agendas, and between recipient governments and aid donors. In Chapter 14, *Mark Robinson* explores the extent of policy coherence in the formulation and implementation of such policies through an analysis of interactions among aid donors, foreign policy establishments, and recipient governments. He argues that political sensitivities, donor self-interest and problems of implementation will inevitably frustrate the attainment of increased policy coherence and better co-ordination among donors. Policy incoherence is an innate feature of donor policies in this field of activity, and evidence of coherence is the exception rather than the rule. Efforts to enhance policy coherence and improve co-ordination will be undermined by pressures that cause fragmentation and weaken coherence.

In the early 1990s, Rwanda and Burundi were caught up in a wave of major political instability and ethnic violence, which spread into eastern Congo and beyond. As a major bilateral donor (and the former colonial power) Belgium was a prime witness, and inevitably also an important international actor, in the unfolding events.

In Chapter 15, *Johan Debar, Robrecht Renard and Philip Reyntjens* describe Belgium's reactions to the crisis in its foreign policy and its development co-operation policy, and assess the outcomes. They argue that efforts were made to attain coherence of policies pursued by the departments of foreign affairs and aid, both within the two policy areas and between them, especially with regard to political conditions set for aid. Although some successes can be recorded, the final outcome was disappointing; it is argued that better results might have been achieved. The political instability was not neutralised and the violence was not stopped. On the contrary: the region witnessed one of the worst genocides Africa has ever experienced.

Under the existing circumstances it may be questioned whether an external intervention would have been able to stop the downward spiral in the region. It may also be argued, from a Belgian perspective, that more powerful actors with different agendas were involved – especially France and, at a later stage, the United States – and that other donors, such as the United Kingdom and the Netherlands, stepped in when Belgium applied the brakes. However, considerable internal weaknesses also undermined Belgium's efforts to play an active role in resolving the crisis, including the administrative and political difficulties of adapting traditional aid instruments to the new circumstances, and the fear of a public opinion backlash after the murder of ten Belgian paratroopers in Rwanda in April 1994.

*

The research and publishing programme has received much help and goodwill. The Swiss Agency for Development and Co-operation in Berne has generously contributed to the project by covering the major expenses involved in organising the workshop in Geneva and the costs related to the production of a camera-ready manuscript. This grant is acknowledged with pleasure and appreciation. We are also indebted to the institutes with which the authors of the component studies included here are associated for their valuable contributions in kind to this project. Special thanks are due to the Institut universitaire d'études du développement (IUED) in Geneva and the EADI Secretariat for its hospitality, in opening its premises for the workshop in late April 1997. The fertile interaction between administrators and researchers at that workshop resulted in a significant strengthening of almost all the papers that are now presented in this volume.

From the very beginning, the project has had the privilege of being integrated in the research programmes of the IUED in Geneva and the Norwegian Institute of International Affairs (NUPI) in Oslo and has benefited from their institutional support. The project has, in its final stages, benefited from the editorial support of Eilert Struksnes and the efficient secretarial support of Liv Høivik, who has produced the camera-ready manuscript. Warm thanks also go to Wendy Davies for language revision and assistance in editing the present volume.

1

Coherence of Policies Towards Developing Countries: Approaching the Problematique

JACQUES FORSTER AND OLAV STOKKE

I. INTRODUCTION

In the early 1990s, the issue of policy coherence towards developing countries came to the fore in the international donor community. In December 1991, a high-level meeting of the Development Assistance Committee (DAC) of the Organisation for Economic Co-operation and Development (OECD) called for development concerns to be taken into consideration in all dimensions of North–South relations: macro-economic policies, trade, export credits, tied aid, direct investments, agriculture, the environment, migration (including policy on refugees), the arms trade and drugs [*OECD, 1992: 31 ff*]. The perspective was, necessarily, that of donor governments. The main concern was that aid should be effective and that the policies and the aid-giving practices of different donors *vis-à-vis* a recipient government should be coherent and not conflicting. However, policy coherence does not operate in a political vacuum; the objectives set for a coherent donor policy constitute the most crucial issue.

Nation states have increasingly become interdependent. Although the tendency towards globalisation and that towards regionalisation may entail competing perspectives, both processes produce interdependence, especially within the economic area. The outcome of the Uruguay Round both demonstrates the increasing globalisation of economies and accentuates this process. Within a globalised economy, regional interdependence has grown even tighter, as exemplified by European economic and political integration, with the European Union (EU) as the dynamo. Similar processes have taken place within the political domain and even within the cultural field, triggered, in particular, by the information technology revolution.

Within the political and cultural areas, however, autonomous mani-festations are more widespread and potent.

Although all nation states are involved in these processes, some are more affected than others. While some national and regional systems are quite autonomous, others – particularly the weakest countries in the South – are vulnerable. Integration of these systems into the glo-bal (market) economy has been seen as the best, if not the only, way out of poverty and maldevelopment from the perspective of the pre-dominant development ideology of the 1980s and 1990s.

However, perspectives differ with the setting and immediate and long-term interests of stakeholders and decision-makers. Govern-ments operate on their own as well as within regional and global arenas in pursuit of what they perceive as their national interest. How-ever, institutions at these various levels tend to become actors in their own right. This applies to both global organisations, such as the Bretton Woods institutions (BWIs) and the various United Nations (UN) organisations and agencies, and to regional organisations, such as the European Union (EU). Organisations may exert an influence on policy outcomes beyond that of their separate members [*Cohen et al., 1972*]. However, some governments have greater influence over the policies of these organisations than others; in some cases, this is reflected even in the constitutions of these organisations.

Within national political systems, framework conditions and main actors differ from those of the international level with variations from one national system to another, too. Political processes are character-ised by competition (and co-operation) between stakeholders repre-senting different values and interests. As in international systems, not all actors carry the same political weight, nor do they have equal access to decision-makers at various levels. And the arena for deci-sion-making may differ from one policy area to another, each arena having actors who may share a world view that emerges from the spe-cialised agenda and predominant objectives set for the particular pol-icy area. Achieving policy coherence within the complex setting of an open, pluralistic political system is therefore a demanding challenge.

In most systems, the political and administrative leadership at the centre aspires towards coherence, although more so within national political systems than within international and regional systems, where government representatives tend to represent competing natio-nal stakeholders rather than the core of the organisation. The same is true of regional organisations that have reached a high degree of economic and political integration, such as the EU, with the administration in Brussels constituting the core, although more manifest for some EU member governments than for others. Tension exists between the centre's aspiration towards coherence and centrifugal forces at lower levels of the political and administrative system. Increased policy coherence may strengthen some values and interests and weaken others, affecting the various stakeholders differently. In turn, this may influence their attitude towards coherence as well as their preference of arena for decision-making.

It follows that attainment of policy coherence will be affected by systemic factors such as, in particular, a coherent norm system, procedures for the implementation of these norms, including negotiation, mediation and conflict resolution, and institutions responsible for policy decision-making, monitoring and enforcement of the norms set. Such regime factors are poorly developed when it comes to policy coherence within the political-administrative systems both of donor states and of regional and international organisations; they are, almost by definition, least developed within international (multilateral and regional) organisations [Krasner, 1982; Young, 1991; Keohane, 1993].

In 1991, the high-level DAC meeting recognised the need for effective participation by developing countries in the global economy and their co-operation in confronting global challenges and in solving regional security issues. Enlightened self-interest was made explicit, particularly the longer-term interest of OECD countries in an effective functioning of the global economy and the solving of other problems that are global in scope, including the threat to environmental sustainability, and those associated with orderly political and economic transitions in many parts of the globe. In the view of the DAC, such conditions could not be obtained without substantial political, economic and social development in the South. Development co-operation, in the form of financial and technical assistance to help these countries in building national capacities, remained essential. Because of their significant impact, it was also considered crucial that OECD macro-economic, trade, financial and others policies towards the South were part of an integrated approach in support of developing countries. The DAC opted for broad coherence across this range of OECD country policies as a central feature of a larger economic and political framework for managing global challenges over the coming decades [OECD, 1992: 31]. This common ground is further elaborated in a strategy report adopted five years later, Shaping the 21st Century: The Contribution of Development Co-operation [OECD, 1996a].

Development co-operation, although governed by overall objectives, covers a broad spectrum of relations and issues. Within a donor country, policy coherence may be sought within the framework of the aid policy. This, however, constitutes only one pillar of the donor country's relations with developing countries; coherence may also be sought within the broader framework of trade, migration, global climate, and other policies, and in other aspects of the domestic and foreign policy. At the international level, coherence may be sought within the framework of donors' policies, involving both their aid policies and their broader policies towards the developing countries. The DAC called for coherence in each of these domains. Coherence may be sought between donor and recipient policies, too; it is opted for this in the rhetoric of donor governments.

The concept of policy coherence may be new; but what it is about, aims and some of its implications, are well known. In this Chapter, the various notions associated with the concept will be explored in search of a definition (section II). The rationale will be identified (section III), the main obstacles explored (section IV), and the main mechanisms associated with the search for greater coherence at various levels discussed (section V). Potentials and limitations, achievements and shortcomings will be discussed in the concluding section (VI).

II. DEFINING THE CONCEPT AND ITS CONTEXTS

Policy coherence is not yet an established concept in the literature. However, if one accepts the observation by Fukasaku and Hirata [*1995: 20*] that '"policy coherence" refers to the consistency of policy objectives and instruments applied by OECD countries individually or collectively in the light of their combined effects on developing countries', it becomes clear that policy coherence has been on the agenda since aid was introduced. The focus has been on the overall impact of policies of industrial countries and regional and multilateral organisations on developments in the South. Policy co-ordination has been considered a major instrument to achieve increased coherence. In this volume, the concept is broadened to include policies of the recipient side of the development co-operation relationship.[1]

(1) A Rational Choice Approach

There is no set definition of policy coherence. This is demonstrated by the authors of this volume who between them focus on policy coherence in different contexts, primarily that of national and regional donor policies. However, there is broad agreement as to the need to

---

1. Sections II–V draw on Stokke [*1999:chaps 2–5*].

specify a number of parameters in order to make the concept opera-tive. These parameters relate to

(1) the ultimate objective of policy coherence – coherence for what and for whom?
(2) coherence between the various stages of policy formulation and implementation – between motives and objectives, between objectives and strategies and mechanisms for policy implementa-tion, and between motives and objectives and actual outcomes and impacts; and
(3) the levels at which coherence is to be achieved.

Coherence is often conceived of within a rational choice model related, in particular, to a defined administrative system. The core features are that, within this particular system,

(a) *objectives* should be formulated in clear terms and harmonised. The implication is that objectives within a policy framework, for instance the development co-operation policy, should be inter-nally consistent. Objectives pursued within other policy frame-works of the system – for instance trade, the environment, migra-tion, security – should be attuned to each other or, as a minimum, not be conflicting;
(b) *strategies and mechanisms* should be attuned to the objectives and, as a minimum, not conflict with them or the intentions and motives on which they rest; and
(c) the *outcome* should correspond with intentions and objectives or, as a minimum, not conflict with them.

(2) Four Systemic Frameworks of Policy Coherence
Applied to relations with developing countries, policy coherence or incoherence relates to four more or less distinct systemic frameworks, two of which relate to policies established within the national system of a donor country (although affecting its foreign policy) and the remaining two to policies established within various international systems, involving bilateral, regional and multilateral arenas.[2]

---

2. In this book, authors have established a typology of levels and types of policy coherence adapted to the specific needs of their research. Paul Hoebink led the way in this respect with a paper presented to the sessions of the Working Group on Aid Policy and Performance during the EADI General Conference in Vienna in Septem-ber 1996, when this project was launched (*[Hoebink, 1996]* – a revised version is included as Chapter 10 of this volume). The typology that follows is that of the editors of this volume. It does not attempt to reflect the diversity of conceptual approaches contained in subsequent chapters.

(a) Coherence of aid policy. The aid of a donor country is channelled through many different systems. Distinction may be made between the following:

- state-to-state bilateral aid, provided directly to a recipient government, or rather to many governments, each with framework conditions that may be specific to that country, and with different aspirations, objectives and priorities;
- bilateral aid, which is also channelled through the private sector and non-governmental organisations (NGOs) – in particular, donor country firms and NGOs, but also international non-governmental organisations (INGOs) and even recipient country NGOs;
- multilateral aid, provided through several regional and global international organisations. Distinction may be made between the United Nations system and the development finance institutions. In the case of many European donor countries, a substantial share of their aid is channelled through the European Union (EU).

The effectiveness of these various systems, in realising the objectives set and agreed upon, varies extensively. This constitutes part of the coherence problematique: good intentions alone are insufficient; lack of ability or capacity often represents constraints both on the aid-providing side and within the recipient systems. At times such constraints may be prohibitive. In aid relations, the donor may be able to improve its own delivery capacity through better planning and quality control (monitoring, evaluation). The means to improve these qualities within recipient systems are more limited (and constitute an objective for aid, *inter alia*, in terms of support for institutional development). In some cases the very rationale for aid may constitute a stumbling block; from the perspective of policy coherence, an explicit poverty-orientation for aid (in terms of directing state-to-state aid to the poorest countries) may be considered dysfunctional if aid effectiveness is the prime concern since a weakly developed public administration is part of the poverty syndrome.

Aid is also provided for a host of different purposes: some are related to a particular sector (health, education, water, communications, agriculture, etc.); others are cross-sectoral (rural development, environmental improvement); still others are related to particular groups (the poor, children, women). It goes without saying that aid provided for one purpose may impact negatively on others. For aid within sectors, the perspective may easily be narrowed down to sector-specific objectives; what may make sense given the perspective of one sector may well conflict with policies within other sectors, thus creating a coherence problem. Cross-sectoral issues are less exposed to such inconsistencies.

(b) Coherence of policies towards the South. Aid constitutes only one dimension of a donor country's relations with countries in the South; several of its policies within other areas affect developing countries (trade, migration, arms sales, etc.), directly or indirectly. Even policies considered entirely domestic – related to the internal distribution of resources, such as subsidies for domestic agricultural or industrial production – influence these relations: they may improve the ability of home production to compete favourably with imports, thereby reducing the income that developing countries derive from exports.

Policies outside the realm of aid relations may counteract objectives pursued through aid and therefore, by definition, be incoherent from the perspective of development co-operation. The aid policy may, by the same token, be considered incoherent from the perspective of institutions with a responsibility for non-aid relations with developing countries. For instance, guidelines set for aid (such as one prescribing that aid should be targeted to poor social strata in the least developed countries (LLDCs)) may be considered incoherent from the perspective of the donor's trade interests. Exporters and investors will not consider these countries as the most attractive business partners: restrictions in the use of ODA may therefore be considered incoherent from the perspective of business promotion. What might appear coherent from one perspective (promotion of social and economic development in the South) may appear incoherent from another (promotion of the donor's trade). The perspective therefore matters.

Some aspects of these 'other' policies (trade, environmental concerns, peace and conflict prevention, etc.) have increasingly been integrated in the objectives set for aid. This further complicates the issue, particularly when a new objective is included to facilitate domestic vested interests. The declared aim of these aspects of other policies is to promote development in the South. It becomes necessary to transcend a rhetoric which may camouflage incoherent policies.

At the level of international relations, two frameworks are particularly relevant in our context:

(c) Coherence of donors' policies towards the South, and of aid policy in particular. We started out from this framework, with particular reference to the DAC high-level meeting in 1991. As for the individual donors, we may distinguish between

- policies that affect the South directly, in that they concern various dimensions of the international relations of industrialised countries (such as trade, migration, foreign investment, sales of military equipment, human rights); and
- domestic policies that affect the South only indirectly, in that, although they are not specifically geared towards developing countries, they may have an effect on their development. Domestic environmental, agricultural, defence and human rights policies are examples of policies of this type.

At this level, the credibility of industrial countries *vis-à-vis* developing countries is also at stake as well as their legitimacy as intervening donors. Important gaps can exist between recommendations made to developing countries and the policies followed by industrialised countries in the same areas (environmental policies or the opening-up of certain sectors to international competitors are cases in point). Global, regional or bilateral levels are involved with reference to these policies.

(d) Donor–recipient coherence, with particular reference to development policies. This applies to bilateral state-to-state relations involving development assistance, to relations between regional donor institutions and governments and regional institutions in the South, and to such relations involving global multilateral institutions – whatever the degree of integration.

It follows that objectives pursued within one of these policy frameworks may contradict objectives pursued within others, resulting in policy incoherence. As a general rule, the more stakeholders there are involved, the greater the probability of a conflict of interest, resulting in incoherent policies. We will return to this in section IV.

(3) Policy Coherence: State-of-Affair and Process Perspectives

In the above, policy coherence and incoherence is implicitly considered as *a state of affairs*: at a certain point in time, policies within a policy area or between different policy areas, within national or international frameworks (four have been identified), may or may not be coherent. Policies within one policy area or between different policy areas may be mutually supportive or may conflict with each other. Coherence may, accordingly, be defined as a policy whose *objectives*, within a given policy framework, are internally consistent and attuned to objectives pursued within other policy frameworks of the system – as a minimum, these objectives should not be conflicting; where *strategies and mechanisms* are attuned to the objectives, they should, as a

23

minimum, not conflict with the objectives or with the intentions and motives on which these are based; and where the *outcome* is corresponding to the intentions and objectives, it should, as a minimum, not conflict with these.

This definition would, at a general level, guide what to look for, with particular attention directed to inconsistencies. Although the two perspectives overlap to some extent, *a process perspective*, where the focus is on the organisational set-up ('regime') to attain policy coherence, adds a dynamic dimension.

Objectives would also be the point of departure in a process perspective: they should be formulated in clear terms and harmonised both within a given policy framework and between different frameworks. Then the main focus changes from the content of policies to the governmental aspects: the rules set, and the institutions and procedures for forming and implementing the policies. To what extent is the need for policy co-ordination explicitly woven into the system in terms of procedures and regular or ad hoc committees which represent the main concerns (stakes) at work within a particular policy area or between different policy areas? To what extent is a system for monitoring policy coherence established? To what extent are procedures in place to solve conflicts between competing or conflicting concerns (for instance, between ministries with different primary objectives, which may even be conflicting in given contexts)?

Both perspectives may help to illuminate trends. If policies, as stated and implemented, constitute the point of departure for assessing trends, the state of affairs of these policies may be compared at different points in time and indicate the direction: towards increased coherence or incoherence. Likewise, the institutional set-up may reflect the determination of a government – or an international (global or regional) organisation – to follow rhetoric with action: after a statement of commitment to greater policy coherence, have the institutional competence and capacity to follow up been improved?

III. THE RATIONALE

Policy incoherence constitutes the main rationale for seeking coherence. Conflicting interests and values are the main cause of incoherence within most systems and at most levels. Such conflicts are often replicated – and reinforced – at the level of public administration, making incoherence rather than coherence the rule. Some (government) policies may be deliberately incoherent in order simultaneously to accommodate conflicting values or interests. A distinction may therefore be made between intended and unintended incoherence. Although decisions by governing bodies may be considered rational within the context of decision-makers seeking compromises between conflicting parties, outcomes may not be considered rational from a broader, systemic perspective where effectiveness of goal attainment is the major justification for seeking policy coherence or, as a minimum, ensuring that policies are not conflicting.

(1) Compartmentalisation of Politics: Perspectives Differ from One System to Another

Policy formulation and implementation at an international or national level involve many systems which may relate to each other both horizontally and vertically. Within each system, a predominant 'world view' prevails, based on the overall objectives pursued and an ever-shifting balance between the values and interests of major stakeholders. These systems are themselves part of wider systems. What is considered a rational choice will be system-specific and may, accordingly, vary from one system to another.

The point of departure therefore becomes all-important. In the previous section, four contextual frameworks have been identified, all of them containing a large number of separate systems. The complexity was indicated only with regard to one of the frameworks, the aid policy of a donor country, where reference is made to the various channels of the aid delivery system and the different purposes and target groups to which aid is directed. Although overall objectives are set for aid, the various systems through which aid is channelled may be founded on widely different world views. The same may be said of the aid administration itself, including the aid agency: for example, the predominant world view within a section concerned with promoting human rights may differ markedly from that prevailing in a section concerned with promoting exports through mixed credits. Predominant world views influence decisions along with values and interests, and constitute a framework for rational choices.

Politics is compartmentalised. The predominant logic within the sub-systems reflects perceptions, interests and values of the actors within the particular system unit. It follows that the various systems (such as administrative units) within the hierarchical order (such as an aid administration) may represent different logics. However, they are also part of a wider system, also with a distinct logic, expressed in terms of overall justifications and objectives for the total activity; this logic represents the outcome of decision-making processes that have involved a different set of actors.

From a top-down perspective (from which, to a large extent, but not exclusively, the concern for policy coherence is driven), the logic of sub-systems may represent constraints to policy cohesion at higher systemic levels. To illustrate the point: an administrative unit concerned with human development, such as health, education or refugees, may find it frustrating to follow up expectations from the top to make use of services or commodities purchased at a high cost at home in order to promote domestic exports or employment if this would reduce the benefits for recipients (less health or relief for money). This may, in turn, affect the actual follow-up, particularly if such discrete signals from the top run contrary to the rhetoric or stated policy. From a bottom-up perspective, the logic of the wider system may, by the same token, represent constraints to policy cohesion within the sub-system.

It follows that policy coherence may not be easily achieved even when systems within a hierarchical order are involved, particularly because of the compartmentalisation of politics and public administration. The challenge becomes even greater when systems at the same (horizontal) level are involved and where the hierarchical order is weak and diffuse, if present at all. This is the reality that confronts most efforts towards policy coherence. In our context, it applies within all four frameworks identified, particularly, in rising order, for the national policy of a donor country *vis-à-vis* developing countries, the policy of donor countries, and the coherence of donor–recipient policies.

(2) The Rationale for Coherence of Donors' Policies Towards Developing Countries

Policy coherence in development co-operation was first made an important theme at the level of donor co-operation. Reference has been made to the high-level meeting of the DAC in 1991 and the follow-up through the strategy paper five years later [*OECD, 1992; 1996a*]. The policy was driven by a core institution for donor co-operation.

This was not an entirely new policy on the part of the OECD nor for other donor 'owned' organisations such as the Bretton Woods institutions (BWIs). Throughout the 1980s and the early 1990s, donors made efforts to co-ordinate their policies towards developing countries. During the 1980s, the BWIs were at the helm, planning and implementing this co-ordination, with particular reference to first-generation conditionality related to structural adjustment policies. In the late 1980s and early 1990s, they played a less prominent role in forming and implementing second-generation conditionality related, in particular, to democracy, human rights and good government. The initiative moved increasingly to major bilateral donors and the European Community, with the DAC playing a role, too [*Stokke, 1995; Hewitt and Killick, 1996*].

By introducing the new concept of policy coherence, the OECD succeeded in ensuring a prominent role for itself in its old drive for increased co-ordination of donors' policies and in setting the agenda for this co-ordination. The issue has been driven by the DAC ever since; it has been given prominence in the yearly reports of the DAC Chair.[3] There will always be competition between institutions in setting the international agenda; taking the lead in policy co-ordination, therefore, also serves a self-promotional purpose. However, the rationale for policy coherence, from the perspective of the DAC, is much wider – although complex.

The justification given for a policy should always be taken seriously, even if, as is usually the case, there are also hidden agendas. From a DAC perspective, the stated rationale of policy coherence relates to rational choice concerns from a political and administrative perspective. The development assistance of donor governments (and multilateral agencies) should be better co-ordinated in order to be more effective and efficient *vis-à-vis* its developmental objectives. Waste through duplication should be avoided and the development assistance of one donor should not counteract that of another. This applies not only to their aid and aid policy, but also to their policies within other areas such as trade, investments and security [*OECD, 1992; 1996a; 1997*].[4]

---

3. See, for instance, the overview of the DAC Chair in the 1996 DAC report [*OECD, 1997: 8–10*], subsequent to the 1996 strategy document. The commitment to greater co-ordination and coherence is explicitly related to the objectives set out in the strategy document – 'the vision'. In his 1997 report [*OECD, 1998a: 14*], 'the basic need to bring development co-operation squarely within a coherent policy environment in relations between industrialised and developing countries, and a need to give development objectives far greater weight than at present' is listed among the four priorities for 1998.
4. The commitment of the DAC members to policy coherence is summed up as follows [*OECD, 1996b: 18*]:

> We should aim for nothing less than to assure that the entire range of relevant industrialised country policies are consistent with and do not undermine development objectives. We will work with our colleagues in the broad collaborative effort now underway within the OECD to examine linkages between OECD Members and the developing countries, building on the promising work on this theme completed in 1994 [*OECD, 1995*]. We are confident that we can do more than just avoid policy conflict. We will work to assure that development co-operation and other linkages between industrialised and developing countries are mutually reinforcing.

However, aspirations go beyond considerations of effectiveness and efficiency. The vision takes as a point of departure that in the year 2000, four-fifths of world's population will be found in the developing countries. Although conditions will be improving for most, the number in absolute poverty and despair will still be growing. The industrialised countries have a strong *moral imperative* to respond to the extreme poverty and human suffering that still afflict more than one billion people, and a strong *self-interest* in fostering increased prosperity in developing countries. 'Our solidarity with the people of all countries causes us to seek to expand the community of interests and values needed to manage the problems that respect no borders – from environmental degradation and migration, to drugs and epidemic diseases. All people are made less secure by the poverty and misery that exist in the world. Development matters' [*OECD, 1996b: 1*]. Three objectives are highlighted [*ibid.: 8–11*]:

(1) *Economic well-being*: The proportion of people living in extreme poverty in developing countries should be reduced by at least one-half by 2015;

(2) *Social development*: There should be substantial progress in primary education (universal primary education in all countries by 2015), gender equality (*inter alia*, eliminating gender disparity in primary and secondary education by 2005), basic health care and family planning; and

(3) *Environmental sustainability*: There should be a current national strategy for sustainable development, in the process of implementation, in every country by 2005, so as to ensure that current trends in the loss of environmental resources – forests, fisheries, fresh water, climate, soils, biodiversity, stratospheric ozone, the accumulation of hazardous substances and other major indicators

---

In his 1997 report, the DAC Chair gave high priority to more intensive efforts to improve co-ordination and coherence within the OECD [*OECD, 1998a: 14*]:

This will involve addressing questions of coherence and consistency between bilateral and multilateral channels of co-operation, between public and private financing for development and, most difficult of all, between the development policies of industrial countries and their policies concerning investment, trade, agriculture, the environment, arms sales and other aspects of relations with the developing countries.

At the DAC 1991 high-level meeting, which initiated this process, attention was directed to the following seven specific issues of policy coherence [*OECD, 1992: 38–46*]: environment, migration, science and technology, military expenditure, export credits and tied aid, and regional co-operation.

– are effectively reversed at both global and national levels by 2015.

These objectives are linked to more qualitative objectives such as a commitment to promote social integration by fostering societies that are stable, safe and just and based on the promotion and protection of all human rights, democratic accountability and the rule of law as key elements of integrated development strategies. 'Investment of development resources in democratic governance will contribute to more accountable, transparent and participatory societies conducive to development progress' [*OECD, 1996b: 11*].

The substance of the policy which is established as a basis for policy coherence involving DAC countries, in terms of objectives, strategies and guidelines, was first outlined by the high-level meeting in 1991 and further developed in the strategy paper of 1996. Development concerns loom large, although the overall foreign policy concerns of DAC governments are also involved. However, the overall perspective is that of development in the South, based on the objectives traditionally set for aid refined by those coming to the fore in the late 1980s and early 1990s: poverty alleviation being the major concern along with human rights, democracy (with an emphasis on participation), and good government. The hegemonic ideology of the day, market liberalism, is also part and parcel of the policy. Still, an important observation deserves to be highlighted: a developmental perspective prevails over conflicting, self-centred concerns [*OECD, 1992; 1996a; 1997*].

At the level of regional co-operation in Europe, policy coherence in development co-operation becomes particularly important because of the institutional arrangements: aid from EU member states is partly provided bilaterally through national aid agencies and partly channelled through the EU Commission (and global multilateral agencies). This structure makes policy incoherence particularly visible and inconvenient. It also illuminates the core problematique of policy coherence when several systems are involved and where the hierarchical order is diffuse, if it exists at all. The concern for policy coherence therefore also becomes instrumental for the European project and is used for that purpose by the centre in the effort to forge a common foreign and security policy. From the EU perspective, this may constitute as important a rationale for policy coherence as the traditional justifications outlined above with reference to the DAC.

(3) The Rationale for Coherence of Policies Towards Developing Countries of Individual Donor Countries

At the level of global politics, governments remain the main actors – although major international non-governmental organisations (INGOs) increasingly enter the stage and transnational corporations carry weight. This also applies at the level of regional politics in Europe although some authority is transferred to or shared with Brussels. As noted, organisations at both levels carry an influence of their own over and above that of their individual members [*Cohen et al., 1972*]. The strong influence over evolving development ideology by international organisations, through their major publications, may illustrate the point with reference to the development discourse; this applies especially to the World Bank (the annual *World Development Report* in particular), the United Nations (the annual *Human Development Report* in particular) and the OECD (the annual DAC report *Development Co-operation* in particular). However, ultimate power still resides with national governments.

At the level of national politics the main rationale for policy coherence is much the same as the one identified above with reference to the global level – a concern for effectiveness in attaining overall policy objectives related to developing countries and North–South relations. However, objectives at this level, even developmental objectives, may be different from those agreed upon at the global level; the political environment, major stakeholders and decision-makers are different, too, involving government institutions as well as civil society and, ultimately, voters.

At the level of public administration, sub-systems, mostly along sectoral political and administrative dividing lines, are at work – each with its specific overall objective, stakeholders and decision-makers. Within a predominantly horizontal government structure, the Prime Minister (and the PM's Office) represents the hierarchical dimension along with a few other ministers (and ministries), such as finance and foreign affairs. For most of the other ministries, perspectives differ; for the most part, these perspectives are linked to domestic interest groups with which the sector ministry interacts.

The rationale of these separate units differs and may conflict with the logic of the national system in the area under scrutiny. For instance, the trade interests of a donor country may, at the international level, compete or conflict with similar interests of other donor countries; these interests may also conflict with the development interests of recipient countries. Furthermore, the domestic export interests of a donor country may successfully compete with recipient interests for aid monies.

A wide range of policies of a donor country, administered by separate ministries, affect developing countries and North–South relations in general, directly or indirectly. In most donor countries, the administration of development assistance is also divided between several administrative units, even several ministries, with a weakly developed hierarchical co-ordination.

From the perspective of the political and administrative leadership of the policy area concerned – the minister of foreign affairs or of development co-operation (and the PM) – it makes little sense that policies pursued by the various units under her or his responsibility are at odds. Nor does it make sense that autonomous actors through whom aid money is channelled – such as those of the private sector, including NGOs – should pursue policies that are at odds with each other or with those pursued in bilateral state-to-state co-operation or within multilateral agencies. From this perspective, particularly that of a minister for development co-operation, it does not make sense that other ministries should pursue policies that are at odds with the aid policy.

(4) The Rationale for Donor–Recipient Policy Coherence

We have already discussed the rationale for policy co-ordination among donors at global and regional levels, involving donor governments. There is a similar rationale for policy coherence between donor and recipient governments. In both cases, policy co-ordination involves politics among nations. The problematique involving donor–recipient co-ordination is different from the former for one major reason: the inherent asymmetrical power relationship, particularly when aid is involved.

From a donor perspective, it makes sense that aid, which is supposed to fulfil overall objectives generated in the donor country, is attuned to objectives and priorities set by the recipient government. If this problematique is not confined to the art of aid rhetoric, quite serious problems arise, not least because economic, social, cultural and, accordingly, political framework conditions are so divergent between donor and recipient governments, particularly where the LLDCs are involved.

From the donor and recipient perspective alike, the rationale for policy coherence is clear: aid is most effective and efficient if integrated with the development plans and priorities of the recipient government as an additional resource to those generated domestically.

This is in accordance with current mainstream philosophy; during the 1990s, aid providers have subscribed to the need for participation and 'ownership' on the part of recipients – as reflected in the drive for coherence within the DAC, too [*OECD, 1992; 1996a; 1997*]. The sustainability of aid-supported activities is also involved; if not integrated in the recipient's priorities, the activities would fade away when aid ends.

However, for a variety of reasons, the optimal situation seldom prevails. On the donor side, domestic concerns may set a 'national interest' stamp on aid that conflicts with 'development interests', even 'national interests', as conceived on the recipient side. The recipient government may still agree to the aid because it is considered a 'free' resource. On the recipient side, a self-seeking administration may be in place – corrupting power as well as aid. The development perspectives and ideologies of donor and recipient may differ, too. Rhetoric cannot make such unpleasant realities dwindle. What – if any – is the answer?

In the early 1970s, some Scandinavian governments went quite far in living up to their rhetoric of recipient-oriented aid in their implementation: for utilitarian reasons referred to above, coupled with ethical reasons associated with the sovereignty principle, they deemed that those affected by aid should also decide on its uses. Looking back, Gus Edgren [*1984*] referred to the 'flower-power period' of Swedish development co-operation. Although the rhetoric lingered on, the realities of the 1980s and 1990s look quite different: in stark contrast to the rhetoric and lessons learned[5], donors prescribed policy reforms by recipient governments as a condition for aid, first related to their economic policy and then to their administrative and political system – in the first place, structural adjustment, human rights, democracy and good government. This adds up to a policy coherence on premises set by the donors.

If this is the reality hidden behind the demand for increased policy coherence among donors and a rhetoric of recipient ownership and participation, question marks are queuing. What is the sustainability of a policy that is governed from the outside – good intentions aside? As observed by Martin Doornbos [*1995*], one effect of the various

5. See, for instance, the 1996 DAC strategy paper which, under the sub-heading 'Making Aid Work Better', observes that '... one of the key lessons about development co-operation is that donor-driven initiatives rarely take root and that developing countries and their people must be at the centre of any effective system' [*OECD, 1996b: 15*]. In line with this analysis, the DAC governments commit themselves 'to better co-ordinate our aid efforts in line with the strategies of our partner countries. ... [The] developing country should be the co-ordinator of development co-operation wherever possible' [*ibid.: 17*].

external initiatives and involvements in providing 'good governance' might, paradoxically, be that the capacity for policy-making and implementation of Third World governments will be weakened rather than strengthened as a consequence of their loss of policy initiative. And what about the internal coherence of a donor policy which aims at promoting democracy and at the same time removes the power of the recipient government to decide over the most vital questions on the political agenda – in first-generation conditionality, the economic policy to be pursued?

The crucial point is not the rationale for coherence between policies (aspirations, objectives, strategies and means) on the donor and the recipient side; both sides of a development co-operation relationship might agree on this point. What matters is who has the upper hand: who should be the co-ordinator? The donor, or the recipient? And on what conditions? The ideal situation would presuppose identical objectives on the part of donor and recipient. This seldom applies, if at all. In practice, the asymmetrical power relationship is at work to strike the balance in favour of donor co-ordination, but also utilitarian and ethical concerns are at work on the donor side.

IV. OBSTACLES: CONFLICTING PERSPECTIVES, INTERESTS AND VALUES

Perspectives differ with the context. In section III, which explored the rationale for policy coherence, the main message was that when operationalised in concrete contexts, it differs from one system to another and from one level of a complex system to another. Predominant aspirations, objectives, strategies and means are system-specific and may therefore vary from one system to another. The compartmentalisation of politics implies that different stakeholders, representing different interests and values, are at work within the various policy arenas. The analytical framework established in section III constitutes the framework for the discussion in this section, too. We will focus on structural aspects in an attempt to identify the main obstacles to a coherent policy within and between the four frameworks identified – the development co-operation policy of a donor country, the policies of a donor *vis-à-vis* the South, donors' aid policies and donor–recipient policies.

(1) Politics Among Nations and Competing National Interests

Common overall objectives for the main donor governments are set out in the 1996 DAC strategy document. To a large extent these aims reflect the stated objectives pursued through first- and second-generation aid conditionality. In addition to the traditional development objectives set for aid, such as economic growth and social development, attention has increasingly been directed towards environmental concerns, human rights, democracy and good government. The main emphasis is increasingly on poverty alleviation.

On the surface, therefore, bilateral donors and multilateral agencies to a great extent agree on aspirations, objectives and strategies. This is nothing new; as shown by Göran Hydén [1994], paradigms tend to change and move in the same direction at almost the same time for all donors although, as argued elsewhere [Stokke, 1996], a development paradigm may continue to exert influence after it has lost its hegemonic position to a competing ideology – development paradigms tend to live parallel lives.

However, development assistance is part of the foreign policy of donor governments and used to promote national interests. This applies, in particular, to major governments aspiring towards global or regional hegemony; during the cold war period, the aid policy of the superpowers was driven by security interests and can best be explained within the dominant paradigm of international relations after the Second World War, that of realpolitik, with roots that stretch back to Hans Morgenthau [1948]. Although the aid policy of some Western middle powers can be better explained within the paradigm of humane internationalism [Stokke, 1989a; 1996], elements of self-interest are at play even if they may have a longer-term perspective and be more related to global or international common goods than is the case for the major powers.

The national interests of individual donor countries, pursued by means of development assistance, may differ, compete and conflict. In addition to the declared policy reflected in the OECD strategy paper [1996a], bilateral donor governments have hidden agendas where less lofty interests are pursued. Attaining policy coherence may therefore be difficult when interests conflict. This applies to the multilateral system, too. Member governments also pursue their national interest within these systems; in addition, the various multilateral organisations compete among themselves for influence and resources.

The urge for more co-ordination is not confined to aid policy; as noted, the DAC's ambition is that development objectives should be taken into consideration in all areas that affect North–South relations (such as trade, investments, migration, environments and refugees). Within this broader framework, conflict between interests is multiplied. Although norm-setting has taken place at the 'global' level, involving donors, the actual follow-up takes place at the level of regional co-operation (EU) and at the national level of donor countries.

Regional co-operation within the EU, involving aid donors who between them provide more than half of all development assistance, finds itself at a crossroads. The centre and most major member governments are opting for a common foreign and security policy; however, the national interests of member governments are at play both at national and union levels. These national interests and values are not confined to the development agenda, nor necessarily pulling in the same direction.

(2) Competition between Interests and Values within Donor Countries

Within the national setting of a donor country, there are competition for ODA resources. Competitors do not even have to disguise their claims with the justification that the activities are conducive to development in the South. Promotion of exports or employment at home may be equally effective justifications, particularly when the economy is under pressure. Adaptation to such pressures may conflict with the overall objectives set for development co-operation. It may even change the focus of the aid policy – from development needs in poor countries to pressing domestic concerns at home – giving the development co-operation concept a new flavour. The urge for greater policy coherence may well be used for this purpose, too.

Sectoral policies tend to have their own logic, as outlined in more detail in the previous section, and these may be conflicting. To avoid conflict, policies generated and implemented within systems that are compartmentalised need to be co-ordinated. Co-ordination, and accordingly coherence, is not easily obtained between systems that relate to each other horizontally and where hierarchical mechanisms are not in place or are weakly developed: in such systems the sectoral logic will persist. This is the more or less 'normal' state of affairs in most government administrations. However, hierarchical mechanisms of various kinds are also at work in all government systems. The centre, the PM (or President) and the PM's (or President's) staff in particular, plays a crucial role in this regard. In fact, policy coherence at the national level is almost totally dependent on the authority and dedication of the centre in curbing centrifugal forces, not least those emerging from interests and values based in sectoral logic.

How difficult this moderating and co-ordinating role may be in actual practice, when interest groups are involved, may be illustrated through a few examples related to policies towards developing countries. Donors feel that developing countries are using all too large a share of their scarce resources on maintaining a military capacity; for this reason, reduced spending for such purposes has been established as one of the criteria for aid allocations by some donors [*Stokke, 1995*]. For small and medium-sized industrial countries that run arms industries, exports become a necessity because of economics of scale: large production series are found necessary. Thus, two logics, driven by different interest groups, may be conflicting.

A similar, classic conflict often appears between 'ideal' values and 'commercial' interests. In the 1990s, democracy and political and civil human rights have become prominent objectives of both the foreign and development co-operation policies of several donor governments. In the early 1990s, some of the largest-growth economies (such as those of China and Indonesia), attractive from the perspective of exports and investments opportunities, had a poor performance with regard to democracy and human rights. Aid (in the form of mixed credits and the like) and technology transfers always lend an element of support to the regime of the day. This recognition has not prevented donor governments from supporting and promoting the efforts of industrialists and exporters to pursue their interests in these countries – also involving aid money.

At the end of section III, we commented on the rationale for policy coherence between donor and recipient governments. When it comes to policy implementation, the logics of the two perspectives easily conflict since it is perceptions, values and interests of different stakeholders that are at stake; such conflicts are often camouflaged by general, overall objectives and rhetoric. The main conflict, which has fundamental implications, remains unsettled: outside the realm of rhetoric, who is to decide what the policy and priorities should be – donor or recipient authorities? When aid is involved, on what conditions, if any, should aid be provided (or accepted)? The answers to these questions are bound to affect aid relations fundamentally.

Conflicting perspectives and interests between donor and recipient authorities can be illustrated at a somewhat less fundamental level, involving the value and substance of aid: namely, procurement tying of aid. It has been calculated that tying reduces the real value of aid in financial terms by 15–30 per cent [*Jepma, 1996*]. In addition, tied aid may be complicated and costly for the recipient to administer. The now classic case from Kenya, where a water development programme received 18 different types of pumps supplied by different donors who had tied their aid, may illustrate the point: the problems involved in running such a programme when servicing and spare parts are required are easily imaginable. Ill-adapted technologies may turn tied gifts into heavy real costs for a recipient.

So much for the economics of tied aid. In addition, aid tied to commodities or services of the donor may, at worst, have negative development effects in recipient countries since it is provided 'free' and may out-compete local products, producers, entrepreneurs and providers of services. This may apply to other mechanisms, too, such as that of mixed credits – the subsiding of donor country exports through the aid programme.

Aid-tying and mixed credits are both elements in a protectionist policy. Donors apply more direct measures in this regard in their trade policy, which may also affect development negatively and conflict with the interests of the recipient.

From the perspective of the development objectives set for aid, such manifestations represent policy incoherence both within the framework of the aid policy of the donor country concerned and within the framework of donor–recipient coherence. They provide good examples to sustain the main argument throughout this section: perspectives differ from one setting to another because the actors involved and the values and interests at stake differ and may conflict.

(3) Discrepancy between Commitments and Deeds: Weak Hierarchical Structures

Donors have, none the less, established a common framework for a coherent policy towards developing countries based on a common understanding of their best, long-term interest. What may be identified as the best overall interest from a long-term perspective may conflict with the immediate interest of some stakeholders within the system. The 1996 DAC strategy paper is viewed as a key document because the major donor countries are members of the OECD and the DAC is entrusted to play a central role in establishing norms and monitoring performance within this policy area. Norms, in terms of overall, long-term objectives, may facilitate action; however, in themselves they do not guarantee that a follow-up will take place. What mechanisms are in place to ensure follow-up?

In reality, at the OECD level very few mechanisms exist, other than the monitoring instrument. As already stated, it is up to the member governments to follow up DAC recommendations in their bilateral policy and in their capacity as members of regional (such as EU) and multilateral institutions. Few institutions that involve hierarchical co-ordination are at work at the 'global' level.

At the level of individual DAC member governments, relevant institutions include the cabinet, the Prime Minister and the PM's Office, and a few ministers (and ministries) with overall responsibility, such as finance and foreign affairs. However, hierarchical structures are weakly developed at this level, too. In most countries, the administration of development co-operation is concentrated in one ministry (foreign affairs or development co-operation), which ensures hierarchical co-ordination; however, as noted, compartmentalisation takes place even in such an organisational set-up (although exceptions exist, as illustrated with reference to France by Philippe Hugon in Chapter 4 of this volume).

Within the framework of donor–recipient co-operation, donor governments and multilateral aid agencies, including the World Bank (WB), give emphasis to 'ownership' by the recipient government and participation by those involved in the development process, concepts that are seen as preconditions for development. In actual practice, however, relations – and an eventual policy coherence – reflect asymmetrical power relations. This applies whether policy coherence is agreed bilaterally between governments or settled within contexts dominated by donors, for instance in consultative groups set up for each aid-recipient country, where representatives of the recipient government meet with the major donors under the chairmanship of the WB. Asymmetrical power relations also impact on non-aid relations, such as trade.

V. MECHANISMS TO ATTAIN POLICY COHERENCE

Confronted with the centrifugal forces that we have identified and structures that favour policy incoherence, what mechanisms are at work to ensure policy coherence – or may be established in order to attain policy coherence – within our four systemic frameworks? A key to the answer is provided when we consider centrifugal forces and structures that may make incoherence the 'normal' state of affairs: in order to obtain coherence, these processes have to be reversed. Competing and conflicting interests and values will not disappear by themselves; as far as possible they will have to be accommodated or harmonised. Such harmonisation has to be context-specific.

(1) Opting for an International Development Regime
Objectives constitute the crucial point of departure. Objectives may be taken for granted, as in the case of those established within a

38

certain framework at a certain point in time. In a setting where objectives are settled, the question is narrowed down to finding the ways and means of realising these objectives across systems and policy areas. Most discussion on policy coherence implicitly, if not explicitly, takes this point of departure. However, objectives are themselves context-specific and may indeed constitute the core problem: basically, incoherence stems from conflicting objectives. The question therefore is: how can joint objectives be achieved, across policy areas and policy frameworks? It follows that objectives cannot be taken for granted over time: the process aiming at increased coherence of the policies towards developing countries may lead to objectives far removed from those prevailing when the process was initiated. This may lead to some stakeholders 'dropping out', choosing instead to stick to their original objectives.

What mechanisms would enable agreement on objectives, strategies and means within a given system or policy area and also ensure follow-up? Regime theory may give guidance by identifying factors of critical importance: a regime is defined as a system of norms, objectives and rules formalised through some sort of agreement between most actors within the policy area, including the major ones; procedures for the implementation of these rules, including mediation and conflict resolution; and institutions responsible for policy-making, monitoring and enforcement of the rules set.[6] In our case, the problem is not limited to a specific issue-area; several issue-areas are involved. The coherence problematique may be issue-area specific, but the core problem consists of harmonising several issue-areas across a variety of systems.

The most crucial observation is that, at the level of international politics including development co-operation, only fragments of a global regime are presently at work. However, in some issue-areas, several components are established. This applies, for instance, to the new trade regime which is emerging after the Uruguay Round of negotiations – institutionalised with the World Trade Organisation (WTO) as the core.

Several components of a human rights regime have also been established. Rights have been codified in the Universal Declaration of Human Rights adopted by the UN General Assembly in 1948 and in a

---

6. For a mainstream definition, see Krasner [*1982: 185*]: 'International regimes are defined as principles, norms, rules and decision-making procedures around which actor expectations converge in a given issue-area.' See also Keohane [*1993: 28*]: '... regimes can be identified by the existence of explicit rules that are referred to in an affirmative manner by governments, even if they are not necessarily scrupulously observed.'

series of universal and regional charters and agreements ratified by governments.[7] International institutions exist to monitor performance and follow up on these rights. However, governments interpret rights and principles differently and give different priority to the various rights. From an international regime perspective, the basic weakness is that residual powers reside with individual governments: it is up to each government to monitor and follow up on violations – not comforting if the roots of the problem can be traced to the government itself.

Within several other issue-areas of relevance to the development agenda – such as democracy, environment, good governance – very few regime components are at present established even at the conceptual level. Let us take democracy as an example: at a high level of generalisation, democracy is broadly considered a value. This value is alluded to in the DAC 1996 strategy document. Political participation is the key word. However, there is no global consensus on the concept. Some interpret it in narrow terms, separating the political system from the economic and social system to which it is joined, and insisting that economic and social democracy should be separated from the question of governmental structure. Others find a definition that excludes the economic and social reality from the political totally unsatisfactory, omitting what is considered the most important task of democratic regimes.[8] Although broad agreement exists among DAC members about a 'minimalist' concept of democracy – such as the value of free and fair elections – there exist no joint programme for attaining these values world-wide and no institutions with competence or capacity to realise the norm.

---

7. The Universal Declaration of Human Rights was followed by the International Covenant for Civil and Political Rights and the International Covenant for Economic, Social and Cultural Rights. In addition, other treaties deal with specific categories of people, such as children, women and the mentally ill, or malpractice, such as torture, discrimination and disappearances. These treaties are ratified by most governments although some have expressed reservations with regard to individual sections.
8. For a 'classical' definition, separating the political system from the economic and social system to which it is joined, see Diamond *et al.* (eds.), [*1988-90, I-IV; II:xvi*], 'a system of government that meets three essential conditions: meaningful and extensive *competition* among individuals and organized groups (especially political parties) for all effective positions of government power, at regular intervals and excluding the use of force; a highly inclusive level of political participation in the selection of leaders and policies, at least through regular and free elections, such that no major (adult) social group is excluded; and a level of *civil and political liberties* – freedom of expression, freedom of the press, freedom to form and join organizations – sufficient to ensure the integrity of political competition and participation'. The authors admit (in line with Robert Dahl's concept *polyarchy* [*Dahl, 1971*]) that, confronted with the real world, the definition presents a number of problems because systems which broadly satisfy the criteria nevertheless do so to different degrees.

The same is true of other core objectives on the agenda for development co-operation and the wider agenda for North–South relations – including the very concept of development, defined as a human right.[9] Development theory and development paradigms have shifted over time [*Stokke, 1996*]; there is no globally agreed programme, nor a global regime capable of implementing such a programme.

However, there are fragments of a global development regime – particularly on the donor side. As observed above, DAC members have agreed on some basic objectives, norms and targets and most of them have also committed themselves to transfer resources (ODA) to developing countries. However, these commitments take the form of recommendations to the member governments. It is up to these governments to interpret and follow up on the recommendations: the DAC itself has no financial means to follow up its 'vision', it can only monitor the follow-up of member governments based on reports from these governments and its own research. Basically, therefore, these commitments by member governments may be withdrawn unilaterally – as demonstrated in the case of the internationally agreed volume target set for aid, 0.7 per cent of GNP. Few governments have ever met this target, and development assistance has declined steeply since the end of the cold war.[10] This does not imply that the commitments are without any value; it means, however, that the regime to bolster them is extremely fragile.

(2) In the Absence of a Fully-Fledged International Development Regime

At a less ambitious level, norm-setting occurs in the form of policy assessment, discussion, consultation and co-ordination, resulting in agreed advice and recommendations. At the level of global institutions, particularly the UN system, both the North and the South are

9. The concept of development, itself controversial, is given a variety of definitions. For a definition which commands a high degree of international consensus, see the UN General Assembly vote adopting the Declaration on the Right to Development (Resolution 41/128,04.12.1986): '... development is a comprehensive economic, social, cultural and political process, which aims at the constant improvement of the well-being of the entire population and of all individuals on the basis of their active, free and meaningful participation in development and in the fair distribution of benefits resulting therefrom' (Preamble, paragraph 2). The resolution was adopted by 147 votes to one (the United States) with eight governments abstaining.
10. While the DAC average performance in 1964 was 0.48 per cent of GNP in official development assistance (ODA), it had dropped to 0.30 per cent by 1994. In 1997, total aid was down to US$47 864 million, 0.22 per cent of GNP. Only four of the 21 DAC member countries met the 0.7 target – Denmark, Norway, the Netherlands and Sweden (only 21 of OECD's 29 member countries are members of the DAC, the EC making up its 22nd member) [*OECD, 1998b: 4*].

involved. There are several forums for policy co-ordination within this system, with particular reference to development co-operation; the UNDP is explicitly given this role and UNDP Roundtables are one of the instruments in this regard. However, overall policy co-ordination, involving all relations with countries in the South, is poorly developed: rhetoric aside, compartmentalisation seems strongly developed, as reflected in recent complex emergency operations, although joint committees and task forces are established to ensure policy coherence.

The development finance institutions have also taken on an active role in seeking policy coherence, again with particular reference to development co-operation, involving both bilateral and multilateral donors. The consultative groups established for individual recipient countries by the major donors, meeting in Paris under the chairmanship of the World Bank, represent an important instrument in this regard. Recommendations emerging from these meetings may be followed up by action (aid conditionality), if that should be necessary in this asymmetrical power relationship where the many aid providers are meeting the one recipient government; if the recipient country is small, poor, debt-ridden and aid-dependent, the asymmetrical power relationship is extreme. The regional development banks also represent meeting places for the co-ordination of aid between donors and governments of aid-recipient countries, involving norm-setting as well.

Norm-setting among donors takes place, in particular, within the framework of the DAC, where most industrialised donor countries are members, and in donor-owned global institutions such as the BWIs. As noted, even some follow-up of norms may occasionally take place within these institutions. At the global level, there is no lack of meeting places for donors and recipients to co-ordinate policies; donors also have several forums for policy co-ordination. However, as an international regime, donor co-ordination is weakly developed beyond norm-setting.

As noted earlier, the regional co-operation that is evolving within the EU finds itself in a process where the union institutions are increasingly sharing responsibility with those of member states in the area of foreign and security policy, including development co-operation. Although basically a form of co-operation where residual powers remain with member governments, the level of integration between the participating countries is higher and outcomes of policy co-ordination more committing than is the case in global, multilateral organisations – the prospect is that more 'regime factors' will be at work within the confines of EU donors.[11]

(3) Policy Coherence at the Level of Individual Donor Countries

The governments of nation states, therefore, hold the key to political coherence at the level of international politics (global and regional – including donor co-operation (DAC)) as well as in national politics. Important policy positions in global and regional organisations are decided at government level, as are national policies that may affect developing countries and North–South relations directly or indirectly. In reality, however, much is left to the discreet judgement of the government administration. Moreover, government powers are circumscribed, or are at least in open, active democracies where the voters are final decision-makers. Political influence is also exerted by the so-called civil society, institutions and organisations that actively seek to influence the turn of events in general or within specific issue-areas in particular – this applies especially to the main employee and employer organisations, active in the national arena.

(a) The crucial role of the political and administrative centre. In the analytical framework established in previous sections, the roots of the coherence problem within national confines have been indicated. To attain policy coherence within these confines presupposes a strong government. This does not necessarily imply an authoritarian government: paradoxically, such a government, although it may sway policies its way, may not be effective in ensuring consensus on policy objectives, which affects sustainability, and the policy as such will not necessarily be coherent. It refers to the ability of the regime to formulate and implement a coherent political programme in which conflicting concerns driven by particularistic (sectoral) interests and values are adapted to some overall policy aspirations, objectives and principles. Within a parliamentary system, this may imply the existence of a comfortable and reliable majority in Parliament. It follows that a government based on a single political party (with a declared programme) will, in general, constitute a more solid basis than a coalition government based on political parties with separate programmes. As noted, the authority of the PM, and her or his commitment to policy coherence, is of crucial importance.

---

11. See contributions by Paul Hoebink and Andrea Koulaïmah-Gabriel (chapters 10 and 11 in this volume). For an overview of the evolving EU project, see also Wallace and Wallace [1996].

In view of the compartmentalisation of politics, policy co-ordination is necessary across sectoral boundaries, between ministers and ministries; this applies to both policy formulation and implementation. Overall policy declarations by the government may be helpful to a certain degree: they point to the general direction, but tend to be less precise on ways and means. However, governments have numerous opportunities to be more precise – in medium-term plans, white papers on particular sectors, issue-areas, or cross-cutting issues, and annually through the budget. Whereas white papers are usually prepared by the sectoral ministry that is assigned the main responsibility for the area, the budget represents the outcome of a process where all ministers (and ministries) are involved, co-ordinated by the minister (ministry) of finance, usually in close co-operation with the PM (PM's office) – and priorities are expressed not only in words but also in hard figures. The national budget proposal therefore represents the prime opportunity for a government to co-ordinate policies and attain policy coherence – if it so wants.

However, policy coherence is not achieved in one stroke even if the will is there. The national budget – as amended in the process before it is adopted – represents a majority compromise at a certain point in time; it does not imply that conflicting interests have not been at play (they have), nor that they have not had their day, resulting in incoherent policies. Some of these inconsistencies emerge from a deliberate choice to accommodate conflicting interests. What mechanisms might help in reducing such policy inconsistencies, which are not deliberate choices from the perspective of the national centre?

(b) Inter-ministerial and intra-ministerial restructuring and co-ordination. At the institutional level, inter-ministerial restructuring may be one mechanism to ensure policy coherence among neighbouring policy areas: they may be brought together under one political and administrative leadership in a super-ministry; alternatively, more specialised ministries may be established for particular issue-areas, such as development co-operation. Both solutions have strengths and weaknesses. As noted in an OECD paper on public management [*OECD, 1996b: 20-21*], while a large, multi-sectoral ministry can help integrate related policies in a more coherent framework, there are limits to the number of internal conflicts that can be internalised. And it may reduce the political accountability, too: conflicts are solved internally by civil servants rather than at the political level by ministers. Issue-specific ministries, on the other hand, may focus on specific problem areas and constituencies. However, they may make overall co-ordination difficult and increase fragmentation.

44

Intra-ministerial restructuring is a mechanism at hand for seeking policy coherence at that level. Such restructuring may imply that the aid policy (aid administration) is integrated in a broader administrative context, usually that of the ministry of foreign affairs, in order to ensure greater coherence in the foreign policy (including aid). It may also take the opposite direction: a policy area may be given a more distinct administrative setting with some autonomy *vis-à-vis* the political and administrative leadership – as an aid agency with a separate, government-appointed board – to ensure greater internal coherence within the particular policy area. In the 1990s, the trend has been in the direction of greater intra-ministerial co-ordination, described in greater detail and discussed in several of the case-studies (chapters by Ashoff, Pratt and Stokke in this volume).

This raises a core problematique in our context: would development concerns be best served within a separate administrative unit (a separate minister/ministry of development co-operation/an autonomous aid agency; there exist various combinations) or would they be best served if integrated in larger units – such as a ministry of foreign affairs, which deals with all foreign affairs relations? The answer will depend on perspectives and the particular context. From his perspective, Cranford Pratt (Chapter 3 in this volume) finds that, in the case of Canada, reorganisation in order to integrate development co-operation administratively in the ministry of foreign affairs has affected development concerns negatively – 'narrowly self-interested trade and international political objectives' have come to determine both non-aid and aid policies. From this perspective, the drive for coherence has negatively affected 'real aid'; accordingly, a more autonomous aid administration emerges as a better alternative. We will return to this discussion in the concluding section.

Inter-ministerial co-ordination aiming at policy coherence may be improved through participation in decision-making and communication. Although such devices will not necessarily remove conflicting interests and values, they may contribute towards building bridges between conflicting 'world views' and create more 'legitimacy' for policy outcomes. Such co-ordination can take place at the level of political office-holders (deputy ministers) or at various civil service levels, involving ministries with stakes in the particular issue-area in regular meetings, task forces or issue-specific ad hoc meetings. The mechanism of a 'hearing system' fits in here; concerned ministries are invited to provide their comments on a proposed new policy initiative or issue to the responsible ministry before the proposal is finalised. Such mechanisms may also improve intra-ministerial policy coherence.

45

However, there is a wider setting which also matters: civil society, the private sector, and the extra-ministerial expertise on issue-areas under consideration that exists elsewhere in the society – in universities and the research community in particular. Interest- and value-based concerns in society are, of course, aggregated through the normal political processes through the political parties; bearers of these concerns (institutions, organisations) may also be included in extended hearing systems. Inclusion in decision-making through the mechanisms of communication and participation adds legitimacy to policy outcomes, which have a bearing on policy coherence, too.

VI. POLICY COHERENCE: VISION OR REALITY?

Words may mean different things; the context may allow for different interpretations. It is clear from the discussion in previous sections that this also applies to policy coherence: its content depends on the context, and contexts differ. What may be perceived as coherence within one framework may be considered incoherence in another.[12]

(1) The Fertile Ground

The OECD Development Assistance Committee (DAC) has acquired a kind of ownership by creating a new concept for a familiar notion. This, in turn, adds flavour to the concept: it reflects the perspective of the industrialised, Western donor community at a crucial point in time – the cold war over and the old bipolar world order in the process of being replaced by a new order. The needs of the South are viewed from the North, that is, from the perspective of an organisation of which all Northern governments are members, not necessarily from that of each individual member government. When the concern for greater coherence of their policies *vis-à-vis* developing countries was voiced in 1991, these governments were already accustomed to a policy of interference in the internal affairs of developing countries: for more than a decade, economic policy reforms had been prescribed as a condition for aid (first-generation conditionality), followed up, from 1989–90 onwards, by second-generation conditionality which prescribed both systemic reform (democracy) and policy reform (good governance, human rights).

Against this background, it is not surprising that a common approach by donors is considered a necessity in order to obtain results. Policy co-ordination is the very rationale of the OECD; for

---

12. This section draws on Stokke [*1999: Ch. 9*].

years, the DAC has been arguing for more co-ordination of the development co-operation of its member governments. The trick, in 1991, was to shift the focus from means to ends: emphasising the need for policy cohesion. The demand for coherence came as a response to the incoherent policies of DAC governments, triggered by their particular interests and their conflicting interests as well.

The ground was fertile for the 'new' demand for coherence of donor policies. The international system transformation evolving in the late 1980s and early 1990s, ending the bipolar East–West cold war which had dominated international relations since Second World War, also had implications for North–South relations: in many ways, it was a prerequisite for the coherence debate to take place and created the space for policy dialogue on new issues. Although the motives for promoting economic and social development in the South varied among donor governments, the aid of the two superpowers was driven by security concerns, both parties attempting to contain the influence of the other by supporting friends and allies. For these powers, the main rationale for aid faded away with the end of the cold war. On the other hand, the change in the world order paved the way for a new concentration on such issues as democracy, human rights and good governance, as well as the traditional objectives set for aid – poverty alleviation in particular.

The demand for policy coherence came at a time when resources made available for aid were dwindling. Foreign aid from the East disappeared almost overnight with the disintegration of the USSR. Aid from the remaining superpower was further reduced in the 1990s. At the same time the scarce resources had to be distributed to a larger number of recipients including several countries of the former Soviet Union and East and Central Europe. Shrinking ODA funds were in demand for a host of new activities, including the promotion of democracy and human rights.[13] The need to achieve more with fewer resources puts pressure on policy-makers and aid agencies to improve efficiency. By purporting to avoid policies at cross-purposes [*Kruger, 1993*], policy coherence was considered conducive to a more efficient use of public funds and, more generally, well attuned to improve public management.

---

13. The gradual redefinition of ODA by the OECD may indicate this development. Newcomers on the list of what is defined as ODA include the following: aid for democratic development; contributions to combat narcotics; participation in UN peace-keeping operations (excluding purely military components); assistance to demobilisation efforts; the lion's share of contributions to the Global Environmental Facility (GEF); and a share of the costs involved in accommodating asylum seekers and refugees from developing countries in the industrial country hosting them.

Another factor which may have facilitated the demand for increased policy coherence at this level is the growing recognition of the effects of globalisation on several countries of the South. Donor-driven policies, such as structural adjustment programmes, have opened up the economies of many developing countries. The outcome of the Uruguay Round accentuates these processes. As a consequence, the impact of the trade, financial and monetary policies of industrialised countries on developing countries will increase drastically. The effects of contradictions between the objectives of the various policies *vis-à-vis* developing countries have therefore become greater than in the past. The need to review policies from the perspective of their impact on development in the South is therefore more necessary than ever.

The increasing diversity and complexity of North–South relations does not result only from the integration of developing countries in the world economy. 'New' global problems[14] have appeared on the international agenda and attracted public awareness and increased political attention. They include environmental problems (air and water pollution, use of non-renewable resources, management of global commons), production, distribution and consumption of narcotics, international crime, epidemic diseases, and international transfer of weapons – all of which cross national borders. The growing interdependence, and increasing awareness of the threat to the security and welfare of humankind caused by these global problems, are driving the new concern of governments of the industrialised countries for a more coherent policy towards the South.

Two aspects of the DAC's prevailing drive for increased coherence of policies *vis-à-vis* developing countries are of particular importance. First, the perspective set out from the very beginning was explicitly to promote development in the South. This is considered an end in its own right as well as being in the long-term interest of the North. From this perspective, pursuance of self-centred, short-term interests that counteract the prime objective becomes dysfunctional. And second, the drive for policy coherence is combined with a policy programme. The trade mark of this programme is a concern for development in the South. A flavour that reflects the prevailing *Zeitgeist* within the OECD area is easily discernible, too: a predominantly mar-

---

14. 'Global problems' can be defined as problems that combine the following characteristics:
– they affect global security and welfare;
– their negative effects carry an impact beyond the areas in which they originate; and
– they can be solved or alleviated only by way of international co-operation.

ket-oriented ideology in combination with the main concerns associated with second-generation conditionality, namely democracy, human rights and good governance. The member governments have agreed on both the need for more coherence and on the policy to be pursued.

(2) The Follow-up at the International Level: What is the Strength of the International Development Regime?

Does coherence, at this level, work? If not, what are the necessary preconditions for it to work? The first question cannot be answered by a simple yes or no; it has succeeded to a certain degree. By focusing on the need for coherence, justified by rational choice arguments (effectiveness in terms of attaining goals), the DAC has succeeded in drawing attention to and gaining acceptance for greater co-ordination of policies *vis-à-vis* developing countries. The ground was fertile and the timing right. Since the early 1980s, the trend had been towards greater donor interference in the political affairs of recipient countries. The values promoted by second-generation conditionality, cherished in most donor countries, turned even governments previously opposed to interference into unreserved supporters of committed policy co-ordination among donors – as illustrated in the case of Norway (Stokke, Chapter 7 in this volume). Moreover, a programme for a coherent policy has been established by an organisation consisting of all the major donor countries and given the role of setting norms and monitoring the performance of donors *vis-à-vis* the norms agreed.

Do the norms work, however? A donor country has interests *vis-à-vis* developing countries which compete or conflict with the interests of other donor countries. Promotion of such interests may also affect development in the South negatively. Such interests do not just disappear. Against this background, what is the capacity of the DAC to make the norms work? Apart from norm-setting through agreement among member governments on general recommendations (in itself important), the DAC has few means at its disposal, except that of monitoring performance and making new general or specific recommendations to governments based on these findings. The DAC is a government-driven enterprise and its monitoring of performance relies to a large extent on inputs from member governments.

Such weaknesses from a regime perspective aside, what has been achieved represents an important step on the road to increased coherence of policies towards developing countries. Governments are expected to report on their performance *vis-à-vis* agreed norms, and this process directs their attention to the issue-area. However, it is entirely up to member governments whether or not to follow up on recommendations, and to what extent. The commitments and follow-up procedures such as reporting on achievements and monitoring of performance create expectations. The importance of such mechanisms on performances should not be ignored.

None the less, from the perspective of regime theory, the DAC appears as a weak organisation; the first rung of the ladder (overall norms and a programme) and the second rung (monitoring) are in place, while the remaining rungs are missing. It has no financial resources at its disposal to follow up norms. Individual member governments' commitment to the agreed norms, geared from within or inspired from outside, will therefore be decisive for the outcome.

The OECD is not the only organisation in which norm-setting within this area takes place. Donor governments also co-ordinate their policies *vis-à-vis* the South in broader contexts where they hold the upper hand, particularly in the BWIs, which, in addition to norm-setting, may also follow up through resource allocations. The inter-national trade regime, further developed in the Uruguay Round of negotiations, sets norms which will increasingly affect developing countries in new issue-areas; this regime also has procedures and instruments to accommodate and settle conflicts and powers to enforce decisions, if necessary.

The regional co-operation within the EU, including donor governments that provide about 56 per cent of total aid[15], has not so far been particularly close in the area of development co-operation; member governments have, by and large, pursued their bilateral policies independently of the EU, although a fairly high share of their total aid has been channelled through EU institutions. However, to the extent that a common foreign and security policy may be realised, closer policy co-ordination among member governments is envisaged. Policy outcomes from this co-ordination may also affect the policy positions and strategies of the donor community generally. However, as already noted, although aspirations among member governments vary and powers are increasingly vested in the Brussels-based institutions, residual powers remain with member governments.

---

15. In 1997, EU member governments provided US$26,620 million in ODA. The European Community is the world's second largest multilateral channel of development assistance (after the World Bank) and its combined programmes (US$5261 million) are the fifth largest among the 22 members of the DAC (after Japan, USA, France and Germany), with a growing trend during recent years while most donor countries have shown a declining trend [*OECD, 1998b*].

Is the conclusion therefore that we are back to square one? The positions of individual donor governments and the power play within national arenas will be decisive for the outcome of policy co-ordination by donors, with particular reference to DAC – although with a difference: governments tend to relate to internationally agreed norms and even adapt their policies accordingly.

The DAC flavour notwithstanding, policy coherence as a concept has come into universal use. It has been adapted to other systems, including complex systems such as the two national frameworks we have focused on: the policy of individual donor countries towards developing countries and their development co-operation policy. As will be seen from the following chapters, several governments have made strong commitments to greater coherence both within their development co-operation policy and, generally, with regard to their policies *vis-à-vis* developing countries.

(3) The Follow-up at the Level of Individual Donor Countries: Capabilities, Constraints and Opportunities

Within the arena of national politics, domestic stakeholders with various interests and values co-operate, compete and conflict; they are closer to decision-makers and, to a greater extent than in international arenas, they are able to make an impact on decision-makers. Clearly, they hold the upper hand whereas stakeholders in the South rarely participate directly in the political process, being 'represented' instead by domestic actors with their own vested interests and values. Norms and commitments agreed at regional or global levels also impact on decisions [*Stokke, 1989ab*].

In contrast to most international organisations, the 'regime' factors identified earlier are in place and at work when it comes to individual donor states, although not necessarily within the two policy frameworks identified earlier. Generally, they are well developed within the framework of aid policy, in particular if it is organised as a separate political and administrative unit (minister and/or ministry); in practice, the structure varies from one country to another. In most cases, development co-operation is administered by the ministry of foreign affairs; however, in some countries responsibility is divided between several ministries. Within the wider framework – of policies *vis-à-vis* the South and others that may affect developing countries or North–South relations – the 'regime factors' are less developed, mainly because of the compartmentalisation of politics and administration. Responsibility for these policy areas is usually divided between various ministries, with little horizontal co-operation and weak hierarchi-

51

cal co-ordination – although this may vary from one system to another.

Of greatest importance is agreement, at government level, on policy objectives and priorities. Overall objectives are in place for most donor countries, at the least derived from international commitments. However, whereas these may give general direction, they may be interpreted in many ways when it comes to policy implementation. For this reason, they have to be operationalised and adapted to the various policy areas and spelled out in terms of strategies, principles and guidelines – even means.

Policy coherence requires a clear commitment at government level: conflicting interests and rationales between and within policy areas mean that it cannot be taken for granted. Development co-operation itself is a very complex policy area which, in recent years, has witnessed a proliferation of objectives.

There is, furthermore, a need for procedures to resolve or accommodate conflicts between the various issue-areas. Even guidelines may be conflicting: for instance, the principle of poverty-orientation of aid (aid should go to poor groups in the poorest countries) and that of recipient-orientation of aid (aid should be integrated in the priorities of recipient governments) may be at odds, since not all recipient governments give priority to poverty alleviation. A hierarchical organisation, usually in place for a policy area, is conducive but insufficient in itself. The competition for resources between the various policy areas may be resolved through the national budget, but this alone does not prevent conflicting policies; the budgetary process itself is important for the outcome. The ability to reach decisions is all-important; however, decisions alone do not create coherent policies. Transparency, communication and inclusiveness *vis-à-vis* stakeholders (participation) in decision-making within the system are key elements in the process of achieving sustainable policy coherence.

Co-ordination of policy areas across political and administrative borders (for instance, between different ministries) aiming at policy coherence represents an even greater challenge for the reasons described and discussed in previous sections. Here, the hurdles are higher and hierarchical co-ordination is weaker than within a policy area. The rationales of the various ministries with primary responsibility for the numerous policy areas that affect, directly or indirectly, developing countries and North–South relations, may differ quite substantially. In a very real sense the rationales of sectoral ministries reflect vested interests of the donor country within this sector and the main stakeholders have direct access to decision-makers and are able to influence outcomes. The rationale of a ministry of trade illustrates the point. The ministry of foreign affairs is also geared towards the promotion of domestic interests and what is considered the national interest in particular. The traditional culture in which the civil servants of this ministry are bred means that their first question is naturally 'What is in this for us?' The perspective will not necessarily be that of long-term interests.

Yet, the answer to this challenge is much the same as for the specific policy area of development co-operation: a government programme in which the primary objectives of the various policy areas are harmonised and integrated, and for which priorities are set. This programme needs to be operationalised. The major stumbling blocks should be identified, with guidance as to how to address the problems involved. An explicit government commitment to policy coherence would be a *sine qua non*. Performance *vis-à-vis* the policy prescriptions – overall objectives and coherence – should be monitored. This, in turn, presupposes operationalised targets, institutions for monitoring, and procedures for follow-up and for accommodation of conflicts between ministries – outside or within the government (cabinet).

As noted earlier, the PM (and the PM's office) has a crucial role to play in ensuring inter-ministerial policy coherence. From a process perspective, inter-ministerial permanent committees and ad hoc task forces at political or civil service levels are among the mechanisms that may facilitate coherence. Transparency, communication and participation in decision-making are crucial to inter-ministerial co-operation. Although some of these elements are in place in most government administrations, more in some donor countries than in others, they are more weakly developed within the institutionally 'artificial' policy area called 'policies towards the South' than in more conventional, institutionalised policy areas such as 'development co-operation'.

Co-ordination to attain policy coherence means that compromises have to be made. The more actors there are – in terms of stakeholders as well as decision-making and administrative structures – the more compromises will be necessary. The compromise decisions reached will, obviously, not be the first choice of all parties involved; there may be winners and losers, too. The crucial question therefore is: who co-ordinates who? Whereas the DAC has placed development concerns (as they perceive them) first, DAC member countries – in so far as they have sought to co-ordinate national policies *vis-à-vis* developing countries – have by and large been primarily concerned to ensure the coherence of their foreign policy. Co-ordination has taken place within the framework of the ministry of foreign affairs and aid policy has been adapted to general foreign policy concerns. This setting is not conducive to making traditional development concerns – real aid – the winner.

From the very beginning, development co-operation has been a 'special case', driven, to a large extent, by altruistic motives and less by short-term selfish interests. Self-interest has always played a part in the aid business, more explicitly in the policy of some donor countries than of others; however, it makes little sense to explain the rationale for aid exclusively in such terms, even in the case of the superpowers during the cold war. The basically altruistic motivation for aid may explain why donor governments, when initiating this activity, set up a separate organisation to administer it – an aid agency with some autonomy *vis-à-vis* the ministry of foreign affairs – in order to visualise its 'ideal' purpose *vis-à-vis* recipients and safeguard its aims from the more interest-based concerns vested in a ministry of foreign affairs.

However, the dilemma involved in making aid a special case is obvious: values and norms become confined to this particular policy area while it is business as usual within others areas which may be of even more importance for development in the South. The broader perspective was given much greater emphasis in the mid-1970s, with the call for a new international economic order, and it was in this programme that the rationale of policy coherence (the DAC version) was first provided. This is the rationale for the 'development constituency' within donor countries when arguing for policy coherence: policies within other areas should not conflict with, but be adapted to and help facilitate, the development objectives set for aid policy.

From this perspective, integration of aid in the broader context may seem more rational – and more appealing – than to treat it as a special case. But a dilemma appears: traditional preoccupations of other policy areas may gain the ascendancy. The outcome of an integrative approach is not necessarily foreseeable; it will depend on the relative strength of the various stakeholders and of predominant norms. As already noted, Cranford Pratt (Chapter 3 in this volume), examining trends in Canada, clearly recommends the 'special case' administrative solution in preference to the integrated approach which has resulted in development concerns losing out to vested business and foreign policy interests. In the case of Norway, Olav Stokke (Chapter 7 in this volume) detects similar trends, but observes that the 'development constituency', since the early 1990s, has argued strongly for policy coherence from a development perspective and has succeeded as far as overall objectives set for policies towards the South are concerned. However, the drive for greater policy coherence has primarily affected the ODA budget.

Conflicting interests and values cannot be waved away with a magic wand. The relative weaknesses or strengths of different interest groups will be all-important to the outcome of an integrated approach. In a national political setting where the values of humane internationalism hold a weak position, in general or at a crucial point in time, it may seem rational for the 'development constituency' to go for a 'special case' type structure to administer development co-operation. However, a weak position in domestic politics is not the best basis for a pressure group to obtain its preferred solution, particularly in this case, where the international community (DAC) is recommending an integrated approach. It follows that in a national political setting where the values of humane internationalism are more entrenched in the polity, the 'development constituency' may be tempted to take a bolder position: to opt for integrating development concerns in the broader policy. Of course, a bold position is no guarantee of success, but a favourable political environment may increase the chances of success.

From an overall perspective, the focus on policy coherence may contribute to a more systematic policy-making process. Given the original DAC perspective, where the concern for greater coherence is combined with a policy programme that reflects development concerns, such a focus may, first, enable the impact of various policies on developing countries to be identified, and, second, lead to a discussion of the extent to which the policies are compatible with the overall objectives set by industrialised Northern countries for development in the South. It may also create more transparency both in the policy-making and the implementation of policies vis-à-vis the South, and in North–South relations generally, particularly if the DAC and individual member states make serious efforts to operationalise performance criteria and establish institutions for monitoring and follow-up. It is widely assumed that a positive correlation exists between transparency and accountability; so the focus on policy coherence may lead to increased accountability, too.

For the OECD, making recommendations to its members is probably the realistic extent of its capacity to follow up on the policy coherence agenda set by the DAC. However, this would be no small achievement: recommendations may even work, since member governments are involved both in the process leading to the recommendation and required to report on their performance. Within a regional setting such as the EU, there will soon probably be no such limitation; however, at present there is. Within the national setting, member governments themselves decide how best to achieve policy coherence.

REFERENCES

Cohen, M.D., J.G. March and J.P. Olsen, 1972, 'A Garbage Can Model of Organisational Choice', *Administrative Science Quarterly*, Vol. 17, No. 1.

Dahl, Robert A., 1971, *Polyarchy: Participation and Opposition*, New Haven: Yale University Press.

Diamond, Larry, Juan J. Linz and Seymour Martin Lipset (eds.), 1988-90, *Democracy in Developing Countries*, Vols I-IV, Boulder: Lynne Rienner Publishers.

Doornbos, Martin, 1995, 'State Formation Processes under External Supervision: Reflections on "Good Governance"', in Stokke (ed.).

Edgren, Gus, 1984, 'Conditionality in Aid', in Stokke (ed.).

Fukasaku, Kiichiro and A. Hirata, 1995, 'The OECD and ASEAN: Changing Economic Linkages and the Challenge of Policy Coherence', in Fukasaku *et al.* (eds.).

Fukasaku, K., M. Plummer and J. Tan (eds.), 1995, *OECD and the ASEAN Economies: The Challenge of Policy Coherence*, Development Centre Documents, Paris: OECD Development Centre.

Hewitt, Adrian and Tony Killick, 1996, 'Bilateral Aid Conditionality and Policy Leverage', in Stokke (ed.).

Hoebink, Paul, 1996, 'Coherence and Development Policy: The Case of the European Union', paper presented at the 8th EADI General Conference, Vienna, September 1996.

Hydén, Göran, 1994, 'Shifting Perspectives on Development: Implications for Research', in Mette Masst, Thomas Hylland Eriksen and Jo Helle-Valle (eds.), *State and Locality*, Oslo: Norwegian Association for Development Research and Centre for Development and the Environment.

Jepma, Catrinus J., 1996, 'The Case for Aid Untying in OECD Countries', in Stokke (ed.).

Keohane, Robert O., 1993, 'Analysis of International Regimes: Towards a European-American Research Programme', in Volker Rittberger (ed.), *Regimes in International Relations*, Oxford: Clarendon Press.

Krasner, Stephen D., 1982, 'Structural Cause and Regime Consequences: Regimes as Intervening Variables', *International Organization*, Vol. 36, No. 2.

Kruger, A.O., 1993, *Economic Policies at Cross-Purposes. The United States and Developing Countries*, Washington, D.C.: Brookings Institution.

Morgenthau, Hans, 1948, *Politics Among Nations*, New York: Knoph.

OECD, annual, *Development Co-operation*, Paris: DAC, OECD.

OECD, 1992, *Development Co-operation, 1992 Report*, Paris: DAC, OECD.

OECD, 1995, *Linkages: OECD and Major Developing Economies*, Paris: OECD.

OECD, 1996a, *Shaping the 21st Century: The Contribution of Development Co-operation*, Paris: DAC, OECD.

OECD, 1996b, Building Policy Coherence. Tools and Tensions, Public Management Occasional Papers No. 12, Paris: OECD.

OECD, 1997, *Development Co-operation, 1996 Report*, Paris: DAC, OECD.

OECD, 1998a, *Development Co-operation, 1997 Report*, Paris: DAC, OECD.

OECD, 1998b, OECD News Release, SG/COM/NEWS(98)93, 1 October 1998. Paris.

Stokke, Olav, 1989a, 'The Determinants of Aid Policies: General Introduction', in Stokke (ed.).

Stokke, Olav, 1989b, 'The Determinants of Aid Policies: Some Propositions Emerging from a Comparative Analysis', in Stokke (ed.).

Stokke, Olav, 1995, 'Aid and Political Conditionality: Core Issues and State of the Art', in Stokke (ed.).

Stokke, Olav, 1996, 'Foreign Aid: What Now?', in Stokke (ed.).

Stokke, Olav, 1999, *Coherence of Policies Towards Developing Countries: Aspirations and Realities*, Oslo: NUPI.

Stokke, Olav (ed.), 1984, *European Development Assistance*, Volume 2, *Third World Perspectives on Policies and Performance*, Tilburg: EADI Book Series 4.

Stokke, Olav (ed.), 1989. *Western Middle Powers and Global Poverty*, Uppsala: Scandinavian Institute of African Studies.

Stokke, Olav (ed.), 1995, *Aid and Political Conditionality*, London: Frank Cass, EADI Book Series 16.

Stokke, Olav (ed.), 1996, *Foreign Aid Towards the Year 2000: Experiences and Challenges*, London: Frank Cass, EADI Book Series 18.

UNDP, annual, *Human Development Report*, New York, N.Y./Oxford: Oxford University Press.

Wallace, Helen and William Wallace, 1996 (third edition), *Policy-making in the European Union*, Oxford: Oxford University Press.

World Bank, annual, *World Development Report*, Washington, D.C.: World Bank.

Young, Oran, 1991, Report on the 'Regime Summit', held at Dartmouth College, November 1991, Hanover: Institute of Arctic Studies.

2

The Shifting Grounds of Policy Coherence in Development Co-operation

GÖRAN HYDÉN

I. INTRODUCTION

The concept of coherence may be a new term in the study of policy, as Paul Hoebink notes in a recent review of challenges to development co-operation in the contemporary setting (Hoebink, this volume, Ch. 10). It does not yet have a place in the literature as do more established terms such as co-ordination or control. It is significant too that it has emerged as a professional and political concern not in the United States but in Europe, reflecting a difference between the two places in terms of how politics is being conducted. In the pluralist political system of the United States, coherence is, if not anathema, nonetheless a peripheral matter. In Europe with its long tradition of democratic corporatism, however, coherence is both a practical and intellectual concern.

In spite of this difference in political and intellectual tradition between the US and Europe, it is important to recognise that at least in the field of development co-operation neither is the divergence between the two places as great as it may be in other fields nor is the concept such a novelty. Development co-operation is a unique political and bureaucratic activity in that it takes place between countries. For organising inter-state activities governments always consider themselves as having the ultimate voice. Thus, the United States is no exception. Its development co-operation has been organised along very similar lines to that of European countries. Secondly, if coherence is meant to refer to the extent to which intended policy objectives are attained or not, the concern is not fresh even if the term may be. The effort to be consistent and coherent in the use of foreign aid is as old as the activity itself. Policy actors have always strived for active implementation according to plan. They have also tried to eliminate or reduce the influence of forces antagonistic to a preferred policy option.

Coherence, therefore, has always been an issue in the field of development co-operation, but it is still important to ask why this term has emerged as significant and relevant only in recent years. To appreciate this fully, it is worth examining how the ground for policy coherence in the field of development co-operation has shifted since the 1960s and subsequently discuss its usefulness in the current context. Before embarking on this exercise, however, it will be necessary to define the subject matter of this chapter and address some introductory questions about the concept of policy coherence.

II. DEFINING THE SUBJECT MATTER

As indicated above, policy coherence as used in this chapter – and in the rest of this volume – refers to the consistency found between policy intention and policy outcome. In this respect, policy coherence is a measure of institutional effectiveness. Using the concept, however, has its own difficulties because policy differs in scope and occurs at different levels in organisational hierarchies. For example, coherence is likely to be easier to achieve within a narrower than a broader policy scope because it involves fewer objectives or instruments. Similarly, it is likely to be easier whenever fewer actors are involved. More concretely, it is easier to achieve coherence in the field of development co-operation than it is in the overall policy field involving another country. Security, trade or cultural policies may go against specific objectives or values pursued in development co-operation. It is also easier to achieve internal coherence, within a single organisation, than external coherence, which involves other actors. In the field of development co-operation, for example, there is often a choice between achieving coherence in the bilateral relations between donor and recipient on the one hand, and between donor organisations on the other. As will be discussed further, choices along these lines have different implications for the nature of development co-operation.

Coherence is not the only value that policy-makers and implementors will pursue. Although it is often prioritised, implementational practice typically interferes to render coherence problematic. For example, one may expect that divergent interests will be brought to bear on the extent to which a particular policy is really executed as intended. Groups of actors which find a policy adverse to their own interests may intervene so as to divert its original intentions. Policy coherence, however, may also be threatened by lack of information. Few policies, if any, are made with perfect information. There is always going to be an information gap which will limit the extent to which policy coherence can be achieved. This is what Hoebink refers to (Hoebink, this volume, Ch. 10) as 'unintentional' reasons for incoherence.

It may be worth recognising also that some problems of incoherence are structural, while others are caused by the actors involved. In many instances when policy coherence is being pursued, existing institutional arrangements are such that however well intentioned individual policy actors are, their intentions are sabotaged by rules and regulations over which individual actors have no control. For example, policy coherence in the field of development co-operation often falls short of expectation because it involves co-ordination between institutions in two separate sovereign states. Even when conditionalities are applied, the difficulty remains. In this case it might be said that it is a given that policy coherence is going to be hard to achieve. In other instances, however, lack of coherence in policy is the result of unexpected rivalry between institutions. Such rivalry may stem from misunderstandings or battles over control of specific mandates or resources. These may not have been intentional but have become, none the less, a factor in policy implementation.

Drawing on this brief discussion, it may be said that policy incoherence rather than policy coherence is likely to be the normal thing. What policy actors typically do is to reduce the levels of potential policy incoherence rather than pursue some form of optimal or perfect policy coherence. What we have tried to do so far is to indicate that this task can be defined in relation to two parameters: the first referring to actor *intention*, the other to actor *autonomy*. With the help of the following matrix it is possible to identify at least four general reasons for policy incoherence.

This map of causes of policy incoherence summarises in an abbreviated form the kind of challenges that policy actors find in achieving higher degrees of coherence in their activities. But it is important also to address additional questions: (1) why is policy coherence important? (2) how is policy coherence achieved? and (3) for whom is coherence being sought?

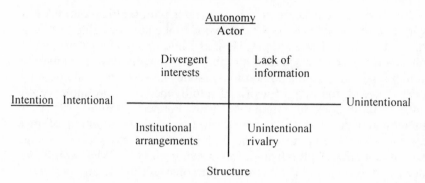

FIGURE 1
CAUSES OF POLICY INCOHERENCE

III. DIFFERENT ASPECTS OF POLICY COHERENCE

Interest in policy coherence may be justified on many grounds but foremost is typically the issue of legitimacy. Policy implies a public choice in favour of one alternative over another which, if not achieved, indicates to the public one of two things. Incoherence, or lack of success in implementing policy, may be due to the lack of will to achieve it or inadequate means of power to put it into practice. In either case, the impression rendered is one of shortcoming, something that usually translates into questions of legitimacy. Is a government really serious in trying to get things done? Does it really have the means to solve societal problems? The question of why policy coherence is important to a political actor or a student of politics, therefore, is based on its significance for credibility and, indirectly, for public support.

Another issue of interest to the student of policy is how coherence may be achieved. The basic distinction in the literature is between rationalists and realists [*Bobrow and Dryzek, 1987*]. The former place greater emphasis on how a policy is designed. They have faith in scientific rationalism and the prospect that the answers to problems facing humankind lie in the realms of professional expertise. To that extent, they are even prepared to isolate other factors from the equation of how to get things done so as to reduce the risk of a planned intervention becoming side-tracked or undermined. This effort at insulating the actual implementation of public policy from social or political forces rests on the assumption that facts and values can be separated and that politicians, once they have decided in favour of a

particular policy alternative, are ready to leave the task of implementation to the 'experts'.

Further, rationalists are positivist in their philosophical outlook but
vary in their belief as to how far they may take their doctrine of scientific rationalism. For example, Herbert Simon recognises that human
rationality is always bounded and that we typically have to settle for
suboptimal yet 'satisfising' options. None the less, he is also confident that with the help of artificial intelligence, we may improve on
current limitations to rationality. Karl Popper's notion [1963] of
incremental problem-solving advocates a cautious adoption of this
approach because the greater the faith placed in it, the greater too the
risk that political pluralism is rendered irrelevant. Why would we
need a polyarchy or democracy if the answers to all our problems
may be found in science?

Realists oppose rationalists precisely because they lack a sense of
the significance of politics. The technical or professional task of
working out a solution to a particular problem is only a first step and
cannot be done in isolation from a process in which potential stakeholders may participate. In short, realists accept that without ground-
ing a particular approach to solving a problem in the minds of the
public (or at least those most directly affected), this would stand little
chance of becoming reality. Coherence, therefore, is not sought in the
sphere of rationality, but in the political realm.

No one has more consistently put forward this view than Charles
Lindblom who, ever since first coining the phrase, 'the science of
muddling through' [Lindblom, 1959], has questioned the extent to
which scientific probing really provides answers to vexing societal
questions. Instead, he has argued that at least in democratic polities,
what counts is the political process. Coherence is the result of working out a political consensus that ensures there is commitment to
seeing a policy through from beginning to end [Lindblom, 1991].
Another realist version is provided by Cohen, March and Olsen
[1972] with their 'garbage can' model of problem-solving, according
to which decision-makers have to balance three separate streams of
problems, policies and politics in order to achieve a degree of coherence that ensures successful implementation. The question of how to
achieve policy coherence, therefore, is one which is characterised
both by great diversity and by controversy.

A third issue of relevance here is the question of coherence for
whom. Ultimately, the justification for a given policy rests with the
ability to serve the public or a particular client group. Consequently,
effective policy implementation is a matter of reaching specific

targets set in relation to identifiable, often quantifiable objectives. Ends, however, are not considered in isolation from means. Policies are assessed also in terms of the costs of the means to achieving the ends. Efficiency is set against effectiveness. In this situation, the issue of policy coherence may be defined in terms of the interests not of the clients but of the implementing organisation. One aspect of policy coherence may get in the way of another as, for example, Cranford Pratt (this volume) indicates.

Another interesting case in point comes from the airline industry where Delta Air Lines in the United States, facing increased competition in 1994, engaged in a cost-cutting exercise. In a survey conducted among its 58,000 employees two years later, however, nearly half the workforce said that Delta's customer service was worse, they did not trust management and they felt they had no ownership in the company [*Tampa Tribune*, 12 March 1997]. The ensuing public perception had been no better. The airline's image of being customer-friendly was lost. In an attempt to deal with this deteriorating image, the company began rehiring customer service agents and mechanics.

In this case, the challenge of achieving policy coherence on the terms of the organisation's own management was pushed too far. Being lean meant also being mean, an impression that a service company competing with others could ill afford. As this and other cases illustrate, to understand fully the many dimensions of policy coherence it is necessary to examine in whose interest such coherence is being sought. It may even be in some cases that a certain measure of policy incoherence is necessary to achieve a greater degree of policy coherence at another, and more important, level.

IV. POLICY COHERENCE IN DEVELOPMENT CO-OPERATION

This latter point is of particular relevance to the field of development co-operation. Foreign aid is justified on the grounds that it improves the living conditions of people in the poorer regions of the world. Support for such acts of solidarity has been remarkably strong and consistent over a long period of time in many European countries. Such support notwithstanding, however, the policy situation in development co-operation is peculiar in that the beneficiaries or stakeholders do not constitute a domestic constituency in the donor countries. Since the beneficiaries are located in a foreign country, the task of achieving policy coherence is particularly challenging. The risks of incoherence are especially great as many more factors enter into the process of getting a policy implemented. These factors are on the side of both donors and recipients. As I will demonstrate below, the ratio-nale for achieving policy coherence in the relationship between donors and recipients has changed considerably over the almost 40 years that development co-operation has been in existence as an inter-national phenomenon.

Coherence in development co-operation is also influenced by pol-icy scope. A single-sector focus is likely to ensure policy coherence more easily than a strategy entailing work in many sectors. In the latter scenario, more than one organisation is typically involved, thus creating the possibility of institutional or bureaucratic rivalry at the expense of cost-effective implementation. How to mitigate such ten-dencies has always been on the agenda for development co-operation organisations, but it has proved difficult to improve policy coherence. It is not surprising, therefore, that the search for coherence has con-tinued and in recent years been intensified.

With the help of the questions (a) at what level and (b) within what scope policy coherence is being sought, it is possible to identify four separate positions that have characterised development co-operation in the past 40 years. This typology is admittedly somewhat arbitrary and does not do justice to all questions that can be raised about the concept and its operationalisation. None the less, the purpose here is to provide a sort of road-map that helps us understand the concern we have today with the need for policy coherence.

A look at this figure suggests that policy coherence has been pre-sent as a genuine concern in development co-operation ever since the 1960s when the notion of comprehensive national development plan-ning was expected to guide inputs by outside donors. It has since shifted in a zigzag fashion via 'integrated development' in the 1970s and 'structural adjustment' in the 1980s to our current preoccupation with governance and democratisation. Each period has been charac-terised by its own challenges, reflecting some of the issues already raised above. I shall now analyse each period and the specific chal-lenges to policy coherence that they have generated.

(1) Comprehensive Planning

In the early years of development co-operation there was never a question about the priority of the recipient's own policy objectives. Foreign aid was a mere complement to the inputs provided from dom-estic sources. External assistance was meant to accelerate national development by being focused on those sectors that were most critical and where domestic resource constraints were greatest. Particularly in

FIGURE 2
TYPES OF POLICY COHERENCE IN DEVELOPMENT CO-OPERATION

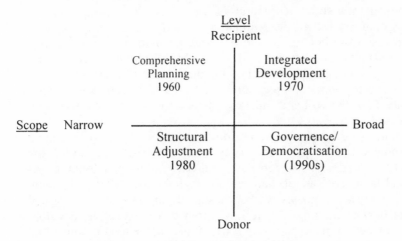

African countries where the private sector was very weak, it was also granted that the state needed to play a pivotal role in guiding and promoting economic and social development. What really made the task of achieving policy coherence appear relatively easy was the insistence on a national development plan. This document was envisaged as a plan not only for the public but also for the private sector, an all-encompassing guide for national development.

Donor governments appeared to have no problem in accepting this set-up which gave particular prominence to economists. The national development plan was endorsed by the ruling party and the government in power, but the process of arriving at certain types of priorities did not involve the various segments of the population, not even organised interests. Producing the national development plan, therefore, was primarily a bureaucratic exercise involving economic expertise in sectoral ministries and in the body with overall responsibility for this exercise, typically a ministry of development planning. Because everyone tended to view development in economistic terms, few questions were asked about the extent to which it was legitimate that a single group of professionals would be allowed to exercise such a great degree of influence. In fact, because many of the economists involved were expatriates provided by individual donor countries, they were seen more than anything else as a guarantee of reliable and realistic development targets.

What analysts in those days tended to overlook was the fact that the national development planning exercise was insulated from reality by the bureaucratic structures within which it was taking place. In most places, planners lacked the political clout that was necessary to keep the process from being hijacked by particular interests vested in sectoral ministries. The latter not only tended to dictate the specific content of the plan but also controlled the implementation process. Thus, the extent to which policy coherence was achieved was usually dependent on the will and capacity inherent in the individual sectoral ministries.

Donors were reluctant to question the sovereignty of the recipient government and its priorities. They were satisfied with having the opportunity to design projects that would fit into these national priorities and thus serve as mechanisms for realising overall development objectives. The emphasis was on design. If the design was correct, results would automatically follow. From this perspective, development looked simple. There was little, if any, bureaucratic politics on the donor side, because development co-operation in those days was typically conducted through a central agency. Even where this was not the case as, for example, in the case of Germany and the Netherlands, the existence on the recipient side of an authoritative national plan document reduced the risks of incoherence.

What was not appreciated by the donors was the fact that development was about more than producing well-designed projects. Incoherence could not be prevented by merely technocratic or bureaucratic means. As the 1960s proceeded, therefore, it became increasingly apparent that the implementation of development projects was itself a politically contested process. Even though the notion of policy coherence was not used in those days, it was challenged, particularly on the ground in recipient countries.

(2) Integrated Development

Integrated development became the principal method of dealing with policy incoherence in development co-operation in the 1970s. It emerged from the experience with project-based work, which often amounted to little because it was scattered. Furthermore, there was often rivalry among agencies involved in such work, thus exacerbating tendencies towards policy incoherence. The philosophy behind integrated development activities was that it would be possible to bring together divergent policy objectives under a single institutional umbrella, thereby reducing the risks of conflict in bringing about economic and social development objectives. Two separate approaches to integrated development evolved in response to this challenge. One was centred on the establishment of an independent integrated development project or programme based in a particular geographical region of a country. The Chilalo Agricultural Development Unit in Ethiopia, funded by the Swedish International Development Authority (SIDA), was the pilot effort that eventually led to projects based on this approach in Ethiopia and elsewhere in Africa. A second approach focused on incorporating the idea of integration into existing government services by strengthening regional and district administration through deconcentration of authority from central-line ministries. The first, and in many respects the most ambitious, of these efforts was implemented by the government of Tanzania in collaboration with McKinsey & Co, the international consulting firm. It was followed by similar programmes in other African countries, such as Kenya and Zambia.

The scope of these integrated development programmes was deliberately multi-sectoral. The previous approach may have been integrated at the level of planning and design but when it came to implementation it was disconnected. The new approach was meant to bring planning and implementation closer together in the hope that it would increase policy effectiveness. The idea of having everything – agriculture, education, public health and infrastructure – under one roof appealed to politicians and experts alike. With access to a broader range of development activities, the former liked integrated development because it enhanced their chances of gaining legitimacy for their government and themselves. The latter approved of the measure because it was an administrative reform that brought civil servants closer in touch with their clients, thus improving the prospect of greater policy coherence.

During the 1970s, the assumption continued to prevail that foreign aid was a complement to local efforts in recipient countries and that it was the responsibility of the government in these places to provide the policy and institutional framework for channelling outside assistance. The role of national development plans remained significant and provided the overall framework within which integrated development activities were pursued. For example, what happened in Tanzania and Zambia was that foreign donors were invited to 'adopt' a particular region or district and concentrate their input on a geographically confined area where it would be easier to demonstrate and evaluate the results of their efforts. This appealed to the donors who were increasingly anxious that their assistance should be meaningful and effective. Although donors varied in terms of their acceptance of the development policies of individual recipient countries and some were favoured over others, the principle that foreign aid was being given within a framework provided by a sovereign national government was never questioned as long as this approach enjoyed support in the international community.

The concept of integrated development, however, did not survive beyond the 1970s because it became increasingly apparent that it had its own serious inadequacies. Particularly grave was the growing bureaucratisation that accompanied this approach. To ascertain the integrated nature of development, and thus policy coherence, it was deemed necessary to establish elaborate management structures that were not only costly but also proved to be unwieldy. Instead of leading to greater autonomy on the part of local officials to respond to spontaneous development demands, these individuals were confined to operating within rigid administrative regulations that limited their ability to be effective. Integrated development induced the creation of an administrative superstructure that tended to contradict the very reason for its establishment in the first place, namely that of bringing government closer to the people and thus enhancing the prospect of greater policy coherence. The costs rather than the benefits of this approach were beginning to concern the donor community more and more as the 1970s drew to an end.

(3) Structural Adjustment

Structural adjustment brought a whole new way of looking at policy coherence in development. The turning-point was the World Bank's report on how to accelerate economic growth in African countries by relying more on the market than the state as the prime mover of development [*World Bank, 1981*]. Accompanying this effort was the call for reform of public finances so as to ensure a climate in which investments would be safeguarded from inflation and other financial management shortcomings. Structural adjustment meant bringing economics back in. The rallying call in international development circles became that of 'getting prices right'.

The new approach changed the parameters of development co-operation in two major ways. The first was the insistence on macro-economic reform in developing countries which previously had relied heavily on political mobilisation and bureaucratic administration to implement policy. In the 1980s everything else was going to be subordinated to specific macro-economic reform demands. Developing countries were told to stop living beyond their means and were painfully reminded of this as increasing interest rates quickly raised the burden of repaying debts for projects which in the 1960s and 1970s had failed to produce intended outcomes. Generous funding for basic social development programmes in the fields of education and health was coming to an end as governments were compelled to reduce spending to levels closer to those of domestic revenue receipts. Governments were also told to reduce the number of servants on their payroll. In many African countries, for instance, the personnel function had deteriorated to a point where large numbers of people on the official payroll were fictitious individuals who did not exist in reality. Downsizing the public service, therefore, became mandatory as a means of getting public finances in better shape. The most controversial part of this set of reforms, however, was associated with realigning the value of local currency. By opening up African economies to global market forces, the typical effect was a devaluation of the local currency. In many places, the devaluation was considerable and had to be carried out gradually in order to reduce the risks of political upheaval. In some countries such as Ghana and Zambia, management of the process still could not prevent street demonstrations.

Deregulation of the economy had the effect of creating new terms of trade for rural and urban residents. While before, it had been beneficial to live in the urban areas where food and sometimes other basic necessities were subsidised, the gradual removal of subsidies in the 1980s made life in urban areas increasingly expensive, forcing most able-bodied residents to engage in complementary small-scale economic activities. This 'second' or 'informal' economy has continued to be a prominent part of the African scene ever since. At the same time, the terms of trade for people living in the rural areas improved, particularly where government taxation of peasant produce was being reduced or removed. Their gains, however, never proved as great as anticipated because higher prices on imported goods limited the extent to which the rural population could improve its living standards. Furthermore, with both education and health-care now becoming increasingly subject to payment by individuals, the cost of living for most villagers was going up and not down.

Governments in developing countries, particularly in sub-Saharan Africa, had great difficulty in accepting the structural adjustment packages that were being forced upon them. Because of their own economic weakness, there was little they could do but 'drag their feet'. The most vociferous and consistent ideological opposition to structural adjustment came from Tanzania's president, Julius Nyerere, but by the middle of the decade he had to give up too, especially after his few remaining friends in the Nordic countries told him that he had no choice but to accept the terms of the International Monetary Fund and the World Bank.

The second way in which development co-operation changed in the 1980s was the decision by all major donors to adopt unanimously the call for structural adjustment. There were some laggards – in particular, the Nordic governments – but by 1984–85 the neo-classical version of economics inherent in the structural adjustment approach reigned supreme in the international community. This meant not only general agreement about the elevation of macro-economic reform above everything else in development co-operation, it also implied that the terms were no longer set by recipient governments through national development plans but at a supranational level. The 'Washington consensus' rendered the annual meetings of the IMF and the World Bank increasingly important. Additional mechanisms for holding recipient governments accountable for their efforts at reform were developed under the auspices of the Organisation for Economic Co-operation and Development (OECD) and the so-called Paris Club.

Policy coherence prospects were strengthened in the 1980s as donor governments took a common stand and used their economic power to induce or coerce developing country governments to adopt structural adjustment. It is no coincidence, therefore, that implementation of structural adjustment policies has been quite successful in the formal sense. This does not mean that people in these countries have necessarily benefited from these policies, nor does it imply lack of opposition to them. None the less, some quite remarkable structural changes have taken place in the economies of most developing countries since the beginning of the 1980s. Policy coherence in development co-operation may never have been greater than in the heyday of structural adjustment in the second half of the 1980s. Even the 1990 report of the South Commission, which was chaired by President Nyerere, accepted the inevitability of neo-classical economic thinking [*South Commission, 1990*]. This is in sharp contrast to the report ten years earlier by the North-South Commission, which still argued for the creation of a new international order that bore the features of government-controlled economies [*Brandt Commission, 1980*].

(4) Governance and Democratisation

In the 1990s structural adjustment had to take second place to concerns with political reform. These have crystallised around two key concepts: governance and democratisation. The former is largely an invention of the World Bank, which, according to its own official

70

mandate, cannot talk about politics in a way that may be interpreted as partisan and prefers to create its own code words that loosely refer to the same thing. Thus, governance in the perspective of the World Bank refers to the use of political reforms to strengthen the prospect of effective policy implementation. In this way, governance is closely related to the concept of policy coherence. Governance is also used by other donors but bilateral agencies often prefer to 'call a spade a spade' and some shy away from it in favour of direct reference to democratisation. Regardless of which term is used, multilateral and bilateral donors agree on the substantive need for political reform to strengthen public accountability and participation in public affairs, respect for human rights and the principle of the rule of law, and preventive efforts to reduce the risk of bloody intra-state conflicts. The assumption here is that these things go together: that greater political openness also fosters greater respect for the rule of law and reduces the risk of civil war.

For a long time politics and development were kept apart. Development co-operation was being insulated from political issues. This has changed in recent years as analysts increasingly realise that politics is not so much an instrument for solving problems as the root of the problem itself. For instance, in African countries the neo-patrimonialist tendencies among rulers have limited the extent to which economic reform really benefits the public. By imposing their own unofficial rules with regard to access to officially open markets, they are able to extract bribes from economic actors, leaving the latter exposed to their opportunistic political whims. Calls for greater transparency and public accountability, therefore, tend to centre on the need for reducing corruption in public office. Consensus about the need for political reform has been facilitated by the end of the cold war which has made individual donor governments less ready to accept forms of government that do not resemble their own.

Policy coherence, therefore, continues to be sought on terms set by the international community or, more specifically, the principal donor governments. The difference from the 1980s, however, is that the scope within which coherence is sought is broader. Furthermore, the challenges of achieving coherence are being exacerbated by the increased number of actors participating in development co-operation. The agenda for such co-operation is quite complex today, involving both economic and political reform at the national level in recipient countries. This means that the demands on governments in these countries are even heavier than before, but the simultaneous combination of economic and political reform requirements may give

71

recipient-country governments more leeway in dealing with the donor community [*Stokke, 1995*]. We have seen, for instance, that performing well with regard to either economic or political reform is often enough to lower the demands with regard to the other. This is particularly true if the country has clout in international politics as the cases of China and Indonesia illustrate, but Uganda is also a case in point. President Museveni's government has been hailed as committed to economic reform and has managed its own structural adjustment programme quite successfully. This relative success is definitely one factor that explains why the same government has been able to get away with a constitution that rules out multi-party democracy (at least in the short-to-medium run). The relationship between the Kenyan Government and donors has also been characterised by the ability of the former to use economic reform to soften the demands for political reform. What seems increasingly clear is that donor demands for democratisation have not increased the prospect of policy coherence but may, if anything, have lowered it.

The problems of achieving coherence have been compounded by the fact that development co-operation is no longer merely a government-to-government affair nor one that involves only bilateral arrangements. Furthermore, development itself has been redefined in ways that nowadays emphasise the role of the private and voluntary sectors. This means, first of all, that not only is there a development co-operation ministry involved, but there are often other administrative agencies that have a stake in what is going on in developing countries. Some countries, such as Sweden, have tried to keep all matters of development co-operation under one roof, but it is increasingly difficult to do so, particularly because of the role played by private enterprise and non-governmental organisations. These are difficult for governments to control and their agenda is often different from that of governments. What they set out to do sometimes contradicts official government policy. To this complication should be added yet another, which stems from the accelerated efforts in the 1990s to strengthen the European Union. As Hoebink (this volume, Ch. 10) argues, there are increasing instances of incoherence in policy outcome resulting from divergencies in approach between the European Union, on the one hand, and individual member governments, on the other.

It is easy to see that compared to previous decades when policy coherence was taken for granted because the institutional set-up was relatively simple, it has become a more manifest concern in the 1990s since so many factors tend to undermine efforts to achieve better results from development co-operation activities. Policy-makers believe that coherence is a key determinant of policy success, and this concern has grown with the increased public scepticism in most countries about the usefulness of foreign aid. The question, therefore, is what, if anything, can be achieved intellectually and practically through this new focus in development co-operation? It is to this question that the remainder of this chapter turns.

V. PUTTING POLICY COHERENCE TO FURTHER USE

The review of previous efforts at accomplishing greater policy coherence in development co-operation is instructive in the sense that it confirms that these have tended to emphasise the extremes rather than the middle ground. During the 1960s and 1970s the political framework on the ground in recipient countries – whether or not it was a democratic one – was accepted as the basis for development co-operation. The sovereignty of the recipient government was generally respected and foreign aid was treated largely in technocratic terms as an effort that complemented domestic initiatives. Since 1980 the philosophy behind development co-operation has shifted almost half-circle: aid is now being given on terms set by the donors and current conditionalities are not only economic but also political. The frustrations of the first two decades have given way to the scepticism (if not cynicism) of the 1990s. It does not need too much imagination to suggest that these are not conditions congenial to constructive development co-operation and, therefore, greater policy coherence.

There is a great risk in the current situation, particularly in relation to sub-Saharan Africa, that what we grandly call 'development co-operation' may degenerate into a form of neo-colonialism or simply fizzle out, owing to lack of patience with what is happening on the ground in Africa. Current efforts by the European Union, on its own, or in collaboration with the United States, to co-ordinate programme initiatives to deal with the rising number of human emergencies in Africa and elsewhere often show scant regard for the social and political forces on the ground, the assumption being that these efforts are strong enough to effect a change for the better. Although the experience in Somalia in the early 1990s should not be overgeneralised, one lesson to be learnt is that an outside expeditionary force is no guarantee of success.

Large-scale interventions, even if well co-ordinated among many actors, contain too many uncertainties to have much prospect of success. Yet, there is a tendency both at national and intergovernmental levels in Europe to concentrate and co-ordinate programme initiatives on the premise that these stand a better chance of being both efficient and effective. For example, Sweden has proposed a major programme initiative in the Great Lakes region of Africa which sets aside US$500 million for a five-year period. This is at least in part justified with regard to the need to avoid what are seen as incremental and scattered projects and programmes where the tangible impact may be of limited publicity value. In this kind of situation it is easy to lose sight of the broader rationale for policy coherence, namely the extent to which local stakeholders in the recipient country are involved and can articulate their views. The broader political aspects are abandoned in favour of what may become bureaucratic tinkering with the concept of coherence within the donor organisations. Bureaucratic politics replaces representative interests as key determinants of policy outcomes. The means become an end in itself, a sure recipe for decline in public confidence and support for development co-operation.

Development co-operation may still have a future and policy coherence may still be a concept worth working with, but it is likely that the answers to our questions of how to ensure greater coherence will have to be sought in new places. Development co-operation itself is already beginning to change in the margins as a result of frustrations with what are viewed as current mainstream approaches. Donors are increasingly seeking ways of developing and safeguarding the political space that is needed for local initiatives to flourish. One example of this concern is the tendency to place donor money in funds that allocate them to local organisations – governmental or non-governmental – in recipient countries. Although the experience of working through such funds is mixed, some lessons have emerged which could have direct relevance to the question of how to achieve greater policy coherence in development co-operation. One such lesson is that these funds become mechanisms of pursuing political patronage if they are controlled by the political executive. Another is that when controlled by the donor they fail to encourage local accountability. Yet another is that when established within a subnational as opposed to a national scope, they easily become parochialised or hijacked into building ethnic or religious constituencies [*Hydén, 1995*].

Drawing on these experiences, there are currently efforts under way to improve the fund model. Particularly significant in this context has been the initiative jointly taken by the African Association for Public Administration and Management (AAPAM) and the Dag Hammarskjöld Foundation to explore the possibility of setting up autonomous development funds for channelling donor contributions to economic and social activities in recipient countries [*Dag Hammarskjöld Foundation, 1995*]. This model foresees joint ownership and control of these funds by recipient governments, civil society in these countries and the outside resource providers. Rather than serving the expectations of individual donors the funds would be sectoral institutions, incorporated in the recipient countries, and would thus help facilitate local accountability. Their lending or grant facilities would be open to both governmental and non-governmental organisations, competing among themselves for development finance. Decisions to allocate grants or loans would be made on grounds of feasibility and professional merit, with the tripartite ownership of the funds serving as the best guarantee of their not being turned into mere patronage tools.

The advantages of this model for the purpose of strengthening policy coherence are many. First of all, it allows donors and recipients to share responsibility on an equal basis not only for implementation but for deciding how resources should be allocated. Because the collaboration takes place in the context of boards of directors of locally incorporated institutions, it has an authoritativeness in the recipient country that is lacking in contractual donor arrangements with individual ministries or corrupt government institutions. Secondly, it reduces the number of levels at which co-ordination needs to be sought. With representatives of both outside resource providers and domestic stakeholders brought together in a set of institutions with responsibility for allocating development funds in a professional and non-partisan manner, the risks of contradictory moves by individual donor- or recipient-country institutions are minimised. Thirdly, by providing a general development policy framework within which recipient-country institutions can apply for financial support, these funds make it possible for organisations outside central government to have easier access to development finance. Fourthly, by insisting on professional criteria for allocation of resources, the funds are likely to encourage constructive competition to improve performance, among both governmental and non-governmental organisations. Finally, the autonomous development fund should in the long run have the effect of reducing the need for costly foreign aid bureaucracies in donor countries, a concern that is increasingly being voiced not only in the United States but also in many European countries.

All these factors should have the effect of giving development co-operation a new lease of life. They would also help bring about conditions in which the task of achieving policy coherence is facilitated. By reducing the risk of policy coherence being merely a prerogative of the donors, autonomous development funds should make decisions about resource allocation better understood in recipient-country circles and thus enhance the prospect that policy intentions are put into practice in ways that have eluded development co-operation to date.

VI. CONCLUSIONS

Much of this discussion has placed development co-operation at the centre of things. We must realise, however, that this activity no longer enjoys the same degree of priority as in previous years. In many countries, foreign aid is increasingly subsumed under other broader policy objectives. This degradation of development co-operation in the context of overall governmental policy objectives is likely to make the task of achieving policy coherence more difficult in the future. There is also an attendant and growing risk of internal coherence within the donor government itself becoming the overriding policy concern, rendering coherence in relation to recipient countries a matter of only secondary importance.

The situation is not, however, entirely gloomy. There are initiatives under way to identify, safeguard and expand the political and social space available to actors in the recipient country. Clearly, though, any reorganisation of the institutional formulas for development co-operation requires both political vision and the political will to sustain the activity. New funding models offer a good opportunity to restore the credibility of development co-operation activity at a time when it badly needs to demonstrate some successful outcomes of the emphasis on improving governance practices in recipient countries, especially in Africa where problems of governance are particularly serious. There is cause, then, for cautious optimism. Actor intention and autonomy in the field of development co-operation are still real concerns and the enterprise cannot only be salvaged but developed into a positive contribution to relations between countries in the North and the South. If policy coherence is to be achieved, however, it must be sought increasingly with the institutional requirements of the recipient country in mind, rather than primarily within the donor bureaucracy, whether at governmental or intergovernmental level.

REFERENCES

Bobrow, D.B. and J. Dryzek, 1987, *Policy Analysis by Design*, Pittsburgh, PA: University of Pittsburgh Press.

Brandt Commission, 1980, *North–South: A Program for Survival, Report of an Independent Commission on International Development Issues*, Cambridge, MA: MIT Press.

Cohen, M.D., J.G. March and J.P. Olsen, 1972, 'A Garbage Can Model of Organizational Choice', *Administrative Science Quarterly*, Vol.17, No.1.

Dag Hammarskjöld Foundation, 1995, *Autonomous Development Funds in Africa. Report from an Expert Consultation in Kampala, Uganda, 4–6 April, 1995*, Uppsala: Dag Hammarskjöld Foundation.

Hydén, G., 1995, 'Reforming Foreign Aid to African Development: A Proposal to Set up Politically Autonomous Development Funds', *Development Dialogue*, No.2.

Lindblom, C.E., 1959, 'The Science of Muddling Through', *Public Administration Review*, Vol.19, No.1.

Lindblom, C.E., 1991, *Inquiry and Change: The Troubled Attempt to Understand and Shape Society*, New Haven, CT and London: Yale University Press.

Popper, K., 1963, *The Open Society and Its Enemies*, Princeton, NJ: Princeton University Press.

South Commission, 1990, *The Challenges to the South, The Report of the South Commission*, Oxford: Oxford University Press.

Stokke, O. (ed.), 1995, *Aid and Political Conditionality*, London: Frank Cass.

Tampa Tribune, 12 March 1997, Tampa, FL.

World Bank, 1981, *Accelerating Development in Sub-Saharan Africa*, Washington, DC: World Bank.

3

Greater Policy Coherence, a Mixed Blessing: The Case of Canada

CRANFORD PRATT

Greater coherence in the policies of developed countries towards the developing countries is assumed, understandably, to be important and desirable by many who are committed to sustained and equitable international development. The Canadian experience suggests at least that a more nuanced judgement may be called for.

In Canada greater policy coherence has been emphasised at different times in three quite different ways. Greater coherence between the macro-economic policies of recipient governments and those advocated by international financial institutions was emphasised in the 1980s, in the hope of lessening the risk that good aid programmes would be undermined by faulty economic policies on the part of recipient governments. Greater policy coherence within the Canadian International Development Agency (CIDA) was championed, particularly in the early 1990s, as a means of increasing the development impact of Canadian aid. Finally, greater coherence between CIDA's policies and other Canadian policies that have had an impact on the developing countries has been advocated as almost self-evidently desirable. This chapter subjects these expectations to critical analysis.

I. GREATER COHERENCE BETWEEN THE MACRO-ECONOMIC
POLICIES OF RECIPIENT GOVERNMENTS AND THE DEVELOPMENT
STRATEGY FAVOURED BY CIDA

The Canadian International Development Agency (CIDA) has sought

The research on which this chapter is based was made possible by a research grant provided by the Social Science and Humanities Research Council of Canada. Portions of this chapter appeared in an earlier version in *Canadian Foreign Policy* 5 (2), 1998.

to influence the macro-economic policies of governments receiving Canadian aid only quite late in the day.[1] Both CIDA officials and Canadian diplomats had largely refrained from such efforts, fearing that they might jeopardise the goodwill created by Canada's aid programmes. Moreover, for most of its recipients, Canadian aid was not sufficiently important for CIDA reasonably to aspire to significant policy influence. To illustrate: in 1989, excluding ten small Caribbean island states in which Canada was also a major presence, only three countries – Ghana, Bangladesh and Colombia – received more than ten per cent of their total bilateral aid from Canada [*Groupe SECOR, 1991, 90–140*]. This comparative disinterest in using aid as leverage for policy reform began to shift in the mid-1980s. It then changed dramatically in 1989 with the reappointment of Marcel Massé as President of CIDA.[2] Again and again he repeated this message:

> There is clearly a change in the way we have to look at development policy. ... The influence of the domestic economic policies swamps away the influence of all the aid flows ... and therefore conditionality on macro-economic policies ... is essential to us.[3]

Massé was a firm neo-liberal. He was in no doubt that Canada should add the weight of its influence to the great pressure being applied on the major aid recipients by the International Monetary Fund (IMF) and the World Bank to ensure that they accepted the packet of structural adjustment policies prescribed for them by the IMF.

CIDA's use of aid to exert pressure on governments to implement structural adjustment programmes was by far the most persistent effort undertaken by Canada to advance policy coherence with its aid recipients. These efforts can be viewed positively only if one completely discounts the importance of recipient governments fully 'owning' the development policies they pursue, and accepts that the minimal government neo-liberalism then being pressed on Third World governments is in fact essential to sustained development in their countries. These are highly contentious propositions and hardly a solid foundation from which to champion the advantages of greater policy coherence.

---

1. For a careful appraisal of these efforts, see Burdette [*1994*].
2. Marcel Massé had previously been an Executive Director of the IMF for five years and before that Deputy Under-Secretary of State for External Affairs. He had also been President of CIDA from 1980 to 1982.
3. From a transcript of an address by Massé to Canadian directors of the IFIs, meeting in Ottawa, 29–30 Oct. 1990.

II. GREATER POLICY COHERENCE WITHIN CIDA

It might nevertheless seem reasonable to assume that greater policy coherence between CIDA's various programmes and projects would improve its overall impact on development. There are obvious instances where greater coherence is called for. It cannot but be detrimental, for example, for Canadian food aid to undermine the prospects of success of Canadian assistance to local food self-sufficiency. Yet, the advantages of increased policy coherence within CIDA, the most plausible of the several types of coherence that have been promoted, lose their self-evident quality when one examines two of the most significant ways in which CIDA actually sought to increase the internal consistency of its various activities.

(1) The Strategic Management Review of 1990–91

A wide range of organisational and managerial problems within CIDA led Marcel Massé in 1990 to commission a major strategic management review [*Groupe SECOR, 1991*].[4] One of the issues which Massé wanted to be addressed was the lack of firm central policy direction within CIDA. Certainly the main instruments that might have been the vehicle of effective presidential direction were underdeveloped and underused. The President's Committee spent little time on policy development and its members, the vice-presidents and branch heads, tended to defend their own turfs and were very respectful of the domains of their colleagues. Major planning documents were not regularly drawn up and when they were, they often focused on current activities rather than strategic considerations. The overriding preoccupations were process, probity and prudence. As a result, Groupe SECOR concluded the branch and country programmes acted like separate fiefdoms, each with its own parochial culture and each resourceful in preserving its autonomy away from central direction [*Groupe SECOR, 1991: 4–38*].

To rectify this lack of policy leadership, the report recommended the creation of a high-powered corporate office surrounding the president, to be staffed by persons highly trained in policy research and strategic analysis. This office was to have final responsibility for the allocation of resources, issuing mandates, determining aid strategies and relations with other donors as well as recipient governments. There were to be training programmes for middle-rank officers so that

---

4. Groupe SECOR's report is discussed at length in Pratt [*1992: 595–613*] and in Rawkins [*1994: 168–82*].

they would understand and appreciate the objectives and strategies devised by the corporate office.

The coherence which Massé was after and which the SECOR report hoped to achieve was one substantially obtained through a decidedly top-down style of management. The report was unconcerned about ensuring the upward flow of detailed knowledge of the countries receiving assistance and had little appreciation of what would be lost if those who knew most about the needs of recipient countries were excluded from the process of planning country and regional programmes. What was neither acknowledged nor provided for was the need to weld together a strengthened policy branch at the centre with programme planning at the country and regional levels.[5] It is small wonder that the SECOR report generated much unease in CIDA.

In the end, largely because of a major controversy triggered by another aspect of the SECOR report, much of the report was abandoned (see section IV). What is relevant to the argument of this section is the widely held judgement, shared by this author, that policy coherence achieved in the manner proposed and without recognition of the value of a diversity of inputs into policy planning would have been disastrous.

(2) CIDA's NGO Responsive Programme and Greater Policy Coherence

A second more specific but nevertheless important example of a mistaken overvaluation of the advantages of policy coherence occurred a few years later. CIDA authorities had decided that, with the agency's resources so severely cut, every effort should be made to ensure that Canadian aid was not 'frittered away'. They therefore decided that all CIDA-assisted activities should contribute to the accomplishment of the priorities, country by country, which CIDA set for its aid. A number of senior officials and, in particular, a key vice-president, were determined that this guideline should be extended to include CIDA's programmes with Canadian NGOs. They therefore pressed that no NGO programme or project should be supported save those that fell within CIDA's Regional and Country Policy Frameworks [*CIDA, 1995*].

---

5. The Groupe SECOR team was so preoccupied with addressing Massé's emphasis on the need to achieve closer policy control that it totally ignored a reform which many saw as desirable – much fuller consultations in the preparation of the country planning documents with the authorities in the countries concerned and with NGOs and other non-governmental institutions working in these countries.

81

What was at issue was CIDA's responsive programme for Canadian NGOs. Under this, CIDA supported many activities proposed to it by NGOs without regard to whether these activities were within or outside the quite narrow parameters of these policy frameworks. Many within CIDA were strongly opposed to any serious curtailment of this programme and the NGO community rallied vigorously in its defence.

There were many secondary arguments for the responsive programme. These ranged from its contribution to the vitality of Third World civil societies to its contribution to development education in Canada. However, the primary case for maintaining the programme, a case never doubted by many within CIDA and finally accepted by the agency as a whole, was that a genuine measure of pluralism, rather than full policy coherence, was preferable when pursuing objectives as fraught with uncertainties and complexities as how best to meet basic needs, or to promote human rights and democracy, or to encourage the full participation of women in the sustainable development of their societies, to name three CIDA priorities with regard to which Canadian NGOs have long had an honourable record.

III. GREATER COHERENCE BETWEEN AID POLICIES AND OTHER COMPONENTS OF CANADIAN FOREIGN POLICY 1968–95

(1) The Issue More Closely Identified

The greater policy coherence which many in the development community most emphasise is coherence between development assistance policies and the wide range of non-aid policies that has significant impact on international development. Their concern is to ensure that non-aid policies reinforce rather than undermine the development objectives of aid policies.

However, it should not be assumed that if this greater policy coherence is achieved, it will represent a triumph of development objectives. In many important ways, governments deliberately maintain policy incoherence. For example, the contradictions between Canadian aid and immigration policies have long been obvious: CIDA assists educational development and local entrepreneurial initiatives in many developing countries, while at the same time Canadian immigration authorities seek to attract from these same countries immigrants with capital to invest and with skills and professional qualifications which are in short supply in Canada. The Canadian government has never sought greater coherence between Canada's aid and immigration policies. The two policies are accepted as coexisting components of Canada's overall policy towards developing countries.

A similar acceptance of incoherence has always existed with regard to aid policies and other components of Canadian foreign policy. CIDA has never had significant influence on the trade or other foreign policies of the Canadian government. However, the reverse has not been true. The pursuit of development objectives by CIDA has been tempered from the start by commercial and international political considerations. Illustrations are numerous and obvious: Canadian bilateral aid has always been significantly tied to Canadian goods and services; the selection of the agricultural products to include in Canadian food aid has long been a political decision; the choice of countries receiving Canadian bilateral aid and the size of each country programme have also been politically determined decisions[6] as were decisions on the comparative importance of multilateral and national instruments in the disbursement of Canadian ODA. It has never been seriously imagined within CIDA that it could itself have primary responsibility for these decisions or that they would be taken in response only to development considerations.

Achieving greater overall foreign policy coherence has in fact never been championed by CIDA. CIDA's central concerns were rather how best to ensure that development implications were adequately considered by the political leadership when taking major, parameter-determining decisions which inevitably have remained in its hands. Further, the concern was how to achieve for CIDA a genuine and significant measure of operational autonomy so that, within these politically determined boundaries, it could then be substantially free of pressures that would further diffuse the development focus of its work. The real dynamics of the issue of greater foreign policy coherence are therefore best revealed through a study of the institutional relationship between CIDA and the Department of Foreign Affairs and International Trade.[7]

---

6. Until 1994 these decisions were taken by cabinet on the recommendation of the Secretary of State. In that year André Ouellet, the Secretary of State, decided that these decisions were within his authority and their reference to cabinet ceased.
7. The Department of Foreign Affairs and International Trade was called before 1995 the Department of External Affairs and International Trade and, before 1981, the Department of External Affairs. More simply the department is referred to as External Affairs or Foreign Affairs.

(2) Relations between CIDA and the Department of External Affairs to 1989[8]

The central insight that determined the initial and long-lasting institutional arrangements for the management of Canadian development assistance was that of the first president of CIDA, Maurice Strong. He opposed the creation of CIDA as an autonomous public corporation, or as a separate department, or as a division or branch within External Affairs. He was convinced that the development objectives of CIDA would be best served if CIDA were an agency of External Affairs, headed by a president with the status of an under-secretary of state and responsible directly to the political minister, then the Secretary of State for External Affairs.

Strong thus acknowledged that the political ramifications of Canadian aid were such that it would be unrealistic for CIDA to aspire to the fully autonomous status of a public corporation – unrealistic because no cabinet would be willing to relinquish political control either of activities of such significance to Canadian foreign policy or of the spending of such substantial sums of public monies. Strong wanted nevertheless to protect CIDA's operational autonomy. He therefore insisted that its president be given the rank of a deputy minister. This ensured that while his administrative decisions and his policy advice could be overruled by his minister, they could not be set aside by a fellow official, however senior.

In Strong's view, it was important that the minister responsible for CIDA should be the Secretary of State for External Affairs. This would ensure that once the president of CIDA had convinced 'its' minister of the necessity of any policy, that policy would be unlikely to be successfully challenged at cabinet, a happy circumstance not at all ensured if the responsible minister were a separate, and inevitably quite junior, minister for international co-operation.

Most observers agree that from about 1977 until the late 1980s there was a gradual erosion of CIDA's policy autonomy. In 1977, the President of CIDA, Michel Dupuy, in an important communication to CIDA staff, wrote:

> the recent evolution of the Canadian economy as well as its short and medium term prospects, require that CIDA strive to ensure that its activities maintain or generate employment and economic benefits in our own country. We must also aim at strengthening

---

8. David Morrison has just published a detailed and authoritative history of CIDA [*Morrison, 1998*]. I have recently dealt at some length with the development of CIDA policies [*Pratt, 1996: 334–70*].

mutually beneficial bilateral relationships between our developing partners and Canada (as quoted in Morrison [*1994: 135*]).

Having unequivocally affirmed this position, Dupuy then, but only
then, added: '(T)his goal must be achieved while not neglecting our
essential mandate which is international development' [*ibid.*].
    From then on, CIDA came under increasing pressure to ensure that
its policies brought trade and international political advantages to
Canada. A few years later, Margaret Cately-Carlson, Dupuy's successor, aptly summarised the role that CIDA had come to accept: 'CIDA
is a policy-taker, not a policy-maker' [*Rawkins, 1994:162*]. CIDA
policies and other Canadian policies towards the developing countries
were becoming more coherent, to the advantage, not of CIDA's putative primary objective of reaching and helping the poorest countries
and people, but of non-development objectives that had been thrust
upon it.
    In 1987 the Standing Committee on External Affairs and Inter-
national Trade (SCEAIT) of the House of Commons sought to rectify
this. In an important report on Canadian development assistance, *For
Whose Benefit?*[9] [*House of Commons, 1987*], the committee, though
not recommending any major changes in the institutional framework
within which Canadian development assistance operated, did seek to
ensure that CIDA, within that framework, would be better able to
resist bureaucratic and political pressures to diffuse and dilute its
development mandate. 'The aid program', it wrote, 'is not for the
benefit of Canadian business. It is not an instrument for the promotion
of Canadian trade objectives' [*House of Commons, 1987:8*].
    The committee's recommendations included: that central emphasis
be given to human resource development, with a primary focus on the
poor; that aid be deployed more actively to protect and promote
human rights; that the tying of Canadian aid be significantly reduced;
that great caution mark any effort to link aid to trade promotion; that
a Development Charter be legislated; that a legislated commitment be
given that the level of aid would not fall below 0.5 per cent of GNP;
and that an International Development Advisory Council be created to
advise on long-range policy issues.
    Had these recommendations been genuinely welcomed and vigor-
ously implemented, much of the earlier erosion of the development
focus of Canadian aid policies might have been reversed, and a better
balance struck between development, commercial and foreign policy

9. Often referred to as the Winegard report, after the chair of the committee,
William Winegard.

considerations. However, they were not. Instead, in its detailed official response, *To Benefit a Better World* [*Government of Canada, 1987*], and in CIDA's new strategy paper, *Sharing Our Future* [*CIDA, 1987*], the government carefully protected those elements of the aid programme, such as parallel financing with the Export Development Corporation (EDC), which it wished to retain but which were clearly not endorsed by the report. Further, the various safeguards to protect Canada's development assistance which the Winegard report had recommended were all ignored, as indeed was, soon after, the whole of the strategy paper.

(3) CIDA's Seeks Greater Policy Autonomy, 1989–92

In 1989, under Marcel Massé's direct leadership, CIDA made a major effort to increase its control of its own policies and to widen its influence within government. CIDA did not dispute that it should serve Canadian foreign policy objectives but, under Massé, it sought to shift the balance of power between CIDA and External Affairs in its favour. In effect, Massé tried to accomplish a fuller realisation of Strong's perception of CIDA's role, that is, as a powerful policy-making and implementing body, responsible to the Secretary of State, operating within boundaries broadly set by the government, sensitive to political and foreign policy objectives that were important to the government but largely free of detailed overview by External Affairs.

In retrospect, four related strands to this 'Massé project' can be identified.[10] First, the policy-making capabilities of a high-powered corporate office immediately around the president were expanded, adding research and analytical skills and strength in macro-economics and in newer policy areas such as social policies, human rights and democratic development. Through this office, Massé hoped to equip CIDA to play a more important policy role and to exercise much closer policy direction over the agency's operations.

Second (as discussed above), effective policy leverage on governments which were recalcitrant towards IMF/World Bank structural adjustment programmes became a major CIDA preoccupation. This served greatly to increase the ideological harmony between CIDA and both Finance and External Affairs. Nevertheless, it was not tactical in purpose; Massé was in fact a true believer.

Third, a discussion paper, *Sustainable Development*, was published in June 1991 by CIDA's Policy Branch [*CIDA, 1991*]. Massé hoped that it would be approved by cabinet as a new CIDA mission statement. The statement reaffirmed a neo-liberal approach to economic

---

10. This subsection draws heavily on Pratt [*1993–94; 1994–95; 1996*].

development but embedded it within a wider policy framework ('the five pillars of development') that was defined within broad and general terms. Had it become a cabinet statement, almost any policy that CIDA might wish to pursue could easily have been justified as falling within a cabinet-approved mission statement. CIDA would therefore have been more strongly placed to resist pressure from External Affairs on policy issues.

Fourth, accompanying this assertion of a greater policy role for CIDA was an increased responsiveness within CIDA to Canadian foreign policy objectives and trade interests. In particular, CIDA's Asian Branch was susceptible to this tendency. The Canadian government had come to recognise the great asymmetry between the growing economic and political importance of the countries of South-East Asia and China and the weakness of Canadian links with their economies, their governments and their peoples. It became an important objective of Canadian foreign policy to lessen this asymmetry. CIDA responded to the challenge, rapidly expanding its programme in Thailand, Indonesia, the Philippines and China. In close collaboration with External Affairs, CIDA came to see its task primarily in terms of creating mutually valuable relationships between important business, governmental, educational, scientific and social organisations in these countries and their Canadian counterparts [Rudner, 1994].

There were other major examples of CIDA's increasing concern to reflect major foreign policy and trade interests. These were not dictated by External Affairs, but CIDA had itself internalised these foreign policy objectives and made them its own. It was as if CIDA wanted to prove to External Affairs and to cabinet that it could be trusted with decisions that had important commercial and foreign policy dimensions.

CIDA seemed well placed in 1992 to accomplish its self-transformation. It had increasingly sought to placate External Affairs and Finance by taking initiatives that these powerful departments might otherwise have insisted on. It had been sensitive to the interests of Canadian investors and exporters, so that it faced no serious threats from that quarter. It could not expect totally to win over critics of the new approach who were within CIDA itself or within the NGO community. However, its leadership was confident that it could contain its internal critics and that as many of the larger NGOs and most of the non-governmental institutions (NGIs)[11] were by now so dependent on

---

11. CIDA uses the term non-governmental institutions to refer to such organisations as universities, co-operatives and trades unions in contradistinction to non-governmental organisations which are popularly based voluntary organisations primarily engaged in development-related work.

CIDA funding the agency would be able easily to isolate its critics in the voluntary sector.

(4) The Crisis Over Policy Coherence, 1993–95

Massé's ambitious aspirations to win for CIDA far greater policy competence and autonomy were in fact confounded by External Affairs itself.[12] Both the minister, Barbara McDougall, and the department wanted a redefinition of the CIDA–External Affairs relationship that would significantly increase External Affairs' control of Canadian aid policies. McDougall therefore decided that the CIDA paper would not go to cabinet and, instead, asked External Affairs to prepare an international assistance policy update paper.[13]

This paper, the Carin paper (after its author, Barry Carin) revealed the use that External Affairs hoped to make of the greater powers to which it aspired. It set out several options for CIDA's bilateral programme. Under the preferred option, the programme would be divided into four activities (Canadian dollars throughout):

(1) traditional development assistance to some eight to ten countries – $170m;
(2) assistance to the former Soviet Union and Central and Eastern Europe – $200m;
(3) economic co-operation programmes in some six to eight countries 'to position itself for long-term market penetration into priority markets' – $246m;
(4) four foreign policy thematic funds:
    (a) an economic co-operation fund – $328m,
    (b) a human rights, democratic development and governance fund – $110m,
    (c) an environment fund – $110m,
    (d) a reserve fund – $75m.

There could hardly have been more dramatic evidence that External Affairs was far more preoccupied with commercial and foreign policy concerns than with any commitment to reach and help the poorest peoples and countries. Equally significant was the precedent that the policy update paper sought to establish that External Affairs would

---

12. This section summarises an analysis which I have developed elsewhere [*Pratt, 1994; Pratt, 1996*].
13. This document was prepared by Assistant Deputy Minister Barry Carin on McDougall's instructions. In the fierce infighting that then occurred between External Affairs and CIDA, the paper was leaked to the NGO community. For a fuller discussion of this paper and the whole crisis which then followed, see Pratt [*1994; 1996*].

now set the main heads of expenditures in the aid budget and therefore the overall orientation of the aid programme.

This paper was not an ill-conceived aberration.[14] For several weeks McDougall insisted that it be implemented. Many Canadian NGOs were for a while ambivalent over the whole dispute, for they had been strongly critical of major features of CIDA policies under Massé's leadership. However, the Carin paper seemed so unreasonable and pre-emptory that the national association of Canadian NGOs, the Canadian Council of International Cooperation (CCIC), led a major campaign against it. With an election close at hand, the Prime Minister, Brian Mulroney, finally put the whole issue on hold. Thus, at the time of the October 1993 election, it was as yet unresolved whether External Affairs would be granted the greater control of development assistance policies that it had long desired.

(5) The Resolution of the Crisis, 1993–95

Given the demoralising consequences of this continuing indefiniteness, one might have expected at least that CIDA's future as an institution would be quickly resolved after the election, and in a sense it was, but not all that succinctly. The report of the 1994 Special Joint Parliamentary Committee Reviewing Canadian Foreign Policy lacked the authority of the Winegard report. Nevertheless, what it proposed for CIDA's primary purpose, 'to reduce poverty by providing effective assistance to the poorest people, in those countries that most need and can use our help' [*House of Commons, 1994: 48*], the definition it offered for CIDA's basic policy framework and the six priorities and the various safeguards it suggested demonstrated a determination that CIDA's development mandate should not be easily set aside.

Canada in the World [Government of Canada, 1995], the 1995 official government statement on Canadian foreign policy that followed the committee's report, built Canadian foreign policy around the pursuit of three objectives: jobs and prosperity; common security; and Canadian values and culture. It is categorical that Canadian development assistance is an integral component of foreign policy and an instrument serving these three integrating national interests. It recognised Foreign Affairs' interest in a range of policy areas that overlapped with CIDA's interests by announcing the creation of a new global issues branch in Foreign Affairs. However, by deliberately not announcing any changes in the institutional relationship between

---

14. Less authoritative but certainly symptomatic of the same ideological mind-set is a paper published at about the same time by Foreign Affairs [*Dimic, 1995*].

CIDA and Foreign Affairs,[15] the official statement effectively confirmed that while development assistance would continue to be integral to Canadian foreign policy, CIDA would retain a significant measure of operating and policy autonomy.

(6) Conclusions on the 1992–95 Crisis over Policy Coherence

The government of Canada thus took a deliberate decision in 1995 to value a measure of diversity within the foreign policy-making process. It deliberately chose to maintain a measure of policy incoherence, rather than create machinery that would better ensure policy coherence. The greater policy coherence that Foreign Affairs had sought through a fuller subordination of CIDA to it was not in any way intended by those advocating it, to make Canadian foreign policy more responsive to the development needs of the poorest countries. On the contrary, it was intended to ensure that CIDA policies and programmes would more fully serve Canadian trade and international political interests. It is small wonder then that most commentators see the failure of this effort in increasing the coherence of Canadian foreign policy as beneficial to the quality of Canadian aid policies.

IV. THE RENEWED DRIVE FOR GREATER FOREIGN POLICY COHERENCE, 1996–97

(1) Continuing Tensions in CIDA–Foreign Affairs[16] Relations 1996–67

With the publication of *Canada in the World*, the Canadian government reaffirmed its preference for the institutional framework that had existed before both Massé's attempt to increase the policy autonomy of CIDA and the counter-effort of External Affairs to assert an expanded authority over Canadian aid policies.[17] CIDA would continue to be a department of government administering some 75 per cent of the International Assistance budgetary allocation. It remained under the authority of the Minister of Foreign Affairs, with a president whose status was that of a deputy minister. Its own specific mandate, very largely drafted initially within CIDA and reflecting existing

---

15. The new liberal government changed the name of the Department of External Affairs and International Trade to the Department of Foreign Affairs and International Trade.

16. The long-standing title of the Canadian foreign minister, the Secretary of State for External Affairs, was at this time changed to the Minister of Foreign Affairs.

17. This section draws heavily on Pratt [*1998*].

policies, was part of the official government statement, *Canada in the World*.

It was thus reasonable for CIDA to assume that it would be free, for a period of time at least, from any further initiatives to change the balance of power between itself and Foreign Affairs. However, almost from the start, a major effort to bring CIDA under its closer control gathered momentum within Foreign Affairs. This effort provided another opportunity to assess the likely consequences for Canadian development assistance of that greater coherence sought by Foreign Affairs, between Canadian aid policies and other components of Canada's foreign policy.

In significant part, the new crisis in the relations between CIDA and Foreign Affairs resulted from the fact that a wide range of non-military international issues, now commonly called global human security issues, have become more important to Canadian foreign policy since 1989. In 1995, as already noted, Foreign Affairs created a new branch, now named the Global and Human Issues Branch, to develop policies in this regard. Its several divisions reveal how extensively its interests overlap with issues addressed by CIDA: Economic and Social Development, Environment, Human Rights and Justice, Migration, Population and Humanitarian Affairs, and Peace-building and Democratic Development. When this branch was established, the hope was that there would be some degree of synergism between it and the Policy Branch of CIDA, with Global Issues addressing broad foreign policy themes, immediate issues on which policy was needed because of a ministerial interest, a new international crisis or the requirements of forthcoming international conferences, and CIDA's Policy Branch focusing on how Canada's long-term development interests could be related to these new concerns.

However, whatever the early expectations, these arrangements have generated only frustration. Global Issues is responsible, within the department, for policy in subject areas that are increasingly salient in foreign policy, but with regard to which CIDA has both an established interest and ongoing programmes. The frustration results, in part, from differences of points of view over policy. Primarily it stems from the fact that only CIDA has budgetary resources with which to finance initiatives in these fields. Foreign Affairs has therefore had to depend on the co-operation of CIDA whenever there have been significant budgetary implications to initiatives which it has wished to recommend.

The relationship between CIDA and Foreign Affairs has been further complicated since Lloyd Axworthy became Minister of Foreign Affairs in 1996. His ambition is that Canada should play a more prominent role in issues of common human security. His style is spontaneous, the focus of his interests shifts frequently, and he expects rapid and co-operative responses from the bureaucracy. However, many of his concerns fall within CIDA's orbit. To finance the initiatives he desires, CIDA has been pressed then to move funds away from activities that are integral to existing programmes.

These difficulties have been compounded by the fact that coincidental with the appointment of Axworthy as Minister of Foreign Affairs was the appointment, for the first time, of a separate minister for international co-operation with responsibility for CIDA. The motives for this seemed unrelated to any consideration of what would make for a more effective aid policy. For domestic political reasons the Prime Minister wished to add Pierre Pettigrew to the Quebec membership in the cabinet. Pettigrew thus became Minister for International Co-operation, and also Minister Responsible for la Francophonie.

As Axworthy was less than fluently bilingual, this new appointment had the further political advantage that a francophone would speak for Canada on all matters pertaining to la francophonie. It also perpetuated a long-standing practice, honoured by both the liberals and the conservatives, that a francophone would have final control over the allocation of CIDA contracts, an important instrument in the continuing political struggle in Quebec between federalists and separatists. When the Prime Minister then moved Pettigrew to a different portfolio some eight months later, he did not return responsibility for CIDA to Foreign Affairs but, instead, named Donald Boudria, another francophone, as Minister for International Co-operation and Minister Responsible for la Francophonie.

That a separate minister is now responsible for CIDA, with final ministerial authority over its activities and its expenditures, has inevitably further complicated relations between CIDA and Foreign Affairs. It has added the dimension of a contest for turf and limelight between two ministers. Foreign Affairs and its minister can now influence CIDA policies only indirectly through interdepartmental and interministerial consultations. It is small wonder then that the appointment of a separate minister for international co-operation is viewed by Foreign Affairs and its minister as a serious obstacle to the development of a fully coherent foreign policy.

(2) Some Illustrations of Recent Strains in CIDA–Foreign Affairs Relations

Four examples may help to make this discussion more concrete. First, after the landing of substantial American forces in Haiti in 1994, the then minister, André Ouellet, for easily identifiable political reasons, decided that there should be major Canadian participation in the second phase of this operation, and that it should include both the despatch of Royal Canadian Mounted Police (RCMP) officers to Haiti and the training of Haitian police in Quebec.

CIDA initially resisted the suggestion that it should pay for this. These programmes had not been part of its aid strategy for Haiti; they would clearly be very expensive (the figure of $12m was suggested to me as the likely annual cost); and CIDA judged that if sums of that order were to be spent in Haiti, they could finance major basic needs projects of much higher priority. Nevertheless, CIDA recognised the strength of the minister's commitment and finally accepted that it would pay the total cost of this police project, devoting to it most of its discretionary resources for the whole year.

Second, late in 1996, the deputy Prime Minister and the Minister for Foreign Affairs were determined to restore to Radio Canada International the resources that the Minister of Finance had announced would be cut. CIDA was prevailed upon to find $4m as a contribution to an institution-saving packet, accepting a very unconvincing rationalisation that this was legitimate development expenditure.

Third, the minister, having decided to defy the US Helms-Burton law, was anxious to demonstrate that Canadian interests in Cuba were principled rather than merely commercial. He therefore wanted to be able to argue that Canada agreed with the US on the central importance of improvements to human rights in Cuba, but that Canada believed that maintaining trade relations with Cuba facilitated Canadian pressures for the alleviation of human rights abuses there.

Although the previous minister, Ouellet, had sought to widen the range of Canadian activities in Cuba, there were in fact very few CIDA projects in Cuba, save those that were trade-related. For example, in 1995–96, bilateral aid to Cuba had totalled a mere $160,000, while that branch of CIDA which promotes greater trade relations with developing countries, its Industrial Cooperation Branch, had spent a total of $700,000 [*IDIC, 1997: 57*]. Even more relevant, CIDA reported no human rights and democratic development projects at all in Cuba, not even small ones financed from the Canada Fund at the Havana embassy.[18] CIDA was nevertheless

---

18. Canada Funds had been created from CIDA resources in many embassies in developing countries to finance local projects identified by these embassies. As a result of Ouellet's interest, there were some small projects related to human rights which were financed from the Canada Fund at the Havana embassy but which were reported under a different label, so as not to complicate relations with the Cuban government.

required suddenly to demonstrate an involvement with human rights and democratic development in Cuba and a CIDA team hurried off to Havana to see what might be done.

The fourth example relates to Axworthy's emphasis on the appropriateness and desirability of a major Canadian role in peace-building, that is, in healing the hatreds, easing the fears, reviving the economies and reconstituting the governments of societies ravaged by civil wars. Initiatives of this sort are desperately needed in a significant number of countries. Neither Global Issues in Foreign Affairs nor CIDA could possibly be expected to have in hand detailed plans of how Canada might best contribute to peace-building. Deciding where Canada might play a role, what that role should be and then actually implementing what was decided, require inputs not only from Foreign Affairs and CIDA, but also from major Canadian NGOs and from such other departments as Defence, Justice, the RCMP and Elections Canada.

The question of how such activities would be financed was always close to the surface. Foreign Affairs, which sees itself as the lead department on these matters and, indeed, is, had few resources of its own for these purposes. Although it might seem appropriate that savings within the Defence budget should finance peace-building activities, the government and Foreign Affairs accepted that CIDA was politically the only feasible primary source. After some extended sessions, CIDA agreed to devote $10m for a Peace-building Fund, with a further $1m coming from Foreign Affairs. The fund is administered from within CIDA by the director of its International Humanitarian Assistance Division (MHA). However, policy is made by a joint CIDA/Foreign Affairs committee at assistant deputy ministerial level,[19] a committee that is serviced jointly by MHA and Global Issues.

The fund is hardly adequate for the initiative the minister requires. $11 million will permit limited rapid responses to some crises but other resources will be needed very soon thereafter to extend the first inputs and to permit new commitments. Much more inter-departmental manoeuvring must be anticipated.

These four examples of tensions between Foreign Affairs and CIDA make it easy to see why relations have grown more complicated between them. However, it is harder to decide whether these difficulties expose fundamental problems which call for radical surgery.

---

19. NGO participation in this committee was sought by the Canadian Peacebuilding Coordinating Committee but rejected by government.

(3) A Renewed Advocacy of the Subordination of CIDA to Foreign Affairs

By early 1997, many who had been or were officials in the Global Issues Branch of Foreign Affairs, and others as well, were advocating that full policy coherence between CIDA and Foreign Affairs should be accomplished by reducing CIDA to a policy-neutral agency which would implement development assistance policies as determined by Foreign Affairs. It was widely believed that this major change was supported by Axworthy.

Three key moves were seen as sufficient to accomplish this transformation:[20]

(1) CIDA's Policy Branch would need to be integrated into the Global Issues Branch of Foreign Affairs;

(2) the separate cabinet position of Minister for International Co-operation would need either to be scrapped or to have its authority significantly redefined to ensure that final ministerial responsibility for aid policies is returned to the Minister of Foreign Affairs; and

(3) less essential but clearly consistent with the purpose of the change, the president of CIDA would need also to be appointed an Assistant or Associate Deputy Minister of Foreign Affairs in order to establish her/his subordination to the Deputy Minister of Foreign Affairs.

No fuller integration of CIDA into Foreign Affairs was seen by the proponents of radical change as necessary or desirable. No one in Foreign Affairs wanted the department itself to *manage* international assistance programmes.[21] What Global Issues and Axworthy were after was that Foreign Affairs should indisputably *be responsible for aid policies* with authority, when it wished, to determine project and programme selection.

The proposed changes would have ensured that result. Stripped of its policy branch, CIDA would quickly have become merely an implementing agency, for it would be without the competence to be more than that. M. Hugette Labelle, the president of CIDA, would be

---

20. What follows is a summary of the advocacy of a policy-neutral CIDA as it was offered to me in several extended interviews with senior officials in Foreign Affairs in April 1997.
21. A precedent for these arrangements was established in 1995 when the administration of international assistance to the former Soviet Union and to central and eastern Europe was transferred from Foreign Affairs to CIDA, with Foreign Affairs retaining policy responsibility for these programmes.

without the staff essential for her to provide policy leadership and to advise whichever minister was responsible for CIDA. She would be reduced *de facto* to a chief administrative officer. The coherence of Canadian aid policies and the other components of Canadian foreign policy would have been substantially ensured.

(4) Assessing the 1996–67 Effort to Achieve Greater Policy Coherence between CIDA and Foreign Affairs

The Context Contrasted with 1993: The discussion of the effort in 1992–93 to subordinate CIDA more fully to Foreign Affairs concluded that the greater policy coherence that it was intended to promote would have significantly lessened Canadian assistance to the long-term development needs of the world's poorest countries and peoples.

This earlier conclusion cannot simply be transposed to the fresh efforts in 1996–97 to accomplish greater policy coherence. Much has in fact happened that threatens CIDA as a development agency with a mandate to 'support sustainable development in developing countries'. Cold-war considerations no longer provide hard-nosed foreign policy reasons to continue foreign aid. Responsiveness to the needs of the poorest within Canada is declining, a trend that impinges also on public and governmental concern about global poverty. Pressures from the private sector, the Prime Minister's office and Foreign Affairs and International Trade continue to ensure that much Canadian aid is deployed to advance Canadian trade interests. Public confidence that Canadian aid actually reaches and helps the poorest has eroded, as has confidence that Canadian aid has 'made a difference'. Many new areas of international co-operation have become important, further marginalising official interest in Foreign Affairs in traditional development assistance. In these new circumstances, the possibility that the institutional subordination of CIDA to Foreign Affairs may contribute to, rather than detract from, the responsiveness of Canadian foreign policy to the overall needs of the developing countries must therefore be freshly assessed.

The Case in 1997 for Greater Policy Control by Foreign Affairs: The objective of the proposed fuller subordination of CIDA to Foreign Affairs which has been canvassed most recently has been in part to overcome the difficulties being experienced in their relationship. With these changes, there would no longer be a separate minister responsible for CIDA whose co-operation would need to be won for aid policy initiatives desired by the Minister of Foreign Affairs. The bureaucracy of Foreign Affairs would therefore be able to respond far more swiftly to ministerial instructions. The president of CIDA could, of course, still champion CIDA's preference in any disagreement but at some point, (s)he could be overruled by the deputy minister.

A further organisational improvement was also anticipated by the supporters of this change. The merging of the two branches would create a larger critical mass of officials working together on the new global security issues. Moreover, as the officials would now all be members of a single policy unit, disagreements should be fewer and, if they did emerge, should be more easily resolved. Finally, it was argued that these issues were unavoidably foreign policy issues. Foreign Affairs should, therefore, be responsible for policy with regard to them.

The subordination of CIDA to Foreign Affairs has been sought, however, for reasons far more substantial than their possible contribution to bureaucratic efficiency. Advocates of the integration of CIDA's Policy Branch into the Global Issues Branch of Foreign Affairs have seen it as a further step towards fuller overall policy integration within that department. Global Issues does not as yet play a central policy role within Foreign Affairs. Its concerns overlap significantly with those of other branches in the department which, moreover, also have strong policy capabilities. As a result, the influence of Global Issues is often less than its supporters would wish. For example, the human rights and justice division of Global Issues has not played a significant role in determining Canadian trade policies towards highly repressive regimes and it is the Trade and Economic Policy Branch, with its dominant orientation towards Canadian trade interests, not the Global Issues Branch, that has been permitted to develop competence relating to development assistance and to trade policies towards the developing countries.

The transfer of CIDA's Policy Branch into Global Issues is supported by some who are primarily interested not so much in aid issues as in augmenting the strength and status of Global Issues within Foreign Affairs in order to increase thereby the department's responsiveness to the new global human security issues.

A final argument favouring the greater subordination of CIDA to Foreign Affairs is quite different in character. It is offered by individuals who are anxious that Canadian foreign policy should be *more* responsive to the needs of Third World countries, but who no longer feel that much reliance should be placed on CIDA. I present here this argument in what seems to me its most persuasive form.[22]

---

22. What follows brings together a number of separate considerations presented to me in interviews with proponents of greater Foreign Affairs policy control. It is a fuller presentation of this argument than any one of them presented to me but is, I think, consistent with their own individual developments of it.

CIDA has long compromised its commitment to its putative first objective of helping the development efforts of the poorest peoples in the globe's poorest countries and has instead been responsive in a major way to Canadian trade and foreign policy interests. Moreover, the cuts to CIDA's budget have been particularly severe so that even at best, it can contribute less and less to the welfare and development of the globe's poorest. The era of development assistance is effectively over. The case for greater responsiveness to the needs of the less developed countries must be championed with regard to a far wider range of policies than just aid. It therefore must have its advocates *within* Foreign Affairs; concern over Third World poverty should not be sidelined into an ever-weakening CIDA.

The absortion of CIDA's Policy Branch into Global Issues and the explicit broadening of its mandate to include international development would provide at least the chance that it could become a 'Trojan horse', internal to Foreign Affairs, advocating Canada's long-term interest in equitable and sustained development in the less-developed countries. Turning that possibility into a reality, rather than 'saving CIDA', should be the primary objective of those concerned to retain some measure of humane internationalism in Canada's relations with the less developed countries.

Some Good Reasons for Caution: Neither the efficiency arguments nor the broader public policy arguments for the fuller subordination of CIDA to Foreign Affairs are as persuasive as their advocates maintain.

Two considerations tell against the bureaucratic efficiency arguments, one quite specific and the other more general. The specific point is easily stated. Policy-making must build on knowledge and experience. The conversion of CIDA into a policy-neutral agency would greatly lessen any significant feedback from the policy-implementing branches of CIDA to the policy-makers, who would, under the proposal, all be absorbed into Foreign Affairs.

The more general consideration is more complex. An increasing number of government departments, from the Department of Defence to the Department of Fisheries, now contribute to Canadian policies beyond its borders. Greater coherence in Canada's overall foreign policy is certainly an important objective. However, it cannot be accomplished by conceding to Foreign Affairs responsibility for setting the foreign policy components of the activities of these other departments. What was being proposed with regard to CIDA, its subordination to Foreign Affairs, follows an older and increasingly inappropriate model. It could not be extended to the many other departments involved in overseas activities of one sort or another. What is needed instead for issue after issue, is effective *horizontal* consultative machinery, involving Foreign Affairs, but with the choice of the lead department depending on which department has the most appropriate concentration of expertise.

There is a further basic public policy argument against the greater subordination of CIDA to Foreign Affairs: it would be likely, quickly, to lead to a marked decline of any substantial Canadian commitment to long-term sustainable human development in the world's poorest countries. It is true that activities which would promote long-term development in these countries certainly qualify as contributions to global human security. However, officials moulded in the traditions of the Department of External Affairs would be likely unduly to filter out development considerations too early in the decision-making process. Other global human security objectives, such as containing the drug trade, influencing destructive environmental policies, rebuilding stability in societies destroyed by civil war, advancing good governance in countries of political or economic importance to Canada and strengthening the capabilities of regional powers, would be more likely to be favoured by Foreign Affairs, seeing them as having a more immediate impact in the recipient countries, and winning for Canada more approval and influence than activities to help meet the development needs of the world's poorest countries and peoples. Indeed, the subordination of CIDA has been sought precisely to facilitate a shift of Canadian development assistance away from development and poverty-focused objectives towards common global security projects.

There is a final major reason for caution. It cannot be assumed that the proposed subordination of CIDA to Foreign Affairs would mean that global human security concerns would in fact determine the newer expenditure patterns. Foreign Affairs is overwhelmingly concerned to strengthen Canada's internationally competitive economic position. Activities to promote Canadian trade and investment rather than efforts to augment global human security could easily end up as the principal beneficiary of any further subordination of CIDA to Foreign Affairs.

The Crisis Resolved? The appointment of a new federal cabinet following the Canadian national election on 2 June 1997 provided the newly re-elected Liberal Prime Minister, Jean Chrétien, with an opportunity, had he wished to take it, to ensure greater policy

99

coherence between CIDA and Foreign Affairs. He could have decided to scrap the Ministry for International Co-operation and to restore to the Minister of Foreign Affairs his formal responsibility for CIDA policies. He could have gone further and also approved the substantial transfer of the policy branch of CIDA to Global Issues in Foreign Affairs.

He did neither of these. Instead he appointed Diane Marleau, the previous Minister of Health, as Minister for International Co-operation and Minister Responsible for la Francophonie. It would be naive to see this decision as significantly influenced by the various arguments for caution towards the subordination of CIDA to Foreign Affairs. Rather, domestic political considerations, which had originally led to the decision to create the separate ministry, have continued to predominate. However, the immediate result is that, for whatever reasons, Chrétien has opted to continue to place authority for CIDA in the hands of a separate minister and to leave the institutional relationship of CIDA and Foreign Affairs unchanged.

V. FINAL REFLECTIONS

The story just told certainly illustrates, as did the account of the 1992–95 crisis in CIDA–Foreign Affairs relations, that the Department of Foreign Affairs is recurrently aroused to seek greater authority over Canadian development assistance policies. However, in this instance as in the former, it is reasonable to conclude that, had Foreign Affairs achieved the greater policy coherence it was after, the quality of Canada's contribution to long-term, equitable international development would have diminished rather than improved.

Canadian experience thus suggests that greater policy coherence, as it has actually been pursued, has not been the self-evident advance that it is sometimes assumed to be. Section I points out that greater coherence between the macro-economic policies of the governments receiving Canadian aid and the neo-liberal development strategy favoured by Canada may in fact have diminished rather than improved the Canadian contribution to the development of the economies and the welfare of the populations of the developing countries. Section II comes to a similar judgement about the likely consequences of the efforts of the CIDA leadership in recent years to increase coherence between the various separate activities supported by CIDA.

Section III argues that the greater coherence of Canadian aid policies and Canadian foreign policy, which the Department of Foreign

Affairs hoped to accomplish by seeking a greater subordination of CIDA to it, would almost certainly have diminished the quality of Canada's international development assistance had its effort succeeded. Finally, section IV considers the fresh efforts by Foreign Affairs in 1997 to increase the coherence of Canadian aid policies with Canadian foreign policy. As well in this instance, it seems very likely that, had greater policy coherence been achieved through the conversion of CIDA into a policy-neutral agency subordinate to Foreign Affairs, there would have been a further deterioration of Canada's commitment to the long-term development of the least developed countries.

Such a deterioration in the quality of a country's development assistance is not an inevitable consequence of a greater subordination of the national aid agency to its foreign ministry. The Canadian case suggests that the key variable is the comparative importance that the government and its foreign ministry attach to the country's aid programme. In those countries where the aid programme is widely viewed by the public and by the government and its ministries as a central and attractive feature of foreign policy, there is no reason to expect that a greater subordination of the aid agency to the foreign ministry will have adverse implications for the aid programme. However, as the Canadian case illustrates, where the government itself and more particularly its foreign ministry have other foreign policy preoccupations which easily displace the promotion of equitable long-term development, greater overall policy coherence between aid policies and foreign policies is much more likely to lead to the further predominance of trade and political considerations in the shaping of aid policies.

Consciously accepted contradictions in fact abound within the foreign policies of most, if not all, OECD states. The promotion of human rights and democratic participation, for example, is an important objective of many of their development assistance agencies, at the same time as their governments foster trade, diplomatic and even military relations with states whose governments are highly oppressive but economically or geopolitically important. Even more relevant for our argument, many aid agencies typically compromise the integrity of their commitment to development by responding also to domestic demands that they be sensitive to the trade interests of national exporters and to other foreign policy objectives.

It is therefore, perhaps, imprecise and confusing when those of us concerned with promoting sustainable human development and greater international equity identify greater policy coherence as an important policy objective. A *full* congruity in any developed country between the whole range of its policies towards developing countries and the development objectives of its aid policies is an impossible objective, owing to the multiple characteristics of foreign policy objectives. Even more relevant, *greater* policy coherence between aid and foreign policies can be achieved, and in most OECD countries may in fact be more likely to be pursued, not by bringing trade and other national foreign policies into line with development objectives for the South, but by ensuring that aid policies more fully advance the trade and international political objectives of the developed countries.

It is, thus, perhaps more effective for those concerned with advancing equitable international development to stress the importance, not of greater policy coherence, but of giving greater weight to development considerations as against narrowly self-interested trade and international political objectives in the determination of both non-aid and aid policies.

REFERENCES

Burdette, Marcia, 1994, 'Structural Adjustment and Canadian Aid Policy', in Pratt (ed.).
CIDA, 1987, *Sharing Our Future: Canada's International Development Strategy*, Ottawa: Canadian International Development Agency, Supply and Services.
CIDA, 1991, *Sustainable Development*, Discussion Paper, Hull: Canadian International Development Agency.
CIDA, 1995, 'The Role of the Voluntary Sector in Development and CIDA's Relationship with Canadian Voluntary Organizations: CIDA Framework', Canadian International Development Agency, zeroxed memorandum.
Dimic, Nicolas, 1995, *The Geographic Distribution of Canada's Bilateral Assistance: An Alternative Approach*, Policy Staff Paper 95/15, Ottawa: Department of Foreign Affairs and International Trade.
Government of Canada, 1987, *To Benefit a Better World*, Ottawa: Supply and Services.
Government of Canada, 1995, *Canada in the World: Government Statement*, Ottawa: Department of Foreign Affairs and International Trade.
Groupe SECOR, *Strategic Management Review: Working Document* (publisher and place of publication not indicated but 1991).
House of Commons, 1987, *For Whose Benefit? Report of the Standing Committee on External Affairs and International Trade on Canada's Official Development Assistance Policies and Programs*, Ottawa: Supply and Services.
House of Commons, 1994, *Canada's Foreign Policy: Principles and Priorities for the Future, Report of the Special Joint Parliamentary Committee Reviewing Canadian Foreign Policy*, Ottawa: Parliamentary Publications Directorate.
International Development Information Centre (IDIC), 1997, *Statistical Report on Official Development Assistance: Fiscal Year 1995/96*, Ottawa: CIDA.
Morrison, David, 1994, 'The Choice of Bilateral Aid Recipients', in Pratt (ed.).
Morrison, David, 1998, *Aid and Ebb Tide: A History of CIDA and Canadian Development Assistance*, Waterloo: Wilfred Laurier University Press.

Pratt, Cranford, 1992, 'Towards a Neo-Conservative Transformation of Canadian International Development Assistance: the SECOR Report on CIDA', *International Journal*, Vol.47, No. 3.

Pratt, Cranford, 1993–94, 'Canadian Development Assistance: Some lessons from the last review', *International Journal*, Vol. 49, No.1.

Pratt, Cranford, 1994–95, 'Development Assistance and Canadian Foreign Policy: Where we now are', *Canadian Foreign Policy*, Vol.2, No.3.

Pratt, Cranford, 1996, 'Humane Internationalism and Canadian Development Assistance Policies', in Pratt (ed.).

Pratt, Cranford, 1998, 'DFAIT's Take-Over Bid of CIDA: The Institutional Future of the Canadian International Development Agency', *Canadian Foreign Policy*, Vol.5, No.2, Winter.

Pratt, Cranford (ed.), 1994, second edition 1996, *Canadian International Development Assistance Policies: An Appraisal*, Montreal and Kingston: McGill-Queens University Press.

Rawkins, Phillip, 1994, 'An Institutional Analysis of CIDA', in Pratt (ed.).

Rudner, Martin, 1994, 'Canadian Development Cooperation with Asia: Strategic Objectives and Policy Goals', in Pratt (ed.).

4

The Coherence of French and European Policy in International Development Co-operation

PHILIPPE HUGON

Aid donors seek to improve the co-ordination and coherence of bilateral and multilateral development co-operation policies in the light of the wasteful implementation of aid and of its scarcity. Coherence relates to the external effects of policies on areas other than development co-operation, but also among its various components. Co-ordination refers to greater information transparency and complementarity, in the policies of recipient countries, and between these policies and those of various donor countries.

These objectives are primarily stated in the Maastricht Treaty (Section XVII of the Treaty). The principle of complementarity relates to the sectors in which the European Community shares its competency (as is the case with development co-operation), thereby implying a division of tasks enabling the actors to complement one another. The principle of subsidiarity applies to the sectors where the Community has legal competence [*EPCDM, 1994*].

The term, aid policy coherence, is, however, ambiguous. Expressed as objectives, at least four levels of coherence can be distinguished (Forster, this volume, Ch. 9):

– Internal coherence between all aspects of bilateral policy in order to reduce divergences between the various facets and aims of each policy and to increase complementarity between the desired effects of a policy and the actual outcomes;

Many thanks to G. Chedeville Murray, Ministry of Foreign Affairs, J. Forster and O. Stokke for their helpful comments.

- Internal coherence between bilateral and multilateral policies which aims to reduce the contradictions existing between the aims and procedures of different donors;
- Coherence between the policies of donor countries;
- North–South external coherence which aims to minimise the contradictory or negative effects of aid on recipient economies.

As for the latter, one can apply Sens's entitlements theory, as suggested by Morrissey (this volume, Ch. 12). Incoherence would result from counter-productive effects of aid policy on a country's ability to meet and provide for basic needs, thereby generating a negative impact on local production and trade. In other words, aid (considered as an external entitlement) has a negative effect on the recipient country's direct entitlement tied to production (by competing with local food production) or on its exchange entitlement which is tied to trade (by reducing external trade or having a negative effect on the terms of trade).

The notion of coherence thus touches upon several levels and brings to light several types of problems: legal (the problem of sharing jurisdiction), organisational (problems resulting from the multiplicity of decision-makers and procedures), economic (problems of compatibility between divergent interests) and financial (the problem of setting up a coherent financial framework). It reflects interdependencies between decision-making levels which give rise to tangled or interactive hierarchies. Relations among donors may be of a hierarchical nature (with one country as the leader of the hierarchy), co-operative (with a sharing of competencies) or competitive (with more or less captive markets). Relations with recipient countries may be centred around conditionality (with more or less supervision or benevolence) or based on partnership. As a result the coherence of multi-faceted bilateral and multilateral policies takes on a multiplicity of forms.

TABLE I
THE DIFFERENT TYPES OF COHERENCE IN DEVELOPMENT CO-OPERATION POLICIES

Ties between donors and beneficiaries	Hierarchical	Co-operative	Competitive
Conditionality	Imposed coherence	Coherence with shared competencies	Coherence through multilateral supervision
Partnership		Coherence through mutual responsibility	Coherence through mutual responsibility

Nonetheless, it may seem that the objective of *coherence* is largely utopian if one considers that policies reflect a compromise between aims and means, which tend to be conflicting and contradictory. To fulfil the objective of *co-ordination* is very difficult, considering the great numbers of decision-makers involved, even if it is facilitated by the de facto leadership of the Bretton Woods institutions. The effects of aid policies differ from the expected results or initial objectives. Political decisions often represent a compromise between various lobbies. Development proceeds by trial and error and is further limited by the challenges that oblige decision-makers to reform their policies. Short-term incoherences can therefore become coherent in the long term, or vice versa. A high degree of coherence could only be sought either through a totalitarian and technocratic approach or through unwavering faith in the market's invisible hand.

The coherence and co-ordination of aid policies are even more difficult to achieve considering that various factors come into play in different situations.

In France, for example, the development co-operation system is very complex and involves numerous decision-makers. The internal coherence of bilateral policy becomes all the more tenuous as an increasing share of aid is allocated to multilateral institutions. Furthermore, criticism of aid, or 'aid fatigue', has given rise to growing conflicts over its objectives and procedures and has called into question its original orientations.

At the European level, there are several complicating factors. The region is seeking to increase its strength and influence through the construction of a European Union, since it is obviously easier to speak with one voice when the number of speakers is limited. Europe suffers from high unemployment, and its close neighbours to the East and South are undergoing economic crisis. One must also place the issue of the convergence of economic policies and the co-ordination of development co-operation within the context of recession and strong competition to win markets. Finally, since the fall of the Berlin Wall, Europe's centre of gravity has been shifting towards the centre and the east. Member states have different views on priorities and on what is to happen after the Lomé IV Treaty; ACP countries (Africa, the Caribbean and Pacific) received 65 per cent of external financing provided by the sixth EDF (European Development Fund) but their share had fallen to 33.5 per cent by the time of the eighth EDF.

Traditional recipients (ACP countries) have visibly lost their bargaining power since the fall of the Berlin Wall, the emergence of strong economies among Asian countries and the normalisation of the situation in South Africa. There are, moreover, growing conflicts of interest between the North and the South and among Southern countries, as indicated, for instance, by the differing opinions expressed in the World Trade Organisation (WTO). These conflicts have arisen in spite of new opportunities within the context of democratisation and structural adjustment [*EPCPM, 1994*]. The weak growth of recipient countries and the spread of what some have called the 'aid disease' [*Gabas and Sindzingre, 1996*] have led to a questioning of the value of development aid. Numerous assisted countries continue to play on the rivalry existing between the main donor countries and consider aid as a rent-like source of income to be appropriated.

Since incoherences of development policies reflect simultaneously conflicts of interest, different kinds of procedures and diverse objectives, it may seem illusory to imagine a situation of full coherence. On the other hand, it is possible to reduce contradictions, to define possible synergies and areas of concerted action and negotiation, on the basis of common objectives, such as the long-term economic development of countries (which are partners of the European Union). This would help reduce the 'lack of co-ordination, articulation, expression and impulse, which is characteristic of the Community' [*CEE, 1992: 1*].

We will discuss successively: (1) the new context of French and European development co-operation, (2) the problem of the lack of coherence in French policy, (3) the problems of poor coherence and co-ordination between French and European policy.

1. THE NEW CONTEXT OF DEVELOPMENT CO-OPERATION POLICY

Since the establishment of official development assistance after the Second World War, the world has undergone profound changes.

Development assistance policy has to respond to numerous demands and challenges emanating from the South such as rapid population growth, migratory pressures, the destruction of ecosystems and the lack of capital and competencies in the fight against poverty. It is also placed in a new context of globalisation, more specifically in its financial dimension, and in the long-term indebtedness of numerous developing economies. It must take into consideration the fact that its partners are increasingly following different paths and that the international environment has undergone profound transformations.

Aid policy continues to be guided by diverse and even contradictory objectives on the part of the North, which have been evolving since the fall of the Berlin Wall and which include, for example, geopolitical interests, the search for markets, and – in the case of France – the spread of the French language. It finds itself in a context of growing unemployment in Europe and budgetary convergence prior to the launching of the Euro.

These various factors have an important impact on French development co-operation policy, traditionally oriented towards Africa, and on Europe's development co-operation, directed primarily towards ACP countries.

(1) Contrasts in the ACP's Evolution

In a world undergoing a process of globalisation, marked by a rise in international competition and regional tensions in several subcontinents, sub-Saharan African and ACP countries continue to be privileged partners in French and European development co-operation. However, they remain poorly integrated in regional and global dynamics. Despite liberalisation policies which also affect its international economic relations, Africa is marginalised with regard not only to commercial flows but also to technological and financial flows; as a result, it is being 'disconnected' from the world economy. The share of imports from outside the European Community, originating from ACP countries, dropped from 6.7 per cent in 1976 to 2.8 per cent in 1994. The share of direct foreign investments in Africa, as a percentage of the total investments in LDCs (excluding China), which amounted to 6 per cent in 1985, fell to 4 per cent in 1995. Thirty years ago, the average income for African countries represented 14 per cent of the average income of developed countries, whereas it is 7 per cent today; moreover, Africa controlled 3 per cent of world trade as opposed to just 1.5 per cent today. The exhaustion of 'rentier' regimes is evident, characterised by the logic of redistribution. The State is unable to fulfil its minimal functions of maintaining security and territorial control. It is overrun from the top by the Bretton Woods institutions which have instigated a transfer of power and from the bottom by the widespread informal functioning of society. However, a slight resumption of growth and private investments is observable, having doubled in volume from 1994 to 1996, reaching US$ 12 billion. However, this growth originated in South Africa and in petroleum investments, and the increase, Africa's share of direct foreign investments, fell from 3 per cent in the early 1980s to 2.3 per cent in 1996.

(2) The Permanent Indebtedness of African Countries

Since the beginning of the 1980s, numerous African countries have been caught up in the vicious cycle of *permanent indebtedness* which has backfired on domestic financial systems. Credit must be guaranteed against the growth of real assets and exports which would allow for repayments. However, inadequate external resources led, up until the beginning of the 1990s, to a (self-sustained) growth in external indebtedness due to the accumulation of arrears, rescheduling and new loans. Numerous borrowing countries, among the LDCs, have become insolvent debtors. The rescheduling of payments, and access to credit to repay interest, have merely perpetuated the problem. Debt has been feeding itself.[1]

Debt stabilisation has not provided these countries with long-lasting means of rebuilding their financial systems. Multilateral debt, which for a long time could not be rescheduled, particularly where the creditors were the Bretton Woods institutions, has become an increasingly greater part of external debt.[2] This external indebtedness has had a crucial impact on countries receiving foreign aid and on the terms and conditions of development co-operation:

- It has affected internal debt and has greatly increased public debt, the accumulation of overdue wages and payments to enterprises. It has also spread to the domestic financial system.
- Repayment transfers were made independently from debt transfers.
- African countries have to manage a regressive process: they increased their debt by acquiring additional loans to ensure debt servicing, in an international context of low prices; this often led to a deflationary adjustment process.

The permanent indebtedness of African countries has placed them under tutelage, thereby reducing the responsibility of their governments. Except in a few exceptional cases, the market was unable to play the role it did in Latin America following the Brady Plan. Aid, in the form of projects, was to a large extent replaced by budgetary assistance and adjustment loans.

---

1. The external debt of sub-Saharan Africa (excluding South Africa) thus rose from US$ 95 billion to 185 billion in 1990; it tripled between 1980 and 1990, representing 12 per cent of the total debt of developing countries. At the end of 1993, Africa's overall long-term debt was estimated to be US$ 240 billion, of which 181 billion were official credits and 22 billion were funded by financial institutions. Total debt was equal to US$ 278.8 billion. Debt service represented 25 per cent of exports in 1993.
2. It rose from 96 per cent to 362 per cent of goods and services exports. Debt service, which was actually disbursed, went from 10.9 per cent to 22.1 per cent, half of which represented interest payments.

(3) The Growing Significance of Public Aid and the Fading Presence of Private Creditors

In Africa, official development assistance (ODA) has replaced reluctant private credit and investment.[3] At the international level, peace dividends (savings of US$ 800 billion) did not lead to an increase in official development assistance. Besides a few sector-related vested interests, Africa does not represent major long-term or short-term economic stakes. Since the fall of the Berlin Wall, it is of no interest for geopolitical (Cold War) reasons. The international context is, moreover, characterised by a decline in ODA resources.

However, sub-Saharan Africa remains the subcontinent which receives the most aid.[4] From 1980 to 1993, 11 per cent of its average GNP came from development co-operation. This region which represents 12 per cent of the world population receives 37 per cent of the ODA of DAC member countries. Multilateral aid has increased from 18 per cent in 1980 to 36.5 per cent in 1992. With diminishing private flows, ODA has taken over (amounting to US$ 30 billion in 1992, or 8 per cent of its GDP). Although financial transfers to Africa have remained positive, financial transfers from the International Monetary Fund have been negative since 1990 and net transfers from the World Bank have been decreasing. The Community (including its member states) has spent nearly 0.5 per cent of its GNP on aid to developing countries; this represents more than 40 per cent of the total aid they receive. Africa receives a little more than half of the Community's aid.

(4) The Significance of Aid for Adjustment

The nature of aid has changed; it has assumed greater macro-economic scope, with quick-disbursement mechanisms (Stabex funds, structural adjustment loans and counterpart funds) being favoured. Adjustment aid has gained importance *vis-à-vis* project aid. As a result, the objectives, procedures and co-ordination of international aid have changed.

---

3.   In 1991, positive financial transfers were equal to US$ 2 billion. Long-term financial flows decreased from US$ 10 billion in 1982 to 4.7 billion in 1990. On the other hand, private investments, at 2.5 billion in 1991, were below their 1985 level. They increased to US$ 5 billion in 1994, 9 billion in 1996 and 11 billion in 1997, which can be primarily attributed to South Africa and petroleum-exporting countries.
4.   In terms of the GNP percentage of DAC (Development Assistance Committee of the OECD) member countries, ODA dropped from 0.35 per cent in 1982–84, to 0.29 per cent in 1993. Furthermore, the share of aid allocated to the least developed countries went from 31 per cent in 1981–82 to 25 per cent in 1992. Meanwhile the annual growth rate of ODA in US$ was equivalent to 0.5 per cent during the 1980s; it went down to -2.4 per cent between 1990 and 1994.

In 1994, over one-third of French foreign aid was devoted to debt alleviation and nearly 10 per cent was allocated to programme aid, as against 33.1 per cent to infrastructure projects and 27 per cent to programmes in other sectors [*CAD, 1996*].

The European Union, which since the Lomé IV treaty has accepted the principle of adjustment, has greatly modified its doctrine and methods of allocating aid. General import programmes and counterpart funds (related to adjustment, Stabex and Sysmin funds or food aid) ease the foreign currency constraints of those countries not in the Franc Zone. This leads to targeted budgetary assistance in priority sectors (education, health, food security, road infrastructure). By implementing rapid disbursements of financial assistance, the European Union has changed its modus operandi: instead of stabilising economies, it seeks to adapt them to the world market; conditionality has become a substitute for partnership; projects have been to a large extent replaced by programmes; targeted budgetary assistance has become part of a coherent financial framework [*Coussy, 1997*]. Stabex, Sysmin or adjustment funds represented over 30 per cent of the seventh and eighth EDF. This aid, in the form of grants, has safeguarded priority sectors which were burdening public budgets. It led to an increase in net transfers unlike those of the World Bank whose loans generate debt servicing.

The logic of aid has been greatly modified by the implementation of adjustment and debt management. Financial stabilisation, macroeconomic conditions and the institutional framework (good governance, political or institutional conditionality) have now become priorities. The objective of salvaging what exists overrides long-term projects.

Adjustment has also promoted the convergence of donor countries, in liberalist doctrines as well as their methods of managing debt and adjustment under the leadership of the Bretton Woods institutions. To be eligible for aid, a country has to be 'on track' when negotiating with these institutions [*Duruflé, 1997*]. One can speak of a partially co-operative aid oligopoly, headed by a leader [*Coussy, 1997*] and therefore of a co-ordinated hierarchy. The European Union can nonetheless influence the World Bank (by privileging the budget). There seem to be divergent positions on conditionality and aid eligibility.

Thirty years after the independence of African countries, foreign aid is still vital to their societies. Aid, development co-operation and technical assistance help in controlling situations of crisis. They help maintain the minimal provision of public services but they lead to the perpetuation of high-cost technical assistance with limited transmission of know-how. They often generate counter-productive effects and can also lead to the African governments' loss of autonomy and responsibility. Instead of being a provisional transfusion, aid has transformed itself into a permanent perfusion which has allowed states to guarantee their minimal security and territorial control functions and to finance public investments.

On the financial side, what used to be exceptional and provisional is now structural; short-term loans multiply themselves to create a long-term perspective, but in a short time frame. Aid continues to be concentrated in capitalistic sectors and hardly affects the poorest or the actors in civil society. It remains to a great extent tied to short-term commercial interests or debt settlements.

(5) Globalisation and Multilateralism

The globalisation of markets is accelerating. Transnational flows blend with decision-making centres; deregulation and progress in telecommunications are leading to a single market for goods and capital flows. Transnational firms weave among themselves worldwide networks; they act on strategic markets and conclude between themselves agreements on a global scale rather than on a regional level.

There are new hierarchies of comparative advantage, and centres of gravity have shifted towards new regional poles, especially Asian ones. Moreover, the productive system has been restructured on the basis of new technologies, goods and services. The growth rate of world trade in manufactured goods and services is twice as high as that of mining products and four times that of agricultural commodities. The relative prices of commodities tend to decrease in the long term compared to goods and services, which are a source of technological revenue, as well as a source of creativity and of added value when exchanged in non-competitive markets. In a competitive world, African and Asian, Caribbean and Pacific countries remain inadequate in terms of specialisation and have weak diversification of export products.

The system promoted by the Uruguay Round and the World Trade Organisation has become highly incompatible with generalised systems of preferences and numerous protections which continue to be characteristic of aid policies (multifibre agreements, price subsidies, tied aid). The aim is to:

- generalise the principle of the most favoured nation clause;
- integrate into the GATT logic those sectors (agriculture and textile) hitherto excluded from negotiations (on services, intellectual property) or outside their scope;

112

- reduce tariffs and, more importantly, eliminate new trade barriers and all measures that limit competition (subsidies, dumping);
- reform the internal functioning of the GATT in order for it to become an organism of conciliation and dispute arbitration.

In a context of globalisation, the debate is much less centred on trade versus aid or on the complementary or competitive role of aid with regard to savings or exports (two-deficits model, absorption models or aid disease). The main aim remains to foster an auspicious international environment which would reduce risks and uncertainties, create a feeling of trust, and attract capital.

In a world undergoing profound transformation, former French and European development co-operation policies are greatly called into question.

II. LACK OF COHERENCE IN FRENCH DEVELOPMENT CO-OPERATION POLICY AND INSTITUTIONAL REFORMS

(1) The Objectives and Particularities of French Co-operation

Development co-operation was set up at the time of Africa's decolonisation. Common interests were created through the prolongation of historical and geographic factors, the former being mostly related to colonial history. Development co-operation policy was elaborated and implemented on the basis of principles other than those of multilateralism and free trade. It was a matter of managing the transition of former colonies towards viable economic systems that would foster development. It was acknowledged that the premise for the implementation of free trade between the North and the South had not been laid down. As a result it was deemed necessary to set up a protective and compensatory legal right to development. Development co-operation was considered to be a priority.

Three main geographical areas can be distinguished, corresponding to different objectives:

- Sub-Saharan Africa is dominated by cultural, geopolitical and humanitarian concerns. Nonetheless, there are economic interests in certain sectors (mining and petroleum) on the part of certain companies that have found a 'niche', especially in the Franc Zone, which has remained a privileged area.
- In the Mediterranean Basin, commercial and financial concerns as well as the need to control migratory pressures, are deemed to be more important.

113

- In the remaining countries of the South, aid instruments are, to a greater extent, tied to export promotion, the support of French companies and, to a large extent, the promotion of the French language.

There is a great diversity of development co-operation instruments. They range from technical and cultural assistance, numerous kinds of economic aid, financial support – especially adjustment aid – to project loans. French aid is made up of several components:

- *military*: which aims to avoid tensions and guarantee security;
- *cultural*: which seeks to promote the French language and French culture;
- *economic*: which attempts to gain access to strategic products such as petroleum and to develop external markets (tied aid);
- *social* (emergency assistance, the social dimension of structural adjustments);
- *political* (human rights, democratisation, institutional development).

(2) Calling into Question the Main Elements of French Development Co-operation

The main elements that in the past guaranteed a certain level of coherence of French policy are today called into question.

There is much controversy over the areas in which French aid is deployed. Nonetheless, aid continues to be concentrated on former colonies ('pays du champ') but new trends are appearing.[5] Private economic actors are attracted by new promising markets, especially in Asia. There is much debate and conflict over which interests should be privileged. Some people defend economic interests that can be served by leaning towards promising markets; others favour geopolitical and cultural interests in linguistic and geographical zones of proximity. French policy remains torn between a worldwide vocation, accompanied by the redeployment of firms in the context of globalisation,

---

5. In 1996, according to the Prime Minister's Office, French development co-operation (including Overseas Territories) amounted to 38.1 billion francs, of which 49 per cent was allocated to Sub-Saharan Africa (18.7 billion); 15 per cent went to North Africa (5.7 billion); 12 per cent to the Pacific (4.6 billion); 5 per cent to South Asia (1.6 billion); 7 per cent to America (2.5 billion); 3 per cent to the Middle East (1.23 billion); and 2 per cent to southern Europe (748 million); of which 30.5 per cent, in 1994, was tied aid and 81.8 per cent allocated in the form of grants. ODA's share of GDP tends to decrease. It went down from 0.5% in 1995 to 0.45% in 1996 (not including Overseas Territories).

and a regional strategy, focusing on Africa, which reinforces cultural, political and geopolitical policies. Whether or not to maintain the Ministry of Development Co-operation, whose area of competence does not extend beyond the former colonial territories, exemplifies this debate.

As for the *instruments*, it may be noted that technical and cultural co-operation has been greatly reduced and that macro-economic loans, tied to structural adjustments, have increased. The presence of the military has also been reinforced. Elementary education and basic health have become priorities; however, in 1990, only 4 per cent of French development assistance was allocated to grassroots education, health care and nutrition. French aid continues to be tied (over 40 per cent) and does not always have to do with development [*Marchand, 1996*]. An increase in emergency aid and decentralised development co-operation[6] is also evident. This is less conducive to an overall, long-term coherent vision and tends to lead to a case-by-case approach. As a result there are marked contradictions which are accentuated by the plurality of decision-making bodies.

(3) The Plurality of Decision-making Bodies

The situation has been described by some as institutional chaos. The institutional system is, in any case, highly complex. This complexity is detrimental to transparency and to the visibility of the country's global contribution to development co-operation [*Marchesin, 1993*]. Although ODA appropriations are decided by Parliament, the distribution of aid among different ministries makes it impossible to have an overall picture.

In 1987, there were no fewer than 14 ministerial departments involved with development co-operation. As Cazes [*1987: 7*] has pointed out, 'credits and procedures are determined by the Treasury, whereas the Foreign and Development Co-operation Ministries are responsible for political legitimacy'. The actors in this multipolar system are: the Treasury, the Ministries of Development Co-operation, Foreign Affairs and DOM-TOM[7], as well as the 'technical' ministries, the French Fund for Development (CFD) and research institutions such as CIRAD and ORSTOM. When it comes to Africa, strategic decision-making takes place at the presidential policy-making unit at the Elysée Palace.

---

6.   Decentralised development co-operation is that which is implemented by French local authorities such as city councils, departmental or regional councils.
7.   Ministry responsible for French Overseas Departments and Territories.

TABLE 2
FRENCH INSTITUTIONS INVOLVED IN DEVELOPMENT CO-OPERATION

Multilateral aid	Bilateral aid
Ministry of Economics and Finance	Ministry of Foreign Affairs Ministry of Development Co-operation Other ministries
→ IBRD, European Union, regional development banks, special funds, other agencies	→ Grants
Ministry of Foreign Affairs	CFD/Treasury
→ United Nations	→ Loans and grants

Until the 1998 reform (in February), bilateral aid was under the juris-diction of Ministry of the Economics and Finance, the Ministry of Development Co-operation, the Ministry of Foreign Affairs and the French Fund for Development. One was obliged to include the techni-cal ministries. The Ministry of Economics and Finance has been gain-ing in importance with regard to debt cancellations, which make up most 'non-project' aid. The Fund for Aid and Co-operation (FAC) of the Ministry of Development Co-operation benefits 32 former colo-nies ('pays du champ'). Its extension to ACP countries is under con-sideration. The French Fund for Development (CFD), which used to allocate loans, operated the same way as the FAC, that is, on the basis of tied aid. The State Secretary of Development Co-operation and the CFD delt with the political and administrative dimensions of co-ope-ration with African countries. The Treasury delt with commercial and financial matters, focusing on Asia and Latin America. The Ministry of Foreign Affairs was in charge of bilateral technical assistance for countries other than former colonies (as was the situation in June 1997).

Multilateral aid was mainly administered by the Ministry of Econo-mics and Finance and the Ministry of Foreign Affairs.

This piecemeal approach made it difficult for French aid policy to be coherent and gives rise to duplications in the field. Despite numer-ous white papers on development co-operation drafted by committees under the responsibility of eminent personalities (Jeanneney, Vivien, Hessel, Marchand), the French system of development co-operation had not been modified for a long time [*Vernières, 1995*]. For instance, the idea suggested by Hessel of setting up a High Council for deve-lopment co-operation, as an autonomous organism directing and evaluating aid, was not taken up. For a long time, the idea of creating a large development co-operation agency was the subject of much debate but became obsolete after the hesitations of the 1980s and the

1995 presidential elections. In 1996, several decisions were made public: these included the creation of an inter-ministerial committee of development assistance, which was to improve co-ordination within the administration and further the search for new coherence in budgetary procedures. The scope of intervention of the Ministry of Development Co-operation had been enlarged and now includes ACP countries and South Africa. The scope of intervention of the French Fund for Development (CFD) was extended to the same ACP countries while progressively eliminating government protocols. This should have given rise to better co-ordination with the European Union's field of intervention (as long as the ACP countries are the same as those stated in the Lomé IV Convention), but failed to do so.

There are four major actors: the Ministry of Economics and Finance which controls over half the aid (22.8 billion francs), the Ministry of Development Co-operation (5.4 billion), the Ministry of Foreign Affairs (4.6 billion) and the French Fund for Development (3.1 billion); total disbursements amounted to of 35 billion francs in 1994.

The reform that took place in February, 1998, has given rise to important changes in the system of French development co-operation. It aims at increasing aid coherence, strengthening the convergence of bilateral and multilateral aid policies as well as reinforcing their complementarity. It leads to the normalisation of relationships with African countries. The 'Ministry for Africa' will become part of the Ministry of Foreign Affairs. The French Development Fund will become the French Development Agency, acting as a central operating body. An inter-ministerial committee of international development co-operation has also be created, along with a priority area of solidarity. French development co-operation policy is, henceforth, centred around two major poles: the Ministry of Foreign Affairs and the Ministry of Economics, Finance and Industry.

(4) Calling into Question the Legitimacy of Development
  Co-operation

Finally, 'aid fatigue' and criticism of the system of development co-operation have called into question its objectives and procedures. Recipient countries continue to take aid for granted. Several authors (Bayart, Gabas, Marchesin, Medart) have denounced the patrimonial and clientelist nature of French aid. Even though development co-operation is supposed to be based on conditionality (where efficiency is a priority), control and contracts, it often remains tied to short-term interests. The reverse flows are not negligible. They are estimated at 67 per cent for the FAC, 76 per cent for the CFD and 100 per cent for the Treasury's loans.

Attempts have been made to move from paternalistic relations to partnerships, but personal relations are still maintained with African heads of state. In 1997, the events that took place in Central Africa (former Zaire, Congo) indicated the failure of this policy.

Finally, French development co-operation policy continues to be strong, despite its contradictions and lack of coherence, but it has to take more account of the Bretton Woods institutions. The extent of multilateral debt, which could not be rescheduled (until the 1997 measures regarding Uganda), the leadership of the Bretton Woods institutions in structural adjustment, the search for greater rationality in the allocation of funds, have often placed France in a secondary role *vis-à-vis* the World Bank or the International Monetary Fund (as was illustrated by the doctrine advocated by the government of the Ivory Coast on the Franc Zone, according to which the Treasury is no longer to be the last-resort lending institution). French aid policy must also fit with the aid policy of the European Union and its member states. There is a growing problem of co-ordination, particularly with regard to the compatibility of the Franc Zone and the institution of the Euro.

III. THE PROBLEMS OF COHERENCE AND CO-ORDINATION BETWEEN FRENCH AID POLICY AND THE EUROPEAN UNION

The objectives of the European Union Treaty, mentioned in articles 130u (objectives of development co-operation) and 130x (relations with member states), are as follows:

- eonomic and social sustainable development, with an emphasis on the most disadvantaged countries;
- gradual and smooth integration into the global economy;
- the elimination of poverty;
- democratisation;
- upholding thce rule of law and human rights.

The Treaty also attempts to take into consideration the international context, the role of the United Nations and international organisations.

(1) Problems of Co-ordination between French and European Aid Policies

Several reasons explain the differences and even the conflicts of interest between EU member states:

- historically, the Yaoundé and, later, the Lomé conventions were much more advantageous to former colonial powers than they were to European states with no colonial history;
- bilateral tied aid corresponds to national commercial interests;
- transfers of sovereignty or policy co-ordination are even more difficult to undertake because of the great number of national decision-makers who have neither the same objectives nor the same development co-operation procedures. As seen earlier on, France has the most complex system of development co-operation of all European Union members. Concerted action, at the European level, is particularly difficult to achieve because of the multiplicity of decision-making centres; it often leads countries to protect their own sovereignty;
- as decentralised development co-operation grows and as actors from civil society (firms, micro-projects, NGOs, associations) play an increasingly important role, it seems even more difficult to reach coherence and co-ordination;
- to go even further in the transfer of sovereignty, into the field of development co-operation, would require public opinion to be willing to accept the political cost of such a transfer.

In reality, the national development co-operation policies of member states often diverge as much by their principles as by their methods. States differ in the importance they ascribe to, for example, subsidiarity. One can identify conflicts of national policies by sectors, regions and countries. The process of transferring sovereignty takes place slowly, meets with opposition and does not impinge much on development co-operation policy. Thus other European countries are not as concerned as France is with the evolution of the Franc Zone and, more generally, by privileged relations with Africa. The definition of priority countries, in the post-Lomé framework, is not the same: France and certain countries of the South wish to maintain privileged relations between France and Africa, whereas northern Europe would like to establish privileged ties with the least developed countries. Some countries have expressed their scepticism regarding the very usefulness of coherence, even though they recognise the fact that a minimal degree of co-ordination would help avoid duplication or conflicts [*House of Lords, 1993*].

Policy co-ordination was considerably easier when the number of member states was limited, when partners from the South were fewer and when the Community clearly upheld a specific position.

History has led the European Community to abandon progressively the specificity of its development co-operation policy. Europe has had to deal with tensions between its privileged ties to countries with which it has historical and geographic ties (ACPs and Mediterranean countries) and its dynamic economic interests, which have been pushing Europe towards new industrialised countries, especially in Asia. The Community's preference scheme has progressively become obsolete. As the European Community has grown and became stronger, it has also become increasingly globalised, thereby relatively loosening its commercial and financial ties with ACP countries and the Mediterranean world. Considering the ACPs' severe financial crisis, stabilisation and structural adjustment policies have modified the Community's methods, which have departed from its initial principles, and favoured the leadership of the Bretton Woods institutions. Several member states uphold multilateralism and free trade, which have become reference objectives.

Member states have different positions on the fundamental question of whether to promote free trade or Community preferences; the Community no longer upholds the position it had originally maintained on this issue.

Developing countries also have divergent interests on this question and there is no agreement among member states to reinforce the preferential treatment of the poorest countries and therefore to set up a protection hierarchy according to geographical areas.

(2) The Post-Lomé Debates

The risks of incoherence between European policies and development co-operation policy are all the greater, considering that the latter is presently under review. Historically, an increasing amount of money has been allocated to the Community's international programmes of action, and member states have delegated part of the responsibility for financial assistance to the Community. Emergency aid, food aid, trade promotion, development financing, support for specific activities (with NGOs, in research and development, the environment, AIDS, etc.) are the main instruments. The EEC/ACP agreements are based on principles that illustrate a less liberal approach than that of GATT. The first convention (in 1975) was perceived as an innovation in North–South relations and a first step towards a new international economic order: autonomous control of expenditures, an advantageous exchange regime, concerted action in decision-making, partnership, preferential measures and various forms of aid. The principles guiding EEC/ACP agreements sought to uphold mechanisms of stabilisation and co-operation: liberalisation (generalised systems of preferences), specific guaranties (on prices and quantities for sugar), compensating mechanisms for the fluctuation of export revenues (Stabex, Sysmin), access to the EDF's aid programmes and 'contractuality'.

The outcome of Lomé presents a mixed picture. The most positive outcome is that of the sugar protocol which promoted the industrialisation of Mauritius, thanks to the productive investment facilitated by sugar revenues. Jamaica, Zimbabwe and Kenya were also able to develop their industries thanks to the Lomé agreements. Contrary to what was intended, ACP countries were unable to modify and diversify their specialisation on primary products. They were unable to keep up their market shares even though they had free access to the European market for up to 95 per cent of their export of agricultural products. Industrial concessions, the measures tied to transfers of technology or to the promotion of private investment had little impact. Stabex or Sysmin allowances were insufficient to correct imbalances caused by falling prices. They financed state budgets more than they were able to promote diversification or to rebuild export-oriented activities. They generated rents and, at best, supplied public budgets with oxygen. D. Bach [1993] talks of a charitable, clientelist and income-generating scheme and considers the Lomé Convention to be a *drifting anchorage*. The Community has been highly criticised for its over-complicated administrative and sluggish decision-making procedures and its failure to reduce the financial burden of aid.

The principles of the Lomé Convention were also incompatible with GATT's and the WTO's trade multilateralism and with structural adjustment. Financial aid policy has changed greatly since the Community set up structural adjustment loans and used counterpart funds, which must be managed in a coherent, financial framework. Adjustment policies call for greater co-ordination, not only among member states, but also with the Bretton Woods institutions. Policy co-ordination has therefore been enhanced, in terms of the management of counterpart funds and greater concerted action on structural adjustment.

As a result there has been more coherence in the way funds have been used (imposed coherence); however, external coherence, requiring mutual responsibility, has greatly diminished. Short-term financial coherence has won over long-term coherence.

(3) The Impact of the Maastricht or Amsterdam Treaty

According to the Maastricht Treaty, which has become the Amsterdam Treaty, the Community and member states must co-ordinate their development co-operation policies and consult each other on their aid programmes.

In the European Union's aid policy, there is no subsidiarity principle. State members compete with one another and bilateral aid is an instrument of commercial competition (Morrissey, this volume, Ch. 12).

A certain transfer of power has taken place at the European level. Trade policy today is dealt with solely at the Community level. It was the Community rather than individual European countries that participated as such in the GATT negotiations, as it is now doing in the WTO negotiations. Through the Lomé Convention, there is an entire delegation for trade co-operation. However, co-operation between Europe and developing countries continues to be shaped by the bilateral policies of member states. The Community does not have the attributes of a nation state, master of its foreign policy. By contrast, France has privileged relations with its former French-speaking colonies and plays a leading role among countries of the Franc Zone.

Several conflicts or diverging objectives come to light. We will look at a few examples:

- An important point is that the adoption of a European norm may have an impact on primary products. Some European countries (Denmark, Ireland, Great Britain) have obtained derogations regarding the use of cocoa butter in chocolate (allowing them to use 5 per cent of non-cocoa butter or vegetable oil products in chocolate). If this derogation became the rule, the European demand for cocoa would drop by 200,000 tons which would affect, first and foremost, Africa. As for vanilla and vanillin, the ecological label or the prohibition of additives, the same stakes are involved.
- The evolution of the European Union, as foreseen by the Maastricht Treaty, now known as the Amsterdam Treaty, will have an impact on the monetary and financial situation of developing countries; it should promote a greater stability of interest and exchange rates. New questions come to light such as whether or not the monetary European Union will be able to co-exist and co-operate with the Franc Zone. The institution of a single currency is no doubt compatible with maintaining the rules of the Franc Zone, as budgetary choices will continue to be under the jurisdiction of individual sovereign states; furthermore monetary development co-operation agreements are the responsibility of the French Treasury and not of the Bank of France. It seems

nonetheless obvious that changes will take place and that the question of co-ordinating community assistance to countries outside of the Franc Zone, with the assistance provided by the French Treasury to the Franc Zone, will become an acute problem.

– Another problem is the divergence between member states, especially between southern Europe (France, Italy, Spain) and the others, over *tied aid,* which is barely consistent with the logic of development [*Marchand, 1996*]. Tied aid undoubtedly involves supplementary costs, compensated by high levels of conditionality; it also increases the volume of aid. The shift from bilateral to untied, multilateral aid would, in all likelihood, reduce the global volume. It should also be mentioned that the share of tied American aid is increasing.

IV. CONCLUSION

What are the possibilities of achieving greater coherence and better co-ordination in the Community's development policy?

The coherence and co-ordination of national policies – notably in the case of France – and Community policies, only make sense if there is a general consensus on a few major principles and if coherence is based on areas where there is a convergence of interests and principles. Europe must choose clearly between two options:

– expansion of the Union and further integration into the world economy, with an acceptance of operating as an economic community with weak co-ordination of economic policies; or
– becoming a federal political union, which would imply transfers of sovereignty and greater co-ordination of development co-operation policies.

To define a clear position on development policy is obviously a prerequisite to establishing coherent and well co-ordinated policies. Community policy and that of member states could be distinguished in the long run according to strategic sectors, such as food, health, education and training, energy, support for regional integration or the environment, which could come under the jurisdiction of the European Union.

We have privileged several possible areas of convergence. A development co-operation policy intended to facilitate development would call for greater flexibility in resource allocation, a diversification of partners, simple conditionalities linking aid to the ACPs' ability to become more responsible. This implies that the principle of conditionality must be accepted, that decentralised development co-operation must be promoted and that European policy needs to be assessed on a permanent basis.

This would imply taking into consideration not only the market rules but also geopolitical interests in an attempt to integrate history and geography and identify areas of conflict and solidarity in order to establish new interdependencies. A minimal agreement on development policy, in a globalised world, can be an integrating factor for Europe as was the common agricultural policy in the past. Europe must increase its bargaining power towards the Bretton Woods institutions. It can also set up a co-ordinated conditionality, which would render its aid more effective.

The new interdependencies between Europe and the South (on issues such as trade, environment, population, drugs and AIDS) cannot be dealt with, effectively and in the long term, at the bilateral level. Each one of these areas is tied to problems of sovereignty transfers and implementation of the principle of subsidiarity, and requires co-ordination in bilateral development co-operation policies.

It would therefore be necessary to:

- shift from short-term preoccupations with stabilisation to the resumption of medium- and long-term financing of productive and social investments;
- create a stabilised environment which would encourage investment and favour the reconstitution of states, grounded in their basic functions. The promotion of private investments requires significant public investments and the creation of an institutional environment which fosters trust, security and credibility;
- differentiate between adjustment aid and political aid and suspend the latter in the case of serious violations of human rights;
- take into consideration the plurality of types of democracy and privilege respect for the rule of law;
- promote debt alleviation in order to end structural adjustment under strict supervision and restart a credit cycle in which money creates wealth.

Thinking of development in a long-term perspective would allow for the reconciliation of contradictory interests and for greater coherence in development co-operation policies. It is in the interest of Europe and France that peripheral and neighbouring areas expand their markets and increase their income, as was the case with Japan in East Asia and with the United States in the Americas. Aid can only be effective if it is in support of dynamic domestic forces and if it is integrated into coherent policies, which have been conceived at the level of recipient countries.

In the post-Lomé framework, four options can be envisaged:

- maintenance of the status quo: non-reciprocity, differential treatment, contractualisation and priority access to the market. This scenario is highly unlikely and is at variance with that promoted by the World Trade Organisation;
- a global agreement, complemented by bilateral agreements. The trade dimension of the Lomé Convention would be eliminated by Europe's integration into the generalised system of preferences (the GSP); it would be superseded by an aid system in which preferential treatment towards the least developed countries could be increased;
- the ending of the Lomé Convention with the institution of free trade agreements with ACP countries, on a regional basis. Reciprocity could be uniform, following a transitional period;
- reorientation of the agreements towards the poorest ACP and non-ACP countries, independently of former colonial ties.

There are important arguments in favour of a subsidiarity that would give priority to the European Union in several areas of development assistance (including economies of scale, reduction of transaction costs and of misuse of resources, increased bargaining power, especially *vis-à-vis* the Bretton Woods institutions). The financial clout of the European Union, compared to that of the World Bank, can reduce the weight of the leader of the 'aid oligopoly', even if the European Union's human resources and institutional capacities remain insufficient. However, the national interests of member states remain strong and divergent. Development co-operation policy is, thus, along with the issue of a single currency, a crucial stake in the construction of the European Union.

REFERENCES

APRODEV/EECOD/CIDSE, 1994, [Seminar] 'Towards Coherence in North/South Policy: The Role of European Union', Brussels, No. 19–21 OI (contributions by J. L. Dubois, G. Frisch, B. Goudzwaard, P. Hugon, P. Hilton, M. Steinke and C. Robinson).

Bach, D. (ed.), 1993, 'L'Europe et l'Afrique. Le maillon manquant', *Politique africaine*, No. 49.

CAD, 1996, *Coopération pour le développement. Rapport du Président du CAD*, Paris, OCDE.

Cazes, 1987, *L'aide francaise au Tiers Monde*, CAP, Ministry of Foreign Affairs, (March).

CEE, 1992 (May), *La politique de coopération au développement à l'horizon 2000*, Brussels.

CEE, 1996, *Livre vert sur les relations entre l'Union européenne et les pays ACP à l'aube du 21ème siècle. Défis et options pour un nouveau parténariat*, Brussels, mimeo.

Cerruti, P., P. Hugon and S. Collignon, 1992, *La coopération monétaire en Afrique Sub-saharienne. Le rôle des arrangements régionaux de paiements*, Brussels: CEE.

Coquet, B., J.M. Daniel, I. Fourmann; D. Bach (ed.), 1993, 'L'Europe et l'Afrique: flux et reflux', *Politique africaine*, No.49.

Coussy, J. and P. Hugon (eds.), 1991, *L'intégration régionale et l'ajustement structurel en Afrique Sub-saharienne*, Paris: La Documentation Française.

Coussy, J., 1997, *L'appui de l'Union européenne aux ajustements structurels*, Paris, GEMDEV, mimeo., February.

Davenport, M., 1990, *Europe 1992 and the Developing World*, London: ODI.

Duruflé, G., 1997, *Evaluation de l'appui à l'ajustement structurel de l'Union européenne au Cameroun*, Paris, GEMDEV, mimeo., February.

EPCDM, 1994, *La politique européenne de développement après le traité de Maastricht. La revue à mi parcours de Lomé IV et le débat sur la complémentarité*, Maastricht.

EPCDM, 1996, *Au delà de Lomé IV. Pistes de réflexion sur l'avenir de la coopération ACP/UE*, June.

Faber, G., 1993, *Toward More Coherence in EC Policies*, note (mimeo), CEE.

Forster, J., 'The Coherence of Policies Towards Developing Countries: The Case of Switzerland', this volume, Ch. 9.

Fukasaku, K. and D. Erocal, 1993, *The Challenges of Policy Coherence in Development Co-operation*, Paris: OCDE, July.

Gabas, J.J. and A. Sindzingre, 1996, *Les enjeux de l'aide dans un contexte de mondialisation*, GEMDEV Seminar, Paris, September, mimeo.

Grilli, E., 1993, *The European Community and the Developing Countries*, Cambridge: Cambridge University Press.

Hewitt, A., 1996, *La convention de Lomé: diagnostic, méthodes d'évaluation et perspectives*, Paris: GEMDEV.

Hoebink, P., 'Coherence and Development Policy: The case of the European Union', this volume, Ch. 10.

Hommes, E.W. (ed.), 1993, *Towards more Coherence in EC Policies*, The Hague: NAR.

House of Lords, 1993, *European Community Development Aid*, 21st Report, London.

Hugon, P., 1984, 'French Development Co-operation: Policy and Performance', in Stokke, O. (ed.), *European Development Assistance*, Vol. 1, Tilburg: EADI.

Hugon, P., 1993, *L'économie de l'Afrique*, Paris: La Découverte.

Hugon, P., 1994, *L'Europe et le Tiers Monde*, Special Edition, *Tiers Monde*.

Hugon, P. and P. Robson, 1991, *La dimension régionale de l'ajustement dans les ACP*, Brussels: CEE.

Hugon, P., G. Pourcet and S. Quiers Valette (eds.), 1993, *L'Afrique des incertitudes*, Paris: PUF.

Jadot, Y. and J.P. Rolland, 1996, *Les contradictions de la politique européenne à l'égard des pays en développement*, Solagral, mimeo.

Jospin, L., 1998, *Le nouveau dispositif français de coopération*, Conférence de presse. Paris (February).

THE COHERENCE OF FRENCH AND EUROPEAN POLICY

Lafay, G. and Unal-Keneci, 1993, *Repenser l'Europe,* Paris: Economica.
Marchand, Y., 1996, *Une urgence: l'afro-réalisme,* Paris, Rapport au Premier Ministre.
Marchesin, P., 1993, *Le mystère des chiffres ou l'opacité du système français d'aide au développement,* Paris: Observatoire permanent de la coopération française, mimeo.
Mayes (ed.), 1993, *The External Implications of European Integration,* Hemel: Hampstead.
McDermott, I. and S. Alee (eds.), 1993, *Africa and the European Community after 1992,* Washington DC: World Bank, Economic Development Institute.
Morrissey, Oliver, 'Aid and Trade Policy (In)Coherence', this volume, Ch. 12.
OCDE/CAD (1991): *La coopération pour le développement et le défi de la cohérence des politiques dans le nouveau contexte international,* Paris.
Page, S., 1990, *Some Implications of Europe of 1992 for Developing Countries,* Paris: OCDE.
Sideri, S. and Sengupta (eds.), 1992, *The 1992 Single European Market and the Third World,* London: Frank Cass.
Stevens, C., 1990, 'The Impact of Europe 1992 on the Maghreb and Sub-Saharan Africa', *Journal of Common Market Studies,* Vol. 29, No. 2.
Stokke, O. (ed.), 1984, *European Development Assistance,* Vol. 1, Tilburg: EADI.
Stokke, O. (ed.), 1996, *Foreign Aid Towards the Year 2000: Experiences and Challenges* London: Frank Cass, EADI book series No. 18.
Tovias, A., 1990, The European Communities' Single Market: The challenge for Sub-Saharan Africa, Washington DC: World Bank.
Vernières, M., 1995, *Nord-Sud – Renouveler la coopération,* Paris: Economica.

5

The Coherence of Policies Towards Developing Countries: The Case of Germany

GUIDO ASHOFF

I. INTRODUCTION

(1) Aim of the Chapter

The aim of this chapter is twofold. First, addressing an international readership, it will present several cases of policy incoherence between development co-operation and other policies that have attracted public attention in Germany in the last few years. The intention is to explain briefly the specific incoherence in each case and to point to the debate which the issue has triggered in Germany.

Second, the chapter will deal with the question of how donor countries may achieve more coherence between development co-operation and other policies that affect developing countries: how they may prevent the goals of development co-operation being neutralised, or indeed impaired, by the impact of other policies. The question is prompted by the observation that while the call for greater policy coherence seems in principle undisputed, at least among the actors involved in development co-operation, it is less clear how it may be translated successfully into political practice. Even the Development Assistance Committee (DAC) of the OECD, which made policy coherence one of the central issues of its 1992 Chairman's Report on Development Co-operation [*OECD, 1992*], did not specifically deal with ways to implement greater coherence.[1] As a

---

1. This is also the case with an issues paper on policy coherence submitted by the OECD's Development Co-operation Directorate (DCD) and the DAC in 1994 [*OECD, 1994*]. Meantime the OECD Public Management Service (PUMA) has analysed the issue in greater detail and distilled the experience of OECD countries into practical lessons, but it did so without explicit reference to development co-operation [*OECD, 1996a*].

means of advancing the debate, it seems therefore worthwhile to look at the corresponding experiences of, and attempts by, individual donor countries. This chapter presents the case of Germany.

(2) Definition of Policy Incoherence and Scope of the Chapter

Throughout this chapter, the term 'policy coherence' refers to the coherence between German development co-operation and other German policies that affect the development of developing countries (that is, external coherence as termed by Hoebink (this volume, Ch.10). This largely corresponds to the DAC's understanding of the term in the above-mentioned 1992 Report. The chapter will therefore not deal with coherence within German aid policy, that is, the consistency of its goals, instruments, programmes and projects (internal coherence), except in one respect that will be explained in section VI. The chapter deals neither with coherence between the aid policies of Germany and other donors (which is to do with donor co-ordination) nor discusses coherence between German development co-operation and the policies of recipient countries (which is to do with policy dialogue). None the less, the issues of donor co-ordination and policy dialogue will enter the arena at a certain stage in the analysis of policy coherence.

Defining policy coherence in this manner requires a further comment. Other policies may impair development co-operation in two ways. In the first case, other political goals or interests assume predominance at the implementation stage of development co-operation, provoking inconsistencies between the stated goals and the practice of development co-operation. Initially, this might be construed as a case of internal incoherence (according to the above-mentioned terminology), but since the inconsistency is due to the influence of other policies it should and will be considered here (see section III), albeit very briefly, since it is not the focus of the current debate on policy coherence. In the second case, development co-operation is implemented in accordance with its goals, but neutralised or impaired by the impact of other policies, without the latter having necessarily intended to do so. That is, as it were, the 'classic' case of (external) policy incoherence which will be dealt with in sections IV and V.

(3) Structure of the Chapter

This introduction is followed by some conceptual remarks which aim at a realistic and politically meaningful understanding of the issue of policy coherence (section II). Sections III and IV deal with the

129

evidence of and the debate on policy incoherence in Germany. Section V draws several conclusions with regard to different types of policy incoherence, the role of non-governmental organisations (NGOs) in heightening public awareness of policy incoherence, the importance of donor co-ordination and the co-responsibility of developing countries. Section VI outlines the current procedures practised in Germany to achieve policy coherence. Section VII presents several proposals to improve policy coherence that have been advanced in the German debate and concludes by briefly assessing the proposals in the light of the conceptual remarks made in section II.

II. SOME CONCEPTUAL REMARKS ON THE ISSUE OF POLICY COHERENCE

(1) Policy Coherence and the Question of Overriding Objective

Policy coherence as defined in this chapter means that different policies that have an impact on developing countries ideally reinforce, or at least do not neutralise or impair, each other. From the point of view of governance, policy incoherence entails the risk of ineffectiveness (goals not being met), inefficiency (scarce resources being wasted) and loss of credibility. In times of increasing pressure to improve public management, the need for policy coherence has unsurprisingly been recognised as urgent. Enhancing policy coherence is undoubtedly a matter of appropriate public management, but it should not be reduced to that alone. Equally important is the question of how objectives are set and their hierarchy, otherwise the problem of incoherence might be solved simply by following the line of least resistance, or by looking for the smallest common denominator of different policies.

Policy incoherence is often (though not always; see below) due to the fact that different policies (in their stated concept or by their implementation) aim at different or even mutually exclusive objectives. The call for greater coherence thus raises an important question as to which objective should be overriding: for example, promoting the economic and social development of developing countries or defending jobs in the donor countries. This is particularly true when different policies, such as development co-operation, economic policy and foreign policy, are represented by ministers with full cabinet rank as in Germany. Depending on how the question is answered, the plea for greater coherence might be directed against development co-operation with the demand that it should itself become coherent with other policies by subordinating its objectives to those of other policies.

On a conceptual level, this problem (perhaps, trap) can only be avoided if there is an overriding objective that can be used as a guideline to judge which policy should be changed in order to achieve greater coherence. Clearly the overriding objective that should govern different policies of donor countries and, in principle, the policies of recipient countries as well can be defined only in general terms. It is important, however, to recall that a worldwide consensus on such an overriding objective was reached in 1992 during the United Nations Conference on Environment and Development (UNCED): namely, the objective of 'safeguarding our global future'. More specifically, OECD donor countries agreed that a more coherent strategy towards relations with developing countries should: first, enable developing countries to enhance their political, social and economic development and to participate effectively in the global economy; and second, adjust the OECD policies with a view to strengthening the openness and stability of the world economy and the basis for constructive co-operation to meet regional and global challenges [*OECD, 1992: 34*].

(2) Reasons for Policy Incoherence and Consequences for a Politically Meaningful Understanding of Coherence

To gain a politically meaningful understanding of policy coherence, it is important to register the reasons that may cause incoherence, since the scope and direction of efforts to resolve policy incoherence largely depend on the factors causing it. There are several reasons for policy incoherence:

Complexity of socio-economic and political development processes: Although there is increasing international consensus on the principles of 'sustainable development', we still need to acknowledge the high complexity of socio-economic and political development which is beyond any deterministic understanding. Although we are called upon to broaden our understanding of development and constantly review concepts against the background of experience, we cannot hope to conceive, once and for all, a complete and universally accepted theory of development from which definite strategies, clear-cut targets and consistent policies could be inferred. Political decisions will always have to be taken under uncertainty. Consequently no definite *ex ante* analysis of the potential incoherence of policies is possible that goes beyond assessments of plausibility. It is, however, both possible and necessary, at least in grave cases of manifest incoherence, to conduct an accompanying or *ex post* evaluation in order to change the relevant policies and to draw any possible conclusions for the future formulation of policies [*Kürzinger, 1996: 2*].

Lack of information: Even if in principle sufficient knowledge is available to ascertain and assess the impact of a given policy on other policies, basic problems concerning information may still exist. Actors in other policy areas are often not aware of the repercussions their decisions may have on developing countries and development co-operation. Political decisions and instruments applied may cause unintended negative effects because their possible developmental impact has been insufficiently explored or relevant information available elsewhere has not been utilised. It is therefore necessary (though not sufficient), first, to enhance the understanding of the possible developmental impact of other policies and, second, to encourage a better flow of information and greater transparency between different policy areas. Developing analytical capacities and information systems is becoming crucial [*OECD, 1996a: 9; Schmieg, 1997a*].

Divergent political interests: Policy incoherence is not just the outcome of an incomplete theoretical understanding of the development process or insufficient information; it is also most frequently the result of divergent and often conflicting political interests that seek to shape the formulation of policies according to their own ends. Hence coherence – or lack of it – is highly political. Compared with other policies, development policy tends to be somewhat weak, since it serves no specific, powerful interest group in the donor countries. Consequently, striving for greater coherence between policies affecting developing countries needs efforts to mobilise public support for the sake of development co-operation.

Organisation of the policy-making system: Theoretically, the head of state or government has prime responsibility and the political power to ensure coherence between the different policies pursued by members of his or her government. In addition, most governments have inter-ministerial regulations and procedures to discuss and co-ordinate different policies. Nevertheless, depending on the way the policy-making system is organised and the extent to which it is compartmentalised, the structure of competences and responsibilities has a great influence on the extent of policy coherence or incoherence. The plea for more coherence therefore also requires a look at the way in which political decisions are taken and may be influenced within government.

Division of political competences between the European Union (EU) and the EU member states: In the case of Germany and other EU member states, an additional source of policy incoherence should be noted. Member countries have transferred their political responsibility in certain areas (such as foreign trade, agriculture and fisheries) to the supranational level of the EU, whereas other policies continue to be formulated and implemented predominantly at the national level (including development co-operation).[2] The division of competences between different policies increases the possibility of policy incoherence since the common policies of the EU are influenced by actors not only in one member state but in all member states. This source of possible incoherence might be regarded as constituting a case for better co-ordination between different donors, which is therefore outside the scope of this analysis. However, it will be considered here because the EU is more than just another third party to member states. Decisions on EU policies are taken by the Council of Ministers (in co-operation with the European Parliament) on which each member state is represented. The plea for more coherence between policies that affect developing countries means, therefore, that the governments of EU member states should keep in mind not only their national policies but also the EU policies for which they share political responsibility.

In drawing conclusions from these remarks, it should be stressed that complete policy coherence is neither theoretically conceivable nor practically feasible. A realistic and politically meaningful goal, therefore, is to end the most salient cases of policy incoherence; another is to strive for greater coherence by deepening the understanding of how different policies affect the process of development, and by mobilising a growing public and political consensus with regard to the need for more coherence given the stated overriding objective. To some extent this will remain necessarily a trial-and-error process.

---

2. Development co-operation has not become a common policy within the EU. The development co-operation policy pursued by the EU coexists with the national development co-operation policies of the EU member states and, according to the Treaty of Maastricht, is complementary to them.

(3) The Co-responsibility of Developing Countries

The issue of policy incoherence is frequently discussed in a way that assumes that developing countries are merely victims of incoherent policies of donor countries. It should not be overlooked, however, that developing countries in some cases have some room for manoeuvre to reduce the negative impact of incoherent donor policies. If, for instance, donor countries attempt to dump subsidised agricultural surpluses on the markets of developing countries, threatening their domestic agricultural production, the potential importing countries may choose to what extent they actually want to import the cheap surpluses, and whether it might be useful to impose a countervailing import levy to compensate for the subsidy applied by the exporting countries. Of course, such decisions would be highly political, and contingent on the interests of different groups in the importing country. Decision-makers in the development co-operation administrations of donor countries should, therefore, raise the issue of policy coherence both in discussions with their cabinet colleagues at home and in dialogue with their partners in recipient countries (governments or NGOs).

III. POLICY INCOHERENCE I: INCOHERENCE BETWEEN THE STATED
GOALS AND THE PRACTICE OF DEVELOPMENT CO-OPERATION DUE
TO THE INFLUENCE OF OTHER POLICIES

This type of policy incoherence occurs when development co-operation is linked with or subordinated to other policies in such a way that the implementation of development co-operation differs from its stated goals. The basic question in this context concerns the relationship between the goals and interests of development policy and those of other policies.

The declared goal of German development co-operation has consistently been to support economic and social development in recipient countries through strategies aimed at 'help for self-help', and thereby contribute to improving living conditions (although the concepts in pursuit of that goal have changed). At the same time, the Federal Government has always regarded development co-operation as part of its overall foreign relations. Moreover, development policy, like every other government policy, is subject to the constitutional imperative to benefit the German people and to avoid endangering them, and therefore obliged to serve German interests.

The definition of German interests is decisive. In view of growing unemployment, budget constraints and the influx of refugees and asylum seekers, German development co-operation has come under increasing pressure in the last few years to justify itself in terms of German self-interest. The guidelines for German development co-operation defined by the Federal Ministry for Economic Co-operation and Development (BMZ) in October 1996 [*BMZ, 1996a*] are, in part, a response to that pressure. They emphasise that a development policy that is committed to the goals of sustainable development and safe-guarding our global future is entirely in Germany's self-interest. If the latter, however, is interpreted in terms of another (short-term) foreign policy, foreign trade or domestic interests, goal conflicts sometimes arise with development co-operation.

In fact, concrete self-interest has always influenced and also partly impaired the practice of German development co-operation. A few examples may serve as illustration:

Foreign policy: Throughout the 1950s and 1960s, German develop-ment co-operation was closely linked with foreign policy in two ways. The Hallstein Doctrine prescribed termination of diplomatic relations and development co-operation with countries that officially recognised former East Germany. As a consequence, economic and development co-operation with several countries (such as Cuba, former Ceylon, former Tanganyika and Zanzibar) was stopped, while other African countries were prevented from recognising East Ger-many [*Bodemer, 1974: 113–25; White, 1965: 72–3*]. On the other hand, the foreign policy interest in image-building prompted the Federal Government to extend development co-operation to almost every developing country, thus applying what critics have labelled a 'watering-can approach'. From the viewpoint of efficiency and effec-tiveness of aid, concentrating scarce resources on fewer countries might prove a more appropriate policy. A current point of conflict concerns human rights. In 1991 BMZ established five basic allocation criteria[3] in spite of reservations by the Ministry of Foreign Affairs. In the case of several countries violating the criteria (such as Haiti, Sudan, Zaire, Togo and Kenya), German development assistance was reduced or stopped [*Lingnau and Waller, 1996: 8–9*]. However, in the case of China, for foreign policy and economic reasons, BMZ has

---

3.   The five criteria are: respect for human rights, participation of the population in political decision-making processes, guarantee of the rule of law, creation of market-friendly economic conditions, development commitment of the government (largely synonymous with good governance as discussed at international level).

been unable to apply the criteria with the same rigour, despite the unsatisfactory or even deteriorating human rights situation there. As a result, there has been critical debate in Germany on the credibility of BMZ's policy.

Export and employment policies: The well-known issue in this respect is tied aid which has long been part of the development policy debate in Germany. According to DAC statistics, about 40 per cent of German bilateral official development assistance (ODA), excluding technical assistance and administrative costs, was tied in 1995 [*OECD, 1998: A 50*]. This was one of the highest shares among 15 DAC member countries for which figures on the tying status of aid were available.

Domestic policy (refugees and asylum seekers): At the time of writing, there is a debate under way in Germany to reduce or stop development co-operation with countries which are unwilling either to take back citizens whose demand for asylum has been rejected or to co-operate with the German authorities in verifying the identity of refugees and asylum seekers without a passport.

In comparison with other donors, when it comes to the relationship between development policy and specific self-interest, Germany stands mid-field. It has never subordinated its development co-operation policy to foreign and security interests with the same blatancy shown by the United States, nor, as Japan has done in the past, to foreign trade interests. On the other hand, Germany has never sought a developmental profile as distinct as various 'like-minded countries', for example, some Scandinavian countries and the Netherlands, have achieved in the past [*Ashoff, 1996: 31*].

IV. POLICY INCOHERENCE II: THE IMPACT OF DEVELOPMENT CO-OPERATION IMPAIRED BY OTHER POLICIES

(1) Development Co-operation and Foreign Trade Policy

The relationship between German development co-operation and the common foreign trade policy of the EU probably provides the most long-standing example of policy incoherence. At the conceptual level there is no contradiction between trade policy and development policy. From the beginning, one of the goals of German development co-operation has been to encourage the integration of developing countries into the world economy. In 1966, the first German minister for development co-operation, Walter Scheel, made it clear in a statement on new ways of development co-operation that the credibility of the donor countries would depend on their willingness to open their markets to exports from developing countries [*Scheel, 1966: 15*]. The Basic Principles of German Development Co-operation, adopted in 1986 by the Federal Government and still valid, recognise that exports are the principal source of foreign exchange for the developing countries. The document stresses the need for industrialised countries to provide Third World countries with easier access to their markets as well as the need for developing countries to reduce their dependence on commodity products by diversifying their production. Accordingly, the Federal Government declared its willingness to support proposals for comprehensive trade liberalisation and to support the developing countries' efforts to diversify their production and exports [*BMZ, 1986: 16*].

The policy incoherence results from two contradictory facts: German development co-operation has promoted the exports of developing countries to Germany and the EU for a long time both indirectly and directly.[4] At the same time, the EU's common foreign trade policy continues to be characterised by a number of protectionist elements (escalating tariffs, tariff ceilings, quantitative restrictions, import levies, self-restraint agreements, anti-dumping measures) against 'sensitive' imports from developing countries (such as beef, bananas, textiles and clothing), despite the trade preferences accorded them in the framework of the Generalised System of Preferences, the

---

4. German development co-operation promotes the exports of developing countries *indirectly* by a wide range of instruments aiming to improve the competitiveness of the private sector in the partner countries. There are three levels of approach: the state, intermediary institutions and individual enterprises. German development co-operation starts by assisting partner governments to create a competitive system which stimulates economic activity. Furthermore, it supports the private sector in setting up self-governing bodies (including business associations and chambers of industry and commerce) which are then qualified to provide effective services to their members and represent their interests. Various instruments assist implementation: these include advisory services extended to governments, partnerships between German chambers and business associations and similar self-governing bodies in the developing countries, several types of advisory services for enterprises (integrated experts, senior experts), provision of equities and long-term loans by the German Investment and Development Corporation (DEG) and technology transfer (support of technology centres and research institutes). Direct export promotion is provided through PROTRADE (a trade and trade fair promotion programme) and the Integrated Advisory Services (IAS) for the private sector. The approaches and instruments of German development co-operation in the area of private sector development are explained in BMZ [*1996b; 1996c*].

Lomé Convention and the agreements with the southern Mediterranean countries.

While it is true that in Germany, too, some economic sectors have advocated a certain level of protection against competitive imports from developing countries, Germany has always adopted a relatively liberal stance within the EU with regard to its common foreign trade policy, although it eventually accepted compromises reflecting the more restrictive views of some other EU member countries. The incoherence between German development co-operation and the common trade policy of the EU has therefore attracted particular attention in Germany and has been criticised by a broad coalition of economic and development research institutes, NGOs engaged in development co-operation, and BMZ. In the above-mentioned Basic Principles, the Federal Government explicitly acknowledged that the increasing protectionism of the industrialised countries had inhibited development in the Third World and held up the integration of developing countries into the world economy.

The prospects of the EU's foreign trade policy are mixed. In the face of persistent structural unemployment in most EU member countries, there are likely to be more calls for protectionist measures against 'unfair trade practices' on the part of low-wage countries. On the other hand, the successful conclusion of the Uruguay Round has reinforced international obligations for market liberalisation. It is for this reason that development policy should urge that those obligations be implemented in the common foreign trade policy of the EU. This holds particularly true for the agreed phasing out of the existing restrictions against textile and clothing imports from developing countries and the opening up of the EU's agricultural market since the inclusion of the agricultural sector in the GATT regime [*Kürzinger, 1996: 4*].

Particularly sensitive are issues arising of the interface between trade, environmental, and development policy. As consumers and legislators in the EU tend to place increasing environmental and health-related demands on domestic and imported goods, developing countries failing to meet the demands quickly enough may be faced with new trade restrictions. It is possible for development policy to take on an important intermediary function in the conflict between the goals of trade policy and environmental policy, thus providing its own contribution towards greater coherence. Development co-operation has two potential roles: to influence national environmental and trade policy in such a way as to ensure that consideration is taken of the capacity of developing countries to adapt their production processes and exports to new product-related requirements; and to support the efforts of developing countries to make the required technical and organisational adjustments, thus obviating any possible trade conflicts stemming from differences in environmental standards [*Kürzinger, 1996; Wiemann, 1993; Scholz, 1996*].

(2) Development Co-operation and Agricultural and Fisheries Policies

The debate on policy incoherence has been propelled by the impact of the EU agricultural and fisheries policies on developing countries and development co-operation. The most notorious stumbling blocks have been the subsidised beef exports of the EU to West Africa and recently to South Africa and the fisheries agreements that the EU has concluded with a number of developing countries. Other causes for concern are the subsidised EU exports of sugar, wheat, tomato paste and milk powder [*Schmieg, 1997b; Deutsche Welthungerhilfe and Terre des Hommes, 1997*]. The basic problem is the negative impact on the development of agriculture and fisheries in the partner countries. The specific problem lies in the fact that the EU counteracts its own development co-operation efforts. The following sections refer only to cases where projects of German development co-operation have been impaired by EU policies.

(a) Subsidised beef exports.[5] Following an evaluation of a large German project on grown cattle fattening in the Ivory Coast, there was a presumption among insiders in German development co-operation from 1984, that the financial viability of the scheme would be undermined by imports of frozen beef from the EU. Subsequently rising imports made this assessment increasingly plausible, and a similar view was taken by other donors. However, only after German and European NGOs had started campaigning against the subsidised beef exports to West Africa in April 1993 and informed the media, was the issue discussed fully both at national and EU levels and steps taken to alleviate the situation. As a result of the NGO campaign and several initiatives by the Dutch minister of agriculture, supported by his German colleague, the EU Council of Ministers and the European Commission lowered the export subsidies in four steps by almost 30 per cent between June 1993 and January 1994.

Early in 1994, BMZ, supported by the Federal Ministry of Agriculture, commissioned, with the German Development Institute, an in-

---

5. This section is largely based on Brandt [*1995a; 1995b*].

depth study on the impact of the subsidised beef exports on the domestic markets of the West African countries. The study [*Brandt, 1995b*] showed that in the case of the Ivory Coast, which during the period 1985–90 had taken up more than 50 per cent of all EU exports of beef to West Africa, the domestic price level for beef would have been between 20 and 30 per cent above the recorded level if no beef at all had been imported. The effect on price was sufficient seriously to impede the development of economically profitable feed-lot operations in the Ivory Coast. Furthermore, because of the strongly price-correlated regional market, the Ivory Coast's liberal import policy for meat had a negative impact on the producer prices of the nomadic cattle farmers in Mali and Burkina Faso and the cattle exports from the two Sahel countries. There were similar effects due to increasing imports of frozen meat from the EU in Benin and Ghana, which had liberalised their import policies at the beginning of the 1990s. Conversely, other West African maritime countries (for example, Senegal and Nigeria) largely excluded beef imports from overseas through quantitative and tariff restrictions.

(b) The fisheries agreements between the EU and developing countries.[6] In many developing countries, the fishing industry is of great importance for nutrition, employment and trade. According to estimates of the Food and Agriculture Organisation of the United Nations (FAO), however, two-thirds of all maritime fisheries are fully fished or overfished. Consequently, more balanced fisheries policies are required to prevent overexploitation and ensure a sustainable stock management.

German development co-operation currently supports the fishing sector in a number of developing countries.[7] Most projects concern artisanal fishing and provide advice on appropriate technology development, sustainable resource management and strengthening the capacity for self-help. This approach is in line with the overriding objective of poverty alleviation, to which German development co-operation is committed, since fish harvested by artisanal means is an

---

6. This section (except the paragraph on Mauritania) is largely based on Brandt [*1995c*].
7. Development co-operation projects concerning artisanal fishing are being implemented on the coast in Madagascar, Cape Verde, Papua New Guinea and the Dominican Republic; and inland in Brazil, Malawi and Nigeria. There are fish-breeding projects, for instance, in Burkina Faso, India and Brazil, and small-scale aquaculture projects in Malawi, Benin, Syria and Sri Lanka. In Mauritania and Namibia assistance is provided at sectoral level. There are also German NGOs like Brot für die Welt and MISEREOR which support artisanal fishing, for example in Senegal.

indispensable source of protein for low-income population groups in many coastal countries.

There is a risk of policy incoherence due to the common fisheries policy of the EU or, more precisely, the fisheries agreements that the EU has concluded in the last few years with about 20 developing countries (for the most part ACP countries). The agreements grant the EU fleet, which suffers from overcapacity, fishing rights in the 200-mile zone of the partner countries in exchange for financial compensation (and development assistance according to the most recent 'second-generation' agreements). Although the agreements are supposed to avoid threatening the capacity for regeneration of the fishing grounds, a possibility of overfishing remains, resulting either from contravention of fishing rights (due to insufficient monitoring and sanctions) or from overestimation of sustainable fishing yields (due to faulty biological stocktaking and/or shortcomings in the partner countries' fishery policies).

In 1997, BMZ asked the German embassies in 35 coastal developing countries to collect information on the fishery policies pursued, the impact of fisheries agreements concluded with third countries (including the EU) and the partner countries' capacity to monitor the compliance with the agreements. According to the information obtained, there is evidence that in a number of countries the fisheries agreements contribute to overfishing. Many countries lack both the basic statistics to establish sustainable fishing quotas and effective means to monitor the agreements and impose sanctions in the case of contravention of fishing rights. In addition, in several countries the fishery policies seem to be geared to short-term foreign exchange and fiscal interests rather than long-term sustainable resource management.

BMZ is currently concerned about the fisheries agreement recently concluded between the EU and Mauritania. Mauritania depends heavily on fishing as a source of both foreign exchange and income for the poor population. The fishery sector is a focal area of German development co-operation with Mauritania. Germany financed the purchase of a control vessel to monitor foreign fleets operating in the 200-mile zone and provides technical assistance to develop the sector and improve the monitoring capacity. According to BMZ, the agreement with the EU might provoke the overfishing of certain species, thereby endangering the Mauritanian fishery sector and counteracting German assistance. The Federal Government has repeatedly raised the issue in the 'fishery group' of the EU member states and the Commission. The Federal Ministry of Agriculture, which is responsible for fisheries in the German government, is open-minded about BMZ's view because Germany, in contrast to the Iberian countries, has no particular fishing interests along the West African coast. A special feature of the negotiations between the EU and Mauritania was the former's offer to finance, as part of the compensation for fishing rights, investments in the monitoring system; the latter, in view of its difficult budget situation, insisted on an entirely disposable financial compensation [*Schmieg, 1997b: 40*].

German and European NGOs have made several demands on the governments of EU member countries and the European Commission: to base new agreements on a careful stocktaking of fishing grounds and the yields of coastal fishing industries, to reserve the 12-mile zone for artisanal fishing, to involve the latter in the negotiation of the agreements, to provide for an effective monitoring system and to support the local fishery sectors [*Hazeleger, 1997*]. On the other hand, the fisheries agreements highlight the co-responsibility of the partner countries: it is primarily their function to design appropriate fishery policies. It is clear that these may be shaped by quite different interests (for instance, high financial compensation leading to far-reaching fishing rights versus more restrictive fishing rights in support of a sustainable exploitation of the fishing grounds).

(3) Development Co-operation and Corruption

Corruption provides another example of policy incoherence which can be observed in several OECD countries but is particularly manifest in Germany. The incoherence results from the way corruption is dealt with in development co-operation compared with other government policies.

From a development viewpoint there is no doubt about the negative impact of corruption: it undermines good governance, wastes scarce development resources, undermines the credibility of and public support for development co-operation, and compromises open and transparent competition on the basis of price and quality [*OECD, 1996b*]. Consequently, the fight against corruption is an indicator used by BMZ to assess the development commitment of the governments of developing countries which, for its part, is one of the five basic criteria for the allocation of German ODA to recipient countries established by BMZ in 1991. The effect of the five criteria is twofold: ODA to countries severely violating the criteria is supposed to be (and in several cases has actually been) reduced or stopped (negative conditionality). Conversely, German ODA supports the partner countries in attempts to create development-conducive economic and political framework conditions (positive measures). This includes assistance to fight corruption.

In contrast to development co-operation, German criminal law, tax legislation and official export credit insurance (Hermes) tolerate and even enhance corruption in the form of bribery of foreign public officials:

German anti-bribery laws apply only to bribery of domestic public officials: bribery of foreign public officials is not a punishable offence. Other OECD countries are more restrictive in this respect. The US Foreign Corrupt Practices Act explicitly prohibits bribery of foreign public officials. In Canada, New Zealand, Norway, Sweden, Switzerland, Turkey and the UK, the general anti-bribery laws are sufficient to cover the bribery of foreign public officials [*Geiger, 1995: 16–17*].

German tax regulations encourage the bribery of public officials by allowing bribes to be deducted from taxable income. If the recipient is German, he or she has to be named to the tax authorities; however, no such provision exists for bribes paid to foreign public officials. In 1996 the rules for the deductibility of illicit payments to German recipients were tightened somewhat. Bribes to foreign accounts, however, remain fully deductible from taxable income without the recipient's name having to be divulged to the German authorities. According to Rainer Geiger, deputy director for finance, taxes and business affairs with the OECD, the only OECD countries with similar regulations are Belgium, Luxembourg and Greece, while the great majority of OECD countries apply stricter rules. Bribes are generally not deductible in the USA, Canada, Japan, Finland, Norway, Sweden, Denmark, Italy and the UK. In Australia, Austria, France, Ireland, the Netherlands and Switzerland, bribes can be deducted from taxable income provided the recipient (domestic or foreign) is named [*Geiger, 1995: 16–17*].

The official German export credit insurance (Hermes) may *de facto* encourage bribery, although its regulations stipulate that insurance will not cover damages if the exporting firm has violated domestic or foreign laws. Since bribes paid to foreign officials can easily be concealed in the purchase price, it is quite possible that they will be covered by insurance in practice. Though this incentive to bribery is less important than the tax deductibility, it should not be overlooked [*Eigen, 1995: 78*].

For a long time only insiders were aware of the incoherent treatment of corruption in German policies. It was primarily the initiative of NGOs that brought the issue to the public. In 1995 the Joint Conference Church and Development (Gemeinsame Konferenz Kirche und Entwicklung, GKKE) and the Society for International Development (SID) organised a hearing in Bonn on 'Corruption as an Obstacle to Development' with keynote speakers from the OECD, the Council of Europe, the Ministry of Foreign Affairs and almost all political parties represented in the Federal Parliament (Bundestag) (for the proceedings see Holtz and Kulessa (eds.) [1995]). A second hearing on the same subject was organised in 1996 by the GKKE and Transparency International (TI) with delegates from several federal ministries (including BMZ), the political parties, the Association of German Chambers of Industry and Commerce (Deutscher Industrie- und Handelstag, DIHT) and the German Taxpayers' Association (Bund der Steuerzahler) (for the proceedings see Waller and Kulessa [1996]). TI has been particularly active in raising public awareness of the issue. Other NGOs, such as the Deutsche Welthungerhilfe and Terre des Hommes, have repeatedly referred to corruption in their annual reviews of German official development assistance (for instance, Deutsche Welthungerhilfe and Terre des Hommes [1995; 1996]).

It is interesting to note that the debate on corruption as an obstacle to development coincided with a much broader political debate on fighting corruption in Germany. Since 1995 there have been political initiatives by the Social Democratic Party (SPD) and the parties of the governing coalition, and legislative initiatives by the Upper House (Bundesrat) and the Federal Government to fight corruption in Germany. Although the SPD and TI have called for additional provisions to end the preferential treatment given to corruption in international business transactions, the anti-corruption law eventually passed by Parliament in June 1997 remains silent on international corruption. Hence, neither the initiatives by NGOs nor the domestic policy debate on corruption have been sufficient to end the incoherence in the treatment of domestic and international corruption.

There is hope, however, that this will be achieved as a result of growing international pressure. The USA has long urged other OECD countries to follow the example of its Foreign Corrupt Practices Act of 1977 and take effective measures against corruption in international business transactions. Major progress was made in this respect in 1994 when the OECD governments agreed to take collective action to tackle the problem and adopted a Recommendation on Bribery in International Business Transactions, followed by another Recommendation on the Tax Deductibility of Bribes to Foreign Public Officials in 1996. The recommendations call on the OECD member countries to take effective measures to deter, prevent and combat bribery of foreign public officials.

While most OECD countries were willing to follow this line, Germany and France insisted on a binding international convention (whose negotiation, however, would take considerable time). A compromise was reached in May 1997 when the OECD Council of Ministers recommended that member countries should criminalise the bribery of foreign public officials in an effective and co-ordinated manner by submitting proposals to their legislative bodies by 1 April 1998 and seeking their enactment by the end of 1998. The OECD Council decided, to this end, to open negotiations promptly on an international convention to criminalise bribery in conformity with agreed common elements, the treaty to be ready for signing by the end of 1997, with a view to its entry into force twelve months thereafter.

Against this background, the German Parliament (that is, the parties of the governing coalition and the SPD), when passing the above-mentioned anti-corruption law, adopted a resolution urging the Federal Government to implement the OECD recommendation of May 1997 and to participate actively in the negotiation of the international convention according to the agreed timetable. In December 1997, the OECD convention was signed. It is a major step forward though it neither covers the bribery of foreign political parties nor explicitly commits the member states to abolishing the tax deductibility of bribes paid to foreign public officials. Now it is the member states' task to ratify the convention by April 1998 and to transform its provisions into national law by the end of 1998. This might become difficult in Germany because in September 1998 the next Bundestag will be elected.

In August 1997, BMZ decided to include an anti-corruption clause in the summary records of future government negotiations with developing countries on development co-operation. BMZ thereby followed a recommendation adopted by the DAC High Level Meeting in 1996. The DAC recommendation was part of the OECD's efforts to fight corruption.

(4) Development Co-operation and Arms Exports

From the point of view of development co-operation, the issue of arms exports to developing countries has become increasingly critical for two reasons: First, Germany (like many other donors) considers the development commitment of the partner countries' governments a prerequisite for development co-operation and an important criterion for the allocation of aid. Excessive military expenditure, going beyond the needs of legitimate self-defence and by far exceeding social expenditure, is regarded by BMZ as indicating questionable development commitment. Second, the number of civil or inter-ethnic wars in or between developing countries has multiplied: apart from their immediate impact (killings of sometimes genocidal dimensions, emergencies, refugees), these wars destroy past development achievements and jeopardise current development efforts. Over the last ten years, emergency aid has captured a growing share of German and other donors' development assistance, withdrawing scarce resources from 'classic' development co-operation. Dealing adequately with the conflicts has become a major challenge for development co-operation and has prompted BMZ to elaborate a strategy paper on development co-operation and crisis prevention [*BMZ, 1997a*].

Against this background, arms exports by donor countries to developing countries give rise to the suspicion of serious policy incoherence. In Germany, three circumstances have reinforced the debate on arms exports and development co-operation in recent years:

first, the information that Germany had, in 1994, become the world's second most important arms exporter;

second, the Federal Government's decisions of May 1994 and May 1996 to liberalise the regulations on arms exports in case German firms supply components to common military production projects of firms having their headquarters in EU or NATO member states or in countries considered on a par with NATO members, with a view to facilitating private co-operation in military production that is of German or NATO interest (for a summary of the decisions see BMWi [*1996a: 28–30*]);

third, the liberalisation of the German regulations governing the export of dual-use goods in 1995 in line with harmonisation efforts at the EU level (the list of countries outside NATO to which dual-use goods intended for conventional weapon projects must not be exported without prior government approval was reduced from 32 to 12 countries).[8]

The Churches and other NGOs have viewed this development with great concern, fearing a turning away from the restrictive principles of German arms exports policy (see, for instance, Brock (ed.) [*1996*]), and have urged the government to strive for a global policy of conflict prevention and peace-building and to make stringent reductions in German arms exports [*Deutsche Welthungerhilfe and Terre des Hommes, 1995: 29; 1996: 16–17*]. In October 1996, the Committee for Economic Co-operation and Development of the German Parliament organised a hearing of experts on the issue of development co-operation and arms exports (a former hearing on the same subject had been organised in 1984).

The experts' statements presented at the hearing [*Deutscher Bundestag – Ausschuß für wirtschaftliche Zusammenarbeit und Entwicklung, 1996*] and a close look at the available statistics show that the issue is more complicated than the public debate suggests and that the call for greater policy coherence requires careful analysis in the German case. The following points can be made:

German regulations on arms exports are among the strictest worldwide. The Political Principles for Arms Exports adopted by the German government in 1982 forbid arms exports to countries outside NATO[9] in which there is a danger of armed conflict or where German arms exports might exacerbate existing armed conflicts.[10] Germany

---

8. On 1 July 1995, the former country list H of the German Foreign Trade Regulation was replaced by a new country list K comprising the following countries: Afghanistan, Angola, Cuba, Lebanon, Libya, Iran, Iraq, Mozambique, North Korea, Somalia, Syria and former Yugoslavia [*BMWi, 1996a: 30*]. The list may be changed. The countries that were taken off the former list H were: Albania, Algeria, Bulgaria, Cambodia, China, Egypt, the Autonomous Territories of Gaza and Jericho, India, Israel, Jordan, Kuwait, Mauritania, Pakistan, Rumania, Qatar, Saudi Arabia, South Africa, Taiwan, Vietnam and Yemen [*BMWi, 1998: 27*].
9. German arms exports policy treats a number of third countries on a par with NATO member states. This refers not only to some other developed countries (Australia, Austria, Ireland, Japan, New Zealand, Sweden and Switzerland), but also to the member states of the Association of South-East Asian Nations (ASEAN), that is, Brunei, Indonesia, Malaysia, the Philippines, Singapore and Thailand (Vietnam being excepted) [*BMWi, 1996b: 2*]. Although the decision to include the ASEAN countries dates back to the era of the cold war (the motive being to support anti-communist countries), it has not been reversed since then.
10. German arms exports to Turkey (a NATO ally) and Indonesia (treated on a par with NATO states) have repeatedly given rise to public debate because of the violation of human rights and the armed conflict with minorities in both countries (Kurds in Turkey and East Timor in Indonesia).

has agreed to the eight criteria on arms exports adopted by the EU at the summits of Luxembourg (1991) and Lisbon (1992): arms exports are conditional on the situation in the recipient countries on a basis including regard for human rights, peace, security and stability in the region and the possible misuse of arms (however, the criteria are interpreted and applied by the individual EU member countries). Germany has also agreed to the principles for the transfer of conventional weapons adopted by the Organisation for Security and Co-operation in Europe (OSCE) in 1993 and is a member of the Wassenaar Arrangement on multilateral export controls of 1996 which aims at a comprehensive exchange of information on arms transfers (including export licences issued and export bans imposed by the member states).

In relation to arms exports, a clear distinction should be made between three product categories: first, conventional weapons and weapons systems (a frequently used definition being the one of the UN Register of Conventional Arms;[11] the corresponding term in German legislation is 'war arms' whose definition goes somewhat beyond the UN Register); second, small arms, ammunition and military equipment; third, dual-use goods that can be used for both civil and military purposes. In Germany, exports of war arms are subject to the Law on the Control of War Arms (Kriegswaffenkontrollgesetz) and need to be authorised by the Federal Ministry of Economic Affairs; exports of small arms, ammunition and military equipment (not covered by the Law on the Control of War Arms) and dual-use goods require a licence by the Federal Export Office (Bundesausfuhramt) in accordance with the Foreign Trade Act (Außenwirtschaftsgesetz) and the Foreign Trade Regulation (Außenwirtschaftsverordnung).[12]

German overall arms exports (three categories mentioned before):
The most comprehensive and internationally comparable data on arms

---

11. The definition of the UN Register of Conventional Arms comprises the following seven weapons or weapons systems: battle tanks, armoured combat vehicles, large-calibre artillery systems, combat aircraft, attack helicopters, warships and missiles or missile systems.
12. Since 1 July 1995, exports of dual-use goods have been subject to a common EU regulation, while exports of conventional weapons and small arms, ammunition and military equipment continue to be subject to national regulations (according to Article 223 of the EU Treaty). The EU regulation on exports of dual-use goods is a first step toward harmonising the different export policies of the EU member states, but it still leaves scope for divergent or additional national regulations (the aforementioned German country list K being an example).

exports are published by the US Arms Control and Disarmament Agency (ACDA) whose statistics on arms transfers cover conventional weapons and weapons systems, small arms, ammunition and other ordnance and dual-use equipment when its primary mission is identified as military [ACDA, 1997: 189].[13] According to these statistics, Germany is – on an international scale – no more than a small exporter and only a marginal supplier to developing countries. In the period 1990–95, Germany accounted for 4.7 per cent of total arms exports worldwide (ranking fifth after the United States, Russia, the United Kingdom and France) and 1.7 per cent of total arms exports to developing countries (ranking sixth after the United States, Russia, the United Kingdom, France and China). A similar picture emerges when the shares of major suppliers' arms exports going to developing countries are compared: in the period 1990–95, 22 per cent of German arms exports went to developing countries (China 97 per cent, Russia 92 per cent, United Kingdom 85 per cent, France 73 per cent, United States 47 per cent) [ACDA, 1997: 156].[14]

German exports of conventional weapon systems (first product category): There are two main international sources of information on the transfer of conventional weapons: the UN Register of Conventional Arms and the statistics of the Stockholm International Peace Research Institute (SIPRI).[15] According to the SIPRI statistics, Germany became the world's second most important exporter of major conventional weapons in 1994 (ranking third in 1992, 1993 and 1995) (quoted from Rohde [1995: 3; 1996: 1]). This much-discussed surge of German arms exports is due to the large-scale export of second-hand weapons of the NVA (the army of the former German Democratic Republic) and surplus weapons of the Bundeswehr (the West German army), the great bulk of which was supplied to NATO and Scandinavian countries [BICC, 1997: 121–2; Rohde, 1996: 3]. In the

---

13. ACDA points out that the data on countries other than the United States are estimates by US Government sources and tend to be understated [ACDA, 1997: 190].
14. ACDA's definition of developing countries differs slightly from DAC's definition. For example, South Korea and South Africa are considered developed by ACDA and developing by DAC [ACDA, 1997: 185; OECD, 1998: A 101].
15. The UN Register of Conventional Arms is based on information provided by the reporting countries according to the definition mentioned in footnote 11. The SIPRI statistics differ from the UN Register in the definition of conventional weapons, the sources and the method of compiling. The SIPRI arms transfer data cover six categories of major weapons or systems (aircraft, armoured vehicles, artillery, guidance and radar systems, missiles and warships) and are compiled from information contained in about 200 publications from throughout the world [SIPRI, 1995: 4–6]. For a comparison of the two sources see Rohde [1995: 19–22].

period 1992–95, only a small fraction of German exports of conventional weapons went to developing countries: 1.2 per cent according to SIPRI and 1.7 per cent according to the UN Register [*Rohde, 1996: 1*]. On the whole, therefore, it is fair to conclude that the German regulations governing the exports of conventional arms have been applied restrictively in relation to exports to developing countries. However, the following German exports of conventional weapons to developing countries should be noted (period 1992–95): 30 warships to Indonesia, 18 armoured combat vehicles to Thailand, 15 armoured combat vehicles to Kuwait, three submarines to South Korea, two attack helicopters to Bahrain and one submarine to India.[16]

German exports of small arms, ammunition and military equipment: A different picture emerges when this product category is taken into consideration. Then the share of German exports going to developing countries tends to be much higher. Unfortunately, there are no official data on actual exports. The only evidence that is available is provided by the statistics on the licences issued by the Federal Export Office in accordance with the Foreign Trade Regulation.[17] Although the values registered in the licences are not identical with the actual export values, they give a first indication of the export policy pursued by the German government.[18] In 1995, the last year for which information was published, the Federal Export Office issued licences for the export of arms, ammunition and military equipment (section A of the

---

16. According to the UN Register of Conventional Arms (quoted from Büttner *et al.* [*1996: 24*]), the SIPRI statistics reveal further German exports of major weapons to developing countries: for instance, the supply of three military transport aircraft to Columbia and Thailand, respectively, and five Wiesel 'scout cars' to Indonesia; and licences for 60 coast guard navy aircraft to India, six submarines to South Korea and four submarines to Brazil [*SIPRI, 1997*].

17. The German government publishes detailed information on its arms export policy (including statistics on the export licences issued) only when it is explicitly requested to do so by Parliament, that is, usually the opposition parties, which have the possibility to introduce so-called 'small or great parliamentary questions'. The Government's answers to the questions constitute one of the most important and sometimes the only published source of information on the practice of German arms export policy.

18. On the other hand, a number of applications for exports of arms, ammunition and military equipment to developing countries were rejected by the Federal Export Office in recent years [*BMWi, 1998: 11–12*]. It is difficult exactly to measure the restrictiveness of the arms export policy pursued. The Federal Government, for instance, admits a high 'approval ratio' (the share of export applications approved in the total number or value of export applications submitted), but points out that this result merely reflects the fact that arms exporters tend not to submit applications that are unlikely to be approved [*ibid.: 10*].

Foreign Trade Regulation, which does not include conventional weapons covered by the Law on the Control of War Arms) worth almost three billion German marks, with licences for exports to developing countries (DAC's definition) accounting for about 26 per cent of this value (20 per cent if Turkey as a NATO ally is excluded). Major countries of destination (apart from Turkey) were: South Korea, Brazil, Saudi Arabia, Thailand, Indonesia, Malaysia, Morocco, Egypt, India and South Africa [*BMWi, 1996b: Annex Tables 1–3*].

German exports of dual-use goods (third product category): Much the same can be said of German exports of dual-use goods to developing countries. In the first half of 1995 (the only recent period for which detailed statistical information is available), the Federal Export Office issued licences for the export of dual-use goods worth 3.4 billion German marks; licences for exports to developing countries accounted for at least 27 per cent of this value.[19] Major countries of destination were Malaysia, South Africa, Iran, Egypt, China, India, Brazil, Thailand, Argentina and Indonesia [*BMWi, 1996b: Annex Tables 7–18*].[20]

German arms exports and the official German export credit insurance (Hermes): The opposition parties in the German Bundestag (SPD and Greens) and NGOs have repeatedly criticised the Federal Government for insuring arms exports under the Hermes scheme and called for an end of this practice. Although, according to the Federal Ministry of Economic Affairs, the share of arms exports in the total exports covered by Hermes is very small (one per cent in the period 1990–93) and, as a rule, only arms exports to NATO countries are accepted for insurance, several cases of arms exports to non-NATO countries which had been covered by Hermes were reported in recent years (for instance, exports to Argentina, Indonesia, the Philippines, Botswana

---

19. Until 1 July 1995, when the common EU regulation on dual-use goods came into force, dual-use goods that were subject to the Foreign Trade Regulation were listed in four sections: B (nuclear products), C (strategic products according to the former CoCom list), D (chemical products) and E (biological products). Since 1 July 1995, the four lists have been integrated into the new common EU list C of dual-use goods. The 27 per cent share of developing countries in the licences issued for German exports of dual-use goods in the first half of 1995 is the average share registered in the four sections B, C, D and E. The correspondent shares of licences for exports to developing countries in each section are as follows: B: less than one per cent, C: 43 per cent, D: 70 per cent, E: 50 per cent [*BMWi, 1996b: Annex Tables 7–18*].
20. As in the case of small arms, ammunition and military equipment (see footnote 18), it has to be noted that a number of applications for exports of dual-use goods to developing countries were rejected in recent years [*BMWi, 1998: 14–15*].

and Swaziland) (for the critical debate on the issue see Käpernick and Kulessa (eds.) [*1994: 89–90*]; Strecker [*1997*]).

By way of summary, four main conclusions may be drawn with regard to the issue of policy coherence: First, German arms exports to developing countries are far less important than the public perception tends to assume, particularly if Germany is compared with other major arms suppliers. Second, there is no evidence that German arms export policy has permitted the supply of arms to those developing countries (mostly in sub-Saharan Africa) that have been involved in civil wars in recent years and absorbed increasing resources of development co-operation for the purpose of emergency and post-conflict aid. Third, among the major Third World recipients of German conventional weapons, small arms, ammunition, military equipment and dual-use goods, there are several countries that are part of areas of tension (for instance, Turkey, South Korea, India, Iran, Egypt, Morocco) or involved in intra-national armed conflict (for example, Turkey and Indonesia). Arms exports to such countries may be highly counter-productive in terms of development progress. Fourth, although in the case of German arms exports the evidence of manifest policy incoherence is less clear than, for example, in the cases of subsidised beef exports or the fisheries agreements of the EU, the available information on German arms exports going to developing countries should be sufficient for BMZ to undertake a careful analysis, case by case, to ascertain the possibility of policy incoherence.

(5) Development Co-operation and Domestic Environmental Policy

At the 1992 UN Conference on Environment and Development (UNCED) in Rio de Janeiro, the industrialised and developing countries assumed a common but differentiated responsibility for global sustainable development. It was recognised that the industrialised countries were largely responsible for environmental problems with global impacts – such as the threat to the world climate – and that their current production and consumption patterns are unsustainable and should not become generalised in view of the grave environmental burden entailed [*Kürzinger, 1996: 6*]. Hence the industrialised countries should not confine themselves to supporting environmental projects in developing countries by means of development co-operation: they need to reorient their own development in line with the demands of sustainability.

The issue of policy coherence thus becomes central. As BMZ has explicitly pointed out, efforts of development co-operation to promote sustainable development in the South are neither credible nor ultimately effective without similar efforts in the North [*BMZ, 1990: 33*]. Not surprisingly, the relationship between development co-operation and domestic environmental policies has gained increasing attention in Germany since the Earth Summit in Rio. In fact, German development co-operation has accentuated its environmental profile in the last few years, whereas progress towards sustainable development in Germany, according to many observers, is lagging far behind what is deemed necessary.

Development co-operation:. In 1991, BMZ made protection of the environment and natural resources one of three leading priorities of German development co-operation (with poverty alleviation, and education and training). This priority is reflected in each of BMZ's five 'regional concepts' for co-operation with (sub-Saharan) Africa, North Africa and the Middle East, Asia, Latin America and Central Europe and the Newly Independent States as well as in most of BMZ's 'country concepts' which define assistance strategies with regard to individual recipient countries. It is, of course, difficult to verify the precise proportion of ODA resources actually earmarked for environmental projects and programmes since protection of the environment and natural resources is a cross-sectoral task. According to estimates by BMZ, the proportion amounted to 20–25 per cent of bilateral financial and technical assistance in the period 1990–96 [*BMZ, 1997b: 156*]. At the multilateral level, Germany is the third-largest contributor to the Global Environment Facility (GEF) behind the United States and Japan with a proportion of 12 per cent [*BMU, 1997: 81*]. German development co-operation displays a number of innovative and forward-looking approaches, particularly in relation to capacity-building (for example, networking and strengthening of the relevant actors at all levels) [*BMZ, 1997c*] and the introduction of economic instruments and alternative forms of conflict resolution (in addition to command and control policies). These approaches sometimes go beyond the practice in Germany [*Kürzinger, 1996: 7*].

Domestic environmental policies: Germany is often regarded as a pioneer in environmental policies and, compared to many other industrialised countries, claims for this role are justified to some extent. Germany, for instance, went beyond the industrialised countries' commitment (included in the UN Framework Convention on Climate

Change) to return greenhouse emissions to 1990 levels by the year 2000: deciding to cut its carbon dioxide emissions by 25 per cent from 1990 levels by 2005, it launched a climate protection programme comprising more that 100 measures [*BMU, 1997: 24*]. This goal is also more ambitious than the international agreement reached at the UN Climate Conference in Kyoto in December 1997 according to which the industrialised countries are to reduce their greenhouse emissions by 5.2 per cent (EU: eight per cent) from 1990 levels in the period 2008–2012.

Critics, however, emphasise that, in view of the pressing environmental problems, current efforts are far from sufficient effectively to restructure prevailing production and consumption patterns; they are also losing momentum in view of increasing budget constraints, high unemployment levels and the present standstill of reforms.[21] A salient example is the failure to reform the tax system in keeping with environmental needs. Environmental concerns in Germany are not exclusively – and probably not even primarily – voiced by those actively engaged in development co-operation, but their contribution is significant in heightening public awareness of sustainable development as a challenge not only for developing countries but also for Germany. In order to outline briefly a recent debate, three critical reviews of Germany's environmental policies may be relevant:

In 1996 the Wuppertal Institute for Climate, Environment and Energy published a comprehensive study entitled 'Zukunftsfähiges Deutschland' ('Sustainable Germany') initiated by BUND (Bund für Umwelt und Naturschutz Deutschland), which is an environmentally oriented NGO, and the Catholic relief organisation MISEREOR [*BUND and MISEREOR, 1996*]. The study shows in detail that Germany's resource utilisation and emissions are actually unsustainable and suggests reform in many areas such as energy, transport, industry and agriculture which ultimately involves far-reaching change to the economic and social system and the prevailing lifestyle.

Similar conclusions are drawn in the 'Alternative Indicators Report' on Germany's sustainability [*Forum Umwelt und Entwicklung,*

---

21. According to two comparative studies of the environmental policies of 25 countries, Germany had – on an international scale – become a pioneer country in the 1980s, but dropped back within the group of progressive countries in the 1990s [*Jänicke and Weidner, 1997: 15, 19*].

1997a]. The report anticipates, and is intended to stimulate, an official report which Germany agreed to elaborate on the basis of 134 indicators proposed by the UN Commission for Sustainable Development (CSD): these assess the sustainability of development in different countries (Germany is one of 20 pilot countries in this project and has agreed, together with its partner country Brazil, to put forward a report by 1999).

On the occasion of the Special Session of the UN General Assembly held in June 1997, five years after the Rio conference, the Forum Umwelt und Entwicklung[22] presented a critical review of progress and set-backs in German and international environmental policies [*Forum Umwelt und Entwicklung, 1997b*]. The report criticised the German government, *inter alia*, for having so far failed to conceive a national strategy for sustainable development as stipulated by Agenda 21, for standstills or even set-backs in the implementation of measures to reduce the emission of greenhouse gases and for reductions in German ODA.

If the developing countries are to be discouraged from losing interest in environmentally relevant measures, particularly as regards efforts of global benefit, it makes little sense to negotiate more and more new international conventions or to cut back on environment-oriented projects and programmes of development co-operation. Instead, Germany should reclaim the pioneering role in the protection of the environment that it so often signals publicly [*Kürzinger, 1996: 7*].

V. SOME CONCLUSIONS FROM THE EVIDENCE

The preceding sections allow the following conclusions to be drawn:

(1) The different cases of policy incoherence suggest two distinctions:

(a) The first distinction should be made between what might be called 'single-issue incoherence' versus 'systemic incoherence'. A common feature of issues such as subsidised beef exports, the EU fisheries agreements, corruption and arms

---

22. The Forum Umwelt und Entwicklung (Forum Environment and Development) was founded shortly after UNCED 1992 by 35 NGOs and Third World groups which joined together to stimulate the post-Rio debate in Germany.

exports is that it is relatively easy to bring the incoherence with regard to development co-operation into focus both analytically (though each case requires a careful and sometimes complicated analysis) and politically. Not surprisingly, a great deal of the public debate on policy incoherence in Germany has concentrated on these clear-cut issues which lend themselves to campaigns by NGOs and Third World groups intended to arouse public awareness. In contrast, the incoherence between development co-operation and environmental policies at home has more of a 'systemic' nature since the call for greater coherence ultimately means that domestic production and consumption patterns need to be questioned from the point of view of sustainable development. The problem of achieving more policy coherence in this case is multifaceted and cannot be reduced to a single pithy juxtaposition, such as 'support to cattle-raising versus subsidised beef exports'.

(b) The second distinction refers to the incoherence between national development co-operation and either other principally national policies (such as treatment of corruption) or other policies that are designed and negotiated at the EU level (such as foreign trade and agricultural policies). Achieving greater policy coherence in the latter case requires co-ordination not only with other national ministers involved but also with other EU member countries and is therefore more difficult.

(2) Even when policy incoherence appears to be self-evident (as, for example, in the case of arms exports), a careful analysis of each case is indispensable, particularly in relation to the role of different policies, the asserted impact of the incoherence and the level of political decision-making (at national compared with EU level). Failure to do so will restrict those politically responsible for development co-operation in devising a well-founded line of argument for talks with representatives of other policy areas, and NGOs and Third World groups in attempts to launch credible campaigns.

(3) The examples of subsidised beef exports and corruption show that in some cases policy incoherence was known to insiders for some time, becoming matters of public and political debate only after NGOs started to inform the media and the public and to

address members of parliament or parliamentary committees both at the national and the EU levels. NGOs and the media can play a major role in raising public awareness of policy incoherence and mobilising political opposition to it and this makes them a potentially important ally for development co-operation in efforts for greater policy coherence. However, the success of any such alliance depends on the extent of NGO and media campaigns as well as other factors such as the strength of the political interests involved and the general situation which may be more or less conducive to achieving greater coherence (for instance, the conclusion of the Uruguay Round and the gradual reform of EU agricultural policy since 1992 have made it easier for the EU to reduce export subsidies for beef exports to West Africa; in addition, the devaluation of the CFA franc in 1994 helped to mitigate the negative impact of the subsidised beef exports on development co-operation projects).

(4) Achieving greater policy coherence sometimes requires joint action by different donor countries. This frequently leads to complications, particularly if governments hide behind the alleged need for co-ordination with other countries; however, in some cases joint action actually supports the efforts towards more coherence.

  (a) Joint action (or donor co-ordination) is obviously necessary when the policies causing the incoherence come within EU responsibility – for instance, common foreign trade and agricultural policies – but it can also be observed in policy areas which, strictly speaking, are of national concern only. A typical example is the setting of standards (for example, environmental standards or treatment of corruption) for nationals (particularly for national firms operating in international business), where governments seek to harmonise national regulations in order to create equal conditions for international competition. It is for this reason that Germany has so far refrained from defining and enforcing certain environmental standards on its own, seeking instead to achieve common, but possibly less strict, EU standards, and thereby laying itself open to criticism by environmentalists and those calling for more coherence between German development co-operation and domestic environmental policies. It is clear that achieving more policy coherence becomes a complicated, time-consuming and perhaps frustrating process when it involves harmonising the policies of different countries on the basis of a smallest common denominator that falls short of the original national objective.

(b) Governments sometimes hide behind the alleged need for an international harmonisation of policies or donor co-ordination rather than change certain domestic policies on their own. The German government put forward this argument to explain why it had not included bribery of foreign public officials in the new and stricter anti-corruption law passed in June 1997, pointing to the consensus to be sought within the OECD (actually, the consensus had already been found when the law was passed). The United States had long before made bribery of foreign public officials a punishable offence, however, demonstrating that a national decision on this issue would have been entirely possible.

(c) The debate on the incoherence between development co-operation and treatment of corruption in Germany provides another interesting experience: actors of German development co-operation (BMZ, members of the Parliamentary Committee for Economic Co-operation and Development, NGOs) were unable to mobilise the political support needed to end policy incoherence, and were unable to benefit from the domestic policy debate on fighting corruption in Germany to achieve a policy change. International pressure to deal with bribery in international business transactions, exerted mainly by the US and supported by the OECD, alone prompted the German government to consider the issue fully.

(5) The example of subsidised beef exports of the EU shows clearly that the developing countries in some cases are able to mitigate the negative impact of policy incoherence on the part of the donors by adjusting their own policies. To what extent this actually occurs, of course, depends on the economic and political interests involved. Not surprisingly, NGOs in donor countries campaigning against policy incoherence have tried to mobilise and support NGOs in the recipient countries in order to raise public awareness there. In some cases, such as donor trade and environmental policies, however, the developing countries can do little to counteract the negative impact of policy incoherence.

VI. CURRENT PROCEDURES TO ACHIEVE POLICY COHERENCE IN GERMANY

Germany, in contrast to most other donor countries, has a full-fledged ministry for development co-operation (BMZ).[23] Hence development co-operation enjoys full cabinet rank and is in a privileged position to bring its voice and knowledge to bear in the government's discussions and decision-making and to foster policy coherence. Achieving policy coherence, however, is complicated by the fact that responsibility for the German policies affecting developing countries is split between a number of other ministries. Furthermore, even within development co-operation, BMZ shares responsibility with other ministries. The call for policy coherence, included in the Treaty of Maastricht, has given additional momentum to the discussion of this issue. The following sections briefly describe the competences of BMZ and other ministries whose policies affect developing countries, the procedures of co-ordination within the Federal Government, BMZ's position on policy coherence and the measures taken to improve policy coherence.

(1) Distribution of Competences for Policies Affecting Developing Countries

Political responsibility for development co-operation rests largely, but not exclusively, with BMZ.[24] In rough terms, BMZ is responsible for bilateral financial and technical co-operation as well as for multilateral development co-operation (that is, contributions to most UN organisations and funds providing development assistance, the European Development Fund (EDF), the World Bank Group and the regional development banks). In the last few years, about 70 per cent

---

23. BMZ was founded in 1961 (several years after German development assistance had started) for three reasons: (1) The Foreign Ministry, the Ministry of Economic Affairs and other government departments responsible for development co-operation had co-ordination problems which could not be solved. (2) Parliament had campaigned for an impartial ministry, thus following a trend already evident in the early 1960s among Third World groups. (3) During the coalition negotiations preceding the formation of a new government, the leader of the Liberal Democratic Party (FDP), Walter Scheel, pressed for an additional ministry for his party [*Claus and Lembke, 1992: 282*].
24. Strictly speaking, political responsibility within the area of development co-operation is only relevant from the point of view of internal policy coherence as defined in section I and is therefore not within the scope of this chapter. Nevertheless, it is mentioned here because it is closely related to the basic question of how different ministries responsible for the whole range of policies affecting developing countries can achieve more policy coherence. Some of the proposals to improve policy coherence aim at a redistribution of ministerial responsibilities (see section VII).

of German ODA reported to the DAC came from the BMZ budget [*BMZ, 1997b: 60*]. The Ministry of Foreign Affairs is responsible for emergency aid, equipment aid, humanitarian mine clearance, democratisation assistance and cultural co-operation with developing countries. The Federal Ministries for Research and Technology, Economic Affairs, the Interior, and Family, the Elderly, Women and Youth finance minor development co-operation programmes. Financial contributions to the institutions (not to specific assistance programmes) of the following UN organisations and programmes come not from BMZ but from other ministries: UNICEF, UNRWA, UNHCR and UNESCO (Foreign Ministry), FAO (Agriculture), WHO (Health), UNEP (Environment). The development co-operation programmes and institutional contributions to UN organisations of these ministries amount to about five per cent of German ODA.[25]

A special case is EU development co-operation. Within the Federal Government, responsibility rests with the Ministry of Economic Affairs for historical reasons. However, German contributions to the EDF come from the BMZ budget, and BMZ represents Germany on the European Council of development co-operation ministers and on various development co-operation committees at EU level. Finally, the Ministry of Foreign Affairs takes the chair on behalf of Germany in negotiations between the EU and third parties (for example, the Lomé Convention).

BMZ maintains that in practice co-ordination with other relevant ministries is part of its routine. However, because of the complicated and somewhat idiosyncratic distribution of the responsibilities for development policy and the fact that the other ministries tend to use their own specialists for aid activities under their competence, BMZ, in spite of being the official ministry for development co-operation, has to expend part of its strained capacity for co-ordination with other ministries just to ensure policy coherence within the area of development co-operation.

Outside development co-operation, ministerial responsibilities concerning relations with developing countries at the Federal level are distributed as follows: Economic Affairs covers foreign trade policy including WTO, trade preferences and the Multifibre Agreement, commodities, promotion of German exports and direct investments

---

25. The remaining 25 per cent of German ODA reported to the DAC comprise the development co-operation of the Federal States [*Länder*] (costs of university places for students from developing countries; specific development co-operation programmes), the expenditure of the municipalities on refugees and asylum seekers from developing countries and Germany's financial share in EU development co-operation and food aid financed from the EU budget.

and the official export guarantee scheme Hermes, including Hermes debts of developing countries; Finance is responsible for ODA debts and co-operation between the IMF and developing countries; Agriculture covers EU agricultural and fisheries policies and FAO; Environment covers global environmental problems; Foreign Affairs is responsible for the UN General Assembly and ECOSOC and for UN peace-keeping missions in co-operation with Defence; the Interior covers refugees and asylum seekers. The situation is probably not completely different from that observed in other donor countries, but it inevitably complicates the business of inter-ministerial consultation and co-ordination.

The UN World Conferences held since the early 1990s complete the picture. Within the Federal Government, political responsibility was distributed as follows: World Conference on Children (New York, 1990): Family, the Elderly, Women and Youth; World Conference on Environment and Development (Rio de Janeiro, 1992): Environment; World Conference on Human Rights (Vienna, 1993): Foreign Affairs; World Conference on Population and Development (Cairo, 1994): the Interior; World Social Summit (Copenhagen, 1995): Labour and Social Affairs; World Conference on Women (Beijing, 1995): Family, the Elderly, Women and Youth; Habitat II (Istanbul, 1996): Construction, Regional and Urban Development; World Food Summit (Rome, 1996): Agriculture. This distribution of responsibilities was formally correct: Germany, in conjunction with the other participating countries, attended the World Conferences as member of the UN family and not merely as donor country. However, the responsible ministries needed to rely heavily on BMZ for expertise and co-ordination, since the majority of the conferences dealt mainly with problems in developing countries. As a consequence, Germany's preparation for the conferences required complicated, time-consuming and not always optimal inter-ministerial co-ordination.

(2) Consultation and Co-ordination within the Federal Government

Theoretically the German Constitution (Grundgesetz) ensures that the Federal Government pursues a coherent policy. Article 65 of the Grundgesetz is explicit in this respect: the Chancellor defines the political guidelines; within these guidelines each minister is responsible for his or her portfolio; disagreements between different ministers are settled by the cabinet. The procedural rules of the Federal Government (Geschäftsordnung der Bundesregierung) require each responsible ministry to co-ordinate its policy with all other ministries concerned. Each ministry is obliged to go through inter-ministerial consultation and co-ordination for policy initiatives and decisions, and each ministry that considers itself affected by the policy of another ministry is entitled to be involved in consultations and co-ordination. The political responsibility of an individual minister is therefore limited by the principle that each decision rests ultimately with the Federal Government (cabinet discipline). The political responsibility of a ministry mainly comprises the right to take initiatives in its area of competence, to prepare and chair consultation and co-ordination with other ministries, to implement the decisions taken, and to represent the Federal Government in domestic or international negotiations.

Inter-ministerial consultation and co-ordination take place at different levels depending on the political importance of an issue (ranging from the level of desk officers to that of division chiefs, directors and deputy ministers, up to the level of ministers and finally – albeit rarely – cabinet level). The representatives of the ministries concerned meet either on an *ad hoc* basis or regularly, and for some issues permanent committees have been created. BMZ is represented, for instance, on the Hermes committee (dealing with official export guarantees and chaired by Economic Affairs) and the co-ordination committee for humanitarian and emergency aid (chaired by the Foreign Ministry and including NGOs); but it is not a member of the Federal Security Council (responsible, *inter alia*, for basic questions of German arms exports policy and chaired by the Chancellor's Office), despite several efforts to obtain membership.

To settle conflicts and achieve coherence between policies that impair each other, a fundamental requirement is thorough information on the impact of the conflicting policies and sound factual arguments directed towards finding the most appropriate rather than the smallest common denominator. Information alone, however, is not sufficient. Of course, the way policy conflicts are actually settled is a highly political matter. Which common denominator is found and which policy wins through against other policies depends also on factors such as the political interests involved, the political commitment, leadership and bargaining power of the parties concerned, public awareness and support and, not least, the level of interest maintained by a ministry in fighting for greater coherence, in spite of the potential for a good deal of additional work and an uncertain outcome. Each desk officer, division chief, director, deputy minister and minister willing to push through his or her ministry's position in interdepartmental consultations may insist on the view taken, but risks being overruled at the next level (and ultimately in the cabinet). In practice, therefore, most issues are not pushed to the highest level, and sometimes ministries appear to prefer a tacit understanding: by not intervening in the business of other ministries, it is hoped that the latter will behave in the same way.

The examples of policy incoherence presented in section IV show that German development co-operation has had to work alongside incoherent policies in several areas up to now, although in others progress has been achieved. The examples, however, inevitably fail to show the daily efforts towards policy coherence undertaken by BMZ at different levels, which are an important part of its current work.

(3) BMZ's Efforts to Improve Policy Coherence

Policy coherence did not become an explicit issue on the agenda of development co-operation until the 1990s – either internationally or in Germany. The Basic Principles of the Federal Government's Development Policy of 1986, for instance, while stressing the need for policy dialogue with the partner countries and better co-ordination among donors to improve the effectiveness of aid, did not consider the issue of policy coherence. The only reference made was that the goals of development policy should be given greater emphasis in other areas falling within the European Community's sphere of competence, such as agriculture, trade and industry [*BMZ, 1986: 35*].

The increasing attention paid to policy coherence in Germany since the early 1990s is due to four main factors: first, growing public and political awareness of the cross-border character of development problems: ultimately, they affect global human security and require coherent policy responses, making development policy an essentially cross-sectoral and inter-ministerial task; second, the need for increased efforts to improve the impact of development assistance in view of growing budget constraints; third, a public debate on grave cases of policy incoherence (such as subsidised beef exports) triggered by NGO campaigns; fourth, the Treaty of Maastricht which, for the first time, gave the call for policy coherence legal expression: Article 130v stated that the EU should take account of its development co-operation goals in the implementation of policies likely to affect developing countries; although this article refers to EU policies only, it has given additional momentum to the debate on policy coherence in Germany.

BMZ has stressed the need for greater policy coherence in a number of official statements and documents: for example, in the Ninth and Tenth Reports on Development Policy submitted to Parliament on behalf of the Federal Government [*BMZ, 1993; 1995*], in several memoranda on Germany's development co-operation forwarded to the DAC for its aid reviews and in the most recent conceptual guidelines of BMZ [*BMZ, 1996b*].[26] In the Ninth and Tenth Reports on Development Policy, the Federal Government explicitly criticised the industrialised countries' protectionism and the EU's subsidised beef exports; it also confirmed the consensus, expressed in several debates of Parliament by the government and all parliamentary parties, that promotion of development should be considered a cross-sectional task in the overall framework of German policies [*BMZ, 1993: 59; BMZ, 1995: 47–8*].

BMZ specifically raised the issue of the EU's subsidised beef exports. In addition to commissioning an in-depth study on their impact, BMZ raised consciousness within the Federal Ministry of Agriculture, which supported the decision taken by the EU Council for Agriculture in 1993 to lower the export subsidies. The German presidency in the EU Council for Development in 1994 provided an opportunity to call for greater harmonisation between the agricultural and development policies of the EU. As regards the fisheries policy of the EU, BMZ, based on the results of the survey it has undertaken among German embassies in 35 coastal countries, stresses the need to design the fisheries agreements in a way that ensures a sustainable management of fish resources, and to assist the partner countries in strengthening their monitoring capacity.

BMZ has taken several administrative and organisational steps in recent years to improve policy coherence [*Schmieg, 1997a: 3–4*]:

BMZ has initiated and chairs an inter-ministerial working group on 'policy coherence' which convenes to discuss relevant issues on an ad hoc basis at the request of one of the participants (usually BMZ). The EU fisheries agreements have been a particularly important issue discussed in this working group.

Since 1992/93, BMZ's planning division has designated one person to deal with coherence issues.

Following the latest reorganisation of BMZ in January 1997, the sectoral divisions of BMZ have been given explicit responsibility for monitoring issues of policy coherence in their respective areas.

---

26. For a survey of official statements by the German government and the political parties on the need for policy coherence see Wissing [*1994*].

VII. PROPOSALS TO IMPROVE POLICY COHERENCE IN GERMANY

(1) Overview

In view of the concrete experience of policy incoherence discussed in sections III and IV and BMZ's own claim that development policy is ultimately a cross-sectional task serving the aims of sustainable development and global human security, critical observers consider the existing mechanisms of inter-ministerial consultation and co-ordination insufficient and offered different proposals to achieve greater policy coherence. Summing up the debate of the last few years, one can identify seven different proposals (which sometimes have been presented in conjunction): (1) to enhance the status of development co-operation by basing it on a specific law; (2) to create a Development Cabinet; (3) to strengthen BMZ's co-ordinating and monitoring role within the Federal Government; (4) to expand the sphere of competence of BMZ; (5) to merge BMZ with the Ministry of Foreign Affairs; (6) to subject all policies to a development impact assessment; and (7) to utilise fully BMZ's existing scope of action and to increase sensitivity in other ministries as regards the development impact of their policies.

It is interesting to note that the issue of policy coherence plays a prominent role in the political debate on future development co-operation that is currently going on in Germany in view of the next parliamentary elections at federal level in September 1998 (much the same could be observed before the last Bundestag elections in 1994). Several of the aforementioned proposals to enhance policy coherence were voiced in two issues papers on future development policy presented by the Development Co-operation Committee of the Christian Democratic Union (CDU) in August 1997 [*Bundesfachausschuß Entwicklungspolitik der CDU, 1997*] and the Forum One World of the Social Democratic Party (SPD) in September 1997 [*Forum Eine Welt der SPD, 1997*].

Policy coherence is also an important topic of the 'Memorandum 98: Toward a Policy of Sustainability – Development Policy as International Structural Policy. Demands Addressed to the Bundestag and the Federal Government' published in April 1998 by representatives of NGOs and members of different development co-operation institutions [*Deutscher et al., 1998*]; a similar initiative had been taken in 1994 with the 'Memorandum: Strengthening North–South Policy in the Activities of Parliament and Government. Demands Addressed to the Parties in the New Bundestag' [*Deutscher et al., 1994*]. Currently, there seems to exist a remarkable consensus among the development co-operation advocates of the SPD, CDU and Greens in the German Parliament in relation to the need to strengthen the role of development policy and to improve policy coherence (although this consensus is not necessarily shared by the majority of the three parties).

None of the seven proposals (except perhaps the last one) has to date been accepted by the Federal Government and its coalition in Parliament, either because the proposals are considered factually inappropriate or because of a lack of political will needed to give development policy the political weight demanded by critics. The following sections briefly present the proposals and conclude with a short assessment.

(2) Enhancing the Status of Development Co-operation by Basing It on a Specific Federal Act

In common with most other OECD donor countries (but in contrast to the United States, Austria, Denmark, Sweden and Switzerland), Germany has no specific development co-operation or foreign assistance act [*Claus et al., 1989: 31–8; Thiel, 1996*]. The legal basis of German development co-operation is provided by the annual budget laws and commitments Germany has assumed under international law. The call for a specific Federal Development Policy Act is included in the two memoranda of 1994 and 1998 and a motion concerning the reform of German development policy tabled by the Greens in 1995 [*Eid-Simon et al., 1995*]. It has been a particular matter of concern of the opposition SPD which introduced drafts of such an act during the last and current term of Parliament [*Hauchler et al., 1995*] and renewed the demand in the issues paper of 1997.

The advocates of a specific law have advanced, among others, the following arguments for their initiative [*Hauchler et al., 1995: 10*]: first, serving no domestic interest groups, development co-operation is in danger of being subordinated to the goals and interests of other policies and therefore needs a legal basis that defines (and protects) its principles, aims, priorities and instruments. Second, development co-operation should be conceived as a cross-sectional task of all policy areas, requiring a coherent approach towards developing countries. Hence, according to the proposed law, all policy decisions should be subjected to a development impact assessment. Third, development co-operation needs broad societal consensus and support; this should be enhanced through greater involvement of Parliament in development policy decisions (to be ensured by an ombudsman for development policy and BMZ's obligation to submit its annual financial, sectoral and regional planning to Parliament for approval) as well as closer co-operation between public and private actors.

In a hearing organised by the Parliamentary Committee for Economic Co-operation and Development in March 1994, the SPD initiative was supported by former BMZ Minister Erhard Eppler, representatives of the Churches and several experts. Critics, however, questioned the usefulness of a law to ensure policy coherence – a highly political matter – and whether it would be appropriate to require a development impact assessment of all policies (see below). The draft was rejected by the governing coalition in Parliament. The Federal Government argued that the legal basis for development co-operation was sufficient and a specific development policy law would restrict scope for action and possibilities for a quick response to changing circumstances. Moreover, the chances of succes for the draft were limited by the fact that it had come from the main opposition party.

(3) Creating a Development Cabinet

The proposal of a Development Cabinet is an old one. It was renewed in the Memorandum of 1994 and the two issues papers of CDU and SPD published in 1997. The basic idea is that the Chancellor takes responsibility for the co-ordination and coherence of all policies that affect developing countries (initial understanding of policy coherence) or are relevant in view of the overriding objective of 'safeguarding our global future' (recent and more comprehensive understanding of policy coherence). According to the SPD initiative, which is somewhat more explicit than the other ones, the Development Cabinet should be chaired by the Chancellor and meet several times a year to define and monitor the goals of German foreign, development and security policies.

For a Development Cabinet to play the expected role, the crucial point is the political will of the cabinet to accept 'safeguarding our global future' as the overriding objective of all policies rather than the institutional mechanism itself. Strictly speaking, a Development Cabinet of this type would be completely in line with the existing provisions for inter-ministerial consultation and co-ordination described above and would leave unchanged the roles and responsibilities of the ministries concerned. Basically, it would act as a permanent inter-ministerial committee. Its potential advantages are: first, to increase awareness among the different ministries with respect to the need for greater policy coherence; second, to stress the importance of policy coherence by an institutional arrangement; and third, to secure the automatic involvement of the Chancellor's Office.

The idea of a Development Cabinet has hitherto not been taken up by the Federal Government, a frequent argument being that the existing provisions for inter-ministerial consultation and co-ordination are sufficient. Actually, however, the concept of development policy as a cross-sectional task of all policies does not yet enjoy the political support needed to give a Development Cabinet real momentum. In addition, BMZ has never advocated a Development Cabinet, fearing undue interference from other ministries in its affairs.

(4) Strengthening BMZ's Co-ordinating and Monitoring Role within the Cabinet

A common proposal to improve policy coherence, included in several initiatives mentioned above, aims at an enhanced co-ordinating and monitoring role of BMZ within the Federal Government. The 1997 issues papers of CDU and SPD proposed a co-ordination committee chaired by BMZ and comprising all relevant ministries: the committee should support the Development Cabinet either by co-ordinating the policies of the different ministries on the basis of guidelines to be defined by the Development Cabinet (SPD proposal) or by monitoring all policies with regard to their development impact (CDU proposal). According to the Memorandum of 1998, the Federal Government should define guidelines for a policy of sustainable development that are binding for all ministries; BMZ should monitor the compliance with the guidelines and, to this end, have the right to a say (including the right to a suspensive veto until a cabinet decision) in other policy areas such as international environmental policy, international monetary and debt policies, international trade, investment and agricultural policies, arms exports policy and cultural policy. The CDU and SPD papers called for BMZ's membership in the Federal Security Council.

These proposals contain three new elements: first, the idea of guidelines that commit all ministries to the objective of sustainable development; if such guidelines are to have a real impact rather than be a mere declaration of intent, they will require not only a clear understanding of what sustainable development means in each policy area, but also considerable efforts toward a political consensus among quite different interests; second, BMZ's monitoring role; in order to play this role effectively, BMZ will have to to create the necessary monitoring capacity which it currently does not have (see section VII); third, BMZ's reaffirmed right to a say in other policy areas (including a suspensive veto) and membership in the Federal Security

Council. Although the proposals are less radical than one might presume (as explained above, BMZ, like any other ministry, can demand to be involved in inter-ministerial consultation and co-ordination and push an issue up to the Cabinet level whenever it considers itself concerned), they would enhance BMZ's standing within the Cabinet and facilitate its endeavour toward greater policy coherence in the current business of inter-ministerial consultation and co-ordination.

(5) Expanding BMZ's Sphere of Competence

There have been two variants on this proposal. The first one, included in most of the aforementioned initiatives, aims at transferring to BMZ the responsibility for all aid-related policies presently looked after by other ministries. This approach, labelled 'development policy in one hand', would integrate within BMZ: humanitarian and emergency aid, equipment aid, democratisation assistance, European development policy, international environment issues, responsibility for all UN organisations and programmes engaged in development assistance and, finally, responsibility for international conferences dealing mainly with developing countries. A positive side-effect of this proposal, if implemented, would be to expand the mandate of the specialised Parliamentary Committee for Economic Co-operation and Development, allowing it to strike a more equal balance in relation to the powerful Budget Committee.

The second and more ambitious variant, proposed by the Greens before the parliamentary elections in 1994, aimed at creating a Federal Ministry for International Co-operation and Sustainable Development. This would be responsible for all aid-related policies with the addition of international debt and commodity issues, technology transfer between the North, South and East and core areas of international agricultural policy [*epd-Entwicklungspolitik, 1994: 9; Fues, 1994*].

None of these proposals has materialised so far: the existing distribution of ministerial responsibilities reflects historical circumstances, departmental interests and coalition considerations rather than factual arguments of development policy.

(6) Merging BMZ with the Ministry of Foreign Affairs

The aforementioned proposals have two things in common: they seek to enhance policy coherence by strengthening the role of BMZ and development policy in the cabinet; and they have strongly been advocated by the SPD, or more precisely, by the 'development policy wing' of the party. Interestingly enough, however, during the election

169

campaign at the federal level in 1994, the former leader of the SPD and candidate for the post of Chancellor, Rudolf Scharping, announced that on his election the SPD would incorporate BMZ in the Ministry of Foreign Affairs as the department for development co-operation following the pattern of a number of other OECD donor countries. The then secretary-general of the SPD explicitly justified this approach, stressing the need to increase the political importance of development policy and to achieve greater policy coherence. According to him, only a strong ministry could give development policy the momentum required in view of the global character of development problems [*Verheugen, 1994*].

The public response to the announcement was disastrous. Development specialists and activists from all parties represented in Parliament (including the SPD), from the Churches, NGOs and development co-operation institutions almost unanimously rejected the idea for fear of development co-operation being subordinated to other interests and losing its societal support. Of course, the controversy is to some extent a matter of faith. What is really important is the kind of development policy that is pursued. The existence of a separate ministry is very useful to enhance the political standing of development policy and to underpin its possibilities of expression in the Cabinet, but it cannot compensate for a lack of political leadership and development commitment on the part of government. Other donor countries where development policy is under the responsibility of the Ministry of Foreign Affairs do not necessarily pursue a less convincing development policy. It should also not be forgotten that BMZ owes its existence more to 'coalition arithmetic' than to conceptual wisdom.

(7) Subjecting All Policies to a Development Impact Assessment

The memoranda of 1994 and 1998, the SPD draft of a Federal Development Policy Act, the motion concerning the reform of German development policy tabled by the Greens in 1995 and the 1997 issues papers of CDU and SPD called for the introduction of a development impact assessment (DIA). According to the draft submitted by the SPD (which has made the most comprehensive proposal in this respect) the Federal Government should examine in particular all projects in the fields of financial and monetary policy, economic, agricultural and trade policy, environmental and technology policy in terms of their economic, social and ecological impacts on the developing countries [*Hauchler et al., 1995: 8*]. The term 'development impact assessment' is derived from the environmental impact assessment

(EIA) introduced into German development co-operation in 1988. The proposals give no details as to how DIA is to be applied in practice.

In a study commissioned by SPD members of the Parliamentary Committee for Economic Co-operation and Development, the German Development Institute (GDI) critically reviewed the idea of a DIA and concluded that any one-to-one transfer of the concept of EIA to the far more complex field of policy coherence was bound to run into a number of methodological and political problems [*Kürzinger, 1996*]. The study pointed out four main difficulties of DIA:

The use of DIA presupposes sound knowledge of at least partial cause and effect relations, and, in view of the great complexity of socio-economic and political development processes, even presumes a universally accepted understanding of development: such an understanding does not as yet exist. Even among the different political parties there is no general agreement on what is to be understood by 'development'. Within a given spectrum, different development goals may exist side by side – for example, poverty alleviation, economic growth, sustainable development – all of which may result in different criteria for the use of DIA.

The EIA as currently practised is above all a project-specific procedure, of particular relevance for investment projects. DIA, however, is intended to be applied to entire policy areas or to assess the development compatibility of activities that do not correspond to clearly defined projects. This is a methodological claim more ambitious by far. The discussion on more comprehensive approaches and instruments geared to identifying the environmental impact of policies (a current topic is 'strategic environmental assessment') is, even in the comparatively advanced area of environment, only in its initial stage.

DIA is likely to be unpracticable for aid administration. All donors have created significant administrative structures and procedures designed to conduct EIAs. In view of the complexity of policy coherence and the number of developing countries to be considered, this would be even more necessary for a DIA procedure. The process associated with a formal DIA would entail collecting and processing an unmanageable supply of documents from a number of ministries. There is a danger that the management of this complex procedure would assume dimensions that left little time for any substantive issues. Moreover, in view of present budget constraints, it is virtually inconceivable that the additional staff needed could be hired.

Perhaps the most important argument against a DIA as a mechanism for achieving greater policy coherence is the inadequacy of administrative procedure to settle conflicts of a political nature. It is essentially for politicians themselves to heighten the interest accorded to development-related views and provide for a more development-oriented balance between the various political interests; this should not be delegated to administration. In addition, a bureaucratic procedure is only as effective as the underlying political decision-making and support on which it depends.

(8) Pragmatic Approaches to Enhancing Policy Coherence

In contrast to DIA, the aforementioned GDI study [*Kürzinger, 1996*] proposed two pragmatic approaches to enhancing policy coherence.

The first is both relatively easy to put into effect and not over-risky: an incremental approach that limits itself, at first, to selected issues. BMZ might, for instance, concentrate initially on one or two policy fields of high importance for developing countries (such as agricultural, trade or environmental policies). It should be provided with the necessary financial resources and staff (including sectoral technical expertise and travel expense for participating in negotiations) to exhaust fully the framework defined by existing responsibilities and to introduce high-quality coherence-related inputs into relevant political processes (through expert commentaries on documents, preparation of briefing and background papers from the perspective of development co-operation, active presentation of these perspectives in inter-ministerial co-ordination processes and in international discussions and negotiations). This effort should go in conjunction with BMZ focusing more closely on the design and practical application of conceptual guidelines for the implementing agencies, thus strengthening the core functions of BMZ. Conducive to monitoring this process would be the establishment of a BMZ 'policy coherence study group' comprising representatives of the political, regional and sectoral departments and experts from implementing agencies and research institutes.

In order to increase awareness of the need for greater policy coherence in other policy areas as well, the issue should be discussed more intensively – with a focus on results – by the scientific advisory boards of the ministries concerned, by Parliament, and by public institutions concerned with development co-operation. It will only be possible to obtain the required co-operation of actors in other policy fields if they have gained at least some initial insights into the reasons for and advantages of avoiding negative impacts on developing countries and if they understand that increasing policy coherence touches upon their own (enlightened) self-interest. Policy coherence will be regarded as a 'debt owed' by a given ministry to BMZ only when development policy, or BMZ as the 'facilitator', insists on a case-by-case discussion of serious cases of policy incoherence and calls for concrete commitments aimed at gradually eliminating the problem. In this way development policy could be established as a cross-sectional task and a one-sided delegation of 'development compatibility' or DIA to BMZ avoided. The process of calling in the 'debt owed' might be facilitated by a discussion of coherence problems in the existing scientific advisory boards of the ministries concerned; by a 'Coherence Report' to be prepared by the advisory boards and designed to sensitise political decision-makers, administrators and the public; and by technically competent and critical 'small' or 'great parliamentary questions'.

(9) Conclusions with Regard to the Proposals to Improve Policy Coherence in Germany

The following conclusions briefly review the aforementioned proposals to improve policy coherence in the light of the conceptual remarks made in section II. More precisely, the question is to what extent the different proposals contribute to overcoming the various reasons for policy incoherence. In general, it has to be stressed that all attempts to achieve greater policy coherence by legal, administrative or bureaucratic measures cannot invalidate two basic reasons for possible policy incoherence: the complexity of socio-economic and political development processes and the existence of divergent political interests. A particularly clear example in this respect is the idea of achieving policy coherence by means of a strict development impact assessment of all policies. Policy coherence is highly political by its very nature and ultimately should be dealt with in the political arena. Nevertheless, the proposals referred to above could be helpful, albeit to a varying degree, in reducing the impact of the different factors that cause policy incoherence.

Complexity of socio-economic and political development processes: As stated above, it is hardly possible to conceive a complete and universally accepted theory of development. However, a less ambitious – albeit important – goal is to better understand the complexity of socio-economic and political development and the likely impact of different policies. In this respect, four of the aforementioned proposals can be helpful: (1) creation of a Development Cabinet, provided it actually succeeds in sensitising other ministries with regard to the development impact of their policies; (2) strengthening BMZ's monitoring role provided BMZ develops the necessary monitoring capacity; (3) development impact assessment (DIA) of policies on condition that it is not applied as a strict bureaucratic procedure; DIA has a useful role to play if it is construed as an attempt to understand and discuss the complex development impacts of different policies and to break new analytical and methodological ground; (4) pragmatic approaches aimed precisely at stimulating BMZ and other ministries – and their advisory boards – to reflect on development impacts of their policies.

Lack of information: These four proposals, if implemented, would clearly promote a better flow of information and greater transparency between different policy areas and might even induce efforts to develop further the analytical capacities of the ministries concerned. Expanding BMZ's sphere of competence could equally improve the flow of information: responsibility for aid-related policies currently split among a number of ministries, would be transferred to a single ministry, with a subsequent reduction in time-consuming inter-ministerial consultation and co-ordination. The same would apply to integration of BMZ into the Foreign Ministry. Nevertheless, improving the inter-ministerial information system will remain an important task aimed at adequately dealing with the complex issue of policy coherence.

Divergent political interests: A specific Development Policy Law or Foreign Assistance Act could not neutralise divergent political interests, but it could clearly enhance political and public awareness of development policy by confirming its importance and overriding goal (that is, to help promote sustainable development and safeguard our global future) and by stressing that this goal corresponds to a clear national self-interest that should not be confused with or subordinated to other domestic interests. In principle, the latter should be served by other specifically designed policies. A Development Policy Law, however, should not blur the dividing line between Parliament and Government by obliging BMZ to submit its detailed annual financial, sectoral and regional planning to Parliament for approval, as the SPD draft suggested. Creating a Development Cabinet, strengthening

BMZ's monitoring role and expanding BMZ's sphere of competence could make an equal contribution to enhancing awareness of the importance of more coherent policies towards developing countries, provided the political will to give greater weight to development policy exists or can be generated.

Organisation of the policy-making system: On the whole, the organisation of the German policy-making system is relatively conducive to policy coherence: Germany has a fully-fledged ministry for development co-operation and the procedural rules of the Federal Government ensure that each ministry is entitled to put on the agenda all issues of inter-ministerial consultation and co-ordination. Against this background, the proposals to create a Development Cabinet or to expand the BMZ's sphere of competence would amount to an incremental rather than a fundamental improvement. In the practice and routine of government action, however, such an improvement could enhance the chances for greater policy coherence.

Division of political competences between the EU and EU member states: The proposals presented above refer to the national level in Germany. As stated at the beginning, the division of political competences between the EU and its member states is a prominent source of policy incoherence. Basically any progress towards more policy coherence at the national level will increase the pressure to strive equally for greater policy coherence at the EU level.

REFERENCES

ACDA, 1997, *World Military Expenditures and Arms Transfers 1996*, Washington, DC: US Arms Control and Disarmament Agency.
Ashoff, Guido, 1996, 'The Development Policy of the Federal Republic of Germany', *D + C (Development and Co-operation)*, No.5, Berlin: Deutsche Stiftung für internationale Entwicklung (German Foundation for International Development).
BICC (Bonn International Center for Conversion), 1997, *Conversion Survey 1997*, Oxford: University Press.
BMU (Bundesministerium für Umwelt, Naturschutz und Reaktorsicherheit = Federal Ministry for the Environment, Nature Conservation and Nuclear Safety), 1997, *Auf dem Weg zu einer nachhaltigen Entwicklung in Deutschland. Bericht der Bundesregierung anläßlich der VN-Sondergeneralversammlung über Umwelt und Entwicklung 1997 in New York*, Bonn: BMU.
BMWi (Bundesministerium für Wirtschaft = Federal Ministry of Economic Affairs), 1996a, 'Exportkontrollpolitik bei Rüstung und rüstungsrelevanten Gütern', Antwort namens der Bundesregierung auf die Große Anfrage der Fraktion BÜNDNIS 90/DIE GRÜNEN, *Deutscher Bundestag – 13. Wahlperiode, Drucksache 13/5966*, 6.11.96.

BMWi, 1996b, 'Statistische Angaben zum bundesdeutschen Export von Rüstungs- und rüstungsrelevanten Gütern', Antwort namens der Bundesregierung auf die Kleine Anfrage der Fraktion BÜNDNIS 90/DIE GRÜNEN, *Deutscher Bundestag – 13. Wahlperiode, Drucksache 13/5680, 2.10.96*.

BMWi, 1998, 'Rüstungsexportkontrollen in der Bundesrepublik Deutschland – Sachstand und Perspektiven', Antwort namens der Bundesregierung auf die Große Anfrage der Fraktion der SPD, *Deutscher Bundestag - 13. Wahlperiode, Drucksache 13/10104, 11.3.98*

BMZ (Bundesministerium für wirtschaftliche Entwicklung und Zusammenarbeit = Federal Ministry for Economic Co-operation and Development), 1986, *The Basic Principles of Federal Government's Development Policy*, Bonn: BMZ (original German version: 1986, English translation: 1989).

BMZ, 1990, *Achter Bericht zur Entwicklungspolitik der Bundesregierung*, Bonn: BMZ.

BMZ, 1993, *Neunter Bericht zur Entwicklungspolitik der Bundesregierung*, Bonn: BMZ.

BMZ, 1995, *Zehnter Bericht zur Entwicklungspolitik der Bundesregierung*, Bonn: BMZ.

BMZ, 1996a, 'Entwicklungspolitische Konzeption des BMZ', *Entwicklungspolitik aktuell* No. 072, Bonn: BMZ.

BMZ, 1996b, 'Privatwirtschaftsförderung in den Partnerländern des BMZ. Sektorübergreifendes Konzept', *Entwicklungspolitik aktuell* No. 071, Bonn: BMZ.

BMZ, 1996c, *Memorandum on the German Development Policy 1996/97 for the DAC Aid Review*, Bonn: BMZ.

BMZ, 1997a, 'Entwicklungszusammenarbeit und Krisenvorbeugung', *Entwicklungspolitik aktuell* No. 079, Bonn: BMZ.

BMZ, 1997b, *Journalisten-Handbuch Entwicklungspolitik 1997*, Bonn: BMZ.

BMZ, 1997c, *Die Fähigkeit zum Umwelt- und Ressourcenschutz in Entwicklungsländern stärken. Beiträge der Entwicklungszusammenarbeit*, Bonn: BMZ.

Bodemer, Klaus, 1974, *Entwicklungshilfe – Politik für wen? Ideologie und Vergabepraxis der deutschen Entwicklungshilfe in der ersten Dekade*, München: Weltforum Verlag.

Brandt, Hartmut, 1995a, 'The Effects of EU Export Refunds on West African Countries' Beef Sectors', *Economics*, Vol. 52, Tübingen: Institut für wissenschaftliche Zusammenarbeit (Institute for Scientific Co-operation).

Brandt, Hartmut, 1995b, *Auswirkungen von Exporterstattungen der Europäischen Union auf die Rindfleischsektoren westafrikanischer Länder*, Berlin: Deutsches Institut für Entwicklungspolitik (German Development Institute).

Brandt, Hartmut, 1995c, *Prospects for Development Co-operation in the Fishing Industry*, Berlin: Deutsches Institut für Entwicklungspolitik.

Brock, Lothar (ed.), 1996, *Rüstungsexportpolitik im Dialog. Entwicklungen und Möglichkeiten einer Kontrolle nach Ende des Ost-West-Konfliktes*, Dokumentation der Aktivitäten der Gemeinsamen Konferenz Kirche und Entwicklung 1992–1996, Materialien zum GKKE-(Gemeinsame Konferenz Kirche und Entwicklung)-Dialogprogramm, No. D 16, Bonn: GKKE.

Büttner, Veronika *et al.*, 1996, 'Stellungnahme zum Fragenkatalog für die Öffentliche Anhörung des Ausschusses für wirtschaftliche Zusammenarbeit und Entwicklung zum Thema Rüstung und Entwicklungszusammenarbeit' am 16. Oktober 1996, Ausschußdrucksache 13/111, Bonn: Deutscher Bundestag – Ausschuß für wirtschaftliche Zusammenarbeit und Entwicklung (Sekretariat).

BUND and MISEREOR (eds.), 1996, *Zukunftsfähiges Deutschland. Ein Beitrag zu einer global nachhaltigen Entwicklung*, study prepared by the Wuppertal Institut für Klima, Umwelt und Energie, Basel: Birkhäuser Verlag.

Bundesfachausschuß Entwicklungspolitik der CDU, 1997, *Thesen zur Entwicklungszusammenarbeit als Beitrag einer Welt-Zukunftspolitik*, Bonn: CDU.

Claus, Burghard *et al.*, 1989, *Co-ordination of the Development Co-operation Policies of Major OECD Donor Countries*, Berlin: Deutsches Institut für Entwicklungspolitik.

Claus, Burghard and Hans H. Lembke, 1992, 'The Development Co-operation Policy of the Federal Republic of Germany', in Ippei Yamazawa and Akira Hirata, eds., *Development Co-operation Policies of Japan, United States and Europe*, Tokyo: Institute of Developing Economies.

Deutsche Welthungerhilfe and Terre des Hommes, 1995, 1996, 1997, *Die Wirklichkeit der Entwicklungshilfe. Dritter Bericht 1994/95; Vierter Bericht 1995/96; Fünfter Bericht 1996/97. Eine kritische Bestandsaufnahme der deutschen Entwicklungspolitik*, Bonn and Osnabrück: Deutsche Welthungerhilfe and Terre des Hommes.

Deutscher, Eckhard *et al.*, 1994, *Memorandum zur Verankerung der Nord-Süd-Politik in Parlament und Regierung. Forderungen an die Fraktionen im neuen Bundestag*, Bonn (reprinted, for example, in Uwe Holtz and Eckhard Deutscher, eds., *Die Zukunft der Entwicklungspolitik. Konzeptionen aus der entwicklungspolitischen Praxis*, Bonn: Deutsche Stiftung für internationale Entwicklung, 1995).

Deutscher, Eckhard *et al.*, 1998, *Memorandum '98. Für eine Politik der Nachhaltigkeit – Entwicklungspolitik als internationale Strukturpolitik. Forderungen an Bundestag und Bundesregierung*, Bonn.

Deutscher Bundestag – Ausschuß für wirtschaftliche Zusammenarbeit und Entwicklung, 1996, 'Stellungnahmen zu der öffentlichen Anhörung zum Thema Rüstung und Entwicklungszusammenarbeit' am 16. Oktober 1996, Ausschußdrucksachen 13/111 und 13/112, Bonn: Ausschuß für wirtschaftliche Zusammenarbeit und Entwicklung (Sekretariat).

Eid-Simon, Uschi *et al.*, 1995, 'Antrag zur Reform der bundesdeutschen Entwicklungspolitik', *Deutscher Bundestag - 13. Wahlperiode, Drucksache 13/246, 18.1.95.*

Eigen, Peter, 1995, 'Vorschläge von Transparency International (TI) zur deutschen Gesetzgebung und/oder Praxis', in Uwe Holtz and Manfred Kulessa, eds., *Korruption als Entwicklungshindernis. Läßt sich Korruption durch rechtliche Maßnahmen in Deutschland unterbinden?*, Teil II, Materialien zum GKKE-Dialogprogramm, No. D 12, Bonn: GKKE.

epd-Entwicklungspolitik, 1994 (No. 20/21) = Informationsdienst des Evangelischen Presse-dienstes (epd), Frankfurt.

Forum Eine Welt der SPD, 1997, *Reformvorschläge zur Struktur der Entwicklungszusammenarbeit und Entwicklungspolitik – Angebot zum Dialog*, Bonn: SPD.

Forum Umwelt und Entwicklung (ed.), 1997a, *Fünf Jahre nach dem Erdgipfel. Wie zukunftsfähig ist Deutschland? Entwurf eines alternativen Indikatorensystems*, Bonn: Forum Umwelt und Entwicklung.

Forum Umwelt und Entwicklung (ed.), 1997b, *Fünf Jahre nach dem Erdgipfel. Umwelt und Entwicklung – Eine Bilanz*, Bonn: Forum Umwelt und Entwicklung.

Fues, Thomas, 1994, 'Ein neues BMZ? Die grüne Vision einer reformierten Nord-Süd-Politik', *blätter des iz3w*, No. 200, Freiburg: Informationszentrum Dritte Welt.

Geiger, Rainer, 1995, Statement made during a hearing on corruption and development co-operation in Bonn in June 1995, in Uwe Holtz and Manfred Kulessa, eds., *Korruption als Entwicklungshindernis. Läßt sich Korruption durch rechtliche Maßnahmen in Deutschland unterbinden?*, Teil II, Materialien zum GKKE-Dialogprogramm, No. D 12, Bonn: GKKE.

Hauchler, Ingomar *et al.*, 1995, 'Entwurf eines Gesetzes zur Entwicklungspolitik der Bundesrepublik Deutschland', *Deutscher Bundestag – 13. Wahlperiode, Drucksache 13/2223, 30.8.95.*

Hazeleger, Barend, 1997, 'Fisch der Armen für die Reichen. Die EU gefährdet im Senegal die Fischerei und das Einkommen vieler Menschen', *Der Überblick*, No. 2, Hamburg: Arbeitsgemeinschaft Kirchlicher Entwicklungsdienst.

Holtz, Uwe and Manfred Kulessa, eds., 1995, *Korruption als Entwicklungshindernis. Läßt sich Korruption durch rechtliche Maßnahmen in Deutschland unterbinden?*, Teil I und II, Materialien zum GKKE-Dialogprogramm, Nos. D 11 and 12, Bonn: GKKE.

Jänicke, Martin and Helmut Weidner, 1997, 'Zum aktuellen Stand der Umweltpolitik im internationalen Vergleich – Tendenzen zu einer globalen Konvergenz?', *Aus Politik und Zeitgeschichte – Beilage zur Wochenzeitung Das Parlament*, No. B 27, Bonn: Bundeszentrale für politische Bildung.

Käpernick, Ralf and Manfred Kulessa, eds., 1994, *Der deutsche Hermes in der Einen Welt. Die staatlichen Hermes-Bürgschaften in der entwicklungspolitischen Diskussion*, Materialien zum GKKE-Dialogprogramm, No. D 8, Bonn: GKKE.

Kürzinger, Edith, 1996, 'Entwicklungsverträglichkeit', Berlin: Deutsches Institut für Entwicklungspolitik (mimeo).

Lingnau, Hildegard and Peter P. Waller, 1996, 'Förderung von Menschenrechten und Demokratisierung im Rahmen der Entwicklungszusammenarbeit', *africa spectrum*, No. 31, Hamburg: Institut für Afrika-Kunde.

OECD, 1992, *Development Co-operation. Efforts and Policies of the Members of the Development Assistance Committee. 1992 Report*, Paris: OECD.

OECD, 1994, 'Coherence of Members' Policies toward Developing Countries: Concrete New Needs and Opportunities', issues paper submitted by the Development Co-operation Directorate and the Development Assistance Committee, Paris: OECD (DCD/DAC(94)34).

OECD, 1996a, 'Building Policy Coherence: Tools and Tensions', OECD Public Management Service Occasional Paper No. 12, Paris: OECD.

OECD, 1996b, Draft Recommendation of the DAC (concerning the issue of corruption), Paris: OECD (DCD/DAC (96)11/REV 1).

OECD, 1998, *Development Co-operation. Efforts and Policies of the Members of the Development Assistance Committee. 1997 Report*, Paris: OECD.

Rohde, Joachim, 1995, *Der deutsche Rüstungsexport 1992–1994*, Ebenhausen: Stiftung Wissenschaft und Politik (SWP).

Rohde, Joachim, 1996, 'Die Trendwende: 1995 schrumpfte der deutsche Rüstungsexport gegenüber dem Vorjahr auf weniger als ein Sechstel', *SWP aktuell*, Ebenhausen: Stiftung Wissenschaft und Politik (SWP).

Scheel, Walter, 1966, *Neue Wege deutscher Entwicklungspolitik*, Bonn: BMZ.

Schmieg, Evita, 1997a, Comments to the presentation of the German case during the International Workshop on Policy Coherence in Development Co-operation, organised under the auspices of the Working Group on Aid Policy and Performance of the European Association of Development Research and Training Institutes (EADI) in Geneva, 24–26 April 1997 (mimeo).

Schmieg, Evita, 1997b, 'Coherence between Development Policy and Agricultural Policy', *Intereconomics*, Vol.31, No.1, Hamburg: Hamburg Institute for Economic Research (HWWA).

Scholz, Imme, 1996, 'Trade, Environment and Development Co-operation', study for the OECD Development Co-operation Directorate, submitted to the DAC Working Party on Development Assistance and Environment, 14th meeting, Paris, 23–24 April 1996.

SIPRI (Stockholm International Peace Research Institute), 1995, *SIPRI Factsheet*, http://www.sipri.se/pubs/Factsheet/sipdat.html.

SIPRI 1997, *Yearbook 1997. Armaments, Disarmament and International Security*, Oxford: University Press.

Strecker, Sebastian, 1997, 'NRO-Forderungen zum Hermes-Instrumentarium', *NORD-SÜD aktuell*, Vol.11, No.3, Deutsches Übersee-Institut (German Overseas Institute).

Thiel, Reinhold E. (ed.), 1996, *Entwicklungspolitiken – 33 Geberprofile*, Hamburg: Deutsches Übersee-Institut.

Verheugen, Günter, 1994, 'Grundsätze zur Neuorientierung der Entwicklungs-zusammenarbeit', *Nord-Süd Info-Dienst*, No.66, Bonn: Aktionskreis Nord-Süd und Parteivorstand der SPD.

Waller, Peter P. and Manfred Kulessa (eds.), 1996, *Korruption als Entwicklungs-hindernis. Läßt sich Korruption durch rechtliche Maßnahmen in Deutschland unterbinden?*, Teil III, Materialien zum GKKE-Programm, No. D 14, Bonn: GKKE.

White, John, 1965, *German Aid. A survey of the sources, policy and structure of German aid*, London: Overseas Development Institute.

Wiemann, Jürgen, 1993, 'Umweltorientierte Handelspolitik: Ein neues Konfliktfeld zwischen Nord und Süd?', in Benno Engels (ed.), *Perspektiven einer neuen internationalen Handelspolitik*, Hamburg: Deutsches Übersee-Institut.

Wissing, Thomas, 1994, *Entwicklungspolitik als Querschnittsaufgabe. Vorstellungen der Bundesregierung und der Parteien zur Kohärenz der Entwicklungszusammen-arbeit – Auswertung entwicklungspolitisch relevanter Äußerungen*, Materialien zum GKKE-Dialogprogramm, No. D 4, Bonn: GKKE.

6

Coherence and Development Policy in the Netherlands

PAUL HOEBINK

Policy coherence – or the goal of achieving an integrated policy towards developing countries – has played an important role in Dutch development policies from the 1970s onwards. Particularly in the 1990s, the concern has come to the forefront of the debate in relation to the Netherlands' foreign and economic policies and to European Union policies. Coherence of policy could and should be found on many levels of internal and external policies. To limit the terrain covered by this chapter, a limited number of policy issues has been selected; these are issues that public and parliamentary debate in the Netherlands have identified as particularly important in demonstrating incoherences in policy, coinciding with subjects identified by DAC/OECD to be of major importance for policy coherence.[1]

I. DUTCH DEVELOPMENT POLICY AND COHERENCE: SOME HISTORICAL LINES

Before giving a short historical sketch of the place of 'coherence' in Dutch development policy, it is necessary to outline some aspects of the concept and bring it to workable proportions.

This chapter has benefited from research assistance by Annelies Haijtink.

1.   For this purpose, the official parliamentary records (Handelingen van de Tweede Kamer/Handelingen van de Eerste Kamer), among other sources, were searched on the concept of 'coherence' as well as the older term 'integral policy', likewise on some policy issues evident from the public debate or arising from an interview on policy coherence with Mr Jan Pronk, minister of development co-operation of the Netherlands (1973–77, 1989–97) on 24 March 1997. Some of the issues dealt with here have featured in DAC reports for a long time (tied aid) or are highlighted in the report of 1992, which had a special focus on coherence (environment, military expenditure) [DAC/OECD, 1992: Ch.6].

(1) 'Internal'/'External', 'Horizontal'/'Vertical' Coherence

If we define policy coherence as 'the non-occurrence of effects of policy that are contrary to the intended results or aims of policy' (Hoebink, this volume, Ch.10), it is clear that a chapter on policy coherence and development policy might well have to address very broad policy issues. It would also be possible to look at the question from a very narrow perspective.

This narrow perspective may be defined as *internal coherence*: the effects of a certain part of development policy should not be contrary to the intended results or aims of the same or other parts of development policy or foreign policy. Development policy in itself should be consistent. This need for consistency applies to a range of policy instruments, as well as levels of policy. It implies coherence in the rationale behind development co-operation, in goal-setting and prioritisation, between dialogue and implementation, between different types of aid, between various donor programmes, and between donor's policies, multilateral policies, aid recipient and NGO policies (Figure 1). Since development policy is part of foreign policy the second type of 'internal coherence' concerns coherence within foreign policy: development policy *vis-à-vis* foreign or trade policy. It is related to the place of development co-operation within the whole construct of foreign policies and within the bureaucracies that deal with foreign affairs and trade issues.

The broad perspective could be called *external coherence*, in which goals and activities in a given policy sector should not be at odds with policies in another sector, in this case development policy. Of relevance to development policy are market policies, policies that privilege certain economic sectors (for example, by means of subsidies), migration policy, and environmental policies, among others. Thus, external coherence calls for examination of relations between government bureaucracies, the hierarchy between these institutions, differences in ideology and, in the final analysis, power relations within a given context.

Since development co-operation is a part of foreign policy defining 'internal coherence' is somewhat problematic. If we look at policy content, internal coherence with regard to development policy may well be found in all aspects or terrains of foreign policy; however, if we look at organisational structures it could well be argued that we are addressing matters of 'external coherence', since policy decisions are taken in different departments, often without consultation or co-ordination.

FIGURE 1
INTERNAL AND EXTERNAL COHERENCE
IN DEVELOPMENT POLICY

Internal Coherence (1) Conflicting themes	Internal Coherence (1) Conflicting issues
Motives vs. motives	Economic interests vs. humanitarian considerations Strategic interests vs. humanitarian considerations Trade promotion vs. poverty alleviation Trade promotion vs. economic self-reliance
Motives vs. goals	Economic self-reliance vs. poverty alleviation
Goals vs. goals	Economic self-reliance/poverty alleviation vs. aid dependency Economic self-reliance/poverty alleviation vs. charity (NGO goals) Poverty alleviation vs. export-led growth (multilateral organisations' goals/recipient government's goals)
Goals vs. aid instruments/types	Economic self-reliance/poverty alleviation vs. aid intrusion
Internal Coherence (2) Conflicting themes	Internal Coherence (2) Conflicting themes
Development policy vs. foreign policy	Humanitarian goals vs. human rights violations
Development policy vs. trade policy	Economic self-reliance vs. protection
External Coherence Conflicting themes	External Coherence Conflicting issues
Development policy vs. domestic agricultural policy	Economic self-reliance vs. protection and subsidies
Development policy vs. migration policy	Humanitarian goals vs. immigration restrictions

A second distinction could be made between 'horizontal' and 'vertical' coherence. Both 'external coherence' and 'internal coherence' relate to another typology: in one category, coherence is sought between the policies of various organisations at the same level (horizontal), for example ministries or government organisations; in another, (in)coherence comes into play at different levels (vertical), for example between the policies of the donor government and private sector aid organisations, bilateral and multilateral donors, and donors and recipient governments.

(2) 'Integral Policies'

In the 1970s we see for the first time a more articulated effort to look for policy coherence with regard to development policy in the Netherlands. The term 'coherence' itself is not used, but words such as 'structural policy', 'integral' and 'integrated' appear frequently. In the first substantial White Paper of 1966 it had been stressed that foreign aid was at first seen as a temporary phenomenon, a sequel to decolonisation. Thus the developed countries tried to restructure their international trade, agriculture and industries, 'mostly without paying attention to the consequences for the less developed countries' [*Nota hulpverlening aan minder ontwikkelde landen, 1966: Ch.IV*].[2] Poverty reduction in other parts of the world could be achieved by means of surpluses through transfer of knowledge and capital. A structural policy which aimed at 'a gradual integration in the world economy' was the new way to address the problem and thus development policy had to be 'an integral part of general national policy', 'an essential element of all political activities'. The White Paper did not go much further than this statement, other than saying that co-operation in the UN, the EEC and the OECD was a precondition for this 'international structural co-operation'. An interdepartmental consultation took place, involving all the relevant ministries but dealing mostly with aid issues. Only in the preparation for major international conferences (such as UNCTAD) were other development problems discussed, and in this the ministry of economic affairs mostly took the lead.

In the first White Paper of Minister Pronk the emphasis was on the 'integration' of different aid instruments: technical and financial, bilateral and multilateral, project and programme aid should not be channelled through closed circuits, but should as far as possible be connected [*Nota Bilaterale Ontwikkelingssamenwerking, 1976: 17–18*]. In the budget papers, however, the 'integral structural approach'

---

2. Translations of quotes from reports and White Papers are mostly provided by the author, with the exceptions of the 1990 and 1993 White Papers.

was promoted. Trade and aid issues should be dealt with simultaneously, the government stated in 1974. It complained about the lengthy decision-making process in the EEC, the principal forum for debating and formulating structural policy on aid and trade since decisions on trade had been transferred to Brussels.[3] The so-called 'oil crisis' made raw materials – and the guarantee of a continuous supply and stable prices – the major issue for several years.

The Netherlands supported the call for a New International Economic Order (NIEO) in the Special General Assembly in 1974: a change in international structures was necessary to diminish the large differences in wealth, according to the government. In the budget paper of 1977 this 'integral policy' was again given emphasis, against the background that international development policy was in an impasse. 'Integral' meant a single co-ordinated approach towards policy on the transfer of financial flows, debt, raw materials, trade, industrialisation and agriculture. 'Unity of foreign policy' was required to guard against the use of 'incompatible instruments'. The document concluded that it had reached an 'optimal combination of different foreign policy goals in which the relative growth of wealth of the Third World got larger emphasis'.[4] From these words it should be clear that in Pronk's view the climate in the cabinet for working on these issues was very good.[5] The focus thus was strong on foreign policy in all its aspects, but not on coherence between internal (European) and development policies.

The change of government in 1977 did not initially result in a major alteration of policy. In the main White Paper of this period, 'Development co-operation in a world economic perspective' [*Nota ontwikkelingssamenwerking in wereldeconomisch perspectief, 1979*], Minister De Koning explained his ideas on development problems and on the solutions for the 1980s. Key concepts in this report were: 'the existing mixed economic system' and the 'increased interdependence between rich and poor countries'; De Koning also stated that it would not be permissible to shift 'the consequences of national problems onto the shoulders of the weakest'. The problems of developing countries were approached from these three angles. The report was thus to an important degree an extension of the line of thought introduced into the policy documents under Pronk. This continuity is

---

3. Tweede Kamer, session 1974–75, 13 100, Ch. V, No.2, Sept. 1974, pp. 62–3. Also interview with Jan Pronk.
4. Tweede Kamer, session 1975–76, 14 100, Ch. V, No.2, Sept. 1975.
5. Interview with Jan Pronk, Minister for Development Co-operation, 24 March 1997.

also reflected in the approval that De Koning gave to the Brandt report when it was presented in the Netherlands. However, the government acknowledged that concrete agreements on raw materials and capital markets were lacking and that, in effect, decisions on these concerns were taken in other fora, often against the interests of developing countries.

In the years to follow, as a result of the debt crisis and conservative world leadership, these issues vanished from the international agenda. This, in combination with the rather weak position of new ministers for development co-operation in the cabinet, resulted in retrogression *vis-à-vis* the attention paid to the position of developing countries in the world market, and to 'integral' or 'structural' policies. In the 1980s, development co-operation policy became narrower and was restricted mainly to aid policy. For example, the debt crisis – the most important problem facing many developing countries – was not dealt with at all in the budget papers, and a government report on the crisis was entirely a ministry-of-finance affair [*Hoebink, 1987: 29–45*].

(3) Coherence and 'Decompartmentalisation'

The concept of coherence, however, appeared for the first time in government documents at the end of this lean period. In the White Paper on the quality of aid [*1989*] a short paragraph is dedicated to 'coherent policy', stressing the necessity of integrating policy on aid and also on trade, international finance, etc. In the budget paper for 1990 (Jan Pronk's first budget since being back in office) the same words are repeated almost verbatim. The budget paper also refers to the establishment of a subcouncil of the cabinet, the Council for Development Co-operation, in order to improve interdepartmental co-ordination. According to the minister this had been fruitful. The agenda had been mainly taken up with EC development co-operation, the GATT Uruguay round and the OECD. According to Jan Pronk, this council, like the interdepartmental consultations that took place in the 1960s and 1970s, had little influence and dealt with development co-operation issues only (interview, 24 March 1997).

The major White Paper of 1990 – 'A World of Difference' – gave a broad analysis of development problems. It analysed the crisis in the development process, both theory and policy. It sought to identify the fading frontiers, the greater risks and the narrower margins. It did not come up with any new proposals for a more 'structural policy', although issues such as the restructuring of debt and the untying of aid were put on the agenda. In his second, much more pessimistic, White Paper – 'A World in Dispute' (1993) – Pronk brought coherence to the fore, introducing the concept of 'decompartmentalisation'. The analysis was that the tone of 'A World of Difference' had been too optimistic: instead of peace after the end of the cold war, we had seen conflicts spread like bushfire around the world. In the letter to parliament in which he presented this White Paper Pronk wrote: 'Its main conclusion is that the contemporary world calls for the "decompartmentalisation" of approaches and policies, both within development co-operation itself and between it and other dimensions of foreign and international policy.'

In the concluding chapter it was stated that 'fourteen priority areas for a development co-operation policy' had been identified, 'whose content must differ radically in the remaining years of this century from the preceding three decades'. This decompartmentalisation meant that development policy was 'no longer the "soft" sector of foreign relations' and was leading to a broader form of international co-operation, with consequences for the financing of aid programmes and for the choice of countries. In terms of finance, it meant that Pronk (the aid budget) had to pay for the growing influx of asylum seekers, for Dutch language courses and for a transport aircraft for military interventions. Overall, these austerity measures and budget cuts brought the volume of Dutch aid back from about one per cent of GNP in 1989 to around 0.8 per cent in the mid-1990s. As ex-Minister De Koning stated: 'It is nice to talk about decompartmentalisation, but when you go into the cabinet you have to remind yourself that you enter into the company of pickpockets.'

Decompartmentalisation was the aim of the organisational change proposed in the review of foreign policy carried out by the Labour government of Wim Kok which came to power in 1994. A White Paper in 1995 spelt out the need for decompartmentalisation: 'In today's world there is a growing tendency for problems to be interrelated and multidisciplinary in nature. ... In short, policy fields are merging. This means that a greater amount of co-ordination and integration is needed, both in policy terms and in organisational terms.' Two major organisational changes were that embassies in aid-receiving countries should have greater autonomy in the preparation and implementation of development projects and that the new regional departments inside the ministry should be responsible for integrating all aspects of foreign policy. 'Uniformity and consistency of policy will thus be assured', the paper argued, 'and effectiveness and decisiveness enhanced, since knowledge and instruments can be pooled and deployed to better effect' [*The Foreign Policy of the Netherlands: A Review, 1995: 51*].

II. INTERNAL COHERENCE AND AID

With regard to coherence between different aid programmes and instruments, two issues have been the focus of debate in the Netherlands: first, the mix of motives and the implications thereof for aid effectiveness; and, second, the choice of aid-receiving countries. One of the main aspects debated has been the relation between human rights policy and development policy, which will be dealt with in the next section. The prominence of the economic/commercial motive, symbolised as well as given form by tied aid, is the subject of this section.[6]

The Dutch bilateral aid programme began in the 1960s in response to pressure from the employers' federation. The main exporting firms, represented in the Commission for Developing Countries, complained about the 'false competition' they had to face, because other European countries were giving soft loans under their bilateral aid programmes whereas the Netherlands was not. The government had been quick to respond to Truman's plea for foreign aid in Point Four of the 'New Bold Programme', contained in his inaugural speech of January 1949.[7] But this aid was multilateral and technical, so it offered few opportunities for Dutch exporting firms. Another part of the aid programme was destined for the colonies, particularly Dutch Papua New Guinea, and largely used for the salary bill of the colonial service. In two position papers in 1960 and 1964 the employers thus urged the government to begin its own bilateral programme. They found support from the ministries of agriculture and economic affairs. The Netherlands joined the aid consortia for India and Pakistan and finally, in the White Paper of 1965, the employers' federation got what they wanted – a bilateral aid programme. Within a few years the bilateral part of the aid programme was three times the volume of the multilateral.

The establishment of the bilateral aid programme could be seen as a victory of the economic/commercial motive behind foreign aid over the humanitarian/ethical motive. Ethical considerations have been stressed in all the main White Papers and government reports on Dutch aid since the 1950s, whereas trade and investment interests are mostly played down or not mentioned at all. Since the Netherlands is

---

6. Strong arguments against tied aid are provided by, among others, Stichting Onderzoek Multinationale Ondernemingen [*1981*] and Herfkens and van der Lans [*1986*].
7. For a more detailed description of the history of the foreign aid programme of the Netherlands by the present author see: Hoebink [*1988*]; Hoebink [*1994*]; Hoebink [*forthcoming*].

not a major power within Europe, political and strategic motives have only partly found their way into the country's aid programme: in its aid relations with (former) colonies and in the recent inclusion of IMF and World Bank voting group members in the aid programme (and thus, by holding the directors' posts, continuation of influence in those organisations). These ties with former colonies led to a problematic relationship with Surinam (see below), but also to incoherence: officially, Dutch aid should go to the poorest countries. In effect, only around 28 per cent of aid goes to the least developed countries, and the rather rich Dutch Antilles feature among the three most favoured states.

Bilateral financial aid was initially administered by the ministry of economic affairs, representatives of which visited the aid-receiving countries to negotiate aid disbursements, and carrying 'shopping lists' in their bags. Although the stated goal was to integrate developing countries into the world economy and thus to alleviate their poverty, promotion of Dutch exports was clearly the most important, if unstated, goal.

From 1973 onwards this changed dramatically. With the Den Uyl government (1973–77) dominated by the Labour Party, responsibility for all aid programming and instruments was given to the minister for development co-operation. In its one and only goal that 'aid should as much and as directly as possible ameliorate the position of the poorest of the poorest', the humanitarian/ethical motive gained ground. Furthermore, aid became partially untied, meaning that contributions for procurement were also possible from developing countries. Even a conservative government in the mid-1980s, emphasising the role of private enterprise in the foreign aid programme, was unable to reverse this trend. The backflow percentage (that is, the percentage of bilateral aid spent on goods and services from the Netherlands) gradually was reduced from some 90 per cent at the end of the 1960s/beginning of the 1970s, to 75 per cent at the end of the 1970s, to 55 per cent in the mid-1980s, to 45–50 per cent in the 1990s. Most recent figures state that the backflow is around 65 per cent. Moreover, in the country programmes it is the needs of aid recipients that determine aid disbursements in most cases. For some time, the tying status of Dutch aid has been favourable compared to that of other DAC donors, with about 10 per cent tied, 45 per cent partially tied and about 30 per cent multilateral.[8]

---

8.   See the annual reports of the Development Assistance Committee [*DAC/OECD, several editions*].

The tying of aid, which indicates the economic/commercial motivation behind – or rationale for – the aid programme, has been seen as a major reason for low aid effectiveness. In a review of a study with this conclusion, Jan Pronk argued that aid-tying was the reason that many projects were white elephants, with little – if any – development relevance.[9] An evaluation, entitled 'Aid or Trade?', of a special fund to finance trade opportunities for Dutch companies, the so-called 'programme for developmentally relevant export transactions', came to more or less the same conclusion regarding this controversial programme: half of the projects had no financial and economic sustainability; the technological integration of most projects was problematic; export income created was insufficient to cover debt service; and employment creation was minimal [*IOV, 1990*].[10]

This led Jan Pronk to make a major effort to reduce aid-tying. As stated in *A World of Difference* [*1990*], the Dutch government would take action in international fora, such as the DAC/OECD, to promote discussions on aid-tying and to achieve the untying of aid within the EU and, preferably, within the OECD too.[11] Five years later the minister had to conclude that his efforts showed no results and that he had to put his ambitions with regard to this issue on ice.

Aid-tying did not lead to an increase in Dutch exports to developing countries. On the contrary, despite a generous aid programme, these steadily declined to less than ten per cent of total exports – under half the OECD average. Traditionally, Dutch agricultural and chemical exports are more directed to Europe. This tendency seems to have been reinforced during the last decade. Furthermore, only a small number of exporting firms profited from aid procurement. Traditionally, Dutch exports to developing countries are dairy products, textiles and textile machinery. Exports financed by aid included trucks, aeroplanes, machinery for the food industry, medical equipment, dredging ships and tugs, fertiliser and services. Only consultancy firms seemed to have used Dutch aid as a springboard to enter new markets.[12]

---

9. This was a review of this author's doctoral dissertation [*Pronk, 1989*].
10. Later country reports on Tanzania, Mali and India show the same results for projects and programmes that had their roots more in business interests than in developmental considerations.
11. It is funny to see that one of the policy incoherence issues mentioned by the DAC as far back as the 1960s is taken up by one of the donor countries at such a late stage.
12. On this subject see Hoebink and Schulpen [*1990*]. The first paragraph is based on an analysis of export figures for concentration countries, as demonstrated in Hoebink [*1988*].

Instruments to promote Dutch investments evolved from the beginning of the 1960s out of a programme to give Dutch companies that had lost their possessions in Indonesia other chances in developing countries. A programme to finance joint ventures, insurance against political risks, and from 1974 onwards a fund to subsidise the restructuring of labour-intensive industries (textiles, electronics) in developing countries have all been tried. None of them was very successful and they mainly served as export-promotion instruments.[13] Dutch foreign investments (excluding the tax haven, the Dutch Antilles) fell back from about 30 per cent of total foreign investments to less than 10 per cent, in a period when OECD investments were still more than twice as much. If one were to deduct investment in oil and chemicals (Royal Dutch Shell), investments in the least developed countries would be next to nothing.[14]

III. DEVELOPMENT POLICY AND HUMAN RIGHTS

Until the 1970s, the Netherlands had virtually no human rights policy.[15] In 1948, during the negotiations on the Universal Declaration of Human Rights, it had objected to the right to self-determination. The Netherlands also abstained in votes on anti-apartheid resolutions, reasoning that this was an internal affair of the government of South Africa; at the same time, the Dutch government supported the USA in its Vietnam war. The long-standing minister of foreign affairs, Joseph Luns, a conservative Catholic, refused to condemn any human rights violations, particularly not in the case of NATO allies such as Portugal and Greece. The most glaring absence was any condemnation by the Netherlands of Suharto's 1965 *coup d'état* and the subsequent mass killings in Indonesia. In effect, the minister of foreign affairs, Joseph Luns, and the leader of the Labour Party both welcomed the change in power. The Netherlands soon

---

13. An organisation established to finance joint ventures – the Financierings Maatschappij voor Ontwikkelingslanden – was only able to broaden its portfolio when it dropped the principle that a Dutch company should provide capital in a business venture. The history of these investment instruments is still unwritten. For some examples of FMO investments see Dalmeijer [*1987*]; Dalmeijer [*1995*]. For an evaluation of the 'restructuring programme' see, for example, Netherlands Economic Institute [*1990*].
14. See Van Nieuwkerk and Sparling [*1985*]; Kox and van Velzen [*1985*]. Recent analysis on Dutch foreign investment is not available.
15. This section is, apart from white papers and parliamentary records, based on Verloren van Themaat [*1981*]; Visser [*1983*]; Malcontent [*1996*]. For a more general overview of Dutch human rights policies see Kuitenbrouwer [*1996*].

started its new aid programme in Indonesia and even became chairman of the Inter-Governmental Group for Indonesia (IGGI), the only aid group led by a bilateral donor. In his memoirs, the minister for development co-operation at that time makes no mention of human rights violations in Indonesia.[16]

In the Labour-dominated cabinet of Prime Minister Den Uyl this changed drastically. The Labour Party's minister of foreign affairs, Max van der Stoel, had championed human rights and opposed the Greek junta in the Council of Europe. The stand taken on human rights issues by the minister for development co-operation, Jan Pronk (also Labour Party), received firm support from the Labour left wing, whose (informal) representative in the cabinet he was.

However, human rights policy was not very coherent. Pronk decided to enter into aid relations with Cuba and Vietnam with the aim at ending their isolation and facilitating 'dialogue' also on a number of issues including human rights. Pronk favoured a strong line on Indonesia, where the situation of political prisoners was the main human rights issue.[17] Van der Stoel's focus was more on eastern, and to a lesser extent, on southern Europe. He was in favour of a cautious line on Indonesia. Both ministers, as well as Pronk's successor, De Koning, were against suspending aid as a means of showing opposition to gross violations of human rights and trying to effect change. However, aid to Uganda was suspended in 1972 because of the reign of terror of Idi Amin; in September 1973 aid to Chile was also suspended after the *coup d'état* of General Pinochet. In his choice of aid-receiving countries Pronk stipulated a redistribution criterion (his third criterion), stating that the aid-receiving country should have a policy that would guarantee that aid would improve the situation of the entire population. Additionally it was stated that the protection of human rights should be an integral part of this policy. At the end of his first term Pronk prepared a short report for the cabinet in which further steps against Indonesia were prepared, although, in

---

16. However, Udink spends one chapter on the renewal of relations with Indonesia [*Udink, 1986*]. For Luns's points of view see van der Plas and Luns [*1971*].
17. Pronk's involvement in these issues has caused resentment for many years: in the 1970s, on the part of conservative liberals and christian democrats, and in the 1990s from conservative christian democrats, particularly at the time of breaking-off of the relations with Indonesia. It even influences the positions of scientists. Kuitenbrouwer [*1996*] as well as Malcontent [*1996*] accuse Pronk of one-sidedness (not criticising Cuba and Vietnam and putting pressure on Indonesia), ignoring his way of reasoning, as well as his criticisms of the Cuban and Vietnamese governments.

retrospect, his policy with regard to the release of political prisoners can be considered quite successful.[18]

Pronk's successor De Koning adopted a more cautious approach. He was quick to change the policy of concentrating on specific developing countries. The degree to which human rights were being respected replaced Pronk's criterion that aid-receiving countries should have a redistribution policy. Thus Pronk's ('famous') third criterion had been toned down, if only slightly so, and there was a new criterion (human rights) which Pronk had seen as part and parcel of his third criterion. Cuba had already been removed from the list immediately upon De Koning's coming into office, because of the presence of Cuban troops in Angola, and especially in accordance with the election promises of the VVD (the conservative liberal party). Aid to Vietnam was reduced to humanitarian aid alone after the Vietnamese military action in Cambodia. Criticism of human rights violations in other countries was clearly toned down.

In the first White Paper, 'Human Rights and Foreign Policy' (1979), a large chapter is devoted to human rights and development co-operation. It stressed that initially aid was given without any political conditionality, but that gradually more strings were attached, since 'by giving foreign aid one in fact contributed to the prolongation of repressive regimes'. The choosing of programme countries is seen as a moment to test the human rights situation in the given countries. On the other hand this government, in the same White Paper, stressed that it did not want to use aid as an instrument to reward or punish governments for fostering or violating human rights [*Nota De rechten van de mens in het buitenlands beleid, 1979*]. In its most recent progress memorandum on this White Paper (1997) the Dutch government reported on the positive developments with regard to human rights since the end of the cold war. It was still worried about countries engaged in civil war and about Asian reluctance to embrace human rights fully. It called for special attention to be paid to the rights of children, women, minorities and indigenous peoples [*Ministerie van Buitenlandse Zaken, 1997*]. With regard to aid-receiving countries it stated that the Dutch government is giving more attention at the moment to positive and encouraging measures (education, support for elections) than to sanctions.

---

18. In 1976, the Indonesian government announced it was to release a large number of political prisoners. In Amsterdam in 1973, during the meeting of the Indonesian aid group, IGGI, Pronk for the first time in the history of this aid group discussed human rights, such as the destiny of political prisoners. For a detailed study see Baneke [*1983*].

In the right-wing cabinet of the mid-1980s under Minister Eegje Schoo, human rights policy was demoted to third place, as was evident in the cases of Sri Lanka, Pakistan, and, most especially, Indonesia, which had provoked the former governor of Djakarta to strong criticism of Eegje Schoo, when he called her 'a minister in special service in Suharto's cabinet to ameliorate public relations'.[19] Executions of political prisoners who had been in gaol for 18 years brought the Dutch government no further than issuing statements of concern and grief.[20] Only in the case of Surinam was there strict adherence to the human rights criterion. Discussions on aid were postponed after President Chin A Sen's retirement from office in February 1982, and aid was suspended after what came to be called the 'December killings' in that same year. In the following years, and until Schoo's successor, Piet Bukman, visited Paramaribo in 1988 for lengthy negotiations, Surinam was provided only with disaster relief [*Hoebink, 1982; van der Werf, 1985*]. This not only indicates the ambiguity of Dutch policy towards Surinam, but also the ambiguity of the human rights policy within development co-operation as a whole.

In November 1991, the Indonesian army had opened fire on demonstrators in Dili, the capital of East Timor, territory occupied by Indonesia. According to the Indonesian authorities, 50 people had been killed, while local church groups spoke of at least 120 dead. In reaction to this, Canada, the Netherlands and Denmark had provisionally cancelled all new aid activities. In January 1992, after the Indonesian authorities had published the results of an investigation into the events and had announced their intention to punish the officers involved, Denmark and the Netherlands revoked the cancellation.

On 25 March 1992, the Indonesian government announced in a strongly worded letter that it no longer wished to receive development aid from the Netherlands, that the projects would have to be transferred to the Indonesian authorities within slightly more than a month, and that Dutch experts and volunteers would have to leave within

---

19. Elseviers Magazine, 14 June 1986.
20. Violations of human rights and executions of political prisoners have been discussed in the Dutch parliament on several occasions (sometimes one gains the impression that just before the visit of the minister for development co-operation and IGGI Chairman a prisoner was executed). See, among others, Handelingen Tweede Kamer (Proceedings of the Second Chamber), Vergaderjaar (budget year) 1981–82, 17 100, Ch. V, No.90; Vergaderjaar 1983–84, 18 100, Ch. V, No.86; Vergaderjaar 1983–84, 18 100, Ch. V, No.111; year of session 1984–85, 18 600, Ch. V, No.126; Vergaderjaar 1985–86, 19 200, Ch. V, No.74; year of session 1986–87, 19 700, Ch. V, No.141; etc. In both 1990 and 1993 the ministers of foreign affairs were obliged to produce special reports on human rights in Indonesia.

several months.[21] Indonesian students in the Netherlands would either be recalled or would henceforth receive their money from the Indonesian government. Aid to private organisations would also be discontinued. What is more, the aid consortium for Indonesia (IGGI) which was chaired by the Netherlands, would be dissolved and replaced by a consultative group under the leadership of the World Bank.

Earlier on, President Suharto had announced that he had little appreciation of the use of aid withdrawal as a threat in relation to the issue of human rights. Nevertheless, the cancellation in March 1992 came as a complete surprise and a great shock to Dutch diplomatic circles – Dutch diplomacy had already had to cope with a number of severe setbacks in the period just before this. The policy on human rights was heavily criticised by the private sector and by a number of professors in Wageningen whose projects had been discontinued. Like India, Indonesia was a country with which the Netherlands experimented with the so-called 'broadening' of aid relations, fitting these increasingly into existing trade relations. In parliament, which had fanned the flames of the 'Dili debate' itself, Pronk was also strongly criticised by the christian democrats, although almost all the daily papers noted that this was done in order to save the face of Van den Broek, the minister responsible for human rights policy. The other parties almost unanimously demonstrated their support for Pronk's policy.

In summary, Dutch human rights policy towards developing and aid-receiving countries can be divided into three categories: one for the larger developing countries, particularly Indonesia, towards which a generally cautious approach was taken in the case of human rights violations; a generally stricter attitude towards small developing countries; and, finally, a particularly strict policy towards Surinam. One could not stop to imagine that Dutch business interests steered Dutch goverment's cautiousness in the case of larger developing countries.

Because democracies are usually not criticised for severe human rights violations, the ultimate consequence of every type of human rights policy will be that dictatorships will say 'be off with your aid', as President Sukarno did to the Americans, the government of Malaysia to the British, President Mobutu to the Belgians and the government of Kenya to the Norwegians. The irony is that the country

---

21. Articles on this episode are: Schulte Nordholt [*1995*]; Baehr [*1996*]. Both articles tone down the role of Minister Van den Broek in the affair, and leave out a comparison with the other 'boycotters', Canada and Denmark.

which received the softest treatment form the Netherlands in relation to human rights abuses – the 'former pearl in the crown' – was most sensitive to the criticisms.

Incoherences are in this respect not confined to human rights policy itself. Looking at the lists of major recipients of aid from the Netherlands, we see that Indonesia is by far the most important recipient in the 1970s and still holds the first position in the 1980s. In the top ten during those years we also discover Pakistan, the Sudan and Kenya, and, by the end of the 1980s, China.[22] Only in four cases did severe human rights violations cause a discontinuation of the aid relationship: Chile (1973), Uganda (1975), Cuba (1979) and Surinam (1982). On the other hand, criticism by the liberal/christian democrat coalition government at the end of the 1980s of the Sandinista regime in Nicaragua did not lead to major changes in aid disbursements.

IV. DEVELOPMENT POLICY AND THE ENVIRONMENT

That environmental problems have an important role to play in development policy has long been acknowledged in the Netherlands. Already at the beginning of the 1970s Dutch governments also accepted that to solve global environmental problems developing countries should be supported, also by financial means. Still, it took a long time before environmental policies with regard to developing countries and development policy took shape.[23] Apart from this internal incoherence within development policy itself, an inconsistency vis-à-vis Dutch environmental policies could also be detected.

Preventing and combating environmental disasters was the prime motivation for convening the Stockholm Conference (1972), which resulted in the Action Plan and Declaration of Stockholm. This conference and the meeting in Founex before it, the foundation of UNEP (1972), the Report of the Club of Rome (1972), and the UN Conference on Desertification (1977) each had some repercussions for Dutch development policy at first, but interest in ecological problems declined rapidly. A review of government memoranda reveals that the above events have not led to substantial attention being paid to such problems in policy-making or in the implementation of aid programmes. One could summarise Dutch policy up to the 1990s in the phrase 'little said, less done'.

---

22. See DAC/OECD [*several editions*]. Table 42/43 in recent years (in earlier editions these tables had other numbers) have given, since 1982, figures on major recipients of aid from individual DAC members.
23. This paragraph is partly based on Hoebink [*1991*].

POLICY COHERENCE IN DEVELOPMENT CO-OPERATION

Minister Pronk's memorandum, 'Improving the Quality of Dutch Aid' (1976), goes no further than to say that an 'ecological approach' must be introduced alongside the distributive aspect: the effects of projects on the natural environment should be considered [*Nota Bilaterale Ontwikkelingssamenwerking, 1976, nr. 3:5, 22*]. Although the question of distribution and the fight against poverty are elaborated in various parts of this memorandum, there is only this one reference to the ecological component. In 1978, the first recommendations from the National Advisory Council for Development Co-operation on ecology and development co-operation appeared [*NAR, 1978*]. This quite short 'advisory letter' was the result of an initiative by the Dutch branch of the International Union for the Conservation of Nature and Natural Resources (IUCN), the influence of which was clearly discernible. The Council, among others, pointed out that the Netherlands had signed a good number of international agreements on the environment, dating back to 1969, but had not ratified them. After 1978 there was a long period of silence, and it was not until 1990 that the National Advisory Council again made environmental considerations part of an 'advisory letter'.[24] The lack of influence of the 1978 recommendations, and the incompleteness of the 'ecological approach', became apparent in the year following the report's publication. In 1979, in a Memorandum on the Improvement of the Quality of Bilateral Aid, issued by Minister de Koning, improvement in aid quality was – as far as environmental aspects were concerned – concentrated on just one question in the assessment of projects, namely 'what is the effect on the ecology? Is it necessary to have a special preliminary inquiry?'[*Nota Verbetering van de kwaliteit van de bilaterale hulp, 1979, nr.3: 182*].

It was not until July 1982 that the minister for development co-operation reacted to the NAR report, although he had been called upon to do so by parliament in the autumn of 1981. The memorandum 'Ontwikkelingssamenwerking en Ecologie' (Development Co-operation and Ecology) [*1982*] gave a concise survey of ideas about the environment and development, and described the activities of UNEP, as well as Dutch policy and aid in this field. Dutch policy seemed to have made little progress. The memorandum contained little more than a few general statements, which for the most part concerned aid policy in a general sense. Around 20 projects were mentioned among the financed activities in the field of nature and environment

---

24. See 'Briefadvies Milieu en handel' (Advisory letter on environment and trade), Den Haag, 15 May 1990; and shortly thereafter 'Briefadvies Tropisch regenwoud' (Advisory letter on tropical rainforest wood), Den Haag, 15 May 1990.

protection and conservation, and these were mostly integrated rural development programmes and forestry projects.

The so-called 'Herijkingsnota' (Reverification Memorandum), the main policy document of Minister Schoo, dated 1984, combined energy and ecology in one short section of only half a page. Reference was again made to the policy recommendations of the CECOS (Committee on Ecology and Development Co-operation), which was supposed to come up with a more precise position. For the first time, environmental problems were mentioned (erosion, deforestation, soil deterioration), as were some causes (the cutting of timber, extension of cultivation, overgrazing). At the same time, the separate budgetary category for 'ecology and energy' was abolished.

In 1986, CECOS produced its long-awaited recommendations, which were transmitted to parliament by Minister Bukman in October, without much comment [*Commissie Ecologie en Ontwikkelingssamenwerking, 1986*]. The Committee identified three types of environmental problems which can adversely affect the essential functions of ecosystems in developing countries: exhaustion through over-use, pollution and disturbance through industrialisation and urbanisation, and damage and destruction through exploitation of resources. This resulted in a first recommendation, that the Netherlands, together with the recipient country, should develop an ecologically responsible policy for each country and region. Environmental profiles and basic environmental documentation (a kind of sectoral policy programme) should form the basis of such policy. An environmental section should be included in the policy programmes for all countries. With respect to personnel, environmental policy should be strengthened by the recruitment of more environmental experts, the establishment of a central point for environmental affairs within the ministry, and the provision of courses for officials. Finally, the number of environment-oriented projects should be increased, and support should also be given to non-governmental organisations working to promote responsible environmental policies.

Parliament was not satisfied with Minister Bukman's accompanying letter, and the minister had to provide a more detailed plan. The government's response was also rather short.[25] The minister declared that 'the integration of environmental considerations' into policies was 'an essential factor in the struggle to improve quality', and that

---

25. Regeringsstandpunt inzake Milieu en Ontwikkelingssamenwerking, Tweede Kamer, Vergaderjaar 1986–87, 19 767, No. 2, 13 May 1987 (Position of Government concerning Environment and Development Co-operation, Second Chamber, budget year 1986–87).

the policy on this 'would be continued and, where necessary, intensified'. Environmental profiles for regions in which aid was concentrated would be drawn up, and an attempt would be made to improve the level of knowledge of personnel. The minister did furnish further information a year later, in reply to questions from, and in discussion with, parliament. In a memorandum, Minister Bukman replied to the criticism of aid policies that had been expressed the year before [*Nota Kwaliteit, 1989*]. The ministry recruited its first ecologist in 1984: a lone ecologist, who also had to give half his time to the energy programme. In parliament, there were references to the 'half ecologist', and Minister Bukman spoke about the 'poor ecologist'.[26] Nevertheless, the minister was at first very unwilling to add to the personnel. Only in the memorandum, 'Kwaliteitsverbetering' (Improvement in Quality), did he announce the recruitment of environmental experts for the Sectoral Policy and Technical Advice Department (Directie Sectorbeleid en Technische Advisering). In 1989 a second ecologist was appointed. From 1985 onwards annual one-day courses on the environment were held, each for 20–30 ministry personnel.

In 1985, Minister Schoo had stated that funding in her budget for environmental management, in particular forestry, should be doubled: in five years there should be an increase to 100 million guilders. In his reaction to the CECOS recommendations, Minister Bukman stood by this intention. In 1989, the first National Environmental Policy Plan announced a further expansion of funding. An extra 50 million guilders a year would be made available for environmental projects and for the energy sector in developing countries. The overall figure was set to reach 250 million dollars in 1994, half of it to be devoted to combating the greenhouse effect in developing countries [*Jaarverslagen Ontwikkelingssamenwerking, 1988 and 1989*]. In 1982, Minister van Dijk could list only 22 projects with an environmental component, whereas in 1987 Minister Bukman could refer to 111 projects which 'alongside structural combating of poverty' had 'restoration, conservation or management of the natural environment, or the reduction of existing pollution, as a goal of major importance'.[27] These constituted five per cent of the total number of projects. The

---

26. Vaste Commissie voor Ontwikkelingssamenwerking/Vaste Commissie voor Milieubeheer, 68ste uitgebreide commissievergadering, Vergaderjaar 1987–88, 20 June 1988, pp. 28–29 (Permanent Commission for Development Co-operation/Permanent Commission for Environmental Protection, 68th extensive session, budget year 1987–88).
27. Ecologie en Ontwikkelingssamenwerking, Lijst van Antwoorden, Tweede Kamer, Vergaderjaar 1987–88, 19 767, No.4, 20 April 1988, p.1 (Ecology and Development Co-operation, List of answers, Second Chamber, budget year 1987–88).

majority of the projects were aimed at conservation, management and restoration. Four environmental profiles were completed in 1988, and another seven were being prepared.[28] Between 1985 and mid-1988, three reports on environmental effects were drawn up in relation to the building of a dam in Bangladesh, a wetland project in Indonesia and a canal construction project in Colombia.[29] Since the projects list in each of these years ran to more than 2,000 projects, it could be said that this form of reporting was not employed extensively.[30]

In September 1990, Minister Pronk published his 'A World of Difference'. For the first time there was now some evidence of an integrated development co-operation and environmental policy. One chapter outlines the growing risks to which humankind and the earth are exposed, but analyses of environmental problems are to be found in other chapters too, for example those dealing with regional problems. To combat poverty in a sustainable manner is the central goal of Dutch policy. According to the memorandum, sustainable development has three component parts: first, economic growth (development); second, a fair distribution of wealth (combating poverty); third, conservation of the eco-scope (ecological sustainability). Real sustainability, geared to the renewal of both natural and manufactured capital, is the overall aim.

This memorandum led to the announcement of a number of measures designed to overcome the negative ecological consequences of aid projects and programmes and to promote international co-operation in the field of environmental conservation. In the first of these categories are to be found: the development of environmental planning modalities in the environment area, such as environmentaleffect reports and environmental profiles, and the systematic checking of all

---

28. See also de Wit et al. [1990].
29. Ecologie en Ontwikkelingssamenwerking, Lijst van Antwoorden, Tweede Kamer, Vergaderjaar 1987–88, 19 767, No.4, 20 April 1988, p. 5 (Ecology and Development Co-operation, List of Answers, Second Chamber, budget year 1987–88).
30. The same picture of scant regard for environmental effects can be gained by reading the answers to written questions addressed to Minister Bukman by the Labour (PvdA) Member of Parliament, Verspaget, about the supply of fertilisers. A criticism of the extensive supply of fertilisers as part of Dutch aid, from the ecological point of view, is that artificial fertilisers can promote erosion and acidification, P. Hoebink [1988:134–9]. Two questions referred to these possibly harmful negative effects. In his answer, Minister Bukman said that the possible acidification effects of the use of artificial fertiliser were mentioned in evaluations whenever there was reason to do this. Two passages from evaluation reports were annexed as evidence: the effects were discussed in a positive sense in just a few lines. The minister did not deal with the promotion of erosion by artificial fertilisers [Tweede Kamer, Vergaderjaar 1988–89, Aanhangsel bij de Handelingen, pp. 1459–60] (Second Chamber, 1988–89, Appendix to the transcripts).

projects for their environmental effects. The second category consists of guidelines for the inclusion of environmental considerations in natural resource agreements, trade and investment regulations and structural adjustment programmes. A special spearhead programme for the environment was introduced (alongside those for women and development, research and urban poverty). A staff of 10 was attached to the programme office, to work on the global ecological problem, the development of policy at both national and international levels, the development of competence, etc. The spearhead programme received funding of 125 million guilders in 1991; a sum which increased to 275 million in 1994 – 25 million more than was promised by previous ministers.

The Netherlands was one of the countries that promised, at the UNCED in Rio de Janeiro in 1992, to spend an extra 0.1 per cent of GNP on environmental protection. However, the labour/liberal cabinet of Prime Minister Kok, formed in 1994, failed to follow up on this promise in the government programme for 1995–98. During the discussions on the reverification of Dutch foreign policy, the leader of the Labour parliamentary group also failed to include this in the agenda of the so-called homogenous group for international co-operation spending. This lack of action was not even taken seriously by Jan Pronk. Finally the 0.1 per cent figure for environmental co-operation with developing countries was included within the target of 0.8 per cent for development aid.

With the so-called 'Sustainable Development Treaties', Pronk tried to develop a new instrument to foster environmental co-operation. Treaties were made with Costa Rica, Benin and Bhutan. In 1995 they were ratified by parliament, after some heated debates. Reciprocity was built into the treaties, but met with hard parliamentary resistance. It was inconceivable to some senators that the Dutch environmental movement should invite ecologists from these countries to criticise the new development of Schiphol airport, and pay for the visit out of the development budget.[31] The effort to link other ministries to an ecological development policy and build in some policy coherence through these treaties has clearly failed.[32] So far the treaties seem to be more of a new travel circuit for the environmental movement than a new, sustainable and efficient development instrument.

It could be argued that, until 1990, Dutch development aid policy lacked an integrated vision of the relationship between the

---

31. As was planned by one of the major Dutch environmental groups, Milieudefensie. See records of the First Chamber, 21 May 1996.
32. *Trouw*, 14 March 1997.

environment and development, and the manner in which ecological and development problems should be reflected in the implementation of policy. There were some vague policy ideas and standpoints, and some first moves towards establishing environmental conservation goals in the execution of policy. However, the ministry was inadequately equipped, in terms of both personnel. and procedures, for environmental conservation and protection to have any real chance of being taken into account in policy implementation. With the second arrival in office of Minister Pronk, and after the publication of the memorandum 'A World of Difference', a major change took place in environmental and development policy, bringing to an end major incoherences in this area. The memorandum's analytical section on this topic was widely praised, and was seen as breaking the existing pattern.

Translating the analysis into policy, however, raises questions, not only because financial inputs did not match policy intentions and international promises. These questions relate not so much to the specific policy area of development co-operation, but to penetration into the internal policies of the Netherlands. A major incoherence still exists here, related to production systems and consumption patterns in the Netherlands. It is argued that the high-input agriculture of the Netherlands causes depletion of resources and makes a significant contribution to the greenhouse effect. Furthermore, the Netherlands uses agricultural land in developing countries (Brazil, Thailand) for fodder production for its intensive livestock sector – land that could be used for local food production in these countries. Calculations indicate that to meet his consumption needs, every Dutchman uses 1.5–3 times as much agricultural land worldwide than is at his disposal in the Netherlands itself.[33] CO_2 emissions caused by horticultural production in greenhouses will rise by 50 per cent by the year 2020. Along with energy consumption by industry and transport this amounts to an extra emission of greenhouse gases of between 40 and 80 per cent. European policy and international agreements should force the Netherlands to a reduction of 20 per cent [*RIVM, 1997*]. The present level of greenhouse-gas emissions together with the high consumption of other depletable resources and the limits this imposes on developing countries, growth could be said to make policy intentions on environmental issues, such as those expressed in 'A World of Difference', meaningless. In the discussion on the extension of

33. The ecological footprint of the Netherlands is in one case calculated at 4.7 ha/cap, while available ecological capacity is 2.8 ha/cap. FAO calculations come to three times the ha/cap. See, among others, de la Court [*1991*], Wackernagel [*1997*].

Schiphol airport, for example, it was argued that 'poor countries had to bleed for the sake of a less noisy airport'.[34]

V. DEVELOPMENT POLICY AND ARMS TRADE

Another issue with a long history, and the subject of fierce debate about incoherences between trade policies on one side and development and human rights policies on the other, is that of Dutch arms exports to developing countries. The Netherlands figured among the 20 largest exporters of arms in the 1970s and 1980s, climbed to a place in the top ten in the 1990s, and reached seventh place in the first half of the 1990s, with a total export of US$2 billion [*SIPRI, 1995*]. Over the years about 40 per cent went to non-NATO members. The exporting of arms to developing countries, in particular, has met with criticism both in and outside parliament.[35] However, arms production is only between 1.2 and 1.4 per cent of total industrial production in the Netherlands.

The first government report in which arms exports were touched upon was the White Paper on 'Disarmament and Security' of 1975 [*Nota Ontwapening en Veiligheid*]. It stated that considerations of peace policy would prevail above commercial interests in the selective arms export policy of the Netherlands. In particular, the exporting of arms to regions or countries in conflict would be rigorously scrutinised, and careful consideration of the kind of equipment requested would form part of the assessment. It has been said that these policy papers were codifying rather than prescriptive: they clarified existing policies, but did not formulate clear policy lines for the future [*Colijn and Rusman, 1984*]. Given its effect on the Dutch economy, arms exporting to authoritarian regimes is clearly open to discussion. A parliamentary resolution in 1983 was more strict, though, and prohibited arms exports to those countries that systematically and flagrantly violated human rights. Employment in endangered industries was officially seen as an important factor too. This was particularly important for the shipbuilding and aircraft industries.

After the end of the cold war the government felt it necessary to come up with a new White Paper that would replace the 1975 report. 'Arms exports policy' was presented to parliament in 1991. The political examination of arms exports would, according to this White

---

34. J. Kortland, 'Arme landen bloeden voor stil Schiphol', in *De Volkskrant*, 23 May 1997.
35. This paragraph is, apart from parliamentary records, based on Breuker *et al.* [*1971*]; Colijn and van der Mey [*1984*]; Everts [*1985*].

Paper, be based on the criteria of human rights and military tension, as well as on international embargoes. With regard to the military tension criterion it was stressed that the Dutch government would not necessarily refuse exports to countries that were victims of unprovoked aggression. The human rights criterion is explained as 'the danger of military goods being used for the repression of a country's own population' [*Nota Wapenexportbeleid, 1991*]. This was the way the criterion had been already interpreted since 1975. The government reported that it had not been possible to refine both the human rights and the military tension criteria, meaning that each case should still be examined in its own right.

In the parliamentary debate on the report the human rights criterion was, as in earlier discussions about arms deliveries, the centre of criticism. Several members of parliament wanted to put a stop to all exports to regimes that systematically violated human rights. Particularly the parties of the left asked the government to draw up a blacklist of countries that were excluded from arms exports, so as to avoid always having to explain the criteria, which might differ from one occasion to another. The other reason for these parties' request was that the government had indicated that a formal refusal of export licences was in practice never given. However, the government did not want to define the human rights criterion further, neither to draw up a blacklist of countries.[36]

Since the 1970s it has been agreed that the minister for development co-operation is asked for advice on all major arms deliveries to programme countries. In practice, this procedure has often not been followed. Jan Pronk cites the export of corvettes to Indonesia as an example (Interview, 24 March 1997). According to Mr Pronk this contract was reconfirmed in 1983 and 1989 at the start of new labour/ christian democrat governments. During the term of the last two cabinets the advice of the minister for development co-operation has not been asked for either, for example in the recent cases of the export of helicopters and armoured cars to Tchad and Egypt. In the case of the sale of old Leopard tanks to Botswana the negative advice of Mr Pronk was passed over.[37]

It was the arms deliveries to authoritarian regimes and human rights violators that gave rise to most discussion in the 1970s and

---

36. Tweede Kamer, zittingsjaar 1991–92, 68ste en 70ste vergadering, 31 March/2 April 1992 (Second Chamber, budget year 1991–92, 68th and 70th session).
37. Interview, 24 March 1997. Also: *De Volkskrant*, 7 Feb. 1997. The delivery was vetoed by Germany, the original producer of the tanks, but the Netherlands exported trucks and artillery to Botswana. It received protests from the government of Namibia.

1980s. Corvettes, frigates, helicopters and armoured cars to Indonesia (1976, 1979, 1981, 1985), submarines to Taiwan (1981), and starfighters to Turkey (1983) were among the most debated arms exports. The war in East Timor and in Irian Jaya made Indonesia, in the eyes of left-wing MPs, a country that should not receive any Dutch arms, according to the criteria set out in the aforementioned policy papers. The same was stated for the war in Kurdistan in the case of Turkey. In all cases the interests of Dutch wharfs and Fokker, often hit by recession, seem to have weighed heavier than criteria coming from humanitarian considerations.[38]

In December 1990, parliament agreed to a resolution in which the government was not only invited to discuss excessive military expenditure with aid-receiving countries, but also to take this into account in the distribution of Dutch foreign aid.[39] In the years that followed the Dutch government continuously stressed in letters to parliament or reports of DAC and World Bank meetings that it saw military expenditure as an integral part of the concept of 'good governance' and that it considered aid groups and aid consortia to be the right fora in which to discuss this issue.[40] In a long letter to parliament the minister for development co-operation also gave an extensive overview of the international discussions in the DAC, World Bank, UN and EU on this issue. Mr Pronk acknowledged that data on military expenditure were old and not very reliable, and also that some of the concepts (legitimate self-defence needs, reasonable sufficiency) were not well defined. He wrote that military expenditures were part of country memoranda and were discussed in the policy dialogue with all the main programme countries.[41]

VI. DEVELOPMENT POLICY AND TRADE: THE LEAST DEVELOPED COUNTRIES AND THE CASE OF COCOA

As stated above, from the 1960s onwards trade has been seen as one of the terrains in which a coherent development policy could be

---

38. One illustration is the parliamentary debate on 15 Feb. 1988 on Wilton Fijenoord, one of the wharfs building naval ships, but in economic trouble: Tweede Kamer, Vergaderjaar 1987–88, 20 444, No.1 (Second Chamber, budget year 1987–88).
39. Tweede Kamer, Vergaderjaar 1990–91, 21 813, No.20 (Second Chamber, budget year 1990–91).
40. See among others: Tweede Kamer, vergaderjaar 1991–92 (Second Chamber, budget year 1991–92), 22 300 V, No.96, 16 March 1992; idem, 22 300 XII, No. 52; idem, Vergaderjaar 1992–93 (budget year 1992–93), 22 800 V, No. 49; idem, 1993–94, 20 298, No. 16.
41. Tweede Kamer, Vergaderjaar 1991–92, 22 300 V, No.125, 24 June 1992 (Second Chamber, budget year 1991–92).

discerned. Members of conservative parties in parliament regularly used the 'trade not aid' slogans in pleas for a decrease in the aid budget. Through the years the connection between aid and trade has been used as a sort of bible text. Throughout the 1970s, the Netherlands supported developing countries' campaigns for an NIEO and for more just trading practices. It was also in favour, during the Paris North–South Conference (1976–79), of the creation of a Common Fund, which would enable developing countries to be compensated for losses following declines in raw material prices. Furthermore, it shared the opinion that IMF compensation funds should be extended.[42] And, finally, from the mid-1970s it had been prepared to give balance-of-payments support or programme aid to those countries suffering from rising oil prices and falling raw material prices. However, in its 'structural policy' the Netherlands was bound by EC actions and – as was the complaint already in the 1970s – decision-making was slow. One could also say that the Netherlands was not very active, apart from in some UNCTAD conferences in the 1970s, in coming up with new proposals or canvassing support for new initiatives. The negative effects of European internal policies or subsidies, particularly agricultural policy, seemed to have been out of sight all of the time. At least in none of the official documents on trade issues and trade with developing countries was any reference made to these forms of European protectionist policies.[43]

An example might be the critique of the development co-operation policies of the labour/christian democrat cabinet of Joop den Uyl in the 1970s. It is acknowledged by nearly all informed observers that for the first time a so-called 'integral development policy', including not only financial but also industrial, technological and trade relations, was fostered by the government. On the other hand the Netherlands was seen as one of the most protectionist European governments in the negotiations on the Multi Fibre Arrangement [*Bos,*

42. A clear example of this support is the white paper on development co-operation from a wider world economic perspective [*Nota Ontwikkelingssamenwerking in wereld-economisch perspectief, 1979*]. In an extensive letter to parliament, Minister De Koning compared his white paper with the Brandt report and the Action Programme for a New International Economic Order, concluding that there were few differences between the three (Brief aan de Tweede Kamer, Tweede Kamer, Vergaderjaar 1979–80, 15 800, Ch. V, No.117, 20 June 1980 / Letter to parliament, Second Chamber, budget year 1979–80).
43. An example might be that in the government paper on development co-operation and employment no reference at all is made to European (trade) policies or even Dutch policies to stimulate exports from developing countries. See *Nota Ontwikkelingssamenwerking en Werkgelegenheid* [*1984*] (White Paper, 'Development Co-operation and Employment'). It is one of the conclusions with which Jan Pronk also agreed in the interview for this article.

1977], as being locked into European points of view and gradually drifting towards the defensive attitude of rich countries [*Coppens, 1977*]. Pronk [*1977*] agreed to some of these points of criticism and conceded that such outcomes were related to power relations in the Netherlands at the time, but he denied that the development dimension had lost influence during this period.

In recent years we have seen some changes here. At the WTO conference in Singapore in December 1996, the secretary of state for international trade, Anneke van Dok, came up with an initiative to give the least developed countries preferred access to Western markets. During the preparatory negotiations, the European Union had taken a defensive attitude towards the Action Plan for the LLDCs; the Netherlands pushed for duty- and quota-free access for these countries. During the conference itself, the EU softened its position, mainly in reponse to the Dutch government's arguments. The Dutch agricultural sector sounded loud protests against the government's position, fearing the competition in this sector from LLDCs.[44]

A second example of the changed attitude relates to the case of cocoa.[45] The harmonisation of the European market in 1992 formally ended the situation of the UK, Denmark and Ireland having an exceptional position (being allowed to use vegetable fats and more milk in chocolate than the original EC member states). The chocolate producers have been lobbying for a long time for the adaptation of European rules towards UK directives. The Maastricht Treaty made harmonisation a top priority. The Netherlands is a major cocoa importer and cocoa butter producer, as well as a chocolate producer: Amsterdam is the largest cocoa harbour in the world; the Zaan region has the largest cocoa-manufacturing industries in Europe; and Mars has the largest European chocolate-producing industry in the southern part of the Netherlands. All the industries, as well as Dutch NGOs and even the cardiac diseases foundation, took part in lobbies for and against a harmonisation in the direction of the British regulations. This struggle was reflected in a bureaucratic fight between the ministries of economic and foreign affairs, in which the position of economic affairs was somewhat ambiguous. The Netherlands turned out to be a defender of the interests of cocoa-producing countries on this issue. The European Commission proposal of April 1996 leaves

---

44. Tweede Kamer, Vergaderjaar 1996–97, 25074, nos.1, 2, 3 and 4, 21 Oct. 1996, 29 Nov. 1996, 21 and 22 Jan. 1997 (Second Chamber, budget year 1996–97).
45. For this section the following texts were used: Elshof [*1994*], van Putten [*1996*], Bowen [*1997*]; see also Mr Pronk's statement on the issue in *IS Informatie*, No.11, 25 May 1994.

decisions on vegetable fats content to the member states; but this proposal has not yet been accepted by the member states. Since there is no consensus between the member states, it is expected that the case will be pending for some years.

VII. SOME CONCLUSIONS

Coherence of development policy has been discussed in official reports and parliamentary debates in the Netherlands from the mid-1960s onwards. In general, internal coherence in a type 1 (within development policy itself, and between motives/goals/instruments/types of aid) was less an issue here than internal coherence in a type 2 (between several parts of fóreign policy). On the question of external coherence (between development policy and internal policies) there has been no discussion at all, although in some fields (agriculture, migration, environment) serious incoherence existed and still exists. The main issue with regard to internal coherence in type 1 has been the role of the economic/commercial motive, specifically of tied aid. Incidentally, conflicting goals within development policy and between development policy and foreign policy have also been addressed. The discussion on external coherence has for a long time addressed only the dichotomy between foreign policy goals and instruments, focusing on conflicts between human rights and development policy, trade interests and developmental goals.

Looking back at some of the most frequently debated issues, we could conclude that in terms of policy coherence there have been very mixed results. The influence of different interest groups, the status of the minister for development co-operation in the cabinet, the importance of the issues raised, all make outcomes difficult to predict, when the demands of a consistent policy are taken into consideration. It is clear that in the 1970s and 1990s, under ministers like Pronk and De Koning, coherence was more at the centre of the debate than in the 1960s and 1980s. However, in important dossiers (concerning, for example, human rights in 'important' countries, or arms exports) these two ministers, too, seem to have had greater difficulty in reaching some coherence than when they addressed policy issues of 'minor relevance' (such as human rights in small countries and tied aid).

Public interest had a limited role to play here. It is impossible to remember the government of certain legal texts in relation to policy coherence. Loss of development policy coherence can sometimes be a gain in employment, meaning that support might go either way. But if issues are raised in so-called 'smart coalitions', as in the cocoa case, it may be possible to change the balance in favour of developing countries' interests. It is interesting to note that these successes were not achieved with the help of much public debate or media attention, but were more a clever 'lobby affair' in the back rooms of political debate.

REFERENCES

Baehr, P., 1996, 'Mensenrechten en ontwikkelingshulp: Nederland en Indonesië' (Human Rights and Development Aid: The Netherlands and Indonesia), in P. Everts, *Dilemma's in de Buitenlandse politiek van Nederland*, Leiden: DSWO Press.

Baneke, P., 1983, *Nederland en de Indonesische gevangenen: Een studie naar de effectiviteit van de Nederlandse bemoeienis met mensenrechten* (The Netherlands and the Indonesian Prisoners: A Study on the Effectiveness of the Dutch Involvement in Human Rights), Amsterdam: Wiardi Beckman Stichting.

Bos, H.C., 1977, 'Balans van een beleid' (Balance Scale of a Policy), *Internationale Spectator*, Vol.31, No.9, Sept.

Bowen, B., 1997, 'A clone is being proposed': It would be false chocolate, Brussels: European Fair Trade Association.

Breuker, J., G. Koolstra and L. Reijnders, 1971, *Het militair-industrieel kompleks in Nederland* (The military-industrial complex in the Netherlands), Nijmegen: SUN.

Colijn, K. and L. van der Mey (eds.), 1984, *De Nederlandse wapenexport: beleid en praktijk – Indonesië, Iran, Taiwan* (The Dutch Arms Exports: Policy and Practice – Indonesia, Iran, Taiwan), Den Haag: Clingendael.

Colijn, K. and P. Rusman, 1984, 'Het Nederlandse wapenexportvergunningenbeleid' (The Dutch Policy on Licences for Arms Exports), in Colijn and van der Mey.

Commissie Ecologie en Ontwikkelingssamenwerking, 1986, *Advies Milieu en ontwikkelingssamenwerking*, Amsterdam: Koninklijk Instituut voor de Tropen (Commission on Ecology and Development Co-operation, 1986, Advisory Letter on the Environment and Development Co-operation).

Coppens, H., 1977, 'Pronk is/was nog maar halverwege' (Pronk is/was Only Halfway), *Internationale Spectator*, Vol.31, No.9, Sept.

Court, T. de la, 1991, *Verschillende werelden: Ontwikkelingssamenwerking in de jaren '90* (Different Worlds: Development Co-operation in the 1990s), 's Hertogenbosch: Bijeen-Boek.

DAC/OECD, 1992, *Development Co-operation: Efforts and Policies of the Members of the Development Assistance Committee*, Paris: OECD.

DAC/OECD, *Development Co-operation: Efforts and Policies of the Members of the Development Assistance Committee* (several editions), Paris: OECD.

Dalmeijer, M., 1987, *Ervaringen van Nederlandse bedrijven in ontwikkelingslanden* (Experiences of Dutch Companies in Developing Countries), Den Haag: COB/ SER.

Dalmeijer, M., 1995, *Geld en nog veel meer: 25 jaar beleid en praktijk van investeren in ontwikkeling* (Money and Much More: 25 Years of Policy and Practice of Investing in Development), Den Haag: SDU.

Elshof, P., 1994, *Cocoa Butter and Alternatives: The Substitution Debate*, Den Haag: Nederlandse ontwikkelingsorganisatie SNV, April.

Everts, Ph., 1985, *Controversies at Home: Domestic Factors in the Foreign Policy of the Netherlands*, Den Haag: Martinus Nijhoff.

Herfkens, E. and N. van der Lans, 1986, *Ontwikkelingshulp en de rol van het Nederlandse bedrijfsleven – Solidariteit in ontbinding?* (Development Co-operation and the Role of the Dutch Business Community – Solidarity in Dissolution?), Amsterdam: Evert Vermeer Stichting.

Hoebink, P., 1982, 'Suriname en de twee Nederlands maten' (Surinam and the Two Dutch Measures), *Derde Wereld*, Vol.1, No.2, Nijmegen: Stichting Derde Wereld Publikaties.

Hoebink, P., 1987, 'Nederland en de schuldenkrisis' (The Netherlands and the Debt Crisis), *Derde Wereld*, Vol.6, No.2, Nijmegen: Stichting Derde Wereld Publikaties.

Hoebink, P., 1988, 'Geven is nemen: de Nederlandse ontwikkelingshulp aan Tanzania en Sri Lanka' (To Give is to Take: The Dutch Development Aid to Tanzania and Sri Lanka), Ph.D.thesis, Catholic University Nijmegen, Nijmegen: Stichting Derde Wereld Publikaties.

Hoebink, P., 1991, 'Dutch Development Cooperation and the Environment: Little Said, Less Done', *Internationale Spectator*, thematic issue: *Environment and Development – the Road to Rio Janeiro*, Vol.45, No.11, Den Haag: Nederlands Instituut voor Internationale Betrekkingen Clingendael.

Hoebink, P., 1994, 'Of Merchants and Ministers: A Short History of the Foreign Aid Programme of the Netherlands', in F. Schuurman (ed.), *Current Issues in Development Studies: Global Aspects of Agency and Structure*, Saarbrücken: Breitenbach Verlag GmbH.

Hoebink, P., forthcoming, 'From Export Promotion to Supporting Developmental and Humanitarian Needs: The Humanitarization of the Foreign Aid Programme of the Netherlands', *The European Journal of Development Research*.

Hoebink, P. and L. Schulpen, 1990, *Adviesburo's en Ontwikkelingssamenwerking: verslag van een enquête* (Consultancy Bureaus and Development Co-operation: A Report of a Survey), Nijmegen: Derde Wereld Centrum, Occasional Paper 20.

IOV (Inspectie Ontwikkelingssamenwerking te Velde), 1990, *Hulp of handel? Een evaluatie-onderzoek van het programma Ontwikkelingsrelevante Exporttransacties*, Den Haag: Ministerie van Buitenlandse Zaken (Inspectorate Development Co-operation, Aid or Trade? An Evaluation of the Programme for Developmentally Relevant Export Transactions).

Jaarverslagen Ontwikkelingssamenwerking (Annual Reports, Development Co-operation), Den Haag: Voorlichtingsdienst Ontwikkelingssamenwerking, 1988 and 1989.

Kox, H. and L. van Velzen, 1985, *Kapitaalexport vanuit Nederland* (Capital Exports from the Netherlands), Amsterdam: SOMO.

Kuitenbrouwer, M., 1996, 'Nederland en de mensenrechten' (The Netherlands and Human Rights), in M. Kuitenbrouwer and M. Leenders (eds.), *Geschiedenis van de mensenrechten: bouwstenen voor een interdisciplinaire benadering*, Hilversum: Verloren.

Malcontent, P., 1996, 'Nederland en de mensenrechten in de Derde Wereld 1973– 1981' (The Netherlands and Human Rights in the Third World 1973–1981), in M. Kuitenbrouwer and M. Leenders (eds.), *Geschiedenis van de mensenrechten: bouwstenen voor een interdiscipliniare benadering*, Hilversum: Verloren.

Ministerie van Buitenlandse Zaken, 1997, *Derde Voortgangsnotitie over de rechten van de mens in het buitenlands beleid*, Den Haag: Ministerie van Buitenlandse Zaken (Ministry of Foreign Affairs, Third Progress Memorandum on Human Rights and Foreign Policy).

NAR (Nationale Advies Raad voor Ontwikkelingssamenwerking), 1978, *Advies Ecologie en Ontwikkelingssamenwerking*, Adviesnr. 57, Den Haag: Staatsuitgeverij (National Advisory Council for Development Co-operation, Advisory letter on Ecology and Development Co-operation).

Netherlands Economic Institute, 1990, *Evaluatie Herstructureringsprogramma* (Evaluation of the Restructuring Programme), Rotterdam: NEI.

Nieuwkerk, M. van and R. Sparling, 1985, *De internationale investeringspositie van Nederland* (The Position of the Netherlands in International Investments), Deventer: Kluwer/De Nederlandsche Bank.

Nota Bilaterale Ontwikkelingssamenwerking – Om de kwaliteit van de Nederlandse Hulp, 1976, Begroting 1977, Tweede Kamer, 14 300, hfst.V, Buitenlandse Zaken, bijlage 4, Sept. (the White Paper 'Bilateral Development Co-operation – Improving the Quality of Dutch Aid', 1976, Budget 1977, Second Chamber, 14300, Ch. V, Foreign Affairs, annex 4, Sept.).

Nota De rechten van de mens in het buitenlands beleid, 1979, Handelingen Tweede Kamer, vergaderjaar 1978–79, 15 571, No.1–2, May 1979 (the White Paper 'Human Rights in Foreign Policy', 1979, Proceedings of the Second Chamber, budget year 1978–79).

Nota Een wereld in geschil: De grenzen van de ontwikkelingssamenwerking verkend, 1993, Tweede Kamer, vergaderjaar 1993–94, 23 408, nr. 1–2, Sept. 1993 (the White Paper 'A World in Dispute').

Nota Een wereld van verschil – Nieuwe kaders voor ontwikkelingssamenwerking in de jaren negentig, 1990, Tweede Kamer, vergaderjaar 1990–91, 21 813, nr. 1–2, Sept. 1990 (The White Paper 'A World of Difference', 1990).

Nota Herijking bilateraal beleid, Tweede Kamer, 18 350, vergaderjaar 1983–84, 1 mei 1984 (Memorandum on the Reverification of Bilateral Aid Policy, 1 May 1984, Proceedings of the Second Chamber, budget year 1983–84).

Nota hulpverlening aan minder ontwikkelde landen, 1966, Den Haag, Ministerie van Buitenlandse Zaken, 1966 (the White Paper on 'Aid to Less Developed Countries'), Tweede Kamer (Second Chamber), 8800, Ch. V, No.3, July 1966.

Nota Inzake de verbetering van de kwaliteit van de bilaterale hulp, 1979, Rijksbegroting 1980, hfdst V, Buitenlandse Zaken nr. 3, bijlage 2a, Sept., p.182 (the White Paper 'On the Improvement in Quality of the Bilateral Aid', 1979, national budget 1980, Ch. V, Foreign Affairs, No. 3, annex 2a, Sept.).

Nota Kwaliteit: een voorzet voor de jaren '90 (the White Paper 'A First Move for the 1990s'), Den Haag: Directoraat Generaal Internationale Samenwerking, July 1989, p.22 (34).

Nota Ontwapening en Veiligheid, Tweede Kamer, vergaderjaar 1974–75, 13 461, nr. 1–2 (White Paper on 'Disarmament and Security', Second Chamber, budget year 1974–75).

Nota Ontwikkelingssamenwerking en Werkgelegenheid, Tweede Kamer, vergaderjaar 1983–84, 18 503, No. 1–2, Aug. 1984 (White Paper on 'Development Co-operation and Employment').

Nota Ontwikkelingssamenwerking in wereldeconomisch perspectief (White Paper on 'Development Co-operation in a World Economic Perspective'), Begroting 1980, Tweede Kamer, 15 800, Ch. V, Buitenlandse Zaken (Foreign Affairs), bijlage 1, Sept. 1979.

Nota Wapenexportbeleid, Tweede Kamer, vergaderjaar 1990–91, 22 054, nr. 1–2, 28 maart 1991 (the White Paper 'Policy for Arms Exports').

Notitie Ontwikkelingssamenwerking en ecologie, 1982, Tweede Kamer, zitting 1981– 1982, 17 502, 15 July 1982 (Memorandum on Development Co-operation and Ecology).

Plas, M. van der and J. Luns, 1971, *Luns: 'Ik herinner mij ...'* (Luns: 'I remember ...'), Leiden: Sijthoff.

Pronk, J., 1977, 'Naschrift' (Epilogue), *Internationale Spectator*, Vol.31, No.9, Sept.

Pronk, J., 1989, 'De linker- en de rechterhand in de Nederlandse ontwikkelingshulp' (The left and the right hand in Dutch development aid), *Derde Wereld*, Vol.8, No. 3, Nijmegen: Stichting Derde Wereld Publikaties.

Putten, M. van der, 1996, *Chocolade, wie bijt?* (Chocolate, Who Bites?), Amsterdam: Evert Vermeer Stichting, Oct.

RIVM (Rijksinstituut voor Volksgezondheid en Milieu), 1997, *Nationale Milieuverkenning 4 1997–2000*, Alphen aan den Rijn: Samsom/Tjeenk Willink (National

Institute for Public Health and Environment, National Exploration Environmental Issues 4 1997–2000).
Schulte Nordholt, N., 1995, 'Aid and Conditionality: The Case of Dutch–Indonesian Relationships', in O. Stokke (ed.), *Aid and Political Conditionality*, London: Frank Cass.
SIPRI, 1995, *SIPRI Yearbook 1995*, Oxford: Oxford University Press.
Stichting Onderzoek Multinationale Ondernemingen, 1981, *Wie helpt wie? Ontwikkelingshulp aan het Nederlandse bedrijfsleven*, Odijk, Sjaloom (Foundation for research on multinational corporations, 1981, Who is Helping Who? Development Aid to the Dutch Business Community).
The Foreign Policy of the Netherlands: A Review, The Hague: Ministry of Foreign Affairs, Sept. 1995, White Paper.
Udink, B.J., 1986, *Tekst en Uitleg. Over sturen en gestuurd worden, ervaringen in politiek en bedrijf* (Text and Explanation. About Steering and Being Steered, Experiences in Politics and Business), Baarn: Anthos.
Verloren van Themaat, J.P., 1981, 'Ontwikkelingssamenwerking en de rechten van de mens' (Development Co-operation and Human Rights), in Ph. Everts and J. Heldring, *Nederland en de rechten van de mens*, Baarn: Anthos.
Visser, C.J., 1983, 'Nederland en het opkomen voor mensenrechten' (The Netherlands and Standing Up for Human Rights), in S. Rozemond, (ed.), *Het woord is aan Nederland – Thema's van buitenlands beleid in de jaren 1966–1983*, Den Haag: SDU.
Wackernagel, M. *et al.*, 1997, *Ecological footprints of Nations*, San José: Earth Council/Centre for Sustainability Studies.
Werf, S. van der, 1985, 'Opschorting van Nederlandse hulp aan Suriname: hoe lang nog?' (Suspension of Dutch Aid to Surinam: How Much Longer?), *Derde Wereld*, Vol.4, No.1, Nijmegen: Stichting Derde Wereld Publikaties.
Wit, E. de, M. Marchand and G. A. Persoon, 1990, 'Milieuplanning in ontwikkelingslanden' (Environmental Planning in Developing Countries), *Milieu – tijdschrift voor milieukunde*, Vol.5, No.4, Meppel: Boom.

7

Development Co-operation and Policy Coherence: The Case of Norway

OLAV STOKKE

I. INTRODUCTION

In the 1990s, a widely shared conviction emerged among donors that their policies should become more coherent than in the past. In 1991, the Development Assistance Committee (DAC) of the Organisation for Economic Co-operation and Development (OECD) expressed the need for coherence and outlined some basic elements of a coherent policy [*OECD, 1992: 31ff*].[1] In Norway's stated policy towards the South, including aid policy, coherence has emerged as a key concern.[2]

A preliminary draft of this chapter was presented at an international workshop organised, under the auspices of the EADI Working Group on Aid Policy and Performance, by IUED and NUPI in Geneva in April 1997. I am grateful to participants, in particular Mr Dag Nissen, Assistant Director-General, MFA, for comments. I am also grateful to several senior administrators for their time and insights shared with me in a series of interviews (*infra*, note 8). I am particularly indebted to Professor Jacques Forster, Mr Helge Kjekshus, Special Adviser with the MFA, and Professor Cranford Pratt for constructive comments on later drafts. The usual disclaimers apply!
1.   For a definition of coherence, see Chapter 1 (this volume). Basically, objectives and instruments within a policy area should be consistent with each other or, as a minimum, not be inconsistent, and the outcome should not conflict with the intentions. This also applies to a donor's and donors' various policies towards developing countries. The common ground is further elaborated in a strategy report adopted in 1996 [*OECD, 1996b*].
2.   In the mid-1980s, successive governments produced white papers on development co-operation [*Report No. 36, 1984; Report No. 34, 1987*]. In 1987, Parliament set the policy on this basis but found the broader North–South policy neglected in these white papers [*Recommendation No. 186*]. It took the government almost five years to respond [*Report No. 51*]; in the meantime, there had been demands, particularly from the Conservatives, for a major review by an independent commission of experts. In 1993, the government appointed a Commission on North–South and Aid Policies (hereafter referred to as the Commission) which delivered its report two years later [*NOU, 1995: 5*]. The government followed up with another white paper later that year [*Report No. 19*], provoking an intense debate, and even leading to one of the opposition parties producing a counter-report [*Christian Democrats, 1996*]. In mid-1996, Parliament set the policy after an extensive process which included hearings of experts [*Recommendation No. 229*].

Coherence is identified as a virtue and as an effective instrument to attain the overall aims set for aid.[3]

The new international environment of the 1990s made policy-making more complex than before. New concerns related to the South came to the fore; within a humane internationalism tradition, poverty alleviation and development remained a major concern but other concerns, such as human rights, democracy and the environment, attracted more attention. Old conflicts, contained in the old order, flared up and became more visible; they caused human suffering and the disintegration of societies, even of states. Old problems, such as migration and drug trade, became burning issues more than ever.

Responses to many of these 'new' challenges have been handled by the aid administration, but they impinge closely on ministries of foreign affairs and pose more complex issues of policy co-ordination than 'traditional' activities financed from the aid budget. Many of the 'new' concerns that require international action are non-developmental issues and are handled by other institutions; however, there is growing pressure to use ODA finances even for these purposes.

Political processes are characterised by competition between stakeholders representing different interests and values. Not all actors carry the same political weight; nor do they have equal access to decision-makers at various levels. The arena for decision-making may differ from one policy area to another. And an organisation may exert an influence of its own on policy outcomes beyond that of its separate members [Cohen et al., 1972]. However, in contrast to the scenario of competing interests, the debate on policy coherence tends to conceive of decision-making within a public administration framework. In this study, the two perspectives will be combined in an attempt to explore how the emphasis given to coherence has affected Norwegian foreign policy in general, and aid policy in particular.

Achieving coherence within the complex setting of an open political system is no easy matter. Although the political and administrative leadership at the centre aspires towards coherence in most systems, policies tend to become incoherent for a variety of reasons. Interests and values vary, resulting in conflicting objectives, which are also pursued in different political and administrative arenas. Some arenas are specialised, giving stakeholders operating within them considerable influence over decisions. Other arenas cover broad fields,

---

3. In this chapter, the terms official development assistance (ODA), foreign aid, development assistance and development co-operation are used as more or less synonymous, although there is a time sequence in their coinage which may reflect different connotations. Most often, the short term (aid) will be used.

involving stakeholders with a wide variety of values and interests and therefore resulting in tougher competition. However, both national and international politics is to a large extent compartmentalised, reinforced by a compartmentalisation of administrative structures.

Tension exists between the centre's aspirations towards policy coherence and centrifugal forces, particularly at lower levels of the political and administrative system. Increased policy coherence may strengthen some values and interests and weaken others. Thus different stakeholders are affected differently which, in turn, influences their attitude towards the norm of policy coherence as well as their preference of arena for policy decisions – the narrow or the broader one. Although often expressed in neutral, technical terms, demands for increased policy coherence do not operate in a political vacuum.

Attainment of policy coherence may be influenced by systemic factors such as, in particular, a coherent norm system (do the various policy objectives, guidelines and mechanisms coincide or are different, even conflicting, objectives and norm systems at work?), procedures for the implementation of these norms, including negotiation, mediation and conflict resolution, and institutions responsible for policy decision-making, monitoring and enforcement of the norms set.

In this context, a distinction may be drawn between frameworks which involve national politics and those involving regional, multilateral and international relations.[4] The main focus here will be on national frameworks, that is, the internal coherence of Norway's aid policy, and the coherence of its various policies towards the South. The broader frameworks – coherence of these policies, aid in particular, *vis-à-vis* the policies of other donors and *vis-à-vis* the recipients' policies – will not be dealt with in depth; however, the declared policy will be briefly described and discussed.

Policy coherence will be analysed within this setting of conflicting concerns and priorities. Focus will also be directed towards regime factors; to what extent are mechanisms identified above established and at work? An overriding question will be how the demand for increased policy coherence has affected the aid policy, if at all. The questions posed are:

(1) What are the main features of the *declared* coherence policy? The emphasis will be on the stated policy evolving in the 1990s;

---

4. For definitions and discussions of an international regime see, *inter alia*, Krasner [*1982*], Young [*1991*], and Keohane [*1993*].

(2) How has the stated policy been *followed up*, if at all? The emphasis will be on changes in the institutional framework, in the stated policy (objectives) and in the implementation of aid, particularly changes which indicate new priorities (changes in the distribution of attention and resources); and

(3) Who have been the main *determinants*? What norms, interests and stakeholders have been best served by the demand for increased coherence of the policies towards the South, in particular the aid policy?

In section II, prescriptions with regard to policy coherence will be identified, based on the key policy documents of the 1990s. In section III, the follow-up will be described from a process perspective: to what extent have mechanisms established to ensure policy coherence been strengthened and new ones created? In section IV, the effects of the policy prescription on policies towards the South will be explored, with particular reference to aid policy. The declared and implemented policy will be scrutinised for its elements both of continuity and of change. In section V, an attempt will be made to identify which stakeholders have benefited from the demand for increased policy coherence and which have been the losers.

II. POLICY COHERENCE: THE STATED POLICY

Policy coherence has been defined as a negation, '[t]he non-occurrence of effects of policy that are contrary to the intended result or aims of policy' (Hoebink, this volume, Ch.10). From a process perspective, coherence may also be conceived of in positive terms, based on a prescription that the various policies should be cohesive and mutually supportive of each other.

Distinctions are made between (1) the internal coherence of aid policy, the core area of this study, (2) the coherence of national policy towards the South generally, which in addition to aid also includes any policies affecting the South or North–South relations, directly or indirectly, (3) the coherence of donors' policies affecting the South or North–South relations, and (4) coherence between the policies of donor and recipient. What may appear as a coherent policy within one of these frameworks may be incoherent from the perspective of another. The perspective chosen is therefore significant.

What are the policy prescriptions that emerge from the main policy documents of the 1990s?

215

(1) The Internal Coherence of Norway's Aid Policy

The 1992 White Paper repeats what has been stated before, namely that the overall objectives set for development co-operation should govern all aid, whether provided directly (state-to-state) or channelled through multilateral aid agencies, international organisations, the private sector or non-governmental organisations (NGOs). It admits, however, that the various objectives will not always coincide and that in the implementation of policy it may be necessary to prioritise between different objectives and concerns [*Report No.51: 177*].[5] The 1995 White Paper states that all aid should be part of a coherent strategy [*Report No.19: 6*].

(2) A Coherent National Policy Towards the South

The 1992 White Paper is also clear about policy at the national level, stating as the government's objective: 'a coherent [helhetlig] Norwegian North–South policy, where our efforts within the various North–South areas (macroeconomic relations, debts, trade, primary commodities, resource issues and global environmental problems) and our development co-operation are co-ordinated as well as possible' [*Report No.51: 56*]. In 1995, the government emphasised that Norwegian policy *vis-à-vis* developing countries should adapt to the challenges and opportunities facing these and the international community generally [*Report No.19: 5*]. And Parliament agreed: Norwegian aid policy should be considered in a broader North–South political context, particularly related to international relations affecting the economy, debt and trade. However, it argued that increased coherence between the various components of the policy towards the South should affect not only aid, but foreign policy and trade policy as well [*Recommendation No.229: 7–8*].

The practice, which I will return to, may look different, however. A broader approach means there will be more stakeholders and, from the perspective of aid policy objectives, less chance for internal aid policy coherence. However, the overall objectives for policy towards the South established by Parliament in 1996 were much in line with the overall objectives established for aid policy.

---

5. The policy 'should guide Norwegian attitudes towards development issues that are debated in bilateral and multilateral fora, the allocative practice to be followed as regards disbursement of aid, and the implementation of aid-financed activities in our programme countries and other recipient countries. The policy we seek to promote in international fora is to be reflected in our bilateral development co-operation in the same way as bilateral efforts are to supplement what the multilateral organisations do' [*Report No.51: 177*]. Please note that direct quotations from official Norwegian documents, with the exception of Report No.19, 1995, are translated by the author and are not official versions.

(3) Coherence of Donors' Policies

Co-ordination of aid among donors has been on the international agenda almost as long as aid itself. The main rationale has been to improve aid effectiveness by avoiding duplication and waste. Competing vested interests among donors have made co-ordination of aid difficult to attain on the part of both bilateral and multilateral donors.

Norway's attitude to international co-ordination of aid has been ambivalent for slightly different reasons [Stokke, 1995b: 184]. Until the mid-1980s, its attitude may at best be described as lukewarm, mainly because it was assumed that the common ground would be established by the major Western donors, and it was felt that this would differ from the objectives and priorities set for Norwegian aid. In addition, the guideline prescribing recipient orientation of aid was held in high esteem, at least in the rhetoric; co-ordination of aid by donors was perceived as a 'ganging up' against weak recipient governments.

In the mid-1980s, however, a change took place in relation to first-generation conditionality; in the case of Tanzania, the Nordic governments associated themselves with the policy of the Bretton Woods institutions. In terms of policy content, the objectives of second-generation conditionality – promotion of good governance, democracy, human rights – were conducive to a more favourable attitude towards increased co-ordination of donors' aid and aid policies.

However, a certain ambivalence remained, not least because donor co-ordination was felt to increase the asymmetrical power relationship between the two parties. The guideline which prescribed that aid should be recipient-oriented, that is, adapted to the objectives and priorities of the recipient governments and integrated in their development plans, underpinned this uneasiness; aid should be steered by the recipient government, not by the donor(s). The most pressing need, therefore, was the co-ordination of aid on the recipient side by the recipient government itself. How did the major policy papers of the 1990s deal with this ambivalence?

According to the government's 1992 White Paper, Norway should make every effort to influence the policies and practices of multilateral institutions towards Norwegian positions on development co-operation. However, '[a]t the same time it is important that Norwegian bilateral aid supports what has been agreed upon in international fora as priority areas for the 1990s' [Report No.51: 56]. The reference was explicitly to the controversial issue of the structural adjustment programmes of the IMF and the IBRD.

217

At the level of declared overall policy, this statement seems to settle the ambivalence. The rhetoric presents a situation that implies mutuality; it would, however, be quite optimistic to expect a small donor to be able to sway the mainstream policy of multilateral agencies. The pledge to bring Norwegian policy into line with that of multilateral institutions, particularly the Bretton Woods institutions, is confirmed in the government's presentation of its recent policy in this area.[6]

A similar attitude is stated with reference to related policy areas: North–South policy positions that are promoted internationally should be consistent with those held at the national level. Special reference is made to trade policy *vis-à-vis* developing countries; internationally co-ordinated arrangements (for instance, within the GATT) are considered more effective than national arrangements undertaken unilaterally [*Report No.51: 56*]. The international arena is considered to be paramount; it follows that contributions to the international decision-making process are held to be the best means of tackling issues related to improving framework conditions for developing countries.

Although this may be a realistic position, the approach may be questioned: a forceful stand in bilateral relations when the practical opportunities are much better might be a good alternative or, at least, a complementary approach, particularly with regard to aid. Within an international (trade) negotiation regime, generosity towards third parties is limited; parties tend to protect and promote their own immediate and long-term interests, even when committed to more lofty objectives within a humane internationalist framework.[7]

The Commission provides guidance towards a stronger humane internationalism commitment. It made a strong plea for a more integrated policy towards the South and found its various elements to be interlinked. It argued for more committed international co-operation in decision-making by supranational bodies, particularly on global environmental issues. It was appropriate that the South be given greater influence in the decision-making processes of such bodies. The political leadership of the MFA should renew its efforts to build

---

6. The government claims [*Report No.19: 186–7*] that Norway has actively participated in forming a new international development agenda for the 1990s, in accordance with the Norwegian policy on development and aid and changed conditions in the developing countries, and that there has been, since the beginning of the 1990s, considerable coherence between Norwegian policy and the international demands set for aid.

7. See several contributions to 'The Western Middle Powers and Global Poverty Project' [*Pratt (ed.), 1989; Stokke (ed.), 1989; Helleiner (ed.), 1990; and Pratt (ed.), 1990*], in particular the contributions by Gerald K. Helleiner [*1990*] and, analysing the Norwegian case, Helge Hveem [*1989*].

bridges across the North–South divide, the Commission argued, indicating that initiatives should be taken to develop a 'like-minded' attitude on a broad spectrum of policy issues affecting the South and advocating the use of 'meeting places' rather than formal institutions [*NOU, 1995: 5: 33–4,124*]. It was a modest plea in the right direction.

The DAC's strategy document from 1996 [*OECD, 1996b*] represents an important statement of donor co-ordination and coherence. It has been conspicuously absent from the Norwegian debate. Is this an indication of continued ambivalence?

(4) Coherence between Donor and Recipient Policies

A different kind of ambivalence characterises Norwegian aid policy in this area. The dilemma is illustrated, at the level of stated policy, by the inherent contradiction between overall objectives set for aid (poverty alleviation, with particular reference to exposed groups such as minorities, women, etc.) and the guideline set for bilateral development co-operation prescribing that aid should be recipient-oriented, that is, adapted to the priorities and development plans of the recipient government. In 1984, the government modified the guideline; equal weight was to be given to the overall objectives set and the guideline; outside the country programmes, overall objectives might be pursued even when not given priority by the recipient government – with reference, *inter alia*, to programmes for women in development, minorities and human rights. Norwegian aid was not to be automatically allocated in accordance with preferences and plans on the recipient side [*Stokke, 1989: 200–205*]. How did the major policy documents of the 1990s affect this dilemma?

The dilemma is discussed elsewhere [*Stokke, 1989; 1995b*]. Norms – formalised as guidelines – carry weight, but vested interests often exert an even greater influence on policy implementation. The strong position of the guideline derives not only from the power of norms but also from the institutional setting established for bilateral development co-operation. Aid is concentrated on a few selected regions and programme countries with which long-term development co-operation is established through rolling, multi-year country programmes and an annual policy dialogue and negotiations. Although the system provides the donor with ample room to pursue vested interests, it also gives the recipient an opportunity to take the initiative in shaping the programme within the agreed financial frame, and the legitimacy to do so, too, strengthened by the established guideline set for Norwegian aid.

The ambivalence continued into the 1990s. NORAD initiated a policy change by combining the guideline prescribing recipient orientation with a new one prescribing recipient responsibility: the ultimate responsibility for initiating an activity financed by aid and for planning and implementing it should rest with the recipient. The implication was that if the activity did not live up to expectations, the allocation of future aid would be affected: more effective or efficient systems would be preferred [NORAD, 1990; Stokke, 1991a].

In 1992, the government followed up on the twin principle. The emphasis, however, was clear:

> our development co-operation should increasingly be based on the recognition that aid primarily is useful in a setting where it is used effectively by the recipient as a supplement to domestic resources. Norway will therefore support continued change in the national policy of developing countries in order to establish conditions for economic growth, sustainable development, social distribution and improvement of the living conditions of particularly vulnerable groups [Report No.51: 56].

This position was restated by the government-appointed Commission which took a negative view of aid agencies which bypass the state by building up alternative administrative structures and argued that the capacity of public authorities to implement a development-oriented policy should be strengthened. Recipient countries and their instituti- ons should be responsible for their own development [NOU, 1995:5: 14–15, 30]. In Report No.19 [1995: 6], the government agreed that aid should increasingly be directed towards capacity building and institutional development.

However, rhetoric and practice may represent different worlds. In practice, country programmes have been reduced while a growing share of total ODA has been allocated to special funds implanted out- side recipient structures.

III. THE FOLLOW-UP: ESTABLISHED AND NEW MECHANISMS

To what extent and in what manner has the strongly stated commit- ment to coherence been followed up? One way of approaching this question would be to focus on the process of achieving increased policy coherence: to what extent have procedures and mechanisms already in place to ensure policy coherence been strengthened or weakened, and new procedures and mechanisms created?[8]

---

8. Institutions and procedures established within the government administration in order to co-ordinate policies and facilitate coherence are not easily assessable from

(1) The Setting

The drive for policy coherence is triggered by a state of incoherence: conflicting interests and values and a compartmentalisation of political decision-making and administration. Politics within one policy area or sector attracts one set of stakeholders and decision-makers, representing a set of values, interests and concerns, and tending to generate a 'world view' and set of objectives which differ from those of other, similar settings. Increased coherence between different policy areas covering common ground is, therefore, not easy to achieve.

In the international setting, co-ordination among donors takes place within the Development Assistance Committee (DAC) of the OECD. This organisation, through the monitoring of norms and objectives jointly agreed by its members, plays an 'independent' role in improving policy coherence in general and within more specific core areas.[9] Within the regional context of the European Union, similar mechanisms are at work, with effects that often go beyond member states. The consultative groups, co-ordinated by the World Bank, serve a similar purpose, and have an executive function. The Roundtables, organised by the United Nations Development Programme (UNDP), also serve a co-ordinating function, although the political muscle is less visible, if it exists at all. All these mechanisms influence the 'institutional philosophy' of donor aid agencies in the direction of policy convergence; the large degree of convergence is indicated by the phases in the development discourse as systematised by Göran Hydén [1994].

---

policy documents. In describing evolving patterns and assessing their impact (subsections 3–6), I have greatly benefited from interviews with Ambassador Oddmund Graham, Special Adviser (formerly Secretary-General), Ministry of the Environment; Mr Kjell Halvorsen, Director-General, Global Department, MFA; Mr Nils Haugstveit, Deputy Director-General (Development Co-operation Policy Section, which includes budget and NORAD), Bilateral Affairs Department, MFA; Ambassador Ole Kristian Holthe, Special Adviser for Sustainable Development and the Environment, Department of Resources and the Environment, MFA; and Ms Gerd Wahlstrøm, Director-General (Management), NORAD.

9. Two examples may illustrate the point. Since the early 1980s, an expert group on evaluation has been at work, composed (usually) of the heads of the evaluation units of the member states (and those of some multilaterals, too). Obviously, this initiative has an effect on the norms set for evaluation which, in turn, affect aid policy, too [Stokke, 1991b]. In the early 1990s, when promotion of democracy, human rights and good governance became the clarion call for development co-operation, the DAC established a similar working group on participatory development and good governance. A working group has been established to improve coherence, too [OECD, 1996a].

My primary concern here, however, relates to the national political system, where the main responsibility for creating a coherent policy is vested in the Prime Minister (PM) and the government, and the degree of success depends, in the first place, on the political centre's commitment to policy coherence and on its follow-up capacity and authority. However, within this very institution, the seeds of policy incoherence are sown: ministers are vested with the double responsibility of being part of a collegium and representing sectoral concerns. Although committed to a joint political programme and to the *gemeinschaft* of the collegium, they also represent the positions of an administration for which they carry the responsibility. Coalition governments, comprising political parties with primary commitment to different programmes, start out with a handicap that may give greater autonomy to individual ministers and, accordingly, may result in greater incoherence.

Similar tensions apply at lower levels in the administration, down to the units responsible for a circumscribed activity (sector), in their relations with higher levels: the heads represent positions prepared by the units for which they are responsible but also operate in a setting with broader, even competing, concerns. It is not surprising, however, if their first loyalty is to the unit; however, promotion in the system is linked to their flexibility in broader contexts.

Another dimension, reinforcing compartmentalisation and consequently the probability of policy incoherence, should be mentioned. The Norwegian system has a tradition of 'hearings' with stakeholders before conclusions are drawn. Organised vested interests interact with 'their' ministry (or unit of a ministry) in order to form norms and influence policy implementation. In the process, vested interests are internalised in the sectoral ministries.

These are general features in policy-making, although the political culture may vary and make a difference. What then are the responses?

Important elements in a strategy to create greater coherence include agreed norms, objectives, procedures for implementation, monitoring and conflict resolution. An agreed political programme, where objectives are set in clear and operational terms and prioritised, constitutes a necessary basis. Institutions which include the most important concerns involved (stakeholders) across sectoral borders are helpful. However, what matters is the way these institutions work (the process), which brings us back to the prevailing political and administrative culture of the system and its separate units.

The Ministry of Foreign Affairs carries the ultimate responsibility for all official development assistance (ODA). However, it has also the responsibility for a multitude of other foreign relations, involving security, trade and international co-operation in general, which draw in other sector ministries as well. Competence and expertise within areas of importance in development co-operation (ODA) or in the broader policy towards the South are, on the other hand, situated in sectoral ministries; these ministries may also carry the ultimate responsibility for such areas (the MFA has the last say when ODA is involved).

Looking at the follow-up, with reference to ODA, what are the procedures and mechanisms established to ensure intra-ministerial coherence between policies administered by the major departments of the MFA? In the 1990s, political responsibility for various ODA-financed activities was shared between the Minister of Foreign Affairs and the Minister of Development Co-operation, both situated in the MFA; co-ordination between departments under different political leadership attracts particular interest. Within the agency implementing bilateral aid (NORAD), responsibility for the various components is also vested in separate administrative units, which calls for co-ordination. What mechanisms are there to ensure horizontal coherence between policies administered by different ministries? And what mechanisms are there to ensure vertical coherence between, in particular, the centre (PM's Office) and sectoral ministries responsible for particular components of the broader policy towards the South and, in the specific area of aid policy, between the MFA and NORAD? The focus here will be on institutional frameworks.

(2) Inter-ministerial Restructuring

Several ministries and even more ministers are involved in setting the norms and implementing the various components of the policy towards the South, in particular the Ministry of Foreign Affairs, the Ministry of Industries and Trade, and the Ministry of the Environment. Other ministries and public institutions are also drawn in; in general, norm-setting involves the Ministry of Finance or, for more particular aspects, the Ministry of Agriculture, when imports of agricultural products from the South are on the agenda.

Administrative restructuring is a strategy often applied in order to ensure policy coherence between neighbouring policy areas: these may be brought together under one political and administrative umbrella in a super-ministry or, alternatively, more specialised ministries may be established. What have been the patterns in the Norwegian case?

In 1984, when the Ministry of Development Co-operation was established, the latter strategy was chosen. In the late 1980s, when the

Ministry of Trade and the Ministry of Development Co-operation were merged with the MFA, the former strategy was followed, although the political responsibility for the areas concerned remained vested in separate ministers.

From the perspective of policy coherence, each solution has its strengths and weaknesses. As noted in an OECD paper on public management [*OECD, 1996a: 20–21*], while a large, multi-sectoral ministry may help integrate related policies in a more coherent framework, there are limits to the number of policy conflicts that can be internalised. With its many internal divisions, it risks reproducing on a smaller scale problems found in the government as a whole. It may reduce the political accountability for policy-making as well: conflicts are resolved internally by civil servants rather than at the political level by ministers. Issue-specific ministries, on the other hand, may provide flexible structures capable of focusing on specific problem areas and constituencies; however, they may make co-ordination problematic and increase fragmentation.[10]

In 1996, a new inter-ministerial restructuring moved most trade issues to a new ministry of industries and trade. However, the prime responsibility for most aspects of the policy towards the South remains vested in the MFA.

(3) Intra-ministerial Restructuring and Co-ordination

Administrative restructuring has been a recurrent instrument to ensure intra-ministerial coherence. A new round of restructuring within the MFA, which took place in September 1997, had the overall objective of improving the coherence of foreign policy generally. It follows that aid policy was to be brought into line with overall policy towards the South, which in turn was to cohere with the broader concerns of foreign policy, and vice versa.

Within the new structure, bilateral relations with the South are administered by a department with several sections, four for the regions and one for NORAD and cross-cutting aid. 'Global' issues are administered in another department with sections for the UN, the international finance institutions, and human rights and humanitarian aid. Trade policy issues remaining with the MFA after the inter-ministerial reorganisation of 1996 (multilateral trade policy, import

---

10. There is a temptation to seek structural solutions in order to solve policy co-ordination problems (*inter alia*, creating or dismantling ministries). Experience increasingly seems to point to the limitations of such solutions: restructuring is disruptive and policy issues and their interlinkages change too rapidly to allow timely structural adaptations [*OECD, 1996a: 20–21*].

policy and import/export control) are administered by a third department. Global environmental issues are dealt with in a fourth department (resources and the environment) by one of the sections; and relations with Russia and the CIS countries are administered by a department for security policy, including OSCE.

Although reflecting 'functional' concerns too, the main principle guiding the reform seems to be that of 'geography', particularly as far as bilateral development co-operation is concerned. The main instrument in ensuring policy coherence *vis-à-vis* individual countries is the 'desk' system established in the department in charge of bilateral relations. There are desks for Africa, Asia, Latin America and the Middle East, and these are supposed to cover all bilateral relations (not only development co-operation) and to communicate with other departments of the MFA (foreign policy, foreign economic policy) and NORAD. The global department also relates directly with the functional units (health, education, etc.) of NORAD.

Intra-ministerial co-ordination within and beyond the line organisation may be promoted through institutional devices, such as regular 'staff meetings' among heads of departments (with the political leadership present or absent) or, more specifically, between heads of departments which cover a common ground. Ad hoc task forces for cross-cutting issues would serve a similar function, involving civil servants at lower levels. To what extent are such mechanisms at work?

At the civil service level, the Secretary-General and three assistant secretaries-general – for foreign policy issues, foreign economic policy issues and development co-operation – constitute the leadership group and are expected to play a policy co-ordinating role. A unit for planning, research and evaluation, reporting directly to the Secretary-General, may also have a role in ensuring intra-ministerial policy coherence; a strategic use of the evaluation mechanism might facilitate such a role.

Weekly meetings also take place between the heads of the two departments mainly concerned with aid, the global and bilateral departments, attended also by the head of section responsible for NORAD and by the heads (or representatives) of departments for administration, legal affairs, culture and information, and the secretariat of the minister of international development and human rights. These meetings are chaired by the assistant secretary-general for development co-operation.

Outside the formal line structure, and the regular meetings of heads of department referred to, no special arrangements have been made to ensure intra-departmental or intra-ministerial policy coherence; the 'visible hand', in terms of well-established norms for aid policy and internal communication, is expected to do the trick.[11]

Relations between the MFA and NORAD constitute a particular case: the aid agency is governed by the MFA through the Development Co-operation Policy Section.

'Geography' is the predominant organising principle of the NORAD system too: overall, objectives are to be adapted to the prevailing conditions of a programme country and operationalised within this framework. The mix may therefore vary from one country to another. A functional department and its units become involved when the activities are planned.

A 'memorandum of understanding' is worked out between the MFA and the recipient government; in this process, the Norwegian embassy (where the aid administration, previously a separate NORAD Resident Representative Office, is integrated) plays a central role. This memorandum also represents the major instrument by which to ensure donor–recipient coherence, since it is expected that the 'understanding' will reflect the priorities of the recipient.

A strategy for the individual programme country, based on this understanding, is the major instrument in aid implementation; it is operationalised for each embassy in a plan for the activities and a budget. A dialogue with the recipient side on performance and future plans takes place every year; in this, new objectives and priorities may be introduced.[12]

Co-ordination of direct state-to-state bilateral aid (country programmes) on the one hand, and aid for particular activities

---

11. As stated by one of my respondents (Director-General, MFA), 'in my department, all know what is to be done, guided by an aims/means/result-oriented approach and priorities based on overall objectives that have been established for many years and internalised in the staff. Regular meetings take place within the department and within the sections, communications are circulated, and I have encouraged informal cross-sectoral communication' (interview, 18 Feb. 1998).

12. The status of the country strategy is that of an internal working document, although it is in English and communicated to the recipient government; the brief 'Memorandum of understanding', in contrast, is signed by the two parties.

Responsibility for planning and decisions is vested in the bilateral affairs department (MFA); in practice, however, the system has decentralised features: the country strategy is prepared by the embassy, with NORAD participating in working groups and commenting on drafts. Although the strategy is expected to govern all Norwegian-funded aid, multilateral aid is not easily integrated nor are several special grants, and aid channelled through NGOs enjoys flexibility. The Norwegian delegation to the yearly dialogue on performance and future co-operation is usually headed by a high-ranking MFA official (at times a NORAD official, depending on the main theme); on special occasions, the minister of international development and human rights or the state secretary may head the delegation.

administered by other units of the MFA or NORAD (relief, human rights, democracy, industrial co-operation) or NGOs on the other, has to a large extent been left to the embassy situated in the countries concerned. However, NORAD is to be consulted with regard to aid channelled through the larger Norwegian NGOs to programme countries. In special cases (aid to Guatemala is a case in point), ad hoc arrangements may be established to ensure exchange of information between implementing agencies operating in the same area. However, the general pattern is that little co-ordination takes place: the various activities are run by the separate administrative units in charge. Part of the explanation is that the kind of aid referred to, in particular humanitarian aid, is channelled to countries outside the group of programme countries.

Intra-ministerial policy coherence is also facilitated through joint participation by the relevant departments (global and bilateral) and NORAD in external frameworks: advisory or governing bodies of particular major programmes, such as the Special Programme for Africa. These units also participate in meetings on projects financed from the aid budget, and are included in delegations to international conferences.

Participation in such processes also facilitates policy coherence among donors; this applies, in particular, to meetings of the consultative groups on individual recipient countries (co-ordinated by the World Bank) and Roundtables (co-ordinated by UNDP).[13] The bilateral affairs department is in charge; NORAD participates in the preparations and the meetings and has occasionally headed the delegation. However, other departments of the MFA, such as Resources and the Environment, are not involved in the process and barely kept informed.

Assessment of a structural reform in the making belongs to the future. From a policy coherence perspective, however, the new organisation looks more promising than the former, particularly with regard to the desk system and the integration of humanitarian aid into one of the 'aid' departments. However, the risk of incoherence is

---

13. Consultation among donors takes place also on a regional basis; for Norway, formal and informal consultations involving harmonisation of policies have been particularly close within a Nordic setting. The traditional meetings (up to the early 1990s) of heads of Nordic aid agencies twice a year are now to be resumed. An interesting reminiscence of the former group of non-aligned countries, active in the late 1970s and early 1980s to push new international economic order policies [Løvbræk, 1990], may be mentioned too: in the case of Bangladesh, a core group (Canada, the Netherlands and the Scandinavians) has met in Dhaka to co-ordinate their positions ahead of the Paris consultative group meetings on Bangladesh – and separate meetings have taken place in Paris too.

easily identified: large units may achieve greater policy coherence within their confines but at the same time they run the risk of encouraging compartmentalisation, with effects of the kind indicated above [*OECD, 1996a*].

(4) Inter-ministerial Co-ordination

The government (cabinet) is the ultimate forum for inter-ministerial co-ordination, although informal, bilateral communication between colleagues often sorts out problems that arise. Before an important issue is raised, the government is informed by the relevant ministry in a formal note. And major policy conclusions are, in turn, also discussed in the government on the basis of formal notes by the ministry in charge before the issue is presented to Parliament in a governmental proposition or report.

Traditionally, the MFA has carried a co-ordinating and advisory function *vis-à-vis* the other parts of the central administration in matters involving foreign policy relations. Only the PM and the Minister of Foreign Affairs could represent the state internationally; within the government, the responsibility for foreign policy and relations with other states and international organisations is still vested in the Minister of Foreign Affairs. However, other ministers (such as the ministers of finance, trade, defence, fisheries, the environment) carry responsibility for issues where solutions have increasingly to be sought internationally; this in turn makes co-ordination necessary. Although within most areas technical knowledge rests with the sectoral ministry, the responsibility for co-ordination is usually vested in the MFA.[14]

Inter-ministerial co-ordination may also be achieved through joint committees on a permanent basis or ad hoc task forces. To what extent are such instruments at work, at political and civil service levels, involving ministries that interact on the policy towards the South, the MFA, the Ministry of Industries and Trade and the Ministry of the Environment in particular? To what extent, for instance,

---

14. The problematique is dealt with in Report No.11 [*1989: 68ff*], where guidelines are established and the MFA is given the main responsibility for the preparation, co-ordination and implementation of the foreign policy. However, the government may decide to place the responsibility for a particular case with foreign policy implications or an international meeting with another ministry. The sectoral ministries and the MFA are instructed to keep each other mutually informed and to invite points of view on matters that concern the foreign policy or may have such implications. The primacy of the MFA is reflected in the concluding guideline [*ibid.:71*]: 'In those cases where another ministry is given the responsibility for an issue with foreign policy implications, this responsibility is to be implemented in close consultation with the Ministry of Foreign Affairs.'

have other ministries been involved when the MFA has formulated the objectives, priorities, strategies and major instruments of aid policy (and of policy towards the South in general)? Equally relevant, to what extent is the MFA involved when other ministries formulate major policies within their sectors that are of relevance for the South or North–South relations?

At the political level, meetings of state secretaries (deputy ministers) of 'neighbouring' ministries take place when major policy issues are reviewed; these are chaired by the state secretary of the ministry with responsibility for the policy area. The PM's Office is also represented. The meetings are also attended by the key civil servant(s) of the host ministry. An inter-ministerial committee on North–South issues was at work when the Labour government prepared the 1995 White Paper;[15] however, the new coalition government has not established a committee on international development and human rights. As noted, coalition governments confront particular problems. The present coalition has met this challenge by combining ministers and state secretaries from different parties: all three parties in the coalition are represented with state secretaries in the PM's Office and two parties in the MFA.

The main mechanism to ensure inter-ministerial policy coherence, however, is the system of 'hearings': white papers or major government policy papers are, as a matter of routine, distributed to affected ministries for comments before the policy is finalised by the ministry and agreed by the government.

In many donor countries, a source of incoherence in policy towards the South (and development co-operation) is that responsibility for the various components of the aid policy is vested in different ministries, with little co-ordination (the case of France may illustrate the point – see Hugon, this volume). Up to the mid-1980s, this was also the case with Norwegian aid: policies pursued within the bilateral country programmes were not always attuned to policies advocated in the Bretton Woods institutions, which reflected macro-economic concerns predominant within the Bank of Norway and the Ministry of Finance. The move towards greater coherence resulted, more than institutional reform, from a change in development philosophy and, in particular, bilateral development co-operation policy, which brought Norwegian positions more in line with the predominant trend in the

---

15. This pattern is well established: the state secretaries of more or less the same ministries (and the PM's Office) also constituted a reference group when Report No. 36 was prepared in 1984 under a coalition government. The state secretaries meet also more informally at a weekly lunch where current issues are brought up.

1980s (a macro-economic perspective; more 'market', less 'state'); the change of policy towards Tanzania in the mid-1980s by the Nordic governments exemplifies the point.

Although responsibility for ODA is vested in the MFA, this ministry shares with the Bank of Norway (Ministry of Finance) responsibility for policies vis-à-vis the Bretton Woods institutions (BWIs): the MFA is responsible with regard to the World Bank (ODA) and the Bank of Norway with regard to the IMF (monetary policy). However, there is no joint 'co-ordinating committee'; in my opinion, such a committee might facilitate policy coherence and contribute to mutual understanding on complex issues between the institutions involved which, particularly in the past, have represented conflicting cultures, perspectives and concerns. Policy co-ordination to a large extent takes place within an extended Nordic framework; occasional conflicts on policy positions or priorities between the MFA and the Bank of Norway are therefore left to be 'resolved' within this wider setting.[16]

Global conferences on particular issues – which in the 1990s have focused on children, the environment, human rights, population, social affairs, women and habitat – tend to influence the priorities set for both bilateral and multilateral aid; for cross-cutting issues, as most are, such meetings also fulfil an ad hoc policy coherence function in both a national and an international framework. Inter-ministerial committees prepare reports on national performance and policy positions; several ministries, in addition to the lead ministry, may be included in the delegation. The MFA often has an overall co-ordinating role even when the relevant sector ministry is in charge. Although several of these meetings relate to development issues, with particular reference to the South, NORAD has not always been involved in the process, although it has been more often than not.

Similar co-ordination takes place more regularly on particular agencies or programmes that involve several ministries. The MFA is not necessarily the lead ministry; in the case of the FAO committee, for example, the Ministry of Agriculture is in charge and the Ministry of Church, Education and Research is in charge of the UNESCO committee. However, while ad hoc groups are established to co-ordinate Norway's positions at important global meetings, it is exceptional that standing inter-ministerial committees are established to facilitate co-ordination and policy coherence. There is ample room for improvements in this regard.

---

16. The Nordic governments share an office in Washington and an Executive Director whose appointment rotates between the countries. Policy is to a large extent co-ordinated through this office which communicates with the Nordic capitals.

Cross-cutting issues constitute a particular challenge to inter-ministerial co-operation; environment is a case in point involving several ministries. The political responsibility for the issue is vested in the minister of the environment. In the 1970s and 1980s, negotiations on 'local' environmental issues (acid rainfall, polluted seas) were handled by the Ministry of the Environment (ME). In the late 1980s and early 1990s, however, 'new' issues (the ozone layer, climate, bio-diversity), regional or global in character, came to the fore; they affected vital parts of the economy (energy, natural resources) and attracted the attention of several ministries. Sector ministries affected, including finance, energy and communications, and the PM's Office, were involved in preparing Norway's negotiation positions on conventions on climate and biodiversity, with the ME at the wheel and heading delegations.

International environmental issues became prominently placed on the political agenda by governments headed by Ms Brundtland (Labour) and by the centre–conservative coalition government as well. In the 1990s policy positions were in a very real sense decided at government level; the ministers of the environment and foreign affairs were particularly involved and the PM was taking an active part (interview, Ambassador Graham). An inter-ministerial committee of state secretaries was established for environmental policy (the PM's Office and the MFA were included), chaired by the state secretary of the ME.

The ME played an active role in the follow-up of the Brundtland Commission. Its administrative capacity to deal with this cross-sectoral issue, including an international department, was strengthened. National and international research milieus were mobilised. The organisation of national research was affected (environment and development were combined in one of the six research areas within the Research Council of Norway) and the national research capacity in this field, particularly applied climatic research, was strengthened; this involved the ministry responsible for research. Important aspects of environmental policy were the responsibility of other ministries: for international aspects, the MFA was responsible for aid for sustainable development.

The division of labour and responsibilities between the two ministries was settled at cabinet level. Responsibility for international environmental policy (global issues, including climate and biodiversity) remained with the minister of the environment. The MFA was given responsibility for inter-ministerial co-ordination of sustainable development. Two inter-ministerial committees have been established: a national committee for international environmental issues with a mandate to supervise the follow-up on Agenda 21, chaired by the ME; and an inter-ministerial committee with a mandate to co-ordinate policies pursued in the Commission on Sustainable Development (CSD) and report back to the authorities at home with a responsibility for the follow-up, chaired by the MFA.[17] The ME is the lead ministry for the UN Environmental Programme (UNEP), including funding.[18] Responsibility for other international development agencies and funds allocated for bilateral environmental activities in the South is, however, vested in the MFA. Responsibility for the broader policy area is therefore shared between the minister of the environment and the minister of international development and human rights.[19]

A parallel, low-key inter-ministerial structure operates too; a contact group on environmental aid is established. It is co-ordinated by the MFA through the Department of Resources and the Environment and attended by representatives from two other departments of the MFA (Global; Bilateral), NORAD and the ME. The contact group serves in an advisory capacity, and decisions are taken by the relevant line organisation; all activities are funded from the ODA budget (MFA).

Few other inter-ministerial structures exist of the kind established to co-ordinate environmental policy across ministerial dividing lines; however, the cases cited illustrate how intra-policy coherence may be sought by way of institutional arrangements. Another inter-ministerial group involved with the policy towards the South has recently been

---

17. The ministries and government agencies represented in the two committees are identical [*MFA, 1997c*]: the Prime Minister's Office, Foreign Affairs, Environment, Finance, Fisheries, Agriculture, Petroleum and Energy, Local Government and Labour, Industries and Trade, Transport and Communications, and Church, Education and Research. The inter-ministerial CSD committee, appointed by the government on 4 Sept. 1997, also included NORAD. Political responsibility for CSD is vested in the MFA (the minister of international development and human rights) and administered by the Department for Resources and the Environment.
18. Even here, responsibility is shared: overall responsibility, involving the status, reform and future of the UNEP, is vested in the MFA (global department) with the ME as the implementing ministry. Funding responsibility is shared, too: basic funding (the UN budget) and financing of particular programmes are provided from the MFA budget; the UNEP fund is financed from the ME budget.
19. The organisation to co-ordinate CSD policies is new; by the end of February 1998, the inter-ministerial CSD committee had met twice. Working groups have been established to prepare Norwegian policy positions in fields where international CSD meetings are planned, viz. for energy and climate (2001), oceans and live marine resources (1999), fresh water (1998) and industrial co-operation (combined with aid) (1998). Since the funding of these various activities comes from different sources, the work is to be decentralised; the idea is that responsibility should be spread and ownership created (interview, Ambassador Holthe).

established with the purpose of generating new ideas on industrial development for the 1999 ODA budget.[20]

Most inter-ministerial mechanisms of the kind initiated by the MFA relate to the use of aid monies. If the stated policy (*supra*, section II) is to be taken seriously, representatives from the 'aid' administration should also be included when committees are set up to formulate or execute policies not financed from the aid budget which, directly or indirectly, affect the South or relations with the South.

(5) Formalised Policy Objectives and Strategies

Within all four frameworks, stated policy objectives and strategies are important to attain policy coherence. In the Norwegian setting, such objectives are established in a medium-term perspective in the government's long-term plans every fourth year. The annual budget also contains objectives with a range beyond its time perspective. These documents are based on inputs from the sectoral ministries and represent a synthesis; however, this is no guarantee against conflicting objectives. As noted, government policies are also hammered out in major white papers which cover broader or more specific fields.

Clear-cut objectives constitute a precondition for the attainment of intra-policy coherence too, particularly in cross-cutting policy areas. Formalised strategies reinforce such objectives. The major white papers produced since 1984 include formalised strategies on several cross-cutting policy areas. In addition, more specific strategies have been elaborated and revised; these include the strategy for women in development [*MFA, 1997a*], first formulated in 1985, and for aid and the environment [*MFA, 1997b*]. In one sense, the formalised Norwegian policy establishes a good basis for policy coherence; however, overall objectives are expressed in broad terms that may permit a variety of interpretations. Some inconsistencies are also recognised in government white papers.

Overall objectives are satisfactory in so far as they provide general direction, but they need to be operationalised within specific contexts. This is where the real problem starts. Objectives tend to remain at a high level of generalisation and provide weak guidance as to priorities, even in those cases where sectoral strategies have been worked out.

---

20. This group is chaired by the state secretary for international development and human rights (MFA), and is made up of representatives from three MFA departments (Bilateral, Global, Trade), NORAD and the Ministry of Industries and Trade.

(6) Involving the Wider Community

The process in which policy is created is also important. Intra-ministerial and inter-ministerial co-ordination is usually an essential component in the process, but the involvement of the wider community also matters. To what extent are stakeholders outside government structures integrated in the process that determines objectives, strategies and major instruments?

Broad participation in the preparatory phase of policy formulation is ensured by means of the aforementioned 'hearing' system that gives a voice to public institutions, NGOs and private sector interests deemed to have a stake; this system is often activated also in the process of fine-tuning policy. Moreover, the so-called 'corporative state' involves direct and close interaction in the implementation of policy between institutions representing vested interests and 'their' sectoral ministry.

Private sector consultants have been extensively used in the preparation of policy positions. The major humanitarian NGOs have increasingly been integrated in the aid delivery system and have become major instruments, particularly in the implementation of humanitarian aid. Networks based on this kind of co-operation have been established for policy discussions of common interest; NGOs and public institutions (directorates) with particular technical competence are cases in point. NGO representatives are often included in official delegations to international meetings along with representatives of employer and employee organisations within the private sector.

However, important means of ensuring the participation of the wider community have been neglected in recent years. Since the early 1980s, the predominant philosophy has been to rid public administration of 'unnecessary' boards and advisory committees in the name of efficiency. Until 1984, when it was included as a department of the Ministry of Development Co-operation (MDC), NORAD had an executive board appointed by the government; it also had a Council elected by Parliament, with representatives from public institutions, NGOs and the private sector. In 1984, the council was replaced by an MDC-appointed advisory council which was dissolved later in the 1980s.

For years, therefore, the development co-operation administration, with close relations to vested interests and pressure groups, has had a predominantly closed, technocratic/administrative profile. The major NGOs active within this field, particularly in providing humanitarian aid, are in a way an extended part of the system, with vested interests involved too. Unlike many other aid administrations, the Norwegian one has not been provided with the opportunity systematically and regularly to draw on and seek strength from the insights and judgements of the wider community. The Netherlands demonstrates how this 'capital' may be utilised in formulating, renewing and implementing an active policy towards the South.[21]

In the Norwegian setting, the government has found it useful to draw on the insights of an advisory council for disarmament and arms control composed of independent experts. With the cold war behind us, and with Norway outside the European Union, it would be a good idea to establish a broader advisory system on international relations. The model established by the Netherlands could provide useful guidance!

IV. POLICY OBJECTIVES AND IMPLEMENTATION: TRENDS IN THE 1990S

How coherent have policies towards the South been in the 1990s? How and to what extent has the norm calling for greater policy coherence influenced policies? These questions will be addressed in this section, with particular reference to aid policy. Focus will be on the current state of affairs as well as major trends: changes in attention and in the use of resources involving the various components of the policy. The direction of such changes with regard to objectives and priorities is especially important.

The actual follow-up of the stated objectives through resource allocations is part of the coherence problematique. However, the extent to which they indicate actual coherence or incoherence is not easily assessed since objectives are seldom given a price tag; within the aid policy, this applies both to 'traditional' objectives and 'new' objectives. Objectives are usually expressed in broad terms too, allowing for broad and varied interpretations.

Policy changes are influenced by many factors, including changes in social, economic and political environments and in perceptions of vested interests; effects of the prescription calling for policy coherence are not easily isolated. Causality is therefore hard to establish

---

21. For years, the Dutch National Advisory Council for Development Co-operation, with a tiny secretariat in the MFA, has been active in policy research and advice. In 1997, a major reorganisation took place, further expanding these activities: the Advisory Council on International Affairs (AIV) was established, with four commissions – Human Rights, Peace and Security, European Integration and Development Co-operation. The advisory function involves several ministries. For an overview of how 17 European countries (Norway is not among these) have organised such advisory boards, see Annemiek Kooij and René Mevis [*1994*].

through this approach, even when coherence is given as the justification.

Stakeholders may use the coherence argument in pursuit of their interests and values. Those outside the specific policy area may use it in an attempt to change the objectives, priorities and allocation of resources established within the core area in order to serve their own interests better. A classic case in our context are efforts to adapt aid objectives and implementation so as to promote exports to, or investments in, the South. Likewise, stakeholders within the core area may use the coherence argument to attempt to change the objectives, priorities and the allocation of resources within other, 'neighbouring' policy areas so as to bring them closer to their own policies. In our context, this might imply efforts to change the trade policy (for instance, norms governing imports and exports) to serve better the needs of partners in the South or development in the South in general.

The demand for policy coherence, therefore, becomes an integral part of the ordinary political competition between stakeholders representing different values and interests. This competition takes place both within a particular policy area (involving the various, at times conflicting, policy objectives set within this area) and between policy areas with different, and conflicting, primary objectives. The outcome is reflected in the policy, as stated and implemented, and changes in this policy.

Against this background, what are the most important changes during the last decade that have taken place in Norwegian policy towards the South in general and in aid policy in particular? In what direction have these changes carried the aid policy? To what extent have the various policies – as stated and implemented – been coherent? The focus will be concentrated on two parameters: first, the relations between traditional objectives set for development co-operation and the competing 'new' ones (democracy and human rights in particular), and second, the relations between development and the 'new' concern for peace and conflict prevention.[22]

(1) 'Traditional' and 'New' Objectives

Successive Norwegian governments and Parliament have emphasised altruistic motives for development co-operation: the moral obligation

---

22. Two other parameters are well suited for assessing continuity and change in Norway's policy related to our problematique: the evolving relationship between development objectives and the 'new' environmental concerns and between development objectives and commercial concerns. They are explored elsewhere [*Stokke, 1999*], and a few conclusions emerging from this discussion are referred to in the concluding section.

to help human beings in distress emerges as the most powerful incentive. Aid has been conceived of as an instrument to promote international common goods: international stability and peace, and other internationally shared interests (economy, health, ecology). For a small country this reflects enlightened self-interest. More self-centred interests have also been discernible, but these have been of secondary importance in the declared policy. The overall objectives have reflected these justifications: in 1962, promoting economic, social and cultural development in the South was set as the main objective, fairer income distribution being added ten years later. Poverty alleviation and attaining social justice emerged as the primary tasks [*Stokke, 1984; 1989: 169–74*]. These concerns were confirmed in 1984.[23]

In subsequent years, what changes have taken place in the declared policy? To what extent has there been follow-up in the allocation of resources: is there a discrepancy between words and deeds?

(a) Trends in the declared policy. In 1987, before the cold war had come to an end and before policy coherence had come to the fore, a gradual change of emphasis took place. The Labour government confirmed the overall objective set in 1984 by its predecessor and gave prominence to five sub-objectives: responsibility in the administration of natural resources and the environment; economic growth; improvements in the conditions of the poorest, in particular women; support for social, economic, and political human rights; and the promotion of peace between nations and regions.[24]

In the 1990s, *human rights and democracy* were increasingly emphasised. In the 1992 White Paper, the furtherance of human rights was given as an objective in its own right within the framework of development co-operation. The Labour government saw a close connection between respect for human rights and the development of a democratic system based on pluralism and popular participation [*Report No.51: 213*]. In the 1995 White Paper, these positions were maintained, this time coupled with peace-promoting and peacekeeping activities [*Report No.19*], to which I shall return.

---

23. In 1984, the overall goal is 'to assist in creating lasting improvements in the economic, social and political conditions of the people in developing countries. Development assistance shall be used in a way that maximises its development effects for the poor sections of the population. Aid shall in the first place be directed to the poorest developing countries and be provided in a form that creates as little dependence on continued aid as possible' [*Report No.36: 20*].
24. In accepting the five objectives proposed in the 1987 White Paper, Parliament emphasised that these had to be assessed according to their capacity to contribute to fulfilling the core objective set in 1984. Alone, they could not justify aid projects [*Stokke, 1989: 173–4*].

(b) Promotion of democracy and human rights – the follow-up. How and to what extent has the added emphasis on human rights and democracy been followed up? What strategies and mechanisms have been employed? What priority is given to the 'new' objectives in terms of aid allocations?

This policy has to a large extent been formulated within a Nordic framework. The twofold strategy outlined was:

(i) to integrate efforts to strengthen civil and political human rights and democracy in the 'ordinary' aid programmes most of which were intended to improve living conditions for the ordinary people, that is, to promote economic and social development. A first imperative was to ensure that aid activities should not *damage* human rights. Involving local people actively in the planning and implementation of aid projects was seen as the best way to avoid such damages;

(ii) to channel aid to projects that strengthen the democratisation process and human rights, directly or through Norwegian and international NGOs and institutions or groups within recipient countries.

In the major policy documents, dialogue with recipients and a jointly agreed and mutually binding development contract have been presented as the main instruments in bilateral state-to-state development co-operation. The emphasis has been on supportive efforts, although conditionality has not been totally excluded: in certain contexts, where the authorities tolerate, assist in or are directly responsible for severe violations of human rights, a redistribution, reduction or even the termination of aid might be considered, according to the prescriptive norms. This raises the issue both of alternative channels (*inter alia*, NGOs) and forms (*inter alia*, humanitarian aid).

At the institutional level, posts as special adviser for human rights were established – one in NORAD and two in the MFA (one of which was within the aid administration). This mechanism had been used earlier in order to follow up on high-profile policies within cross-cutting areas – first (in the mid-1980s) to promote gender issues which, in the 1990s, became part of the human rights package (in fact, a major part of the funds allocated for human rights went to projects to improve conditions for women). For a variety of reasons, the creation of this post only marginally influenced policies, although it signalled that the issue was considered important.[25]

In bilateral relations, Norway has kept a low 'democracy–human rights' profile. Although the norms have been communicated in general terms to its main partners in bilateral development co-operation, increasingly since the mid-1980s, conditionality has only exceptionally been applied and then only mildly. The Wamwere incident, which made Kenya break diplomatic relations with Norway in 1990 (Norway, in turn, terminated state-to-state aid to this programme country) might appear to indicate the opposite; however, the outcome was unintended from the Norwegian side. Norway has participated within the consultative group framework co-ordinated by the World Bank in cases involving pressure for policy reform [*Stokke, 1995b: 182–97*].

Another mechanism established is a fund for the promotion of democracy, also intended to strengthen civil society (churches, trade unions, humanitarian organisations and other institutions).

Since 1984, a fund at the disposal of the MFA, established in the early 1970s in order to provide humanitarian aid to victims of the apartheid regime in South Africa and to support liberation movements in southern Africa, has increasingly been used to promote democracy and human rights. Its size, however, has remained modest (US$2–8 million a year).

In 1992, an aid-for-democracy strategy [*MFA, 1992*] brought these varied activities together within the aid framework. The strategy was designed to support national and regional efforts for peace and stabilisation, electoral processes and elected assemblies, judicial protection and the rule of law, economic planning and control, decentralisation and organisational pluralism, and the promotion of mass media and information. Norwegian expertise within these areas has been drawn upon, *inter alia*, through a resource bank for democratic development and human rights (NORDEM), administered by the Norwegian Institute of Human Rights. A Nordic group on human rights and

---

25. The advisers were outside the 'line' organisation that planned and implemented aid, had unclear mandates and no money at their disposal – which turned the institution into an appendix. In a 1996 memorandum NORAD's human rights adviser acknowledged that no coherent strategy existed to define and operationalise the human rights component as part of the aid policy and proposed means of filling this gap: the policy statements should be interpreted as calling for more than a mere increase in the number of aid-supported projects within the human rights area; promotion and protection of human rights should become an integral part of all development co-operation. However, this approach has been questioned, primarily because the existing competence and capacity within the administrative system (the MFA and NORAD) is found to be very limited [*Selbervik, 1997: 21–3*].

development, established in 1990, was initially given a co-ordinating role in these various efforts. United Nations activities – the work of an office to guide and implement democratic elections and of the UN High Commissioner for Human Rights – have been supported as have Norwegian institutions and NGOs which have co-operated with these UN bodies and local partners.

A clear picture of the resources actually spent on the promotion of democracy and human rights is not easily arrived at. A large number of small and some larger activities have been organised by different administrative units, the resources being drawn from several budgetary items, including humanitarian aid, refugees, aid for women, along with more specific budgetary items for democracy and human rights. The various activities have often been intertwined with peace promotion activities and run by separate administrative units with little overall co-ordination. Support for the activities has been pro-active. It is estimated that the support for democracy and human rights projects increased from 0.55 per cent of total aid in 1990 to 3.73 per cent five years later [*Selbervik, 1997: Appendix 1*].[26]

(c) *Concluding remarks.* Promotion of democracy and human rights became a high-profile part of Norway's foreign policy in the 1990s. It also became an integral part of the declared aid policy. From the perspective of overall foreign policy objectives, therefore, policy coherence has applied. The pursuit of the 'new' objectives has not, it seems, conflicted with or affected negatively the pursuance of 'traditional' objectives set for aid, competition for financial resources aside.

However, what would be a proper balance between a high-profile objective and the use of resources? Only a small share of the ODA budget has actually been used in pursuit of the two interlinked high-profile policies although the trend during the first half of the 1990s pointed upwards. What would be the proper share for a new priority concern? Four per cent of total aid? Ten per cent?

How consistent has the policy been? Norway has kept a low profile in the dialogue with programme countries on these issues although overall objectives set for aid and norms guiding aid allocations have been conveyed in general terms; in a few instances, negative performance has also influenced allocations [*Stokke, 1995b: 189ff*].

Norway has supported internationally co-ordinated pressure for democratic reform and human rights *vis-à-vis* small, aid-dependent

---

26. Aid for democracy and human rights increased from NOK 42 million in 1990 (involving 102 activities) to NOK 172 million (318 activities) in 1993, and NOK 295 million (386 activities) in 1995 [*Selbervik, 1997: Appendix 1:9*].

countries in southern Africa, participating in a consultative group context for the countries concerned. However, trade and investment in fast-growing economies in the South have been actively promoted by the government with little, if any, regard to their democracy or human rights record; the PM has served as an effective door-opener for Norwegian exporters and industrialists both in China and Indonesia. ODA has been used in these efforts too. The rhetoric has been adapted to this drive: concern for human rights and democracy is best served by active participation and dialogue, not by withdrawal.

Much of the financial support for human rights and democracy has been pro-active; it came in response to a wide variety of applicants on the recipient side, mostly outside the state sector. This may conform with the guideline prescribing that aid should be recipient-oriented in order to be effective. It may be asked, however, whether support for hundreds of small, scattered projects, without any overall co-ordination in terms of strategies adapted to different political, social, economic and cultural environments, and with little evaluation, is the most effective way of pursuing laudable objectives.

(2) Development and Peace and Stability

In the 1990s, 'new' conflict patterns have come to the fore. Whereas in the bipolar post-Second World War era, inter-state conflicts were in the focus, the ending of the cold war brought the focus more towards intra-state and trans-state, regional conflicts. Conflict has increasingly been seen as a threat to development. Since development depends on an enabling environment that includes the absence of violent conflict, the link between development and peace is obvious. To what extent and in what ways has this recognition been reflected in Norwegian development co-operation policy in the 1990s – as stated and implemented? Are there problems of policy incoherence involved?[27]

(a) The declared policy. In 1987, promotion of peace was identified as one of the five sub-objectives set for aid by the Labour government [*Report No.34*]. In the 1995 White Paper, it became an objective in its own right, coupled with human rights and democracy and with humanitarian aid – preventing and alleviating distress arising from conflicts [*Report No.19: 5–6,10*]. Poverty and ecological problems in the South have increasingly been recognised as a security problem; if

---

27. The theme of violent conflict prevention and development co-operation is explored and discussed in Stokke [*1997*]. This sub-section draws heavily on section VII of that study.

not solved peacefully, they may take on violent forms. According to the 1992 White Paper, development co-operation and improved framework conditions for developing countries may help to reduce these problems in the long term; in the short term, however, many latent conflicts in the South may flare up into armed conflicts and create huge human and material losses. Stability and peace constitute a condition for development. The government, therefore, will contribute to the prevention and solution of conflicts in the South by supporting, for example, peace-promoting efforts and co-operation across boundaries, protection of democracy and human rights, various forms of mediation, and UN peacekeeping operations. Peacekeeping operations should be followed up by peace-promoting development efforts in order to stabilise the situation after a violent conflict [*Report No.51: 56*].

In the 1995 White Paper, the government restated its integrated approach: peace, reconciliation and democracy are important for economic and social development. Support for conflict resolution is regarded as an integral part of Norwegian humanitarian aid and relief aid and as an important element of long-term development co-operation too. Short-term humanitarian aid, peace efforts and promotion of democracy should therefore as far as possible be viewed in conjunction with long-term development co-operation, and the two aid forms should be co-ordinated. Since many of the relief efforts take place in countries with which Norway has no long-term bilateral co-operation agreements, the government would ensure that the UN system plays an active role in co-ordinating short-term and long-term aid efforts [*Report No.19: 1*]. In 1996, Parliament agreed: humanitarian aid should be considered in close connection with efforts to promote peace and prevent conflicts, and efforts to promote peace should be considered also in conjunction with long-term development co-operation [*Recommendation No.229: 22–3*].

(b) The follow-up. To what extent and how has the stated policy been followed up? Some trends can be identified.

(i) Increases in relief aid. During the 1990s, the ratio of 'aid for long-term development' to 'relief aid' has increasingly moved in favour of 'relief aid'. In 1986, 9.9 per cent of total aid was allocated to relief, international humanitarian aid, refugees and human rights; this share increased to 11 per cent in 1990 and 17.2 per cent in 1996. Although corresponding with a general trend internationally, it is almost three

times higher than the DAC average [*Report No.51: 238; Proposition No.1, 1997: 161; OECD, 1996c: Table 2*].

Linkages with Norwegian NGOs have been strengthened and regulated; the government refers to this close co-operation as 'the Norwegian model' [*Report No.19: 19*]. Most humanitarian aid has been channelled through the four largest humanitarian organisations and the UN system.[28] Linkages with the private sector have been similarly improved; since 1991, a system that ensures deliveries of Norwegian commodities and services at short notice to emergency areas (the Norwegian Emergency Preparedness System, NOREPS, co-ordinated by the Norwegian Export Council) has been created and further developed. In 1995, a group of specially trained aid workers prepared to go to disaster areas at short notice was established (NORTEAM).

It would be premature to conclude that this development results from the quest for greater policy coherence. The strong focus on the human suffering in central Europe and the increased number of refugees from this and other areas of conflict probably provide a better explanation. Although part of an integrated approach for peace promotion and conflict prevention, it should be noted that humanitarian aid has always been part of the ODA concept.

However, the expansion cannot be explained as a result of increased demand alone. Since the early 1990s, the combination of peace and relief operations has increasingly become a high-profile component of Norwegian foreign policy. Responsibility for humanitarian aid (ODA) has been split between the aid administration and the traditional foreign affairs administration; this split has probably facilitated the rapid increase of the humanitarian aid component in the early 1990s and kept it at a high level in recent years because it became part of a high-profiled foreign policy. Personalities count too; until the recent change of government, responsibility for the activity was vested in a dynamic deputy minister (MFA), Mr Jan Egeland, who previously held high positions in humanitarian organisations, including executive positions in the Norwegian Red Cross.

(ii) Aid as a follow-up to foreign-policy peace initiatives. In a few cases, Norway has for various reasons played a role in conflict resolution. Chief among these is the long-standing conflict in the Middle

---

28. About 25 per cent of ODA is channelled through NGOs. Humanitarian aid in 1996 amounted to NOK 1,546 million, of which 64 per cent was channelled through NGOs (in particular, the Norwegian People's Aid, the Norwegian Red Cross, the Refugee Council, Norwegian Church Aid) and the remaining 36 per cent through the UN (in particular, UNCHR) [*Proposition No.1, 1997*].

East between Israel and the Palestinians, where the conflicting parties found it useful to involve the good offices of Norwegian diplomacy (the so-called Oslo agreement). The agreement between the conflicting parties in Guatemala, and support for the Mandela government in South Africa, are two further cases in point.

Each of the three cases has its particular background. The common denominator is that the recipients were not among those countries chosen for bilateral development co-operation; however, extensive aid was used to follow up on previous foreign-policy initiatives.

In the case of the Israeli–Palestinian accord, long-standing and close relations between the Labour parties (and trade unions) of Norway and Israel, together with an evolving recognition of and support for the PLO, explain why the two parties decided to make use of the Oslo channel when they found the time ripe for negotiations. The relationship of trust between the Norwegian government and the US administration was an additional asset. Norway followed up with generous ODA grants to the new PLO administration, although Palestine was not among the geographical areas identified as recipients of Norwegian bilateral development assistance.[29] It also agreed to co-ordinate international aid-pledging to Palestine and, in 1993, itself pledged NOK 1,000 million over a five-year period, a commitment it has fulfilled.

In the Guatemalan peace accord, an NGO (Norwegian Church Aid) prepared the ground that at a later stage involved Norwegian diplomacy in tandem with the United Nations. The mediating role was followed up with ODA commitments and the upgrading of Norway's diplomatic presence. Guatemala did not satisfy the poverty criterion and was not among the countries selected for development co-operation, but Norwegian NGOs had been active in the country for some time. However, Central America had been identified as a region to which Norwegian aid was to be channelled, though with particular reference to Nicaragua.

The South African case is different: extensive aid came as a logical consequence of long-standing support for the liberation struggle and humanitarian aid to the victims of the apartheid regime, since the mid-1970s a high-profile component of the foreign policy. ODA has been provided in order to sustain peace and stability at a critical point in time for the new regime (the aid has been tailored to support the

---

29. In 1995–96 (average), the Palestinian-administered areas ranked third among Norway's top ten recipients of bilateral aid (US$45 million) [OECD, 1998: 104].

democratisation process and Norwegian exports). South Africa does not meet the poverty criterion set for Norwegian aid.[30]

This picture of an active role in peace promotion and conflict resolution is dampened by another case – that of Mozambique – illustrating the importance of two structural aspects which influence policy. First, the administrative setting and its predominant perspective matters. Mozambique has been among the programme countries since 1976, in the 1990s among those receiving most bilateral aid. For years, the relations had been handled almost exclusively by the aid administration; the primary perspective, accordingly, was towards development, although the conflict had for years made it almost impossible to pursue 'normal' long-term development. A recent evaluation of Norway's aid to Mozambique [*CMI, 1997*] confirms what might be expected: the policy was rooted in the general principles of aid. It was an expression of political support for the partner government – an indirect declaration of solidarity and help with cushioning the government against the intrusive donor presence, enhancing its autonomy.

However, the evaluators were strongly critical of the MFA's role in the peace process: they found no involvement from the MFA in the negotiations that set the strategic terms for peace and development in the transition period.[31] Lack of capacity and competence within the MFA to deal with the security issues involved may be both the primary and a sufficient explanation, illustrating the second point: competence and capacity are preconditions for an active role and the resources at hand were very limited.

The case illustrates the need for an integrated approach. What emerges as coherent within the old setting may seem less convincing given the new internal aid policy setting that gives priority to peace efforts and, even less so, from a foreign-policy perspective.

Should the trend indicated by the three first cases be attributed to the new quest for coherence or are there other equally convincing explanations? The probability is that 'normal' concerns would have

---

30. Additional cases where political or humanitarian engagements have resulted in more long-term aid commitments include Eritrea, Ethiopia, Namibia, the Sudan, Zimbabwe and ex-Yugoslavia.
31. The evaluation report was critical to the role of the MFA in the peace negotiations: 'While opportunities for influencing those terms arose during the course of implementation, the Norwegian government generally did not respond, and then clearly not in a proactive manner' [*CMI, 1997: x*]. Given Norway's role as a major donor, 'it is striking that there was virtually no engagement by high-level officials in the Ministry of Foreign Affairs in the Mozambican peace process' [*idem*]. 'Overall, Norway's role in the Mozambican peace process was that of a reliable source of finance to programmes whose strategic terms were set by others' [*ibid.: xi*].

led aid in these directions without even the emphasis on policy coherence. ODA has been supplied to fragile democracies emerging after years of authoritarian and repressive rule on earlier occasions too, although the country in question may not have qualified according to the poverty criterion set for the selection of main recipients of bilateral aid. In the mid-1970s, this was clearly demonstrated in the case of Portugal.

The three cases referred to are success stories which, so far, have earned political prestige internationally and (equally important) nationally, which, in turn, reinforces the approach. In several cases, NGOs have been instrumental in preparing the ground before the MFA stepped in. This strategy involves dangers too: as observed by Tvedt [*1995*], important foreign-policy initiatives are taken and implemented by NGOs which, since they are operating with public funds (ODA), may be considered acting on behalf of the state. However, this is not always the case; in some conflicts, different NGOs have pursued different, even contrary, policies. Risk-taking is part of this game; however, initiatives that are unco-ordinated run the risk of backfiring, with repercussions both for peace promotion and development assistance.

In the three cases, ODA has been used extensively to follow up foreign-policy efforts geared towards peace and conflict prevention; the probability is that the support for rehabilitation in conflict-ridden former Yugoslavia will tax future ODA budgets even more severely. Much of the political energy and capacity on the foreign-policy side (to distinguish these activities from the 'ordinary' aid delivery system) have been focused on these cases, in addition to emergency aid. However, most projects within the general area of peace and conflict prevention are of a different kind: hundreds of small projects under the democracy, human rights and peace promotion umbrella, with little, if any, co-ordination. If the democracy and human rights projects referred to above (section IV) are included, this support increased from less than one per cent of total ODA in 1990 to almost five per cent in 1995. The effects of scattered, small projects within this area are seldom evaluated [*Selbervik, 1997; CMI, 1997*].

(iii) ODA and peacekeeping operations. Since the early 1960s, Norway has been strongly committed to UN peacekeeping and has contributed extensively to such operations both financially and 'in kind', providing mediators, observers, health personnel and soldiers. The many conflicts of the late 1980s and early 1990s, most of which erupted within the borders of established states, confronted international society, and the UN in particular, with the challenge of restoring and

maintaining peace. Responding to such demands has been back-breaking for the UN financially; it has also placed a heavier burden on those governments which took part in the operations, including the Norwegian government. To what extent did this situation affect the aid budget?

Peacekeeping and development co-operation have been considered different activities and financed from different sources. The costs resulting from participation in UN peacekeeping operations have been financed from the defence budget, and to some extent been refunded by the UN; one exception has been that the costs arising from Norway's participation in peacekeeping operations in the Lebanon (UNIFIL) were shared equally between the Ministry of Defence and the MFA. However, the monies drawn from the aid budget were not reported as ODA in the DAC statistics (and did not qualify as such). In 1987, Parliament relieved the aid budget of these expenses (and reduced the budget accordingly), the argument being that what could not be recorded internationally as aid (according to the criteria laid down by the DAC) should not be included in the aid budget; this applied to some expenses related to export promotion as well [*Stokke, 1989: 208*]. The decision was rooted in a concern for real aid: to protect ODA from being used for purposes other than those for which it was intended, particularly from potentially resource-demanding activities such as the two identified – peacekeeping and the promotion of Norwegian exports.

Such battles are seldom won decisively. The financing of Norway's military participation in the NATO-led implementation force (IFOR) in Bosnia-Herzegovina may serve as a case in point. Confronted with costs beyond those arising from commitments to UN peacekeeping operations in the region (UNPROFOR), the Brundtland government (Labour) proposed that, in addition to reallocations in the defence budget, some resources should be drawn from the aid budget [*Proposition No.1, Add. No.11, 1995*].

This provoked protests, both from within Labour and from some of the opposition parties. The rebellion within the Labour parliamentary group ended in a compromise which Parliament accepted against the votes of the opposition parties in the centre and on the left.[32]

---

32. The President of Parliament, Ms Kirsti Kolle Grøndahl (Labour), formerly a Minister of Development Co-operation, had stated publicly that the government proposal to use aid money for military purposes came close to immorality. The compromise meant that the 1996 aid budget was not to be touched, while the proposed amount from the 1995 budget (NOK 120 million, not used in 1995 but transferable to 1996) was to be reallocated for IFOR [*Budget Recommendation No.7, Add. No.1, 1995*].

However, policy coherence was not invoked as a justification in any of the main policy documents, nor in the debate in Parliament [*Proceedings of Parliament, 1995*].

What conclusions may be drawn from this case? Aid monies were in fact allocated for military peacekeeping. However, the longer-term outcome may probably be the opposite of what can be concluded on this evidence. The previously established distinction between aid objectives and peacekeeping was re-established in budgetary terms as far as Labour was concerned. It is rather dramatic when the Labour group in Parliament does not support a proposition forwarded by a Labour government, partly justified on ethical grounds. Neither the 1996 aid budget nor the subsequent aid budget were taxed. However, other – complementary – tasks related to peace and stability in the affected region, including relief aid, aid for refugees and rehabilitation, have been a heavy burden on the aid budget. For some years ex-Yugoslavia has been the largest recipient of Norwegian bilateral aid.

(c) Summing up. Since the mid-1980s, aid has become increasingly 'politicised' both at the level of declared policy and of implementation. Promotion of peace and prevention of conflict have become objectives for development co-operation in their own right and not only as part of general policy towards the South; they have also become part of a high-profile foreign policy.

In the declared policy, no incoherence is indicated between this new component of the aid policy and other components. However, added emphasis to one activity means less elsewhere, affecting the distribution of resources as well. To what extent, for instance, has the poverty profile been affected?

The strong emphasis on relief has dramatically changed the flow of aid away from the South to Europe, and away from long-term development to short-term crisis management. Although the poverty profile may be retained, it is a different poverty profile from the one envisaged for development co-operation. Humanitarian aid, relief assistance, support for refugees and rehabilitation have increased dramatically during the 1990s, far beyond the OECD average; in 1996, relief aid alone amounted to 17.2 per cent of total aid.

Other aspects of the new emphasis have affected the poverty profile negatively and removed aid from developmental concerns; ODA for peacekeeping operations illustrates the point. Questions have been raised about whether humanitarian aid always contributes to conflict resolution, or whether it may sometimes exacerbate the problems [*Stokke, 1997*]. The effects on development of this type of aid have also been questioned sometimes.

However, although it has increased during the 1990s, the share of total aid allocated to conflict prevention remains modest – in the area of five per cent in 1996, distributed to a host of small, scattered projects with little overall planning and co-ordination. Is this share consistent with the high profile accorded to it in the declared policy?

V. ANALYSIS AND CONCLUSIONS

Policy co-ordination was considered a virtue long before coherence became a major concern. In the preceding sections, several conclusions have been drawn with regard to the current state of policy coherence from the perspective of development co-operation. In this concluding section, attention will therefore be directed to the more fundamental question posed: what can policy changes in the 1990s tell us about the determinants? Who have emerged as winners and who have been losers?

(1) Democracy and Human Rights: Foreign-Policy Coherence, High-Profile Rhetoric and Modest Resource Allocation

Democracy and human rights have emerged as objectives for development co-operation in their own right. However, although the resources allocated have been increased, the promotion of these objectives has not been a heavy burden on the aid budget. Modest financial resources have allowed the government to maintain a high foreign-policy profile nationally and internationally.

Promotion of these values, human rights in particular, has previously been pursued through international institutions other than those concerned with development and has been pursued by departments in the MFA other than those concerned with development co-operation (see, *inter alia*, Report No.93 [*1977*]). This division coincided with patterns in the international system: human rights and development were considered different activities, with responsibilities vested in separate institutions. Up to the mid-1990s, this specialisation continued: there were three special advisers for human rights – one on the staff of the Minister of Foreign Affairs, one on the staff of the Minister of Development Co-operation and one in NORAD. Little co-ordination and co-operation took place between these advisers and, as far as the aid advisers were concerned, the mandates were not very clear.

The integration of human rights in the aid policy, which started in the mid-1980s, represents a big step towards national foreign-policy coherence. Increased emphasis on human rights made life somewhat more complicated for the aid administration, particularly in respect of bilateral relations; human rights performance became an issue in the dialogue, albeit at a very general level. The value of raising the issue in this setting has been questioned, however, since those who might exert some influence on the human rights situation in the recipient country were not around the table when the aid programme was discussed [Stokke, 1995b].

Who have been the winners and who the losers? The winners in the Norwegian arena are a wide variety of humanitarian NGOs, including the churches, from which development co-operation has obtained the strongest backing traditionally. It is more difficult to identify the winners abroad, since small contributions have been thinly spread over a variety of purposes and organisations. If the declared policy is followed up, the most exposed and poor people in countries with repressive regimes might be affected negatively because of withdrawal of aid. However, guidelines provide means of accommodating this concern. State-to-state aid may, for instance, be switched to NGOs or INGOs and aid may be targeted to specific purposes or social groups. Humanitarian aid is usually exempt from such restrictions.

The potential losers among Norwegian stakeholders are business interests oriented towards countries with repressive regimes. However, the new hurdles are not high, if they exist at all, as demonstrated by business-driven aid to China and Indonesia. The potential losers in the South are authoritarian, repressive regimes which violate human rights extensively and systematically, particularly if the countries are poor and not commercially attractive; it is even less probable than before that such regimes will be included or retained as recipients of bilateral state-to-state aid.

This situation is not entirely new. In 1976, respect for human rights was made a criterion in the selecting of new recipients of bilateral aid. Then as now, adherence to such principles by recipient governments only marginally affected the flow of ODA resources, particularly when commercial interests were involved [Stokke, 1989: 191–200; Stokke, 1995b: 169–76].

A coherence problem is involved. The consistency of Norwegian policy on this account is weak even when aid money is involved. Confronted with industrial and business interests in expanding markets, lofty values do not have the upper hand: the government has strongly supported Norwegian industrial and export interests in China and Indonesia, also from the aid budget (mixed credits, the environmental package) [Stokke, 1999: Chapter 7, 2 and 3]. From the perspective of development co-operation policy, and even from a foreign policy perspective, this may be considered an expression of policy incoherence. From the perspective of narrow trade policy objectives, however, it may be considered an expression of coherence; trade interests are the winners.

In the mid-1990s, the Labour government's rhetoric was adapted to accommodate trade interests; the argument advanced was that such values as democracy and respect for human rights are best served through economic interaction, co-operation and dialogue, not by moral condemnation or boycott. The then Prime Minister did raise human rights questions in the dialogue at high levels, a tricky thing to do in the context of promoting trade; politicians of a less impressive stature than Ms Brundtland might not have had the nerve to do so or might have considered that their vested interests would be in jeopardy. This is all the more so with those who are directly involved in expanding their businesses. In either case, the strength of the argument remains to be proved and the effects are not easily traced.

The subsequent centre coalition government followed up on its predecessors' record; ahead of the King's visit to China in late 1997, human rights were flagged up even more overtly: they were to be pursued in the dialogue even at the cost of business contracts.[33] The government strengthened the human rights profile by appointing, within the MFA, a minister of international development and human rights, a move which may also affect the integration of the two perspectives.

(2) Environments: Foreign-Policy Coherence and Weakening of the Poverty Profile of Aid

Since the mid-1980s, environmental concerns have become objectives for development co-operation in their own right. Except for the case of particular projects, it is difficult to assess the priority given to this concern in financial terms. Until the mid-1990s, its institutional basis within the aid administration has been relatively weak.

The inclusion of ecological concerns as an objective for development co-operation is another expression of increased coherence at the level of foreign policy. Responsibility for global environmental issues is shared between the MFA and the Ministry of the Environment; responsibility for aid for sustainable economic and social development in the South resides within the MFA, with the Minister of International Development and Human Rights, and with NORAD as an implementing agency.

---

33. For the intentions, see Frafjord Johnson [*1998*]. The minister refers to contacts with China as a good example: a human rights dialogue may be pursued at the political level, supported by economic and technical assistance.

Who are the winners and losers? It is difficult to identify the losers, and the obvious winners in the national arena are advanced industries which have been able to make their technology and products attractive as exports promoted by aid under the umbrella of the environment [*Stokke, 1999: Chapter 7, 2*]. However, at the level of recipient countries, the poverty profile of aid has been negatively affected since the recipients are mostly middle-income countries in the South, not the poorest countries (LLDCs, LICs), the traditional partners in Norwegian development co-operation.

(3) Aid and Trade: Foreign-Policy Coherence with Business as the Winner?

Aid and trade have always been connected, although particularly so when the economy has been under pressure or stagnating. The link between aid and Norwegian export interests (commodities and services) has been particularly strong, however, aid tying has been moderate and the return flow small in relative terms.[34]

The linking of aid and exports represents a manifestation of incoherence from the perspective of development co-operation. Most ODA resources earmarked for this purpose have been allocated to mechanisms the primary purpose of which is to promote Norwegian industrial and export interests. The efforts to ensure a high return flow have pursued the same objective. The value for money on the recipients' side has thereby been reduced. However, some of the mechanisms referred to seek to promote development in the South. The priorities reflected in the actual use of resources cannot be portrayed as foreign-policy coherence, given the objectives Parliament has set in its policy towards the South. From a trade policy perspective, however, the concessions to Norwegian export interests, compromising development objectives, represent a manifestation of policy coherence. Concessions the other way around are scarce.

Who are the winners and losers? On the national scene the winners are industrial and business interests, increasingly so in recent years. The various mechanisms direct ODA towards countries different from those chosen for development co-operation, thus weakening the poverty profile of the bilateral aid programme on this account. This is not by coincidence: the mechanisms have explicitly been exempted from the guideline established to ensure the poverty orientation of aid.

---

34. Commercialisation of aid has been a contentious issue in the aid debate, centred around the concept of real aid, with altruism and self-interests as the two poles. The issue is discussed, from the perspective of policy coherence, in Stokke [*1999: Chapter 7, 2 and 3*]. See also Eriksen [*1987*] and Stokke [*1984, 1989, 1991a*].

(4) Conflict Prevention and Peace Promotion: Humanitarian NGOs and International Humanitarians as the Main Winners

Long-term development co-operation and conflict prevention *cum* peace promotion, including peacekeeping, have traditionally been considered different and separate activities. In the 1990s, this changed, particularly in relation to so-called complex emergencies: peace and stability have increasingly been seen as a precondition for development, and vice versa. Moreover, ODA has increasingly been used to promote peace. Humanitarian aid, always considered part of the ODA package, although with a primary objective of its own, constitutes the main link. However, although the border line between international peace operations and development co-operation has become blurred, a distinction remains: ODA is not to be used for military operations with the purpose to restore or keep peace. Responsibility for the two activities is vested in different ministries.

Efforts to establish and sustain peace and stability, to relieve human suffering and to assist in creating sustainable, long-term development are increasingly considered to be complementary activities. Development assistance may represent a necessary follow-up to the other two in facilitating reconstruction and getting a crisis-ridden society and economy back on track again. In pursuing its 'traditional' objectives, development assistance is also seen as an instrument for preventing conflicts from turning violent. In actual practice, however, aid, particularly humanitarian aid, may also be instrumental in creating conditions ripe for conflict, triggering violent conflict and prolonging war and human suffering [*Stokke, 1997*].

No mutuality is involved: it is almost inconceivable that long-term development activities should be funded from the defence budget, even if such efforts might prevent conflicts from becoming violent. The evolving coherence of foreign policy is therefore at the expense of 'traditional' long-term development co-operation objectives.

Who are the winners? In a limited sense, NGOs and INGOs specialising in humanitarian aid and recipients of this kind of assistance, including refugees: to a large extent, dramatically increased relief aid has been channelled through such organisations. The geographical distribution of aid has been affected too. In the 1990s, an increasing share of ODA has been used in Europe for refugees and relief aid. Bosnia-Herzegovina became the largest single recipient of bilateral aid and Mozambique, another country ridden by violent conflicts, became the second largest. Long-term development co-operation has been the main loser.

(5) The Major Trend-setters: DAC and the Multilaterals?

Norway is committed to adapting its policy towards the South, with aid in particular, in line with positions agreed by multilateral institutions, including the Bretton Woods institutions. This commitment is matched by another: to participate actively in these organisations in order to move agreed policy in the direction of Norwegian positions.

How consistent is this position at the level of declared aid policy? As indicated, donor co-ordination may further increase the asymmetric power balance inherent in the aid relationship. In a situation where aid is increasingly used in order to reform policies on the recipient side – as illustrated by the objectives set for first- and second-generation conditionality [*Stokke, 1995a*] – these aspects become of vital importance: a weak developing country is left with virtually no alternative to the policy prescription given by the donors. Although not all recipients of aid are small and/or weak, many are, and aid-dependent as well. A borderline is crossed therefore: advice is in practice transformed into dictates.

To what extent is this in harmony with the objectives set for Norwegian aid and norms and guidelines set for the development co-operation with bilateral partners? And how are these guidelines adapted to serve the new imperative, if it is an imperative?

The commitment to donor co-ordination may run contrary to the guideline prescribing Norwegian aid should be recipient-oriented, the way it was conceived of when first introduced in the early 1970s. As adapted in the early 1990s, when the principle of recipient responsibility was introduced, the two approaches have become more consistent. However, the change of policy is clear, although camouflaged somewhat by the rhetoric (recipient orientation was maintained as a guideline, but made conditional). The main justification provided for the original guideline was based on the normative stance that every country is responsible for its own development. 'Aid neither can nor should replace a country's policy; the role of aid is to support the recipient country's own development efforts. It is not the task of Norwegian aid to counteract a country's own priorities or to repair the effect caused by the policy' [*Report No. 51: 219–20*].[35] However, it follows that in those cases where the authorities pursue a policy that runs contrary to the overall objectives set for Norwegian aid, the continuation of the aid relationship had to be reassessed. The main

---

35. As before, additional justifications were given, including a utilitarian one (if not based on development plans and priorities of the recipient government, no lasting effects would be attained by aid) and one explicitly based on international law: respect for the sovereignty of the recipient country.

mechanism in implementing the dual guidelines of recipient orientation and recipient responsibility, with due regard to the justifications given, was the concept of mutually agreed and binding development contracts between donor and recipient.

How may a commitment to donor co-ordination, with the implications outlined, and the twin guidelines of recipient orientation and recipient responsibility, reflect an internally consistent policy? In the policy documents it is repeatedly stated that the government aims to strengthen the capacity of recipient authorities to steer and co-ordinate foreign aid themselves. However, this, too, may contradict the stated overall policy of donor co-ordination, so perhaps the old ambivalence lingers on in the declared policy?

The basic elements of policy coherence, as outlined by the DAC, include the following objectives [OECD, 1992: 34]: to enable developing countries in the context of a global market economy to:

- build economies and institutions and apply policies which create broad-based political, social and economic development, improving the standard of living for their people;

- participate effectively with mutual benefit in world trade, investment and technology flows; and

- participate effectively according to their diverse capacities in the constructive solution of regional and global problems.

These objectives, according to the DAC, translate into corresponding requirements for OECD policies which provide a frame of reference both for judging the coherence of policies and for formulating proactive strategies:

- strengthening the emphasis of development co-operation on institutional and economic capacity-building in line with the aims and objectives of participatory development;

- strengthening the openness and stability of the world economy;

- strengthening the political and institutional basis for constructive co-operation and partnership with developing countries in order to confront regional and global challenges.

Objectives at this level of generalisation may of course be given greatly varied content when implemented. The various elements are outlined in greater detail in the 1992 report and in more specialised reports dealing with some of the basic dimensions, such as participation and other objectives associated with good governance, democracy and human rights, and elaborated in the strategy for future development co-operation adopted by the DAC in 1996 [*OECD, 1996b*].

If overall objectives at this level of generalisation are taken as the point of departure, however, the Norwegian aid policy finds itself consistent with the norms established.[36] However, norms and overall objectives, although important, represent only the first step in a process towards a coherent policy; the remaining rungs on the ladder are missing.

(6) Donor–Recipient Coherence: The Poverty Profile as the Loser?

The discussion on donor coherence affects donor–recipient coherence as well. Norway is committed to seeking coherence between its bilateral aid policy and the policies and priorities of recipient governments. In the 1990s, however, it is taken almost for granted that the objectives and priorities set for Norwegian aid should constitute the primary basis for development co-operation.

The 1992 White Paper reflects a determination to influence the national policies of the recipients of aid in accordance with what the government (or rather the donor community) deems to be good policies, according to the conventional wisdom of the day. However, some ambivalence remains, as reflected in the justifications given for the twin guidelines of recipient orientation and recipient responsibility.

The insistence on policy coherence on the objectives and priorities set by the donor has several implications for the implementation of aid, which in turn lead to policy dilemmas. This insistence is not entirely new; it is reflected in the rationale behind the criteria established in the early 1970s for selecting the main recipients of bilateral development co-operation: in addition to the poverty criterion, these countries were to have authorities who pursued a development-oriented and socially just policy to the benefit of all sections of society, particularly the worst-off groups of the population. At the time, the primary justification was utilitarian: aid would be more effective if it worked along with the priorities set by the recipient

---

36. In its self-appraisal, the government finds its own policy in conformity with the policies of other Western donors [*Report No.19: 186–7*].

government than against. Another guideline prescribed that long-term commitments should govern aid relations with the countries chosen for bilateral co-operation. The strategy, therefore, had to accommodate changes in the policy too.

In the 1990s, a normative justification was added to the utilitarian one, as reflected in that for the twin guidelines of recipient orientation and recipient responsibility, with the concept of a mutually binding development contract as major instrument. The logic of this stated policy is that when there were important policy diffences between donor and recipient, the continuation of the relationship might be affected. For a development contract to function, the same logic would apply, and if the recipient government did not honour its commitment, then the aid would be discontinued.

This has several implications which might profoundly affect the aid policy, for the aid relationship would not be conceived of as a long-term commitment by the donor: the recipient's policy and performance would be decisive. This might, in turn, affect the planning system (country programmes, with a multi-year plan horizon), and even the very system of having programme countries.

The concept of a development contract never materialised in operational terms. However, the 1995 White Paper [*Report No.19*] proposed a new system geared towards greater flexibility for the donor: country programmes should be limited to the basic needs sectors (human development), and governments in the selected regions should compete for funding from regional development funds. In 1996, however, Parliament restored most elements of the old order [*Recommendation No.229*].

These mechanisms might also affect the poverty profile of Norwegian aid (in terms of recipient countries) if working according to their logic: a weak public administration, which affects the government's ability to plan and implement development activities, is part of the poverty syndrome and affects the effectiveness and efficiency in the follow-up. It follows that over time aid would be switched to systems that are more effective in producing the agreed results; this would involve better-off countries in the South.

In practice, the 'old order' which Parliament tried to restore in 1996 has been weakened. The country programmes have never been the only channel of bilateral aid; however, in recent years their relative position has been weakened. Alternative channels have increasingly been used; in the 1990s, humanitarian and 'commercial' aid, often in combination, has increased and special funds have been established for activities outside the country programmes. In 1998, only 35–40 per cent of bilateral aid was allocated to the country programmes, even when 'multi-bi' aid is included [*Development Today, 1997, No. 21*].

As a consequence, the poverty profile of Norway's bilateral aid has been negatively affected: in 1988/89, 89.7 per cent was channelled to the least developed countries (LLDCs) and other low-income countries, in 1994 this share was reduced to 72.2 per cent [*OECD, 1996c: Table 5*].[37] Although the trend shows a sharp decline, Norway still compares well with other DAC members on this account.[38]

It will be interesting to see if the new minority (centre coalition) government, with its basis in some of the political parties which in 1996 restored the 'old order', will be able to reverse the trend.

(7) Summing Up

The main focus here has been on development concerns: how objectives such as social justice, improved conditions for women and minority groups and respect for human rights have been affected. The picture would be incomplete if left at that: as indicated several times, vested Norwegian interests are influencing decisions that steer ODA transfers too.

The improved coherence in Norwegian policy towards the South has almost exclusively taken place in areas that are financed from the aid budget: promotion of new objectives has taken place at the expense of traditional objectives. Sustainable, long-term development has been the loser. This is a logical outcome within a zero-sum game, the new concerns having been pursued within a fixed financial frame. During the period 1986–95, the aid budget increased somewhat in nominal terms but stayed at the same level in real terms – about US$ 1.1 billion at 1994 prices [*OECD, 1997: A 15*].

In the 1990s, aid policy has been under pressure to adapt to other foreign policy concerns. The quest for greater policy coherence has been instrumental in this regard. 'Traditional' actors and their concerns, including humanitarian organisations and business interests, have been influential. The government's interest in increasing its influence in international and multilateral settings, even outside the

---

37. The share of bilateral aid channelled to lower middle-income countries increased from 5.8 per cent in 1988/89 to 17.8 per cent in 1993 and 26.3 per cent in 1994 [*OECD, 1996c: Table 5*].
38. In 1995–96 (average), 0.51 per cent of the GNP was channelled to LICs (0.33 per cent to the LLDCs) while the DAC averages were 0.12 per cent and 0.06 per cent respectively. Denmark (0.49 per cent of the GNP to the LICs and 0.31 per cent to the LLDCs), the Netherlands and Sweden (0.40 per cent (LICs) and 0.23 per cent (LLDCs)), came closest on this account [*OECD, 1998: Table 7*].

core area of development co-operation, has also been among the main determinants.

The various actors have used the coherence argument for different purposes: while proponents of business interests, for example, have argued for the adaptation of aid objectives, guidelines and practices to serve Norwegian exports and investments proponents of more altruistic interests have used the coherence argument for the adaptation of such trade, investments, and other policies affecting the South to the objectives and guidelines set for development co-operation. Both 'parties' have subscribed to a broader policy perspective and policy coherence, but with different aspirations with regard to the outcome.

This position reflects a feeling of self-confidence and strength on the part of the Norwegian 'aid' constituency. The alternative strategy would be to try to isolate development co-operation as a special case politically, and to argue for administrative solutions that separated aid to the extent possible from being spoiled by vested interests in the donor community and by foreign-policy concerns in the administration and with political decision-makers. In countries where the aid constituency feels that its position is weak, it tends to retreat within this strategy. Some of the conclusions already drawn indicate that the manifest self-confidence of the Norwegian aid constituency has not been fully justified at the level of implemented policy. At the level of stated policy, however, it seems to be more justified, with particular reference to the way Parliament has set the policy over the years.

The new foci and changed priorities have followed general trends among donors. The swings in some fields have been even stronger in the Norwegian case than elsewhere; this applies in particular to humanitarian aid. Humanitarian NGOs, on which strong public support for aid has traditionally been based, have been both trustees and beneficiaries. However, the new course, involving the basic perspective and purpose of Norwegian aid, has been contested.

The 1995 White Paper (Labour) may be seen as the end product of a process to adapt aid policy to other foreign-policy concerns. The government placed Norway's policy towards the South, including development co-operation, firmly within a foreign-policy framework, the main task of which was to

promote Norway's interests in relation to foreign countries which includes contributing towards the world community finding common solutions to international problems. Norway's interests are linked to a number of factors which affect our lives, national identity and international position in various ways. In the Government's view, an active South policy is an important element of our overall approach to safeguard these interests' [*Report No.19: 10*].[39]

This statement reflects, overall, a coherent foreign policy at the level of declared policy, making ODA an instrument in this policy, with the primary objective of serving Norwegian interests.

Part of the parliamentary opposition revolted against this perspective, and one party, the Christian Democrats, to which the present Prime Minister and the Minister of International Development and Human Rights belong, even produced an alternative White Paper [*Christian Democrats, 1996*].

Parliament agreed that policy towards the South should be an integral part of a coherent Norwegian foreign policy. It was in Norway's interest to contribute to solving global common tasks in a responsible manner, where conditions are set in a way which made it possible for developing countries to carry their part of the responsibility and to further their own interests. It should be emphasised, the statement went on, that long-term common interests, therefore, are the basic motive for Norwegian policy *vis-à-vis* the South. Development co-operation should in the first place safeguard rights for the weakest, based on the perception that better distribution would create a world that is better to live in for all. The 'long-term and ideal objectives of the aid policy' should remain 'an important point of departure for Norwegian policy *vis-à-vis* the countries of the South'. It is emphasised that 'development for the recipient is the objective of aid. Development must be seen as a process in which the most basic rights for all are safeguarded at the same time as new opportunities are created for sustainable improvements in living conditions and in the quality of life' [*Recommendation No.229: 7–9*].

This was also a plea for coherence, but the perspective is different from that of the Labour government. It argued for international solidarity based on 'traditional' values of development co-operation. The question remains to what extent the present centre-coalition government will be able to live up to the standards set by its member political parties when they were in opposition.

---

39. This is illustrated through the following observations [*Report No. 19:10*]: 'our security is safeguarded by contributing towards preventing and resolving conflicts, our material well-being is strengthened by active involvement in the world economy, including trade, our natural environment is safeguarded by contributing towards the prevention and solution of international resource and environmental problems, our value base is strengthened by making efforts to promote the norms and principles laid down in the UN Charter and international conventions which set out basic rights and obligations.'

Despite reflecting somewhat different positions along an altruism–self-interest axis and somewhat different priorities as far as 'traditional' and 'new' objectives are concerned, both positions are expressions of humane internationalism, to some extent even reform internationalism.

REFERENCES

Budget recommendation No.7, Add.No. 1, 1995 (Budsjett-innst. S. nr. 7. Tillegg nr. 1 (1995–96)), Innstilling fra forsvarskomiteen om endringer i bevilgningen under forsvarsbudsjettet og Utenriksdepartementets budsjett for 1996 i forbindelse med norsk deltakelse i en NATO-ledet implementeringsstyrke (IFOR) for gjennomføring av fredsavtalen for Bosnia-Hercegovina (Recommendation from Parliament's Standing Committee on Defence Issues on Changes in the Allocations under the Budgets of the Ministries of Defence and Foreign Affairs Resulting from Norwegian Participation in a NATO-Led Implementation Force to Implement the Peace Treaty for Bosnia-Herzegovina), Oslo.

Christian Democrats, 1996, KrF (1995–96), KrFs motmelding. Solidarisk sør-politikk (Solidarity Policy Towards the South), Oslo (undated).

CMI, 1997, 'Evaluation of Norwegian Assistance to Peace, Reconciliation and Rehabilitation in Mozambique' by the Chr. Michelsen Institute in association with Nordic Consulting Group (Alistar Hallam, Kate Halvorsen, Janne Lexow, Armindo Miranda, Pamela Rebelo and Astri Suhrke (project leader)), *Evaluation Report* 4.97, Oslo: Ministry of Foreign Affairs.

Cohen, M.D., J.G. March, and J.P. Olsen, 1972, 'A Garbage Can Model of Organizational Choice', *Administrative Science Quarterly*, Vol.17, No.1.

Development Today, Vol.VII, No.21 (12 December 1997), Oslo.

Eriksen, Tore Linné, 1987, 'Bistand og næringsliv: Hjelp til selvhjelp?' (Aid and industry: Help for selfhelp?), in Tore Linné Eriksen (ed.), *Den vanskelige bistanden* (The Problematic Aid), Oslo: Universitetsforlaget.

Frafjord Johnson, Hilde, 1998, 'Menneskerettighetene hjemme og ute' (Human Rights at home and abroad), *Aftenposten*, 10 Feb. (m), Oslo.

Helleiner, Gerald K., 1990, 'Non-Aid Economic Policies towards Developing Countries: An Overview', in Helleiner (ed.).

Helleiner, Gerald K. (ed.), 1990, *The Other Side of International Development Policy*, Toronto, Buffalo and London: University of Toronto Press.

Hveem, Helge, 1989, 'Norway: The Hesitant Reformer', in Pratt (ed.).

Hydén, Göran, 1994, 'Shifting Perspectives on Development: Implications for Research', in Mette Masst, Thomas Hylland Eriksen and Jo Helle-Valle (eds.), *State and Locality*, Oslo: Norwegian Association for Development Research and Centre for Development and the Environment.

Keohane, Robert O., 1993, 'The Analysis of International Regimes: Towards a European-American Research Programme', in Volker Rittberger (ed.), *Regimes in International Relations*, Oxford: Clarendon Press.

Kooij, Annemiek and René Mevis, 1994, *Cooperation of Advisory Structures for Development Cooperation Policy*, The Hague: National Advisory Council for Development Cooperation – NAR.

Krasner, Stephen D., 1982, 'Structural Causes and Regime Consequences: Regimes as Intervening Variables', *International Organization*, Vol.36, No.2.

Løvbræk, Asbjørn, 1990, 'International Reform and the Like-Minded Countries in the North–South Dialogue 1975–1985', in Pratt (ed.).

MFA, 1992, Strateginotat om demokratistøtte i bistandsarbeidet (A Strategy for Democracy Support in Development Co-operation), Oslo: Ministry of Foreign Affairs (mimeo).

MFA, 1997a, Strategi for kvinne- og likestillingsrettet utviklingssamarbeid 1997-2005 (Strategy for Women and Equal Rights-Oriented Development Co-operation, 1997-2005), Oslo: Utenriksdepartementet.

MFA, 1997b, Strategi for miljørettet utviklingssamarbeid (Strategy for Environment in Development Co-operation), Oslo: Utenriksdepartementet (April 1997).

MFA, 1997c, The National Report of Norway to the United Nations Commission on Sustainable Development 1998, Country Profile, Oslo: Royal Norwegian Ministry of Foreign Affairs (Dec. 1997).

NORAD, 1990, *Strategies for Development Cooperation – NORAD in the Nineties*, Oslo: NORAD.

NOU, 1995:5, *Norsk sør-politikk for en verden i endring* (Norwegian South Policy for a Changing World), Report by the North–South/Aid Commission, Oslo: Statens forvaltningstjeneste/Statens trykning.

OECD, 1992, *Development Co-operation, 1992 Report*, Paris: DAC.

OECD, 1996a, Building Policy Coherence. Tools and Tensions, Public Management Occasional Papers No.12, Paris: OECD.

OECD, 1996b, *Shaping the 21st Century: The Contribution of Development Co-operation*, Paris: DAC.

OECD, 1996c, *Development Co-operation Review Series, Norway*, No.14, Paris: DAC.

OECD, 1997, *Development Co-operation, 1996 Report*, Paris: DAC.

OECD, 1998, *Development Co-operation, 1997 Report*, Paris: DAC.

Pratt, Cranford (ed.), 1989, *Internationalism under Strain*, Toronto and London: Toronto University Press.

Pratt, Cranford (ed.), 1990, *Middle Power Internationalism*, Kingston and London: McGill-Queens University Press.

Proceedings of Parliament 1995 (Stortingsforhandlinger (1995–96)), Nr.13, Oslo.

Proposition No.1, Add No.11, 1995 (St prp nr 1 Tillegg nr 11 (1995–96)), Om endringer i bevilgningen under forsvarsbudsjettet og Utenriksdepartementets budsjett for 1996 i forbindelse med norsk deltakelse i en NATO-ledet implementeringsstyrke (IFOR) for gjennomføring av fredsavtalen for Bosnia-Hercegovina (On Changes in the Allocations under the Defence Budget and the Budget of the Ministry of Foreign Affairs for 1996 Related to IFOR). Oslo: Ministry of Defence.

Proposition No.1, 1997 (St prp nr 1 (1997–98)), Utenriksdepartementet (Ministry of Foreign Affairs), Oslo: Ministry of Foreign Affairs.

Recommendation No.186, 1987 (Innst.S. nr.186 (1986–87)), Innstilling fra utenriks- og konstitusjonskomiteen om Norges hjelp til utviklingslandene (Recommendations by Parliament's Standing Committee on Foreign Affairs and Constitutional Matters on Norway's Aid to the Developing Countries), Oslo.

Recommendation No.229, 1996 (Innst.S. nr.229 (1995–96)), Innstilling fra utenrikskomiteen om hovedtrekk i norsk politikk overfor utviklingslandene (Recommendations by Parliament's Standing Committee on Foreign Affairs on Major Features in Norwegian Policy *vis-à-vis* Developing Countries), Oslo.

Report No.93, 1977 (St.meld. nr.93 (1976–77)), Norge og det internasjonale menneskerettighetsvern (Norway and the International Protection of Human Rights), Oslo: Ministry of Foreign Affairs.

Report No.36, 1984 (St.meld. nr.36 (1984–85)), Om enkelte hovedspørsmål i norsk utviklingshjelp (On Some Major Issues in Norwegian Development Assistance), Oslo: Ministry of Development Co-operation.

Report No.34, 1987 (St.meld. nr.34 (1986–87)), Om enkelte hovedspørsmål i norsk utviklingshjelp. Tilleggsmelding til St.meld. nr.36 (1984–85) (On Some Main Issues in Norwegian Development Assistance. Supplementary Report to Report No. 36, 1984), Oslo: Ministry of Development Co-operation.

Report No.11, 1989 (St.meld. nr.11 (1989–90)), Om utviklingstrekk i det internasjonale samfunn og virkningene for norsk utenrikspolitikk (On Trends in the International Society and Effects for Norway's Foreign Policy), Oslo: Ministry of Foreign Affairs.
Report No.51, 1992 (St.meld. nr.51 (1991–92)), Om utviklingstrekk i Nord-Sør forholdet og Norges samarbeid med utviklingslandene (On Trends in North–South Relations and Norway's Co-operation with the Developing Countries), Oslo: Ministry of Foreign Affairs.
Report No.19, 1995 (St.meld. nr.19 (1995–96)), En verden i endring (A World in Change), Oslo: Ministry of Foreign Affairs.
Selbervik, Hilde, 1997, 'Aid as a tool for promotion of human rights and democracy: What can Norway do?', Evaluation Report 7.97, Oslo: Ministry of Foreign Affairs.
Stokke, Olav, 1984, 'Norwegian Aid: Policy and Performance', in Stokke (ed.).
Stokke, Olav, 1989, 'The Determinants of Norwegian Aid Policy', in Stokke (ed.).
Stokke, Olav, 1991a, 'Norsk bistandspolitikk ved inngangen til 1990-tallet' (Norwegian Aid Policy on the Doorsteps to the 1990s), Norsk Utenrikspolitisk Årbok 1990, Oslo: NUPI.
Stokke, Olav, 1991b, 'Policies, Performance, Trends and Challenges in Aid Evaluation', in Stokke (ed.).
Stokke, Olav, 1995a, 'Aid and Conditionality: Core Issues and State of the Art', in Stokke (ed.).
Stokke, Olav, 1995b, 'Aid and Political Conditionality: The Case of Norway', in Stokke (ed.).
Stokke, Olav, 1997, 'Violent Conflict Prevention and Development Co-operation: Coherent or Conflicting Perspectives?', Forum for Development Studies, Oslo: NUPI.
Stokke, Olav, 1999, Coherence of Policies Towards Developing Countries: Aspirations and Realities, Oslo: NUPI.
Stokke, Olav (ed.), 1984, European Development Assistance, Volume 1, Policies and Performance, Tilburg: EADI (EADI Book Series 4).
Stokke, Olav (ed.), 1989, Western Middle Powers and Global Poverty. The Determinants of the Aid Policies of Canada, Denmark, the Netherlands, Norway and Sweden, Uppsala: The Scandinavian Institute of African Studies.
Stokke, Olav (ed.), 1991, Evaluating Development Assistance: Policies and Performance, London: Frank Cass (EADI Book Series 12).
Stokke, Olav (ed.), 1995, Aid and Political Conditionality, London: Frank Cass (EADI Book Series 16).
Tvedt, Terje, 1995, 'Norsk utenrikspolitikk og de frivillige organisasjonene' (Norwegian Foreign Policy and the NGOs), in Thorbjørn L. Knudsen, Gunnar Sørbø and Svein Gjerdåker (eds.), Norges utenrikspolitikk (Norway's Foreign Policy), Oslo: Cappelen, Akademisk Forlag.
Young, Oran, 1991, Report on the 'Regime Summit', held at Dartmouth College in Nov. 1991, Hanover: Institute of Arctic Studies.

8

Policy Coherence Towards Developing Countries: The Case of Sweden

ANDERS DANIELSON

I. INTRODUCTION

For several of the major donor countries, relations with developing countries are complex and multifaceted. Not so for Sweden. With no colonial history, there has been no painful process of transforming colonial links into relations between independent nations. Sweden's long-standing foreign policy of non-alignment implies that there is little need to secure geopolitical advantage in poor countries. Besides, with an import pattern almost exclusively directed towards rich countries, Swedish trade policy does not appear greatly to affect the destiny of low-income nations.

This might suggest that the issue of policy consistency towards developing countries is less relevant in Sweden than in other donor countries. However, this is not necessarily the case. As will be seen below, coherence has many faces, some of which are relevant even for a nation with few non-aid links to poor countries.

The concept of policy coherence is elusive and not easy to measure; it is, therefore, difficult to see what has happened to 'the degree of coherence' over time. As a starting point, we may use Paul Hoebink's (this volume: Ch. 10) definition of coherence as 'the non-occurrence of effects of policy that are contrary to the intended results or aims of policy'. This suggests that policy coherence may be approached from a number of angles. In the following pages I discuss coherence in Swedish policies from the point of view of official development assistance (ODA). Starting with Swedish issues and

Comments on previous drafts by George Andrén, Yves Bourdet, Kiichiro Fukasuku, Paul Hoebink, Göran Hydén, Lars Johansson, Karl-Anders Larsson, Judith Randel, Mark Robinson and Olav Stokke are gratefully acknowledged. The author owes a particular debt to Gösta Edgren who acted as discussant at the Geneva workshop. Petra Menander and Maria Nilsson supplied able research assistance. The usual disclaimer applies.

moving on to international aspects of Swedish policy coherence, I intend to focus in particular on:

- the internal consistency of different development policy instruments;
- consistency between different objectives for development policy;
- development policy *vis-à-vis* other Swedish policies;
- development policy *vis-à-vis* domestic policies in the recipient country;
- development policy *vis-à-vis* development assistance policy in other donor countries or organisations, particularly the European Union (EU).

Although coherence is a fairly recent field for research, it would be wrong to assume that policy-makers have been unaware of it in the past. Writing about Swedish development co-operation in the 1970s, Börje Ljunggren [*1986: 75–6*] notes:

> A main theme was that Sweden could not limit herself to providing aid and then just close her eyes when it came to the nature and effects of all other forms of dependency ... On the concrete level it meant that the impact of such things as Sweden's agricultural, trade or shipping policies on the developing countries must be brought to the surface in order to ensure that such aspects were duly considered when formulating Sweden's policies in these areas. Doing this, one might avoid giving with one hand, simply to take it back with the other ... .
>
> Ideas like these ... were actually presented by a Parliamentary Commission for the Review of Sweden's International Development Co-operation in its main report, submitted to the Government in 1977 and confirmed by Government and Parliament the following year.

A reasonable conjecture, then, might be that Swedish policy coherence *vis-à-vis* developing countries is high, because the awareness in policy-making circles of the possible dangers of incoherence is high. One of the basic messages of this chapter, however, is that while some aspects of coherence seem to have increased over time, others have decreased, so even if it is possible to argue that policy consistence towards developing countries is an issue less urgent in Sweden than in other donor countries it is, through an analysis of Sweden's attitude towards low-income nations, possible to identify areas in

265

which Sweden might improve consistency, and thus efficiency, in its relation with developing countries.

This chapter is organised as follows. In section II a brief overview of Swedish aid is provided, sections III–VII discuss the five aspects of policy coherence listed above, and section VIII offers some concluding comments.

II. SWEDISH DEVELOPMENT ASSISTANCE

In 1968 Parliament decided to increase the aid budget by 20 per cent per annum in order to reach the target of one per cent of gross national product (GNP) in 1974/75 (compared to 0.3 per cent in 1967/68). Even though this objective was not attained,[1] Sweden became the first donor to attain the United Nations' target of 0.7 per cent of GNP in 1975 [*Ljunggren, 1986; Actionaid, 1995*]. Between 1975/76 and 1994/95 at least 0.9 per cent of GNP was allocated to aid every year and the one per cent target was reached on three occasions. However, between 1989/90 and 1994/95, the average annual rate of growth of ODA in real terms was -0.5 per cent and the budget for 1997 announced a further drop of 11 per cent in current prices [*Development Assistance Committee (DAC), 1996b: 32–3*].[2] Furthermore, these figures underestimate the decline in funds available to recipient countries, as administrative costs in Sweden have increased and as increasing shares of ODA are used for asylum costs.

Swedish development assistance is organised in the following way. An annual Bill is prepared by the Department of International Development Co-operation in the Ministry of Foreign Affairs (MinFA) and approved by Parliament. It contains guidelines for overall development assistance policy and an annual budget. After approval of the budget, responsibility for overall policy decisions, multilateral issues (excluding the Bretton Woods institutions and the European Bank for Reconstruction and Development, EBRD)[3] and co-operation with central and eastern European countries rests with the MinFA. The Swedish International Development Co-operation Agency (SIDA) is responsible for planning, implementation and evaluation of bilateral programmes, including humanitarian aid.

---

1. The one per cent target was very nearly reached in 1975/76, with 0.95 per cent of GNP allocated to aid.
2. In 1997 only 0.7 per cent of GNP was allocated to aid.
3. Responsibility for co-operation with the World Bank and the International Monetary Fund (IMF) rests with the Ministry of Finance, except for IDA which is the responsibility of the MFA.

SIDA was formed in 1995 through a merger of five development co-operation entities: the Swedish International Development Authority (SIDA), the Swedish Agency for Research Co-operation with Developing Countries (SAREC), the Swedish Agency for International Technical and Economic Co-operation (BITS), the Swedish International Enterprise Development Corporation (Swedecorp) and Sandö U-centrum (Swedish Centre for Education in International Development). The basic idea of the reorganisation was that recipient countries should have to deal only with a maximum of two entities, SIDA and the MinFA; moreover, both of these were generally represented in embassies.

SIDA was headed by a Board of Directors and a Director General and operates directly under the government. The agency was set up on a matrix basis with a policy department, four regional departments (Southern Africa, East and West Africa, Asia and Latin America) and five sector departments (Social Development, Infrastructure, Environment, Research Co-operation, and Co-operation with non-governmental organisations (NGOs)). The principle was that projects were developed and implemented by sectoral departments (after consultations with regional departments), leaving the latter to concentrate on strategy and planning.

In the early 1970s a country programme strategy was implemented. Programme countries were originally the major recipients of Swedish ODA and decisions on financial frames rest with the government and are determined on an annual basis. Although the share of programmes in total ODA decreased during the 1980s[4] (so that only approximately half of total ODA now goes to support programme countries), this chapter concentrates on programme countries, mainly because the commitments to these are long term and hence perhaps more prone to policy incoherence. Table 1 lists the programme countries and the amounts they received in 1996.

The list of programme countries changes from time to time. Thus, South Africa and the West Bank/Gaza will be included in the list in the future while Lesotho has been dropped. It is clear from the table that Swedish aid is concentrated on sub-Saharan Africa (SSA): in 1994 almost 50 per cent of total Swedish ODA (including non-programme support) went to that region [DAC, 1996b: 37].

Turning now to the composition of ODA, it can be seen in Table 2 that approximately 60 per cent of Swedish ODA is bilateral and, of the remainder, roughly half is multilateral. To the extent that it is

---

4.   Resources outside country frames are allocated to projects for democratisation, humanitarian assistance, NGOs, and balance-of-payments support.

possible to identify trends with regard to aid categories the most obvious one during the 1990s is that multilateral relief aid has increased at the expense of bilateral aid. To some extent non-relief contributions to multilateral institutions have fallen during the 1990s, but Swedish membership of the EU may well compensate for this.

With regard to ODA by purpose, it is clear that Sweden concentrates its efforts on social sectors. Although this seems to suggest that Sweden stands out among DAC members – in 1994/95 Sweden contributed almost one-third of its ODA to social sectors, while the DAC average is approximately 25 per cent (and within the social category, Sweden concentrates on health, almost nine per cent of total ODA compared to a DAC average of 3.3 per cent) – it will be argued later that this is, firstly, a rather recent phenomenon and, secondly, that it represents a convergence with rather than a move away from the DAC average. The major trend identified in Table 2 is that an increasing amount of ODA goes to social sectors and emergency aid at the expense mainly of multi-sector support and programme aid (budget and balance-of-payments support).

TABLE 1
ALLOCATION TO PROGRAMME COUNTRIES 1996 (SEK MILLION)

Recipient	Amount
Africa	*3 368*
Angola	243
Botswana	98
Ethiopia	264
Guinea-Bissau	41
Kenya	156
Mozambique	407
Namibia	111
Tanzania	436
Uganda	218
Zambia	208
Zimbabwe	248
Asia	*2 291*
Bangladesh	190
Cambodia	344
India	107
Laos	118
Sri Lanka	84
Vietnam	307
Latin America	*924*
Nicaragua	332

Source: SIDA [*1997: 11–13*].
Note: DAC [*1996b: 21*] reports budgeted financial frames for 1995/96, which are approximately one-half of the above amounts.

TABLE 2
THE STRUCTURE OF SWEDISH ODA

	1990/91	1991/92	1992/93	1993/94	1994/95
Aid categories (%)					
Bilateral	66.1	63.4	63.1	61.5	61.8
Multilateral	24.4	20.8	21.0	20.0	20.1
Asylum costs	n.a.	5.0	4.6	5.1	5.0
Emergency	6.5	7.6	7.7	9.1	8.5
Multilateral relief aid	3.0	3.1	3.6	4.2	4.5
ODA by purpose (%)					
Social	20.6	24.6	29.2	31.3	33.9
Infrastructure	7.5	7.4	8.4	9.7	9.4
Economic	11.8	17.1	14.1	13.4	12.2
Administration	4.8	3.6	6.0	7.6	5.5
Multipurpose	19.8	10.0	9.2	4.3	5.7
Emergency	12.2	13.7	18.7	22.6	20.8
Programme	19.8	20.3	10.7	7.6	8.3
Other	3.6	3.4	3.7	3.5	4.2
ODA by region (%)					
North Africa and Middle East	1.0	0.8	0.9	1.8	1.3
Sub-Saharan Africa	60.5	56.6	51.1	47.8	46.0
Asia	24.7	23.6	23.7	23.7	28.0
America	11.4	13.8	11.9	14.4	12.5
Oceania	0.2	0.4	0.1	0.0	0.0
Europe	2.2	4.9	12.4	12.3	12.2

Sources: BSD, various issues; DAC [*1996b*]; Bill to Parliament 1994/95: 100, annex 4; Bill to Parliament 1996/97: 1.

Note: As of 1997 the Swedish fiscal year runs from January 1 in contrast to the earlier practice when it started on July 1. As a consequence, fiscal year 1995/96 is 18 months in length and these data are therefore not commensurable with earlier data.

As for the geographical distribution of Swedish ODA, the most important region is sub-Saharan Africa even though the share has fallen in the 1990s. Of the 18 programme countries listed in Table 1, 11 are in SSA; moreover, most of these are classified as the least

POLICY COHERENCE IN DEVELOPMENT CO-OPERATION

developed countries (LLDCs). Another noteworthy feature of the geographical distribution of Swedish ODA is that several programme countries – for instance, Tanzania, Mozambique, Vietnam and Nicaragua – have carried out social experiments where the market mechanism and private initiative have been given only limited room to manoeuvre.

Sweden's performance with regard to aid tying is good in comparison to other DAC members. In 1992/93, approximately half of DAC aid was partially or completely tied while Sweden tied less than 25 per cent. Most of the tied aid is technical co-operation. As for backflows, Andersson and Hellström [*1994*] report a figure of 50 per cent of the untied bilateral assistance, while DAC [*1996b*] finds backflows from multilateral assistance to be around ten per cent.[5]

As noted in the introduction, ODA is but one aspect of the relations between donor and recipient. For Sweden, however, a small country with few historic links with developing countries, ODA is quantitatively by far the most important relation. Imports from SSA (excluding Nigeria), for instance, amounted to a paltry US$61 million in 1993/94 and the trend is negative.[6] Table 3 sets out total financial flows between Sweden and developing countries. The most remarkable feature of this table – apart from the fact that ODA represents some three-quarters of total financial flows – is the steep fall in direct investments over the past decade: from US$229 million in 1983/84 to US$6 million in 1993/94. It will be useful to keep this observation in mind during the discussion of the composition of ODA below.

5. These figures are impaired by grave measurement difficulties, and comparisons with other countries suggest an overestimation of Swedish back-flow: if the back-flow as percentage of total ODA is divided by the percentage of ODA that is tied, the ratio hovers around 1 for most countries. For Sweden, however, the corresponding ratio is almost 2.5 [*Andersson and Hellström, 1994: Table 2.1*].
6. The average annual rate of volume growth between 1983/84 and 1993/94 was - 7.8 per cent. It should also be noted that Sweden's trade surplus with SSA in 1994 was US$240 million, or almost twice the size of imports [*DAC, 1996b: Tables 13–4*]. An analysis of Swedish exports to low-income countries is provided by Andersson and Hellström [*1994*].

TABLE 3
TOTAL FINANCIAL FLOWS TO DEVELOPING COUNTRIES (US$ MILLION, 1993 PRICES)

	1983/84	1988/89	1992	1993	1994
ODA	1,322	1,696	1,881	1,769	1,752
Other official flows	413	0	3	3	0
of which: official export credits	*406*	*0*	*0*	*0*	*0*
Private non-concessional flows	429	561	333	585	404
of which: direct investment	*229*	*124*	*15*	*34*	*6*
of which: private export credits	*200*	*436*	*308*	*551*	*399*
Private grants	109	128	99	130	125
Total non-ODA	951	689	436	717	529
Total flows	2,273	2,386	2,316	2,486	2,281
as % of GNP	1.41	1.28	1.27	1.38	1.26

Source: DAC [*1996b: Table 12*].

III. INTERNAL CONSISTENCY OF SOME AID INSTRUMENTS

Different forms of aid serve different purposes. The most common form of aid – projects – emanates from the idea that the recipient country is poor because it lacks the resources to grow. Ultimately, this idea can be traced back to simplistic Harrod-Domar models in the early 1940s.[7] As donor funds have been pumped into projects in programme countries with little, if any, effect on the rate of growth or poverty, the capital fundamentalism of the 1960s and 1970s has been questioned and the realisation that government policies and macro-economic stabilisation may be important factors in a successful development strategy has led donors to increase the amount of programme support at the expense of traditional, capacity-expanding project aid.

One obvious source of incoherence is that projects are often implemented on the condition that the donor finances the investment (and possibly recurrent foreign exchange costs) while the recipient finances local recurrent costs. This may put strain on the recipient's budget and, hence, jeopardise stabilisation attempts. Even though the principle that donors should not defray recurrent costs of local projects has not been applied very strictly to Swedish aid [*Edgren, 1986: 58*], inconsistencies in the mix between project aid and programme aid have led to an immense waste of donor resources in several programme countries. Thus, for instance, Doriye *et al.* [*1993*] tell the

---

7. It should be noted that while the simple formula that 'increasing investments will increase growth and eradicate poverty' no longer dominates donors' ideology, it still forms an important part of the accounting exercises in the World Bank's Revised Minimum Standard Model. See Tarp [*1993: Ch.4*].

story of Swedish and Norwegian programme aid to Tanzania, something that started in the late 1970s and was triggered off by a realisation that increasing capacity utilisation should have a higher priority than capacity expansion.[8] This is an example when policy incoherence between different types of foreign aid may not only lower the efficiency of aid, but also jeopardise objectives already met.

In rough terms, foreign aid may be decomposed in two dimensions: according to fungibility[9] (that is, programme versus project aid)[10] and according to donor (that is, multilateral versus bilateral). As set out in matrix form in Table 4, this creates four possibilities; each of these improves one particular aspect of coherence. It will be useful to discuss this in some detail.

Starting with aid when fungibility is high, it is necessary to make a distinction between conditionality and no conditionality, at least at the bilateral level. If support comes as programme aid, without attached conditionalities, the recipient is free to spend those resources as it sees fit. Hence, provided that the recipient has a consistent development plan, such aid leads to coherence between the recipient's policies and programme support. If, on the other hand, bilateral programme support is combined with policy conditionality, there will almost by definition be incoherence between programme aid and domestic policies in the recipient country.[11] On the other hand, the donor is free to impose conditionality in order to force the recipient to take those measures deemed necessary in the donor's ideology (trade liberalisation, privatisation, democratisation). However, unless all donors agree on one set of conditionalities (such as the IMF's) interdonor incoherence in policy implementation is a possibility.

Multilateral programme aid – through the EU or the World Bank – is not likely to be given without conditionalities and the type of conditionality imposed may create an inconsistency *vis-à-vis* development ideology in individual donor countries. On the other hand, multilateral programme aid greatly facilitates donor co-operation as the recipient will automatically be faced with only one set of policy conditionality requirements.

---

8. One measure of the efficiency of new investments is the Incremental Capital Output Ratio (ICOR), which measures how many dollars of investment is required to increase current output by one dollar. A normal value of ICOR is in the neighbourhood of 4 to 7. Danielson and Mjema [*1994: Table 5*], albeit on the basis of rather shaky data, calculate an ICOR of almost 40 for the early 1980s.
9. Fungibility is said to exist when it is difficult for the donor to ensure how aid resources are actually spent.
10. Strictly, project aid contains low fungibility only if the donor, rather than the recipient, identifies the project.
11. The existence of such incoherence is the very reason for imposing policy conditionality.

TABLE 4
COHERENCE AND COMPOSITION OF FOREIGN AID

	Degree of fungibility	
	High	*Low*
Bilateral	(a) No conditionality: Favours coherence with respect to recipient's domestic policies (b) Conditionality: Favours coherence with donor's development ideology	Favours coherence with respect to donor's policy objectives (for example, democratisation, gender equality)
Multilateral	Favours donor co-operation	Favours coherence with respect to other donors' policies at a specific level

Turning now to aid characterised by low fungibility, note that conditionality, in the sense in which the term is usually used, is not necessary.[12] Here it is possible for the donor to finance projects that are in line with the donor's development assistance objectives. Thus, for instance, as Sweden has added two new objectives (environmental concern in 1988 and gender equity in 1996), increasing amounts of Swedish bilateral aid have been channelled to finance projects in these areas. The snag, at least in terms of coherence, is that the donor does not necessarily pay attention to the focus of other donors, so, particularly in view of the limited administrative capacity of recipient governments, the possibility of inter-donor incoherence does not seem remote.[13] Moreover, as noted above, bilateral project aid may jeopardise stabilisation objectives endorsed by donor as well as recipient.

Finally, multilateral project aid provides a possibility for improving donor co-ordination. Although the final mix of projects decided in multilateral organisations is the outcome of donor bargaining (so there is a risk that donors with a weak bargaining position may be supporting projects that are not in line with development objectives), it is possible to pool resources and obtain increased coherence between donors. Moreover, multilateral project support focuses to an increasing degree on sectors rather than projects *per se*. This makes it possible for each individual donor to concentrate on projects that are best suited to fulfil development objectives.

---

12. Certain conditions, regarding, for instance, the financing of recurrent costs may still be attached.
13. Thus, for instance, Helleiner *et al.* [*1995: 14–18*] report that some 2,000 projects and around 40 donors are currently active in Tanzania. Moreover, several donors sidestep the government, preferring instead to set up their own project management systems which makes it difficult to take in the total situation.

One important conclusion from the above discussion is that both project and programme aid may increase coherence, so it is impossible to say, from a coherence viewpoint, which is 'best'. A compromise that is used to an increasing degree by both multilateral and bilateral donors is that of sector support. Sector aid is supposed to be used fully in one sector (such as health or agriculture), but is not necessarily given as projects. This has several possible advantages. First, in contrast to pure project aid, there is not necessarily any contrast between capacity expansion and macro-economic stabilisation, because ideally, the government decides how the support should be allocated between project and programme activities. Second, donor co-ordination is facilitated which presumably puts less stress on the government's administrative capacity. Third, although the support is given with conditionalities attached, these are typically less precise than conditionalities for pure programme support, so inconsistencies between the donors' demands and the recipient government's objectives may be less severe than in pure programme support. As the government is given more room to manoeuvre than in traditional project aid, it seems reasonable that the sense of ownership may be increased. In this sense, sector support may serve to restore some of the development co-operation spirit that was largely lost with the advent of structural adjustment programmes.[14]

IV. COHERENCE OF AID OBJECTIVES

Sweden currently has six official development objectives.[15] With year of adoption in parentheses, they are:

- the growth of resources (1978);
- economic and social equality (1978);
- economic and political autonomy (1978);
- the democratic development of society (1978);
- the sustainable use of natural resources (1988);
- equality between men and women (1996) [*DAC, 1996b: 13*].

---

14. This presumes, however, that the donor and recipient governments agree on development objectives and how to reach them. Specifically, the efficiency of sector support will be considerably reduced in the presence of widespread corruption.
15. Note that although the first four objectives were officially adopted as late as 1978, they have served as unofficial objectives since the famous 1962 White Paper (the 'Swedish bible on development co-operation'). Moreover, understanding the Swedish attitude to foreign aid is enhanced if one keeps in mind that poverty eradication, although not part of the official objectives, is the overriding objective.

As Hveem and McNeill [*1994: 39ff*] point out, several of these objectives are in potential conflict. Thus, for instance, the democratic development of society may hamper the growth of output; economic growth is not always compatible with a sustainable use of natural resources. Hence, there is the potential for incoherence between different objectives and this incoherence has probably increased as the number of objectives has increased. It should also be observed that Sweden has no official objective explicitly designed to fight poverty, even though it seems reasonable to interpret poverty alleviation as *the* objective for Swedish ODA and the six objectives listed above as indicators of the principal objective being met.

Moreover, Sweden also has a number of sub-goals, implicit in the acceptance of the Washington Consensus,[16] regarding, for instance, the design of trade policies, the effects of market liberalisation and the proper role of the state.[17] However, as these goals are implicit, and since there is some debate concerning the actual contents of the Washington Consensus, it is difficult to examine the consistency between the main objectives and the sub-goals. This is rendered even more difficult by the fact that the development model behind the formulation of objectives and development policies is not explicit.[18]

However, a more interesting question is if it would be meaningful, or even possible, to formulate development objectives that are internally consistent. This would probably require the formulation of one overriding objective, and all development assistance should then be directed towards the realisation of this goal.[19] Even if one accepts the interpretation suggested above that Sweden's overriding objective is that of poverty alleviation, it should be recognised that this is a complex process and it is possible to travel different routes to accomplish it. Hence, even with one major objective, it is still possible that sub-goals are potentially inconsistent. Moreover, the history of Swedish aid seems to be one where different objectives have been given first

---

16. Most commentators, however, would agree that the 'three pillars' listed further on (section V) form important parts of the Washington Consensus.

17. A potential conflict here is between the Bretton Woods institutions' emphasis on international integration and trade as a vehicle for growth and the Swedish objective of economic and political autonomy. In the 1970s this objective meant that Sweden accepted a development strategy based on industrialisation behind trade barriers, which clearly is at odds with the current ideology of the Bretton Woods institutions.

18. According, for instance, to Hveem and McNeill [*1994: 23*] 'the Swedish government maintains some distance from what has ... become known as the "Washington Consensus" '. I do not agree, mainly because Hveem and McNeill define the consensus narrowly in terms of 'getting the prices right', while I would opt for a less polemical definition.

19. The Tinbergen rule states that one means is needed for every objective. Hence, it is impossible to use ODA simultaneously to fulfil multiple objectives.

priority at different times, mostly due to the current development ideology [*Hveem and McNeill, 1994: 24*]:

> Our survey shows that these goals have had differing emphasis in the Swedish profile over the years. ... One example of a goal which was subject to temporal subsidiarity is democratisation which was a stated goal in the 1962 White Paper but more or less put aside during the sub-period in which autonomy was emphasised.

To the extent that reduction of internal incoherence is warranted, one possibility without rewriting Swedish development objectives is to prioritise explicitly and to evaluate each project with respect to conflicts of interest. To ensure commensurability and consistency between different aid activities, it is probably necessary to assign weights to the different objectives; to be able properly to evaluate aid activities, it is necessary that the authorities are able to answer questions like 'how great an increase in gender inequality are we prepared to accept, given that this project increases income by such and such an amount?' Such a strategy would take Swedish aid authorities into the world of uncertain evaluations and questionable quantifications and it is far from certain that it would serve to enhance Swedish aid coherence.

Perhaps inconsistency between objectives should be interpreted as the price the Swedish aid authorities pay for flexibility. It makes sense to maintain broad goals that do not have to be changed as knowledge of the development process increases or the ideological wind changes. What seems to be important, however, is that the priority of the various objectives is made clear for each aid activity. Such evaluation of coherence between different objectives might be pursued in various ways, including by means of an inspection panel *à la* World Bank, or a 'development impact evaluation' designed along the lines of environmental impact evaluations.[20]

Finally, it should be noted that if one accepts the idea that the interpretation of the objectives changes over time, it would be possible to argue that Swedish aid policies have been blatantly incoherent during the 1990s. The Swedish consensus of giving aid to a selection of the poorest countries in the world and, in particular, trying to assist the poorest strata of the population no longer seems to be the guiding star of Swedish development policies. As we have seen above, Sweden, along with other major donors, cut aid levels in general, and in

---

20. See Hoebink (this volume, Ch.10) for a discussion of different mechanisms for promoting coherence, and their advantages and disadvantages.

particular to the least developed countries in SSA, preferring instead to give relief aid (for instance, in the former Yugoslavia) and support to countries in central and eastern Europe (CEEC) and the newly independent states (NIS) of the former Soviet Union. In addition, the support going to CEEC/NIS focuses, *inter alia*, on common security [*DAC, 1996b: Box 4*], which is not necessarily in line with the official objectives quoted above.

V. TRADE AND AID

To be able properly to assess how Swedish trade policies are linked to Swedish development assistance policies, it is necessary to have a grasp of how Swedish authorities perceive the determinants of economic growth: what kind of model do they have in mind? It has not been possible to find explicit answers to this question, but a recent study by Hveem and McNeill [*1994*] provides some tentative suggestions.

By surveying the annual Bills presented to Parliament, Hveem and McNeill are able to identify trends in Swedish development policies. Four periods can be discerned, roughly corresponding to the decades: international solidarity in the 1960s; North–South polarisation with a structural twist in the 1970s; market-oriented reforms with support for structural adjustment programmes in the 1980s; and continued support for adjustment programmes but with a growing emphasis on poverty alleviation in the 1990s. What makes this survey revealing with regard to Swedish development ideology is that the authors also consider to what extent Swedish development ideology differs from that of other major donors. Their basic finding is that there has been a gradual convergence, particularly after the growing importance of the Bretton Woods institutions (BWIs) in the 1980s, and it is, in the 1990s, difficult to find donor countries that do not endorse the three pillars of the Washington Consensus: the need for macro-economic stabilisation; the need for a larger tradeables sector; and the need for privatisation and deregulation.

One should thus expect, in the 1990s, that those who formulate the official Swedish development assistance ideology should agree with the following statements as a general characterisation of the situation in developing countries, particularly SSA:

(1) macro-economic stabilisation – low inflation and a sustainable external position – is not sufficient but necessary for the sustainability of economic reforms in the longer term;

(2) export expansion is necessary to achieve sustained growth because (a) increased exports release the foreign exchange constraint and lessen the debt burden, and (b) domestic markets are too small to serve as the principal outlets for many of the commodities that are produced. The most efficient policy instruments for attaining export expansion include tariffication of non-tariff barriers (NTBs), general reduction of trade barriers (to the extent that the government's fiscal balance is not jeopardised), and reduction of discrimination against the export sector;

(3) to make resources available for expansion of the export sector, a more realistic exchange rate policy is often necessary;

(4) the government should concentrate on what it does best. Privatisation and deregulation are essential for transferring resources from public to private ownership and for securing a more efficient utilisation of resources.

If we couple this vision of the development process with an analysis of how Sweden's import protection has changed as a result of EU membership, a pattern emerges that does not suggest increased coherence between trade and aid policies. Even though imports from the poorest countries, and programme countries in particular, constitute a tiny part of Sweden's total imports, there are reasons to believe that Sweden, in 1997, trades less with low-income countries than it did five years ago.

Since import legislation in the EU is rather complicated and often based on agreements with individual countries, or groups of countries, and covering specific commodities, it is difficult to see what has actually happened to the average level of protection in Sweden since it joined the EU. However, for textiles, falling under the Multi-Fibre Agreement (MFA), it seems that Swedish membership of the EU has not affected the situation for countries with LLDC status, while discrimination against textile imports from other African-Caribbean-Pacific (ACP) countries has fallen, since Sweden used to levy tariffs on textile imports from these countries (including some of SIDA's programme countries); this is also the case for Latin American states under the extended generalised system of preferences (GSP), while imports from countries in Asia and Latin America covered by the EU's normal GSP agreement are likely to have been the subject of higher rates of protection since Sweden joined the EU [*Laanatza, 1993: 16ff*]. It should be noted that in this group we find three of SIDA's programme countries: India, Sri Lanka and Vietnam.

As for non-textile imports, the picture is less clear. In Table 5 an attempt is made to summarise Swedish trade policy changes with respect to some important commodities. Except in one or two cases, Sweden pursued free trade with these countries prior to joining the EU. With the caveat that the full implications of the Uruguay Round are not yet known, two conclusions seem pretty straightforward. First, Swedish trade policy is in general more protective in 1996 than it was prior to its becoming an EU member. Second, the geographical pattern has changed markedly. For several of the commodities listed in Table 5, the EU imposes higher tariffs, or lower quotas, than did Sweden prior to joining the EU. In particular, the EU consistently favours ACP countries under the Lomé Convention, implying that commodities (such as bananas, rice and sugar) from some of Sweden's traditional import partners now are the subject of substantially higher barriers. Moreover, in the case of textiles (under the MFA agreement) as well as sugar and beef under the respective EU protocols, imports have been substantially more expensive: while deregulation of textile imports in the early 1990s is reported to have saved Swedish consumers approximately US$500 million per annum [*DAC, 1996b: 25*], membership of the EU forced Sweden to reintroduce quotas. In addition, for some commodities (for example, bananas), the Lomé Convention favours varieties that are less in demand in the Swedish market.

The general pattern emerging from this examination of changed trade policies is that low-income countries in the ACP group have been favoured at the expense of non-ACP countries (although not necessarily with higher incomes). A major feature of the Lomé agreement is that ACP countries are granted quotas which they are seldom able to fulfil. To what extent Sweden's changed trade policies should be seen as a move towards or away from increased coherence is largely a matter of interpretation: from the point of view of global efficiency, incoherence has increased since efficient producers of the commodities listed in Table 5 are now subject to higher trade barriers; from the point of view of poverty alleviation, the increased favouring of LLDCs may be seen as increased coherence, particularly since Sweden also endorses structural adjustment programmes. Hence, the acceptance of structural measures to overcome supply rigidities in the ACP countries, coupled with virtually free access to the Swedish market in the case of goods from these countries, does seem a consistent strategy for attaining income growth via export expansion.

POLICY COHERENCE IN DEVELOPMENT CO-OPERATION

TABLE 5
SWEDISH TRADE RESTRICTIONS ON DEVELOPING COUNTRY NON-TEXTILE EXPORTS,[a] 1991
AND 1996

Commodity Group	1991	1996
Grapes	Zero tariff	Tariff 10%–22 %
Lemon juice	Zero tariff	Tariff 12%–42% + fee
Coffee	Zero tariff	Tariff 4% –12%
Bananas	Fee; zero tariff	Import licence (Colombia, Costa Rica, Nicaragua); tariff ECU 750 /ton within quota and ECU 850/ton outside quota
Tobacco	Zero tariff	Quantitative restrictions
Oranges	Zero tariff	Tariff 4%–20%
Avocado, mango	Zero Tariff	Tariff 4%–8%
Rice	Fee; zero tariff	Import licence. Tariff of 55% on difference between intervention price and world market price. Quotas.
Sugar	Zero tariff	Import license. Tariff ECU 390–490/ton.
Rubber manufactures	Zero tariff	Restrictions and SITC 625 exempted from GSP
Ferro-alloys	Zero tariff	Tariff > 8%
Aluminum	Zero tariff	Tariff 6%
Office machines	Zero tariff	Restrictions
Electrical machinery	Zero tariff	Restrictions
Telecommunications equipment	Zero tariff	Restrictions
Passenger motor cars	Zero tariff	Quota
Cycles	Zero tariff	Tariff 17%
Travel goods	Zero tariff	Quotas
Footwear	Excluded from GSP; tariff 14%	Restrictions (China; South Korea); tariff 8%–20%
Watches and clocks	Zero tariff	Tariff 6.3%; restrictions
Toys, sporting goods	Zero tariff	Restrictions; tariff 4.9%–10%
Imitation jewellery	Zero tariff	Restrictions
Tuna fish	Zero tariff (MFN)	Tariff 24%–25%
Canned mushrooms	Tariff 15 %	Tariff 23%
Canned pineapple	Zero tariff	Tariff 12%–15%

Sources: National Board of Trade [*1995*]; Jordbruksverket [*1996*]; Laanatza [*1993*]; EU [*1995*]; Statistics Sweden.

a Significant imports to Sweden, excluding textiles which are discussed in the text. Excluded commodity groups are either relatively insignificant or no changes in restrictions have takes place due to EU membership.

TABLE 6
TRADE WITH DEVELOPING COUNTRIES

(a) Imports from ACP and South Asia (percentage of total imports)			
	1990	1992	1993	1995
France	2.8	2.4	2.4	2.4
Germany	1.7	1.4	1.4	1.3
Spain	3.6	3.1	2.7	2.7
United Kingdom	2.5	3.7	3.5	2.7
Sweden	0.5	0.7	0.6	0.6

(b) Programme countries' exports to Sweden (percentage of total exports)			
	1981	1985	1990	MRE
Angola	0.44	0.27	0	0
Botswana	0	0	0	0.01
Ethiopia	0.05	0.10	0.10	0.09
Guinea-Bissau	0.64	0.36	0.88	0
Kenya	1.74	2.55	2.36	1.72
Mozambique	0.06	1.09	4.96	0.34
Tanzania	1.19	0.34	0.37	0.65
Uganda	0.05	0	0.02	0.01
Zambia	2.67	1.70	0.17	0.15
Zimbabwe	0.42	0.70	0.59	1.08
Total	0.95	0.76	0.42	0.46

Sources: Statistics Sweden; IFS [*1996*].

Note: 0 in Table 6(b) means less than 0.01 per cent.

It should be noted, however, that Sweden's trade relations with LLDCs in general, and programme countries, in particular, are small and have actually been falling over time. As Table 6 shows, around 0.5 per cent of Sweden's total imports emanates from the poorest regions of the world – that is, SSA and South Asia – compared to figures of 2.5 to 3.5 per cent for France, Spain and the UK. The low Swedish figure is most likely a reflection of Sweden's lack of historical links with the developing world (and possibly geographical distance). Moreover, while almost one per cent of the SSA programme countries' export ended up in Sweden in 1981, the corresponding figure for 1993 was less than 0.5 per cent (data supplied by Statistics Sweden). While these figures may seem to suggest that Sweden takes away with one hand, through import protection, what it gives with the other, via ODA, the truth is that countries with least developed country status have virtually free access to the Swedish market, and the dismal performance is explained by two factors: (i) some of their export products are not in demand in Sweden; and (ii) the problem is one of supply in the LLDCs, not of demand in Sweden. As noted above, by combining support for structural adjustment programmes with a policy of zero-tariff imports, Sweden exhibits a coherent combination of trade and aid policy *vis-à-vis* LLDCs.

Protectionism, then, in the usual sense of the word, simply does not exist in Sweden *vis-à-vis* programme countries. What does exist is a subsidised agricultural sector; indirectly, therefore, African food producers are discriminated against. Even though Sweden's agricultural sector has probably become more subsidised owing to EU membership, the Uruguay Round agreed that subsidies to agriculture and exports must be substantially cut. Although fears have been expressed (see, for example, Bach-Friis [*1994*]) that this will lead to increased world market prices for food and thus hurt the poor, food-importing countries of sub-Saharan Africa, it is useful to bear in mind that the estimated gains from agricultural liberalisation greatly exceed the losses, so compensation mechanisms may be devised [*Goldin and van der Mensbrugghe, 1992*]. Moreover, even if food-importing countries are hurt in the short run (by higher food prices), in the longer run liberalisation should stimulate increased production in these countries (particularly if the structural adjustment programmes are successful); hence, it is possible to conclude from the point of view of official development objectives, that it makes sense for Sweden gradually to liberalise its domestic agriculture as this is likely to help secure the achievement of one important goal, namely, the promotion of political and economic autonomy in recipient countries.

Official Swedish development ideology endorses the Washington Consensus where exports play a strategic role. Coherence, then, between trade and aid policies primarily implies access to markets in Sweden. As noted above, Sweden allows virtually all exports from programme countries to enter the Swedish market without trade barriers; Sweden's membership of the European Union does not appear to have changed things all that much. Another aspect that may be of importance for policy coherence in the future is that parts of Swedish trade policies are formulated in the Ministry of Foreign Affairs, which also has responsibility for formulating development assistance policy. Sweden has long relied on informal contacts within and between ministries and agencies to ensure consistency between policies [*DAC, 1996b: 22–4*], even though the transfer of responsibility of certain trade issues to the Ministry of Industry and Commerce may weaken consistency between trade policies and development policy.

VI. SWEDISH AID VERSUS RECIPIENTS' POLICIES

As noted above, official Swedish development ideology (as reflected, for instance, in the annual Bills to Parliament) has changed drastically and frequently since the early 1960s. A rather rough characterisation might be that, in the 1960s, Sweden supported sector and development strategies formulated by the recipient country, while, in the 1990s, it fully endorses the Washington Consensus.[21]

This suggests that the degree of coherence between Swedish development assistance policies and domestic policies in the recipient countries has fallen over time. This impression is strengthened by the fact that Sweden regards a working Enhanced Structural Adjustment Facility (ESAF) between the recipient country and the IMF as a prerequisite for releasing programme support.[22] Policy conditionality may be seen as a means of forcing the government to accept policy measures that it would otherwise not have adopted. Hence, conditionality may be interpreted as an attempt to resolve the problem of incoherence between the Washington Consensus and policy objectives in the recipient country.

However, conditionality as designed by the Bretton Woods institutions also has drawbacks. In particular, a strict enforcement of the conditionality clause may render it more difficult to attain stabilisation objectives and, following the argumentation of the Washington Consensus, make it more difficult to realise longer-term goals. An example will serve to explain this point and to illustrate that Sweden attempts to avoid this obvious incoherence.

In terms of ODA as a percentage of GDP, Tanzania is one of the most aid-dependent countries in the world. At an ODA/GDP ratio of close to 50 per cent in 1992, Tanzania receives significantly more aid in relation to income than do either other countries in SSA or other LLDCs [UNDP, 1995; IBRD, 1996]. Of the US$895 million received in foreign aid in 1994, around US$140 million – some 15 per cent – were in the form of programme aid, mainly budget support.

Now conditionality, as set out in the ESAF agreement, concerns programme support only. In most cases, funds for projects, humani-

---

21. See Anell [1986] for a discussion of the theoretical foundations of Swedish development assistance.
22. The overwhelming majority of donor countries follows this policy. Also note that a running ESAF is necessary for participation in Paris Club negotiations regarding bilateral debt rescheduling. However, although today Sweden accepts policy conditionality as being necessary this is a fairly recent phenomenon. Discussing Swedish attitudes towards conditionality in the 1970s, Edgren [1986: 52] notes 'The Swedish position on policy level conditions has always been that it is improper, if not impossible to impose policy conditions on the government of a recipient country'.

tarian assistance and technical co-operation continue to flow in irrespective of the government's compliance with regard to ESAF conditionality. Conditionality is of the 'all-or-nothing' type, that is, if the terms in the ESAF are honoured, funds for supporting the budget will be forthcoming; if the conditions are not honoured, no funds are available.

It is clear as daylight that this set-up may create a certain irregularity in the financing of Tanzania's budget. It has been calculated [*Danielson, 1996*] that budget support in 1994 amounted to some eight to ten per cent of expected revenues; to put it differently, programme aid financed roughly 80 per cent of the budget deficit. The risk of a vicious circle (or perhaps a Catch-22) is obvious: the country receives no programme aid because it has failed to fulfil policy conditionalities and it cannot honour its obligations as set out in the ESAF because it lacks the funds to do so.

Given that the basic tenet of the Washington Consensus is correct – that macro-economic stability is necessary for the successful completion of adjustment programmes – this policy is obviously incoherent. By refusing to finance the budget deficit by providing programme support, donors may force the country to resort to inflationary financing which, in turn, may render stabilisation (and thus compliance with policy conditionalities) even more difficult to attain.

The problems of 'all-or-nothing' conditionality has been recognised by the Swedish authorities. In an attempt to avoid irregularities that may jeopardise stabilisation attempts and at the same time to retain incentives for the government to honour its obligations, SIDA has proposed a system called 'matching funds'. The basic idea is very simple. Instead of programme aid on an all-or-nothing basis, the proposal is for assistance to be given in relation to the government's performance. If, for instance, one policy condition is that tax revenues should be increased by ten per cent but the government succeeds in increasing them only by seven per cent, Sweden will release 70 per cent of its budgeted programme aid. The idea, of course, is that several donors co-operate – which would be administratively very simple: since programme funds are fully fungible, differences in donor priorities do not enter the picture – so that a substantial part of all programme aid may be released in relation to government performance in order to avoid the implementation of stop-go policies inherent in the current system.[23]

---

23. Although the basic idea of matching funds seems pretty straightforward, there are a number of problems that are not solved yet. Thus, for instance, what indicators should Swedish programme aid relate to? See Danielson [*1996: 25ff*] for a discussion.

Development co-operation – in the sense of 'giving aid' – has, as far as Sweden is concerned, become a more unequal process over time. The general view in the 1960s was that development co-operation was 'mutual influence in a spirit of understanding' [*Ljunggren, 1986: 69*]. Conditionality, as we now understand the term, was not thought to be necessary:

> The idea of country programming as seen by Sweden around 1970 was that one should choose to co-operate only with governments that pursued policies that efficiently served the general development objectives of growth, equity, democratisation and independence. Once you had chosen partners, there was no need to twist their arms in order to change the overall development strategy to suit the Swedish projects – on the contrary, *any attempts to impose policy measures on a recalcitrant government would be counter-productive* [*Edgren, 1986: 52*; emphasis added].

With the growing realisation in the early 1980s that 'the' development problem was probably not one of capital scarcity, Sweden – and most other major donors – moved towards a position where the recipient government's policies were not taken as given but, in many cases, were seen as part of the cause of the problem. Development assistance in the form of programme aid with attached policy conditionality became a lever that was used to change the government's policies towards what in the donor community was perceived to be a sustainable development strategy.

This is not the forum for analysing to what extent the donor community is correct; but it should be noted that Sweden's relations with its programme countries have moved a long way from the buzz-words of the 1970s: 'mutual influence' and 'concerned participation'. One important consequence of the growing incoherence between Swedish aid policies and the domestic policies of recipient countries is that efficiency in the utilisation of foreign aid may have decreased. As recipient governments lose their sense of 'ownership' and when the 'partnership' becomes quite lopsided, there may be a growing realisation in Dar-es-Salaam, Hanoi and Managua that development strategies formulated in the planning ministries and stabilisation plans designed in the treasuries are less important than ideological shifts in the donor community and, ultimately, in Washington.

VII. COHERENCE BETWEEN DONORS: SWEDEN AND THE EU

Even though Sweden seems to have achieved a high degree of coherence between different policies (partly because its non-aid relations with low-income countries, particularly in Africa, are few), much remains to be done. This conclusion is confirmed by the DAC's [*1996b: 26*] review of Swedish development co-operation:

> it is evident that the Swedish government administration has used formal and sometimes informal channels in working towards policy coherence *vis-à-vis* developing countries. The reorganisation of the MinFA, effective as of 1 July 1996, has not at the time of this report been settled, and the location of certain administrative functions remains to be clarified. Much of Sweden's policy coherence has been achieved through *ad hoc* solutions and informal agreements. Against the background of increasing demands in the policy coherence arena, better adapted structures are necessary.

Swedish membership of the European Union has far-reaching consequences for the organisation of Swedish aid. First, 45 per cent of the Community's aid is being allocated through the European Development Fund (EDF) and this necessitates a reallocation of the Swedish aid budget. Second, the Commission is calling for particular co-ordination in the areas of poverty reduction, food security, health and education. Membership requires six per cent of Swedish ODA to be channelled through the EU; this figure is likely to increase to ten per cent in the near future.[24] In addition, there will be an increased demand for staff. Since virtually no funds have been provided, additional funds are required if Sweden is to play an active part in forming and implementing the EU's aid policy – in view of recent cuts in the Swedish aid budget, it seems likely that funds for the EU will be forthcoming by means of cuts in other areas. Third, it has never been perceived as necessary in Sweden to construct preferential trade arrangements as in the Lomé Convention. Even though it is uncertain what will happen after the expiry of Lomé IV in the year 2000, as Table 5 shows, Sweden has had to change its trade policies substantially. Fourth, the objective of EU aid differs from those of Swedish aid and it remains to be seen to what extent Sweden will be

---

24. Approximately US$99 million – of a total ODA budget of US$1,873 million – have been allocated to the EU budget for ODA activities for 1996. So far, allocations to the EU budget have been financed by cuts in the bilateral budget.

able to convince other members of the importance and logic of Swedish objectives. Fifth, the geographical distribution of aid is very different in the case of the EU. Several of the strong members have historical links with countries in Africa, Asia and America; it is quite possible that the objectives for giving aid are less altruistic in the EU: for some countries, commercial policy, security and geopolitical issues, and domestic industrial policy are important determinants of the volume and distribution of aid.[25]

As noted, Sweden currently has six official development objectives. As for the EU, Article 130u of the Maastricht Treaty stipulates the following objectives: sustainable development with particular emphasis on the most disadvantaged; integration in the world economy; participation in the campaign against poverty; and consolidation of democracy, the rule of law, human rights and fundamental freedoms [*DAC, 1996a: 61*].

It is not obvious that the two sets of objectives are compatible. Certainly, as the DAC [*1996b: 23*] notes, the objectives of Sweden and the EU coincide, particularly with respect to structural adjustment, gender issues, democratisation and environmental concerns. However, the Swedish objective of autonomy may well clash from time to time with the EU objective of integration in the world economy.

As for programme countries, the Swedish principle is that it is difficult both to acquire programme country status and to lose it. The idea behind this principle, of course, is to ensure stability in the aid relationship. In 1994, Swedish aid allocations were chosen on the basis of five criteria [*DAC, 1996b: 14*]: development towards the market economy; democracy; respect for human rights; efficiency of aid; and low share of military expenditures in the budget. The fifth criterion has no equivalent in the EU framework, although countries blatantly violating human rights have lost their EU support [*DAC, 1996a: 46*].

---

25. No data are available on the status of tying in the Union, but aid to ACP states is tied to procurement in the 70 ACP states and the 15 EU states and aid to the ALA-MED countries (Asia-Latin America-Mediterranean) is tied to procurement in EU states [*DAC, 1996a: 53*]. Moreover, over three-quarters of Swedish aid was untied in 1993/94 while only half of DAC aid was similarly untied [*DAC, 1996b: 43*].

TABLE 7
GEOGRAPHICAL DISTRIBUTION OF ODA: SWEDEN AND EU (PERCENTAGE)

	Sweden				European Union	
	1983/84	1994	1996		1983/84	1994
LLDCs[a]	48.9	40.9	40.4		54.3	34.3
Other LICs[b]	44.9	25.0	29.2		24.5	13.2
Lower MICs[c]	3.3	32.2	24.9		18.7	48.2
Sub-Saharan Africa	54.0	45.6	34.9		60.1	47.7
Asia	39.6	27.1	19.0		18.3	10.2
Latin America	4.6	11.2	9.9		4.6	10.3
MENA[d]	1.9	4.8	6.7		9.0	16.1
Europe	0	11.3	6.0		2.6	14.7
Others[e]			23.5			

Sources: Figures for 1996: SIDA [*1997: 10–20*]. The rest: DAC [*1996a: Table 11*];
DAC [*1996b: Table 8*].
[a] Least developed countries.
[b] Other low-income countries.
[c] Lower middle-income countries.
[d] Middle East and North Africa.
[e] Includes global assistance, unspecified items and administrative costs.

However, some convergence seems to take place. Table 7 shows the geographical distribution of ODA for Sweden and the EU in 1983/84 and 1994 (and in addition for Sweden in 1996) and it is obvious that the changes in the geographical pattern of ODA are similar. Several trends may be identified. First, the shift away from LLDCs and other low-income countries (LICs) towards lower middle-income countries (MICs). In view of the emphasis put on poverty eradication in both Sweden and the EU, this is somewhat difficult to understand, although disappointment with aid effectiveness in LLDCs may be one explanation (although the drastic fall of Swedish ODA to LLDC observed in the second half of the 1980s seems to have come to a halt during the mid-1990s). Second, the shift away from SSA. For the EU this probably means shifting resources to North Africa and the Middle East (possibly as a result of preferential trading arrangements), while in Sweden's case global allocations have been increased – and to some extent also allocations to Europe. Here, we observe the same trend in the EU, mainly reflecting disaster relief to the former Yugoslavia.

A systematic comparison of the sectoral distribution of ODA from Sweden and from the EU is not possible as the latest available information from the Union relates to 1987. However, since the EU accounts for roughly two-thirds of DAC ODA flows, a comparison between Sweden and the DAC average suggests the possibility that with regard to sectoral priorities, too, Sweden is converging towards the DAC average distribution and hence probably towards the pattern displayed by the Union (Table 8).

While Sweden concentrates more of its efforts on social sectors than the average DAC member, this is a rather recent phenomenon: in the mid-1980s less than 20 per cent of Sweden's ODA was allocated to these sectors compared to a 1992/93 DAC average of almost 25 per cent. In fact, for all the items in Table 8, apart from multi-sector support and relief aid, there has been a convergence in the sense that in those cases where Sweden's share of support in 1983/84 exceeded the 1992/93 DAC average, its subsequent support for that item has diminished, and vice versa.

TABLE 8
SECTORAL DISTRIBUTION OF ODA: SWEDEN AND DAC AVERAGE (PERCENTAGE)

	Sweden		DAC average
	1983/84	1993/94	1992/93
Social sectors	19.3	32.4	24.6
Economic sectors	10.0	13.0	17.6
Production sectors	21.7	13.0	14.5
of which: Agriculture	12.4	10.9	8.2
Industry	8.8	1.9	4.5
Multi-sector	6.5	7.8	4.1
Relief aid	11.5	23.0	5.9
Support to NGOs	3.3	0.1	1.5
Unallocated	23.7	0.1	4.5

Source: DAC [1996b: 36].
Note: Columns do not add up to 100; minor entries excluded.

Historically, Sweden has had few links with low-income countries compared to the major donors in the EU. This means that Swedish development assistance is likely to be less influenced by commercial, security, geopolitical and other considerations than is assistance from some other countries in the Union. This is likely to be one of the major issues as Sweden tries to influence the EU's development cooperation policies: will it be possible for Sweden to maintain its 'clean record' and 'the image of an aid programme untainted by egoistic foreign policy considerations' [Palmlund, 1986: 110]? The evidence in this chapter suggests that the answer is likely to be in the negative: there is a convergence among donors (and Sweden is adapting to DAC averages, not vice versa), both with regard to the geographical and the sectoral distribution of aid, away from the poorest countries and productive sectors and towards lower MICs, social sectors, and temporary aid, such as relief aid. While this is likely to increase coherence between donors, it is not necessarily in accordance with Swedish development policy objectives, particularly not the emphasis on poverty eradication and economic growth. Moreover, the Swedish objective of economic and political autonomy may well conflict at times with the EU's objective of closer integration in the world economy.

As for consistency at the practical level of implementing projects, it is well known that donor co-ordination often leaves something to be desired. Some donors work out project priorities in close collaboration with the recipient government; others avoid the government entirely, either by formulating priorities themselves and simply sticking to these or by supporting NGOs. Moreover, in some recipient countries, particularly in SSA, substantial resources enter the country as commodity support and technical co-operation without passing through the Ministry of Finance.[26] Differences regarding procurement practices, standards for project implementation, responsibilities for field staff, and donor prioritisation render co-ordination even more difficult to achieve.

If donors perceive that co-ordination would be valuable, several simple measures should be considered. First, the meetings of the Consultative Groups (CG) and the Paris Club should be co-ordinated. The CG meetings deal with new aid commitments and the Paris Club with debt relief – two sides of the same coin. Both groups meet in Paris; yet there seems to be no attempt to co-ordinate the outcomes from the two meetings.[27] Second, donors and the recipient government should agree on a core investment plan. Third, it seems that increasing the share of multilateral project aid would be a method for circumventing the fact that donors have their own priorities, not necessarily in accordance with those formulated in the Planning Commission in the recipient country. From this point of view, the falling share of multilateral aid given by Sweden (see Table 2) is worrying, although

---

26. Tanzania is a case in point. See Helleiner *et al.* [*1995: 20ff*].
27. In view of the recent HIPC initiative, it seems even more urgent that debt relief and aid activities are co-ordinated, particularly since HIPC calls for tight conditionality and massive adjustment efforts. For a discussion, see EURODAD [*1996*] and Woodward [*1996*].

membership of the EU may preserve coherence between Swedish and other EU donors' development policies.[28]

VIII. CONCLUDING REMARKS

The basic message of this chapter is that for a long time Sweden has been relatively coherent in its policies towards developing countries. To some extent, this is because its non-aid relations with low-income countries are rather sparse: trade, particularly with the low-income countries of sub-Saharan Africa, is small, and shrinking, and direct investments constitute a tiny part of the resource flow from Sweden to LICs. Moreover, since Sweden has no colonial history, historical links with today's poor countries were virtually limited to missionary contacts (see Heppling [1986] and Andersson [1986] for further information).

However, coherence does not exist in all areas and the most obvious change in Sweden's attitude towards programme countries is probably the move away from giving aid on the recipient's terms. As we have seen, the philosophy in Sweden during the 1960s and 1970s was that the recipient should be allowed to formulate his own development strategy and Sweden assisted with aid (see the quotation towards the end of section VI). The attitude today seems to be that one of the major obstacles to development is bad governance, so policies have to be changed before substantial moves towards Sweden's development objectives can be achieved. In other words, incoherence between Swedish ODA policies and recipient countries' development strategies has increased markedly since the early 1980s. Recent discussions at SIDA, however, concerning forms of conditionality indicate that there is an awareness that IMF-style conditionality may create problems.

---

28. It should be noted, however, that one potential source of incoherence in the future is that while Sweden seems to be moving away from programme aid (cf. Table 2), the Union considers increasing programme aid at the expense of project aid a possible strategy for post-Lomé IV relations with the ACP countries. See, for instance, the European Commission [1996: 71–4]. Although this is not the forum for analysing the pros and cons of the Swedish position in detail, it should be noted that the EU's position most likely is based in the recent surge of foreign direct investments to developing countries: private companies take care of whatever profitable investments that can be identified and bilateral donors concentrate of macroeconomic stabilisation and relief aid. The Swedish position most likely reflects Sweden's focus on Africa: here, foreign direct investments are still negligible and bilateral project aid still has a role to play.

As for the other four questions posed at the beginning of this chapter, the analysis suggests the following answers:

— The mix of aid instruments has changed drastically and it is difficult to generalise as to whether coherence has increased or not — it has to be determined on a case-by-case basis. In any case, stabilisation and capacity utilisation are gaining priority at the expense of capacity expansion. As far as the non-African part of the poor world is concerned, this is probably a logical reaction to the surge in foreign direct investments experienced during the past 15 years or so. For Africa south of the Sahara, however, things look more bleak. Foreign investments are not forthcoming — at least not at rates comparable to those in other parts of the world — and lack of capacity may still be a major problem in several countries. From this point of view, the reluctance of Sweden to follow the World Bank and the EU and, instead, to prioritise programme aid at the expense of project aid, indicates an awareness of the problem and shows coherence with the overriding objective of fighting poverty.

— Official development policy objectives are not internally consistent; this is the price paid for flexibility. To some extent, it reflects the fact that the overriding objective of Swedish ODA is poverty alleviation: since this is a complex process, sub-goals, such as those formulated by Sweden, are, more or less necessarily, mutually inconsistent. To the extent that this inconsistency is perceived as a problem, one possible solution is to make explicit the major objective for each aid activity and, if possible, prioritise the others. It is doubtful, however, to what extent such exercises would solve practical problems.

— Sweden's development policies are relatively coherent with other Swedish policies, mainly because Sweden's relations with programme countries are more or less limited to development assistance. Membership of the EU has turned Swedish trade preferences in favour of countries under the Lomé Convention. Since these countries are often plagued by supply rigidities that hinder them from fulfilling the EU's relatively generous quotas, the combination of Sweden's EU membership and its support for structural adjustment programmes may be perceived as a move towards increased coherence. On the other hand, joining the EU also implies that Sweden has increased tariff barriers *vis-à-vis* imports from non-ACP states. As these seem to be more efficient in producing some commodities traditionally imported by Sweden, EU membership also means a move away from trading with the most efficient producers. This may change as the full implications of the Uruguay Round become known.

– Sweden's development policies have converged towards those in other donor countries, with respect to geography as well as sectors. However, Sweden seems reluctant to substitute programme aid for project aid at the rate suggested by the EU's Green Paper [*European Commission, 1996*]. To what extent Sweden will side with donors or recipients in international organisations (World Bank, IMF, WTO, EU) remains to be seen. However, Sweden is an active proponent of increased donor co-operation, participating in several formal and informal organisations for donors. It is not clear, however, if donor co-operation should take place in international forums or on a country-by-country basis. Given that Sweden is a small country, but a relatively large donor, it may be that the influence of Sweden will be stronger if donors co-operate on a case-by-case basis.

REFERENCES

Actionaid, 1995, *The Reality of Aid 95. An Independent Review of International Aid*, London: Earthscan.
Andersson, C., 1986, 'Breaking Through', in Frühling (ed.).
Andersson, T. and H. Hellström, 1994, *Links Between Development Assistance and Donor Country Exports – The Case of Sweden*, Stockholm: SASDA, Ds 1994:58.
Anell, L., 1986, 'Images of Distant Countries. Reflections on the Theoretical Foundations for Sweden's Development Co-operation Policies', in Frühling (ed.).
Bach-Friis, C., 1994, *Skuespillet – Hvordan u-landerne kan komme i klemme i GATT-aftalen* (The Drama – How the LLDCs May Lose from the GATT Agreement), Copenhagen: Nord/Sydkoalitionen.
BSD, *Bistånd i siffror och diagram* (Foreign Aid in Figures and Graphs), Stockholm: SIDA, annual.
DAC, 1996a, 'European Community', *Development Co-operation Review Series*, No.12, Paris: Development Assistance Committee, OECD.
DAC, 1996b, 'Sweden', *Development Co-operation Review Series*, No.19, Paris: Development Assistance Committee, OECD.
Danielson, A., 1996, *Tanzania: The Impact of Balance of Payment Support*, Macroeconomic Report 1996:10, Stockholm: SIDA.
Danielson, A. and G. Mjema, 1994, 'External Debt and Economic Growth in Tanzania', *African Development Review*, Vol.6, No.2.
Doriye, J., H. White and M. Wuyts, 1993, *Fungibility and Sustainability*, SIDA Evaluation Report 1993/5, Stockholm: SIDA.
Edgren, G., 1986, 'Procedures and relationships in Swedish development assistance', in Frühling (ed.).

EU, 1995, *Trade Relations Between the European Union and the Developing Countries*, March, Brussels: European Commission.

EURODAD, 1996, 'Multilateral Debt: Towards a Solution?', *World Credit Tables. Creditors' Claims on Debtors Exposed*, Brussels: EURODAD.

European Commission, 1996, *Green Paper on Relations Between the European Union and the ACP Countries on the Eve of the 21st Century*, Brussels: European Commission, DG VIII.

Frühling, P. (ed.), 1986, *Swedish Development Aid in Perspective. Problems, Policies and Results Since 1952*, Stockholm: Almqvist & Wiksell.

GATT, 1993, *An Analysis of the Proposed Uruguay Round Agreement with Particular Emphasis on Aspects of Interest to Developing Countries*, Geneva: GATT Secretariat.

Goldin, I. and D. van der Mensbrugghe, 1992, *Trade Liberalisation: What's At Stake?*, Development Centre Policy Brief No. 5, Paris: OECD.

Helleiner, G., T. Killick, N. Lipumba, B. Ndulu and K.-E. Svendsen, 1995, 'Report of the Group of Independent Advisors on Development Co-operation Issues Between Tanzania and its Donors', Copenhagen: Ministry of Foreign Affairs (mimeo).

Heppling, S., 1986, 'The Very First Years', in Frühling (ed.).

Hveem, H. and D. McNeill, 1994, *Is Swedish Aid Rational?* Stockholm: SASDA, Ds 1994: 75.

IBRD, 1996, *Tanzania: Policy Framework Paper, 1996/97–1998/99*, Washington, DC: World Bank.

IFS, *International Financial Statistics, Yearbook*, annual, Washington, DC: IMF.

Jordbruksverket, 1996, *Effekter av import- och exportkvoter i handelsledet* (Effects of Import and Export Quotas in Retail Trade), Rapport 1996:13, Stockholm: Jordbruksverket.

Laanatza, M., 1993, *Vilka handelspolitiska regelförändringar väntar på u-landsområdet vid ett svenskt EG-inträde?* (What Changes in Trade Policy Rules Will Result from Sweden's Joining the European Union?) PM 93-03-05, Stockholm: Ministry of Foreign Affairs.

Ljunggren, B., 1986, 'Swedish Goals and Priorities', in Frühling (ed.).

Majmudar, M., 1996, 'Trade-Liberalisation in Clothing: the MFA Phase-Out and the Developing Countries', *Development Policy Review*, Vol.14, No.1.

McDonald, S., 1996, 'Reform of the EU's Sugar Policies and the ACP Countries', *Development Policy Review*, Vol.14, No.2.

National Board of Trade, 1995, *Det generella preferenssystemet* (The Generalised System of Preferences), Rapport 1995:5, Stockholm: NBT.

Palmlund, T., 1986, 'Altruism and Other Motives. Swedish Development Aid and Foreign Policy' in Frühling (ed.).

SIDA, 1997, *Sveriges internationella utvecklingssamarbete. Statistisk årsbok 1996* (Sweden's International Development Assistance. Statistical Yearbook 1996), Stockholm: SIDA.

Tarp, F., 1993, *Stabilisation and Structural Adjustment*, London: Routledge.

UNDP, 1995, *Tanzania Development Co-operation 1994 Report*, New York: UNDP.

Woodward, D., 1996, 'IMF Gold Sales as a Source of Funds for Multilateral Debt Reduction', *World Credit Tables. Creditors' Claims on Debtors Exposed*, Brussels: EURODAD.

9

The Coherence of Policies Towards Developing Countries: The Case of Switzerland

JACQUES FORSTER

I. INTRODUCTION

Switzerland is among those OECD countries which have, over the past few years, seriously started to address the issue of policy coherence in their relations with developing countries. In March 1994, the Federal Council, that is, the government, submitted to Parliament a report on 'Switzerland's North–South Relations in the 1990s'. This report, which Parliament approved, is better known as 'North–South Guidelines'.[1] Basically, the Guidelines are to:

–   present Switzerland's development policy objectives;

–   recognise that there are contradictions and conflicts of interests between these objectives and other foreign and domestic policy objectives; and

–   suggest that contradictions and conflicts of interest must be identified, clarified through dialogue and, 'if possible, overcome'.

The purpose of this chapter is to:

(a) describe the emergence in Switzerland of this new approach to relations with developing countries (history and rationale);

---

1.   This document complements the government's report on Switzerland's foreign policy in the 1990s published at the end of 1993 [*Conseil fédéral, 1993*].

(b) discuss the objectives of Swiss development policy and the concept of coherence as they are presented in government policy papers;

(c) make a first appraisal of the implementation of this new approach by describing the mechanisms set up to implement it within the federal administration and the role played by other actors.

It is premature to make a global assessment on this new policy. We have therefore chosen to concentrate on a few topical issues where the new approach has been put to the test since 1994. The issues were selected either for their significance for developing countries or for the illustration they provide of the dilemma that confronts governments in their pursuit of greater policy coherence towards developing countries.

II. THE CONCEPT AND LEVELS OF COHERENCE

'"Policy coherence" refers to the consistency of policy objectives and instruments applied by OECD countries individually or collectively in the light of their combined effects on developing countries' [*Fukasaku and Hirata, 1995: 20*]. Consistency of policies therefore requires that these policies all aim at achieving the same objective, that they should be complementary rather than at cross purposes. The important question is, of course, what purpose should coherence serve? In the colonial era, for instance, coherence for the colonial power could have meant the harmonisation of various policy instruments (political, military, economic, population-related, cultural) in order to extract maximum profit and/or influence from the relationship with the colonised territories.

In the present context, the emergence of this concept is related to the concern to promote more efficiently and effectively the economic and social development of developing countries both because official development assistance (ODA) resources are becoming increasingly scarce and because other dimensions of North–South relations are becoming increasingly relevant for these countries as globalisation continues to progress. The growing significance of this concern is indicated by the fact that the topic of policy coherence was on the agenda of the Development Assistance Committee (DAC) High-level Meeting in December 1991 and prominent in the 1992 DAC Report on Development Co-operation [*OECD, 1992*]. Policy coherence may be analysed at various levels:

At the *first level*, the internal consistency of a single policy is ana-lysed. The policy concerned is aid policy, as aid is *the* component of North–South relations the declared objective of which is to promote economic and social development. The pursuit of coherence at this level implies, for instance, the elimination of possible gaps between policy and practice and the reduction of contradictions and inconsist-encies between objectives.

Coherence is, of course, also necessary among donors as well as between donors and recipient countries. At this first level, coherence has always been a key issue that is usually dealt with at various forums (World Bank, UNDP), with varying degrees of success, under the heading of co-ordination and policy dialogue.

The *second level* concerns coherence of various policies in the field of international relations that have a direct impact on developing countries. The 1992 DAC report, which emphasises this level, makes a distinction between interrelated policies that have long been included in the development co-operation dialogue (trade, debt, tied aid and foreign direct investment) and new policy areas (environment, drug addiction, AIDS, immigration, human rights) 'which have added a new dimension to the issue of coherence' [*OECD, 1992: 3*]. This list, to which one may also add international transfers of weapons, indicates that, in the broader approach, the quest for greater coherence encompasses a very wide range of issues and policies and involves practically every ministry and government agency.

At this level, DAC is the only forum to deal with these issues among donor countries. Between donor and recipient countries, the World Bank and UNDP provide the most important multilateral frameworks (the Development Committee and Consultative Groups for the former, Roundtables for the latter).[2]

The *third level* concerns coherence between policies *vis-à-vis* deve-loping countries on the one hand, and domestic policies on the other. Coherence in this case is not only limited to policies that may have an indirect adverse or positive effect on developing countries, but also ones that affect the credibility of industrialised countries in develop-ing countries (that is, the 'do as we say, not as we do' attitude).

---

2. Other forums exist for particular groups of countries such as those of the List of Least Developed Countries (LLDCs); a conference examines periodically a broad range of issues relating to their development and to the role of industrialised countries therein.

Domestic agricultural and industrial policies are examples of the first kind as they may have an indirect impact on developing countries by their effects on the international division of labour.

In other areas such as domestic environmental policy, military expenditure, and the fight against domestic corruption, policies may have no impact on developing countries. Yet, the mere fact that industrialised countries take serious steps to deal with problems for which they advocate action on the part of governments in developing country is likely to enhance the former's credibility in the eyes of the latter and may thus bring about greater commitment to the implementation of international recommendations. The somewhat distrustful atmosphere surrounding North–South discussions as to the priority to be granted to environmental issues in the South would certainly be improved if industrialised countries were to implement at home credible sustainable development strategies including, *inter alia*, a reduction of per capita non-renewable energy consumption.[3]

Agreement on the goal of policy coherence does not preclude differences in view as to which combination of policies is most likely to achieve this goal. These differences may stem from diverse views of what 'development' is to achieve, or from conflicting development theories. For example, to what extent should human rights policy and international economic relations (trade, direct investment) be linked to each other? This question can be answered very differently and lead to varying policy solutions, depending on:

– whether one considers that respect for human rights is a priority irrespective of the 'stage of development' and/or of different cultural values; or

– whether the view is that 'political development' (democratic institutions, respect for human rights) follows economic development.

In the first case, coherence of policies requires that the human rights situation be taken into account by governments of industrial countries

---

3. It is with this purpose in mind that in 1992, the Swiss Aid Agencies Coalition commissioned a 'policy framework paper' for Switzerland designed 'to put our own house in order'. The paper followed a government statement advocating 'symmetrical adjustment policy' for all IMF members. It was drafted by a Ghanaian economist and presented a ten-point programme advocating, *inter alia,* stronger action to combat domestic poverty, to achieve a better gender balance, and to reduce energy consumption and military expenditure [*Mireku,1992*].

when assessing the desirability of granting public support to projects (through ODA and other instruments designed to promote exports and private investment) or when granting developing countries preferential treatment (for example, trade preferences). In the second case, a coherent approach could imply encouraging, or at least not discouraging, such relations, as economic development would eventually induce a more democratic political system and greater respect for human rights.[4]

Thus the quest for policy coherence may be fully supported by development actors having different views on development theory. Their concurring on the need for greater coherence – an objective one can hardly disagree with – would not, however, bring them any closer to shared conclusions on policy prescriptions.

III. THE EMERGENCE OF 'COHERENCE' IN SWISS DEVELOPMENT CO-
OPERATION

In June 1990 while a parliamentary commission debated the allocation of new financial resources to development co-operation, it requested the Federal Council to draft guidelines on the future role of Switzerland in North–South relations with a view to pursuing 'a global and coherent development policy'. The request pointed in particular to the need to gear economic and trade policy increasingly towards development policy objectives. The call for the linking of these two policy areas was relatively new, as Swiss policy-makers had hitherto been rather intent on keeping them apart.[5]

The government readily took on this assignment and entrusted it to a working party comprising of officials from the two most concerned departments of the federal administration: the Swiss Agency for Development and Co-operation (SDC) and the Federal Office for Foreign Economic Affairs (FOFEA). The elaboration of the guidelines met with traditional conflicts arising from the confrontation of

---

4. The successive policies of Western countries towards South Africa during the apartheid era is a good illustration of these two approaches.
5. In 1980, as a revision of the law on the Swiss public export insurance scheme was being discussed in Parliament, some NGOs wanted – out of concern for more coherence – development co-operation criteria to be taken into account if the goods or services insured were to be exported to a developing country. The potential impact of that proposal was severely reduced when Parliament decided to apply it only to the 'most disadvantaged' developing countries, a group of 31 developing countries which, at the time, represented only 0.3 per cent of Switzerland's total exports and 1.7 per cent of its exports to non-European developing *countries* [*Annuaire Suisse–Tiers Monde, 1981: 61*].

different sets of objectives and rationales; this probably explains the length of the process but it did not lead to a resolution of the most controversial issues [*Greminger, 1996:145–6*].

In March 1994, the government submitted to Parliament a report on 'Switzerland's North–South Relations in the 1990s', better known as the 'North–South Guidelines' [*Federal Council, 1994*]. Both houses of Parliament approved the Guidelines, albeit with very little discussion, probably because Parliament was required simultaneously to discuss and approve a multi-year credit of 3.8 billion Swiss francs for the continuation of technical assistance and financial aid programmes. The controversy over the volume of credit all but overshadowed the more far-reaching but less concrete implications of the Guidelines. A 1995–98 Plan of Action for the implementation of the Guidelines was completed by SDC in December 1995.

The issue of policy coherence in Switzerland's relations with developing countries can certainly be traced to before 1990. Since the 1970s, NGOs have steadfastly analysed various aspects of Switzerland's relations with developing countries (trade, direct foreign investment by Swiss transnational corporations, sales of military equipment, transfer of technology, intellectual property rights, etc.), in the light of their overall impact on the social and economic development of these countries and, particularly, on the poorer sections of their populations. As far back as 1975, a commission appointed by Swiss NGOs published a report which explicitly and vigorously raised the issue of coherence, or lack thereof – without using the word – between Switzerland's development policy and other dimensions of its relations with developing countries:

There is a fundamental incompatibility between, on the one hand, a development policy which purports to be at the service of the poorest, and on the other hand, Swiss foreign policy and international economic relations which serve its own interests ... This incompatibility ... must once and for all be recognised and discussed openly. It can only be removed if our economic and financial relations with the Third World are integrated in a global concept of development policy [*Commission des organisations suisses de coopération au développement, 1975: 14*].[6]

In government circles, the concept of coherence emerged in the wake of a global reassessment of Switzerland's foreign policy at the begin-

---

6. Author's translation.

ning of the 1990s. Indeed, issues such as neutrality and relations with the European Union (EU) became very topical at the end of the cold war and with the widening of the EU membership to most Western European countries. Swiss policy-makers were also convinced that since most of the problems the country had to face had an international dimension, it became imperative not only to place international co-operation higher on the country's agenda, but also to increase the awareness of internationally wary Swiss citizens on the significance of these issues.

Some elements of the rationale for this new governmental approach to North–South relations are presented in the Guidelines which argue that the nature of the relationship betwen rich and poor countries has changed with:

– the end of the cold war;

– the increasing awareness of environmental issues and notably of the North–South dimensions of these issues;

– the opportunities and risks related to the globalisation of the world economy; and

– the growing influence of development trends in the South on industrialised countries and vice versa.

Other elements, while not explicitly listed in the document, are nevertheless also relevant to explain the genesis of this approach. A key factor was undoubtedly, as in other countries, the need for development co-operation to acquire a new legitimacy at the end of the cold war and in the face of growing scepticism ('aid fatigue') as to its efficiency and effectiveness. This need was of course compounded by the increasing pressure to cut government spending in various areas, including development co-operation [*Hadorn, 1995: 157–8*]. The timing of the formulation of this new policy was also influenced both by the fact that 'coherence' was on the agenda of the DAC High-level meeting of December 1991 and by the preparation for the Rio 1992 'World Summit' which emphasised new dimensions of North–South interdependence [*Greminger, 1996: 145*].

Finally, in more general terms, one can safely assume that the post-cold war international situation has contributed to giving more prominence to the role of developing countries in world affairs both because of their increasing weight in international economic relations and because of the growing risk of a North–South divide on a number of far-reaching issues such as disarmament, environment, human rights, and the link between trade and labour standards.

The emergence of coherence in Swiss development co-operation represents a major policy shift. Policies referring to, on the one hand, to the promotion of development and, on the other, to external economic relations had hitherto been carefully kept apart [*Forster, 1995*], the main argument being that the universal extending of trade relations was too important for Switzerland to be hampered by other policies (development, human rights). The change was brought about both by pressures emanating from large sections of the public – and their representatives in Parliament – and the realisation that isolation of external economic policy from other dimensions of foreign policy was no longer tenable in the post-cold war international context.

IV. CONCEPT AND LEVELS OF COHERENCE IN GOVERNMENT POLICY

(1) Two Concepts of Coherence: An Unavoidable Coexistence?

Two different concepts of coherence were almost simultaneously put forward by the Federal Council: one relating to foreign policy in general, the other more specifically to relations with developing countries.

Foreign policy: According to its report on Switzerland's foreign policy in the 1990s [*Conseil fédéral, 1993*], the need to improve the coherence of Switzerland's foreign policy is dictated by the need to make it more efficient in defending and promoting the country's national interests.

To achieve this objective, the keyword is co-ordination, which 'can and must be improved in several respects': between foreign and domestic policy; between different areas of foreign policy and between the objectives and instruments of foreign policy. The report recognises that improved co-ordination is necessary to reduce the contradictions that inevitably emerge between various objectives. This is all the more necessary as the field covered by external relations includes an increasing number of policy areas [*Conseil fédéral, 1993: 44*].

Relations with developing countries: In the 'North–South Guidelines' issued a few months later, the call for greater coherence refers to the various dimensions of Switzerland's relations with developing countries. The approach is thus the same as that adopted by NGOs in the 1970s (see section III).

The rationale for enhanced policy coherence is best conveyed by quoting from the report [*Federal Council, 1994: 11*]:

> ... Switzerland must reconsider its relations with the developing countries in a complex and ever changing environment. Development co-operation is no longer the only consideration, but rather the totality of Swizerland's political, economic and social relations with these countries. The traditional dichotomies between environmental and economic policies, between economic and migration policies, between trade and development policies, between domestic and foreign policies can no longer be applied to solve the impending problems. What is required is 'a coherent policy towards the South'. For the formulation of such a policy it is first necessary to highlight potential contradictions between short-term national interests and the longer-term goals of Swiss development policy. Contradictions then need to be clearly tabled in the political decision-making process.

Are the two concepts of coherence complementary or contradictory? In other words, can Swiss national interests be reconciled with those of developing countries? The Guidelines state that the country's external policy objectives apply to relations with industrialised as well as with developing countries and aim at safeguarding Switzerland's long-term interests. Is this to say that these interests coincide with those of developing countries?

This question can to some extent be elucidated by following Fukasaku and Hirata [*1995: 11*] who make a useful distinction between the national and international dimensions of policy coherence:

> 'National coherence' requires that OECD countries' policies help promote, or at least not harm, the economic interests of developing countries ... In addition, policy coherence has an international dimension. In the absence of a world government, the rich countries are primarily responsible for providing 'international public goods' [*Kindleberger, 1986*] such as the open multilateral trading system upon which global welfare depends [*Fukasaku and Hirata, 1995: 20*].

If the concept of international public goods were to be restricted to economic goods (open trading system, guaranteed property rights, etc.), one could question the assumption that the interests of developing countries necessarily coincide with those of industrialised countries. Indeed, on the one hand, the capacity of many developing countries to take advantage of such goods is limited as is, on the other, the extent to which they can exert influence on the content of these international public goods so as to have them correspond to their specific conditions and needs. The very limited role of many developing countries in the Uruguay Round negotiations bears witness to that limitation.

But interdependence is by no means limited to the sphere of international economic relations. Global environmental protection, peace and security, the containment of internationally organised crime including narcotics, control over the spread of disease and of weapons, are issues which require close North–South co-operation. They are also becoming increasingly important international public goods both in the North and in the South even if the governments of the two groups of countries still set different priorities on their agendas.

Policy coherence aiming at the promotion of economic and social development in developing countries – the national dimension of coherence according to Fukusaku and Hirata [1995] – can of course generate decisions that run against the interests of industrialised countries or, to be more precise, against the interests of particular groups in those countries. However, the promotion of 'international coherence' ought in the long run to reconcile the two concepts of coherence to be found in official government papers.

The Guidelines recognise explicitly that there are instances where Swiss national interests cannot be reconciled with the objectives set for the development policy.

> Contradictions may arise between on the one hand, domestic policy objectives promoting employment and economic growth through State-supported export promotion and, on the other hand, development policy aiming at promoting democracy and human rights. These contradictions must be brought out into the open and clarified through dialogue [Federal Council, 1994: 16].

The same document also stresses that 'in a changing and interdependent world' national interests need to be constantly redefined and that a balance has to be struck between short- and long-term interests as well as between national and international interests [ibid., 1994: 12].

Both government reports stress the importance of improving public awareness of these issues. This concern is probably shared by most governments; in Switzerland, however, the requirement is particularly important as the constitutional system enables citizens to vote on foreign policy issues.[7]

(2) The Strategic Objectives of the 'North–South Guidelines'
The strategic objectives presented in the 'North–South Guidelines' logically coincide with those contained in the External Policy Report. They fall under four main headings, each of which corresponds to a specific dimension of development:

(i)   political: 'safeguarding and promoting peace and security, human rights, democracy and the rule of law';
(ii) economic: 'promoting welfare';
(iii) social: 'improving social equity';
(iv) environmental: 'protecting the natural environment'.

In SDC's 'Plan of Action for the implementation of the North–South Guidelines 1995-1998' [*Federal Council, 1994*], each of these strategic objectives is broken down into 15 more specific objectives in different policy areas (see Table 1) which themselves lead to the definition of 47 proposals for action and 150 concrete measures of implementation.

Approximately half the 47 proposals for action distributed among the four policy areas are listed as requiring priority attention.

The proposals for action can be classified in three categories according to the levels of coherence as defined in section II.

(a)   The first level is related to the internal consistency of the development co-operation policy. At this level, the proposals for action aim at improving the implementation (efficiency and effectiveness) of SDC development policy objectives such as:

   –   the promotion of autonomous and participatory development, of a decentralised and efficient public administration;
   –   the improvement of aid co-ordination;
   –   the promotion of private sector activities, particularly of small enterprises;
   –   the reduction of poverty;

---

7. Switzerland is the only country in which the citizens had to vote on issues such as:
   – lending 200 million Swiss francs to the International Development Association (rejected in 1976);
   – membership of the United Nations Organisation (rejected in 1986);
   – membership of the IMF and the World Bank (accepted in 1992);
   – membership of the European Economic Area (rejected in 1992).

- the promotion of gender balance;
- the promotion of sustainable development in developing countries.

At this first level, several government agencies may be involved but their contribution is limited to the formulation and/or implementation of a single policy, development co-operation, whose sole declared objective is to promote development in developing countries.

TABLE 1
STRATEGIC OBJECTIVES OF THE SWISS NORTH–SOUTH GUIDELINES

Strategic Objectives	Policy Areas
1. Safeguarding and promoting peace and security, human rights, democracy and the rule of law	11 Promoting good governance 12 Positive measures to promote human rights, the rule of law and democratic processes 13 Improving international legal assistance 14 Reducing excessive military spending in developing countries 15 Safeguarding and promoting peace
2. Promoting welfare	21 Improving the basic conditions for sustainable growth in developing countries 22 Encouraging the private sector in developing countries 23 Opening the markets of the North to products from developing countries
3. Improving social equity	31 Fighting against poverty and promoting social equity 32 Reducing demographic growth 33 Promoting coherent and internationally coordinated humanitarian assistance.
4. Protecting the natural environment	41 Formulating a sustainable development model for Switzerland 42 Promoting sustainable development at the international level 43 Harmonisation of environment, trade and development policies 44 Striving towards coherent economic, trade, foreign and development policies at the multilateral level.

Source: Federal Council [*1994*].

(b) The second level concerns the coherence of various policies that can have a direct impact on developing countries in relation to the objectives of the development co-operation policy. At this level, issues include:

- respect for human rights, the fight against illegal capital flight and corruption, exporting of arms to developing countries;
- volume of ODA, immigration policy, trade policy (promotion of exports to developing countries, imports from developing countries);
- integration of trade and environmental issues.

These are issues in which conflicts of objectives can arise between development co-operation policy and other policies pertaining to Swiss foreign relations. In all these cases, several government agencies responsible for different policies are involved and there is often a need for conflicts of objectives or of interests to be arbitrated at the political level.

(c) At the third level, that of coherence between domestic policies and policies towards developing countries, the main issues mentioned in the Plan of Action are the following:

- the fight against corruption in Switzerland;
- restricting exports of military equipment and banning certain weapon systems (land mines);
- a sustainable development model for Switzerland.

Some issues may be included at two or even all three levels. The fight against corruption, for example, can be mentioned at the first level in the context of the promotion of good governance in a developing country. It would also appear at the second level if steps are taken to prevent corruption-related outflows of funds from developing countries. Finally, measures taken to combat corruption on the domestic front (in Switzerland) belong to the third level (see also section VI).

SDC's Plan of Action does not shy away from controversial and politically sensitive issues concerning Switzerland's relations with developing countries. This is particularly evident at the third level where, on the basis of the government's Guidelines, calls are made for introducing changes in the legislation to reduce more efficiently both capital flight and corruption and to be more restrictive when it comes to exporting military equipment. As far as immigration policy is concerned, the Plan of Action recommends a revision of the current policy which discriminates against migrants from practically all developing countries[8]: nationals and economies of poor countries should also be entitled to benefit from employment opportunities on the Swiss labour market. Finally the Guidelines clearly state that unless sustainable development strategies are also implemented in industralised countries, these strategies 'cannot be seen as a model for developing countries' [Federal Council, 1994: 24], hence the need to formulate a sustainable development model for Switzerland.

To determine the relative importance granted to the three levels of coherence, each of the 47 proposals for action was ascribed to one or more level. In six cases, a particular measure was simultaneously attributed to levels two and three. This analysis shows that 38 per cent of the proposals for action concern two or more policy areas which have a direct impact on developing countries (level two) and 17 per cent concern coherence between domestic policies and policies towards developing countries (level three). It follows that, altogether, more than half (55 per cent) of the policy measures proposed to improve coherence concern two or more government agencies. This percentage has implications for the implementation of the Plan of Action as it is indicative of the need for efficient inter-agency and inter-ministerial consultation and decision mechanisms (see section V below).

Whereas the Guidelines received relatively little attention in political circles, they were generally acclaimed by the NGO community as a significant step in the pursuit of coherence. According to the Director of the Swiss Coalition of Development Organisations, 'The explicit ... recognition of coherence in the North-South Guidelines is new and represents a milestone in the political struggle for coherence' [Gerster, 1995: 66]. However, the same author queries to what extent this policy will be implemented.

V. THE IMPLEMENTATION OF COHERENCE

The acid test for the best formulated policy lies of course in its implementation. Inadequacy between the ends and the means would in this

---

8. This policy makes a distinction between (a) nationals from EU and EFTA members for whom the objective is eventually to guarantee free access to the Swiss labour market, (b) nationals from the US and Canada, with restricted access conditioned by the needs of the Swiss economy, and (c) nationals from the rest of the world, that is, all developing countries, with practically no access, exceptions for highly qualified personnel notwithstanding [Annuaire Suisse-Tiers Monde, 1996: 101].

context clearly indicate weak political will and lack of coherence. What are the declared ambitions of the Swiss government in this respect? An answer is provided in the North–South Guidelines: to formulate a coherent policy toward the South, 'it is first necessary to highlight potential contradictions between short-term national interests and the longer goals of Swiss development policy. Contradictions then need to be clearly tabled in the political decision making process' [*Federal Council, 1994: 11*]. It would certainly have been unrealistic to aim at eliminating all possible contradictions between short-term national interests and the objectives of development policy. The goal is to see to it that decisions are only reached after a thorough analysis of all their implications for developing countries and of their congruence or conflict with development policy. Referring to a typology put forward by Paul Hoebink, one could say that the Federal Council's ambition is, at least, to avoid 'unintended incoherence' and to be in a position to discuss thoroughly possible instances of 'intended incoherence' (Hoebink, this volume, Ch.10).

A second indication on implementation is included in the Guidelines. It refers to the role of public opinion. 'Implementation of these objectives is neither conceivable nor feasible without the support of the Swiss public', which should accept 'that our long-term welfare also depends on the fate of the South' [*Federal Council, 1994: 11–12*].

The instruments of implementation should therefore include internal procedures to review coherence-related issues within the public administration machinery (within SDC and with other government departments/agencies) as well as external mechanisms designed to involve other actors in the discussion of such issues and thus gain the necessary public support.

The North–South Guidelines do not, however, contain indications as to how to implement this new policy. No reference is made in the report to existing or new implementation mechanisms. Whatever the reason for this omission, it calls upon the administration to rely upon existing mechanisms, but it also leaves room for initiatives by the most directly concerned government agencies.

(1) Implementation within the Federal Administration

Within the federal administration, SDC was instrumental in the promotion of a more coherent approach to North–South relations. It played a major role in the drafting of the Guidelines and followed up their endorsement by Parliament by issuing in December 1995 an 'SDC Plan of Action for the Implementation of the North–South

Guidelines 1995–1998'. Although this document only has the status of an internal working paper, it was widely distributed to SDC's main partners in Switzerland, a group composed mainly of NGOs.

The Plan of Action reflects SDC's priorities and does not purport to commit other goverment agencies. Whilst broadly sharing the views expressed in the Plan of Action, the two agencies most directly concerned by North–South issues (the Federal Office for Foreign Economic Affairs, FOFEA, and the Federal Office for Environment, Forests and Landscape, FOEFL) do not necessarily share the priorities and procedures included in the Plan of Action. However, they have not themselves drafted documents spelling out their priorities for the implementation of the Guidelines.

In spite of its lack of official standing, the Plan of Action ranks high amongst SDC's policy papers; it overrules all other SDC internal policy papers and defines internal responsibilities and deadlines for the implementation of the various objectives. In the many areas where the responsibility lies with other government agencies, the Plan of Action merely defines SDC's objectives or position in the inter-agency policy-making process.

The implementation of certain sets of proposals for action is entrusted to working parties which, according to the topics, are composed of representatives of various government agencies and outside experts. In order not to spread the resources too thinly, not more than six groups are simultaneously at work. The first groups to be set up deal with such clusters of topics as 'human rights and the rule of law', 'donor co-ordination', 'poverty and empowerment', and the 'continuum between emergency assistance and development co-operation'.

To give an example, the working party on 'human rights and the rule of law' is one of the groups working on issues cutting across several policy areas. It includes representatives from five agencies from the federal departments (ministries) of foreign affairs, economic affairs and justice. Its task is to produce a set of guidelines on the promotion of human rights through development co-operation with a view to promoting a more coherent approach within and among government agencies. It is premature to assess the effectiveness of this method of improving policy coherence. Its success will depend on the degree of authority the recommendations enjoy within the administration and on their applicability to day-to-day policy decisions.

The issue of policy coherence provides yet another opportunity to raise the question of the organisation of Switzerland's development co-operation. This is characterised by the shared responsibility of two government agencies, namely SDC and FOFEA. It is clearly recognised [DAC/OECD, 1996] that co-ordination between the two agencies is far from optimal. Policy differences and overlapping competencies entail time-consuming and not always successful attempts at improving co-ordination. Indeed, experienced observers of Switzerland's development policy contend that its main weakness lies in diluted responsibilities on issues where several ministries share competencies. Gerster [*1995: 66–8*] gives as examples of this phenomenon the fact that the chairmanship – and the secretariat! – of the inter-ministerial committee responsible for the follow-up on the 1992 UN Conference on Environment and Development rotate annually betwen the three more closely concerned ministries, and that four government agencies define and implement Switzerland's policy in the Bretton Woods institutions.

While there is certainly room for improvement in the policy-making and co-ordination mechanisms, it can also be argued that the most streamlined and efficient policy-making system will not abolish the contradictions between conflicting policy objectives. Nor should it, as the resolution of conflicts of interests should take place where it belongs, that is, at the political level.

It has been argued that procedures inherent in a collegial system of government, such as that of the Swiss, favour policy coherence 'in that the system guarantees that almost all major decisions are discussed and made by the Federal Council. Thus, in Switzerland, the scope for coherence depends on the political will to be coherent' [*Maurer, 1995: 163*]. This contention would strengthen the case for having various agencies located in different ministries deal with development policy as this would enhance 'development sensitivity' in those ministries. The same author suggests that procedures could be put into place to ensure a systematic 'coherence verification' for major foreign policy decisions concerning North–South relations in the same way as, for instance, this is accomplished to ensure the Euro-compatibility of new legislation. Gerster [*1995: 68*] makes the same proposal.

At this early stage in the assessment of the effects of the 1994 Guidelines on government policy, one has the feeling that in many cases (see also section VI), decisions were made by government as well as by Parliament in full cognisance of possible conflicts with development policy objectives. Whenever incoherence prevailed, it was intended, or at least accepted, in the name of other national interests.

(2) Involvement of Other Actors

When the law on development co-operation was adopted in 1976, a Consultative Commission on Development Co-operation was put into place. It included parliamentarians and individuals from NGOs, business, trade unions, academia and the media. Its task was to advise the government and make recommendations on development co-operation policies and priorities. Its mandate encompassed all dimensions of Switzerland's relations with developing countries as well as transition economies. In the 1990s, sub-commissions were established to deal specifically with issues arising in the Bretton Woods institutions and WTO. The Guidelines are reportedly frequently referred to and used as a framework by the Commission.

Recent debates in Parliament indicate that there is an increasing awareness, at least among the Social Democrats and the Ecologists, of the relationship between development policy and other dimensions of the country's relations with developing countries. To a large extent, NGOs are to be credited for this increased awareness, not only among parliamantarians but also to some extent the public, as NGOs have consistently referred to the coherence policy framework in their information campaigns on a large range of issues (arms exports, domestic sugar production versus imports from developing countries, the fight against corruption, export risk guarantee and human rights, food aid).

So far there has been little evidence that business circles pay much attention to policy coherence in North–South relations. In many recent debates, where immediate business interests have conflicted with development policy, business representatives have staunchly, and not surprisingly, defended the former. However, the sensitivity, particularly of the banking sector, to certain issues of great relevance to North–South relations is certainly greater today than a few years ago. This, however, probably stems more from international pressures to see Switzerland adopt a more co-operative attitude on limiting illegal capital movements than from a concern for policy coherence.

VI. COHERENCE IN PRACTICE: SELECTED ISSUES

Since the Guidelines were approved by government and subsequently by Parliament in 1994, many decisions have been made and legislation passed or proposed which have a direct bearing on developing countries. The purpose of this section is to illustrate with a few examples to what extent the 'policy coherence' approach has had an impact on Swiss policy towards developing countries. The selection of examples is made on the basis of their significance for Swiss development policy and of their capacity to illustrate areas in which short-

and medium-term national interests appear to clash with development policy objectives.[9]

(1) Exports versus Ecology and Human Rights

In 1996, the Swiss government was faced with a decision on an issue which provided a good illustration of the problems encountered in the implementation of a coherent approach to North–South relations. The question was: should the government allow the public Export Risk Guarantee scheme (ERG) to insure the sale of capital goods by Swiss firms in relation to a huge hydroelectric project on the Yang Tse-Kiang river in China?[10]

Conflicts between the promotion of Switzerland's economic relations with developing countries and its development co-operation policy have always been at the centre of the triangular debate between government, NGOs and business. Traditionally, within government circles, the tendency was to avoid as far as possible linkages between these two policy areas, hence a refusal to apply development policy criteria to decisions relating to international economic relations.

The first formal link between this policy instrument and development co-operation policy was established in 1980 when the ERG Act was amended by Parliament to call for the fundamental principles of Swiss development co-operation policy to be taken into account in decisions concerning the 'most disadvantaged developing countries'.[11] This amendment was the outcome of an attempt by Swiss NGOs, strongly opposed by exporters' lobbies, to establish this link for all developing countries. The list of countries considered to be 'most disadvantaged' by the Swiss authorities presently numbers 64 countries, namely, the group of least-developed countries plus 16 other countries, among which are India, China, Indonesia, Egypt and Nigeria.

Two years after this amendment the government was still, however, very reluctant to let the human rights situation in a particular country influence Switzerland's economic relations with that country. In a 1982 report on its human rights policy, the Federal Council stated that universal extension of trade relations was vital in order to

---

9. It would certainly be necessary to undertake a systematic analysis of the 'record' of policy coherence; this is not attempted in this chapter as time and space available did not allow us to embark upon an extensive enquiry.
10. The Swiss Export Risk Guarantee (ERG) programme was established in 1934 to promote exports by insuring exporters against certain risks (non-payment due to political problems, foreign exchange restrictions, inability or unwillingness to pay on the part of public or public guaranteed debtors, etc.).
11. See also note 5 in section III of this chapter.

maintain jobs in Switzerland. This explains why, until recently, Switzerland consistently refused to join international boycotts. In 1985, for instance, Switzerland declared that, although it condemned apartheid, it would not apply economic sanctions against South Africa [*Forster, 1995: 209, 218*].

The 'North–South Guidelines' mark a clear departure from this policy: 'In the risk assessment preceding the granting of an ERG for exports to the poorest countries, it is necessary to put more emphasis on political dimensions and on the respect of human rights in the recipient country. Whenever possible, internationally coordinated action should be sought' [*Federal Council, 1994: 16*].

The request to grant the ERG to Swiss exports related to the Yang Tse-Kiang hydroelectric project thus came as the first major test for the new policy. In October 1996, Asea Brown Boveri introduced a request to benefit from the ERG scheme for the supply of generators to China valued at some 350 million Swiss francs.

Many of the most significant Swiss NGOs undertook a campaign to induce the government to reject this request. Making reference to the provisions of the ERG law and to the Guidelines, they argued mainly that the project would have a negative impact on the environment and that it would entail the forced resettlement of over 1.5 million people. The NGOs maintained that the implementation of such a project required freedom of the press as well as consultation and participation of the people concerned in the decision-making process. They further stated that these conditions do not prevail in China as the pros and cons of the project cannot be discussed openly.[12] Several government agencies were reported to have also recommended that the request be rejected.

In December 1996, the Federal Council nervertheless agreed to grant the ERG to this export of capital goods after having taken into consideration the economic, social and environmental costs and benefits of the project. The Chairman of the ERG Commission stated that having to take into account the fundamendal principles of Swiss development co-operation policy 'did not mean that these principles overrule the main objective of the ERG which is to create jobs in Switzerland'.[13]

---

12. These arguments were expounded in an appeal to the Federal Council, dated 29 October and signed by some 300 people.
13. According to newspaper reports, the ERG Commission, which in that particular case was acting as an advisory body to the government, was divided on this issue. It is noteworthy that the trade unions and SDC representatives on the Commission allegedly disapproved of the recommendation (*Journal de Genève* and *Gazette de Lausanne*, 22 Nov. and 10 Dec. 1996).

The issue, however, was raised in Parliament by the Ecologists who asked the government whether granting the export risk garantee to this project was not in contradiction with the Guidelines and Swiss development policy. The Federal Council replied that, on the one hand, it was difficult to make an objective assessment of the risks and advantages of the project and that, on the other, the economic impact of the project in Switzerland, and particularly its incidence on employment, had weighed heavily in the decision. The government argued, moreover, that a refusal to grant the ERG would not have stopped the project but would have given valuable advantages to foreign competitors. Finally, on the question of human rights the Federal Council took the view that development of democratic structures is a long-term process which can be encouraged by trade, foreign investment and the intensification of relations with the West [*Conseil national, 1996*].

This Yang Tse-Kiang ERG case provides all the ingredients for a perfect case-study although one could argue that the government would seldom be confronted with such a difficult case in view both of the short-term economic interests and the country involved. The conclusions that can be drawn from this example are twofold:

(i)   on the substance, short- and medium-term economic interests, including employment opportunities, took precedence over development policy criteria;

(ii) on the decision-making process, and in comparison to the 'pre-Guidelines era', public discussion, including in Parliament, was probably encouraged by the new government policy which openly recognised the link between the two policy areas. The Guidelines were taken seriously by governmental as well as non-governmental actors with the result that there was no room for 'unintended incoherence'.

(2) Fighting Corruption and Transfers of Illegal Capital: North and South

In the North–South Guidelines, references are made to the necessity to fight 'transfers of capital obtained illegally' and corruption. It is also clearly indicated that action is required in industrialised as well as developing countries. This issue is particularly critical in Switzerland in view not only of the significance of its international role as a capital market, but also of the widespread perception of Swiss banks as the main haven for all kinds of illegal gains. These issues belong to the category that requires co-ordinated action in developing countries as well as in industrialised countries. Attempts to stem corruption in developing countries 'is credible only if we also take on our side the necessary steps to combat this plague' [*Lévy and Greminger, 1997: 11*].

In developing countries, SDC and Swiss NGOs are confronted with corruption in Swiss-funded projects and programmes. SDC supports fully DAC's policy recommendations formulated in 1993 [*OECD, 1994: 34*] and has itself taken specific measures to combat corruption.[14] SDC officials consider, however, that certain forms of corruption, particularly 'petty corruption', cannot be dealt with without taking into account the wider context of poverty (that is, corruption as part of the survival strategies of ill-paid public officers) and the functioning of the judiciary system [*Cart, 1995: 254–7*]. From this perspective, the fight against corruption can only be successfully waged within overall development strategies.[15] SDC also supports Transparency International, a non-governmental coalition against corruption in international business transactions.

As far as domestic policies and measures are concerned, the North–South Guidelines state that 'Switzerland supports the efforts made by OECD to compile codes of conduct concerning the fight against corruption in the industrialized countries' [*Federal Council, 1994: 20*]. A major policy development in this respect was the adoption in May 1994 by OECD governments of a recommendation to member countries to 'take effective measures to deter, prevent and combat the bribery of foreign officials in connection with international business transactions'.[16] Also in this respect, however, the Swiss situation is still far from satisfactory. According to a Swiss expert, 'current legislation is not neutral towards corruption. On the contrary, there are several areas in which Swiss law neglects the existence of corruption or even strengthen conditions conducive to corruption' [*Borghi, 1995: 17*].[17] This author mentions no fewer than nine areas where legislation is inadequate to combat corruption effectively. Among these, SDC officials have identified as priority areas:

---

14. For example, since 1996, SDC and FOFEA have introduced an 'anti corruption clause' in each contract they sign, which covers all dimensions of bribery and not only those aiming at obtaining or retaining business [*Lévy and Greminger, 1997:11*].
15. This does not, however, imply the acceptance of corruption in the name of cultural diversity.
16. Recommendation of the Council of the OECD on bribery in international business transactions, adopted on 27 May 1994 in Paris.
17. Author's translation.

- corruption of foreign civil servants: while the corruption of Swiss civil servants is punishable, this is not the case if the corrupted persons are foreign government officials;[18]

- tax deductibility of bribes paid in order to obtain or retain business;

- enhanced international legal assistance to facilitate prompt and effective return to the country of origin of funds illegally obtained and transferred to Switzerland.

New legal norms to deal more efficiently with these issues have recently been introduced or are being considered.[19] It is generally admitted that Switzerland's traditionally very restrictive attitude in these areas is changing, albeit slowly, in the direction of greater coherence between development policy objectives and domestic practices. This new attitude has been brought about by several factors. The decline and fall of notoriously corrupt Heads of States maintaining 'Swiss bank accounts' and the extension of crime-related capital movements have drawn additional international attention to the Swiss banking system and increased pressure to reform well before the Guidelines were adopted. In fact, on the questions of corruption and movements of illegal funds, the Guidelines do no more than spell out the conclusions that the Federal Council has drawn from this evolution. They provide, however, additional incentives for a systemic approach to these issues by bringing down the walls that hitherto separated domestic practices and development policy.

---

18. Most countries are in the same situation as Switzerland. Only in the US is bribery of foreign officials considered to be a crime.
19. Among the latest developments one can mention the following:
  - A new law on international legal assistance came into force in February 1997. Some progress has been achieved to streamline and accelerate lengthy and cumbersome procedures. In the eyes of specialists, however, much remains to be done.
  - A new law on 'money laundering' was passed by Parliament in Autumn 1997. It aims at applying to all financial institutons, and not only to banks, the rules prevailing for banks. If adopted, this law would put Swizerland's legislation in accordance with recommendations made by the Financial Action Task Force on Money Laundering, which has 28 members. Today only three countries – Canada, Switzerland and Turkey – have not introduced the obligation to report suspicious transactions of non-bank financial institutions to the relevant authorities.
  - In November 1997, Switzerland, like other OECD members, signed an international convention to fight the corruption of foreign officials. The ratification of this convention will be put before Parliament in 1998.

(3) Arms Exports versus Jobs

The recent revision by Parliament of the law on war material, particularly on the export of such material, gave rise to a conflict of interests between development policy on the one hand and foreign trade policy on the other. The Federal Council had proposed the adoption of a rather broad definition of war material; furthermore, in line with the former law and the North–South Guidelines it had linked arms exports authorisations to the human rights situation in the country of destination as well as to Swiss 'development co-operation efforts' [*Conseil fédéral, 1995: 73*].

On both these issues the Federal Council was defeated by Parliament which decided in 1996 to limit the scope of the revised law through a narrower definition of war material and an elimination of references to human rights and development co-operation hitherto included in the law. The main argument of those favouring a more permissive legislation was that one should refrain from putting hurdles in the way of export-oriented firms. An association representing business interests stated that the draft law proposed by the Federal Council 'would seriously jeopardise Switzerland's position as a location for industrial production' [*SDES, 1996*].

The case of an aircraft manufacturer, Pilatus, which exports aeroplanes which can also be put to a military use, is particularly illustrative of the dilemma: business representatives maintained that if Pilatus aircraft were to be included in the definition of war material, as the Federal Council had initially proposed, 900 jobs in a small mountain canton would be jeopardised. On the other hand, NGOs contended that in this area, foreign policy objectives should overrule the interests of the armaments industry. Parliament decided that Pilatus aircraft would not be included in the definition of war material.

The significance of this issue to the Swiss political scene is undoubtedly related to a long-standing and heated debate on the role of the army, military expenditure and export of armaments to developing countries. The North–South dimension of the debate is linked more to a question of principle, that is, of Switzerland's international credibility when it advocates the reduction of military expenditure in developing countries – the third level of coherence defined in section II – than to its actual impact on developing countries which is limited, except for punctual cases, in view of the modest share of Swiss arms exports to developing countries (less than 0.3 per cent of total arms exports to developing countries).[20]

---

20. According to SIPRI figures for 1988–92 quoted by the Federal Council, 1995.

VII. THE POTENTIAL AND LIMITS OF COHERENCE

Judgements on Switzerland's efforts to achieve greater coherence in its relations with developing countries are fairly contrasted. According to the DAC, Swiss efforts are praiseworthy: 'on a comparative basis, it can fairly be said that no DAC Member has gone further in studying and coming to grips with coherence in its relations to developing countries than Switzerland' [*DAC/OECD, 1996: 50*]. The Swiss Coalition of Development Organisations (NGOs) is more sceptical, noting that on several issues, attempts to be more coherent met with limited success in 1995 'when conflicting interests were at stake' [*Weyermann, 1996: 181*]. Both these assessments are not necessarily contradictory, but point to the need to have clear criteria to assess the progress of policy coherence. A starting point could be the declared objectives and ambitions of this approach.

In the case of Switzerland, these can be described as the pursuit of greater coherence of the various policies which, directly or indirectly, have an impact on developing countries. The ambition is not to eradicate all contradictions between development policy objectives and national interests in favour of the former, but to identify clearly these contradictions and, as it were, make a fair attempt at solving them by giving proper consideration to development policy objectives.

As indicated earlier, this concern has a long history, particularly among Swiss NGOs. What then, if anything, is the added contribution of the 1994 government policy paper on North–South relations? In the first place it clearly admits that all dimensions of North–South relations are in one way or another interrelated, in that they have an impact on the development objectives pursued by the Federal Council. It also states that contradictions between development objectives and other national objectives are inevitable and that they are to be ironed out, as far as possible, through dialogue.

In practical terms, as pointed out by Greminger [*1996: 148*], it gives government agencies that share responsibility for the definition and implementation of Switzerland's policy towards developing countries (SDC, FOFEA and, on environmental issues, FOEFL) an enhanced legitimacy within the administration to take initiatives, raise questions and react to policy proposals on a very wide range of topics. It also provides the political actors (political parties, parliamentarians, advocacy-oriented NGOs) with a conceptual framework in which to monitor and stimulate government policy. This is shown by the number of references made in Parliament and in the media to the North–South Guidelines and the coherence requirement on a broad range of issues.

The Federal Council has rightly stressed that public support is a necessary condition for the implementation of its foreign and North–South policy. Support implies awareness of the link between national and international welfare and security (international public goods) even if short-term and specific interests may be conflicting. NGOs play a crucial role as an 'interface' between government and the public: lobbying for coherence while promoting a better understanding through information and education of the complex interrelationships between development in the North and that in the South.

NGOs, however, have been fairly isolated in this advocacy effort. On the whole, the business community does not seem to share this approach to North–South relations. On certain issues mentioned in this chapter, business expresses suspicion that this approach is harmful to the economic interests of Switzerland. Although it is inevitable that such differences of perception persist, the implementation of policy coherence requires that enhanced opportunities for dialogue between the public sector, business and NGOs be provided on a basis enabling discussion of specific issues and a search for solutions with the firms directly concerned. The Federal Office for Foreign Economic Affairs is called upon to play a key role in this respect in view of its close relationship with business representatives.

It is doubtless premature to make an assessment of the impact of this approach on Switzerland's North–South relations. Two provisional conclusions, however, may be drawn on the basis of this limited experience. The first, on the substance of coherence, is that so far, the Guidelines have had little impact, in practical terms, on the outcome of policy-making processes in cases where development policy is confronted with other policies.[21] The two examples given in section VI of this chapter (export risk guarantee for the Yang Tse project and the new law on war material) bear witness to this reality, in the sense that the decisions taken would probably have been the same without the North–South Guidelines.

The second conclusion relates to the process: the objective of exposing possible contradictions and to debate openly on the conflicting interests at stake has to a large extent been achieved. Debate there certainly was, and decisions – right or wrong – were made in full knowledge of their implications for developing countries. Should this be confirmed in the future, one could conclude that the scope for 'unintended incoherence' has been considerably reduced. Ultimately,

---

21. In this chapter, we have not examined the record at the first level of coherence, that is, the internal consistency of development policy.

however, the degree of policy coherence towards developing countries will depend on:

(i) the extent to which development objectives, that is, the progress of developing countries towards the societal ideal defined in the Guidelines (see Table 1), are seen to coincide with the long-term national interests of Switzerland; and

(ii) the development policy framework defined by other industrialised countries, developing countries and international organisations.[22]

In conclusion, the Guidelines can be seen at present as a useful instrument for conducting an ongoing analysis of Switzerland's relations with developing countries, with the aim of eliminating unintended policy contradictions. If their acceptance were to become broader, they could also develop into a means of promoting awareness and debate among all concerned actors on the type of long-term economic development model Switzerland would need to adopt in order to reduce contradictions between its short- and medium-term interests and the requirements of a 'world development policy'.

REFERENCES
Official documents:

Conseil fédéral, 1993, 'Rapport sur la politique extérieure de la Suisse dans les années 90 du 29 novembre 1993', Berne.
Federal Council, 1994, 'North–South Guidelines', Report by the Federal Council on Switzerland's North–South Relations in the 1990s, Berne: SDC (English translation SDC, 1995).
Conseil fédéral, 1995, 'Message concernant l'initiative populaire "pour l'interdiction d'exporter du matériel de guerre" et la révision de la loi fédérale sur le matériel de guerre du 15 février 1995'.
Conseil fédéral, 1996, 'Message relatif à la loi fédérale concernant la lutte contre le blanchissage d'argent dans le secteur financier du 17 juin 1996'.
DAC/OECD, 1996, 'Switzerland', Development Co-operation Review Series No.20, Paris, 1996.
OECD, 1992, *Development Co-operation*, 1992 Report, Paris.
OECD, 1994, *Development Co-operation*, 1993 Report, Paris.

---

22. There is sometimes a tendency to 'Helvetocentrism', that is, to overestimate the influence Switzerland can exert in its bilateral policy dialogue with partner developing countries. The question is whether this tendency is a cause or an effect of the country's reluctance to participate fully in international forums (reminder: Switzerland is not a member of the UN).

Books and articles:

Annuaire Suisse–Tiers Monde 1980, 1981, Genève: IUED.
Annuaire Suisse–Tiers Monde 1996, 1996, Genève: IUED.
Borghi, M., 1995, 'Droits de l'homme: fondements universels pour une loi anti-corruption; le cas de la Suisse', in M. Borghi *et al.* (eds.), *La corruption, l'envers des droits de l'homme,* Fribourg: Editions de l'Université de Fribourg.
Cart, H.-Ph., 1995, 'Principes et limites d'une politique de coopération au développement: que peut faire la DDA?' in M. Borghi *et al.* (eds.).
Commission des organisations suisses de coopération au développement, 1975, *Maldéveloppement Suisse–Monde,* Genève: CETIM.
Forster, J., 1995, 'Conditionality in Swiss Development Assistance', in Olav Stokke (ed.), *Aid and Political Conditionality,* EADI Book Series 16, London: Frank Cass.
Fukasaku, K. and A. Hirata, 1995, 'The OECD and ASEAN: Changing Economic Linkages and the Challenge of Policy Coherence', in K. Fukasaku *et al.* (eds.), *The OECD and ASEAN Economies. The Challenge of Policy Coherence,* Development Centre Documents, Paris: OECD.
Gerster, R., 1995, *Nord–Süd Politik: Abschreiben oder Investieren? Perspektiven der schweizerischen Entwicklungszusammenarbeit,* Zürich: Orell Füssli.
Greminger, T., 1996, 'La cohérence des politiques – un premier bilan de la mise en oeuvre des lignes directices Nord–Sud de la Suisse', in Daniel Fino (ed.), *Impasses et promesses, l'ambiguïté de la coopération au développement,* Nouveau Cahiers de l'IUED, Paris: PUF.
Hadorn, A., 1995, 'La Suisse et les relations Nord–Sud dans les années 90', *Annuaire Suisse–Tiers Monde,* Genève: IUED.
Kindleberger, C.P., 1986, 'International Public Goods without International Government', *The American Economic Review,* Vol.76, No.1, March.
Maurer, P., 1995, 'Réflexions sur la cohérence', *Annuaire Suisse–Tiers Monde,* Genève: IUED.
Weyermann, R., 1996, 'Switzerland Country Profile', *The Reality of Aid,* London: Earthscan.

Unpublished papers and documents, press articles:

Conseil national, 96.1110, 'Question ordinaire urgente Groupe écologiste. Projet de construction d'un barrage en Chine. Pas de garantie des risques à l'exportation (GRE)', 26 Nov. 1996, Berne.
DDC, Section politique et recherche, 'Plan d'action de la DDC pour la mise en oeuvre des lignes directrices Nord–Sud, décembre 1995', Berne (document de travail interne).
Lévy, A. and T. Greminger, 1997, 'Coopération au développement, Comment éviter la corruption?', in *Vers un développement solidaire,* Déclaration de Berne, No.137, Lausanne.
Mireku, E., 1992, 'Switzerland', Policy Framework Paper 1993–2000, Swiss Aid Agencies Coalition, Berne.
SDES, 1996, Documentation, 'Loi sur le matériel de guerre, un contre-projet contesté', No.8, Genève.

10

Coherence and Development Policy: The Case of the European Union

PAUL HOEBINK

The debate on the implementation of the development sections of the Maastricht Treaty can be said to revolve around three Cs: co-ordination, coherence and complementarity. This chapter will deal with one of these three Cs, namely, coherence as defined in Article 130v of the Treaty on European Union (EU). The term refers not only to the coherence of development policy but also to coherence between the development objectives mentioned in the Union Treaty and other policies of the Community. In the first section, the term coherence is explained, the legal basis for coherence of policy described and various forms of incoherence identified. In the second section, the measures taken since 1992[1] and the debate hitherto are outlined and, finally, some mechanisms to achieve greater coherence of development policy in the EU are proposed.

This chapter was originally written in conjunction with the preparation of a report of the National Advisory Council on the Dutch presidency of the European Union in the first half of 1997. The author takes this opportunity to thank the members of the working group which produced the report for their comments on ideas in this text previously presented to them. A later version was presented at the EADI VIII General Conference in Vienna, September 1996. It has also profited from discussions in a seminar on policy coherence at the European Centre for Development Policy Management, Maastricht in March 1997. Needless to say, the author alone is responsible for the ideas and views expressed in this chapter. The advisory report was published in August 1996 under the title *Advies betreffende het Nederlands voorzitterschap van de Europese Unie in 1997* (Recommendation Concerning the Dutch Presidency of the European Union in 1997).
1.   The negotiations regarding the Treaty on European Union were completed during the European Council in Maastricht on 9 and 10 December 1991. The Treaty was signed in Maastricht on 7 February 1992.

POLICY COHERENCE IN DEVELOPMENT CO-OPERATION

I. COHERENCE OF POLICY

Coherence is a relatively new concept both in politics and in the political sciences. There is in fact no mention of it in the standard textbooks on the social sciences.[2] Although the political science literature on policy evaluation notes that a causal link between policy and policy results is often hard to determine, it does not in general deal with the way in which other parts of government policy may interfere with the relevant results or even frustrate the policy altogether.[3] For example, the unintended results of government policy are disposed of in a few standard sentences. The literature on economic policy is an exception in this respect, since here the credibility of government action is linked to its ability to ensure that policy fluctuates as little as possible.

To arrive at a definition we must therefore first consult the dictionaries. These state that coherence is synonymous with consistency.[4] Consistency and coherence of thought and statement therefore mean 'free from self-contradiction'(*Concise Oxford Dictionary; The Wordsworth Concise Dictionary; Van Dale, the Dutch Dictionary*). Coherence of policy could therefore possibly be defined as: 'The non-occurrence of effects of policy that are contrary to the intended results or aims of policy.' For this purpose coherence can be defined either narrowly or broadly. A narrow definition would be that objectives of policy in a particular field may not be undermined or obstructed by actions or activities in this field; and a wide definition would be that objectives of policy in a particular field may not be undermined or obstructed by actions or activities of government in that field or in other policy fields.

---

2.   See, for example, *Blackwell Encyclopedia of Political Thought* (1987), *International Encyclopedia of Social Sciences* (1968, first and later editions), *Political Science Dictionary* (1973), *Handlexicon zur Politikwissenschaften* (1970, first and later editions) and *Piper's Wörterbuch zur Politik* (1985). The same is also true of similar terms such as consistency and inconsistency. Even a search for the rather older term 'unity of policy' fails to produce any workable definitions or references.
3.   One example of this is Blommenstein *et al.* [*1984*]. Nor is this point dealt with in recent literature on political science. See for example Van Deth (ed.) [*1993*].
4.   The Van Dale Dutch dictionary in fact regards coherence as synonymous with cohesion, which is itself defined as intrinsic harmony, this being in turn the definition of consistency. If consistency is regarded as more or less synonymous with coherence, one of the few definitions to be found in academic literature can be seen to be tautological: 'Consistency connotes the need to maintain a coherent policy course over time and across multiple measures' [*Weatherford, 1994: 135–64*]. The definitions of 'inconsistency' in the economic literature are concerned in particular with the way in which economic actors respond to a given policy. See, for example, Kydland and Prescott [*1977: 473–91*], Blackburn and Christensen [*1989: 1–45*].

324

Coherence of policy is in principle important to every field of government policy. First of all, because in the case of incoherence it is possible that certain intended results of policy may be partially or completely frustrated. Second, because the attainment of objectives in a particular policy field could also be hampered by action taken in the relevant field or in other fields, which could produce an adverse effect. And third, because government authorities might lose their legitimacy and credibility if they frustrate or hamper the attainment of objectives in a particular field by means of activities in a different field. It follows that incoherence has the effect of undermining the entire administration. Coherence of policy should therefore be a general objective in all action taken by government.

Notwithstanding the efforts to achieve coherence of policy, incoherence is often a given. First, as government has to deal with many parties and pressure groups, it may well be impossible to find optimal solutions that satisfy all parties concerned and achieve all objectives. Consequently, it is frequently necessary to settle for second-best solutions which may in turn lead to incoherence. Incoherence therefore should not always be regarded as a negative factor and may in some cases be seen instead as a result of clashes and conflicts of interest, in other words, as a compromise in which the relative importance of the actions and actors has been duly weighed.

Second, government is not a unitary whole, but generally consists of a large number of departments, institutions and corporations.[5] These departments and institutions take a large number of policy measures, monitor their implementation and are quite often faced with conflicting interests. It is doubtful whether central government is in a position to keep a grip on the policy of all these different bodies. For example, its supervision of the outcome and results of policy is far from complete.

Third, it is difficult to weigh all the factors and parties and their reactions to an initial policy decision. Consequently, it is often unclear what will be the precise effects of the policy. Finally, administrators and politicians, like academics, tend to be rather short-sighted; in other words they focus entirely on the particular policy field for which they are expected to take measures at the time in question. Sometimes they are also required to be short-sighted and to remedy short-term negative effects at the expense of optimal policy in the long term.

---

5. Weatherford [*1994*], emphasises that in the economic literature government is, however, often regarded as a unitary actor.

All the factors just mentioned apply perhaps in particular to European policy, because not only is the number of parties much greater but there are also many more different types of party. In addition to the cultural, social and economic interests of particular groups or institutions, national interests, as the sum of all these other interests, also play a role in European policy in these fields. It is less easy in European policy than in national policy to find a single forum in which consensus can be reached. In a recent article Hellen Wallace [*1996:28*] noted that there is an 'inherent instability' in European policy. By this she meant that:

> ... it is rarely certain that the outcome of the policy dialogue will produce a clear and consistent line of policy amenable to a sustained collective regime. In other words, European policy regimes are conditional rather than definitive, a consequence of the continuing fluidity of the political setting of less than a policy, pulled between the political territories of the member states and the pressures of global and European influences.

In the same volume Christopher Stevens describes this phenomenon, in an analysis of the EU banana policy, as inherent to the 'crab-like fashion' in which EU policies evolve. As he comments, 'It can easily find itself with mutually incompatible obligations' [*Stevens, 1996*].

Nigel Nugent singles out two important characteristics of European policy: first, 'the differing degrees of EU policy involvement', and second, 'the patchy and somewhat uncoordinated nature of EU policies'. By the latter he means [*Nugent, 1994: 291*]:

> The EU's overall policy framework can hardly be said to display a clear pattern of overall coherence ... The fact is that the considerable national and political differences which exist in the EU make coordinated and coherent policy development that is based on shared principles and agreed objectives very difficult.

This is particularly true of European development co-operation. Different forms of incoherence in this field can be found in the policy not only of the EU but also most certainly of the member states. Nugent argues that the member states think of their own interests first. Whether the relevant policy is politically acceptable is a matter that is considered later. Finally, it is decided whether the EU is the appropriate arena in which to give effect to closer relations between states [*Nugent, 1994: 295*]. At the same time it is necessary to reconcile the differing interests of various national industries or groups. Not surprisingly, development objectives often have to take a back seat. One reason is that the cacophony generated by the member states and pressure groups tends to drown out the arguments of those advocating development objectives, whose voice may therefore be heard only indistinctly or indirectly.

II. THE LEGAL BASIS OF COHERENCE

Article 130v of Title XVII of the Treaty on European Union – the Maastricht Treaty – states that [*CEC, 1992: 61*]:

> The Community shall take account of the objectives referred to in Article 130u in the policies that it implements which are likely to affect developing countries.

This article could be called the Maastricht Treaty's 'coherence article' in the field of development co-operation. Article 130v refers to Article 130u, which sets out the general development objectives for the Community [*CEC, 1992: 61*]:

(1) Community policy in the sphere of Development Cooperation, which shall be complementary to the policies pursued by the Member States, shall foster: the sustainable economic and social development of the developing countries, and more particularly the most disadvantaged amongst them; the smooth and gradual integration of the developing countries into the world economy; the campaign against poverty in the developing countries.

(2) Community Policy in this area shall contribute to the general objective of developing and consolidating democracy and the rule of law, and to that of respect for human rights and fundamental freedoms.

The link between development policy and other policies is, according to the Commission [*1994*], also set down in the Common Provisions of the Union Treaty in Article C:

> The Union shall in particular ensure the consistency of its external activities as a whole in the context of its external relations, security, economic and development policies. The Council and the Commission shall be responsible for ensuring such

consistency. They shall ensure the implementation of these policies, each in accordance with its respective powers.

If these articles from the text of the Treaty are put side by side, the following definition of coherence in relation to development policy can be obtained [*Dubois, 1994: 11*]:

> The articulation between different policies or actions of the Community which aim to minimise or suppress contradictory or negative effects of these policies on developing countries.

In its Declaration on development policy for the year 2000, the EC Council of Ministers of Development Co-operation emphasised the importance of coherence of policy at its meeting of November 1992. The Declaration referred among other things to the 'linkage' between development co-operation policy and other areas of Community policy [*CEC, 1992: Article 27*]:

> The Council recognises the linkage between development co-operation policy and other Community policies. It also recognises the need to take account of their impact on developing countries. The Council urges the Commission to consider how this impact assessment might be carried out more systematically especially with regard to new proposals. It invites the Commission to report in time for the meeting of the Development Council in November 1993 on how it takes account of the objectives referred to in paragraph 18 in the policies that it implements which are likely to affect developing countries.

The relevant report, which will be dealt with in later paragraphs, was presented in November 1994.

It should also be noted that there is already some precedent concerning this article in the form of the Commission's decision on beef export subsidies of May 1994. The Commission stated as follows in this decision:

> It is therefore necessary to take measures to end the serious incoherence that exists between the agricultural policy and the development policy of the Community. Such measures are all the more urgent because this harmonisation is a duty imposed by the Treaty on European Union (Article 130v).

The Commission also proposed measures such as the collection of data and adjustment of the subsidies 'for the purpose of ensuring coherence between the Common Agricultural Policy and the development policy' [*Commission of the European Communities, 1994a*]. As far as coherence relating to the development objectives established in the Union Treaty is concerned, it is possible to draw a certain parallel with Article 130r. This states that [*CEC, 1992: 58*]: 'Environmental protection requirements must be integrated into the definition and the implementation of other Community policies.'

In conclusion, therefore, the term coherence does not appear as such in the Treaty on European Union. Instead the Treaty talks about 'taking account of'. In a later resolution the Council refers to 'the linkage that exists' and to 'the impact'. It was not until the Commission's decision on beef export subsidies of May 1994 that the terms coherence and incoherence were used.[6]

III. COHERENCE AND INCOHERENCE IN EU POLICY

Various types of incoherence can be identified. Three possible classifications are given below. Two of them are institutional (linked with different institutions), one is related to causes for incoherences. There is a classification consisting of three types (external, internal, and what we will call 'inter'). Each of the other two classifications consists of two types (horizontal/vertical and intended/unintended).

The *first classification* (see Figure 1) concerns, as said, three types of incoherence. First of all, there may be incoherence between the development objectives of the Maastricht Treaty and the external policy of the Community (external type). It is called 'external type' because different aspects of foreign policy (development co-operation, trade, foreign policy in general) are brought into this category. In terms of this volume this could be (in)coherence within aid policy, as well as (in)coherence within South policies. It could, however, also involve (in)coherences between development co-operation policies and other elements of foreign policy, not directed specifically at developing countries but indirectly affecting them. Second, incoherence may exist between Community development policy and internal Community policies (internal type). These are policies directed at internal European issues or affairs that might have an (unintended) effect on developing countries. Finally, there may be incoherence between Community development policy and the development policy

---

6. As mentioned in the texts of officials of DG VIII quoted below, Article 130v is referred to as the 'coherence article'.

of the individual member states or between European development policy and policies of developing countries, what I call the 'inter type' (derived from 'inter-European' and 'intercontinental').

FIGURE 1
(IN)COHERENCE BETWEEN DEVELOPMENT POLICY OF THE EU AND OTHER POLICIES
TYPOLOGY 1 (INSTITUTIONAL)

	Development objectives EU		
External Type (1)	Development policy	External policy	Commercial policy
Internal Type (2)	Environmental policy	Agricultural policy/ Fisheries policy	Industrial policy
Inter- (European) type (3)	Development policy of the member states	Policy of developing countries	

An example of the *first type* of incoherence, that is, the external type, is incoherence in European development policy itself. This mainly involves incoherence between the different objectives and/or instruments of development policy. An obvious example is food aid: aid that is sent too late may arrive just at the moment when the local farmers are getting in the harvest. In such circumstances the food aid may limit the scope for them to sell the very produce which they have been encouraged to grow by development programmes.

A second example of this type of incoherence is the overall external activities of the Union in relation to development policy. It was noted in the Benelux memorandum for the Intergovernmental Conference in Turin in March 1996 that there is a lack of 'unity in the external activities' of the Union.[7] Arms export policy is an example of this. Various European member states rank among the world's main arms exporters. A major part of these arms exports is sent to developing countries, where the arms are often used in internal conflicts or for repression. Arms exports of this kind, many of which do not satisfy the criterion of a legitimate need for defence, are contrary to the development objectives of Article 130u and also to the international efforts to reduce defence expenditure.

Finally, the third example of this type of incoherence is between development objectives and commercial policy. If it is the intention to integrate the developing countries gradually into the world economy, they should be given sufficient opportunity to sell their products in

---

7.   It is striking to note in this connection that neither the word 'development' nor the theme of development appears in any of the four preparatory government memoranda for the Intergovernmental Conference [*Ministry of Foreign Affairs, 1994/1995*].

the European market and hence to have as far as possible unrestricted access to it. The objectives of Article 130u should also be taken into account when all kinds of decisions are taken. In practice, many different interests often have to be weighed when such decisions are taken and the internal interests of producers of the member states are frequently given precedence. Examples are the so-called cocoa decision (harmonisation of the internal market by diminishing the cocoa content in chocolate) and the resistance to the importation of cut flowers and tomatoes.[8] Also politicians often have difficulty in weighing the different interests.[9]

The *second type* of incoherence is that between the development policy of the Community and internal European policy. Because this implies a conflict between internal policies and development objectives of the EU, we call this type 'internal'. A first example of this type of incoherence to be mentioned here is incoherence between development policy and environmental policy. Article 130r, which has been referred to above, records that environmental protection requirements must be integrated into other Community policies. This also implies review of the European activities in the area of development co-operation, a 'greening' of European development policy. European policy in this field is still very much underdeveloped: Directorate General (DG) I (external relations, also to Latin America and Asia) and DG VIII (development, particularly the Lomé Convention) have only a small staff for this field, there are still few detailed policy documents and procedures and there is little co-operation between DG I and DG VIII in the development of policy and procedures on environmental impact.

A second form which this type of incoherence could take is that between development policy and other internal Community policies. The most obvious example of this is the common agricultural policy

---

8. If integration of the developing countries into the world economy is an express objective of European policy (according to Article 130u), the Community should provide greater access to products which developing countries can deliver on competitive terms and which compete with those made by European producers. The resistance to the treaty with Morocco in 1996 and the laborious negotiations with South Africa indicate that this objective is often not taken into account.

9. For example, during a debate in the Dutch parliament on the conclusion of a treaty with Morocco, a spokeswoman of the Christian Democratic party opposed the treaty and actually presented a motion against it on the grounds that it would harm the interests of the Dutch horticultural sector (Proceedings of the Lower House of Parliament, 30-2268, 23 November 1996, and 31-2362, 28 November 1996). As the spokeswoman in question also represented her party in development matters, she might have been expected in that capacity to advocate that Morocco should have freer access to the European market.

(CAP).[10] Over a period of several decades, Third World groups have pointed out that subsidising the production of sugar beet and barring cane sugar from the European market are inconsistent with development policy.[11] Another example is the fisheries policy. The absence of measures to reduce the size of the fishing fleets means that the problem of overcapacity has not been tackled and has in fact been spread abroad by the conclusion of catch quotas under fisheries agreements. Two criticisms of these fisheries agreements are that they create problems for the local, small-scale fishing fleets and that there is a danger of overfishing because of the lack of inspections of catches.[12]

A third form of incoherence that could exist is between development policy and industrial policy. The Community could provide developing countries with better access to the European market by means of preferences, yet at the same time give de facto preferential treatment to European industry by means of subsidies or rules, thereby putting it in a better competitive position, or even shield the market altogether and thus, in contradiction with development policy goals, hampering industrialisation of developing countries.

The *third and last type* of incoherence that can be identified in this connection is the inter-European/continental type – that is, incoherence between, at first, the donor policies of the EU and of the member states and, secondly, between donor policies and policies of developing countries (donor coherence and donor-recipient coherence).[13] It is conceivable, particularly in the case of specific projects and programmes, that certain activities which the Union finances or undertakes may be at odds with similar activities of the member states. This could, for example, happen in health care policy if the Union were to wish to encourage primary health care in developing countries whereas a member state, for economic and commercial reasons, is funding projects in hospital health care (donor incoherence). Hospital financing often already takes up an excessively large proportion of the future budgetary resources for health care of the recipient country. The recipient country might have in principle a health policy aimed at

---

10. Some recent studies are: Rolland [*1995*]; SOLAGRAL [*1995*]; Dhondt [*1994*].
11. There is much literature on this subject. See, for example, Stevens and Webb [*1983*]; McDonald [*1996*].
12. See, *inter alia*: FAO Fisheries Department [*1995*]; Greenpeace [*1993*]; CEC [*1993: 91ff*]; European Research Office [*1995a; 1995b; 1995c*].
13. As identified by a former senior official of the Commission: Frisch [*1994*]. This could perhaps better be described as a lack of co-ordination between the Commission and the member states rather than as an example of incoherence.

primary health care, which is redirected by the donor's policy (donor–recipient incoherence).[14]

One of the most important instruments to overcome this type of incoherence is co-ordination. Article 130x of the Maastricht Treaty provides that the Community and the member states should co-ordinate their policy in the area of development co-operation. The article also confers on the Commission a right to initiate policy in this field. An experiment in which the Commission and the member states are endeavouring to co-ordinate their policies in four fields was started in six developing countries in 1994.[15]

A second form which this type of incoherence may take is where the development policy of the Union and/or the member states clashes with a policy of a developing country, which undermines the development objectives of the European Union and hence the assistance that is provided in this connection (donor–recipient incoherence). Policy on investment, prices, industry, agriculture, import and defence are the most obvious factors involving incoherence. Conditionality is one of the answers to the incoherence noted here over time.

FIGURE 2

(IN)COHERENCE BETWEEN DEVELOPMENT POLICY OF THE EU AND OTHER EUROPEAN OR MEMBER STATES' POLICIES
TYPOLOGY 2 (INSTITUTIONAL)

		Vertical		
		International organisations		
Horizontal	DG I (Commerce)	DG I/DG VIII (Development)	DG VI/XIV (Agriculture/ Fisheries)	DG XI (Environment)
		(Ministries) Member states/ Central banks		
		Governments/ Ministries (Developing countries)		

14. In the policy documents on health it is stated: 'The aid provided did not tie in properly with national health policies as it often tended to reflect donors' concerns rather than the needs and priorities of recipient countries ... the aid was very largely focused on investment' [*CEC, 1994b*]. The hospitals built by Belgium and Italy in Cameroon are an example of this. See *De Morgen* (24 Nov. 1995).

15. The countries concerned are Peru, Costa Rica, Bangladesh, Ivory Coast, Mozambique and Ethiopia and the policy fields concerned are poverty relief, food security, education and health care.

FIGURE 3
(IN)COHERENCE BETWEEN DEVELOPMENT POLICY OF THE EU AND OTHER POLICIES
TYPOLOGY 3 (CAUSES)

	Cause	Remedy
Unintended	* interests of developing countries not weighed/left aside * no clear representation of developing countries' interests * knowledge of effects absent	* impact study * mechanisms for better weighing
Intended	* developing countries' interests set aside * member states' interests of more importance * better lobbying by competing interests * no clear assessment available	* impact study * mechanisms for better weighing * compensation * accept incoherence
Structural a. general b. differentiated	* consumers versus producers * producers versus environment * producers versus producers * consumers versus consumers	* accept incoherence * compensation
Temporary	* producers versus producers * producers versus environment	* compensation for modernisation * additional/flanking policy
Fictive	* producers versus producers * consumers versus producers	* mediation * information
Institutional	* cultural differences between institutions * ideological differences between institutions * compartimentalisation of policy departments (horizontal) * lack of co-ordination (vertical)	* transparency/information * co-ordination
Political/ Economic	* conflicting interests (inside member states, between member states, between EU and others) * complexity of issues * deregulation/liberalisation * internationalisation/globalisation	* tolerate incoherence * mitigation * compensation * additional/flanking policy

The *second possible classification* (see Figure 2) of coherence/ incoherence is between horizontal and vertical incoherence. The horizontal type involves the coherence or incoherence of the policies of different Brussels bureaucracies. In other words, cases where the policy on commerce, agriculture and fisheries, the environment and possibly other subjects clashes with the objectives of development policy (this concerns in particular the internal type referred to above but also to a certain extent the external type). The vertical type concerns the coherence of the policy of the member states and developing countries, of the European Commission and of international institutions (financial and otherwise). It includes the inter-European type of coherence as well as to some extent external coherence. Vertical in this instance does not necessarily mean a hierarchy, but is referring to the diverse – from local to global – echelons in decision making. In certain aspects international law and jurisdiction might lead national policies, but great autonomy still exists for 'lower' levels of decision making. Under Article 130r, paragraph 4, the member states are competent to negotiate and conclude agreements in international fora. Yet the Community too may conclude agreements with third parties and act as representative of the member states. The competence problem in this field has not yet been solved.[16] For development purposes, what is particularly important is who acts on whose behalf in the OECD, GATT/WTO and the international financial institutions. For example, European policy on the adjustment and debt problem is relatively incoherent because the different members states and the Community quite often speak a different language.

The *third and last possible classification* of incoherence is that between intended and unintended incoherence. Intended incoherence would be a form in which an authority consciously accepts that the objectives of policy in a particular field cannot be achieved because the policy involves conflicting interests. An example of this is where a government accepts that developing countries will have restricted market access for their exports because domestic employment in certain sectors would otherwise be unduly affected. Compensation may possibly be provided in the form of limited or regulated market access, of concessions in other fields or of cash. A further distinction

---

16. This is the view of Kapteyn *et al.* [*Kapteyn and Verloren van Themaat, 1995: 643–4, 757ff*]. One of the factors that plays a role here is the membership of international organisations which often accept only states as members in accordance with the provisions of their founding convention. In such cases, the Community has 'observer status' at most.

can be made here between an intended incoherence to correct adverse effects in the short term while adhering to the longer-term objectives and an incoherence which is intended purely to remedy certain negative effects for particular parties in the short term. To paraphrase Weatherford, one could call the former incoherence a 'dynamic incoherence' [*Weatherford, 1994:139*], because there is an attempt to establish a balance between two things that are to a certain extent incompatible, between what is good at a given moment and what is good in general.

In the case of unintended incoherence, policies in a particular field frustrate the objectives or results of other policies although this is not noticed because the results of the different policies are never compared. Such an incoherence could frequently occur in the development field because policy produces results at a great distance, which are therefore less visible or are made less visible. An example of this is the meat export subsidies: the effects of these subsidies on the West African market (negative effects from the development point of view) became apparent only when European NGOs revealed them. If, however, subsidised exports were to be resumed because of the growing meat mountain, this would represent a transition from unintended to intended incoherence.

IV. DEBATE AND MEASURES TAKEN HITHERTO

On 18 November 1992 the EC Council of Ministers of Development Co-operation urged the European Commission to make a study of the practical consequences of Article 130v. When the Council met a year later the study had not been presented. And six months on again, in 1994, the Commission had done no more than hold some consultations with external experts. According to officials of DG VIII, the delay was attributable to the dismissive attitude of some member states to this problem. The Commission was also said to be too understaffed to undertake the preparation of a report of this kind [*Dhondt, 1994:93*].

At the end of April 1993 European NGOs started lobbying against the meat exports to West Africa (or rather the subsidies on such exports). They maintained that these exports could be regarded as dumping and that they therefore disrupted the local meat markets [*Eurostep, 1993a; Eurostep, 1993b; Klugkist, 1993/1994*]. This was at odds both with European projects to encourage meat production in some Sahel countries and with European development objectives.[17] The incoherence between European development policy and commercial policy was expressly pointed out by the lobbying parties.

As a result of this lobbying, both the French and the German development ministries commissioned studies of the meat exports and the coherence problem. This increased the pressure on the Commission. Following urgent representations by the Netherlands and Germany, the relevant commissioner (Marin) produced the meat exports report (quoted previously) in which the negative effects were confirmed and adjustments to the subsidies were announced. As mentioned above, this report was the first to include clear references to Article 130v. The Commission announced that it wished to 'ensure coherence' between European development policy and the common agricultural policy.

Thus it was that a report of the Commission was finally produced in which Article 130v was accepted as the 'coherence article'. It was noted that since the Union did not have a comprehensive foreign policy, short-term considerations could often hold sway. As a result, the provision of aid could take precedence over the provision of market access. The job of the Commission in respect of coherence is above all to identify problems in good time and to minimise the negative effects. According to the report, the Commission wishes to concentrate on new policy in order to ensure that the problems remain manageable. No specific proposals were put forward in the Commission document for this purpose. In the debate on the report, the Council therefore got no further than the proposal of the relevant commissioner (Pinheiro) to continue the study and consultations.[18] Although the Netherlands proposed that a mechanism be adopted for identifying present and future problems of incoherence, and Belgium wished to have a joint session of the EC Agriculture and Development Councils, neither suggestion has yet been acted upon. Six months later Denmark submitted a proposal for the design of a system of indicators.

---

17. A German study concluded that the meat exports of Mali and Burkina Faso in the period 1985–93 could have been 20–40 per cent higher if there had been no subsidised exports of frozen meat to Ivory Coast from the EU. See Brandt [*1994*].
18. Statement to the Press, 1849th session of the EC Development Council, Luxembourg, 1 June 1995. The Commission emphasised in a previous meeting of the Directors-General that they would often need to reconcile widely differing interests. The banana file was cited as an example; here the completion of the internal market had to be reconciled with relations with ACP countries, relations with Latin America and requirements in the context of GATT/WTO.

The organisational structure of the new Commission under the presidency of Santer was made 'flatter' in the winter of 1994 to 1995. Different groups of commissioners were instituted for this purpose to co-ordinate certain policy fields. One of these groups concerned the external relations of the Union and consisted of representatives of five commissioners whose portfolio includes foreign policy or aspects of foreign policy. This group has above all a co-ordinating role. In addition, its terms of reference include assuring 'a coherent attitude on horizontal questions, susceptible to affect actions of the Commission in different geographical zones relevant to the responsibilities of the Commissioners'.[19] As far as coherence is concerned, this group is concentrating on new policy and exclusively on foreign policy. The subject of incoherence with internal European policy has not yet (May 1996) been raised.[20]

In May 1996 the European NGOs started a fresh lobbying campaign with regard to Article 130v. On this occasion the campaign concerned the fishing industry. The European Union was blamed for not having reduced the overcapacity of its fishing fleets, and for having simply exported the problem by concluding fisheries agreements. European fishermen, mainly from a few southern member states, are in this way being allocated free fishing rights in the waters of developing countries at the Community's expense. Although the latest generation of these agreements does contain provisions to protect local coastal fishing, there is no adequately equipped inspection service to monitor compliance. As a result, the local small fishermen are suffering. Once again the example comes from West Africa, on this occasion from Senegal.[21]

In the first half of 1997 the Dutch presidency put coherence high on its priority list. In this connection it organised a discussion on 1 March in the Amsterdam Arena on the sectors: conflict prevention, food security, fisheries agreements and migration. The goal was to bring a largely theoretical discussion back to concrete issues.[22] In the Council meeting of 5 June a resolution with regard to coherence of EU policy was adopted. The Commission was urged to report regularly on coherence issues and to present a report in 1998. Furthermore, it should describe questions with regard to coherence in policy

---

19. Groupes de Commissaires, Bruxelles, Commission Européenne, 24 janvier 1995 (O/95/12).
20. Discussions with officials of the Commission in May and June 1996.
21. See, *inter alia*, European Research Office [*1995a; 1995b; 1995c*].
22. Based on Letters to the Dutch Parliament of 26 May 1997 and 5 June 1997, containing the agenda and the unofficial minutes of the Council Meeting of 5 June 1997.

proposals when relevant, and the council concerned should discuss these when the results might be negative for developing countries. In future Councils, trade, environment and agriculture are subjects that will be central in the discussion of coherence.

V. MECHANISMS FOR PROMOTING COHERENCE

It is unclear to what extent Article 130v and its implementation enjoy wide support in the European Union, the Commission and the member states. The article has been repeatedly cited by European NGOs and development aid ministries in connection with the identification of incoherent policy. However, there appears at present not to be much enthusiasm outside these circles for implementing Article 130v. Various proposals have been made in the past to promote the coherence of development co-operation in Europe.

In a recommendation on the Maastricht Treaty, the Netherlands' National Advisory Council for Development Co-operation concluded in 1994 that it would be possible to increase the coherence of policy only in those fields in which the organs of the EU have primary responsibility for common policy [*NAR, 1993*]. In view of the examples of incoherence given here, these fields would be above all the relevant development policy of the Union itself, the commercial policy, the common agricultural and fisheries policy and the environmental policy. The Netherlands' National Advisory Council considered that the Commission should make proposals for increasing coherence. It also recommended that the Commission should report annually to the EC Council and the European Parliament on the progress made in this field, at the same time identifying and describing the problems encountered in increasing the coherence of development policy and other parts of European policy.

In a second report published recently the Netherlands' National Advisory Council concluded that the Commission's November 1994 document on coherence was rather defensive and did little more than describe the problem, without providing instruments that could actually be used to promote coherence. The case-by-case approach advocated by the Commission means that the supervisory role accorded to the Commission in the Maastricht Treaty is in practice being neglected. The Advisory Council once again stated that it was up to the European commissioner, Pinheiro, to make new proposals for procedures. Consequently, it is starting to look very much as though delay is tantamount to cancellation.

In a study of the coherence of development policy and European agricultural policy commissioned by the French development ministry, the French research institute SOLAGRAL proposed a series of measures to promote coherence.[23] First of all, it recommended that a working group of civil servants of different DGs be set up to assess the impact of measures to achieve the development objectives of Article 130u. In addition, it suggested that a group of experts be established to carry out impact and other studies.

Proposals were also made by a church conference held in January 1994. First, it recommended that there should be regular consultations between European and ACP ministers in various relevant policy fields in which it was felt that relations should be clarified and strengthened. The second proposal was that a system should be established for the assessment and evaluation of policies analogous to the environmental clause (Article 130r) [Lutterbeck, 1994]. On the subject of the latter mechanism for achieving coherence, it should be noted that the Commission announced in June 1993 that it would take account of the impact of all its activities on the environment and would have an environmental impact study prepared where the impact was expected to be significant.[24] Each Directorate General would be required to assess the environmental impact of measures or programmes. If necessary, impact studies would have to be carried out. Proposals that could have a major impact on the environment would have to obtain a green asterisk and include a section dealing with the environmental impact.[25]

In addition to these proposals, consideration could also be given to the idea of instituting a complaints procedure comparable to that of the Inspection Panel of the World Bank, as the Netherlands' National Advisory Council suggested.[26] Such a panel could consist of a small number (three or five) of independent members nominated by the member states and the Commission and appointed by the EC Development Co-operation Council. Governments and organisations from developing countries and member states of the European Union could file complaints with such a panel concerning incoherences in European policy. The relevant panel would require the powers and capa-

---

23. See, for example, Rolland [1995]. And the final report: Jadot and Rolland [1996].
24. Integrating the environment into other policy areas within the Commission, Press Communiqué, IP(93) 427, 2 June 1993.
25. Commission document (Sec(93)785/final), 3 June 1993 and Manual of Procedures of the European Commission, paragraph 9.5.4.
26. For a description of the establishment and procedures of the Inspection Panel, see Shihata [1994].

city to investigate and report on complaints systematically. It could then make recommendations to the EC Council for ending or reducing incoherence.

In a reaction to this advice the minister for development co-operation of the Netherlands concluded that he would indeed like to give the initiative in this field to the Commission. Regarding the possibilities for a complaint procedure for NGOs and others, Pronk wanted better access and better information on the existing complaints procedures with the Commission and with the European Parliament. He wanted to foster the debate on coherence by discussions on specific themes (food security, fisheries, migration, conflict prevention).[27] The Danish government also pleaded to give more attention to the issue of coherence by means of discussions on concrete themes, such as food security and the CAP. It expressed its disappointment about the absence of concrete proposals in Commission documents. In an earlier phase it proposed a study on indicators for incoherence, but found no followers in the Council [*Ministry of Foreign Affairs/Danida, 1996: 155–7*].

The various instruments referred to above would have certain advantages and disadvantages. For example, annual reporting and a complaints procedure would be conducive to greater transparency and openness in matters relating to the coherence of policy. On the other hand, an annual report might become nothing more than a ritual with no real value. Another advantage of a complaints procedure would be that the initiatives would not be determined solely by the Commission and could therefore be wider-ranging. However, if no investigative capacity is available or investigations are stonewalled by a lack of openness, such a procedure would have to be terminated because the integrity of the Panel members might otherwise be compromised.

The introduction of a screening test could have various advantages since each decision would have to be weighed. But a disadvantage might be the amount of red tape involved, particularly if it is found in due course that the interests are not even capable of being assessed. The environmental screening test is not yet operating sufficiently smoothly and in all relevant areas, and to date it has not been evaluated.

---

27. Letter from the Minister for Development Co-operation to the Chairman of the National Advisory Council, 30 December 1996.

FIGURE 4
PROPOSED INSTRUMENTS TO FOSTER COHERENCE IN DEVELOPMENT POLICY

	Instrument	Advantages	Disadvantages
National Advisory Council (Netherlands)	Report annually to the EC Council and the European Parliament	* greater transparency and openness	* could be defensive and thus ritualistic * more paper work
National Advisory Council (Netherlands)	Complaints procedure/Insp ection Panel	* greater transparency and openness * initiatives not solely by Commission and therefore wider-ranging	* needs investigative capacity
National Advisory Council (Netherlands)	Screening test	* decisions would have to be weighed	* red tape * window dressing * sometimes difficult to be assessed
SOLAGRAL (French research institute)	Working group of civil servants of different DGs	* decisions would have to be weighed	* lack of transparency * purely bureaucratic
SOLAGRAL (French research institute)	group of experts for assessment studies	* better assessments * solid weighing of decisions	* responsibilities unclear * could be symbolic * could involve unnecessary paper work
Church conference (Germany)	regular consultations between European and ACP ministers	* greater transparency and openness	* ritualistic/not trans-parent * no clear procedures * private initiative left out
Church Conference (Germany)	system for assessment and evaluation	* better assessments * solid weighing of decisions	* no clear responsi-bilities * could be symbolic * could involve unnecessary paper work
Government of Denmark	discussions in Council	* developing set of indicators * discover unintentional concrete cases	* results unclear * behind closed doors, transparency lacking
Government of the Netherlands	complaints procedure Commission	* possibility to present incoherencies	* transparency not secured * investigative capacity lacking
Government of the Netherlands	discussions in Council on food security/fish-eries, conflict prevention, migration	* stimulating debate * discover unknown territories	* results unclear * not leading to instruments/bureau-cratic procedures

VI. CONCLUSION

Coherence of policy is an aspect of government activity that has hitherto received little attention. Nonetheless, provision was made in Article 130v of the Treaty on European Union for coherence of European development policy. Despite the urging of various member states, little has been done to implement this article. The report of the European Commission on this subject is defensive and contains no specific proposals for dealing with incoherence. The Committee on External Relations appears mainly to be concentrating on coherence within foreign policy and coherence of new policy proposals. Consequently, it disregards both existing examples of incoherence and the coherence of development policy and internal European policy. During the Dutch presidency in the first half of 1997, an informal Council meeting in the Amsterdam Arena was dedicated to discussions on policy incoherence in several fields. The official Council meeting in June 1997 did not lead to any concrete proposals to introduce instruments to foster coherence; only new discussions were announced.

None the less, various instruments could be devised to promote coherence. Of the member states, in particular the Netherlands, Denmark and Germany seem in favour of adding new instruments. As far as possible, the effectiveness of new instruments should be weighed in advance. Creating greater openness and fostering clear assessments with a minimum of bureaucracy could be a guideline here. First of all, the mandate of the Committee on External Policy could be expanded to include existing policy and internal policy. The most attractive of the other options would be the annual reporting system and complaints procedure because they can be arranged with this minimum of bureaucracy. In addition, they would ensure greater transparency and provide more scope for supervision.

REFERENCES

Blackburn, K. and M. Christensen, 1989, 'Monetary Policy and Policy Credibility: Theories and Evidence', *Journal of Economic Literature*, Vol.27 (American Economic Association, Nashville).
Blommenstein, H.J. *et al.*, 1984, *Handboek beleidsevaluatie: een multi-disciplinaire benadering* (Policy Evaluation Handbook: A Multidisciplinary Approach), Alphen aan den Rijn: Samsom.
Brandt, H., 1994, *On the Effects of EU Export Refunds on the Beef Sectors of West African Countries*, Berlin: Deutsches Institut für Entwicklungspolitik.

Commission of the European Communities (CEC), 1992, 'Declaration on Aspects of Development Co-operation in the Run-up to 2000', Brussels.

Commission of the European Communities, 1993, 'Common Fisheries and Marine Policy', *Publication of the European Communities*, Nov., Brussels.

Commission of the European Communities, 1994a, *The Coherence of Community Policies with the Objectives of Development Cooperation Policy*, Brussels.

Commission of the European Communities, 1994b, *The Community and the Member States' Policy on Cooperation with Developing Countries in the Field of Health*, Com(94) 77, Brussels.

Council of the European Communities/Commission of the European Communities, 1992, *Treaty on European Union*, Luxembourg: Office for Official Publications of the European Communities.

Deth, J.W. van (ed.), 1993, *Handboek Politicologie* (Political Science Handbook), Assen: Van Gorcum.

Dhondt, P., 1994, *Die Kohärenzproblematik: Zielkonflikte zwischen Agrarpolitik und der Entwicklungspolitik der Europäischen Union: Probleme und Lösungsversuche*, Aachen: Technische Universität.

Dubois, Jean-Pierre, DG VIII, 1994, 'The Question of Coherence: The Impact on Developing Countries', in Gemeinsame Konferenz Kirche und Entwicklung, *Towards Coherence in North/South Policy: The Role of the European Union*, Materialien zum GKKE-Dialogprogramm, Heft D7, Bonn.

European Research Office, 1995a, *An Introduction to EU Fisheries Agreements*, Brussels: Coalition for Fair Fisheries Agreements (CFFA).

European Research Office, 1995b, *Ensuring Coherence in the Fisheries Sector*, Brussels: CFFA.

European Research Office, 1995c, *Structure of EU–ACP Fisheries Agreements*, Brussels: CFFA.

Eurostep, 1993a, *The Subsidised Exports of EC Beef to West Africa: How European Beef Mountains Undermine Cattle Farming in the Sahel*, Brussels: Eurostep.

Eurostep, 1993b, *Briefing Paper on the Campaign of November 1993*, Brussels: Eurostep.

FAO Fisheries Department, 1995, *The State of World Fisheries and Aquaculture*, Rome: FAO.

Frisch, D., 1994, 'Coherence in North/South Policy: The Role of the European Union', Gemeinsame Konferenz Kirche und Entwicklung, *Towards Coherence in North/South Policy: The Role of the European Union*, Materialien zum GKKE-Dialogprogramm, Heft D7, Bonn.

Greenpeace, 1993, *It Can't Go on Forever: The Implications of the Global Grab for Declining Fish Stocks*, Amsterdam: Greenpeace.

Jadot, Y. and J.P. Rolland, 1996, *Les contradictions des politiques européennes à l'égard des pays en développement. Diagnostics dans le secteur agricole et propositions d'amélioration de l'efficacité de la coopération internationale*, Montpellier: Solagral.

Kapteyn, P. and P. Verloren van Themaat, 1995, *Inleiding tot het recht van de Europese Gemeenschappen na Maastricht* (Introduction to the Law of the European Communities after Maastricht), Deventer: Kluwer (Fifth Edition, totally revised).

Klugkist, J., 1993/1994, *First Report on Lobby to Stop the Dumping of EC Beef in West Africa*, 2 June 1993 (Second Report, 17 June 1993; Third Report, February 1994), The Hague/Brussels: NOVIB/Eurostep.

Kydlandt, F.E. and E.C. Prescott, 1977, 'Rules rather than Discretion', *Journal of Political Economy*, Vol.85, No.31.

Lutterbeck, B., 1994, 'Towards More Coherence in North-South Policy: A Summary of Proceedings', in Gemeinsame Konferenz Kirche und Entwicklung, *Towards Coherence in North/South Policy: The Role of the European Union*, Materialien zum GKKE-Dialogprogramm, Heft D7, Bonn.

McDonald, S., 1996, 'Reform of the EU's Sugar Policies and the ACP Countries', *Development Policy Review*, Vol.14, No.2.

Ministry of Foreign Affairs, 1994/1995, *The Netherlands and the Future of the European Union: Four Government Memoranda*, The Hague: Ministry of Foreign Affairs.

Ministry of Foreign Affairs/Danida, 1996, *Plan of Action for Active Multilateralism, Annex Strategies for Individual Organizations*, Copenhagen: Ministry of Foreign Affairs/Danida.

NAR (National Advisory Council for Development Co-operation), 1993, *Recommendation on Development Cooperation after the Treaty of Maastricht*, The Hague: National Advisory Council for Development Co-operation.

Nugent, N., 1994, *The Government and Politics of the European Union*, London: Macmillan, Third Edition.

Rolland, Jean-Pierre, 1995, *Foreign Trade Policy and Regional Trade in Meat and Livestock*, Paris/Montpellier: Ministère de la Coopération/SOLAGRAL.

Shihata, I.F.I, 1994, *The World Bank Inspection Panel*, Oxford: Oxford University Press.

SOLAGRAL, 1995, *Améliorer la cohérence des politiques communautaires pour renforcer l'efficacité de la politique de coopération au développement*, Paris: SOLAGRAL.

Stevens, C. and C. Webb, 1983, 'The Political Economy of Sugar: A Window on the CAP', in H. Wallace *et al.* (eds.), *Policy-making in the European Community*, Chichester: John Wiley.

Stevens, C., 1996, 'EU Policy for the Banana Market: The External Impact of Internal Policies', in Wallace and Wallace (eds.).

Wallace, H., 1996, 'Politics and Policy in the EU: The Challenge of Governance', in Wallace and Wallace (eds.).

Wallace, H. and W. Wallace, (eds.), 1996, *Policy-Making in the European Union*, Oxford: Oxford University Press.

Weatherford, M.S., 1994, 'The Puzzle of Presidential Leadership: Persuasion, Bargaining and Policy Consistency', *Governance: An International Journal of Policy and Administration*, Vol.7, No.2.

11

The EU and the Developing World: Coherence between the Common Foreign and Security Policy and Development Co-operation

ANDREA KOULAÏMAH-GABRIEL

I. POLICY COHERENCE: A VITAL ISSUE FOR THE EUROPEAN UNION

Coherence in European Union (EU) external policies and the effectiveness of the common foreign and security policy (CFSP) were central issues in the preparation of the new Treaty of Amsterdam, signed on 2 October 1997. Coherence has also featured high on the development policy agenda in 1997: both EU Presidencies (the Dutch in the first semester and Luxembourg in the second) attempted to solve some of the inconsistencies affecting the Union's policies towards the South.

Earlier chapters of this volume tend to show that whereas striving for coherence is a good policy guideline, a certain degree of policy incoherence is a fact of life. A report by the Catholic Institute of International Relations [*CIIR, 1996*] reminds us that no government commits itself too firmly to coherence since this is an almost impossible task in a pluralist political system. The difficulty of achieving coherence is aggravated in democratic systems where various interest-based constituencies have divergent interests among which the government needs to find a compromise, or even to arbitrate. Hence the question: why does the EU take such a strong stance, in the Maastricht Treaty and beyond, on coherence? There are three main reasons for the EU stance on coherence:

– *Seeking effectiveness:* The governance structure of the EC is even more complex than that of states and the EC has to live with two levels of compromise-making: between divergent sectorial interests, such as those of consumers versus producers, producers versus environmental groups etc.; and between the interests of the 15 member states. This results in a coherence gap which compromises the effectiveness and credibility of the Union, which still has to prove its usefulness to European citizens.

- *Reaping the benefits of union:* The European Union's added value, or *raison d'être*, both in development policy and in CFSP, is to bring about the convergence or even 'fusion' of the policies of the member states.

- *Playing a role in the international system:* Several authors have seen a potential for the EC/EU to play the role of a 'civilian power'. The EU is seen as an international actor, unable to exert influence by means of traditional instruments but wanting to assert an identity separate from that of the member states[1] and therefore left with 'co-operation' and 'civilian' instruments as means of defending its interests [*Kohnstamm and Hager, 1973; Rummel, 1990*]. In this sense, one could expect (or hope) that the principles underlying EC development co-operation would spill over into the emerging common foreign and security policy, thus limiting the scope for contradictory actions.

In 1992, when concluding the Treaty of Maastricht, the EU set itself a very ambitious agenda, which it has failed to keep up with, mainly because it did not address the root causes for excessive policy incoherence (see sections II and III). However, although both the Maastricht and Amsterdam treaties fail to establish a single comprehensive external relations policy, the gap between development policy and foreign policy is somewhat narrowed (see section IV). The question that remains open is, therefore, how to ensure that this convergence between development and foreign policy takes place in a *development-friendly* manner.

---

1. Other schools of thought see the EU as a mere extension of the member states. For authors like Galtung [*1973*], the EC has the same realpolitik agenda as its component countries: 'take five broken empires, add the sixth one later and make one big neo-colonial empire of it all', was his assessment of Europe's international role. 25 years later, one could argue that more recent developments of the Union, especially its enlargement to small states with no colonial background, challenge the current relevance of his analysis, as new members influence in a non-neocolonial manner European South policies.

II. A 'PRINCIPLE' STANCE ON COHERENCE

Since the Maastricht Treaty, 'coherence' has become a buzz-word in the language of the European Union, especially in the field of external policies and of development co-operation. In the jargon of European development co-operation, there is often mention of the 'three Cs', namely co-ordination, coherence and complementarity. The second of these – coherence – refers to the relation between other EU policies and the development objectives enshrined in Article 130u[2] of the Treaty on European Union[3] (TEU). However, when we look at the overall consistency of the EU in terms of its commitments to developing countries, the other two Cs cannot be disregarded. Coherence between the EU and its member states, including their stance in international organisations, is equally important. Although the treaty does not actually use the term 'coherence',[4] it underlines the principle on three occasions.

First of all, in the common provisions of the treaty, Article C states that:

The Union shall be served by a single institutional framework which shall ensure the consistency and continuity of the activities carried out in order to attain its objectives while respecting and building upon the *acquis communautaire*. The Union shall in particular ensure the consistency of its external activities as a whole in the context of its external relations, security, economic and development policies. The Council and the Commission shall be responsible for ensuring such consistency. They shall ensure the implementation of these policies, each in accordance with its respective powers.

---

2. Article 130u states the objectives of European development co-operation. These are: the sustainable economic and social development of the developing countries; their smooth and gradual integration into the world economy; the campaign against poverty; the development and consolidation of democracy, the rule of law, human rights and fundamental freedoms.
3. At the time of writing, the Treaty of Amsterdam is not yet into force. In this text, the term 'Treaty of Amsterdam' refers exclusively to the new elements introduced at the 1996 IGC, and not to the compiled version of the treaties. The term 'Maastricht Treaty' is used to designate the treaty currently in force, whereas 'Treaty on European Union' describes those references in the Maastricht Treaty that have not been modified in Amsterdam.
4. The English version of the treaty speaks of 'consistency' in Article C, whereas the French version refers to 'coherence'. Beyond the semantics of the Maastricht Treaty, further reports from the Commission and the Council use the word 'coherence'.

Article C is a crucial mechanism of the Maastricht construction as it reflects the compromise made between the urge to bring external economic and foreign policies together, for reasons of efficiency, consistency and transparency, and the reluctance of member states to lose an element of their sovereignty to an integrationist European Community. In order to understand this tension, it is useful to look back at the history of European integration and the building of a common foreign policy.

Co-operation between the member states of the European Community on foreign policy issues started in a very ad hoc and informal manner outside the framework of European Community policies. The member states met in an intergovernmental setting, outside the procedures and dynamics of the EC, excluding, at least in the early years, the Commission. Some progress was achieved with the Single European Act (SEA) in 1987 which added a chapter on European Political Co-operation (EPC) recognising a role for the Commission (to be associated) and for the European Parliament (to be informed). In spite of the word 'Single', the SEA actually comprised two documents: the revised Rome Treaty (an EC document) and the Treaty on European Political Co-operation (an intergovernmental document). The situation was schizophrenic. Organisationally, in an institution like the General Secretariat of the Council of Ministers, the unit dealing with EPC was separate from units dealing with external economic relations.[5] In the European Commission, the Directorates in charge of designing and implementing policies had no competence with respect to EPC matters, which were discretely managed by a unit in the General Secretariat. One can imagine the difficulties arising in the case of economic sanctions, for instance.

Indeed, there was no clear mechanism to ensure that the measures adopted under the Community authority (such as trade or development aid, under the existing regional programmes) would follow the decisions of the member states in the framework of EPC. The example of sanctions is quite illustrative in this respect: member states could agree among themselves that a country, say in the developing world, should no longer receive aid and, more importantly, that the trade preferences it benefited from should be suspended. First, it must be recalled that decisions taken in the intergovernmental framework of European Political Co-operation had no legal implications for the Community. Second, it is often assumed that the

---

5. This separation was symbolically represented by an armoured door which separated the EPC secretariat from the General Secretariat of the Council in the Charlemagne building of the Council.

composition of the two fora (EPC and EC) is identical: this disregards the fact that the Commission and the European Parliament are active participants only in the Community sphere. Concretely, in the case of sanctions, the Commission had to make a formal proposal to the Council of Ministers (which has the same composition in both frameworks) to suspend trade or aid concessions, without being bound by the decisions taken in EPC. This situation inevitably led to tensions between the Commission and the Council on their respective prerogatives.

This artificial separation grew over time, parallel to the development of a 'political' dimension of European external relations. From the point of view of coherence, it became untenable to divide policies that were in fact two facets of a single policy: external relations. Furthermore, by the time of the first Intergovernmental Conference (IGC) – which resulted in the Maastricht Treaty – it was clear that the emerging 'foreign policy' would have to be more substantial than the 'consultative' and 'declamatory' political co-operation. Convergence between the EC and foreign policy became, therefore, a key issue at the IGC. There were (and are) two conflicting schools of thought; the intergovernmentalists, who also argued for a minimalist common foreign and security policy, insisted on keeping the two streams separate. Those favouring greater integration argued for a unified external relations policy. The European Commission, in particular, maintained that all external relations should be unified under one heading, albeit differentiating between trade, development and foreign policy. The compromise was a 'single institutional framework', with a three-pillar structure, in which coherence is to be ensured by the identity of actors (since the Commission is now a full, if weaker, partner of the CFSP) and, in the case of sanctions, by a 'passerelle'[6] between the two pillars.

The objective of 'consistency' as defined in Article C gives no guidelines on how to develop operational tools to achieve it. It gives two institutions the competence to ensure coherence but it does not provide for mechanisms of arbitration, and, most importantly, it does not prioritise amongst the three policies concerned. The unanswered question remains: coherence, yes. But with what?

The second reference that the Treaty makes to 'coherence' is both clearer and more cautious. In title XVII on European development co-operation, Article 130v states:

---

6.   In European legal jargon, the word 'passerelle', borrowed from the French, refers to a clause which acts as a bridge between separate sections of the Treaty, namely between the intergovernmental pillars and the Community pillar of the EU.

The Community shall take account of the objectives referred to in Article 130u in the policies that it implements which are likely to affect developing countries.

This, to some extent, answers the questions posed in Article C. The pursuit of coherence should take place in a 'development-friendly' manner. The burden of compliance rests with other policies such as trade or other external policies of the European Community. Although Article 130v constitutes a clear policy stance, it is undermined by three major weaknesses:

- *The wording is weak:* It requires an obligation in terms of process ('taking into account') but not in terms of result. This makes implementation difficult in view of the limited political weight of a 'soft policy' like development compared with the powerful interests behind trade or agricultural policy. An alternative wording, such as '[article 130u] requirements must be integrated into the definition and implementation of other Community policies'[7], could have been used to strengthen the stance of development policy.

- *Responsibility for compliance rests with the European Community and not member states:* Indeed, articles 130u and 130x[8], which concern complementarity and co-ordination, only apply to member states' policies on development co-operation and therefore do not cover other policies such as foreign affairs, defence or trade in arms which affect developing countries.

- *Responsibility falls on the European Community and not on the European Union:* This is a fundamental distinction meaning that the common foreign and security policy does not have to take into account the development objectives of title XVII.

---

7. This wording is 'borrowed' from that of Article 130r on the objectives and principles of environmental policy. The parallel between the 'coherence' objective of EC development co-operation and the 'integration' principle of EC environment policy has been explored by N. Robins [*1997*].
8. Article 130u qualifies EC development policy as 'complementary to the policies pursued by the Member States': however, this complementarity is currently recognised as having a 'two-way' relation. Article 130x stipulates that 'the Community and the Member States shall coordinate their policies'.

Article 130v's response to the lacunae of Article C is therefore limited to the requirement that within the Community sphere, trade policy and the external dimension of its other economic policies should as far as possible try to be consistent with development policy objectives.

This leaves two questions unresolved: how to achieve coherence between EC development co-operation and EU common foreign and security policy; and, secondly, between the policies of the EU and those of its member states. The degree of coherence in both these areas will determine what kind of international role the EU will play in the future, within the limits that the member states will set. The third reference of the Treaty to coherence can be found in title V which creates a common foreign and security policy. Article J1.4 requires that:

> The Member States ... shall refrain from any action which is con-
> trary to the interests of the Union or likely to impair its effective-
> ness as cohesive force in international relations. The Council
> shall ensure that these principles are complied with.

The motivating force of the common foreign and security policy is revealed in this requirement as well as in the history of European inte-gration: it is to act as a cohesive force in international relations and to overcome the divisions among member states. In other words, internal consensus among member states is given priority above policy out-comes. This search for a common denominator is evident in the unanimity required for CFSP decisions, giving a right of veto to individual member states, and has undermined the effectiveness and credibility of the EU in major international affairs. The unconvincing performance of CFSP since the enactment of the TEU is demonstrated by its responses to the crises in Yugoslavia or Congo-Zaire. This poor record has led the EU to pursue foreign policy through other means, namely external economic policies, including development and humanitarian aid. The latter, in particular, has been referred to as a 'substitute' for an EU foreign policy. It is argued that humanitarian aid is used as a response to crises situations to compensate for the failures of CFSP – due mainly to lack of means and of consensus – and that it is given the high visibility that should correspond to a foreign policy of the EU [*Aptel, 1995*].

The paralysis of the common foreign and security policy and its inward-looking tendency have hindered the pursuit of its stated objectives[9], which are compatible with, and sometimes complementary to, the development policy objectives of the EU:

- to safeguard the common values, fundamental interests and independence of the Union;
- to strengthen the security of the Union;
- to preserve peace and strengthen international security;
- to promote international co-operation;
- to develop and consolidate democracy and the rule of law, and respect for human rights and fundamental freedoms.

The difference 'in principle' between development co-operation and CFSP is not so great. Article C does state that consistency must be pursued in respect for the *acquis communautaire*. It can be argued that since development policy, notably in Africa, was at the origins of the external relations policy of the European Community, the objectives of development co-operation constitute an integral part of the *acquis* that an incipient common foreign and security policy needs to respect.

The reason for the incoherence of CFSP lies, therefore, in its paralysis rather than in an alleged contradiction between its guiding principles and the development agenda. A central theme of the 1996 IGC negotiations, which resulted in the signing of the Treaty of Amsterdam, was the reform of EU foreign policy in order to increase coherence and effectiveness of external actions. The Commission proposed two major objectives of the Treaty revision: 'to bring together the various strands comprising foreign relations into a single effective whole, with structures and procedures designed to enhance consistency and continuity; and to improve the CFSP at all stages of its operation'[10] [*European Commission, 1996a*]. The results of the IGC are disappointing on both fronts. In terms of coherence, the pillar structure has been maintained and progress is limited to the obligation made in Article C for the Commission and the Council to co-operate

---

9. The objectives of the common foreign and security policy are stated in Article J.1 of the Treaty on European Union. They have been slightly modified in the Amsterdam Treaty by increasing the references to the UN Charter and insisting on the security of the Union rather than on that of the Union and its member states (second indent). The wording used in the text reflects the common denominator of the treaties of Maastricht and Amsterdam.
10. The third objective was 'to establish a proper European identity with regard to security and defence, as an integral part of the CFSP'.

in order to ensure consistency.[11] In terms of effectiveness, the major obstacle constituted by the unanimity voting rule was not removed. Why insist so much on procedural issues rather than on content? The EU works in such a manner that objectives matter less than means and procedures to achieve them. The strong stance taken by the EU on coherence is a good thing and since the Maastricht Treaty, a number of positive results were achieved in this field, which will be examined in section IV. These suggest possible strategies for pursuing coherence in EU external relations of the EU, but they are only one part of the story. It is essential to examine the other part, the 'development-unfriendly incoherence', that also results from EU external policies. In the following section, it is argued that the institutional and procedural framework of the European Union is a major source of incoherence.

III. THE COHERENCE DEFICIT OF THE EUROPEAN UNION: AN INSTITUTIONAL EXPLANATION

The pursuit of coherence is a prerequisite for effective and credible governance. However, in a pluralist democracy, absolute coherence cannot be a mandatory requirement. The requirement that 'objectives of policy in a particular field may not be undermined or obstructed by actions or activities of government in that field or in other policy fields' (Hoebink, this volume, Ch.10) can be implemented only by a monolithic governance structure pursuing a single objective, or in the case of a policy which is given absolute priority on any other consideration. Neither is realistic in Western democracies today. A certain level of incoherence is an inevitable result of balancing interests and priorities of different groups in a pluralist society, and when it occurs through an open decision-making process, must be considered 'acceptable'. 'What matters most is not simply whether contrasted policies are being pursued, but whether they are being pursued knowingly or unwittingly' [*OECD, 1996*]. The study by OECD has identified a number of tools for promoting coherence:

– commitment by the political leadership;

---

11. Article C, second subparagraph, as amended by the Treaty of Amsterdam, now reads: 'The Union shall in particular ensure the consistency of its external activities as a whole in the context of its external relations, security, economic and development policies. The Council and the Commission shall be responsible for ensuring such consistency *and shall co-operate to this end.* They shall ensure the implementation of these policies, each in accordance with its respective powers.'

- the existence of a strategic policy framework;
- clear analytical advice for decision-makers;
- capacity for a central overview and co-ordination;
- early warning systems for policy conflicts;
- a decision-making process organised so as to achieve effective reconciliation between policy priorities and budgetary imperatives;
- the ability to adjust policies in the course of implementation;
- an administrative culture which promotes cross-sectoral co-operation and systematic dialogue between different policy communities.

An examination of the European Union governance system, with particular regard to external relations, reveals a clear breach between the decision-making system and the quest for coherence. Without reiterating the eight tools identified by the OECD, it is possible to identify four major bottlenecks:

- the absence of clear leadership;
- the lack of 'acknowledged' strategic capacity;
- fragmentation of the responsibility for co-ordination tasks;
- complex and institutionally differentiated decision-making processes.

The *absence of clear political leadership* in setting priorities for the Union is very detrimental to EU coherence, especially in the area of the common foreign and security policy. The Treaty on European Union states objectives, both in its development co-operation policy and its common foreign and security policy that the EU has been unable, or unwilling, to put into practice. Hence the question: is the European leadership committed to development co-operation and to peace and security? The declarations made both in the CFSP and in the Community suggest that it is in the narrow fields of CFSP and of European development policy. Development policy is supposed to be 'complementary' to that of the member states. In practice, this has meant that 'leadership', as exercised by the Community, is limited to EC development policy, and does not embrace the member states' policies. However, in relation to other policies, development co-operation is clearly not the chief priority of the Community: national concerns and trade or agriculture will be accommodated first.

In the field of common foreign and security policy, the lack of leadership is even more apparent: CFSP is an intergovernmental policy, which requires unanimity of views among member states before any action is undertaken. Advances have been made, since the Maastricht Treaty, to enhance the roles of the European Council and of the Presidency as 'leadership' of the Union. Proposals tabled at the IGC to create a *'Monsieur Europe'*, which would give the Union a higher profile, have resulted in the appointment of the Secretary-General of the Council as 'High Representative for the common foreign and security policy'; unfortunately, as the European Parliament has emphasised, the role and status of this High Representative are not clear [*European Parliament, 1997*]. In any case, this will not be enough to overcome the lack of leadership, unless the member states give the EU, or its High Representative, the instruments and authority to act decisively on the international scene.

The deficit of leadership is also reflected in *the dispersion of information sources for decision-makers to rely on*. The EU so far lacks a central analytical unit that would be at the service of both the EU and the member states. This 'strategic thinking' should be the responsibility of the European Commission. The Commission is independent; it has the role of 'guardian of the treaties'; it does not have vested national interests, but serves the general interest of the Union; and it has an overview of all fields of external relations, at both EC and national level, with the exception of defence. However, doubts have sometimes been expressed about the Commission's capacity for 'strategic thinking'. Although in both development and common foreign policy, these doubts may be justified, this is largely due to the reluctance of member states to give the European Commission a lead co-ordinating or strategic role.

The coexistence of national and EU competence in development policy and CFSP has been used for the retention of national control at the expense of *'collaborative advantage'* [*Metcalfe, 1996*] of co-ordinated strategies. The IGC has agreed to establish a policy planning and early warning unit, which will be the responsibility of the Secretary-General of the Council (who is also High Representative of the CFSP), with personnel drawn from the Council's General Secretariat, the Commission, the member states and the Western European Union. Its objective is to establish 'appropriate cooperation with the Commission in order to ensure *full* coherence with the Union's external economic and development policies' [*Intergovernmental Conference, 1997*] and it is supposed to work, primarily, on issues related or relevant to CFSP. The information and analytical capacity should, therefore, be extended to cover the full range of EU external relations. The role that this unit will play and its credibility will depend on the precise mandate, staffing, and influence in the policy decisions accorded to it by the Council (and the member states).

The responsibility for co-ordination is too fragmented. The Council and the Commission are jointly responsible for co-ordinating external policies, but there is no mechanism to resolve conflicts between the two institutions: in practice, each is ultimately responsible in its field of competence (CFSP or EC). The European Commission paid considerable attention to this issue in its opinion on the IGC [*European Commission, 1996a*]. Under the heading 'Greater consistency in foreign policy', the Commission stated:

> the Union must be able to present a united front. Its foreign policy as a whole will not be effective until there is proper coordination between its various components, for which responsibility is shared among different institutions; the Treaty already requires the Council and the Commission to pursue a consistent foreign policy. But this has not happened under the Treaty as it stands, and the institutions' duties in this respect should be reinforced.

In this respect, the injunction made to the Commission and Council 'to cooperate' in the revised Article C of the Amsterdam Treaty is likely to remain wishful thinking [*Intergovernmental Conference, 1997*].

Fragmentation of co-ordination responsibilities is only the tip of the iceberg. The EU framework, with its two parallel levels of decision-making, its three pillars and its complex procedures has an intrinsic tendency to incoherence.

The coexistence of national and EU competence in the same field of action (development and foreign policy) has already been identified as a source of conflict. Another is the absence of EU competence in certain policy areas where national competence remains untouched: for instance, the policies of some member states on the arms trade clearly contradict the 1991 Council resolution on human rights, democracy and development which condemns the large military budgets of countries receiving assistance from the EC. The inconsistency of the positions adopted by member states leads to contradictions that the EU cannot resolve because of its lack of competence.

If we look specifically at the process of determining EU policies – thus disregarding the relationship between national and European policies – we can see that various players are involved in the design, implementation and funding of the external policies of the Union. The Council of Ministers represents the interests of the member states; the Commission is the guardian of the general interest, and the Parliament sees itself as the 'democratic conscience' of the foreign policy of the Union.

The pattern of interaction between these three institutions in EU external relations varies according to policy areas (trade, development, CFSP), and according to the type of external agreements (trade co-operation, association) which are concluded in the framework of the treaty-making powers of the EC. This generates competition among the various players, who tend to pursue their own agendas at the expense of coherence and unity of action, and leads to confusion for observers and third countries, who deplore the unjustified practices of 'double standards'.

In the field of common foreign and security policy – the second pillar – the interests of the member states clearly predominate. Indeed, the power of initiative is shared by the individual countries and the European Commission, and the role of the European Parliament is purely consultative. The European Parliament has, however, succeeded in intervening in the institutional process of the second pillar through the use of its budgetary powers. This 'bargaining power' makes its participation in the CFSP process more effective than pure consultation; on the other hand, it is a source of tension and policy contradiction.[12] The Council of Ministers decides by unanimity[13] which often results in paralysis of the system since member states' points of view often conflict.

In trade policy, the commercial interest of the Community clearly dominates. This is the policy area in which the Commission has the greatest room for manoeuvre as it has the sole right of initiative: the European Parliament is formally excluded from the process, and the Council of Ministers takes decisions on the basis of qualified majority voting. Multilateral trade negotiations and relations with countries

---

12. An interinstitutional agreement has been concluded between the Parliament, the Council and the Commission providing for a *modus vivendi* on the financing of CFSP. The views of the European Parliament are likely to be given more weight.
13. Article J3 of the Maastricht Treaty provides indirectly for majority ruling: in the framework of a joint action, the Council can decide, unanimously, to put certain matters to qualified majority voting. This facility has not been used. The new Treaty of Amsterdam increases the potential for unanimity: the rule of the revised Article J13 is that decisions need to be unanimous. However, when a common strategy has been adopted, qualified majority voting can be used to implement decisions, joint actions or common positions that result from it. Even in this instance, a member state can block the decision on grounds of 'important and stated reasons of national policy'; the matter can, if a majority of member states so wish, be referred to the European Council (i.e., the level of Heads of State and Government) for a unanimous decision.

such as China or Korea, which do not benefit from Community aid, are governed by the trade chapter of the Treaty, which is not conditional on respect for human rights.

Development co-operation is based on a completely different balance of power, in which the European Parliament has a privileged position. The European Parliament participates in the decision-making process through the 'co-operation procedure'[14], which gives it the right to amend policy proposals by the European Commission. It is notable that the Generalised System of Preferences (GSP), which was governed by the trade chapter prior to the Treaty of Maastricht and subsequently adopted under the provisions of development policy, now includes certain elements of conditionality linked to human rights. In addition, the European Parliament (EP) shares the budget authority with the Council of Ministers on an equal footing: this means that within the limits of the financial perspectives agreed every five years, it has the right to increase certain budgetary posts, regardless of the position of the Council, and even to create new ones.[15] An important exception to this financial power, and another manifestation of incoherence, is the European Development Fund (EDF) which finances the most important development programme of the EC: the Lomé Convention between the EC and countries of Africa, the Caribbean and the Pacific (ACP). The EDF is constituted through national contributions by the member states, and thus falls outside the sphere of competence of the Parliament. The EP has repeatedly tried to gain control by claiming a budgetisation of the EDF, and by promoting budgetary lines which benefit ACP and other developing countries, in areas where it has an interest (such as support for democracy and human rights).

The European Parliament's influence on development co-operation is enhanced by the contractual nature of this policy. The main distinctive characteristic of EU development policy, as opposed to national policies, lies in the existence of co-operation agreements which include common principles and objectives for co-operation, joint institutional mechanisms for monitoring or implementing co-operation, and, in certain cases, preferential trade arrangements and

---

14. The Treaty of Amsterdam changes the procedure to be followed in the sphere of development policy from 'co-operation procedure' to co-decision. This enhances the role of the European Parliament (by giving it a final right of veto on the legislative proposal in question).
15. The European Parliament actually entered the field of external relations of the EC through its budgetary prerogatives. In particular, it initiated a budget line for co-financing with NGOs, in 1976, which has become an important instrument of European development policy.

financial provisions.[16] The assent of the European Parliament is required for these agreements, thus providing it an opportunity for leverage in development co-operation policy. On three occasions, the European Parliament has used the power to veto the Mediterranean agreements to manifest its disapproval of the political situations in the Occupied Territories, Morocco and Syria.[17]

The European Parliament has regularly put forward its 'own independent foreign policy attitude which ... is becoming an important factor in the formulation of foreign policy by the other institutions' [Bieber, 1990]. It is in a position to play this role, unlike the national parliaments, for two reasons: the EP is not confined by a political link (represented by a party majority) with the executive power (shared by the Council and the Commission) that would undermine its independence. Secondly, the EP's budgetary powers are entirely expenditure-related (decisions on the level of income are taken by the member states):[18] this means that the EP has no incentive to reduce the EC budget, and – unlike national parliaments – is not confronted with difficult choices between development co-operation and other expenditures (such as social sectors) in the allocation of funds. The activism of the European Parliament has certainly had a positive impact on European South policies because of its favourable attitude to development co-operation and human rights. However, it has led to increased

---

16. In the past, it was possible to draw distinctions between the co-operation agreements on the basis of the trade and financial provisions: 'preferred' partners of the EC (i.e., the ACP and the Mediterranean countries) benefited from contractually agreed (and binding) trade preferences and financial commitment by the EC. Non-associates (Asia and Latin America) benefited from an EU one-sided non-preferential trade regime known as the Generalised System of Preferences (GSP), and had no legal entitlement to EC aid. Recent changes in EC development policy have blurred these differences: negotiations have taken place for a free trade area with Mercosur; a new trade regime for Mediterranean countries introduces reciprocity, and EC aid to the Mediterranean is no longer contractual. The only exception in both respects is the Lomé IV Convention, which ends in 2000.
17. In 1988 to register disapproval of Israel, and in 1992 of Morocco and Syria. It is unlikely that this situation will occur again as the Maastricht Treaty reduces Parliament leverage. The 'assent procedure', introduced in the Single European Act, required an absolute majority by all EP members of this type of international treaties. The procedure was amended in the Treaty on European Union and now assent is required on the basis of a simple majority.
18. The member states decide regularly on the ceiling to be put on the EC budget: on the entrants' side, this is a percentage of the EU GNP. The current decision dates back to the European Council of Edinburgh (1992). At the same time, the European Council also decides upon 'financial perspectives' for budget growth in the various chapters of the EC budget: administration, internal policies, Common Agricultural Policy, external policies. The favourable economic situation in the EU (especially with its most recent enlargement) has allowed an extension of the financial perspectives until 1999.

fragmentation, especially in relation to the budget: it has multiplied sources of funding, which in turn, need to be executed by separate departments in the European Commission. It may also account for some of the 'double standards' operated by the European Union: countries that depend on EC aid are more likely to be held accountable for human rights abuses.

The following conclusions can be drawn from this institutional explanation for the incoherence of EU policies affecting developing countries:

- the diffusion of responsibilities and the competition between two levels of decision-making and three institutions account for a large part of the incoherence;

- the institutional framework of the EU is constantly evolving: at times, evolution occurs at the expense of coherence;

- there is a growing awareness that the capacity to adopt a defined and coherent external policy will provide a benchmark against which the common foreign and security policy will be tested;

- so far, development co-operation has been the most receptive EU policy to the concerns of developing countries and the one in which the institutional framework has allowed the greatest involvement on the part of the European Parliament. It is, nonetheless, the weakest among EU policies and will need to be strengthened in order to argue its case for an overall foreign policy that is genuinely responsive to developing country concerns.

IV. INTEGRATED APPROACHES AND COHERENCE: BEST PRACTICES
POST-MAASTRICHT

In the four years of implementation of the Maastricht Treaty, there have been a number of experiments to achieve coherence, especially across the pillar structure, which provide some lessons for a future agenda. The creation of a single institutional framework has had some positive practical consequences: first, it has enabled some integrated approaches in areas previously circumscribed by the lack of competence of the Commission in common foreign and security spheres and by the fears of some member states that they would lose sovereignty to the Community. Second, a 'passerelle' clause has been introduced

361

in the Treaty on European Union to adopt economic sanctions. Third, the European Commission and the Council of Ministers have been able to reorganise their internal administration along geographical lines rather than on the basis of a legal competence. For the European Commission, this has meant that the various aspects of foreign policy can be conducted within each of the geographical directorates.[19]

For reasons of efficiency, humanitarian aid was transferred, in 1992, to a newly created European Community Humanitarian Office (ECHO), better able to react promptly than regular directorates-general. However, the portfolios of external relations remain some-what fragmented as five commissioners are primarily responsible for external policies. In addition, some directorates-general, which are primarily internally-oriented also deal with aspects of external policy (such as Fisheries); others conduct policies which have adverse side-effects on development policy (for example, the Common Agricul-tural Policy). Co-ordination between directorates on external relations is achieved through two channels: the general Commission co-ordination mechanisms in the form of inter-service groups and internal consultation, administered by the Secretariat General; and through the RELEX (Relations Extérieures) group of commissioners and cabinet members dealing with external relations. In the Council of Ministers, working groups are organised as follows: a horizontal group deals with development co-operation, and geographical groups conduct specific policies towards regions in the developing world. From the foreign policy side, the same geographic classification has been introduced. However, the coherence between the two sets of geographic groups is not easy to achieve as the Council (and member states) has not, as yet, managed a bridging between the CFSP and development co-operation prerogatives.

(1) Bridging between the Pillars: Practical Opportunities Offered by the Maastricht Treaty

Economic sanctions constitute the only policy area where a direct procedural linkage is made between the common foreign and security policy (the second pillar) and the European Community (the first pillar) through Article 228a.[20] For a long time, this was an area of

---

19. In April 1998, a new department of the European Commission will be created to implement aspects of the various aid programmes of the EU. The exact mandate of this new service and its relation to the external relations directorates-general are not clear at the time of writing.
20. Article 228a (the first pillar) stipulates: 'Where it is provided, in a common posi-tion or in a joint action adopted according to the provisions of the Treaty on European Union relating to the common foreign and security policy, for an action by the

conflict between the European Commission and the Council. Before the Maastricht Treaty was enacted, the Commission had to implement, within the Community framework, decisions taken by the member states in the context of European Political Cooperation. The Commission's position was delicate in a situation of unclear division of competence: measures of an economic nature, whether suspension of aid or embargoes, fall within the realm of Community policies, although the decision to take them is clearly political and belongs to governments.

An example of the way in which the new Article 228a was implemented can be seen in the adoption of sanctions against Haiti in May 1994. The process started with a unanimous political decision, under the provision of CFSP. On the basis of this decision, the EC took measures, in the framework of the first pillar, to suspend certain economic and financial relations with Haiti. The coherence of the decision with other relevant fora of policy-making was ensured by linking EC decisions to UN Council resolutions; and by recommending to the member states that they discontinue economic and financial relations with Haiti, a course of action that was likely to be followed, since the member states themselves brought about the CFSP decision [*Basabe et al., 1995*].

Another example highlighting the way in which consistency through the pillar structure has increased since the Treaty is the control of exports of dual-use goods. These, by definition, fall within the two areas of military security and of trade policy. The existence of the single institutional framework of Maastricht made it possible to regulate this area by adopting a CFSP joint action and a Community trade regulation [*Basabe et al., 1995*].

(2) Conflict Prevention in Africa: Development Policy or CFSP?

The advantage of the single institutional framework is that it allows the European Commission to initiate more integrated proposals that span the two pillars. This is the case, for instance, with the Commission's communication on conflict prevention in Africa. The argument is based on the two-way continuum between development and security in the recipient countries. The communication introduces the concept of 'structural stability' as the ultimate goal of the Union's development policy: 'structural stability could be defined as a

---

Community to interrupt or to reduce, in part or completely, economic relations with one or more third countries, the Council shall take the necessary urgent measures. The Council shall act by a qualified majority on a proposal from the Commission.'

situation involving sustainable economic development, democracy and respect for human rights, viable political structures, and healthy social and environmental conditions, with the capacity to manage change without resort to violent conflict' [*European Commission, 1996b*]. It can be assumed, from the objectives of development co-operation introduced in the Treaty on European Union that since there can be no effective development policy in an unstable environment and no stability without a minimum of social and economic development, conflict prevention is a legitimate area of interest for EU development policy.

The European Commission communication is to be welcomed, especially because the discussion was led from a development perspective: the communication was prepared by the Commission's directorate general for development co-operation (DG VIII), and was debated, under Dutch presidency, by the development ministers of the Union [*Council of Ministers, 1997*]. This is an interesting development since an issue such as conflict prevention would be expected to be addressed within CFSP, because it involves a range of instruments of a political nature: diplomatic demarches, such as the appointment of special envoys to regions in crisis, or even peacekeeping missions. In addition, the adoption by the Commission of this communication has been accompanied by a number of consultations with NGOs and with African organisations, probably as a result of the 'development orientation' of its authors. Significantly, the EU approach to conflict prevention in Africa is characterised by linkages with and support for 'home-grown' African initiatives, such as the creation of a centre for crisis management by the Organisation of African Unity.

Extending EU co-operation with developing countries to 'political' topics such as conflict prevention is positive in that, for example, it allows Africa to rise in the priorities of the European Union, and encourages the adoption of a more comprehensive approach to the problems of the continent. The revised Treaty on European Union [*Intergovernmental Conference, 1997*] extends the activities to be financed under CFSP to include: the deployment of EU envoys, conflict prevention, peace and security processes, and financial assistance to disarmament processes. In principle, this increases the potential for the EU to make a contribution to conflict prevention in Africa, which reflects the importance of EU aid to this continent. There are, however, two opposing risks involved in this evolution: first, that the paralysis which has characterised CFSP during the last five years will undermine EU efforts in Africa; and second, that a 'politicisation' of development policy will lead to a more 'interventionist' attitude towards Africa, and to a greater interference of member states' vested interests in the design of policies aiming at 'structural stability'.

(3) The Geographic Framework for EU External Relations: Towards More Coherent Strategies

Since the conclusion of the Maastricht Treaty, the European Union has had the opportunity to revise in depth most of its external relations. The most striking aspect of this revision is its strategic nature which contrasts with the piecemeal approach characterising 30 years of international co-operation, especially in relation to developing countries. Although the first Lomé Convention in 1975 did correspond, as the comprehensiveness of the agreement reveals, to a certain 'vision' or strategy of the EC and its member states, relations with other developing countries were extremely fragmented. The situation today has been reversed: EU relations with eastern Europe, the Mediterranean, Asia and Latin America seem to follow a certain logic, whereas a sense of drift dominates EU co-operation with the ACP countries. The following section argues that since Maastricht, strategic geographical frameworks have been designed in which the EU has clear objectives, and which bridge the gap between the CFSP and development co-operation to the extent that, in certain cases, development becomes less determining of the establishment of co-operation and the provision of resources.[21]

We begin by looking at the Mediterranean policy of the EC. The Community, since the early 1970s, has been eager to establish good co-operation relations with its immediate southern neighbours, an eagerness which has grown in parallel with the lengthening of its Mediterranean border in 1981 and 1986. Serious obstacles undermined its intentions: the complex political situation in the Mediterranean countries, especially in the Middle East but also in the Maghreb, and the absence of 'political profile' of the EC. Although the member states agreed as early as 1973 to put the Middle East on the agenda of EPC, attempts to present a credible political stance and to establish a political dialogue with the Mediterranean (Arab) countries were unsuccessful for a number of reasons: tensions among member states in agreeing upon a political stance to take in the Mediterranean; friction between some member states and some Mediterranean countries; and competition between southern Mediterranean and north (European) Mediterranean products which made it difficult for the EC to fulfil its southern partners' expectations, in terms of market access.

---

21. This section is based to a large extent on a paper written for the Dutch Derde Wereld Magazine and published by ECDPM [Koulaïmah-Gabriel, 1997].

An examination of EC–Mediterranean co-operation between 1972 and 1992 gives a general impression of a Community that recognises the importance and sensitivity of the region but does not know how to deal with it nor how to address political issues through economic tools.

With respect to the 'rest of the developing world', outside the Mediterranean and the ACP, the European Community had no real strategies. The policy towards those referred to as 'Non-Associates' grew in a very incremental manner, at first through the provision of food aid and later, thanks to the European Parliament's insistence, through co-financing with NGOs. In spite of growing EU interest and the signing of trade and co-operation agreements with several Asian and Latin American individual countries or groups of countries, no clear policy lines were developed on how to relate to such widely differing regions as Asia and Latin America.[22]

Against this background, the reorganisation of EU external relations in the early 1990s has been a worthy achievement. It was greatly facilitated by the existence of a single EU framework, particularly useful in relation to policies towards the Mediterranean and eastern Europe, and by the urge of the EU to position itself strongly and visibly on the international stage. The changes in the various regional programmes of the EC, were, for the most part, launched in 1995–96: new orientations were established in relations with Latin America, a free trade agreement was signed with MERCOSUR, the Euro-Asian summit of Bangkok gave new impetus to these relations, and the Barcelona Conference in November 1995 marked the beginning of the 'Euro-Mediterranean Partnership'. The only exception to this strategic rethinking has been the Lomé Convention: it is taking place now, and the results will be felt only at the turn of the century, when the current convention expires.

European aid recipients emerge as two separate groups with different ranking from the new organisation of EU external relations: the inner circle is occupied by the Mediterranean and by the central and eastern European countries (CEECs) and it follows a logic of geographical proximity [*Delors, 1992*], where political, security and economic concerns are intertwined. In relation to the outer circle, a logic of development aid and of economic interest dominates. Development aid is still the driving force in relations with the poorer countries in Asia; economic (and strategic) motivations guide the relations with successful Asian economies and with Latin American poles of growth

---

22. Commission communications or Council regulations dealing with Asia and Latin America did not even differentiate between the two groups of countries.

(such as MERCOSUR). Relations with Asia and Latin America started to follow separate paths from the mid-1980s. Whereas the Asian programme remains largely economic, EU interests and strategy have a political and cultural slant in Latin America. This is due to a convergence of interest: the EU, especially after the entry of Spain and Portugal, has had an interest in deepening its political ties with the continent, and a democratising Latin America was eager to foster deeper relations with Europe that would act as a counterweight to US hegemony. In practice, this trend led to a positive contribution by the EC and EPC in the mid-1980s to the resolution of the conflicts in Central America ('San José process') and to a structured political dialogue between the EC and Latin America. The coherence between development co-operation and politics, enhanced by the use of EC funds to support democratisation and human rights in Latin America, was due largely to the existence of a genuine willingness on both sides to engage in political dialogue. In contrast, this willingness is clearly not present on the Asian side, and it remains to be seen whether a mutual interest in political dialogue exists, or can be developed, in EU–Mediterranean and EU–ACP relations.

The first circle of EU external developing partners, namely the Mediterranean, offers an interesting example of 'reconciliation' between foreign and development policy, through the existence of a single institutional framework. The opportunity was provided by the start of the peace process in the Middle East. The EU has been more or less successful – depending on the point of view adopted – in using its new CFSP instruments to make a contribution to the process that would be appreciated by at least one of the two parties. It has managed to become 'unavoidable', in spite of the opposition of the USA, by investing in the peace process, diplomatically and financially. This comprehensive approach to the Mediterranean faces several difficulties: some are related to the varying degrees of willingness of the partner countries to give serious consideration to establishing close co-operation links within the Mediterranean, others are related to conflicts of interests between the EU and the southern Mediterranean (especially in terms of trade in agricultural and other sensitive products) or the lack of interest among certain member states in establishing close, and expensive, co-operation with relatively distant countries. The internal EU conflict was resolved, at the European Council in Cannes (June 1995), through a package deal in which financial assistance by the EC to the CEECs, the

Mediterranean countries and the ACP group was negotiated by the member states, on the basis of political and economic interests.[23]

The case of the Mediterranean deserves further attention as it provides a test case for the capacity of the EU to resolve its internal contradictions when dealing with a geographical area to which the EU is extremely sensitive. The current framework of relations is very comprehensive, embracing economic issues such as trade and financial assistance at the same time as political, security, and migration considerations. At a ministerial conference in Barcelona, on 27 and 28 November 1995, the EU and its Mediterranean partners[24] agreed to engage in a partnership based on three pillars: free trade, economic and social development, security and political co-operation. This new partnership is to be implemented through three instruments: a free trade area which is intended to become operative in 2010, association agreements with each of the Mediterranean countries[25], and finally a substantial programme for financial assistance, known as the MEDA programme. The financial protocols have been replaced by a single budget for the Mediterranean, bringing to an end the era of automatic entitlements. MEDA finances projects in the three priority areas[26] that were identified in Barcelona in the framework of guidelines agreed with the partner countries.

The value of the Barcelona process is primarily political: the partnership is conceived as a common enterprise between the EU (and its member states) and its southern partners in which development co-operation is complementary or instrumental to free trade and political dialogue. A major institutional innovation introduced in Barcelona is

---

23. At the Cannes summit, the divergence of interests of the member states was very open. The agreement which was reached resulted from a package deal between three interests: Germany, that wanted to privilege relations with the East; Spain, Italy and to a lesser extent France favoured an expansion of the Mediterranean programme; and France who increased its financial contribution to the European Development Fund in order to maintain the level of financing to the ACP countries.
24. The three Maghreb countries (Morrocco, Algeria, Tunisia), the five Mashrek countries and territory (Egypt, Jordan, Lebanon, Syria, and the Palestinian Authority), Israel, Turkey, Malta and Cyprus. All these countries (except the Palestinian Authority) already had association agreements with the EC. A notable absence from this forum was Libya.
25. At the time of writing, four have been concluded, three are being negotiated and two are at an exploratory stage.
26. The three priority areas are:
  – support for economic transition (preparation of the free trade area, support for the private sector, promotion of European investments, infrastructures).
  – support for socio-economic transformation (social services, rural development, environment, human rights, human resources, support for civil society, and the fight against terrorism, drugs and illegal immigration).
  – support for regional integration.

the provision for dialogue on a wide range of topics (including energy, migration and agriculture) in which the sectoral administrations and ministers are involved. This may help in resolving certain coherence problems, provided that the EC agrees to address with its partners sensitive issues such as the common agricultural policy, and that it is willing to make concessions. The Barcelona partnership will not be easy. There are serious difficulties, stemming from both sides of a complex nature: political, economic and cultural.

Finally, two observations could be made on the reorganisation of EU relations with developing countries through the adoption of comprehensive strategies: the decline in importance of the development co-operation motivation and the tension between the struggle for coherence in external relations and partnership.

First, development co-operation has lost steam as an engine for these relations. The new rationale for EC aid is based on three categories of motivations which determine the nature and intensity of the different regional programmes:

–   political and security concerns: this motivation is clearly dominant in EC policies towards its immediate neighbours, where migratory pressures and risks of instability would directly affect the EC;

–   economic and strategic considerations: the EC as a major trading power is clearly interested in maintaining its presence in booming economic regions. In a world context of globalisation and of multiplication of regional trade arrangements, the EC is eager to position itself strongly in relation to the other economic superpowers;

–   solidarity and humanitarian motivation: these are factors present in the external relations of the EC, especially in terms of assistance to the poorest countries and humanitarian aid.

Second, there is potential tension between the search for coherence and comprehensiveness of EU strategies towards developing countries, and the idea of partnership and international co-operation. Indeed, the current trend in EU external relations indicates that different European-designed patterns seem to be followed within each geographical group. A number of principles guide all sets of EU–developing country relations, such as the inclusion of human rights clauses in all co-operation agreements. This allows for relatively coherent, harmonised and transparent development co-operation programmes and strategies. However, they are also very one-sided, especially since the EC retains more and more flexibility (by keeping control on the financial instruments). On the other hand, EU development policy, contrary to that of the bilaterals, is based on contractual agreements that are supposedly negotiated between the two parties. If the EU comes to the negotiating table with pre-set coherent models, the scope for dialogue with the southern partner will inevitably be reduced.

V. DILEMMAS FOR EUROPEAN DEVELOPMENT CO-OPERATION IN A POLITICISED UNION

In the context of the upcoming revision of the Lomé IV Convention, the interaction between development policy, especially ACP–EU relations, and CFSP constitutes a major challenge. The Treaty of Amsterdam emphasises the need to give greater impetus to the common foreign and security policy, which implies that there is a willingness to reinforce the foreign policy component of external relations. However, the Amsterdam Treaty does not significantly enhance the effectiveness of CFSP, and there is consequently a danger that foreign policy agendas will permeate the external policy agenda. Where does European development co-operation stand in this respect?

The dilemma revolves around whether the development community should fight and lobby for an autonomous development policy based on the objectives of Article 130u, emphasising partnership and contractuality; or whether to pursue an integration of development co-operation in a 'single effective whole'. The 'autonomy' option has the advantage, in a post-Lomé IV context, of retaining a more 'humanitarian' or 'solidarity' approach to development co-operation. However, a total disconnection from foreign policy considerations is not feasible in view of the trends in EU–developing country relations in recent years, and it would risk marginalising both development co-operation and EU–ACP relations.

To overcome this dilemma, three strategies are suggested:

–   to call for a common foreign and security policy which is 'open to the world' [NGDO-LC, 1997] and which effectively promotes human rights, conflict prevention and international co-operation;

–   to pursue an up-grading of the ACP (especially Africa) on the scale of priorities of the European Union, both from a development policy perspective and in political and strategic terms;

– to ensure that in a future EU–ACP agreement, issues of foreign policy such as conflict prevention, trade in arms and security, which have an impact on development, are openly discussed between the ACP and the EU and do not remains solely in the realm of the EU Council of Ministers. Coherence issues, concerning trade or agriculture as well as CFSP [*Tubiana, 1997*], should be subjects for discussion if a 'political dialogue' is to be effective, reciprocal and based on partnership.

REFERENCES

Aptel, C., 1995, *La politique d'aide humanitaire de l'Union Européenne: la création d'ECHO et ses enjeux*, Document de travail du Collège d'Europe No.13, Bruxelles: Presses Interuniversitaires Européennes.
Basabe, F. *et al.*, 1995, 'An Appraisal of the Implementation of the Treaty of Maastricht: Policies, Institutions and Procedures', report for a conference on The future of the European constitution. Perspectives on the implementation and revision of Maastricht, 23–24 June 1995, College of Europe and TEPSA, Bruges.
Bieber, R., 1990, 'Democratic Control of European Foreign Policy', *European Journal of International Law*, Vol.1, No.1/2. (European University Institute, Florence).
Box, L. and A. Koulaïmah-Gabriel, 1996, *Towards Coherence? Development Cooperation Policy and the Development of Policy Cooperation*, ECDPM working paper No.21, Maastricht: European Centre for Development Policy Management.
CIIR, 1996, *Continental Shift. Europe's Policies Towards the South*, London: Catholic Institute for International Relations.
Council of Ministers of the European Union, General Secretariat, 1997, Conclusions of the 2012th Development Council meeting, Luxembourg, 5 June 1997.
Delors, J., 1992, *Le nouveau Concert européen*, Paris: Editions Odile Jacob.
ECDPM, 1996, *Beyond Lomé IV: Exploring Options for Future ACP–EU Cooperation*, Policy Management Report No.6, Maastricht: European Centre for Development Policy Management.
European Commission, 1996a, *Reinforcing Political Union and Preparing for Enlargement*, Opinion of 28 February 1996, Brussels.
European Commission, 1996b, *The European Union and the Issue of Conflicts in Africa: Peace-building, Conflict Prevention and Beyond*, Communication from the Commission to the Council, SEC (96) 332 final, 06-03-1996, Brussels.
European Commission, 1996c, *Green Paper on Relations between the European Union and the ACP Countries on the Eve of the 21st Century: Challenges and Options for a New Partnership*, Nov. 96, Brussels.
European Council, 1996, Presidency Conclusions of the European Council meeting of 21–22 June 1996, Florence.
European Parliament, 1995, 'Fiche thématique sur la cohérence de l'action extérieure de l'Union Européenne au titre du 1er pilier (Communautaire) et 2e pilier (PESC)', Secrétariat Général du Parlement Européen, task-force 'Conférence Intergouvernementale', PE 165.575, Luxembourg.
European Parliament, 1996, *Report of Fernandez Albor, MEP, on Progress in Implementing the Common Foreign and Security Policy (1995)*, A4-0175/96, Brussels.
European Parliament, 1997, *Resolution on the meeting of the European Council on 16/17 June 1997*, Resolution of 26 June 1997, Strasbourg.

European Union, 1993, *Treaty on European Union (signed in Maastricht on 7 February 1992)*, Luxembourg: Office for Official Publications of the European Communities.

Eurostep, 1996, *A Global Foreign Policy for Europe: A Eurostep Briefing for the 1996 European Union Intergovernmental Conference*, Eurostep, Brussels.

Galtung J., 1973, *The European Community: A Superpower in the Making*, Oslo: Universitetsforlaget.

Hill, C., 1993, 'The Capability–Expectations Gap, or Conceptualising Europe's International Role', *Journal of Common Market Studies*, Vol.31, No.3.

Kohnstamm, Max and Wolfgang Hager, 1973, *l'Europe avec un grand E*, Paris: Robert Laffont.

Intergovernmental Conference, 1997, Draft Treaty of Amsterdam, Document CONF/4001/97, Brussels.

Irish Presidency, 1996, 'The European Union Today and Tomorrow. Adapting the European Union for the Benefit of its Peoples and Preparing it for the Future'. A general outline for a draft revision of the treaties. Dublin II, 5 Dec. 1996, CONF 2500/96 CAB, Brussels.

Koulaïmah-Gabriel, A., 1997, *The Geographic Scope of EC Aid: One of Several Development Policies?*, ECDPM working paper No.42, Maastricht: European Centre for Development Policy Management.

Koulaïmah-Gabriel, A. and A. Oomen, 1997, *Improving Coherence: Challenges for European Development Cooperation*, ECDPM Policy Management Brief, No.9, Maastricht: European Centre for Development Policy Management.

Metcalfe, L., 1996, 'Reinventing the Commission', text of a lecture at the Schuman-Seminar: Maastricht in Maastricht, the treaty revisited, 13 May 1996, Maastricht.

NGDO-LC, 1997, *A Europe Open to the World: Civil Society, the IGC, the Union and the South*, Brussels: Liaison Committee of Development NGOs to the European Union.

NCDO, 1997, 'European Conference on Conflict Prevention', background notes and action plan, 27–28 Feb. 1997, Amsterdam.

OECD, 1996, *Building Policy Coherence. Tools and Tensions*, PUMA (Public Management) occasional papers, No.12, Paris: OECD.

Pijpers, A., E. Regelsberger and W. Wessels, 1988, *European Political Cooperation in the 1980s*, The Hague: Nijhoff.

Robins, N., 1997, 'How to Make Soft Policies Bite', paper for an ECDPM workshop on 'Coherence and Cooperation: How to improve the coherence of European development policy', 20–21 Feb. 1997, Maastricht.

Rummel, R., 1990, *The Evolution of an International Actor: Western Europe's New Assertiveness*, Oxford: Westview Press.

Tubiana, L., 1997, 'Le dialogue sur les politiques et le champ géographique de la Convention', presentation at the Brussels Conference on the Future of ACP–EU Relations, 29–30 September 1997, Brussels: European Commission (DG VIII).

12

Aid and Trade Policy (In)Coherence

OLIVER MORRISSEY

I. INTRODUCTION

This chapter develops a general framework in which to approach the relationships between aid and trade policies, and to show how the framework can be utilised in the context of the concepts of policy coherence adopted in this volume (as set out in Chapter 1). Various approaches to aid and trade policy linkages exist in the (limited) literature, but the major ones are implicitly rooted in the two-gap model for aid. One approach starts from the assumption that a principal objective of aid is to bridge a foreign exchange gap in recipient countries. Such a gap could be bridged, or reduced, either by aid (as balance-of-payments support) or by the recipient implementing policies to expand exports. If the manner in which aid is delivered is inconsistent with a recipient export-oriented strategy, then an argument can be made that aid policy conflicts with (recipient) trade policy [*Morrissey and White, 1996*]; this acts against the achievement of donor–recipient coherence. The alternative, within the dual-gap model, assumes that aid is to bridge a savings gap, or more explicitly aid is a source of productive investment. If trade interests encourage donors to link aid to the provision of products that are costly (relative to world market prices) or technologically inappropriate, aid represents a less than optimal investment; hence, (donor) aid and trade policies are in conflict, in the sense that achieving objectives of one undermines achieving the objectives of the other [*Morrissey, 1993*]; this acts against coherence of the South policies (or what Hoebink refers to as external coherence).

This is a revised version of a paper prepared for the International Workshop on Policy Coherence in Development Cooperation, Geneva, 24–26 April 1997. The author is grateful to workshop participants, especially the editors of this volume, for helpful comments.

Another strand in the literature simply considers the conflict between aid and trade policies from the donor perspective [*McGillivray and Morrissey, 1996*]. With respect to incoherence, the issue here is that both aid and trade policy considerations are important in determining aid allocations, but they often pull in conflicting ways, hence trade considerations prevent the optimal aid policy allocation; again, this acts against coherence of the South policies. A fourth contrasting approach would start from the recipient perspective: the strategies, or more specifically reform policies (given conditionality) required to maximise their objective from aid receipts may conflict with the policies that would maximise exports; this is another aspect of donor–recipient coherence. These four variants all reflect inherent sources of policy incoherence: given initial conditions, recipients wish to maximise aid receipts and *their* exports (which under variant one above donors may constrain), while donors wish to optimise the allocation of aid (abstracting from the budgetary decision on volume) and maximise *their* exports.

Although the four approaches outlined above are not inherently inconsistent, in that they all offer an explanation as to why aid and trade policies can conflict, they do not have a common starting point. In particular, the sources of incoherence require either that donors' aid and trade policies conflict *or* recipients' policies towards aid and trade (exports) conflict *or* both, in that there are conflicts within and between both parties. We may all agree that the latter scenario is correct, that is, internal and external conflicts of interest dominate, but the problem then is that the various approaches to the aid–trade policy incoherence issue are not sufficiently general; each is rooted in one specific case (or combination of conflicting interests), and none encompass the entirety. This chapter offers a more general framework.

The general approach is an adaptation of Sen's entitlement theory [*Sen, 1981*], as set out in section II. Section III reviews the 'traditional' approaches to aid–trade policy conflicts, and suggests how these can be incorporated within the more general entitlements-based framework. Section IV considers some evidence for the case of Britain, and section V extends this to consider European Union (EU) policy, in both cases illustrating links to our general approach. We show that acceptance of the aid entitlements approach allows one to interpret information on the incidence of tied aid and the functional and geographical allocation of aid as indicators of the extent of policy incoherence. Section VI offers conclusions.

II. AN ENTITLEMENTS APPROACH TO AID

The essence of Sen [*1981*] is simple. A household's consumption bundle (opportunity set) comprises those items that can be acquired by either: (i) direct entitlements, those they can produce themselves from their endowments; (ii) exchange entitlements, those they can gain by exchanging items produced under (i) or endowments not used in (i); and, to account for any residual needs, (iii) external entitlements, such as social security receipts or other institutionally determined 'awards' (where this is used to encompass entitlements that can be normally expected but are not ensured by actual endowments). Sen was concerned specifically with a household's access to food; it will be useful to sketch his application before turning to our task of applying the approach to countries (rather than households) with the hope that as an 'external entitlement' we can derive a general justification for aid.

The objective of the household is to gain at least enough food to avoid starvation, which can be done in three ways. The first is own production, which represents a direct entitlement as the household endowment set includes an asset, such as land, which can be used to produce food. The second case is exchange entitlement, where the household can trade endowments, such as labour or non-food products, which may be cash crops, for food. If household endowments are insufficient, through direct production and trade together, to gain enough food to survive, they will starve unless there is a non-market entitlement to food. The latter could be village or kin support, or government programmes, or external aid. This is quite easily accepted for a household. In fact, the approach can easily be adapted to make a case for emergency aid in a country (or more normally area) where disaster, such as war and/or famine, has pushed many people into the starvation set. It is less easy to see how the approach could be adapted to the case of a country.

At the level of the country, direct entitlements refer to productive capacity of the economy while exchange entitlements are best interpreted as international trade. At one extreme, there could be exceptionally poor countries which, given their endowments, are unable to obtain sufficient food (through the combination of direct production and trade) to feed their population. Defining internal entitlements as the consumption set that can be obtained from endowments, that is, direct plus exchange entitlements, then such countries can be defined as 'deficient in internal entitlements' and to avoid starvation would be extended external entitlements (of which aid, emergency food relief in this case, is the most obvious example; remittances are another example; the treatment of debt is more complex). It is too limiting to define requirements in terms of food versus non-food; what we want is some generally acceptable measure of needs. In this chapter, we are not concerned with defining the actual measure of national needs; we merely require that such a measure could be agreed: for present purposes, per capita income will suffice (McGillivray and White [1994] offer a route towards a more elaborate measure).

To summarise, we are claiming that one can define a level of needs for a country, and that for present purposes this measure is per capita income (denoted y). A particular level of y is required for 'survival' and we denote this y_s. A country's ability to meet its own needs is its internal entitlements, comprising direct entitlements through production (y_d) and exchange entitlements through trade (y_e). As countries can only exchange what they produce, we require further decomposition: let y_o designate that which is produced and consumed internally, and y_t that which is produced internally but traded internationally (hence determining what can be imported). Thus: $y_d = y_o + y_t$, and $y_e = py_t$ (where p captures the terms of trade effect). Thus, internal entitlements, $y_i = y_o + y_e$. It follows that $y_s < y_i$ implies external entitlements, and for expository convenience we will define this as aid entitlements ($y_a = y_s - y_i$).

The fundamental notion is that one can define aid entitlements, and the implied purpose of aid is to fill the entitlements gap ($y_s - y_i$). In a static framework, this simply represents a criterion for determining how much aid should be allocated to a particular country (in total; there is no implication regarding which donors should provide the aid, nor at this stage is there any direct implication for the form such aid should take). There is a dynamic context in that over time aid flows should have the effect of reducing the entitlement gap (to formalise the approach to a dynamic model would be more complex than warranted by present purposes). Thus, implicit in the approach is that the justification for aid is to fill an entitlements gap whereas the purpose of aid is to reduce the gap over time. It follows that if aid policy, or the interaction of aid and other policies, has effects which serve to increase the gap, these effects are incompatible with the purpose of aid (note that this is a way, but not the only way, in which aid can be ineffective). This contributes to an analysis of conflict between aid and trade policies as we can relate coherence to any policy mix (regarding aid and trade) which has the effect of increasing y_a (effectively by reducing y_i).

Within the entitlements approach, there are two specific ways in which aid and trade policies can interact so as to undermine the purpose of aid; both represent sources of aid failure (to reduce the gap). *Direct failures* arise when the policy mix reduces y_d either by reducing the efficiency of domestic production or distorting the allocation (between what is consumed and what is traded, for example when aid policies effectively discourage export activities). Inappropriate technology or aid that distorts domestic prices could have this effect. Such failures would act against coherence within a donor's aid policy. *Exchange failures* arise from policies which reduce terms of trade (p), such as any effect of tied aid in increasing the price paid for imports or trade policies that discriminate against countries deficient in entitlements. Such failures would act against coherence of the South policies. In the next section we consider how traditional classifications of aid and trade policy conflicts can be related to this framework; in subsequent sections we review some evidence.

A final point to note here is that aid may fail for reasons other than those outlined above. One obvious possibility is inefficient use, or actual misuse, of aid by recipients, so that y_i remains low (or even decreases). Another possibility is that recipients have limited absorptive capacity and are unable effectively to utilise their aid entitlements, although this need not imply that the entitlements gap will increase over time. An implication of these points is that providing the full entitlements in a given year may not be the optimal strategy for reducing the gap over time. It is possible that less aid, which is more easily absorbed and provides fewer incentives for misuse, may be better in the long run. Another possibility is that a country has an unequal income distribution so that while there are no entitlements for the nation as a whole, certain groups or regions would appear to have aid entitlements. We acknowledge these concerns but they are beyond the scope of this chapter.

III. REASONS FOR INCOHERENCE OF AID AND TRADE POLICIES

There are many reasons why one might expect interactions between aid and trade, and a standard approach is to consider how the volume of flows under one policy may influence the volumes under the other [*McGillivray and Morrissey, 1996*]. Aid flows may increase donor exports (trade) either because of the general economic effects on the recipient, or because the aid is directly linked to trade (donors allocate more aid to those countries with which they trade), or because it rein-

377

forces bilateral economic and political links (or a combination of all three); such interactions are unlikely to act against policy coherence. However, each of these reasons can operate in reverse, such that aid reduces trade, which may act against coherence.

Traditional macro-economic theories of aid impact posit that aid supplements domestic savings, leading to higher investment which contributes to higher rates of economic growth than would be the case without aid (which may facilitate the donor exporting more). If aid is effective in this way it increases internal entitlements, and there is no policy incoherence. However, there is only limited evidence for significant positive impacts of aid on growth; this may be because of recipient inefficiencies but it may be partly because aid has distortionary effects. For example, aid tends to fund projects that require the import of capital goods, typically produced by donors; this could lead to direct failures by distorting internal prices, encouraging excess use of imported capital, or encouraging import-substituting rather than export activities. Where such effects can be observed, through an examination of the functional allocation of aid, this is suggestive of a lack of coherence within the aid policy.

The most direct link between aid and trade is formal tying, where the provision of aid is dependent upon the recipient purchasing goods from the donor. In practice this usually means that aid is provided in the form of goods and services procured in the donor country, thus the aid itself is trade (donor exports). In addition to the exports directly financed, tied aid also increases recipient exposure to donor goods and services which encourages follow-on orders and expands, or at least consolidates, commercial ties; in this way aid is used as an instrument of trade policy [Morrissey, 1993]. A less direct form of tying is informal, where donors direct aid towards projects, goods or countries in which its own industries have a strong competitive advantage; in practice it is difficult to distinguish resulting trade from competitive advantage.

For ease of subsequent exposition, we will use the term 'policy incoherence' to refer to any cases where a policy or set of policies act against a particular form of policy coherence; where appropriate, we will identify the specific type of policy coherence involved. Tied aid represents clear evidence of incoherence. If aid was untied, so that the recipients could choose how to spend it, they would have the opportunity to determine their own investment projects, to determine the technology appropriate to these projects, and to purchase imports at world prices [Morrissey, 1993]. Tied aid leads to exchange failures by increasing the price of imports (associated with tying), and direct failures when it limits the ability of recipients to invest using the most

378

appropriate technology; tying may also distort internal prices [*Morrissey and White, 1996*]. Because tying undermines the ability of aid to reduce the entitlement gap, tied aid can be deemed evidence of incoherence within the aid policy.

IV. DONOR POLICY CONFLICTS: THE UK CASE

In section II we defined the essential purpose of aid as meeting and over time reducing recipient needs, in a way that incorporated humanitarian needs and general economic efficiency. In donor countries aid policy is determined within a policy-making process where development interests (typically advocated by NGOs and academics) are weak relative to donor self-interests – government interests (budgetary and strategic) and domestic economic interests, especially business lobbies (although trade unions often take a similar self-interested stance), which tend to capture aid as an instrument of trade policy [*Morrissey, 1993*]. What is in the best interests of donors now may not be best for recipients (that is, may not be effective in reducing their entitlements gap). More generally, where donor interests dominate recipient interests, the potential development benefits of aid are reduced.

As suggested in section III, the most obvious evidence of conflict between donor and recipient interests is found in the extent of tying. The pressures for tying aid to donor trade flows arise at both the micro-economic and macro-economic levels. At the microeconomic level, exporters in the donor country can gain commercial benefits as tied aid supports export orders for some firms, which generally helps exporters in winning contracts in developing countries. Thus, major exporters apply pressure by lobbying the government [*Morrissey et al., 1992*]. From a macro-economic perspective, aid is an outflow of funds from the country for which donors concerned with their balance of payments have an incentive to seek some matching inflow. Tied aid implies that aid outflows are matched by inflows to pay for the exports, which reduces the potential balance of payments deficit. However, tying reduces the value of aid to recipients and can have an effect equivalent to a tariff on imports [*Morrissey and White, 1996*]; in this way, tying can have an effect of reducing internal entitlements. Tied aid is at least less effective than untied aid in reducing an entitlements gap, and the extent of tying can be interpreted as evidence of incoherence within the aid policy.

The level of tying of British aid has remained fairly stable since the late 1980s at over 40 per cent of total aid: DAC [*1985*] reports 41 per

379

cent of British aid as fully tied in 1982/83, while 44 per cent was fully tied in 1989 [*DAC, 1991*] and 1990, although the extent of tying seems to have been reduced significantly to 27 per cent in 1994 (Table 2 below). In fact the evidence in Table 2 suggests that most donors have reduced the degree of tying, often significantly, so that the percentage of total DAC aid fully tied fell from 25 per cent in 1990 to 17 per cent in 1994. This at least suggests that the extent of policy incoherence (measured in this way) has been reduced.

TABLE 1
COMPOSITION OF BRITISH AID, SELECTED YEARS

	1990/91	1992/93	1994/95	1995/96
Total aid (constant £m)	2022	2271	2348	2266
Aid % of GNP	0.31	0.31	0.31	0.28
As % of total:				
developing countries	96.5	90.4	87.4	85.3
multilateral	35.7	44.5	48.8	49.0
As % of bilateral aid:				
Sub-Saharan Africa	50.4[a]	42.3	42.9	37.8
Asia	37.4[a]	35.8	31.8	37.8
Commonwealth		57.8	52.0	55.5
LLDCs		36.3	40.4	35.7
LICs		71.1	68.5	68.5
LMICs		21.2	26.4	26.5
UMICs		7.5	5.0	4.9
By purpose (%):				
public and community services		28.1	32.5	32.7
transport and communications		10.2	5.8	6.9
construction		1.5	1.0	0.5
manufacturing		5.7	8.2	8.4
energy		10.2	13.5	12.9
renewable natural resources		18.1	16.7	14.5
food aid		3.7	3.6	2.4
emergency relief		10.7	17.3	10.4

Notes and sources:
All data from *British Aid Statistics. 1991/92–1995/96* and refer to aid programme. LLDCs are the 48 least developed countries; LICs are 56 low-income countries (1992 per capita GNP below $676); MICs are middle-income countries – L (lower, per capita GNP $676–2695) and U (upper, $2696–8355). Under purposes of aid: public includes education and health; resources includes agriculture and irrigation; emergency relief excludes food aid (allocation by purpose does not total 100 per cent; omitted categories include mining, financial services, and tourism).
a   Refers to 1989/90 and from DAC [*1996: A59–60*].

Other indicators of the influence of business interests over development interests, and hence of potential policy incoherence, are the geographical and sectoral allocation of aid. Table 1 presents some data on the composition of the UK aid budget. While a proper evaluation of business influences would require more detailed data over the period under study, these data serve to make a few points. First, the share of aid allocated through multilateral agencies, which had been fairly stable around 44 per cent in the 1980s, increased gradually to almost 50 per cent by 1995/96 (while the real value of aid fell). Second, the share of aid going to developing countries fell to 85 per cent, implying that an increasing share is allocated to Central and Eastern Europe (CEE) and the former Soviet Union (FSU). Third, and by way of contrast, Britain fares well according to criteria of geographical allocation, with about 35–40 per cent going to LLDCs, almost 70 per cent going to the poorest countries and about 40 per cent to sub-Saharan Africa (SSA), although all of these shares seem to be declining (which may be due to increased allocations to CEE and FSU, most of which are LMICs).

Fourth, there is evidence that the sectoral allocation favours business interests, given the relative emphasis on infrastructure and industry, but this does not imply that the aid is any less effective. Relatively small shares go to construction and manufacturing, a declining share to transport and communications, and energy is the only capital-intensive sector with an increasing share; in total, the share allocated to purposes most likely to support British exports has declined to below 30 per cent. Public and Community Services, which includes health and education, has seen its share increase to almost a third. Emergency aid, which was negligible in the 1980s, has assumed greater importance, while food aid is a small share. On balance, as with the trend in tying, the sectoral allocation of aid has shifted in favour of development interests and we could infer that the quality of British aid has improved.

Table 2 provides some recent self-explanatory data on the largest DAC donors. This allows us to evaluate Britain's performance against that of other donors. We have already drawn attention to the downward trend in the incidence of tying, and remarked that this is a desirable trend (we can note that Germany and Japan, two of the largest donors, are exceptions to the trend).

Some observers may express concern at the general downward trend in the value of aid flows. The nominal increase in DAC net aid, of 11 per cent on 1995 over 1990, is unlikely to have kept pace with inflation; in constant prices total aid fell by about 10 per cent in the period [*DAC, 1996: A15*] and, as a percentage of total GNP, aid has fallen from 0.33 to 0.27. In our entitlements gap approach, this is not necessarily undesirable: if aid is effective, entitlements should fall over time; if countries are growing (which may or may not be due to aid), entitlements should fall; it may even be the case that if absorbtive capacity is low (arguably the case in many African countries), a lower volume of aid would be more effective. Observation of the trend alone does not permit inferences on aid's ability to fill entitlements gaps, although it may be cause for concern (in particular, the almost universal decline in aid relative to donor GNP is worrying); to draw such inferences one would need to identify the gaps (which is beyond the scope of this chapter).

TABLE 2
NET AID FROM DAC DONORS, 1990 AND 1994/95

Donor	Net aid $m[1]		Aid as % of GNP		Tied aid[2]	
	1990	1995	1990	1995	1990	1994
Canada	2470	2067	0.44	0.38	28.4	26.7
Denmark[3]	1171	1623	0.94	0.96	15.8	*n.a.*
France	7163	8443	0.60	0.55	40.8	30.5
Germany	6320	7524	0.42	0.31	38.2	37.4
Italy	3395	1623	0.31	0.15	47.2	18.2
Japan	9069	14489	0.31	0.28	12.5	13.9
Netherlands	2538	3226	0.92	0.81	3.7	2.2
Norway	1205	1244	1.17	0.87	23.2	10.0
Sweden	2007	1704	0.91	0.77	14.5	14.8
UK[3]	2638	3157	0.27	0.28	44.0	26.6
USA	11394	7367	0.21	0.10	19.2	*n.a.*
DAC	52961	58894	0.33	0.27	25.3	17.1

Notes and sources:
1. Volume of net aid refers to the DAC definition of official development assistance in $m at current prices and exchange rates; includes non-aid debt forgiveness in 1990 country figures. From DAC [*1996: A7–8*].
2. Tied aid is the share of total aid 'mainly tied to procurement within the donor country', and may be interpreted as an underestimate; 1990 figures are from DAC [*1992: A–44*]; 1994 figures are from DAC [*1996: A50 and A52*], *n.a.* means not available (excluded from figure for DAC average).
3. Data on tied aid for Denmark and the UK in 1990 relate to 1989 [*DAC, 1991: 206*].

We can also consider trends in aid allocation. In 1989, 25 per cent of total DAC aid was allocated to social and administrative infrastructure, 21 per cent to economic infrastructure, 18 per cent to production (including agriculture), and six per cent to emergency and food aid [*DAC, 1991: 203*]. By 1993/94, the respective shares were 26 per cent, 20 per cent, 11 per cent and, for food aid only, three per cent [*DAC, 1996: A43–4*]. This is remarkably consistent. In 1989/90, 22 per cent of DAC aid was to LLDCs and 54 per cent to LICs [*DAC, 1991: 178*]; by 1994/95, the respective shares were 26 per cent and 52 per cent [*DAC, 1996: A58*], a slight improvement. On criteria of allocation, Britain tends to perform better, being more oriented towards development uses and poor countries than the DAC average, while there is no evidence of an improved allocation of DAC aid in the 1990s.

This overview of British aid policy can be related to incoherence in a number of ways. First, the general orientation of aid towards the poorest recipients and the significant allocation to social sectors and poverty is consistent with an entitlements approach (there is a notion of y_a underlying aid policy). Second, the significant sectoral allocation towards industry, infrastructure, and capital projects in general, can lead to direct failures (in that it can induce domestic distortions which reduce y_t), but the extent of this seems to be falling. This represents incoherence within the aid policy. Third, the evidence of quite significant degrees of tying suggests that prices of imports will be higher than would otherwise be the case (that is, a reduction in p) and may also induce anti-export bias; both cases suggest incoherence of the South policies. The extent of tying has been falling. Thus, while there is evidence of policy incoherence it seems to be declining, such that British aid now is better positioned to fill an entitlements gap than it was in the past. There is therefore no obvious reason to be alarmed by the slight decline in the real volume of aid.

V. SOME IMPLICATIONS FOR EU POLICY

Morrissey [*1993*] reviews trends in aid over the period 1980 to 1990 for the major European donors and concludes that Italy and France adopt the most clearly export-oriented aid policies; their governments are responsive to business demands and, at least in construction, this has helped them maintain or increase their market share in LDCs (given the large decline in Italian aid in Table 2, this is no longer likely to hold for Italy). The UK, Germany and the Netherlands are less responsive to business demands and have made less use of their aid budgets to promote exports. This conclusion is supported by the finding that if EU countries abandoned bilateral tying of aid and allowed procurement from all EU countries, Germany and the UK would be among the gainers while France and Italy would be losers [*Jepma, 1991: 50*]. Morrissey [*1993*] does argue that EU donors use aid as an instrument of trade competition, which is a source of donor incoherence (and the lack of co-ordination between donors imposes costs on recipients).

Article 130u of the Maastricht Treaty includes objectives to integrate developing countries into the world economy, which implies an EU trade policy allowing easier access to goods from developing countries, and objectives to promote poverty alleviation and development, especially in the poorest countries, which implies a coherent development-oriented aid policy. At present, neither policy area is consistent with these objectives. Furthermore, present EU aid and trade policies are incompatible in many respects. A trade policy that allowed easier access to EU markets by exporters from developing countries, and that reduced subsidies under the Common Agricultural Policy which depress world prices of agricultural commodities, would benefit those developing countries able to avail themselves of opportunities for export-led growth. Export expansion is probably a necessary, although not sufficient, condition for economic growth; EU trade policies that restrict exports from developing countries thereby constrain their growth potential. Liberal world trade would make a far more important contribution to economic growth than could aid policies. Hence, EU trade policy does conflict with the objectives of aid policy, by limiting the ability of developing countries themselves to reduce an entitlements gap.

The two areas of policy could be rendered compatible if access to the EU market for developing countries was less restricted, which could fuel economic growth, and aid policy was directed to the development needs of the poorest countries. Economic growth in itself is not the same as development; the latter notion must take into account the distribution of the benefits from growth, the alleviation of poverty and general improvements in living standards and access to social services. EU aid policy could be directed at assisting those countries unable to expand exports immediately to gain easier access to the European market, and at supporting poverty alleviation and investment in human and social capital in all developing countries. In certain respects, trade provides the opportunities for economic growth and aid can be directed at supporting economic and social development. Compatible policies must recognise the interrelationships between these objectives.

There are a number of aspects of European aid policy of relevance to the Maastricht objectives and which contribute to donor incoherence. First is the absence of any rules of subsidiarity: there are no clear guidelines for the role of Community aid *vis-à-vis* the bilateral aid of member states. Second, the aid policies of member states and of the Community are subject to a variety of influences which are often in conflict. The allocation of aid is influenced by foreign policy and trade policy considerations, which can be at cross purposes with the development objectives for a donor, and can be used competitively between donors. Third are the factors determining the total volume of aid. On the one hand, there is domestic pressure to reduce public spending (and aid budgets are vulnerable, as seen from Table 2 above). On the other, there is potential for aid diversion away from traditional recipients and towards the emerging states of CEE and FSU (as witnessed in the case of the UK above); such a trend may or may not be consistent with entitlements-based allocation.

Article 130u of the Maastricht Treaty emphasised that aid from the EU, implicitly including bilateral aid from member states, should be development-oriented. This implies that it should be allocated according to the development needs, and capabilities, of recipients. In practice, aid competition distorts the global allocation of aid. The aid policies of the EU and its member states are subject to internal influences which may undermine the Maastricht objectives for development-oriented aid [*Greenaway and Morrissey, 1993*] and imply donor incoherence.

Briefly, there are three ways in which EU aid policy is at present in conflict with the objectives of Article 130u in the Maastricht Treaty. First, member states use some of their bilateral aid in a competitive manner, notably through tying. Second, the self-interests of member states have a determining influence on EU aid policy. Third, there are no principles to avoid aid diversion and ensure aid allocation in accordance with entitlements. Giving the EU greater control over aid allocations by member states, with established principles of subsidiarity and development criteria for aid policy, would make it easier to achieve development objectives and could offer other benefits to developing countries (especially through improved co-ordination by reducing the number of donors).

The discussion of EU aid policy can be related to our entitlements approach in a manner similar to the case for Britain. First, the principles of Article 130u contain a focus on poverty alleviation and development in the poorest recipients, which is consistent with an underlying concept of aid entitlements. There is also mention of the need to increase the ability of developing country exporters to gain access to the European market, which would be consistent with improving their exchange entitlements (increasing y_e, both by encouraging export-orientation and improving terms of trade). Second, there is evidence of incoherence within the aid policies of member states (our arguments for the UK apply to other donors).

Third, there is incoherence within the South policies of the Community: for example, the Common Agricultural Policy has effects that reduce the terms of trade facing agricultural exporters (reducing p), although this is offset for net food importers who can benefit from subsidised prices (and is also offset for some countries that have preferential access to the EU). Also, there are general aspects of EU trade policy which reduce access to developing countries, hence induce incoherence of South policies. Finally, there is a lack of donor coherence as aid is used as an instrument of trade and foreign policy.

VI. CONCLUSIONS

Recipients benefit from aid but could benefit more if aid policy were more clearly directed at recipient needs rather than donor interests. Aid is structured to benefit donor exporters more than it meets development interests. International and internal political interests, notably public expenditure restraint and trade policy, have been the major determinants of the size and geographical allocation of the aid budget. There are good reasons for business interests to advocate tied aid, and clear commercial self-interested reasons for the government to ·support them. This underlies the conflict between aid objectives and (donor) trade interests, and gives rise to incoherence within aid policy and in donor policies towards the South.

We have advocated an approach to aid based on a concept of entitlements. If, given its resources and ability to trade, a country is unable to meet the basic needs of its populace, that country can be said to have an entitlements deficit, or aid entitlements (the ultimate purpose of which should be to reduce the deficit). Any elements of aid policy, or of policies that interact with aid policy, that have the effect of increasing (or at least not helping to reduce) the deficit can be interpreted as sources of policy incoherence, either within the aid policy or of donor policies towards the South. We have used the cases of the UK and the EU to illustrate how the aroach could be applied to highlight instances of policy incoherence.

We can utilise the three points of inconsistency between EU policies and Article 130u of the Maastricht Treaty to suggest both the relevance and implications of our general entitlements approach. First, the absence of principles of subsidiarity in EU aid and trade policies is relevant because it implies that member states can use policies for competition between each other (which gives rise to donor incoherence). Thus, aid is used as an instrument of trade policy competition. This undermines the developmental effectiveness of aid and induces the various sources of incoherence identified above in relation to Community and member states' aid policies. Subsidiarity would offer no solution in itself, but discussion of how to co-ordinate European aid policy, within members, within the EU, and with respect to other policies, would be helpful to identify, and hopefully reduce, incoherences that we have shown to arise within aid policy, between donors and their South policies.

Second, if our proposal of aid entitlements is accepted, then one would advocate a set of criteria for determining aid allocation: recipients' entitlements, in absolute, will be based on their income. The approach could be extended (with some careful effort) to address cases where distributional inequities in a country, or other defined factors (such as emergencies), confer aid entitlements on specific groups. In this case, but also more generally, the establishment of aid entitlements would be associated with some principles of aid targeting. In establishing entitlements, awareness of sources of incoherence could inform aid policy (and especially any targeting).

Discussion of the volume of aid is less central to our purposes. Apparent ineffectiveness of aid is often used as an argument to reduce the volume, but should really be an indication that perhaps the aid has not been used or allocated effectively. The concept of entitlements in itself does not improve the effectiveness of aid, but it can contribute to such an improvement. However, establishment of entitlements provides an argument that a volume of aid (implicitly defined by the entitlements shortfall) should be provided. Other factors must be taken into account to decide how, and by whom.

REFERENCES

DAC, 1985, *Twenty-five Years of Development Co-operation: A Review*, Paris: OECD, Development Assistance Committee.
DAC, 1991, *Development Co-operation – 1991 Report of the Development Assistance Committee*, Paris: OECD, Development Assistance Committee.
DAC, 1992, *Development Co-operation – 1992 Report of the Development Assistance Committee*, Paris: OECD, Development Assistance Committee.
DAC, 1996, *Development Co-operation – 1996 Report of the Development Assistance Committee*, Paris: OECD, Development Assistance Committee.
Greenaway, David and Oliver Morrissey, 1993, 'Written and Oral Evidence', in the House of Lords Select Committee on The European Communities, *EC Aid and Trade Policy*, London: HMSO (HL Paper 123).
Jepma, Catrinus, 1991, *EC-Wide Untying*, Groningen: University of Groningen, IDE-Foundation.

McGillivray, Mark and Oliver Morrissey, 1996, 'An Empirical Examination of the Link between Aid and Trade Flows', paper presented at the VIIIth General Conference of the European Association of Development Research and Training Institutes, Vienna, 11-14 September 1996.

McGillivray, Mark and Howard White, 1994, 'Developmental Criteria for the Allocation of Aid and Assessment of Donor Performance', University of Nottingham: *CREDIT Research Paper* 94/7.

Morrissey, Oliver, 1993, 'The Mixing of Aid and Trade Policies', *The World Economy*, Vol. 16, No. 1.

Morrissey, Oliver, Brian Smith and Edward Horesh, 1992, *British Aid and International Trade*, Buckingham: Open University Press.

Morrissey, Oliver and Howard White, 1996, 'Evaluating the Concessionality of Tied Aid', *The Manchester School*, LXIV, No. 2.

Sen, Amartya, 1981, *Poverty and Famines: An Essay on Entitlement and Deprivation*, Oxford: Clarendon Press.

13

Development Co-operation in the New Global Economy: The Challenge of Policy Coherence

KIICHIRO FUKASAKU

I. INTRODUCTION

This chapter presents a synthesis of the main results of three studies on policy coherence conducted at the OECD Development Centre and discusses their implications for development co-operation policy. These studies analyse present economic relations between major OECD countries and three developing regions and examine how aid, trade and other pertinent policies of OECD countries are congruent with, and conducive to, sustained growth and development of these regions. The three developing regions are low- and middle-income member countries of ASEAN (Indonesia, Malaysia, the Philippines and Thailand), South Asia (Bangladesh, India, Pakistan and Sri Lanka), and North Africa (Algeria, Morocco and Tunisia).[1]

Underlying these three studies is the growing recognition among policy-makers in major OECD countries that since economic linkages between the OECD countries and the developing regions have become more complex today than some ten years ago,[2] there is a need to reassess development co-operation efforts of OECD member

The author is grateful to Jacques Forster, Andrea Koulaïmah-Gabriel, Olav Stokke and other seminar participants for their helpful comments and suggestions. The opinions expressed in this chapter are, however, those of the author alone and do not reflect those of the organisation to which the author belongs.
1. Because of space limitations, this chapter cannot get into the details of economic linkages between OECD countries and these three developing regions. Interested readers are thus requested to consult Fukasaku, Plummer and Tan (eds.) [*1995*], Fukasaku, Martineau and Solignac-Lecomte [*1998*], and Fontagné and Péridy [*1997*], respectively.
2. See, for example, OECD [*1995*] for a detailed analysis of economic linkages between OECD and major developing regions. See also OECD [*1997*] for a discussion of main features of expected structural change in the world economy in 2020.

countries, which are not limited to aid programmes alone. The issue of coherence – or the lack thereof – between aid and other policies was brought to the attention of donor countries in the 1992 Report of the Development Assistance Committee (DAC) of the OECD. There are two basic reasons for that. First, the supply of aid has been constrained by budgetary pressures in the donor countries, while its demand is expected to increase in many developing (and transition) economies, notably the poorest, in the foreseeable future. A recent rise in private capital flows into the developing countries has been heavily concentrated in a dozen of so-called 'newly emerging economies', and the access to foreign private capital remains very limited for the rest.[3] Thus, enhancing the effectiveness of aid available to them has become even more important today.

Second, a growing number of developing countries have become more outward-oriented in their development strategies, and hence, more closely integrated into the world market. The implementation of the Uruguay Round Agreements, new multilateral initiatives undertaken at the first WTO Ministerial Conference held in Singapore in December 1996 and continued market-opening efforts in various regions all combine to indicate that this reform trend in developing countries will continue in the coming years. As the aid-recipient economies become increasingly open and market-based, it is natural for policy-makers in both donor and recipient countries to take a fresh look at donor countries' economic policies, other than aid, from the standpoint of development co-operation and examine their implications for development.

Having fully recognised these important changes in international financial and policy environment, DAC member countries are now formulating their aid policies for the next century on the basis of the new strategy for development partnership, which was adopted in May 1996 [OECD/DAC, 1996]. The key feature of the new strategy is its proposal of a global development effort to achieve a limited number of policy goals in the time-bound manner. These goals involve specific targets for poverty reduction; promotion of primary education; gender equality in primary and secondary education; basic health care and family planning; and environmental sustainability. In pursuing these goals, the DAC [OECD/DAC, 1996: 2] emphasises the importance of taking individual, country-by-country approaches that reflect local conditions and locally-owned development strategies. At the same time, OECD donors re-emphasise their continued efforts to

---

3. See, for example, Fukasaku and Hellvin [1998] for a detailed analysis of private capital flows to developing countries and their implications.

enhance the coherence between aid policies and other policies which impinge on developing countries.

In section II the notion of 'policy coherence', as used in this chapter, is clarified and the nature of the problems facing OECD donors is discussed. In section III the main results of the three studies that examine in detail present economic relations between major OECD countries and the three developing regions are presented and the coherence issues from the developing-country perspective are discussed. Finally, some concluding remarks are presented in section IV.

II. POLICY COHERENCE: DEFINITIONS AND PROBLEMS

The term 'coherence' generally refers to the consistency between policy objectives and instruments on the one hand, and the consistency among objectives on the other. In the case under consideration, the problem of a lack of coherence arises when there is a serious mismatch between the objectives of OECD countries' different policies and their effects on developing countries.

To avoid misunderstanding about the nature of the problems concerned, it should be noted at the outset that OECD countries' policies are formulated on the basis of their *own* interests, priorities and obligations. Apart from humanitarian aid, the very nature of development co-operation policy makes it inevitable to involve different ministries of donor countries in their respective fields (for example, aid, trade, finance, health, and environment). Mention has often been made of the practical difficulty of co-ordinating different ministries and agencies within the government.[4] For example, Michel [*1997: 33*] states that it is increasingly evident that a comprehensive approach, employing coherent policies across a range of government activities, is essential, and yet officials in aid agencies and trade ministries (for example) often act independently of one another as if aid and trade were independent or even competing policy instruments. The following quotation from Krueger [*1993: 1*] represents an example of policy incoherence of this kind:

When the regime of Ferdinand Marcos was overthrown in the Philippines in 1986, the United States supported the newly elected government of Corazon Aquino. To that end, the U.S.

---

4. In Japan, for example, 19 ministries and agencies are actually involved in the implementation of ODA programmes. This makes it very difficult, if not impossible, to know who is doing what.

Congress authorized $210 million of economic assistance to the Philippines in fiscal year 1987. At the same time, however, U.S. quotas on imported Philippine sugar were being reduced, causing the Philippines to lose $89 million, equal to 42 per cent of the U.S. aid allocation. In addition, Philippine exports of textiles and apparel to the United States were restricted under the Multifiber Arrangement even as the United States was urging the Philippines to remove protectionist trade barriers to stimulate export growth.

Taking a global view of the textile trade policy of industrial countries, UNDP [*1994: 66*] claims that tariffs and non-tariff barriers maintained by industrial countries in their imports of textiles and clothing would cost developing-country exporters US$50 billion a year (at 1992 prices), which is roughly equivalent to total net receipts of bilateral official development finance by all developing countries in the same year (US$49 billion).[5] To deal with the issue of policy (in)coherence more effectively, it is thus essential to make government policies more transparent in terms of their impact on developing countries and expose them to greater public scrutiny at both national and international levels.[6]

Broadly speaking, the coherence issues in development co-operation have two dimensions, national and international. 'National policy coherence' requires that OECD countries' policies help promote, or at least not harm, the economic interests of developing countries; Langhammer [*1995: 213*] puts it as follows:

Developing countries stand to gain if OECD countries fully exploit their growth potential to act as engines, refrain from protectionist measures, provide stable money, export private risk capital and aid to net borrowers, and create fresh human capital that cascades down to lower-income countries and thus keeps world-wide structural change moving.

---

5. Under the Uruguay Round Agreements, MFA quotas are being progressively liberalised over the ten-year period (1995–2005). However, this is not the whole story. See the next section.
6. The periodic review by the DAC of its member countries' aid policies has already started to involve a discussion of policy coherence, but this would require much closer co-operation between the DAC and its member countries on the one hand, and between relevant Directorates within the OECD on the other, if the member countries wish to give more weight to it. See Shigehara [*1997*] for a more general discussion on the role of multilateral surveillance in international policy co-operation.

According to this view, the first and uppermost priority for OECD countries is to 'keep their own house in order'. This refers not only to maintaining macro-economic health but also to increasing structural flexibility in OECD countries. More and more developing economies are determined to follow the footsteps of East Asian 'miracle' economies by exporting their products for which they enjoy comparative advantage *vis-à-vis* the OECD countries and they are more or less dependent on access to the OECD markets. From the developing-country perspective, the capacity (and willingness) of OECD countries to adapt to increased import pressures constitutes an important component of development co-operation efforts. In other words, the open trade policy that OECD countries are advocating for poorer countries requires credible *domestic* policies to foster structural adjustment in their own economies.

Since the OECD countries are (still) dominant as both exporters and importers on world markets, the coherence issues in development co-operation have an international dimension as well; 'international policy coherence' calls upon them to secure collectively the provision of international public goods, such as an open and stable international marketplace, on which the economic welfare of all countries depend. Here, one could see two potential sources of conflict. One is the problem of 'free riders'. Some OECD countries consider that stricter trade rules and obligations should be applied to some more advanced developing countries, as they join the ranks of 'major players' on world markets. This question of 'graduation' is also an important and politically sensitive issue in the context of the DAC discussion concerning ODA eligibility.

Another potential source of conflict is the trend towards regionalism among OECD countries. Regional integration arrangements in Europe and North America can be construed as 'GATT-plus', and thus as stepping stones towards global trade liberalisation. Nevertheless, the proliferation of such regional arrangements inevitably entails an element of discrimination against third countries, particularly poorer ones that are left outside the regional arrangements. In this connection, it should also be noted that the effectiveness of trade preferences, such as the GSP (Generalised System of Preferences) privileges granted to developing countries, has been called into question, as the margin of preferences is being eroded as a result of multilateral trade liberalisation implemented successively under the auspices of the GATT/WTO (see the following section).

Finally, we usually discuss coherence issues with respect to individual donor countries, but this is also an important – and difficult –

subject for the European Union (EU). As a supra-national institution, the EU is still in the process of harmonising and co-ordinating the national policies of its member states. Except for trade, transport, competition, agriculture and coal and steel, common policies do not yet exist in many other areas, including aid and the environment. Policy incoherence is thus a natural topic for the EU whose member states have different historical and cultural backgrounds and policy priorities [*Langhammer, 1995*]. This becomes increasingly important, as the EU is strengthening its political and economic ties with several countries in Eastern Europe, while, at the same time, formulating new external policies towards non-member countries in the Mediterranean region [*Fontagné and Péridy, 1997*].

Today, the 'developing countries' consists of very heterogeneous groups of economies in terms of the level of per capita income, industrial capacity, infrastructure development, human resource base and institution-building. For example, with rapid economic growth, the embrace of outward-oriented development strategies, and improved international competitiveness, several developing economies in Southeast Asia have displayed a remarkable catching up capacity over the past decade, while many developing countries in sub-Saharan Africa risk being marginalised, despite substantial progress made in policy reform in recent years [*Naudet and Pradelle, 1997*]. Many others, again, including those in South Asia and North Africa, are struggling to integrate their economies more closely into the world market. Thus, development co-operation policy needs to be formulated so as to target financial and human resources to meet the needs of developing countries. The three case-studies on which the next section is based provide a comparative perspective in this respect, highlighting the complexity of the problems involved.

III. GROWING INTERDEPENDENCE AND POLICY COHERENCE

This section is organised under three headings: OECD–ASEAN relations, OECD–South Asia relations, and EU–Maghreb relations. Under each heading the main points of discussion will be brought up, which allows us to focus on key coherence issues.

(1) OECD–ASEAN Relations

The workshop volume edited by Fukasaku *et al.* [*1995*] on OECD–ASEAN relations provides an interesting case for examining policy coherence issues.[7] In the postwar years, Western countries shaped economic policies *vis-à-vis* the ASEAN region primarily from the geopolitical point of view, that is, as a counter-force to communist Indochina and a fortress against the 'domino effect'. Today, as East–West rivalry is over and several members of ASEAN have developed into second-tier 'tiger' economies in the Asia-Pacific region, ASEAN countries are increasing their economic weight as OECD countries' trade and investment partners. At the same time, three members of ASEAN (Indonesia, the Philippines and Thailand) are still among the main recipients of ODA from DAC members.[8]

Since the mid-1980s, the governments of four ASEAN countries (the above three countries and Malaysia) have embarked on policy reforms, albeit to varying degrees, towards a more open, market-based economy, and these ASEAN economies, with the exception of the Philippines, have grown at a rapid pace by historical standards (Table 1). Meanwhile, these countries have undergone substantial transformation from natural-resource-based economies to more diversified ones, with increased specialisation in manufactured exports. The combination of strengthened international competitiveness and diversification of their exports to a booming East Asian market, notably China, has made these countries more resilient to the impact of the growth performance of OECD countries [*Fukasaku and Hirata, 1995*]. As a result, the OECD–ASEAN relationship has been evolving away from one based on traditional 'North–South dependency' towards one of 'equal partners'.[9]

---

7. With its membership extended to Viet Nam in July 1995 and to Laos and Myanmar in July 1997, the Association of Southeast Asian Nations (ASEAN) has now come to embrace nine member countries. Among these countries, particular interest is taken in the original ASEAN-4 (Indonesia, Malaysia, the Philippines and Thailand). According to the World Bank, Brunei Darussalam and Singapore are classified as high-income countries so that these countries are excluded from the study.
8. More recently, Viet Nam has emerged as one of the major recipients of ODA from DAC members. See OECD/DAC [*1997: Annex Table 42*].
9. As a regional institution, ASEAN has established regular 'policy dialogue' meetings with several OECD member countries, including those in the European Union. In this respect it should be noted that the Asia–Europe Summit Meeting (ASEM) held for the first time in March 1996 in Bangkok has enhanced significantly the political standing of the institution; its importance as an economic grouping has increased over the past decade.

TABLE 1
GROWTH RATES OF REAL GDP PER CAPITA IN SELECTED DEVELOPING COUNTRIES, 19950–95

	1990	1991	1992	1993	1994	1995	1980–90[1]	1990–95[1]
Southeast Asia								
Indonesia	5,6	5,3	4,8	4,8	5,9	6,6	4,0	5,5
Malaysia	7,2	6,1	5,3	5,8	6,4	7,2	3,4	6,2
Philippines	0,5	-2,4	-1,9	0,0	2,1	2,7	-0,7	0,1
Thailand	9,9	6,7	6,2	6,5	7,4	7,5	6,2	6,9
South Asia								
Bangladesh	4,7	1,2	2,0	2,4	2,4	2,5	2,6	2,2
India	3,6	-1,6	2,5	1,4	3,5	4,5	3,7	2,0
Pakistan	1,7	2,7	5,0	-0,9	0,3	2,5	3,5	1,9
Sri Lanka	4,9	3,3	3,0	5,6	3,9	4,2	2,9	4,0
North Africa								
Algeria	-3,8	-3,6	-0,8	-4,5	-2,6	1,6	-0,3	-2,0
Morocco	2,1	4,0	-6,4	-3,0	9,5	-7,9	1,5	-1,0
Tunisia	5,8	1,8	5,5	0,0	1,5	1,6	1,2	2,1
Memo Item								
China	2,4	7,0	13,1	12,8	11,3	9,1	7,3	10,7

Source: CEPII-Chelem, World Bank.
Note: [1] Average annual growth rates.

One of the main developments over the past decade has been the increased importance of private capital as a source of financing investment funds in developing countries. The share of private capital in total net resource flows to the developing countries jumped from 35 per cent in 1986 to 67 per cent in 1995.[10] Among the developing areas, ASEAN countries have been relatively successful in attracting *both* aid and private flows. Nasution [*1995*] argues that ASEAN's economic value in the international financial market has increased substantially as a result of policy reforms in the 1980s when they undertook sound macro-economic policies and outward-oriented development strategies.[11] In his view, the greatest contribution of foreign aid to ASEAN development was to facilitate pro-market policy reforms, transfer of technology and institution-building. Aid

---

10. In 1995, the total amount of official development finance (ODF) was estimated at US$69.4 billion, accounting for about 29 per cent of total net resource flows to developing countries (US$239.3 billion) [*OEC/DAC, 1997:Statistical Annex Table 1*].
11 See Fukasaku [*1997*] for a detailed discussion of the macroeconomic framework for ASEAN economies.

flows to this region, however, were too small to have any measurable macroeconomic impact.[12]

Speaking of the aid policy of Japan, the largest provider of ODA to ASEAN, Pang [*1995:189*] states:

> Japan's aid to ASEAN countries collectively and individually has played an important part in improving the region's capacity to industrialise and absorb new technology. In particular, the movement of its industries to South-east Asia, which its aid programme facilitated, quickened ASEAN's development of export-oriented industries.

Whether aid has a negative or positive impact on private investment in developing countries remains a matter of debate,[13] but the views expressed by Nasution [*1995*] and Pang [*1995*] about Japan's aid to ASEAN point to the importance of 'policy variables' in evaluating the economic value of aid programmes in recipient countries. Hirata [*1995*] also claims that a heavy concentration of Japan's aid flows to East and Southeast Asia can be justified because of a high degree of interdependence between Japan and these regions.

The ASEAN region has been a highly attractive location for foreign direct investment (FDI) among developing countries in the post-1986 period, as ASEAN's domestic investment climate has improved with economic deregulation, trade liberalisation and foreign investment liberalisation measures. However, Chia [*1995*] argues that there is a need for ASEAN countries to deregulate further foreign investment regimes and rationalise incentive schemes, in order to stay competitive as a location of FDI. The ASEAN countries have so far avoided any attempt to co-ordinate FDI policies within the region and been opposed to establishing any multilateral investment codes that are legally binding. On the other hand, FDI *outflows* from some ASEAN countries are likely to expand in the coming years, and there will be growing scope for international co-operation towards FDI policies.

---

12. Foreign aid has assumed renewed importance in several ASEAN counties, notably Indonesia and Thailand, as their economies adjust to the aftershocks of the 1997 financial crisis.
13. See, for example, Snyder [*1996*] for recent empirical research using cross-country investment regressions based on annual panel data from 36 developing countries over the period of 1977–91. His empirical results show a negative association between aid and private investment (both normalised by GNP and GDP, respectively).

While ASEAN countries have reaped substantial benefits from their adoption of outward-oriented development strategies, their continued growth could be jeopardised by adverse developments in trade policy elsewhere. Increased protectionism and discriminatory regional integration arrangements in OECD countries could lead to a closed and segmented global market-place, potentially impeding future economic development in the ASEAN countries. In particular, the regional integration initiatives in North America – ASEAN's largest export market – are of great concern to ASEAN countries. Plummer [1995] argues that while, in the aggregate, the trade diversion effects of the North American Free Trade Area (NAFTA) do not appear to be of overriding importance for ASEAN countries, at the micro level, several of ASEAN's leading exports (such as textiles, clothing, toys, plywood, palm oil, rubber and sugar) would be negatively affected. In this respect, he points out that priority should be given to strengthening GATT provisions on preferential trading arrangements (Article XXIV) in order to enhance greater policy coherence at the regional level.

Environmental protection is one of the most controversial policy issues facing OECD and ASEAN countries. Ariff [1995] claims that ASEAN countries should learn more from OECD countries' environmental experiences in terms of both mistakes that must be avoided and successes that may be emulated. By adopting a judicious mix of policy measures, ASEAN countries could achieve a level of environmental quality they consider 'optimal' at minimum costs. There are, of course, constraints in applying OECD policy instruments directly to ASEAN environmental problems, largely due to limited administrative and institutional capacities, but some ASEAN countries have already successfully introduced innovative market-based instruments and 'voluntary' mechanisms. Ariff urges OECD countries to help ASEAN countries in their environmental efforts both by providing liberal access to OECD environmental technologies and financial and technical assistance and by stemming the tide of new protectionism that invokes alleged environmental concerns for limiting imports.

(2) OECD–South Asia Relations

The second study [Fukasaku et al., 1998] concerns OECD countries' economic relations with South Asia. This study examines export opportunities for South Asia in the post-Uruguay Round context, with a particular focus on the dismantling of MFA quotas and its implications for the region's textile and clothing sectors. South Asia provides a 'test case' for policy coherence issues, as the governments of the region have embarked on policy reform to make their economies more market-based and outward-oriented over the past five years. The so-called Indian model of self-sustained industrial development through state planning and the adoption of inward-oriented policies in the 1960s and 1970s inspired a sense of 'export pessimism' within the region, a view widely held until quite recently and in a sense still prevailing even today in some official quarters.[14] Four South Asian countries (Bangladesh, India, Pakistan and Sri Lanka) now account for only one per cent of world merchandise trade and less than half the rate in the 1960s. At the same time, health, nutrition and literacy indicators have not significantly improved in the Indian subcontinent, and poverty reduction continues to be a major challenge for the region (Table 2). This challenge will have to be met by attracting more private capital, as official development funds become less available in the region.[15]

Table 3 presents a summary of trade policy reforms in the four South Asian countries since the late 1980s. Despite substantial progress made in the past years, these countries will have to accelerate liberalisation of their trade and FDI regimes in order to compete with East and Southeast Asian economies in an international market-place. This poses a formidable challenge for *both* OECD and South Asian countries. The opening-up of the latter means more trade with the former, since OECD markets purchase 55 per cent (from India) to 82 per cent (from Bangladesh) of merchandise exports from South Asia. Their exports are highly concentrated in a narrow range of labour-intensive products; for example, textiles and clothing alone account for 45 per cent (for India) to 80 per cent (for Pakistan) of their exports. This implies that in the OECD countries, these two industries will have to bear most of the burden of adjustment. Although the Uruguay Round Agreement on Textiles and Clothing provides an important anchor for trade policy-makers on both sides, the 35 years' history of textile trade policy at the GATT suggests that the road towards a quota-free world could be very bumpy.

---

14. At an international seminar jointly organised by the Confederation of Indian Industry and the Centre for Policy Research in New Delhi in March 1995, OECD officials were reminded that 'export pessimism' was still used as an excuse against further opening up domestic markets to foreign competition.
15. The relative importance of this region in total ODA disbursements by DAC members has declined significantly during the past two decades – from 24.5 per cent in 1970–71 to 18.9 per cent in 1980–91 and further to 11.7 per cent in 1994–95 [*OECD/DAC, 1997:Annex Table 42*].

TABLE 2

BASIC ECONOMIC AND SOCIAL INDICATORS IN SELECTED DEVELOPING COUNTRIES

	Population (million) 1994	Population (annual growth) % 1994	GDP[1] (annual growth) %			GDP[2] per capita (OECD=100) 1994	Poverty[3] % 1991	Infant mortality[4] %		Child mal-nutrition[5] % 1993	Illiteracy[6] %	
			1970–80	1980–90	1990–94			1994	1972–94		1994	1972–94
Southeast Asia												
Indonesia	189.9	1.5	8.0	5.5	6.8	17.4	17.0	53.0	-3.4	39.0	16.0	-4.2
Malaysia	19.5	2.4	8.0	6.0	8.4	42.4	16.0	12.0	-5.5	23.0	17.0	-3.8
Philippines	68.2	2.1	6.1	1.6	1.5	11.8	62.0	40.0	-2.1	30.0	5.0	-4.8
Thailand	58.7	1.1	6.8	7.9	8.3	31.9	22.0	36.0	-2.7	13.0	6.0	-5.0
South Asia												
Bangladesh	117.8	2.2	1.5	4.7	4.1	5.3	48.0	81.0	-2.5	67.0	62.0	-0.9
India	913.6	1.7	3.0	5.8	3.4	6.2	25.0	70.0	-2.8	63.0	48.0	-1.4
Pakistan	126.3	2.8	4.7	6.3	4.6	10.6	31.0	92.0	-1.9	40.0	62.0	-1.1
Sri Lanka	18.1	1.3	4.6	4.4	5.1	14.6	22.0	16.0	-4.8	38.0	10.0	-3.5
North Africa												
Algeria	27.5	2.3	6.0	2.6	-0.6	16.5	na	35.0	-5.9	9.0	43.0	-3.2
Morocco	26.6	2.1	5.5	3.9	3.0	18.5	13.0	56.0	-3.5	9.0	51.0	-2.8
Tunisia	8.8	1.8	7.4	3.6	4.3	27.0	14.0	40.0	-4.9	8.0	35.0	-3.8
Memo Item												
China	1,190.9	1.1	6.0	8.8	12.3	16.2	11.0	30.0	-3.2	18.0	19.0	-5.1

Source: World Bank, CEPII-Chelem.

Notes:

1. GDP US$ constant.

2. Constant GDP per capita (1990 prices) in purchasing power parties, OECD (24 weighted average=100.

3. Percentage of population below the national upper poverty line, as defined by the World Bank. Philippines (1988), Malaysia and India (1989), Indonesia and Tunisia (1990), Morocco (1991), Bangladesh and Thailand (1992).

4. Per 1,000 live births; shaded column: average annual change in percentage, 1972–94.

5. Percentage of population under 5. Tunisia (1988), India, Pakistan, China, Thailand, Algeria (1990), Morocco (1992).

6. Age 15 and over; grey column: average annual change in percentage, 1972–94. Except China (1982–94), Algeria (1982–90), Morocco (1985–90), Tunisia (1975–90).

TABLE 3

TRADE POLICY REFORMS IN SOUTH ASIA, 1988–1996

Bangladesh	–	The average non-weighted tariff rate fell from over 100 per cent in the early 1990s to about 30 per cent in 1995, and a
	–	provisional 25 per cent in 1996. The maximum statutory tariff rate was reduced from more than 200 per cent to 45 per cent.
	–	Dispersion remains high, however, due to tariff concessions still in place, and several quantitative restrictions (QRs) remain.
	–	All export duties have been removed.
India	–	Average tariffs – which were among the highest in the world – have been significantly cut. Between 1991 and 1996, the average unweighted statutory tariff on all imported goods was brought from 128 per cent to about 40 per cent. Maximum duty rates have been lowered from 400 per cent to 40 per cent for non-consumer goods and 50 per cent for consumer goods.
	–	However, resistance to trade liberalisation of final goods' industries is actually strong, because of many vested interests involved. While licensing restrictions have been lifted on capital goods, they are still largely in place for consumer goods. Besides, import-weighted average tariffs on the latter are still high (48 per cent, compared with about 30 per cent for the economy as a whole).
	–	Similarly, strong restrictions on trade in agricultural goods remain.
Pakistan	–	The number of items on the Negative List was reduced from 300 to 75 between 1988 and 1994.
	–	Significant cuts were made in import duties and import licences were removed for most goods.
	–	The maximum tariff rate has fallen from 225 per cent in 1988 to 65 per cent in 1996 (against a planned 55 per cent for that year).
Sri Lanka	–	The whole country was declared an export-processing zone in 1992.
	–	The foreign exchange restrictions on current account transactions were removed in 1994.
	–	The average level of tariffs was reduced, but tariff escalation is still high, with effective rates of protection exceeding 100 per cent in certain products (paper, metal products).

Source: Fukasaku, Martineau and Solignac-Lecomte [*1998*].

From the developing-country perspective, the phasing-out of MFA quotas over the ten-year period (1995–2004) is perhaps the most important achievement of the Uruguay Round trade negotiations. Existing studies indicate that while the dismantling of MFA quotas would be beneficial to developing countries as a whole, there would be 'winners' and 'losers'.[16] The MFA has long induced significant distortions in international trade in textiles and clothing, sending misleading signals to both importing and exporting countries. Under the MFA regime, these industries – clothing in particular – have spread widely in developing countries, shifting the location of production from large and more constrained suppliers to small and less constrained ones. However, their economic viability in a quota-free world has yet to be tested.

The econometric analysis of the utilisation of MFA quotas conducted by Fukasaku *et al.* [*1998*] shows that these South Asian countries (except Bangladesh) are indeed among most severely constrained suppliers in both EU and US markets. Therefore, the dismantling of MFA quotas will be much more beneficial for them than for small and less constrained countries. On the other hand, Bangladesh, for example, will have a difficult time of adjustment over the transition period, since the country will lose preferential treatment granted as a least developed country.[17] Thus, how development assistance programmes should be formulated with respect to those developing countries facing greater competition, such as Bangladesh, is an important 'test case' for policy coherence. Any policy initiative to meet this challenge of industrial adjustment must come from *within* the developing countries themselves, but, at the same time, OECD donors can make an important contribution to easing the adjustment pressure by helping them to develop credible economic and social assistance programmes.

More generally, the effect of trade liberalisation on employment and income distribution in developing countries should be a matter of concern for those who are involved in the formulation of aid policy. According to the standard international trade theory, trade opening tends to stimulate the demand for unskilled labour in South Asia where its supply is abundant, thereby narrowing wage gaps between skilled and unskilled labour. However, Robbins [*1996*] casts doubt on this conventional thinking. His empirical work based on labour survey data available in several developing countries in East Asia and Latin America indicates that there is a *widening* of wage differentials

---

16. See Fukasaku *et al.* [*1998*] for a brief review of existing studies.
17. Bangladesh is currently enjoying quota-free access to the EU market.

associated with trade opening.[18] Given a large pool of unskilled labour and a high incidence of poverty in South Asia, the issue of social cohesion will be the main focus of development co-operation in the new policy environment.

(3) EU–Maghreb Relations

The third and final study on policy coherence issues [*Fontagné and Péridy, 1997*] examines the European Union's trade, aid and financial policies towards the three North African countries (Algeria, Morocco and Tunisia – the Maghreb, but not including, in this study, Libya and Mauritania) and discusses their impact and implications for policy coherence. Since 1969, the European Community (EC) – and later the EU – has maintained preferential economic policies towards these three countries to foster their development through *de facto* economic integration with the EU. How much those policies have actually helped to enhance development capabilities in these countries remains a matter of debate, however. This study attempts to bring several coherence issues to the fore in the context of the EU's *New Mediterranean Policy* whose aim is to establish a new partnership between the EU and 11 Mediterranean countries and the Palestinian authorities. As agreed at the 1995 Euro-Mediterranean Conference in Barcelona, the central feature of this policy is to implement bilateral free trade agreements in industrial products between the EU and each of these Mediterranean countries by 2010. This means that the privileged status these Maghreb countries have been enjoying *vis-à-vis* the EU will be lost completely by that time. This profound shift in EU's regional trade policy poses a major challenge for the Maghreb to make significant adjustment to greater competition on the EU market as well as globally, and, at the same time, this would make it inevitable for EU donors to reassess aid and financial policies over the transition period.

Preferential access to the EU market has formed the core of the EU's external policies towards developing countries in the past years. The EU–Maghreb relationship is a case in point. Although the Maghreb countries have been granted *de facto* free access to EU markets, they have faced various non-tariff barriers for food products in which they clearly have a comparative advantage. As far as textiles

---

18. One possible reason is that the accelerated growth of imports in modern machinery and equipment as a result of trade liberalisation would increase the demand for engineers and skilled workers in order to utilise them efficiently even in a labour-surplus economy. Another reason would be increased importance of sales, finance and marketing activities relating to foreign trade, which requires certain types of skilled workers and personnel.

and clothing are concerned, Morocco and especially Tunisia have benefited from the EU's preferential treatment, despite MFA-type quotas imposed on them. According to the quantitative assessment made by Fontagné and Péridy [*1997*], the estimated gains from EU's trade preferences granted to these Maghreb countries (US$3.95 billion in 1991 prices) were far greater than the sum of bilateral ODA provided by EU member countries and EU's Financial Protocols (US$1.37 billion). However, the principle of EU's trade preferences for this region is no longer consistent with the policy trend towards global trade liberalisation. In particular, the dismantling of MFA quotas, as we discussed above, will deprive these countries of their privileged access to the EU market by 2005. At the same time, the EU's Common Agricultural Policy will continue to put them in a disadvantageous position as food exporters, since these Maghreb countries remain excluded from future EU enlargement.

These countries have also enjoyed regular EU financial commitments as part of the EU's preferential policy, in addition to bilateral ODA from EU member countries, notably France, Italy and Spain. However, the authors argue that the EU's financial transfers have met only a small portion of investment needs in these countries, and they appear to be too small to have a significant influence on the EU's direct investment in the region.[19] As discussed above, given the implementation of the EU's *New Mediterranean Policy*, the EU–Maghreb relationship finds itself at a crossroads. For one thing, this policy change signals a clear departure from the past policy inertia that has made the latter financially dependent on the former. For another, it encourages the Maghreb countries to improve significantly domestic supply capability so as to compete in an international market-place and attract private capital more than before. How to help them to achieve this goal is a major task ahead for the aid policy of EU member countries.

A key policy message to European aid communities in this respect is that the gradual establishment of bilateral free trade areas (FTAs) between the EU and each of the Maghreb countries is unlikely to boost exports from the EU's southern neighbours at least in the *short* run. To be sure, this shift in the EU's regional trade policy serves as an important anchor for the Maghreb countries to implement much needed domestic reforms, but the net impact of such bilateral FTAs, as envisaged in the EU's *New Mediterranean Policy*, could involve a

---

19. The EU's financial transfers between 1977 and 1992 amounted to less than US$35 per capita. These amounts were between five and ten per cent of workers' remittance flows to Morocco and Tunisia [*Fontagné and Péridy, 1997: 67*].

deterioration of trade balances on the Maghreb side, as the progressive fall in their import barriers could lead to a significant rise in imports from the EU. The magnitude of adjustment to this new economic environment could be substantial and might have important political and social implications for the aid recipients. The issue of social cohesion in the process of economic opening-up is one of the key areas that require more careful analysis, and donor communities in Europe and elsewhere could play a more active part in addressing this issue in the formulation of aid programmes.

IV. CONCLUDING OBSERVATIONS

A brief discussion of three case-studies in the previous section brings to the fore the complexity of policy coherence issues involved in the new global economy. As concluding observations, I would like to emphasise the following three points:

(1) The notion of 'policy coherence' provides a useful analytical framework in which to evaluate bilateral and regional economic relations between donors and recipients. In order to make it workable in practice, however, the analytical capability of aid agencies as 'development policy advisers' to their governments needs to be enhanced substantially. The relative decline of official aid in net financial transfers to developing countries does *not* mean the declining role of aid agencies as policy advisers and planners in development co-operation.

(2) The contrasting experience of ASEAN and South Asian countries over the past decade suggests that the *domestic* policies adopted by recipient countries are primarily responsible for their own successes and failures. The direct influence of OECD countries' aid, trade and other policies is important but should not be exaggerated. A key message in this respect is that development aid appears to be working better when 'domestic policy variables' in recipient countries are put on the right track than otherwise. The ASEAN countries have been relatively successful in attracting both official and private capital by 'putting policies right'.

(3) The close relationship between aid and trade policies in development co-operation highlights the importance of seeking 'policy synergy' in this respect. As we discussed in the previous section, the future direction of trade policy developments, both domestic and external, has much bearing on the formulation of development assistance programmes for the next century, as examined in

the cases of South Asia and North Africa. A prerequisite for seeking coherent policies is to make policies transparent in terms of their impact on development. The role of policy surveillance at both national and international levels thus becomes even more important to this end. National aid agencies, NGOs and international donor communities, such as DAC, should play a more active role in this process of policy surveillance, which will then help them to develop more comprehensive and coherent policies *vis-à-vis* developing countries.

REFERENCES

Ariff, M., 1995, 'Environmental Policies of the OECD and their Implications for ASEAN', in Fukasaku, Plummer and Tan(eds.).

Chia, S.Y., 1995, 'Towards Greater Coherence in Foreign-investment Policy', in Fukasaku, Plummer and Tan (eds.).

Chia, S.Y. and J.L.H. Tan (eds.), 1997, *ASEAN & EU: Forging New Linkages and Strategic Alliances*, Singapore: Institute of Southeast Asian Studies.

Fontagné, L. and N. Péridy, 1997, *The European Union and the Maghreb: Towards a New Partnership*, Development Centre Studies, Paris: OECD.

Fukasaku, K., 1997, 'Macroeconomic Framework for Sustaining ASEAN's Outward-oriented Growth', in Chia and Tan (eds.).

Fukasaku, K. and L. Hellvin, 1998, 'Stabilisation with Growth: Implications for Emerging Economies', in Hiemenz (ed.).

Fukasaku, K. and A. Hirata, 1995, 'The OECD and ASEAN: Changing Economic Linkages and the Challenge of Policy Coherence', in Fukasaku, Plummer and Tan (eds.).

Fukasaku, K., D. Martineau and H.-B. Solignac-Lecomte, 1998, 'South Asia: A Farewell to Export Pessimism?', Development Centre Technical Papers, Paris: OECD.

Fukasaku, K., M. Plummer and J.L.H. Tan (eds.), 1995, *OECD and ASEAN Economies: the Challenge of Policy Coherence*, Development Centre Documents, Paris: OECD.

Hiemenz, U. (ed.), 1998, *Growth and Competition in the New Global Economy*, Development Centre Seminars, Paris: OECD.

Hirata, A., 1995, 'The Coherence or Lack of Coherence in Japan's Economic Policies Towards Developing Countries', in Fukasaku, Plummer and Tan (eds.).

Krueger, A., 1993, *Economic Policies at Cross-Purposes: the United States and Developing Countries*, Washington, D.C.: Brookings Institution.

Langhammer, R.J., 1995, 'On the Coherence of EC Policies', in Fukasaku, Plummer and Tan (eds.).

Michel, J.H., 1997, 'A New Approach to Development', *The OECD Observer*, No. 204, Feb./March.

Nasution, A., 1995, 'Aid and Development in ASEAN: Lessons from the 1980s', in Fukasaku, Plummer and Tan (eds.).

Naudet, D. and J.-M. Pradelle, 1997, 'A Verdict on Aid to the Sahel', *The OECD Observer*, No. 204, April/May.

OECD, 1995, *Linkages: OECD and Major Developing Countries*, Paris.

OECD, 1997, *The World in 2020: Towards a New Global Age*, Paris.

OECD/DAC, 1996, *Shaping the 21st Century: The Contribution of Development Co-operation*, Paris.

OECD/DAC, 1997, *Development Co-operation: DAC 1996 Report*, Paris.

Pang, E. F., 1995, 'Japan's External Policies and ASEAN', in Fukasaku, Plummer and Tan (eds.).

Plummer, M. G., 1995, 'ASEAN and Economic Integration in the Americas', in Fukasaku, Plummer and Tan (eds.).

Robbins, D.J., 1996, 'Evidence on Trade and Wages in the Developing World', Development Centre Technical Paper No.119, Dec., Paris: OECD.

Shigehara, K., 1997, *Multilateral Surveillance: What the OECD Can Offer*, Paris: OECD.

Snyder, D. W., 1996, 'Foreign Aid and Private Investment in Developing Economies', *Journal of International Development*, Vol.8, No.6.

UNDP, 1994, *Human Development Report*, New York: United Nations.

14

Governance and Coherence in Development Co-operation

MARK ROBINSON

I. INTRODUCTION

Donor policies on democracy and good governance are relatively recent in origin and are still undergoing a process of evolution. Despite attempts to formulate a common interpretation, participatory development and good governance (PDGG) embraces a wide variety of policies and programmes, and official donors vary considerably in the emphasis they give to PDGG policies in their overall aid strategies and country programmes.[1] Aid donors employ a number of different mechanisms to implement such policies, which range from punitive approaches based on aid conditionality through to more positive forms of assistance designed to strengthen political institutions and groups in civil society. Moreover, since PDGG policies focus on domestic policy issues which are politically sensitive, there is potential for conflict between competing aid objectives on the part of individual donors and between recipient governments and donors. For these reasons, one would expect a high degree of policy incoherence and problems of aid policy co-ordination among donors, which renders PDGG highly relevant to a discussion of aid policy coherence.

In this chapter the question of policy coherence within PDGG is examined from a number of different perspectives and levels of analysis. At the global level, it is concerned with policy coherence between international actors, in this case bilateral and multilateral aid donors, and between official donors and sovereign governments as aid recipients. The next level of analysis is concerned with policy

---

1.   In this chapter we use the term Participatory Development and Good Governance employed by the Development Assistance Committee (DAC) of the OECD to refer to policies on democracy, human rights and good governance [*OECD, 1995*].

formulation, in terms of policy coherence within donor governments, between different parts of aid agencies and their host ministries, and between foreign affairs or aid ministries and other government departments. At this level, policies on PDGG can be compared and contrasted with policy agendas and institutional practice within other organs of domestic governance. The third level of analysis addresses the question of implementation by individual donors, in terms of internal policy consistency, and the degree of coherence between policy intentions and policy outcomes.

The analysis rejects the assumptions behind the rational actor model of the policy process where it is assumed that there is a close correspondence between policy design and policy outcomes within bureaucratic organisations. Rather, the arguments developed in this chapter are premised on a more political interpretation of the policy process, where policy decisions are a function of conflict and debate within government organisations, and are subject to public pressure and contending political considerations. Policy outcomes will rarely correspond to policy intentions since the process of implementation is subject to many intervening pressures and complex interactions between recipient governments and donors. Dissonance between policy commitments and policy outcomes is likely to be magnified in an inter-governmental context where PDGG policies are imbued with a high degree of political sensitivity, where other non-aid policy objectives are at stake, and where there are significant imbalances of power and influence inherent within the donor–recipient relationship. Hence, our expectation is that policy incoherence is an innate feature of donor policy on participatory development and good government, and that evidence of coherence represents the exception rather than the norm. In view of such complexities, attempts by donors to enhance internal policy coherence and strengthen co-ordination will be undermined by pressures that promote fragmentation of effort and undermine policy consistency.

The chapter begins with a brief review of the core components of donor aid policies on participatory development and good governance, highlighting variations in policy content and design. The main section of the chapter examines four dimensions of policy coherence, drawing on the experience of bilateral and multilateral aid donors in the PDGG field. The final section begins by examining the mechanisms that have been employed by donors as a means of overcoming problems of incoherence in PDGG policy, and ends with the conclusion that political sensitivities, donor self-interest and implementation problems will frustrate the attainment of increased policy coherence and better co-ordination.

II. THE PDGG POLICY AGENDA

The PDGG policy agenda emerged in the late 1980s in response to a changed global political context characterised by the ending of the cold war and the diminished significance of superpower politics, and a series of political transitions in Latin America, sub-Saharan Africa and Eastern Europe. This was underpinned by a growing realisation that problems encountered in the implementation of structural adjustment policies were attributable to weak and unaccountable states, especially in Africa. Top-down development models were acknowledged to be deficient and participation was identified as a critical ingredient in successful development programmes, as well as an essential facet of democratic politics. Hence, there was a perception among Western donors that development assistance could be used to facilitate democratic political change, enhance civil and political liberties, and improve the functioning of government. Such concerns coalesced around three distinct sets of policies – democracy, human rights and good governance – which constitute the core components of participatory development and good governance as defined by the DAC [*OECD, 1995*].

Not all these policies are new. Several donors, notably Canada, the Netherlands, Norway and the United States, had adopted policies centred on the protection and promotion of human rights over the course of the 1980s. Many donors had developed aid programmes centred on the reform of public administration and capacity-building long before governance became a core policy concern of the World Bank. What changed in the 1990s was the fact that such policies became part of a common set of concerns encapsulated within the rubric of participatory development and good government, and that development assistance was seen as a legitimate means of influencing domestic political agendas in recipient countries. Moreover, a number of donors made high-level public commitments on PDGG policies and increased the volume of aid resources allocated to this end [*ODI, 1992*]. Following the formal adoption of PDGG policies, various donors have been engaged in a process of policy refinement and evolution, and a search for effective interventions and implementation mechanisms [*Crawford, 1995*].

As noted above, democracy, human rights and good governance are the three main areas of concern within PDGG. Donor approaches fall into two broad categories: those which use aid as a lever for pressurising governments to opt for reform, and policies founded on positive measures. The first generally takes the form of political conditionality, where donors suspend, reduce or terminate development assistance pending improved performance on a range of PDGG indicators. The second hinges on a more supportive approach in which aid donors seek to strengthen an ongoing reform process through carefully selected projects and programmes. Within this second category, donor interventions focus on building the political and administrative capacity of state institutions, or on strengthening groups and organisations in civil society.

The process of democratisation under way in a number of developing and transitional countries has attracted a great deal of interest from Western governments and aid agencies anxious to strengthen weak governments and bring about greater political stability. Assistance to fledgling democratic regimes focuses on elections, legislatures, constitutional reform, and support to political parties on the one hand, and aid for civic education, the media, conflict mitigation, and for strengthening the research and advocacy capacity of civil society organisations on the other. In the human rights category, where the focus is on strengthening the rule of law and civil and political rights, programmes include legal, penal and judicial reform, support for paralegal services, human rights advocacy and monitoring. The recipients of such assistance include state institutions, such as law courts, prisons and the judiciary, as well as human rights groups that form part of civil society. Good governance concerns centre on civil service reform, public sector management, decentralisation and reforms of the military, as well as on mechanisms designed to promote accountability and greater participation in decision-making.

It is difficult to quantify the total volume of development assistance allocated for such programmes as there are no comprehensive data available for donor expenditure on democracy, human rights and good governance. Data from the DAC Creditor Reporting System indicate that expenditure on participatory development and good governance has been increasing rapidly in the 1990s, with total expenditure reaching US\$4.0 billion in 1995, equivalent to 8.65 per cent of total official development assistance.[2]

---

2. This category of expenditure includes economic and development planning, public sector financial management, government administration, general government services, legal and judicial development, elections, human rights monitoring and education, demobilisation, post-conflict peace-building, strengthening civil society, and free flow of information.

The United States is the most prominent donor in the field of PDGG activity in terms of expenditure and policy significance, with a particular emphasis on democracy promotion on which it spent an estimated US$500 million in 1995 [*Diamond, 1995: 70*]. Other prominent bilateral donors in this field include Canada, Denmark, Germany, the Netherlands, Sweden and the United Kingdom; among the multilaterals, the EU, UNDP and the World Bank are all significant donors with large PDGG programmes. Data collected on political aid from projects supported by four donors – the EU, DFID, SIDA, and USAID – reveal that well over half the total aid in the form of democracy assistance and promotion of good governance goes to sub-Saharan Africa, whereas Latin America accounts for the largest share of spending on human rights projects [*Robinson, 1996*]. There are significant variations between individual donors in terms of the share of PDGG spending as a proportion of overall aid and regional allocations of PDGG assistance, which will be examined in a later section, as these have a bearing on policy coherence.

III. DIMENSIONS OF PDGG POLICY COHERENCE

The question of policy coherence is especially significant in the context of participatory development and good governance because of its overriding concern with domestic policy issues in recipient countries which have direct political implications. We distinguish between four levels of policy coherence: coherence within aid policy, coherence between policies that affect developing countries, coherence between donor aid polices, and donor–recipient coherence.

(1) Coherence within Aid Policy

The first component of this schema encompasses variations within the PDGG aid policies of individual donors and between PDGG and elements of the domestic and foreign policy agendas. Within this broader schema there are four dimensions of internal coherence: coherence between different components of the PDGG policy agenda, in terms of stated policy commitments and actual resource allocations; coherence between PDGG and other development co-operation policies; coherence between PDGG and other policies towards developing countries; and coherence between PDGG policies and the domestic policy agenda.

The first dimension relates to coherence between different components of PDGG aid policy resulting from the choice of priority areas, aid instruments and delivery mechanisms within individual donors.

Most aid agencies have produced policy statements on democracy, human rights and good governance in which they set out major policy objectives and priority areas. In some cases, donors have indicated a preference for the use of certain types of aid instruments over others (there is usually a stated preference for positive forms of support for democratic political institutions and civil society organisations over political conditionality), and give an indication of their preferred approach (human rights or good governance, anti-corruption measures versus decentralisation, etc.). Since many of these policy statements are conceived in fairly general terms there is not much evidence of incoherence in terms of stated policy objectives.[3] Despite appearances of policy coherence generalised policy statements have a tendency to disguise intra-organisational conflict in terms of the locus of responsibility for PDGG policy within aid agencies and between aid agencies and foreign affairs ministries which is discussed below. The potential for incoherence lies more in discrepancy between policy commitments and resource allocations, and between PDGG policy commitments and domestic policy.

The extent of internal policy coherence is also reflected in the degree of consistency between stated policy commitments and actual resource allocations. As noted earlier, PDGG policies are still undergoing a process of evolution and refinement, and comprise a number of different elements, which donors emphasise to varying degrees. At the same time, in view of the relative newness of the PDGG policy agenda, the significance of actual resource allocations should not be overestimated. Until recently, the British placed particular emphasis on 'good government', and this was reflected in the fact that a high proportion of UK PDGG assistance under the previous government was for civil service and public sector reform [ODA, 1993]. To this extent, there existed a high degree of internal policy coherence. But while good government constituted one of four overarching policy aims, the resources allocated to PDGG activities accounted for a very small share of total aid spending. In 1993 and 1994, UK expenditure on democracy, human rights and good governance totalled £26.7 million, equivalent to 0.8 per cent of its official development assistance. Hence on the basis of expenditure criteria there was a high degree of policy incoherence, in that strong PDGG policy commitments were not matched by correspondingly large resource allocations. By comparison, Sweden spent four times this amount on PDGG, amounting to 5 per cent of its official development assistance.

---

3. See De Feyter et al. [1995] and Crawford [1995] for details.

Sweden emphasises the importance of human rights and non-govern-mental initiatives, and this finds reflection in its spending priorities; human rights projects accounted for one-third of its PDGG expendi-ture, and more than half of this expenditure was channelled through human rights NGOs [*Robinson, 1996*].

The second dimension concerns the degree of coherence between PDGG policies and other aid policies. There is a great deal of poten-tial for incoherence between PDGG and other elements of the donor aid policy agenda, which results in part from the unpredictable politi-cal ramifications of PDGG policies as well as the different aid policy instruments that are employed to advance such policies. The most obvious scope for incoherence lies in the potential conflict between policies designed to promote democratic government and structural adjustment, since the former can create the conditions by which a political party hostile to reform can be voted into power, or opposition groups outside the government can sabotage the reform process through legal strike action and demonstrations. However, conflict between these two policy objectives is not inevitable. For example, evidence from Uganda suggests that political liberalisation creates opportunities for building new coalitions of support for econo-mic reform [*Harvey and Robinson, 1995*].

There is also some degree of incoherence between donor policies on poverty reduction and those on participatory development and good governance. Although some donors stress the advantages of better governance and democratic political institutions for the poor, the link is not always made explicit, and the two sets of objectives can conflict. For example, as noted by Goetz and O'Brien [*1995*] the governance agenda as defined by the World Bank is largely oriented towards improving the institutional environment conducive to market-led development, while the poverty agenda largely focuses on liberalisation of agricultural trade and pricing policy and better target-ing of social sector spending, with little attention to the policies of reorienting public sector institutions to respond to the interests of the poor. The publication of the 1997 World Development Report, *The State in a Changing World*, indicates that considerable progress has been made in reconciling these two agendas.

The third dimension relates to institutional roles and responsibili-ties of bureaucratic organisations concerned with PDGG policy, both in terms of policy coherence among different departments *within* aid agency bureaucracies, and *between* aid agencies and foreign policy establishments. In the former there is scope for incoherence stemming from the division of responsibility for various PDGG policy initiatives within aid agencies. For example, in the case of the UK Department for International Development (DFID), PDGG policy is largely the prerogative of the Government and Institutions Department which is concerned with the role of government and public sector institutions, whereas the Social Development Department tends to stress participation and the role of non-state actors.

There is also potential for policy incoherence within aid agencies and unified foreign affairs establishments where different divisions (geographical and technical) share responsibility for formulating and implementing PDGG policies. In some cases this can lead to an element of competition and internal disagreement about the thrust of key components of PDGG policy. In France and Germany, aid policy is the responsibility of several government departments, each of which has a stake in PDGG policies. Within USAID, the Democracy Center co-ordinates overall policy on democracy and governance issues through a pool of advisers and specialists, but the regional bureaux also have a keen interest in developing approaches that are appropriate in their respective operational environments. For instance, there is a notable difference between the Africa Bureau and the Democracy Center in their understanding of civil society, with the former stressing local-level community initiatives and the latter more concerned with civic advocacy organisations and their potential to influence public policy. Such differences in perspective have important policy implications for the content and thrust of USAID's democracy assistance programmes, which in turn carry significant resource implications.

The European Union presents an especially complicated case of shared responsibility for PDGG policy between different directorates resulting in a plethora of different budget lines for democracy and human rights activity. Overall policy direction on PDGG was established through a resolution of the European Council and the member states in November 1991. Three directorates have some responsibility for human rights and democracy issues within the European Commission: DG VIII (Development) which deals with ACP countries covered by the Lomé Convention, and DG I/A (Foreign Political Affairs) and DG I/NS (North–South Relations), which cover non-ACP countries. The two main budget lines for developing countries (Human Rights and Democracy in Developing Countries and Democratisation in Latin America) are administered by DG VIII and DG I respectively. There are, in addition, at least six other budget lines administered by DG VIII which are not directly related to the promotion of human rights and democracy but which can indirectly support or finance such projects. Seven further budget lines were established in 1992 to support human rights and democracy programmes in Eastern Europe and the former Soviet Union (PHARE and TACIS respectively), managed separately by the European Human Rights Foundation [*Heinz et al., 1995*]. With such a multiplicity of budget lines administered by different directorates the potential for incoherence is very high, though the Commission has sought to address such problems through the formation of an inter-service group in 1993 to co-ordinate EU human rights and democracy projects.

The attainment of coherent policy on PDGG matters can be very complicated when there is a division of responsibility for PDGG policy between an aid agency and the foreign affairs ministry. In the UK, the Department for International Development has responsibility for devising PDGG policies that have clear developmental objectives, whereas the remit of the Foreign and Commonwealth Office (FCO) is to monitor political developments and assume the lead role on human rights. In this respect DFID formulates policies designed to promote accountable and competent government while the FCO channels funds to political parties and human rights groups through the Westminster Foundation for Democracy, among other initiatives. However, while the distinction between political and developmental objectives is becoming more blurred as DFID widens the scope of its PDGG brief, it is attempting to chalk out a distinct position on human rights, emphasising all social and economic rights, rather than civil liberties and political rights which are the principal concerns of the FCO.

A similar situation prevails in Germany where democracy and human rights programmes have traditionally been the remit of the political foundations (Stiftüngen) whose activities are funded by subventions provided by the Ministry of Economic Cooperation (BMZ). In recent years BMZ has been adopting a higher profile in democracy and good governance activity and developing programmes of its own. This has created some tension over the respective roles of BMZ and the traditional mandate of the political foundations.

In the United States a variety of democracy programmes are sponsored by the State Department as well as by the US Agency for International Development (USAID). The State Department has provided grants in aid to the National Endowment for Democracy since its formation in 1983 to support the work of the two party foundations (the International Republican Institute and the National Democratic Institute), the Free Trade Union Institute, and the Center for International Private Enterprise. The State Department also supports the work of the US Information Agency (USIA) which has been engaged in the promotion of democratic values since the Cold war period, involving the training of lawyers and journalists, lecture tours, academic exchanges, and the provision of information on issues such as elections, the rule of law, constitutional reform and civil society. Since the launching of its Democracy Initiative in 1990 USAID has assumed a high-profile role in democracy promotion and allocates a considerable volume of resources for activities ranging from electoral assistance, legislative and constitutional reform, through to support to local government and civil society organisations. The multitude of organisations engaged in democracy promotion in the United States, usually with support from USAID or the State Department, creates the potential for policy incoherence, and has rendered such activity vulnerable to criticism by Republican politicians hostile to a large overseas aid programme [*Carothers, 1995*].

Problems of coherence arising from the respective roles of aid agencies and foreign affairs ministries in PDGG activity do not arise when there is not a separate agency with functional responsibility for aid policy matters. In this respect the closer integration of DANIDA and SIDA with their parent ministries in recent years, and the unified approach to aid policy and foreign affairs in the Netherlands have reduced the potential for policy incoherence resulting from different government ministries having different remits and expectations about their respective roles in PDGG activity.

The fourth aspect of internal coherence relates to donor policies on PDGG and domestic policy concerns. The most obvious area concerns the degree of coherence between donor policies on democracy and human rights overseas and the extent to which such policies find expression in the domestic policy arena. Discrepancies between the types of democratic practices advocated overseas and those followed at home provide examples of internal incoherence. Accusations of double standards and policy incoherence were easily levelled in the case of the previous British government, though Britain is not unique in this regard, and similar examples could be drawn up for other donors. In this respect, an emphasis on legitimate and accountable government in the UK approach to good government sat uneasily with an unelected second chamber in the House of Lords.

Similarly, support for decentralisation and greater budgetary devolution in Africa ran counter to trends towards centralisation and curbs on the financial autonomy of local government in Britain. Overcrowding and deteriorating prison conditions resulting from a harsher sentencing policy were at odds with a stated aid policy commitment to penal and judicial reform. A fourth example was the failure of the Major government to curb the production of arms and military equipment sold to regimes known for their abuses of human rights. On a positive note, one could point to a high level of congruence between domestic policies designed to promote efficient and sound government and the strong emphasis in the British aid programme on similar policy objectives. The new Labour administration came to power in May 1997 on a platform of constitutional reform and political modernisation, with a stated commitment to a more positive stance on human rights overseas. Although the domestic reform programme is still in its infancy, there is likely to be greater coherence between domestic policy orientations and Britain's stance towards the South.[4] However, whether such congruence is actually desirable or appropriate from the point of view of developing countries remains a moot point. We shall return to this question later in the chapter.

(2) Coherence between PDGG and Other Foreign Policy Objectives

The second level of external policy coherence concerns the relationship between PDGG policies and other foreign policy objectives centred on trade, diplomatic, strategic and commercial considerations. While aid policy can be used as a means of advancing foreign policy objectives in any of these spheres, it can also be motivated by altruism [Riddell, 1987]. The multiple objectives of aid policy, which is driven by a combination of altruism and self-interest, can be a source of incoherence in the PDGG field. For example, support for democratisation can be inspired by a variety of motives: the installation and maintenance of a regime favourable to donor interests; the creation of a political environment which is conducive to the successful implementation of economic reforms and a more liberal trade regime; or the creation of new opportunities for marginalised and disadvantaged social groups to participate in the political process. Individual donors might promote democracy in a particular country with a view to advancing all three objectives simultaneously; this is epitomised by the USAID Democracy Initiative, which is driven by a combination of these considerations.

---

4. The British Foreign Secretary, Robin Cook, made explicit reference to the need for greater coherence between an active stance on human rights records of other governments and the Labour government's commitment to democratic reforms across British political institutions, including the House of Lords, in a speech to the annual conference of the Trades Union Conference in September 1997. *The Guardian*, 11 Sept. 1997.

However, there is ample scope for incoherence, in that a more democratic political environment can create the space for governments to be voted into office which are less supportive of donor interests or hostile to foreign investors. Contemporary policy stances may also be greatly at variance with past foreign policy objectives. Hence current concerns with democracy promotion and human rights can be dismissed as inconsistent with US policy priorities in the 1970s and 1980s when emphasis was placed on strategic and diplomatic influence over and above regime characteristics, leading to the familiar yet justifiable charge that the US government lent support to dictatorial regimes until changes in the geopolitical environment rendered democracy a palatable alternative.

Military expenditure is another area where there is great potential for policy incoherence. Hoebink's (this volume, Ch.10) example of the arms export policy of EU member states as a case of policy incoherence assumes even greater force in the context of PDGG policies, where donors are committed to upholding democracy and human rights (and in some cases, reductions in domestic military expenditure) on the one hand while continuing to sanction a high level of arms exports on the other. Britain's attempt to reformulate its relationship with Indonesia with respect to arms sales and human rights reveals the complexity of adhering to a principled stance on human rights when dealing with a powerful Third World government with which it has substantial trade and financial links.[5]

During a visit to Jakarta in August 1997, the British Foreign Secretary announced a six-point plan on improving human rights in Indonesia, designed to combine an ethical foreign policy with practical measures in the form of financial assistance and scholarships to human rights groups and an independent legal aid foundation, open dialogue with human rights leaders, and training by British police officers on non-violent crowd control techniques. The announcement of this new approach followed widespread criticism of the Labour government's decision to proceed with the sale of military aircraft, armoured cars and water cannons to Indonesia which had been approved by the previous government. In an apparent vindication of this new policy stance the Foreign Secretary announced a veto on fresh orders for armoured cars and sniper rifles at the end of September, on the grounds that they could be used for military repression in East Timor.[6]

---

5. UK exports to Indonesia amounted to £828 million in 1996, with imports worth £981 million. Arms sales generated £438 million British firms, while bank-lending to Indonesia amounted to £1,700 million. *The Guardian*, 29 Aug. 1997.
6. *The Guardian*, 26 Sept. 1997.

Donor support in the form of aid for PDGG policies may also vary in accordance with the importance attached to other foreign policy considerations in particular country contexts, which are a further source of incoherence. This is most evident in the case of political conditionality. Experience suggests that aid donors are willing to play down stated policy commitments on human rights when important trade and diplomatic interests are at stake. Donors have been more willing to use political conditionality as means of pressurising governments to reform in the case of relatively weak African states where there are limited trade and commercial interests.

The opposite holds true in East Asia where trade and commercial considerations are major policy considerations for most donor countries. For example, despite a forthright position on democracy and human rights, the United States has consistently resisted adopting an uncompromising stance on these issues in relation to China, either on the issue of the illegal occupation of Tibet or the political clampdown following the Tiannenmen massacre, preferring instead a policy of constructive engagement in which its substantial trade and investment interests are not threatened. In the case of East Timor, most Western governments drew back from a head-on confrontation with the Indonesian government over the massacre of unarmed demonstrators in 1991, despite some strongly-worded expressions of concern. As the only donor to have acted in accordance with its stated policy commitments by threatening to suspend its aid, the Dutch government found itself isolated and its aid rejected by the Indonesian regime [*Robinson, 1993*]. The lesson appears to be that policy incoherence is preferable in relation to PDGG priorities when other, more important, foreign policy concerns are at stake.

(3) Coherence between Donor Policies on PDGG

The third element of the classificatory schema concerns coherence between the PDGG policies adopted by different bilateral aid donor on the one hand, and between bilateral and multilateral agencies on the other. As noted in the previous section, a number of aid donors have issued formal policy statements outlining their broad positions on PDGG which do not contain much evidence of incoherence. However, there is considerable variation between individual donors in terms of the emphasis they give to various components of the PDGG policy agenda, and the focus for PDGG activities. For instance, the UK ODA (now DFID) laid particular stress on governance, especially on measures designed to promote greater accountability, transparency and competence (encompassed by the term good government), which translated into an emphasis on public sector management and civil service reform.

The United States, by comparison, is principally concerned with democracy promotion, and concentrates much of its effort on electoral assistance and measures to promote political pluralism. Sweden tends to emphasise human rights, with a particular focus on human rights organisations and NGOs as the preferred delivery mechanism [Crawford, 1995].[7] Japan is a very different case in point. In contrast with most other donors it desists from adopting a political interpretation of PDGG issues, and maintains a very narrow focus on public sector management. Such a stance has resulted in a high level of coherence between its stated policy position and actions, since it has studiously avoided using political conditionality, but sets it apart from most other donors who emphasise democracy and human rights to varying degrees in their policy statements.

There are also differences in the regional priorities for the PDGG activities of different aid donors. More than 50 per cent of PDGG expenditure by Sweden and the UK is allocated to sub-Saharan Africa, while the EU and the United States divide their PDGG assistance equally between Africa and Latin America. In all four cases, Asia is a relatively minor recipient of PDGG assistance [Robinson, 1996].

What can one conclude from this in terms of policy coherence? At one level such variations in policy priorities and regional preferences are to be expected, since aid donors' priorities tend to reflect historical factors (colonialism and domestic political traditions) and geographical proximity. US emphasis on democracy promotion reflects a long-standing concern with liberal democratic principles and America's mission in the post-cold war era, while Sweden's concern with human rights and organisations in civil society reflects an affinity with a rights-based approach to development and an extension of the Swedish approach to welfare to the international arena. At one level such differences of emphasis and orientation could be treated as evidence of incoherence, but at another level the decision of different donors to emphasise different parts of the PDGG policy agenda reflects comparative advantage and minimises competition and overlap.

---

7. Over half the number of PDGG projects supported by Sweden in 1993 and 1994 fall into the human rights category, while two-thirds of its total PDGG expenditure is allocated through non-governmental channels [Robinson, 1996].

Policy coherence between bilateral and multilateral donors raises different issues from the question of coherence between bilateral aid donors. First, the fact that these multilateral donors depend on contributions from member states, especially from Western governments with large bilateral aid programmes, ensures that their policy agendas are open to influence from this source. For example, EU policy on democracy and human rights was significantly influenced by member states pressing for a more forthright position and for increased support for PDGG initiatives. At the same time, the influence is not one way, since the World Bank's approach to governance has proved to be an extremely important influence in galvanising bilateral aid donors into action and defining the parameters of the PDGG policy agenda. In this respect its influence on the more conservative position adopted by Japan and the UK (in the early 1990s) has been quite marked.

Second, these multilateral donors perform important co-ordination functions within recipient countries (through the UN Roundtable meetings and the Consultative Group (CG) meetings chaired by the World Bank), which are designed to promote greater coherence among donors and, in some cases, joint action on PDGG issues. In the process, there is scope for influential bilateral donors to exercise a significant influence over PDGG policy, with the US playing a significant role in persuading other CG members to agree on political conditionality as the preferred instrument to force the pace of political reform in Kenya and Malawi [*Robinson, 1993*]. Hence it can be seen that the relationship between multilateral donors and bilateral donors in the formulation and design of PDGG policy generally helped to strengthen PDGG policy coherence. The extent to which these donors can and do play an effective co-ordination function as a means of minimising policy incoherence will be examined in the concluding section.

(4) Donor–Recipient Coherence and the Implementation of PDGG Policies

The fourth aspect of coherence is the relationship between aid donors and recipient governments in policy implementation. From a PDGG perspective the issue concerns the implications of aid donors with different policy positions interacting with a single recipient government, or different parts of the same government. It is a central theme in aid policy agenda which is concerned with the role and legitimacy of government institutions. At one level, policy coherence poses a threat to sovereign governments when aid donors can exert collective influence through political conditionality. But donor incoherence can also create difficulties for recipient governments since they adopt differing positions and emphasise different elements of the PDGG agenda. One donor may be seeking progress on human rights, another may stress elections and democratic political institutions, while a third may emphasise public sector reform.

Such policy variations may not be a problem if the government has the capacity to deal with a range of donor policies, but certain types of policy may prove more problematic than others if they are not favoured by the recipient government, which is almost inevitable with the more politically sensitive aspects of PDGG policy. A willingness to engage positively with the donor policy agenda will depend on the degree of perceived threat, and the relative political and diplomatic clout of a recipient government. Strong and politically influential governments may be in a position to exploit donor incoherence and successfully to resist pressure for reform, as the Indonesian case amply demonstrates.

Central to this form of policy coherence is the question of intent, where policy incoherence arises as an intended or unintended consequence of a policy decision. Here the focus is on the extent to which policy intentions are reflected in policy outcomes. According to Hoebink (this volume, Ch.10), 'Intended incoherence would be a form in which an authority consciously accepts that the objectives of policy in a particular field cannot be achieved because the policy involves conflicting interests'. According to this schema, policy emerges out of a rational process of weighing various options in a given context, and necessarily involves trade-offs and compromises. Principled adherence to a PDGG policy package is virtually impossible when commercial and strategic considerations are at stake. Hence, the failure of donors to maintain a consistent stance over PDGG policies is hardly surprising in a context where there is a high probability of adverse reactions on the part of recipient governments which could prejudice trade and diplomatic relations.

But the adoption of lofty commitments to democracy and human rights on the part of donor governments (for example, in President Clinton's 1992 election campaign, or the late President Mitterrand's speech to the Francophone meeting at La Baule in 1991) carry with them the potential for embarrassing compromises when these commitments cannot be realised in practice. Cynics might argue that policy compromises are intentional, especially in the PDGG field, since narrow self-interest will always hold sway over principled altruism. Public commitments to democracy and human rights can be designed for the benefit of certain audiences (for example, as a means of cultivating domestic political support and issuing a warning to regimes hostile to reform) whereas implementation will always entail a significant departure from these commitments in practice.

A less cynical interpretation would reject the rational actor model of the policy process, and begin with the premise that policy implementation inevitably distorts policy intentions when sensitive political issues are at stake. In other words, misplaced expectations about the impact of policy choice are a source of unintended incoherence. An example of this is the outcome of the 1992 Kenyan elections where President Moi was returned to power with a mantle of democratic legitimacy despite donor success in using political conditionality as a means of pressurising the government to hold elections.

Another source of unintended incoherence, where outcomes deviate from policy commitments, stems from inadequate resources, in that donor policy commitments usually presuppose fundamental changes in the structure of governance or the prevailing human rights situation in a given country. Yet the resources allocated to such ends are rarely commensurate with the intended impact and cannot ensure that reforms can be sustained. Allied with this is the short time horizon that governs donor interventions. This is especially notable in the heavy emphasis given to elections by the US and other donors. Furthermore, political reform is contingent and subject to many countervailing pressures. For instance, aid donors may support multi-party elections but find it difficult to ensure that the duly elected government will hold to its electoral promises and adhere to democratic principles. The case of Zambia, where elections ratified by the international community resulted is a handover of power to the opposition movement for multi-party democracy in 1992, is a good example of this phenomenon, since donors now find themselves powerless to prevent the erosion of democratic norms.

The use of political conditionality as a means of advancing the cause of democracy and human rights can have adverse developmental and political consequences which are unintended. For example, in Kenya, the Moi regime deliberately fomented ethnic rivalries as a means of keeping itself in power following donor pressure to force the government to hold elections, resulting in violent clashes between minority ethnic groups. In Indonesia, the decision of the Dutch government to maintain a principled stance on human rights abuses in East Timor prompted a crack-down on Indonesian human rights groups and NGOs, many of which had relied on Dutch aid [*Robinson, 1993*].

Other sources of unintended incoherence include weak implementation capacity on the part of donors and compliance disincentives on the part of recipient governments. Many donors lack the capacity for implementing and monitoring PDGG interventions, either because the interventions are small scale (such as projects designed to strengthen civil society organisations) or because the impact of interventions is difficult to assess since many other intervening variables influence outcomes. One such influence is that of domestic political lobbies who frustrate donor policy intentions by blocking or derailing reform initiatives, especially when reform threatens their power base or political legitimacy. Such opposition often comes from within the recipient government, when PDGG policy initiatives are seen as an affront to national sovereignty or pose a threat to regime continuity which results in compliance disincentives. Hence the failure to anticipate resistance to reform, resulting from incorrect assumptions or imperfect information (bounded rationality), can be a source of unintended incoherence. In the final analysis, policy outcomes are only likely to correspond to policy intentions where the recipient government exhibits some degree of commitment to reform.

IV. CONCLUSIONS

There is an implicit assumption in much of the literature on PDGG issues that policy incoherence is problematic for aid donors and recipient governments. Greater coherence is assumed to result in enhanced effectiveness of PDGG policies. Lack of coherence over objectives, approaches and delivery mechanisms is generally perceived to be a source of poor implementation. Such a perspective emanates from a rational actor model of the policy process which is premised on a close and contingent relationship between policy commitments and policy outcomes. This is not to deny that problems can arise from policy incoherence in the PDGG sphere for recipient governments and organisations. Lack of clarity over policy objectives on the part of aid donors can generate confusion about donor intentions and undermine commitment to reform. Different approaches and operating procedures can stretch implementation capacity and dilute the impact of PDGG measures.

However, greater policy coherence, while potentially desirable for donors, is not necessarily positive from the point of view of recipient governments. Increased coherence between aid agencies and between aid agencies and foreign affairs ministries could be seen as potentially threatening by recipient governments, since donor influence might well increase as a result, leading to greater control over the domestic policy environment and direct intervention in national politics. As we have seen, policy coherence is multidimensional and the desirability of achieving greater coherence in PDGG policy will depend on the level of analysis employed and the interests of the actors that are involved. The point is that policy coherence is not necessarily a good thing for all parties and has to be assessed from the respective positions of aid donors and recipient governments.

There have been a variety of responses to perceived problems of PDGG policy incoherence, especially inter-organisational incoherence. These include the creation of co-ordination mechanisms, within donor agencies, recipient countries and at the supra-national level, enhanced policy dialogue and information exchange, and improved assessment procedures. An example of an internal co-ordination mechanism is the inter-service group established in the European Commission in 1993 with representatives from all directorates to co-ordinate all EC human rights and democracy projects in Western and Eastern Europe and developing countries. Both DG I and DG VIII have steering committees which discuss project applications and make recommendations to the relevant Commissioner. Several bilateral donors have established co-ordination mechanisms as a means of reducing the scope for incoherence though it is difficult to determine their effectiveness. In the United States, where there are numerous government agencies engaged in democracy promotion, a permanent InterAgency Working Group on Democracy and Human Rights was established in early 1994 to consider broad policy issues. Six regional subgroups review the overall democracy plans for particular countries while five functional subgroups meet to discuss policy on the administration of justice, electoral processes, civil–military relations, civil society and the media.

Established in 1993 for a three-year period, the DAC Working Group on Participatory Development and Good Governance was the principal forum for information-sharing and policy dialogue for aid donors engaged in PDGG activity. Thematic seminars on human rights, civil society and decentralisation assisted in the dissemination of ideas about good practice and the policy positions of different donors, and a set of policy guidelines were produced in 1995 to serve as a common reference point [OECD, 1995]. Now that the Working Group has been disbanded there is no longer any official forum for PDGG activity through which information exchange and policy dialogue continue to take place on a regular basis. The European Union is a potential candidate but the absence of a unified focal point for policy initiatives limits its potential role in policy co-ordination for DAC member states.

Within recipient countries there have been a number of initiatives to achieve greater coherence in PDGG policy. The Development Co-operation Directorate of the DAC has been active in identifying mechanisms for strengthening country level co-ordination for PDGG policy. Established consultative mechanisms such as the UN Round-table meetings and the Consultative Groups convened by the World Bank already promote dialogue between aid donors, and have provided the basis for collective donor action in the form of political conditionality. But PDGG issues form a relatively small part of a broader set of discussions on overall aid policy and pledges on the part of individual donors. The aim of the in-country co-ordination exercises is not simply to strengthen donor liaison but to encourage a process of regular consultations involving donors, governments and civil society to promote a wider debate on policy options and concrete initiatives. Several donors have devised formal assessment procedures to assist them in formulating more coherent PDGG policy and these could potentially serve as a basis for bringing together different stake-holders to discuss priorities and propose strategies [OECD, 1996].

Increased co-ordination may help to reduce incoherence in PDGG policy, especially at the country level, but the goal of maximising coherence is probably illusory and potentially undesirable. The evidence presented in this chapter suggests that a high level of incoherence is to be expected in the PDGG policy in view of its political sensitivity, the scope for conflict with other foreign policy objectives, the existence of multiple institutional interests within donor agencies, a diversity of donor interests and priorities and the complexity of implementation. The scope for incoherence is greater the higher the level of political sensitivity, which is partly a function of the choice of aid instrument and the county in question. According to this logic, political conditionality is likely to be a source of incoherence when other commercial and strategic considerations are at stake, whereas positive aid measures designed to promote democracy through elections and strengthening civil society have greater potential for policy coherence, since there is less divergence among donors on the suitability of such measures, and successful implementation is contingent on the commitment of recipient governments.

REFERENCES

Carothers, T., 1995, 'Recent US Experience with Democracy Promotion', *IDS Bulletin*, 26:2.

Crawford, G., 1995, *Promoting Democracy, Human Rights and Good Governance through Development Aid: A Comparative Study of the Policies of Four Northern Donors*, Working Paper on Democratization No.1, Centre for Democratization Studies, University of Leeds.

De Feyter, K. *et al.*, 1995, *Development Co-operation: A Tool for the Promotion of Human Rights and Democracy Assistance*, University of Antwerp, Research Project in the Framework of Policy Preparing Research in the Field of Co-operation in Development, No.4.

Diamond, L., 1995, *Promoting Democracy in the 1990s: Actors and Instruments, Issues and Imperatives, A Report to the Carnegie Commission on Preventing Deadly Conflict*, Washington, DC: Carnegie Corporation of New York.

Goetz, A.M., and D. O'Brien, 1995, 'Governance for the Common Wealth? The World Bank's Approach to Poverty and Governance', *IDS Bulletin*, 26:2.

Harvey, C. and M. Robinson, 1995, 'Economic Reform and Political Liberalization in Uganda', *IDS Research Report* 29, Brighton: Institute of Development Studies.

Heinz, W., H. Lignau and P. Waller, 1995, *Evaluation of EC Positive Measures in Favour of Human Rights and Democracy (1991–1993)*, Berlin: German Development Institute.

Overseas Development Administration (ODA), 1993, *Taking Account of Good Government*, Government and Institutions Department, Technical Note 10, Oct.

ODI, 1992, *Aid and Political Reform*, Briefing Paper, London: Overseas Development Institute.

OECD, 1995, *Participatory Development and Good Governance*, Development Co-operation Guidelines Series, Paris: OECD.

OECD, 1996, 'Draft Policy Note on Strengthening Country Level Co-ordination for Participatory Development and Good Governance', Paris: OECD, DCD/DAC(96) 14.

Riddell, R.C., 1987, *Foreign Aid Reconsidered*, London: James Currey.

Robinson, M., 1993, 'Will Political Conditionality Work?' *IDS Bulletin*, 24:1.

Robinson, M., 1996, *Strengthening Civil Society Through Foreign Political Aid*, ESCOR Research Report, Brighton: Institute of Development Studies.

Stokke, O. (ed.), 1995, *Aid and Political Conditionality*, EADI Book Series 16, London: Frank Cass.

15

Coherent Approaches to Complex Emergencies: Belgium and the Great Lakes Region of Central Africa

JOHAN DEBAR,
ROBRECHT RENARD AND
FILIP REYNTJENS

INTRODUCTION

The Great Lakes region of Central Africa has been in turmoil since the beginning of this decade and has slid into a macabre cycle of violence. Political and ethnic conflict, killings of colossal proportions, huge refugee flows, humanitarian disaster: these have been the fate of Rwanda, Burundi and the Congolese Kivu provinces during the last several years. In this chapter, these momentous events serve only as a background, even if a particularly gruesome one, to the topic we wish to address. Our interest centres on Belgium's foreign policy and development co-operation policies, and in particular the coherence or otherwise of these policies. Rwanda, Burundi and Congo (ex-Zaire) have historically been the major recipients of Belgian aid and the main focus of its diplomacy. The political, social and military upheavals that have taken place in the Central African region have thus been of direct relevance to Belgian foreign policy and aid policy. They have confronted Belgium's bilateral relations, both in terms of diplomacy and development co-operation, with fundamental challenges. A major difficulty has been to respond in an adequate manner to rapidly changing situations: navigating between structural and emergency aid, applying political conditionality in an incremental fashion at a time when this instrument was far from developed,

The authors wish to thank participants at the EADI seminar in Geneva in April 1997 for many helpful comments. Several personal comments on the part of Belgian government officials are also gratefully acknowledged. Needless to say, the authors alone take responsibility for the positions taken in this chapter.

employing diplomacy in the attempt to arrive at negotiated settlements, and even resorting to a military presence which turned out to
be disastrous.

Coherence in policies towards the South is difficult to achieve in
the best of circumstances. But how does it fare in crisis situations?
Belgian aid, for instance, not only had to satisfy its own internal logic
and adapt to the rapidly changing economic and social context in
Rwanda and Burundi, but suddenly became a prime instrument for
achieving difficult geopolitical targets. Can this really work? How
were existing procedures of policy co-ordination between foreign
affairs and development co-operation able to cope with these new
challenges?

In what follows we will try to provide elements of an answer. In
the first section we summarise the major events in the Great Lakes
region of Africa, and how they affected, and were affected by, Western policies. What emerges is a dramatic sequence of events which
swept away much of the development foundations that had been laid
during the three decades since independence. In the second section we
focus on Belgian foreign policy response to events in the region. The
situation we depict is one of a prudent but not incoherent policy
response, yet one unable to have a major impact on the course of
events. In the third section we bring development co-operation into
the picture, and give an overview of the factors that have affected,
positively or negatively, the quality of Belgian foreign policies and
development policies, and in particular their mutual coherence.
Section IV addresses areas of weakness, of which there were several.
Section V contains the conclusion.

I. COMPLEX EMERGENCIES IN THE GREAT LAKES REGION: A BRIEF
   OVERVIEW

(1) Burundi 1988–97: From 'Reconciliation' to Civil War

After the North of Burundi had become the scene of a new round of
violence in August 1988, President Buyoya was under a great deal of
international pressure to embark on a new policy. The stated aim was
to bring the Hutu majority, which had been virtually excluded from
all sectors of state and society since the mid-1960s, into public life
and to pursue a policy of 'national reconciliation'. The appointment
of a government headed by a Hutu prime minister and where Hutu
and Tutsi held an equal number of portfolios, as well as the creation
of a National Commission to study the question of national unity,

430

were significant steps taken in October 1988. The progress made between late 1988 and early 1991 was evident: Hutu entered the state apparatus and were given fairer access to education, even if the Tutsi-dominated army and security services did not support these changes.

Initiated in a single-party context, the process of reform was to continue in quite a different environment from 1991 onwards. Buyoya was reluctantly forced by the 'winds of change' blowing over Africa to accept the introduction of multi-party democracy, with all the dangers this entailed for his efforts at ethnic reconciliation. Indeed many feared that ethnic voting in a competitive system might result in the demographic majority of Hutu emerging as an unassailable political majority.

When in June 1993 free and fair elections were held, this is exactly what happened. Buyoya's challenger, the Hutu Melchior Ndadaye, leader of the main opposition party FRODEBU, convincingly won the presidential election. FRODEBU also won 70 per cent of the votes in the parliamentary elections, with the former single party UPRONA obtaining only slightly over 20 per cent. In ethnic terms, the breakdown in the membership of the National Assembly was about 85 per cent Hutu and 15 per cent Tutsi, an almost perfect match with the demographic situation.

This was a landslide indeed, and it was heavily resented by the existing Tutsi establishment. The new regime was immediately faced with considerable problems: the return of huge numbers of Hutu refugees, the delicate task of ethnically rebalancing the administration, the hostility of a private press generally very close to the former incumbents, inertia and even sabotage on the part of those in the army, civil service and judiciary who were close to UPRONA, and the control of the economy by the ousted elite. During the months following the democratic change, the groups privileged under former regimes grew increasingly upset; and although they were a small minority, they had the monopoly of armed force [*Reyntjens, 1995*].

During the night of 20–21 October 1993, the army staged a coup. President Ndadaye and some of his close collaborators were assassinated, most FRODEBU cadres went into hiding, and massive violence erupted over almost the entire country. Tutsis were killed by outraged Hutus, Hutus were killed by the army and Tutsi civilians. About 50,000 lives were lost, roughly as many Hutu as Tutsi. (On the putsch, the killing of Ndadaye and the ensuing violence, see Human Rights Watch *et al.* [*1994*].)

Although formally the coup collapsed as a consequence of the outbreak of violence in the provinces and the condemnation of the national and international community, by early 1994 two interlinked phenomena had developed [*Reyntjens, 1995*, and update July *1996*]. A creeping coup succeeded in doing what the October 1993 putsch had been unable to achieve: gradually all power was taken away from the elected president and assembly, and effectively transferred to bodies without constitutional legitimacy such as the army and the National Security Council. In fact, the coup which brought Major Pierre Buyoya back to power on 25 July 1996 was just the formal confirmation of an existing situation. The second phenomenon was the gradual outbreak of civil war, which had considerably increased since early 1994. The ethnic purification of Bujumbura and other towns by extremist Tutsi militia, the intimidation and killing of an increasing number of FRODEBU politicians and the creeping coup convinced the former interior minister, FRODEBU leader Léonard Nyangoma, that he should leave the country to set up a new political movement, the *Conseil National pour la Défense de la Démocratie* (CNDD), together with a military wing, the *Forces pour la Défense de la Démocratie* (FDD). Joining forces with older armed movements (PALIPEHUTU and FROLINA), the CNDD-FDD waged an increasingly intense war against the Burundian army and gained control of much of the countryside, where it attempted to organise parallel administrations and to collect taxes. This civil war has claimed significant numbers of human lives. Although the rebel groups have killed civilians, the army in particular has massacred scores of unarmed Hutu. According to certain estimates, over 150,000 people have died in the violence [*Amnesty International, 1996*].

(2) Rwanda 1990–97: From Invasion to Genocide and Violent Dictatorship

In Rwanda, two events almost coincided in the second half of 1990. On the one hand, the country appeared to be embarking on a democratisation process in line with what was happening elsewhere in Africa. On the other, the Rwanda Patriotic Front (RPF), composed essentially of Tutsi refugees who had fled the country in successive waves since the 1959 revolution, invaded the country from Uganda, where many of the attackers served in the National Resistance Army (NRA). The combination of these events was to prove explosive.

Although the initial attack was repelled, the RPF engaged in a campaign of semi-guerilla warfare and was able to capture a small portion of territory in northern Rwanda, which it extended after an offensive in February 1993. In the meantime, the democratisation process continued: a multi-party constitution was adopted in June 1991, a dozen political parties were registered and a transitional government, led by a prime minister from the opposition, took office in April 1992. This in turn allowed negotiations with the RPF to get under way in Arusha (Tanzania). After difficult talks a peace accord was finally signed in August 1993; it provided for power-sharing, the return of the old diaspora and the merger of the government army (FAR) and the rebel force (RPF) [*Reyntjens, 1994*].

In order to oversee the implementation of the Arusha accord, a UN peacekeeping mission (UNAMIR) was sent to Rwanda in November 1993. However, due to an increasing polarisation of the political landscape, the different actors failed to agree on the composition of the transitional institutions. Both the main players – the old regime and the RPF – increasingly returned to a logic of armed confrontation for which they discreetly prepared themselves. And indeed the conflict resumed when on 6 April 1994 President Habyarimana's plane was shot down by ground-to-air missiles, an attack for which guilt has yet to be established. On the morning of 7 April, army units and militia close to the old regime embarked on massive violence: opponents of the Habyarimana regime and the Tutsi generally were the victims of widespread killings. For its part, the RPF resumed the war on the same day. During the period from April to July, probably over a million people were killed in the genocide, political massacres and other violence [*Millwood, 1996*]. Although it is less well documented, the RPF too killed tens of thousands, perhaps hundreds of thousands of civilians.

In July 1994, the RPF took power, and about two million refugees – including the FAR and the militia – fled the country. Although the RPF claimed to adhere to the spirit of the Arusha accord and formed a 'government of national unity', it soon became clear that it alone exercised real power. At the same time it embarked on a systematic policy of 'tutsisation': the civil service, the judiciary, the army and security services, and the economy were increasingly monopolised by Tutsis, most of them members of, or sympathisers with, the RPF. Under the pressure of security concerns caused by increasingly violent raids by ex-FAR and militia from neighbouring countries (Congo in particular), the RPF embarked on a policy that combined forced repatriation, physical elimination and pushing refugees further inland in Congo. Two phenomena emerged as a result. On the one hand, a Rwandan-backed rebellion rapidly spread in eastern Congo, threatening the stability not just of Congo but of the whole region (see *infra*). On the other, far from solving Rwanda's security concern, forced repatriation replaced the threat from outside by a threat from inside;

by repatriating the Hutu refugees, Rwanda imported a civil war, which developed in a way comparable to the situation in Burundi.

(3) Kivu 1994–97: From Ethnic Confrontation to Rebellion

The Congolese Kivu provinces are part of a larger region marked by considerable migratory flows. In particular the presence of large numbers of 'Banyarwanda' – kinyarwanda-speaking Hutu and Tutsi – have caused problems since Congo became independent in 1960. While many of these 'Banyarwanda' are Congolese nationals, others are more recent economic or political immigrants. The political representation of the ethnic groups and the related issue of citizenship have caused conflict both between Hutu and Tutsi and between 'Banyarwanda' (Hutu and Tutsi) and 'natives' (Nande, Bashi, Nyanga, Hunde, etc.). While this was an old problem – there had been so-called 'Banyarwanda revolts' in the 1960s – it became a major issue once again in the early 1990s in the context of the democratisation process, as well as for other reasons, particularly increasing disputes over land. Citizenship again became a bone of contention, as the Banyarwanda had reason to believe that they would be disenfranchised.

Violence erupted in North Kivu during the first half of 1993, leaving thousands dead and over 300,000 displaced. Most of the victims were Hutu and Tutsi 'Banyarwanda', persecuted by Hunde and Nyanga who enjoyed the support of the Congolese army. Although calm returned, the Kivu provinces were again destabilised by the arrival, at the end of 1993, of over 100,000 Hutu refugees from Burundi, and – more profoundly – by the influx of 1.2 million Hutu refugees from Rwanda in mid-1994 after the RPF's victory. The arrival of so many Hutu, tens of thousands of them armed, has profoundly unsettled an already fragile ethnic balance. The alliance between Hutu and Tutsi 'Banyarwanda' has been broken. In late 1995 fighting broke out between Hutu (both 'Banyarwanda' and Rwandan refugees) and Tutsi; so-called 'natives', Hunde in particular, joined in what has amounted to a campaign of ethnic cleansing against the Tutsi. Signs of similar events were visible in South Kivu by early 1996. Violence broke out in September 1996, particularly against the Tutsi 'Banyamulenge' (as the 'Banyarwanda' are known in South Kivu) in the area of Uvira. The difference from the earlier events in North Kivu was that the Banyamulenge and other Tutsi in the region were trained and armed by Rwanda, and that Rwandan army units crossed the border and participated in the fighting, with at least the passive support of the Burundian army [Reyntjens and Marysse, 1996].

This was the beginning of the combination of a rebellion and a regional war. On the one hand, some older and some newly created rebel movements immediately joined the battle against the Congolese army. On the other hand, Rwanda, and probably to a lesser extent, Uganda and Burundi, supported the rebel movement. This allowed Rwanda to create a buffer zone on its western border within Congolese territory, from which it suffered attacks by rebel groups. After Angola joined the fray in February 1997, the insurrection eventually toppled the regime of Marshal Mobutu.

(4) The Perspective of a Regional War

The link to the Sudan is obvious. Southern Sudan was the scene of a complex rebellion and probably the focal point of international and regional alliances. The Khartoum government enjoyed the support of France and China, which were in turn close to Mobutu's Congo and – to put it in a very simplistic way – the Hutu of Rwanda and Burundi. On the other side, the Southern rebellion waged by the SPLA was supported by the US, the UK and Museveni's Uganda, in turn allied – again simplifying – with the Tutsi regimes in Rwanda and Burundi. The potential for an ongoing and expanding conflict was obvious: it involved four government armies, a former government army, over a dozen rebel movements from five countries, all with their own agendas, involved in potentially shifting alliances. As Eritrea and Ethiopia appeared to be increasingly drawn into the Sudanese conflict, a front line stretching from Eritrea to Burundi might well develop.

II. BELGIAN RESPONSE TO DEVELOPMENTS IN THE REGION

Before analysing in some detail Belgium's response to developments in the region, it may be useful to give some indication of the importance of the region for Belgian foreign policy and development co-operation, and of the importance of Belgium in the region. Belgium's postwar African policy has been intricately bound up with the fate of former colony Congo and trusteeship territories Rwanda and Burundi. This can hardly come as a surprise. After decolonisation, Belgian interest in the developing world, and its aid effort, was focused almost exclusively on these three countries. And this is also where its diplomatic and commercial interests lay. Congo, with its huge mineral wealth and its strategic location in the region, was especially the centre of attention. Both politicians and diplomats knew that these three countries in Central Africa constituted the only place abroad where Belgium played any significant role. And the private sector had built up important interests, especially in the rich mining sector of Congo.

Over the years, as development aid spread out to new countries, the relative importance of the three countries gradually declined, but nevertheless remained the cornerstone of African policy. At the beginning of the 1980s the three countries combined still received half of Belgian bilateral aid. By the close of the decade, their share had fallen to about one-third, but was still important. Congo was the major recipient, followed by Rwanda and Burundi, as can be seen in Table 1 in the appendix. In terms of aid per capita, Rwanda came first. More important for our purpose, up to the end of the 1980s, Belgium was the major bilateral donor to Congo and Rwanda, and a close second, after France, in the case of Burundi (see tables 2 and 3 in the appendix). Belgium therefore carried some weight when it came to international deliberations.

The political turmoil and instability of the late 1980s and the 1990s affected Belgium's position in a major way. Relations with Congo deteriorated in the late 1980s, when Belgium tried to apply the 'new political conditionality' that had become fashionable after the fall of the Berlin wall. Mobutu would not have any of it, however, and development co-operation relations broke up in 1990, except for some emergency aid. This made an increase in aid to Rwanda and Burundi possible in the early 1990s, signalling Belgium's support for the efforts at reconciliation. But as the crisis in both countries unfolded and then exploded in 1993–94, aid flows from Belgium eventually diminished there too. In 1993–94 the three countries together received less than one-fifth of Belgian bilateral aid. By 1995 their share had dwindled to less than one-tenth. As other donors have maintained their aid or sometimes increased it, the influence of Belgium in the region has been greatly reduced.

(1) Positive Engagement: Burundi 1988–94 and Rwanda 1990–94

When President Buyoya embarked on his programme of 'national reconciliation' in late 1988, he was encouraged by Belgium to carry on with his reforms by a marked increase in bilateral ODA. When announcing a further package of aid in 1991, Belgium placed it in the context of 'political support for attempts at democratisation and national reconciliation'. When the army killed between 1,000 and 3,000 mainly Hutu civilians in renewed violence in November 1991, Belgium expressed concern and asked for an investigation and the punishment of those responsible. The Burundian authorities were less

436

than forthcoming, but Belgium decided not to press the issue, given the progress in the area of democratisation and in consideration of the fragile position of Buyoya in the face of Tutsi hardliners. Rather, it went on supporting the transition process and helped fund the administrative machinery for the election, including an observer mission, held in June 1993.

The fairness of the elections in Burundi and what appeared initially to be a remarkably smooth transition seemed to vindicate the policy pursued by Belgium and the international community more generally, until the 21 October 1993 military coup whose disastrous consequences we have described earlier. As did other donors, Belgium immediately suspended its co-operation. After a few days the coup collapsed, at least formally, and co-operation was soon resumed, but the Belgian government announced that this would be reoriented, with more emphasis on the strengthening of civil society and the advancement of the rural population. The security situation on the ground was to render development co-operation increasingly difficult. Bilateral efforts to promote political solutions to the rapidly deteriorating situation during 1994–96 steadily withered away.

When Rwanda entered into a period of profound crisis after the RPF invasion of October 1990, Belgium adopted a conditionality policy which rested essentially on three pillars. The first was respect for human rights. Pressure by Belgium and like-minded donors (particularly the US, Switzerland and Canada) was instrumental in the release, in March–April 1991, of thousands of political detainees, arrested for their alleged complicity with the RPF, and in the monitoring of recurrent human rights abuse in 1991–94. When the report of an international NGO mission of inquiry, published in March 1993, pointed an accusing finger at the regime, the Belgian ambassador was recalled to Brussels and the Belgian government threatened Rwanda with sanctions; this was followed by an apparent improvement of the situation.

The second pillar was support for the democratisation process which got under way in the second half of 1990. Belgian pressure was instrumental in the formation, in April 1992, of the first transitional government, in which the opposition obtained the post of prime minister and half the portfolios.

The third pillar was support for the negotiation of a peace agreement between the government and the rebel RPF. This meant active involvement in the Arusha talks which started in July 1992 and where Belgium, together with other donors, was constantly present, offering financial support, keeping open the channels of communication between the parties involved and pledging the funds necessary for the implementation of the accord. When the accords were finally signed on 4 August 1993, Belgium accepted the ultimate consequence of this policy by agreeing to contribute a batallion to the UN peacekeeping mission, UNAMIR, which was to oversee the implementation of the accord.

As described above, the accord collapsed in early April 1994 when President Habyarimana was killed and a vicious civil war erupted overnight. When ten Belgian peacekeepers were brutally murdered by the government army (FAR), Belgium was caught up in the 'body-bag syndrome' and embarked on a piece of panic diplomacy. It uni-laterally withdrew its batallion, a retreat which fundamentally handi-capped UNAMIR, and – with US support – successfully advocated the end of UNAMIR altogether. The UN security council followed this disastrous logic and on 21 April 1994 decided to maintain only a token force in Rwanda. The UN, and also France and Belgium who had had troops on the ground by 9 and 10 April respectively, thus abandoned Rwanda and disentangled themselves from a military intervention which might possibly have avoided the genocide and crimes against humanity that were subsequently perpetrated, and which pushed the country towards the inextricable and violent dead-lock it subsequently faced. This was to be the end of real Belgian involvement, a phase to which we now turn.

(2) Withdrawal: Rwanda 1994–97

Belgium's relationship with the RPF, which took power in July 1994, was bad from day one. For a number of reasons, Belgium was suspec-ted by the former regime to be 'pro-RPF', but this has never been the case and the RPF knew it. Unlike Rwanda's 'new friends' (especially the US, Canada and the Netherlands), Belgium never believed that the new regime was going to bring stability, fearing instead that its narrow political, social and ethnic base would be a major handicap to both medium- and long-term stability in Rwanda.

While most other countries, and the 'new friends' of Rwanda in particular, offered considerable 'genocide compensation' to the new regime in the form of large sums of aid money with almost no strings attached, Belgium attempted to adopt a 'constructive but critical' atti-tude and to attach conditions to its aid and bilateral relations gene-rally. Thus, at the Rwanda Round Table held in Geneva on 20–21 June 1996, Belgium and Switzerland were the only countries to suggest forms of political conditionality, while the US, for instance, towed the Rwandan government's line and did not utter any serious reservations.

It was with the intention of applying a policy of positive political conditionality that Belgium resumed its aid to Rwanda in early 1995. To this end it privileged the sector of justice, involving itself in training of personnel, institutional support for the justice ministry, support for the courts, the prosecutorial offices, the prison system and the bar, and the funding of the UN Human Rights Observer Mission and the International Criminal Tribunal for Rwanda. The commitment made by Belgium in these fields in 1995 and 1996 amounted to about US$12 million, a considerable fraction of total Belgian bilateral and multilateral aid to Rwanda. Other areas of intervention included health care and housing and the provision and distribution of plant seeds.

However, the generous aid provided to Rwanda since 1994 by the US, the UK, Germany and the Netherlands, combined with a marked decrease in its own spending, pushed Belgium back to the fifth place as a bilateral donor, with only 6 per cent of bilateral aid provided by DAC countries (see Table 3 in appendix). Together with the fact that some of those new donors did not seem to attach political conditions, this meant that Belgium was in no position to pursue directly such policy objectives as the promotion of a process of political negotiation between the RPF and groups excluded from power and/or in exile. Relations between the two countries grew increasingly sour. Instead, Belgium attempted to influence the policy of the 'friends of the new Rwanda'. In the wake of the Rwanda-sponsored 'rebellion' in eastern Congo, this was done with some degree of success, particularly with regard to the US. Clearly Kigali was worried about the apparent shift in US attitudes, which it attributed to Belgian lobbying. Rwandan irritation burst into the open after the Belgian foreign ministry alleged that thousands of Rwandan government troops were engaged in Congo: on 29 January 1997 Claude Dusaidi, an advisor to Vice-President Kagame, stated that he believed this showed Belgium had 'gone senile'. However, the outburst did not prevent the US State Department from repeating essentially the same accusation in early February.

(3) Hiding Behind Others' Backs: Burundi 1994–97

Although in resuming its aid to Burundi in early 1994 Belgium intended to stimulate the search for a political settlement of the crisis, the steady worsening of the situation was to make such hopes increasingly illusory. Even the running of a 'food for work'

439

programme, which purported to combine the fulfilment of basic needs and reconciliation at grass-roots level, became practically impossible. By the end of 1995, the security situation had put a virtual end to Belgian development co-operation.

Subsequently, efforts at promoting a political settlement were not pursued directly, but through the EU (the mission of special envoy Aldo Ajello) and the good offices mission of Julius Nyerere, whose work was funded by Belgium throughout 1995 and 1996.

When Major Buyoya resumed power in July 1996, Belgium chose not to condemn the coup outright. Believing the new situation created a possible opening, it gave Buyoya the benefit of the doubt and hoped that he might get negotiations underway. Although that appeared not to be the case, by the autumn of 1996 Belgian and international attention was absorbed by the events in Congo. The civil war in Burundi went on unabated without the slightest move towards meaningful talks, and no one, including Belgium, knew what to do about it.

By early 1997, belief in Buyoya's chances was waning and Nyerere's efforts lost momentum. The mission of UN and OAU envoy Mohamed Sahnoun seemed to offer one of the few opportunities left to back a collective effort.

(4) Humanitarian Rather than Political Involvement: Kivu 1994–97

When Hutu refugees arrived in the Kivu region from Burundi in late 1993 and from Rwanda in mid-1994, an already tense situation was further exacerbated. Instead of seeing this crisis as political – that is, as the consequence of the domestic situation in Congo, Rwanda and Burundi – Belgium adopted a humanitarian and technical response. The questions asked were how to keep the refugees alive and how to get them back to their countries of origin, rather than why they fled these countries in the first place. The consequence was that for over two years, the refugees remained in camps that were both much too large and too close to the borders of Rwanda and Burundi. When war instead of consultation pushed most of the refugees back in late 1996, the cost was massive loss of life and – in particular with regard to Rwanda – the displacement of a security threat from outside to within the county. Never at any moment in time were the refugees themselves involved in the determination of their situation or the search for long-term solutions.

In this, Belgium did not act differently from other international actors. No attempt was made to get the Rwandan government to talk to the refugees' representatives (admittedly, though, Kigali had made it clear that it had no intention of engaging in such talks). The refusal to see the problem as political rather than humanitarian has been very costly. It has been a major contributory factor to the destabilisation of eastern Congo, while it did nothing to reduce the tensions inside Rwanda and Burundi.

III. FACTORS AFFECTING POLICY COHERENCE

In the foregoing we have reviewed the unfolding crisis in Burundi and Rwanda in recent years and Belgium's foreign policy response to it. With respect to the latter, our analysis dwelt on the broad outcome of foreign policy, without distinguishing between the bureaucracies involved, and without dwelling on any differences that may have thus arisen. Nor did we analyse the composition of the three coalition governments that succeeded each other in the period concerned, or the personalities of the cabinet ministers in charge. This omission was warranted to the extent that there was a large degree of agreement, both among departments and among cabinet ministers, and also a fair degree of continuity in policies despite three changes of government. Overall, we argue that Belgian policies were fairly stable all along. From that perspective it can be said that coherence of South policies was broadly achieved.

But it is worth having a closer look. In the following section we look at ambiguities, discontinuities and contradictions that may lie hidden under the surface of an outwardly coherent policy. Our main concern is the role of the minister of development co-operation and his administration, the Belgian Administration for Development Co-operation (BADC), in relation to foreign affairs. Before the Rwanda and Burundi crisis, BADC and the minister for development co-operation had considerable freedom to carry out their role of aid donors as they saw fit. But as the crisis unfolded, the role of both the minister of foreign affairs and his administration became increasingly important. BADC continued with the technical task of running its aid programme, but the volume of aid, and its content and timing, increasingly became matters of foreign policy. How was this shift in emphasis implemented at the operational level? How did foreign affairs and BADC collaborate and co-ordinate? What were the respective roles of the ministers, their entourage, and the administration proper? And how successful was the outcome? Was the aid programme seamlessly integrated into broad foreign policy? And did foreign policy initiatives fully take into consideration the extent to which aid projects and programmes can be used by diplomats as means of political arm-twisting? We try to provide some elements of an answer in the following pages. We do not attempt an overall assessment of Belgian policy in the region as such. Our main interest lies in the contribution of development co-operation to Belgian policy with respect to Rwanda and Burundi.

(1) The Difficult Trade-off between Policy Objectives

It is customary to point to the many inconsistencies in the foreign policy objectives of donors. The development objective does not always fit in with their commercial, political, military, or other ambitions. In the case of Belgian aid to Rwanda and Burundi no major incompatibilities were, in our view, present during the period concerned. Belgium did not have significant commercial interests to defend in the two countries. Admittedly, Belgian aid was to a large extent tied to procurement in Belgium, and this certainly created its own interest groups. Yet, in contrast to the situation in Congo, for instance, or countries in southern Africa, not to speak of some Asian and Latin American countries, there was no strong commercial lobby trying to force the hand of the government. Soft loans, the major instrument of tying and source of lobbying, did not play a prominent role in either country. The new policy of 'co-gestion', which puts much more responsibility in the hands of the recipient, and which was tried out first in Rwanda and Burundi at the end of the 1980s, also considerably reduced the possibility of unilaterally imposed aid projects benefiting Belgian firms to the detriment of the recipient.

That all was not pure and altruistic, however, is illustrated by the following incident. In 1992 Belgium forced Rwanda to accept that part of the aid budget would be used to settle payments arrears to a Belgian firm that had delivered goods to Rwanda in the context of an (untied) multilateral project. The pill was sweetened by the promise to ease the procedures for balance-of-payments support which would now be made available against the simple delivery of documents showing past imports from Belgium. The amount involved was relatively unimportant, and the incident had no other ramifications.

As far as geopolitics is concerned, we have already indicated that it was widely perceived in Belgian political and diplomatic circles that Rwanda and Burundi, together with Congo, were the only countries where Belgium could play a significant international role. Yet not everybody was convinced that this part should be played too enthusiastically. The three countries with which Belgium had historical ties were in fact also the countries where the Catholic Church and Catholic NGOs were strongly present (this was especially true of Rwanda where the Catholic Church was very close to the

442

Habyarimana regime), and where the Belgian Crown showed a keen interest in good relations. Some socialists were especially reluctant to be closely associated with such policies. For the same reasons, the christian democrats felt more inclined to follow a policy of active engagement in the region. Yet this never became a major bone of contention. Socialists were not trying to get these countries dropped from the list of recipients of Belgian aid; they were simply more interested in fostering development co-operation links with other countries that had more socialist appeal. If dissent there was, it came mostly from the political parties of the opposition, notably the franco-phone liberal party whose president voiced very sharp criticism against Habyarimana. The christian democrats became more isolated in their defence of the historical ties with the Rwanda of Habyarimana, and the socialists moved closer to the opposition during 1997 when a parliamentary commission investigated the circumstances surrounding the murder of the Belgian paratroopers in 1994, reported above.

Whenever these countries became the focus of international attention, the traditional Belgian political parties, christian democrats, socialists and the right-of-centre liberals, agreed at least on one thing. They felt that as a former colonial power and important local donor, Belgium understood these countries better than the rest of the world did, and they wanted it to play a role befitting such expertise. Post-colonial nostalgia led to occasional flare-ups of frustration, especially directed against the French who had filled the vacuum left by Belgium and had as it were realigned the two countries, along with Congo (ex-Zaire), bringing them into the francophone sphere of influence.

Apart from the fact that Belgium's geopolitical ambitions were restricted by the country's small size, it is not evident that such ambitions as remained were in conflict with the development objective. The colonial past explained why Rwanda and Burundi were major beneficiaries of Belgian aid, but the main motivation now was the pursuit of development. Belgian policies were certainly not always optimal from a development point of view, but the reasons do not lie in the difficult trade-off between political, commercial, and developmental objectives. The motive for providing aid to Rwanda and Burundi was largely respectable whereas in Congo, right up until the crisis of 1990, Belgium's aid policy was distorted by commercial interests and geopolitical calculations related to (among other factors) the civil war in Angola, in which situation Belgium stood proxy for the US.

(2) Three Changes of Government

If there was reasonable coherence at a broad policy level, maybe some of the frictions reported on further in this chapter were due to the nature of Belgian coalition politics? Table 1 gives an overview of the three Belgian governments in the period under study. All the ministers involved were from the Flemish part of the country, not that this fact is particularly significant on its own. Much more important are the political party, the personality and the experience of the ministers involved. The last column in the table indicates whether, in the authors' opinion, the ministers were more of a 'realistic' inclination or more 'idealistic' in outlook. Any such labelling is inevitably somewhat imprecise and subjective, but we have nevertheless included it. By 'realistic' we mean that a minister will be more keen to use aid to foster non-development objectives. He will tend to play down the trade-off this may involve with the 'pure' development objective of fighting poverty. He will be likewise less committed to risking the lives of Belgian soldiers in operations to support transitions towards more open and accountable political regimes. An 'idealist' minister will, on the contrary, do such things more readily, even if it may entail some risk both for his own political career and for the government.[1] In the last column of the table we also indicate whether or not, to our mind, the ministers were committed to Central Africa as a region. The assessment is again to some extent subjective, even if there are more objective indicators than when assessing the degree of 'idealism'.

The table does not bring out all the important differences. Minister Geens, for instance, had a much more positive opinion of the Habyarimana regime than had his successor, Derycke, and Minister Moreels considers development co-operation as a prime instrument of field diplomacy and conflict prevention, much to the annoyance of foreign affairs. To illustrate how such differences in vision and style affected decision-making in practice we review some of the more important moments in bilateral development relations. In the bilateral

---

1. Another difference is that an 'idealist' minister would fight harder to increase or at least to maintain the development budget. However, on this score, all the ministers concerned were 'realists', so we have not included this particular criterion here. Part of the explanation would seem to be that development co-operation does not carry much weight in Belgian politics, probably even less so than in other donor countries. Ministers of development co-operation have little political weight, and are easily overruled by their colleagues. This is certainly the case when federal budget allocations are being made at a time of fiscal austerity. Even a very idealist minister would just have to accept the verdict of his colleagues, or resign. The distinction between idealism and realism becomes blurred in such cases.

talks of 1991 held with Rwanda, Minister Geens put strong emphasis on the need for more democracy and for reconciliation and peace with the invading FPR. Combined with promises of a generous increase of development aid, the implicit political conditionality was taken seriously. In its 1991 bilateral talks with Burundi, Belgium similarly made use of the carrot of generous aid-spending and the stick of political conditions. As indicated in the table, Geens represented a Flemish nationalist party in the coalition government. His attitude towards Rwanda and Burundi was closer to that of the christian democrats than that of the socialists who were much more reserved. The policy of positive engagement did not last, however.

In 1992 a new minister for development co-operation, Flemish socialist Erik Derycke, was appointed, who took a much more cautious approach, especially with respect to Rwanda. Pressure from Willy Claes, his senior colleague both in the government and in the party, undoubtedly played a role in this. Belgium did not, for instance, support France and Germany in their pressure on the World Bank to speed up the disbursement of aid to tbe country under the Special Programme of Assistance to Africa. In the same year Belgium restricted the use of budget leftovers, which Rwanda proposed to use for balance-of-payments support, and also went back on earlier promises that certain projects would be funded with additional aid money. In bilateral talks with Rwanda in 1992, the Belgian minister emphasised the need for a negotiated settlement to the conflict, more democratic government and the rule of law. He suggested a new domain of co-operation: support for the judiciary and for the organisation of elections. In similar talks in Burundi, the content was the same, but the minister went further in his emphasis on political reform. He visited two human rights organisations, one official, the other non-governmental.

The following year, in July 1993, the mid-term review talks with Rwanda were held without the minister. A high-ranking BADC official headed the Belgian delegation. In his speech he reiterated Belgium's commitment to promoting a peaceful settlement to the conflict, human rights and good governance. There was open talk about political conditionality, however, with the understanding that ongoing projects would not be cut. Sanctions, in the case of non-compliance, would fall on the unspent part of the budget.

TABLE 1
THE POLITICAL SETTING IN BELGIUM, 1991–97

Period	Minister	Political party	Policy
–1991	Foreign affairs: M. Eyskens	Flemish christian democrat	'Realist'; little commitment to Central Africa
	Development: A. Geens	Flemish nationalist	'Realist'; strong commitment to Central Africa
1992–95	Foreign affairs: W. Claes	Flemish socialist	'Realist'; little commitment to Central Africa
	Development: E. Derycke	Flemish socialist	'Idealist'; little commitment to Central Africa
1995–	Foreign affairs: E. Derycke	Flemish socialist	Idealist'; increasing commitment to Central Africa
	Development: R. Moreels	Flemish christian democrat	'Strong idealist'; strong commitment to Central Africa

There was less active involvement from foreign affairs in Burundi, at least up until the October 1993 coup, and consequently Derycke was in a stronger position to set his own agenda there. In 1993, for instance, no high-level talks were held in Burundi. The original timing of the high-level bilateral talks, planned for the first half of 1993, was regarded by development co-operation as inappropriate because of the forthcoming elections. The reasons for this change of heart may seem obvious to aid technicians, but diplomats may have preferred to profit from the occasion, certainly in the context of the upward trend of Belgian aid commitments, to put some political pressure on Buyoya with respect to the elections. But the view of development co-operation prevailed. After the elections and the murder of the elected President Ndadaye, talks became impossible as a consequence of the political chaos and the absence of an effective government. It was not until 1994 that the bilateral high-level talks were finally resumed. By that time, foreign affairs in Brussels was keenly interested in Burundi. Both the Burundian minister of finance, Toyi, and the Belgian minister for development co-operation, Derycke, attended, and both parties intended the talks to send a positive signal to the rest of the donor community. Yet not much came out of them. The message to Burundi was that Belgium was supportive, but could not make any long-term commitment in the face of the political instability that prevailed. Hardly encouraging, and not really helpful.

In 1995 a new Belgian minister for development co-operation took office. In line with his background as a former chairman of the NGO Médecins sans frontières, christian democrat Reginald Moreels was more intent on achieving active development co-operation despite the political turmoil and social and economic degradation in both countries. With Moreels, the style of the bilateral talks changed, especially with regard to Rwanda: in a reversal of pecking order, foreign affairs was now less interested in setting the agenda in Rwanda than it was in Burundi. Annual high-level talks were held, with a strongly involved Belgian minister personally present. Belgium was now more committed but at the same time reserved the right unilaterally to withdraw its aid after each year's evaluation. Political conditionality was explicitly present, linked to political openness and equity.

(3) Co-ordination in Brussels between Foreign Affairs and Development Co-operation

The Belgium Administration for Development Co-operation (BADC) forms part of the Ministry of Foreign Affairs, Development Co-operation and Foreign Trade. However, it has a considerable measure of autonomy, and this is reflected in its administrative organisation. Career-wise, staff do not move freely between BADC and the rest of the ministry, as they do between the departments of foreign affairs and foreign trade, and BADC reports directly to its own minister. At the level of the administration, weekly co-ordination meetings are held under the chairmanship of the secretary-general of the ministry of foreign affairs, but this is mainly to agree on practicalities relating to, say, a visit of a foreign dignitary, rather than to discuss substantial issues of foreign policy. The Ministry of Foreign Affairs has its own Africa division, which operates independently of the Africa desk of BADC. There are of course informal contacts, and officials of the two will meet on occasion, but there is no collaboration in the form of an intense exchange of information or regular meetings. The small size of the Central Africa desk at foreign affairs may have caused it to become overstretched during periods of intense crisis in Rwanda, Burundi and eastern Congo. This may explain at least in part why the pressure exerted by foreign affairs on development co-operation has been uneven over time. Development co-operation had relatively more leeway with respect first to Burundi, and later Rwanda.

The minister for development co-operation may be a senior minister with seats in the council of ministers, as was the case with the first of the three ministers in the period concerned, André Geens.

He came from a Flemish nationalist party which was a junior member in the coalition government of Prime Minister Wilfried Martens. Foreign affairs at the time was in the hands of Flemish christian democrat Mark Eyskens, and this led to occasional frictions which did not, however, impede the formulation of a political consensus. Both his successors were junior ministers without seats in the council of ministers. The first, Erik Derycke, reported to the foreign minister, fellow Flemish socialist Willy Claes, and later to Frank Vandenbroucke, whereas the second, Reginald Moreels, reported directly to the prime minister, fellow Flemish christian democrat Jean-Luc Dehaene. In the meantime Erik Derycke had moved on to become minister of foreign affairs. There was the occasional bickering between the minister in charge of development co-operation and his colleague at foreign affairs, but this was usually settled without it coming out in the media, with some notable exceptions, such as the disagreement in the spring of 1997 regarding attitudes towards the refugee problem in eastern Congo.

There is an accepted division of labour between the two ministers. The minister of foreign affairs takes diplomatic initiatives and wields the axe of political conditionality. The minister of development co-operation dutifully applies any conditionality imposed by foreign affairs in times of crisis, from postponing bilateral talks to with-drawing personnel to interrupting ongoing activities. As long as such political conditionalities, in the way of sanctions, do not apply, BADC is supposed to proceed with the aid business as usual. This is uncontroversial as long as political conditionality is confined to the threat of withdrawing aid. But when Minister Derycke was in charge of development co-operation, he refined the instrument of political conditionality to include positive measures, such as support for the process of democratisation, strengthening the judiciary, and support-ing human rights NGOs. He thus involved BADC in political analysis and a monitoring of political events in the recipient countries, tasks traditionally reserved for the diplomats and officials of foreign affairs. Nor, apparently, was any effort made to ensure effective co-ordination. This would probably have consisted of inviting the specialists of foreign affairs to sit in on meetings at BADC to discuss the desirability and chances of success of projects with policy linkages.

Lack of co-ordination, or at least of consultation, could often also be observed at lower levels of decision-making. There are instances where negative political conditionality was applied at a lower level, on the initiative of the minister for development co-operation, or even at the level of BADC itself. Again there was no involvement of foreign affairs.

When consultation was held between foreign affairs and BADC, it mostly concerned major decisions, not the formulation of BADC policies at the project or programme level. The initiative was normally taken by one of the ministers concerned, and often the consultation was at the level of the personal advisers to the minister rather than at the level of the administration. When the administration was invited to such meetings, only high-ranking officials were involved. As they did not always communicate effectively with the regional desk, internal co-ordination problems were added to external ones. The upshot was that BADC regional desk officers were scarcely involved in broader policy preparation during the Rwanda and Burundi crises. Yet they were the ones who knew most about current projects and programmes, and were well informed about what was happening from their contacts. This lack of communication had different drawbacks. First, the expertise of the geographical BADC desk was not exploited. Officials there could have indicated, for instance, which parts of the portfolio of projects and programmes currently financed would be harmed by political changes, and might have to be discontinued or adapted. They could also have indicated which BADC activities had a chance of benefiting, for instance, those people likely to be the victims of political instability and civil unrest, and who therefore should as far as possible be exempt from political sanctions. In this way they could have helped to draw up a consistent plan for applying different types of political conditionality. They could also have fed back any information obtained about the political situation to those running their own projects and programmes in order to adapt these to the changing socio-political context.

Communication between the minister of development co-operation and BADC was not always ideal either. It was not until 1994 that the first fully spelt-out policy papers for Rwanda and Burundi were produced by the minister's office for use by BADC. And even then they dealt only with the broad orientation of future collaboration, and gave no detailed indications regarding the overall budget or its allocation among the different sectors, let alone identified possible alternative political developments or indicated which projects and programmes might have to be discontinued. Overall, during the period 1990–94 the quality of aid management suffered from a lack of transparency in the communication between the minister and BADC. This led to a considerable degree of frustration and demotivation on the part of staff on the Rwanda-Burundi desk. In 1995 and 1996, Moreels, the new minister for development co-operation, issued memorandums to BADC that were much more detailed and specific.

(4) Co-ordination between Brussels and Embassies and Field Missions

Field-level co-ordination would not at first sight seem to pose major problems. A protocol between development co-operation and foreign affairs from the 1960s regulates the relationship between BADC field missions and Belgian embassy staff. The hierarchical structure is that BADC field missions report to the Belgian ambassador, through whose office all official correspondence with Brussels passes. The ambassador has, of course, the right to add comments addressed to the minister of foreign affairs, but not to refuse his signature. The relationship is asymmetric, in that reports from the embassy to foreign affairs are not routinely communicated to BADC field staff. How it all works in practice depends very much on the personalities involved. It is quite common for an ambassador to convene weekly staff meetings under his chairmanship, involving representatives from both foreign affairs and BADC. Co-ordination is further facilitated by the limited number of staff involved at embassy and BADC field missions and the intensive social contacts among them outside work, especially in small towns such as Kigali and Bujumbura. Yet there is considerable potential for friction. An ambassador is often involved in high-level gatherings with other embassies and the government of the country at which important aspects of development policy are discussed and political commitments made, and he may decide to play an active role on such occasions, without necessarily involving BADC field staff. He may also disagree with the policy of BADC and the minister of development co-operation and use his muscle to get around it. In the case of Rwanda and Burundi in the period concerned in this chapter there are cases both of exemplary collaboration between BADC field mission staff and the embassy, and of lack of mutual understanding and co-operation.

IV. AREAS OF WEAKNESS

(1) BADC Policy

Aid projects are notoriously slow and inflexible. Those administered by BADC do not constitute an exception to this rule. It is not surprising for a project to take two years or more before actual start-up. On the other hand, once they have started, they have a tendency to be perpetuated. Many BADC staff have a strong preference for project aid. The same applies to most of the ministers who have been in charge of development co-operation. Derycke, for instance, saw a reduction of programme aid to Rwanda as a means of avoiding the criticism that Belgium was supporting the by then dubious regime of Habyarimana. Moreels was by background and instinct someone who favoured a micro-oriented project approach. Some of the politicians in charge of development co-operation in the 1980s tended to this same micro-orientation. As a consequence of this shared view between BADC and most ministers of development co-operation, projects and technical co-operation, spread over a large number of activities, dominated bilateral aid in Rwanda and Burundi. In the crisis years of the 1990s this became a handicap, for it proved difficult to adapt such activities to the quickly changing circumstances. Moreover, the presence of expatriate staff in key positions made many projects extra-vulnerable to political turmoil, as expatriate staff were easily withdrawn.

If traditional projects exhibit a tendency to be inflexible, this does not explain fully why there was no real attempt to adapt them to the new context. If one looks at internal BADC documents[2] on Rwanda and Burundi produced during these years, one is struck by the gap between the quality of many macro- and sectoral analyses on the one hand, and that of most project-level reports on the other. It is as if the profound socio-political crisis whose consequences were studied in several macro- and sectoral papers was not perceived to have a major relevance to ongoing projects. There is seldom an answer in project documents to the question of whether the new situation called for some drastic reformulation of the project. To illustrate this: when the BADC field mission in Kigali discussed the desirability of Belgium contributing to demobilisation and rehabilitation in the period preceding the 1994 genocide, there was no apparent effort to review ongoing projects, many of which had become inoperational, and to see which ones might be brought to an end or reoriented in order to free resources.

We do not quarrel with the counter-argument that project aid has another time dimension that cannot without cost be tampered with. For instance, agricultural research into appropriate plant varieties for use by local farmers might not yield immediate results and was therefore of not much help in a crisis situation, but in the longer run it could prove an essential input into sustainable and equitable

---

2. Many BADC documents, even if not confidential, are not routinely available to outside researchers. They are not always internally catalogued, or indeed officially endorsed. This is the reason why they do not figure individually in the reference list.

development. The argument is largely valid, but it does not apply with equal force to all Belgian projects, many of which had only medium-term objectives.

The failure substantially to question ongoing projects was all the more surprising in the light of the fact that many of the regional desk officers involved were trained in the 'logical framework approach' and were applying it keenly. In fact, the Rwanda and Burundi desks had been spearheading the introduction of a new style of project management since the end of the 1980s, in which the logical framework approach was to play an important role as a management tool and policy instrument. The assumptions column of any logical framework of a project in Rwanda or Burundi ought to have contained some reference to government policies or to the general situation in the country, and this should have alerted desk officers and field staff alike to the change in underlying assumptions necessary to make projects successful.[3]

Although our criticism is mostly directed at the project level, not all of the sectoral analyses were of sufficient quality either. With respect to Burundi, one crucial question in particular was inadequately addressed, namely how the strong resistance by the Tutsi elite to the erosion of their economic and other privileges could be overcome. That Burundian senior civil servants and Tutsi ministers could be successful at foiling donor efforts to shift the balance of power in economic and social policy was already clear by the end of the 1980s. We do not think it was too much to ask for BADC to have developed a consistent policy approach to address the matter by the mid-1990s. Yet this was not the case. Among other things, insufficient attention was paid in BADC sectoral documents to the question of whether an explicit political conditionality should apply to certain sectors and not to others, and if it had to be applied, in what form.[4] Sometimes the impression was given that anything that smacked of political analysis was beyond the role of BADC and should be left to the minister and his office, yet in other situations additional conditionality was applied stealthily by the geographical desk, for example by delaying the implementation of certain aid activities. The uneasy relationship in Belgium between BADC and the successive ministers is certainly

---

3. One important reason for the apparent failure to exploit the potential of the logical framework method may have been the fact that under BADC procedures project logical frameworks are made up jointly with the recipient.
4. The education sector, where ethnic inequalities *vis-à-vis* access to higher education were too glaring to ignore, withstands this criticism better than other sectors. BADC tried to apply some sensible conditionalities there.

partly to blame for the lack of an integrated policy vision underlying development co-operation towards the Great Lakes countries.

(2) Development Policy Implementation

Ministers on more than one occasion misjudged the speed, or lack of it, of decisions to grant new aid or to withhold it. In 1992, for instance, the minister decided to put pressure on Rwanda by refusing to grant additional emergency aid requested by the government. Yet such was the backlog of projects and programmes decided on in earlier years that in 1993 the actual disbursements of Belgian aid were the highest ever.[5] Similarly, the Belgian government in 1991 apparently tried to rush through the implementation of a project in Uganda with the aim of keeping a closer watch on the activities of the RPF in southern Uganda. Yet by the time the project would have had a chance of being implemented, the RPF was firmly installed in Kigali.

A more positive point is that Belgium initiated new projects in the legal sector in both Rwanda and Burundi. There was in fact some experience with support to the law faculty at the university, and codification of legislation and legal advisors in both countries. Starting from 1992, new interventions were proposed which were meant to address the specific problems caused by the democratisation process, increasing instability and the civil war situation. The lack of legal expertise at the geographical desk in Brussels and also in the BADC field missions in Kigali and Bujumbura helps to explain why it took so long for these projects to be processed and to come into operation. A first small intervention consisted of not much more than the sending of a legal advisor to the prime minister's office in Rwanda. This was more of a political signal, since the minister belonged to the opposition, and was not expected to yield any tangible results. BADC also decided to fund a crash training programme for lay magistrates with no legal background, intended to start in March 1994. The new minister of development co-operation who took office in 1995 strengthened the same line, but was less reluctant than his predecessor to engage BADC directly in such projects. Several projects demanded by Rwanda to support the working of the judiciary were approved but the minister made this conditional on Rwanda accepting that Belgium give legal support to people facing trial charges for their alleged participation in the 1994 genocide. In Burundi, the Hutu coalition

---

5. This does not show up in Table 2 in the appendix which suggests, rather, that 1992 is the year of highest Belgian spending. This anomaly is probably explained by the fact that some data communicated to the DAC in Paris by BADC referred to commitment rather than disbursement.

partner in the government, FRODEBU, was eagerly expecting Belgium to help in the reform of the Tutsi-dominated judiciary system, but here Belgium was more reluctant to commit itself.

One obvious point of conflict between the technical logic of BADC and the political logic dictated by the evolving situation in Rwanda and Burundi concerned the provision of expatriate experts by BADC. There were vivid memories in Brussels of the way in which the presence of Belgian experts had triggered off costly and risky military interventions in Congo on several occasions in the past. It soon became clear that there were different opinions of how the situation in Burundi had to be handled. In April 1994, in the midst of the geno-cide in Rwanda, the Belgian government, fearing an extension of the ethnic violence into Burundi, decided that BADC experts on Easter holiday leave in Belgium should not be allowed to return to Burundi. In the ensuing months, the positions of foreign affairs and BADC were clearly different. BADC was concerned about the projects and wanted the experts to return, while foreign affairs, supported by the council of ministers, decided against it. First it was decided to wait for the outcome of the high-level bilateral talks finally held in August 1994. In September, the council of ministers decided that only some eight experts would return for the time being. At the end of September, it allowed another seven project staff to return to Burundi. In February 1995, it was decided that a further 23 experts could go back. If we include the three field mission staff who had remained in Burundi all along, the total now amounted to 41, less than half of the 110 present at the beginning of 1994. In the event, the contingent of 23 did not make it back to Burundi because of an internal BADC veto, and this in spite of the insistence from the head of the Bujumbura field mission. The consequences of all these restrictions on expatriate personnel were severe for the projects funded by Belgium, many of which came to a virtual standstill.

Another problem of implementation concerns the decision to increase aid to Burundi in the early 1990s in support of political liberalisation and national reconciliation efforts by the Buyoya government. BADC was unable to mobilise funds through project aid at the speed and on the scale required, and so it was decided, quite logically, to increase programme aid to Burundi instead. Other donors were all doing the same, and Burundi was flooded with easy bud-getary resources, with the result that pressure for macroeconomic reform was considerably reduced. Too much aid therefore weakened Burundi's efforts at macroeconomic reform [*Engelbert and Hoffman, 1994*].

(3) Political Conditionality

One other area in which a lack of coherence within aid policy was felt was high-level communication between Belgium and the recipient countries. Prior to 1994, no policy document was communicated to the recipient in which the overall official Belgian attitude was spelled out. This contrasts with, for instance, the Country Assistance Strategy of the World Bank, and the policy documents issued by USAID. Only in 1994 was such an overall document produced, and even then only for internal, that is, Belgian use. This made it more difficult for recipients to make out the Belgian attitude. A mistake that occurs over and again is that for political reasons Belgium refuses to grant aid, or to start up a project, or to allow an expert to join a project, but without the reason being clearly communicated to the local authorities. What for the Belgian government is clear political conditionality appears to the other side to be a matter of bureaucratic ineptitude. This may be explained as a lack of communication and clarity on the Belgian side. An alternative explanation is that the political conditionality is not so much addressed to the bilateral partner as to public opinion in Belgium.

The problem of communication with the recipient was aggravated by the new approach to bilateral talks on development co-operation, even if in principle this new approach should have improved communication. In fact, from 1991 onwards, the emphasis was increasingly placed on sectoral issues rather than on discussion of individual projects. The intention was to upgrade bilateral talks to the level of a policy dialogue, and thus to improve the quality of communication between donor and recipient governments. Political conditions could be discussed on such occasions. Initially, this worked well in the bilateral talks with both Rwanda and Burundi, as reported above. However, from 1992 onwards, bilateral talks were downgraded to technical review meetings.

How was political conditionality applied to BADC-administered aid? In the case of Rwanda, the first clear signs of political conditionality were in the form of an admonishment by the Belgian minister, combined with a promise of increased aid spending. In 1992, a new minister added another sector: legal co-operation and human rights, which was intended as a form of positive political conditionality. After the negative conclusions of an international human rights commission in 1993, the technical bilateral talks were postponed. This was certainly intended to show to the Belgian public that the government was linking development aid to respect for human rights, and the Rwanda government undoubtedly also got the message. When the talks were eventually held, the Belgian delegation explicitly linked the promises of aid to a positive attitude on the part of the Rwanda government in the concluding round of the Arusha negotiations, and to the institutional amendments that had been agreed upon. In 1995, yet another new minister decided on commitments on a yearly basis, the prolongation being conditional on the twin conditions of respect for human rights and serious efforts to ensure equitable participation of the whole population in the development process. In 1996, the posting of a Belgian expert to the Rwandan planning ministry was postponed in view of the presumed involvement of Rwanda in the civil war in eastern Congo. Here again, it would seem that this political conditionality was essentially addressed to the Belgian public, to show that the government was strict in its dealings with Rwanda. Yet the event passed unnoticed in Belgium, and neither was the political motivation for the delayed departure communicated to Rwanda.

In the case of Burundi, political conditionality also started in earnest in 1991, with positive encouragement of further political liberalisation signalled by a promise of increased aid spending. The new minister in 1992 proposed aid money to be used for reinforcing the legal system and strengthening respect for human rights – very much as he did in Rwanda. After the murder of Ndadaye, aid was temporarily halted. As explained above, in 1994 the return of Belgian experts was made conditional on the fundamental reorientation of Belgian aid. The massacre of Hutu students and the ethnic cleansing at the national university of Bujumbura led to the halting of aid support to the university.

In other cases, Belgium imposed conditions that were difficult to maintain. In one instance in Rwanda in 1993, the imposition of conditionalities led to the ridiculous situation that emergency aid to the local population became dependent on political steps to be taken by President Habyarimana.

V. CONCLUSIONS

Has Belgian policy with regard to the Great Lakes region been coherent or incoherent? In general terms, one could say that it has been both. In the early 1990s, when conflicts in the region appeared manageable, Belgium based its bilateral relations on the pillars of democratisation and respect for human rights, using the stick and the carrot to further these objectives. The fact that Belgium was a small country without apparent geo-strategic interests, combined with it being a major bilateral donor in the region, certainly gave this policy some weight, either on its own or in conjunction with the policies of like-minded partners. However, policies became increasingly incoherent as emergencies grew more complex and apparently less manageable. The tendency to disengage was strongly reinforced in mid-1994 when the security of Belgian citizens in the region became a major concern. The killing of ten Belgian paratroopers and some civilians in Rwanda and the risky and costly evacuation of Belgian expatriates began to preoccupy the minds of policy-makers in mid-1994. The concern for the security of Belgian citizens reinforced the tendency to disengage from what was increasingly perceived as a no-win situation. It thus became hard to resist the temptation to withdraw, or at least to abandon any independent bilateral action and to restrict Belgian involvement to a participation in multilateral operations.

Apart from these political problems, which increasingly made development co-operation subject to (sometimes short-term) foreign policy concerns, the instrument itself was not functioning properly. For a start, the existing aid portfolio, consisting mainly of investment projects and technical co-operation, did not lend itself easily to political sanctions. Moreover, political conditionality, which was new and hardly tested, proved difficult to apply in the extreme and rapidly deteriorating circumstances of the Great Lakes region, where any policy tended to lag behind events. Thus, although support for the reconstruction of the judiciary in post-genocide Rwanda seemed an obvious enough choice for aid, this type of positive conditionality became part of the problem rather than the solution as the regime in Kigali embarked on a practice of 'tutsisation' at all levels, including the judicial system. The fact (or even just the perception) that Tutsi prosecutors and courts were convicting Hutu suspects achieved the opposite of what Belgium (and other donors) had in mind, namely, national reconciliation and justice.

Even more basic problems reduced the effectiveness of Belgian policy. We have stressed the lack of co-ordination between the ministries of development co-operation and foreign affairs, and even within development co-operation itself – that is, between the minister's office and BADC. Disagreement between the two departments was not altogether surprising as ministers' concerns, political leanings and temperaments were far from identical.

The period 1990–91 was one of limited disagreement between the two departments. The ministers were of a similar persuasion (the difference between a right-wing Flemish christian democrat and a middle-of-the-road Flemish nationalist is not that important) and political conditionality was still a relatively new concept, more talked about than effectively implemented. During the period 1992–95, although the ministers were members of the same party, the potential for conflict increased, as 'Realpolitik' and a more moral stance collided. Yet, from 1995 onwards, when Erik Derycke was promoted from development co-operation to foreign affairs, disagreement did not disappear. Although Derycke did not become less 'idealistic', the new minister for development co-operation, Reginald Moreels, former chairman of Médecins sans frontières, was 'hyper-committed', as have been some of his other European colleagues in charge of aid and humanitarian affairs (such as Kouchner in France, Pronk in the Netherlands and Bonnino in the EU commission). Clearly, in periods of acute crisis such as those in Rwanda and Burundi in recent years, foreign affairs thinks in terms of diplomacy and long-term political relations, while development co-operation feels the strain of the humanitarian drama unfolding on the ground.

At lower levels of the two departments, too, coherence was often lacking. This is hardly surprising. Even if we were to assume that the two departments systematically shared the same analysis and agreed on the same mix of objectives, they might still fail to agree on the particular instruments to be used at any given moment in time. And even if all that went well, coherence could still be impeded by poor implementation. BADC was supposed to be in charge of day-to-day development co-operation, while foreign affairs addressed the larger political issues. However, particularly in periods of crisis, these two approaches cannot be realistically separated. As a consequence, there was little articulation between the micro and the macro levels of bilateral relations. Regular consultations on both programme and project management and bilateral politics would have avoided many of the inconsistencies we have described.

Even at BADC level itself, co-ordination was less than ideal. Thus the link between the overall socio-political evolution in the recipient countries and the programme/project level was seldom made, or at least not in the appropriate time-frame (it often takes years to start or end a project). With hindsight, it is quite surprising that clear warning signs of impending and developing crises were not included, or insufficiently included, in the assumptions column of the logical framework applied with regard to Rwanda and Burundi.

Finally, with regard to the instrument of political conditionality which was being developed in the 1990s, obviously it can function only if clear – though not *per se* public – messages are sent to the recipient country. The stick and the carrot have to be shown for what they are: conditionality cannot be implicit. Clearly, on a number of occasions, the Belgian government failed to relay the political nature of a decision, which could then be interpreted by the recipient as merely bureaucratic or linked to other considerations, such as the security situation. Was it because the Belgian minister disliked conveying an unpleasant message or because he hoped that the recipient government would understand the hint? Or because the measure was inspired by a combination of motives, of which conditionality was just one, others possibly being the security of Belgian experts or meeting the demands of certain Belgian lobbies? Another reason for sending mixed messages might well be a fact that is constantly in the mind of Belgian governments, namely the safety of the sizable numbers of Belgian expatriates in the Great Lakes region.

Although we have addressed some incoherences in Belgium's policies towards the South, it should be noted by way of conclusion that the way in which the crises unfolded in the recipient region was such that it would have been difficult if not impossible to influence the situation fundamentally, no matter what measures had been taken. In Rwanda and Burundi, conditionality reached its outer limits. If local and regional actors pursue strategies of confrontation and if mutual fear is their main driving force, bilateral donors' leverage is limited indeed. If, on top of that, the international donor community acts in a less than consistent way, the endeavours of a small country such as Belgium, even if it was among the largest donors to the region at the onset of the crisis, should not be expected to make much of a difference.

REFERENCES

Amnesty International, 1996, *Burundi: Refugees Forced Back to Danger*, Dec. 1996.
BADC, 1996, *1995 Annual Report*, Brussels.
BADC, various internal reports on the bilateral talks with Rwanda and Burundi, Brussels, 1991–94.
DAC, *Development Co-operation Review*, several issues, OECD, Paris.
DAC, *Geographical Distribution of Financial Flows to Aid Recipients*, several issues, OECD, Paris.
Engelbert, Pierre and Richard Hoffman, 1994, 'Burundi: Learning the Lessons', in Ishrat Husain and Rashid Faruqee (eds.), *Adjustment in Africa: Lessons from Country Case Studies*, Washington, DC: World Bank.
Houart, Francis and Rik Coolsaet, 1995, *L'Afrique subsaharienne en transition*, Brussels: dossiers du GRIP.
Human Rights Watch *et al.*, 1994, *Commission internationale d'enquête sur les violations des droits de l'homme au Burundi depuis le 21 octobre 1993. Rapport final*, July 1994.
Millwood, David (ed.), 1996, *The International Response to Conflict and Genocide: Lessons from the Rwanda Experience*, Steering Committee on the Joint Evaluation of Emergency Assistance to Rwanda.

République Rwandaise, 1995, *Plan d'action du Ministère de la Justice*, Ministère des Finances, Kigali.

Reyntjens, Filip, 1994, *L'Afrique des grands lacs en crise*, Paris: Karthala.

Reyntjens, Filip, 1995, *Burundi: Breaking the Cycle of Violence*, London: Minority Rights Group International, March 1995; update July 1996.

Reyntjens, Filip and Stefan Marysse, 1996, 'Conflits au Kivu. Antécédents et enjeux', Antwerp: Centre for the Study of the Great Lakes Region of Africa, Working Paper, Dec. 1996.

APPENDIX

TABLE 1

SHARE OF CONGO (EX-ZAIRE), RWANDA AND BURUNDI IN BILATERAL ODA OF BELGIUM
(PERCENTAGES)

	1970–71	1980–81	1985–86	1989–90	1991–92	1993–94	1995
Congo	52.3	35.4	34.3	20.5	5.9	6.4	4.1
Rwanda	11.8	7.8	6.9	7.5	9.3	7.0	3.1
Burundi	9.7	6.1	5.8	6.1	7.2	4.9	2.3
Total	73.8	49.3	47.1	34.1	22.5	18.3	9.5

Sources: 1970–94: DAC, *Development Co-operation Review*, several issues, OECD, Paris.
1995: BADC, *1995 Annual Report*, Brussels, 1996.
Note: Total refers to the share of all three countries in Belgium's bilateral aid.

TABLE 2

ODA TO BURUNDI, SELECTED DONORS (MILLION US$ AND PERCENTAGES)

	1980	1985	1988	1989	1990	1991	1992	1993	1994
Belgium	27.7	19.2	17.3	17.2	39.5	26.1	52.9	26.3	19.2
France	12.9	22.6	25.7	27.9	37.7	42.2	36.4	28.5	23.0
Germany	10.0	12.6	14.4	20.7	30.4	25.7	20.8	25.4	27.7
US	4.0	9.0	3.0	3.0	18.0	6.0	16.0	18.0	10.0
TOTAL bilateral	59.7	77.2	83.3	89.5	157.6	122.9	148.8	125.7	108.5
EU	12.0	9.5	27.3	35.5	35.7	56.8	65.7	24.0	36.5
IDA	11.6	17.7	44.0	45.0	48.0	39.0	47.7	34.6	25.5
WFP	5.3	1.5	3.2	2.7	3.0	1.6	2.2	5.0	64.2
UNHCR	0.4	0.7	1.7	1.3	0.6	0.9	1.6	0.0	65.9
TOTAL multilateral	53.9	59.1	102.1	113.4	107.6	138.9	163.8	95.0	207.5
% Belgium / grand total	23.6	13.5	9.2	8.3	14.9	10.1	17.0	12.0	6.1
% Belgium/ bilateral	46.4	24.9	20.8	19.2	25.1	21.2	35.6	20.9	17.7

Source: DAC, *Geographical Distribution of Financial Flows to Aid Recipients*, several issues, OECD, Paris.

TABLE 3

ODA TO RWANDA, SELECTED DONORS (MILLION US$ AND PERCENTAGES)

	1980	1985	1988	1989	1990	1991	1992	1993	1994
Belgium	36.2	20.2	29.1	26.7	43.3	55.8	45.5	36.7	29.0
France	15.8	15.4	22.1	17.8	33.9	39.9	26.7	30.3	24.3
Germany	16.8	23.6	25.0	27.2	31.8	40.1	43.6	38.6	46.6
US	7.0	15.0	17.0	9.0	13.0	27.0	7.0	26.0	194.0
Switzerland	5.2	8.4	12.8	9.1	10.2	17.1	13.8	20.2	22.6
UK	0.0	0.1	0.5	0.5	0.9	0.6	0.3	1.2	44.6
Netherlands	4.6	3.0	7.2	5.6	10.7	3.9	6.9	7.2	32.2
TOTAL bilateral	96.6	103.2	137.2	131.7	183.2	232.9	187.5	201.3	487.4
EU	21.4	11.7	39.1	32.5	36.0	21.4	82.5	36.0	45.6
IDA	10.2	29.2	24.0	26.0	21.0	47.0	29.9	36.6	11.1
UNICEF	2.0	1.0	2.0	2.3	2.8	3.8	4.5	0.0	32.3
WFP	2.6	5.9	1.6	1.0	2.0	3.2	7.3	53.9	47.7
UNHCR	0.2	5.1	3.9	1.5	1.5	1.2	1.6	6.1	75.1
TOTAL multilateral	57.5	72.8	112.0	92.3	99.8	127.3	165.5	154.5	226.2
% Belgium / grand total	23.3	11.1	11.6	11.6	14.8	15.3	12.9	10.2	4.1
% Belgium/ bilateral	37.5	19.6	21.2	20.3	23.7	24.0	24.3	18.2	5.9

Source: DAC, *Geographical Distribution of Financial Flows to Aid Recipients*, several issues, OECD, Paris.

TABLE 4

BELGIAN ODA TO BURUNDI, SELECTED CATEGORIES (MILLION BELGIAN FRANCS)

	1988	1989	1990	1991	1992	1993	1994	1995
Technical co-operation and projects	418	444	514	641	1173	450	361	97
Total BADC direct	418	469	1159	641	1394	583	385	107
Total BADC indirect	193	201	203	219	268	291	219	141
Total Belgium	634	694	1394	893	1700	910	641	280

See notes to Table 5.

TABLE 5

BELGIAN ODA TO RWANDA, SELECTED CATEGORIES (MILLION BELGIAN FRANCS)

	1988	1989	1990	1991	1992	1993	1994	1995
Technical co-operation and projects	633	727	589	654	641	525	237	70
Total BADC direct	633	728	839	1304	841	544	558	71
Total BADC indirect	274	320	433	367	367	478	267	276
Total Belgium	1071	1212	1529	1928	1466	1267	969	409

Source: BADC.
Notes: total BADC direct: official co-operation.
total BADC indirect: aid through NGOs, universities, etc.

Glossary

AAPAM	African Association for Public Administration and Management
ACDA	Arms Control and Disarmament Agency – USA
ACP	African, Carribean and Pacific countries, signatories of the Lomé conventions
AIV	Adviesraad Internationale Vraagstukken (Advisory Council of International Affairs) – The Netherlands
ASEAN	Association of South-East Asian Nations
BADC	Belgian Administration for Development Co-operation
BICC	Bonn International Center for Conversion – Germany
BITS	Beredningen för Internationellt och Tekniskt Samarbete (Swedish Agency for International Technical and Economic Co-operation)
BMU	Bundesministerium für Umwelt, Naturschutz und Reaktorsicherheit (Federal Ministry for the Environment, Nature Conservation and Nuclear Safety) – Germany
BMWi	Bundesministerium für Wirtschaft (Federal Ministry of Economic Affairs) – Germany
BMZ	Bundesministerium für wirtschaftliche Zusammenarbeit und Entwicklung (Federal Ministry for Economic Co-operation and Development) – Germany
BSD	Bistånd i siffror och diagram (Foreign Aid in Figures and Graphs) – Sweden
BUND	Bund für Umwelt und Naturschutz Deutschlands (German Association for the Environment and Nature Conservation)
BWI	Bretton Woods institutions
CAD	DAC
CAP	Common Agricultural Policy – EU
CCIC	Canadian Council of International Co-operation
CDU	Christian Democratic Union – Germany
CEC	Commission of the European Communities

CECOS	Committee on Ecology and Development Co-operation – The Netherlands
CEE	Communauté économique européenne (European Economic Community – EEC)
CEE	Central and Eastern Europe
CEEC	Central and Eastern European Countries
CFA	Communauté Financière Africaine (African Financial Community)
CFD	Caisse française de développement (French Fund for Development)
CFSP	Common foreign and security policy – EU
CG	Consultative Group
CIDA	Canadian International Development Agency
CIIR	Catholic Institute of International Relations
CIRAD	Centre international de recherche agricole pour le développement (International Centre for Agricultural Research on Development)
CIS	Commonwealth of Independent States
CMI	Christian Michelsen Institute – Bergen (Norway)
CNDD	Conseil national pour la Défence de la Démocratie – Burundi
CRS	Congressional Research Service
CSD	Commission for Sustainable Development – UN
DAC	Development Assistance Committee – OECD
DANIDA	Danish International Development Agency
DCD	Development Co-operation Directorate – OECD
DEG	Deutsches Investions- und Entwicklungsgesellschaft (German Investment and Development Corporation)
DFID	Department for International Development – UK
DG	Directorate General (of the European Commission)
DIA	Development Impact Assessment
DIHT	Deutscher Industrie- und Handelstag (Association of German Chambers of Industry and Commerce)
DOM	Département d'Outre-Mer (French overseas department)
EADI	European Association of Development Research and Training Institutes
EBRD	European Bank for Reconstruction and Development
EC	European Community
ECDPM	European Centre for Development Policy Management
ECHO	European Community Humanitarian Office

ECOSOC	Economic and Social Council – UN
EDC	Export Development Corporation – Canada
EDF	European Development Fund – EU
EEC	European Economic Community
EFTA	European Free Trade Association
EIA	Environmental Impact Assessment
EP	European Parliament
EPC	European Political Co-operation – EU
EPD	Evangelischen Presse-dienstes – Germany
ERG	Export Risk Guarantee – Switzerland
EU	European Union
FAC	Fond d'aide et de coopération (Fund for Aid and Co-operation) – France
FAO	Food and Agriculture Organisation of the UN
FAR	Forces armées rwandaises
FCO	Foreign and Commonwealth Office – UK
FDD	Forces pour la Défense de la Démocratie – Burundi
FDI	Foreign Direct Investment
FDP	Freie Democratische Partei (Liberal Democratic Party) – Germany
FOEFL	Federal Office for Environment, Forests and Landscape – Switzerland
FOFEA	Federal Office for Foreign Economic Affairs – Switzerland
FRODEBU	Front démocratique du Burundi
FROLINA	Front de libération nationale – Burundi
FSU	Former Soviet Union
FTA	Free Trade Area
GATT	General Agreement on Tariffs and Trade
GDI	German Development Institute – Berlin
GEF	Global Environmental Facility
GKKE	Gemeinsame Konferenz Kirche und Entwicklung (Joint Conference Church and Development) – Germany
GNP	Gross National Product
GSP	Generalised system of preferences
IAS	Integrated Advisory Services – Germany
IBRD	International Bank for Reconstruction and Development/World Bank
ICOR	Incremental Capital Output Ratio
IDA	International Development Association – World Bank

IDS	Institute of Development Studies (University of Sussex, Brighton)
IDIC	International Development Information Centre – Canada
IFI	International Financial Institutions
IFOR	Implementation Force in Bosnia-Herzegovina
IGC	Inter-governmental conference – EU. The first one took place in 1991 and resulted in the signature of the Maastricht Treaty, the second took place in 1996 and resulted in the signature of the Treaty of Amsterdam in 1997.
IGGI	Inter-governmental Group on Indonesia
IMF	International Monetary Fund
INGO	International non-governmental organisation
IOV	Inspectie Ontwikkelinggssamenwerking te Velde (Inspectorate for Development Co-operation) – The Netherlands
IUED	Institut universitaire d'etudes du développement, Geneva
IUCN	International Union for the Conservation of Nature and Natural Resources
KrF	Kristelig Folkeparti (Christian People's Party – Christian Democrats) – Norway
LDC	Less developed country/least developed country
LIC	Low-income country
LLDC	(List of) Least Developed Countries (UN definition)
LMIC	Lower middle-income country
MDC	Ministry of Development Co-operation
ME	Ministry of the Environment
MFA	Ministry of Foreign Affairs
MHA	International Humanitarian Assistance Division (CIDA)
MFA	Multi-Fibre Agreement
MIC	Middle-income country
MinFA	Ministry of Foreign Affairs
NAFTA	North American Free Trade Area
NAR	Nationale Adviesraad voor Ontwikkelingssamenwerking (National Advisory Council for Development Co-operation) – The Netherlands
NATO	North Atlantic Treaty Organization
NBT	National Board of Trade – Sweden
NEI	Netherlands Economic Institute

NGI	Non-governmental institution
NGO	Non-governmental organisation
NIEO	New International Economic Order
NIS	Newly Independent States
NOK	Norwegian kroner (currency)
NORAD	Norwegian Agency for International Development/ now Norwegian Agency for Development Co-operation
NORDEM	Norwegian resource bank for democratic development and human rights
NOREPS	Norwegian Emergency Preparedness System
NORTEAM	Norwegian group of aid workers prepared to go to disaster areas at short notice
NOU	Norske Offentlige Utredninger (Norwegian Public Reviews)
NOVIB	Nederlandse Organisatie voor Internationale Samenwerking (the Netherlands' Organisation for International Co-operation)
NRA	National Resistance Army – Uganda
NTB	Non-Tariff Barrier
NUPI	Norsk utenrikspolitisk institutt (Norwegian Institute of International Affairs) – Oslo
NVA	Nationale Volksarmee (National People's Army) – former German Democratic Republic
OAU	Organisation of African Unity
OCDE	OECD
ODA	Official development assistance
ODA	Overseas Development Administration – UK (now DFID)
ODI	Overseas Development Institute – London
OECD	Organisation for Economic Co-operation and Development
ORSTOM	Institut français de recherche scientifique pour le développement en coopération (French Institute of Scientific Research)
OSCE	Organisation for Security and Co-operation in Europe
PALIPEHUTU	Parti pour la libération du peuple hutu – Burundi
PDGG	Participatory development and good governance
PLO	Palestinian Liberation Organisation
PM	Prime Minister
PUMA	Public Management Service – OECD
QR	Quantitative Restriction

RCMP	Royal Canadian Mounted Police
RIVM	Rijksinstituut voor Volksgezondheid en Milieu (National Institute for Public Health and Environment) – The Netherlands
RPF	Rwanda Patriotic Front
SAREC	Swedish Agency for Research Co-operation with Developing Countries (now a department within SIDA)
SDC	Swiss Agency for Development and Co-operation
SEA	Single European Act – EU
SID	Society for International Development
SIDA	Swedish International Development Authority/now Swedish International Development Co-operation Agency
SIPRI	Stockholm International Peace Research Institute
SPD	Sozialdemocratische Partei Deutschlands (Social-Demo cratic Party of Germany)
SPLA	Sudan People's Liberation Army
SSA	Sub-Saharan Africa
Stabex	Guaranteed stabilisation of export earnings (for ACP countries – Lomé agreements)
Sysmin	Production-support scheme (for ACP countries – Lomé agreements)
SWEDECORP	Swedish International Enterprise Development
SWP	Stiftung Wissenschaft und Politik – Germany
TEU	Treaty on European Union
TI	Transparency International – Germany
TOM	Territoire d'Outre-Mer (French overseas dependency)
UK	United Kingdom
UMIC	Upper middle-income country
UN	United Nations
UNAMIR	United Nations Assistance Mission to Rwanda
UNCED	United Nations Conference on Environment and Development
UNCTAD	United Nations Conference on Trade and Development
UNDP	United Nations Development Programme
UNEP	United Nations Environmental Programme
UNESCO	United Nations Educational, Scientific and Cultural Organisation
UNHCR	United Nations High Commissioner for Refugees

UNICEF	United Nations (International) Children's (Emergency) Fund
UNIFIL	United Nations Interim Force in Lebanon
UNPROFOR	United Nations Protection Force (in Bosnia-Herzegovina
UNRWA	United Nations Relief and Work Agency for Palestine Refugees in the Near East
UPRONA	Union pour le progrès national – Burundi
US	United States (of America)
USA	United States of America
USAID	United States Agency for International Development
USIA	United States Information Agency
USSR	Union of Soviet Socialist Republics
VVD	Volkspartij voor Vrijheid en Democratie (People's Party for Freedom and Democracy – Liberal Party) – The Netherlands
WB	World Bank/IBRD
WFP	World Food Programme
WHO	World Health Organisation
WTO	World Trade Organisation

Notes on Contributors

Guido Ashoff is Head of Department, the German Development Institute, Berlin. He has written extensively on development cooperation and carried out empirical research in Latin America, North Africa and the Middle East.

Anders Danielson is Associate Professor, the Department of Economics, University of Lund, Sweden. Among his publications are *The Political Economy of Development Finance* (1993) and *The Economic Surplus* (1994).

Johan Debar is a macro-economist with the Belgian aid agency (BADC). He has worked for six years in the Central African region for both NGOs and the BADC and was for some time also associated with the University of Antwerp as a researcher in the area of aid management.

Jacques Forster is Professor of Development Economics, Graduate Institute of Development Studies (IUED), Geneva, and previously its Director (1980–92). He is the editor of the *Annuaire Suisse-Tiers Monde*, published by IUED. He was for years a member of the EADI Executive Committee, during 1985–90 the Vice-President. He is a member of the International Committee of the International Red Cross and its incoming Vice-President.

Kiichiro Fukasaku is Research Division Head of the OECD Development Centre, Paris. Before joining the OECD, he was staff economist of the Economic Research and Analysis Unit of the GATT Secretariat (now the WTO) in Geneva (1983–90). He holds M.A. and D.Phil. degrees in economics from Keio University, Japan, and University of Sussex, United Kingdom, respectively. Among his recent publications are *Regional Co-operation and Integration in Asia* (editor, 1995), *Asia & Europe: Beyond Competing Regionalism* (co-editor, 1998), and *Democracy, Decentralisation and Deficits in Latin America* (co-editor, 1998).

Paul Hoebink is Senior Lecturer at the Third World Centre/Department of Development Studies Training College of the Catholic

University of Nijmegen, the Netherlands. He is a member of the National Advisory Council for Development Co-operation of the Netherlands.

Philippe Hugon is Professor of Economics, Paris X Nanterre. He is the Director of the Centre for Research and Economics in the field of development (CERED/FORUM). He has published extensively on development and international economics, including a dozen books, and carried out several international consultancies. He has been a member of the EADI Executive Committee.

Göran Hydén is Professor of Political Science, University of Florida, Gainsville. He has served in teaching positions at several universities in East Africa and also as a Regional Representative for East and Southern Africa of the Ford Foundation. He has published extensively in the field of African studies and development studies, including more than twenty books, and has also served as the President of the (US) African Studies Association.

Andrea Koulaïmah-Gabriel is a Researcher at the European Centre for Development Policy Management, Maastricht, associated with its Dialogue Programme. She is a graduate of the College of Europe, Brugge.

Oliver Morrissey is Associate Professor, Department of Economics, University of Nottingham, Nottingham.

Cranford Pratt is Emeritus Professor of Political Science at the University of Toronto. He is editor and contributor to *Internationalism Under Strain: The North–South Policies of Canada, the Netherlands, Norway and Sweden* (1989), *Middle Power Internationalism: The North–South Dimension* (1990), and *Canadian International Development Assistance Policies: An Appraisal* (1994 and 1996).

Robrecht Renard is Professor of Development Economics, College for the Developing Countries – RUCA, University of Antwerp, Antwerp. He was a member of the EADI Executive Committee for several years (1984–89).

Filip Reyntjens is Professor of Law and Politics, College for the Developing Countries – RUCA, University of Antwerp, Antwerp.

He has also carried out research and teaching on African law and politics at the universities of Leuven and Brussels and worked for several years in Central Africa. He has published extensively, including recent volumes on *L'Afrique des grands lacs en crise* (1994), *Burundi. Breaking the Cycle of Violence* (1995), *Rwanda. Trois jours qui ont fait basculer l'histoire* (1996), and *L'Afrique des grand lacs. Annuaire 1996–1997* (1997). He has been Chairman of the board of the African Studies and Documentation Centre, Brussels, Vice-President of the International Third World Legal Studies Association, New York, and Vice Chancellor of the University of Mbuji-Mayi, Congo.

Mark Robinson is a Fellow of the Institute of Development Studies at the University of Sussex (Brighton) England. His current research interests are on the politics of aid policy, with a particular focus on the impact of foreign aid on civil society organisations in Africa. He has been a Guest Editor of *The European Journal of Development Research* (Volume 10, No. 1. June 1998), a thematic issue on Corruption and Development.

Olav Stokke is a Senior Researcher of the Norwegian Institute of International Affairs, Oslo. He is editor of *Forum for Development Studies* and, since 1979, the Convenor of the EADI Working Group on Aid Policy and Performance.

Index

EADI BOOK SERIES

1. István Dobozi and Péter Mándi (eds.), *Emerging Development Patterns: European Contributions* (1983)
2. Marie Éliou (réd), *Femmes et développment ou les metamorphoses d'un développment au masculin* (1983)
3. Hans-Peter Nissen (ed.), *Towards Income Distribution Policies: From Income Distribution Research to Income Distribution Policy in LDCs* (1984)
4. Olav Stokke (ed.), *European Development Assistance:* Vol. I *Policies and Performance;* Vol. II *Third World Pespectives on Policies and Performance* (1984)
5. Stefan Musto (ed.), *endogenous Development: A Myth or a Path? Problems of Economic Self-Reliance in the European Periphery* (1985)
6. Cecilia Andersen and Isa Baud (eds.), *Women in Development Cooperation: Europe's Unfinished Business* (1987)
7. Olav Stokke (ed.), *Trade and Development: Experiences and Challenges* (1987)
8. István Dobozi (ed.), *Politics and Economics of East–South Relations* (1988)
9. Jaime del Castillo (ed.), *Regional Development Policies in Areas in Decline* (1989)
10. Meine Pieter van Dijk and Henrik Secher Marcussen (eds.), *Industrialization in the Third World: The Need for Alternative Strategies* (1990)
11. Edward Clay and Olav Stokkes (eds.), *Food Aid Reconsidered: Assessing the Impact on Third World Countries* (1991)
12. Olav Stokke (ed.), *Evaluating Development Assistance: Policies and Performance* (1991)
13. Sandro Sideri and Jayshree Sengupta (eds.), *The 1992 Single European Market and the Third World* (1992)
14. Lodewijk Berlage and Olav Stokke (eds.), *Evaluating Development Assistance: Approaches and Methods* (1992)
15. Claude Auroi (ed.), *The Role of the State in Development Processes* (1992)
16. Olav Stokke (ed.), *Aid and Political Conditionality* (1995)
17. Gerry Rodgers, Klárá Fóti and Laurids Lauridsen (eds.), *The Institutional Approach to Labour and Development* (1996)
18. Olav Stokke (ed.), *Foreign Aid Towards the Year 2000: Experiences and Challenges* (1996)
19. Meine Pieter van Dijk and Sandro Sideri (eds.), *Multilateralism versus Regionalism: Trade Issues afte the Uruguay Round* (1996)
20. Meine Pleter van JDijk and Roberta Rabellotti (eds.), *Enterprise Clusters and Networks in Developing Countries* (1997)
21. Claude Auroi (ed.), *Latin American and East European Economics in Transition: A Comparative View* (1998)